eleventh canadian edition

W9-CEA-515

CASES IN

Strategic Management

Paul W. Beamish

Ivey Business School, Western University

McGraw-Hill
Ryerson

McGraw-Hill
Ryerson

Cases in Strategic Management
Eleventh Edition

Copyright © 2015, 2012, 2009, 2006, 2005, 2002, 1999, 1996, 1993, 1990, 1987 by McGraw-Hill
Ryerson Limited. All rights reserved. No part of this publication may be reproduced or transmitted
in any form or by any means, or stored in a data base or retrieval system, without the prior written
permission of McGraw-Hill Ryerson Limited, or in the case of photocopying or other reprographic
copying, a licence from The Canadian Copyright Licensing Agency (Access Copyright). For an Access
Copyright licence, visit www.accesscopyright.ca or call toll-free to 1-800-893-5777.

The Internet addresses listed in the text were accurate at the time of publication. The inclusion of a
website does not indicate an endorsement by the authors or McGraw-Hill Ryerson, and McGraw-Hill
Ryerson does not guarantee the accuracy of information presented at these sites.

ISBN-13: 978-1-25-903051-2
ISBN-10: 1-25-903051-2

1 2 3 4 5 6 7 8 9 0 WEB 1 9 8 7 6 5

Printed and bound in Canada.

Care has been taken to trace ownership of copyright material contained in this text; however, the
publisher will welcome any information that enables it to rectify any reference or credit for subsequent editions.

Director of Product Management: *Rhondda McNabb*
Group Product Manager: *Kim Brewster*
Marketing Manager: *Cathie Lefebvre*
Product Developers: *Catherine Gillespie-Lopes, Jennifer Cressman*
Senior Product Team Associate: *Stephanie Giles*
Supervising Editor: *Cathy Biribauer*
Proofreader: *Laurel Sparrow*
Plant Production Coordinator: *Michelle Saddler*
Manufacturing Production Coordinator: *Lena Keating*
Cover and Interior Design: *Dave Murphy*
Composition: *Aptara ®, Inc.*
Cover Photo: *Courtney Keating/Getty Images*
Printer: *Webcom, Ltd.*

Library and Archives Canada Cataloguing in Publication Data

Beamish, Paul W., 1953-, author
    Cases in strategic management / Paul W. Beamish.–Eleventh edition.
Includes bibliographical references.
ISBN 978-125-903051-2 (pbk.)
    1. Strategic planning–Canada–Case studies. 2. Industrial management–
Canada–Case studies. I. Title.

HD30.28.B3322 2015   658.4'0120971   C2014-904604-9

To the memory of two splendid teachers:

John and Catherine Beamish

About the Author

Paul W. Beamish is Professor of International Strategy at the Ivey Business School, Western University. He is the author or co-author of 55 books, 120 refereed articles, and over 100 case studies. His articles have appeared in *Strategic Management Journal, Journal of International Business Studies, Academy of Management Journal, Academy of Management Review, Organization Science,* and elsewhere. His consulting and management training activities have been in both the public and the private sector for such organizations as Boeing, Cisco, Labatt/Interbrew, The World Bank, the Canadian Foreign Service Institute, and the Harvard Institute for International Development. He has received case writing awards from the European Foundation for Management Development, The Management Development Centre of Hong Kong, The Academy of International Business and the Administrative Sciences Association of Canada. Over 3 million copies of his cases have been studied worldwide. He worked for Procter & Gamble Company of Canada and Wilfrid Laurier University before joining Ivey's faculty in 1987. He is the founding Director of Ivey's Asian Management Institute, and is the Executive Director of Ivey Publishing. He is a Fellow of the Royal Society of Canada, the Academy of International Business, and the Asia Pacific Foundation of Canada. In 2012 he received the International Management Outstanding Educator Award from the Academy of Management.

Contents

Part 1 Strategic Management: Creating Competitive Advantages

Methanex, the world's largest producer of methanol, was a $2.5 billion global company based in Vancouver. Top management at Methanex undertook a quarterly risk analysis that included a systematic review of corporate strategy and the competitive landscape in the methanol industry. The review's primary objective was to identify organizational risks and opportunities and to develop appropriate strategic responses for both short-term profits and long-term growth. Methanex's CEO needed to prepare strategic recommendations and an action plan to present to the board of directors at the next quarterly risk review meeting.

Originally founded in Montreal in the mid-1990s, by 2013 Vice Media was headquartered in New York City. It had assiduously built a global youth brand through unique and seemingly inimitable competitive advantages. While globalizing its operations, Vice Media appeared to have developed expertise in standardizing certain aspects of its business, adapting others to local context and, increasingly, building a global chain. Given Vice Media's explosive growth, how would its global value chain be structured to maintain the carefully cultivated emotional connection the company had created with its audience?

Part 2 Analyzing the External Environment of the Firm

In July 2004, Bombardier Aerospace announced its intention to develop a new family of aircraft called CSeries. By May 2007, the final decision on whether to proceed with the initiative was still pending. Moreover, during this period, the company released several confusing announcements that raised concerns among investors and industry analysts regarding the sustainability of the company's long-term strategy. In the meantime, Brazilian Embraer had invested heavily in research and development and had taken the leadership position in the regional aircraft segment from Bombardier. Consequently, Bombardier was faced with a serious dilemma of whether or not to launch the CSeries project. The decision was expected to have a major impact on the future market positioning of Bombardier.

During the month of November, many men in Canada and around the world participated each year in Movember by growing moustaches and collecting pledges. As a not-for-profit organization, Movember Canada strived to raise both money and awareness for men's health, specifically prostate cancer. The community development manager for Movember Canada faced an interesting challenge. The participation of more women represented a significant opportunity to make a large impact with fundraising, but it also provided an important chance to change attitudes towards men's health. However, many organizations relating to women's health were already well established and successful at reaching out each year for support from female demographics. The manager needed to determine how the organization could attract and involve more women in battling a health issue that was not their own. Compounding the challenge was the efficient and simple campaign it operated which relied on a lean team and low administrative costs.

Case 5 Swimming in the Virtual Community Pool with PlentyofFish   64

Case 6 The Chinese Fireworks Industry   74

Part 3 Assessing the Internal Environment of the Firm

Case 7 Sher-Wood Hockey Sticks: Global Sourcing   86

Case 8 Charles Chocolates   97

Case 9 The Prince Edward Island Preserve Company: Turnaround   110

free-floating selection of cars that allowed customers to pick up or leave vehicles wherever they liked.

Part 6 Corporate-Level Strategy: Creating Value through Diversification

Vincor International Inc. was Canada's largest wine company and North America's fourth largest in 2002. The company had decided to internationalize and as the first step had entered the United States through two acquisitions. The company's chief executive officer felt that to be among the top 10 wineries in the world, Vincor needed to look beyond the region. To the end, he was considering the acquisition of an Australian company, Goundrey Wines. He must analyze the strategic rationale for the acquisition of Goundrey as well as to probe questions of strategic fit and value.

During his 10-year tenure, the president and chief executive officer (CEO) of CIBC Mellon had presided over the dramatic growth of the jointly owned, Toronto-based asset servicing business of CIBC and The Bank of New York Mellon Corporation (BNY Mellon). In mid-September 2008, the onset of the worst financial crisis since the Great Depression threatened to impact all players in the financial services industry worldwide. Although joint ventures (JVs) were uncommon in the financial sector, the CEO believed that the CIBC Mellon JV was uniquely positioned to withstand the fallout associated with the financial crisis. Two pressing issues faced the JV's executive management team. First, they needed to discuss how to best manage any risks confronting the JV as a consequence of the financial crisis. How could the policies and practices developed during the past decade be leveraged to sustain the JV through the broader financial crisis? Second, they needed to continue discussions regarding options for refining CIBC Mellon's strategic focus, so that the JV could emerge from the financial meltdown on even stronger footing.

Part 7 International Strategy: Creating Value in Global Markets

A key requirement to assess a potential international market opportunity is an understanding of basic demographics. At its most fundamental level, the overall size of a national population provides a starting point. There are literally hundreds of potential national markets. These vary greatly in terms of population level, income levels, etc. . . As firms (and managers) consider which markets to enter, a major consideration is experience in the market: "Where They Have Been". This exercise assesses one's exposure to the rest of the world's peoples. A series of worksheets require the respondents to check off the number and names of countries they have visited and the corresponding percentage of world population which each country represents. The exercise can be used as an ice-breaker during the initial class of a module on international strategy or in conjunction with any case study focused on international market entry or selection.

Toronto-based New York Fries' president and executive vice president were preparing for the next biannual meeting of domestic and international franchisees. They planned to provide an update on all aspect of corporate strategy and planning for the year ahead, but they only had a few days to formulate a new international growth strategy. The president and executive vice president were hesitant to expand into new territories partly due to poor experiences in Australia and South Korea, yet international franchisees had encouraged them to investigate promising areas of expansion into China and India.

Complicating matters was the future development of the company's chain of premium hamburger restaurants. While New York Fries was a well-received brand in Canada, it had not yet decided if and how to internationalize the brand. How could the president and executive vice president pursue new opportunities while maintaining their premium brands of French fries and hamburgers?

Part 8 Industry Change and Competitive Dynamics

In late September 2009, the CEO of the Nasdaq-traded solar cell and module manufacturer, Canadian Solar, was at an inflection point in the formation of its strategy. The company had experienced dynamic growth during the past five years buoyed largely by aggressive incentive schemes to install solar photovoltaic (PV) technology in Germany and Spain. The credit crunch, coupled with changes in government incentive programs, caused a major decline in the demand for solar PV technology and analysts were predicting that full year 2009 sales would decline. Furthermore, competition in the industry was fierce with diverse players ranging from Japanese electronic giants to low-cost Chinese producers. Canadian Solar had decided to focus on 10 major markets in the next two to three years where strong renewable policies existed. Students are challenged with deciding if any changes to the company's strategy are necessary.

Part 9 Creating Effective Organizational Designs

The executive vice-president and chief operating officer (COO) of Canadian National Railway Company (CN), wants to change the culture at his organization. The COO has been promoted to his current position after CN purchased Illinois Central, and his first task is to review CN's operations across the country. He notices that employees are leaving work early, a practice called "early quits" that is supposed to reward employees for working harder during the day. He also notices there are other practices, such as late starts that encourage lower productivity. With the goal of improving productivity in mind, the COO elects to tackle the issue of late starts before fixing the early quits problem. This case introduces behavioural science as one of the many management tools that can be used to influence behaviour.

In September 2011, the director of pharmacy services at London Health Sciences Centre (LHSC) faces a major challenge: implementing project HUGO (Health Care UnderGoing Optimization). HUGO is a computerized system that requires a switch from paper and pencil to fully electronic patient records. This project is the most complex and comprehensive one that London area hospitals have ever undergone: the project includes a total of 11 healthcare organizations in London and surrounding region, with expected project costs in excess of $25 million. Implementing HUGO has the potential to save lives in the hospital, where critical errors are often linked to manual processes that involve multiple steps and people. Despite the strong reasons for implementing this project, the director expects significant resistance from nurses, doctors and staff who are used to their way of operating. It is clear that this change challenge involves not just the adoption of new technology but a significant cultural change.

Victoria Heavy Equipment (Victoria) was a family owned and managed firm that had been led by an ambitious, entrepreneurial chief executive officer who now wanted to take a less active role in the business. His son and daughter were not yet ready to succeed him so he wondered what kind of person he should hire to become president. Victoria had been through two reorganizations in recent years, which contributed to organizational and strategic issues which would need to be addressed by a new president. Among these was the need to align the organization design (staffing, structure, systems) to fit the desired strategy.

Part 10 Strategic Control and Corporate Governance

Enerplus Corporation was transitioning from being a buy-and-sell energy trust to a company engaged in exploration and exploitation. It required two new board members and Sue MacKenzie's name was proposed to the CEO by the Enerplus vice president of corporate services. While MacKenzie was intrigued with the idea, she had never actively considered board service as a career step and she now had a new career direction at the Banff Centre. She undertook a thorough assessment of this board opportunity with attention to the career benefits, personal benefits, potential risks, impact on her personal life, and "match" with her new career. Following a series of meetings, MacKenzie was invited to serve on the board and she now had to make a decision: should she accept or decline the invitation?

A successful B.C.-based Canadian road construction and maintenance company is contemplating U.S. market entry via a subsidiary in Texas. The case deals with market entry considerations: speed of entry, the need to invest in learning about a market, and decisions regarding who would manage the subsidiary as well as the proposed governance and control structure.

Part 11 Strategic Leadership: Creating a Learning Organization and an Ethical Organization

By 2013, Sobey's Inc., one of Canada's largest food retailers, planned to develop a sustainable seafood strategy. While data collection, metric selection, employee incentives and customer education were important parts of this emerging strategy, a central decision was what products to choose to sell or not to sell. Certain major competitors had announced that they would sell only "certified sustainable" seafood, an approach strongly advocated by well-known environmental organizations. Sobey's, on the other hand, decided that to abandon uncertified seafood would not only hamper its bottom line but also would eliminate its ability to push the very fisheries that needed more guidance towards better practices. Yet, to continue to sell "red zone" seafood was controversial and could jeopardize Sobey's standing as a leader in sustainable practices. In this context, the vice-president of sustainability had to implement a seafood strategy by year's end.

In September 2009, Brian Lee purchased a computer game developed by a major company and, like other customers, he was experiencing difficulty running it. The source of the problems was a highly restrictive system of digital rights management (DRM), which, while more or less universally disliked, was causing serious technical problems for a minority of users. Lee began to share his experience on the company's message board and was engaging in a debate about online piracy with a company representative. He was curious about piracy in the file-sharing age and wondered why it would be wrong to download a pirated version of the game with the DRM circumvented. The case deals with an ethical issue which resonates with students.

This case examines the giant Canadian mining corporation, Barrick Gold Corporation (Barrick), (called Africa Barrick Gold plc since 2009), and the way it engages in sustainable community developments that surround its mining activities in Tanzania. Following recent organized tensions and heightened criticism from local communities, media, international social lobbyists and local not-for-profit organizations (NFOs), Barrick has attempted to deal with the local communities in a responsible manner. At issue for senior management was whether there was much more that it could reasonably do to resolve the tensions. The case considers: how MNEs seek social license and local legitimacy; the relevance of hybrid institutional infrastructures; the evolving global roles for large corporations and their subsidiaries.

This case traces the establishment and subsequent operation of FIJI Water LLC and its bottling subsidiary, Natural Waters of Viti Limited, the first company in Fiji extracting, bottling and marketing artesian water coming from a virgin ecosystem found on Fiji's main island of Viti Levu. The case reviews the growth and market expansion of this highly successful company. The company has grown rapidly over the past decade and a half, and now exports bottled water into many countries in the world including Canada from its production plant located in the Fiji Islands. In 2008, FIJI Water was the leading imported bottled water brand in the United States. In the context of great marketing success of the FIJI brand, the case focuses on how the company has responded to a number of corporate social responsibility (CSR) issues, including measuring and reducing its carbon footprint, responsibilities to key stakeholders, and concerns of the Fiji government with regard to taxation and transfer pricing issues.

Part 12 Managing Innovation and Fostering Corporate Entrepreneurship

A proposed private-public partnership (P3) involves a Calgary-based private enterprise, Alta Injection Molding (Alta), the Southern Alberta Institute of Technology (SAIT) and the government of Canada. Alta has been chosen to collaborate with SAIT because it developed a unique way to generate revenue throughout its value chain. Alta's strategy towards fostering innovation revolves around a seven-step approach to turnkey innovation. In this P3, Alta would have access to the equipment, while SAIT students would gain exposure to the plastic manufacturing processes and have the opportunity to be connected to company leaders or distribution channels through Alta's large network. Considering the parties involved in this P3, significant differences exist in terms of mindsets, goals and concerns. The president of Alta is wondering whether to participate in the P3, and, if he does, what steps he should take to ensure his business remains viable while not impeding SAIT or the government's goals.

IMAX was involved in several aspects of the large-format film business: production, distribution, theatre operations, system development and leasing. The case illustrates IMAX's use of its unique capabilities to pursue a focused differentiation strategy. IMAX was initially focused on large format films that were educational yet entertaining, and the theatres were located in institutions such as museums, aquariums and national parks. However, IMAX found that its growth and profitability were constrained by its niche strategy. In response, IMAX sought to grow by expanding into multiplexes. Additionally, IMAX expanded its film portfolio by converting Hollywood movies, such as Harry Potter and Superman, into the large film format. This shift in strategy was supported by the development of two technological capabilities—DMR for conversion of standard 35 mm film into large format, and DMX to convert standard multiplexes to IMAX systems. The shift in strategy was partially successful, but carried the risk of IMAX losing its unique reputation.

Preface and Acknowledgements

This book was made possible with the academic and intellectual support from colleagues at the Ivey Business School, Western University, and others across the country. The primary stimulus for this book was the ongoing need for new, high-quality Canadian material.

Having decided to produce a book of cases in strategic management, a number of other decisions were made: (1) to bring together primarily Canadian cases written not only at Ivey, but by faculty across North America, Europe and Asia; (2) to include only decision-oriented cases, which arguably provide the best training for future managers; and (3) to include cases dealing with international business, high-technology industries, service industries, not-for-profit industries, and business ethics.

Much useful feedback was solicited and received on the tenth edition from colleagues at institutions across Canada. This included detailed reviews from the following individuals:

Jeffrey Moretz, UOIT
Siva Prasad Ravi, Thompson Rivers University
Stoney Kudel, George Brown College
Paul Doherty, University of Waterloo
Naheed K. Nenshi, Mount Royal University
Jean-Marie Nkongolo-Bakenda, University of Regina
Barry O'Brien, York University
Clem Ramchatesingh, Humber College
Mark Simpson, George Brown College
Laura A. Thurnheer, Okanagan College
Bernie Williams, University of Lethbridge.

This edition contains 20 new cases (Methanex: Developing Strategy in a Commodity Industry; Vice Media: Competitive Advantage and Global Expansion; Bombardier Aerospace: The CSeries Dilemma; Movember: More Mo Sistas; Sher-Wood Hockey Sticks: Global Sourcing; Charles Chocolates; Entrepreneurs at Twitter: Building a Brand, A Social Tool or a Tech Powerhouse; car2go: Individual Urban Mobility and the Sharing Economy; Sawchyn Guitars: Can an Old Business Learn New Tricks?; Phase Separation Solutions (PS2): The China Question; Cervus Equipment Corporation: Harvesting a New Future; Where Have You Been?: An Exercise to Assess Your Exposure to the Rest of the World's Peoples; Developing an International Growth Strategy at New York Fries; Ethiopian Airlines: Bringing Africa Together; Firstwell Corporation and the Production Mandate Question; Canadian National Railway Company: Culture Change; Project HUGO at LHSC: Leading Urgent Change in Healthcare; Enerplus Corporation: Assessing the Board Invitation; Sobey's Inc.: A Strategic Approach to Sustainable Seafood Supply; and Alta and SAIT: A Potential Private-Public Partnership). New cases were written or selected not only for their ability to achieve the desired pedagogical objectives, but with an eye to retaining student interest. Some of the new cases deal with such topical issues as new media, energy, sustainability, internationalization, and entrepreneurial start-ups.

Professors wishing to delve deeply into certain industries have the option of reorganizing the available material. The book contains multiple cases according to each of the following industry groups or sectors:

- Recreation
- Consumer Products
- Energy
- Mining
- Retail

- Family Business
- Financial Services
- E-Business
- Health
- Transportation

The cases themselves have been organized into the 12 subject areas that follow. These subject areas follow closely the current, mainstream approach to the teaching of strategic management.

1. Strategic Management: Creating Competitive Advantages
2. Analyzing the External Environment of the Firm
3. Assessing the Internal Environment of the Firm
4. Assessing the Intellectual Assets of the Firm
5. Business-Level Strategy: Creating and Sustaining Competitive Advantages
6. Corporate-Level Strategy: Creating Value through Diversification
7. International Strategy: Creating Value in Global Markets
8. Competitive Dynamics and Entrepreneurial Strategies
9. Strategic Control and Corporate Governance
10. Creating Effective Organizational Designs
11. Strategic Leadership: Creating a Learning, Ethical and Socially Responsible Organization
12. Managing Innovation and Fostering Corporate Entrepreneurship

Comprehensive Case Teaching Notes are available to text adopters for all cases from this text's Online Learning Centre.

I am indebted to several groups of people for assisting in the preparation of this book. First, I am grateful to the case contributors from Ivey. From the faculty side I wish to thank Stewart Thornhill, Eric Morse, Andreas Schotter, Chris Williams, Glenn Rowe, Simon Parker and Cara Maurer. In addition, I acknowledge the contributions of the following current doctoral and research assistants at Ivey: Michael Sartor, Ken Mark, Paul Bigus, Jordan Mitchell, Megan Zhang, Meredith Woodwark, Yamlaksira Getachew, and Matthew Wong.

A number of one-time Ivey PhD students who contributed to the cases in this book are now faculty members in their own right. These include:

Nikhil Celly, The University of Hong Kong
Majid Eghbali-Zarch, Memorial University
Anthony Goerzen, Queens University
Louis Hebert, (HEC) Montreal
Nathan Lupton, Fordham University, New York
Kent E. Neupert, Boise State University, Idaho
George Peng, University of Regina
Suhaib Riaz, University of Massachusetts, Boston

Michael Roberts, MacEwan University
Vanessa Strike, University of British Columbia
Jing'an Tang, Sacred Heart University, Connecticut

Case contributors from other institutions include:

John Adamson, Cereson Inc.
Farzad H. Alvi, EGADE Business School, Mexico
Alex Beamish, Writer and Editor, London, Ontario
Daniel Doiron, University of New Brunswick
Carolyn Egri, Simon Fraser University
Travis Guay, Plainsman Manufacturing
Ella Korets-Smith, Immunovaccine Inc.
Michael Maher, University of Calgary
James McMaster, University of The South Pacific, Fiji
Malcolm Munro, University of Calgary
Anil Nair, Old Dominion University, Virginia
Aloysius Newenham-Kahindi, University of Saskatchewan
Jan Nowak, Central European University, Hungary
Michael Parent, Simon Fraser University
Michele Parkin, Western University
Tom A. Poynter, St. John's, Newfoundland
Sharda Prashad, Canadian Business
Davis Schryer, Cervus Equipment Corporation
Daniel Shapiro, Simon Fraser University
Ali Taleb, University of New Brunswick
Shreya Tekriwal, Hacking Health
Charlene Zietsma, York University

The following doctoral and research assistants from other institutions are also acknowledged: Dmitry Alenushkin, Wilfred Cheung, Chris Ellison, Prarthana Kumar, Jeremy Kyle, Adam Mills and Stacey Morrison.

In addition, I wish to thank the various executives who provided the required access to complete the cases in this book, and to recognize those students on whom the cases were tested for classroom use.

I look forward to your feedback.

Paul W. Beamish

Superior Learning Solutions and Support

The McGraw-Hill Ryerson team is ready to help you assess and integrate any of our products, technology, and services into your course for optimal teaching and learning performance. Whether it's helping your students improve their grades, or putting your entire course online, the McGraw-Hill Ryerson team is here to help you do it. Contact your Learning Solutions Consultant today to learn how to maximize all of McGraw-Hill Ryerson's resources!

CourseSmart

CourseSmart brings together thousands of textbooks across hundreds of courses in an eTextbook format, providing unique benefits to students and faculty. By purchasing an eTextbook, students can save up to 50 percent on the cost of a print textbook, reduce their impact on the environment, and gain access to powerful Web tools for learning including full-text search, notes and highlighting, and email tools for sharing notes between classmates. For faculty, CourseSmart provides instant access for reviewing and comparing textbooks and course materials in their discipline area without the time, cost, and environmental impact of mailing print exam copies. For further details contact your *i*Learning Sales Specialist or go to **www.coursesmart.com**.

Instructor Online Learning Centre

Access comprehensive Case Teaching Notes for all cases from the Instructor Online Learning Centre (www.mheducation.ca/olc/beamish).

Methanex:
Developing Strategy
In A Commodity Industry

John Floren, chief executive officer (CEO) of Methanex, looked up from his notes and stared out his office window at the fog gently blanketing the harbour in Vancouver, Canada. It was January 2013. Floren had recently been appointed president and CEO of Methanex, the world's largest methanol producer. Before the 2008 global economic crisis, the senior management team had developed a strategy that had increased annual revenues by more than 30 per cent and earnings by almost 60 per cent. Despite this success, Floren had concerns regarding the sustainability of the corporate strategy's focused scope.

Methanex had been successful in large part due to its cost leadership and reliable delivery, achieved by building multimillion-dollar production facilities in remote, natural gas-rich regions of the world that it supported through its own distribution and logistics system. Unlike many of its competitors, Methanex was not diversified. While Floren believed this lack of diversification allowed his organization to focus singularly and clearly on its strategy, he knew that the company was completely reliant on the stability of the market for methanol. At any time, problems of poor infrastructure and political instability in emerging market economies could result in inconsistent gas supply, crippling Methanex's production and, therefore, impacting its supply chain.

Top management at Methanex undertook a quarterly risk-review process that included a systematic review of corporate strategy and the competitive landscape in the methanol

Adam Mills, Daniel Shapiro, Carolyn Egri and Michael Parent wrote this case solely to provide material for class discussion. The authors do not intend to illustrate either effective or ineffective handling of a managerial situation. The authors may have disguised certain names and other identifying information to protect confidentiality.

This publication may not be transmitted, photocopied, digitized or otherwise reproduced in any form or by any means without the permission of the copyright holder. Reproduction of this material is not covered under authorization by any reproduction rights organization. To order copies or request permission to reproduce materials, contact Ivey Publishing, Ivey Business School, Western University, London, Ontario, Canada, N6G 0N1; (t) 519.661.3208; (e) cases@ivey.ca; www.iveycases.com.

Copyright © 2013, Richard Ivey School of Business Foundation   Version: 2013-06-11

One time permission to reproduce granted by Richard Ivey School of Business Foundation on April 22, 2014.

IVEY | Publishing

industry. The primary objectives were to identify organizational risks and opportunities and to develop appropriate strategic responses. The Methanex board of directors had taken a keen interest in the strategic positioning of the firm and had requested Floren present his strategic recommendations and action plan for the future of Methanex later that morning. The issue of strategy direction was particularly important in light of the market valuation of the company being only two-thirds of the replacement value of its assets.

Among Floren's many concerns were the impact of the global recession and, in particular, threatened production facilities in Egypt and Chile. In Egypt, unpredicted and unpredictable social unrest threatened production from a brand new $870 million[1] facility. In Chile, once one of the firm's major production centres, 2.86 million tonnes of plant capacity sat idle because of the Argentinian government's ban of natural resource exports. While these risks were substantial, Floren also saw an opportunity for Methanex to expand in China. China was becoming a significant player in the global supply and demand for methanol due to two recent discoveries for alternative methanol use: as a component of dimethyl ether (a substitute for propane as household fuel) and for conversion into olefins to make polypropylene plastic. However, Methanex had little presence in China and no significant investments in these new local applications. Although the potential rewards were high, so were the entry risks.

Floren knew the board was particularly concerned with strategic options for the future. With a $2.5 billion organization under their control, he and the board would need to carefully weigh their options for both short-term profits and long-term growth.

METHANOL

Methanol was a widely traded chemical commodity consumed in all major regions of the world. Also known as methyl alcohol, methyl hydrate or wood naphtha, methanol was a simple form of alcohol that was used as a base ingredient in the production and manufacturing of a multitude of products globally. While methanol occurred naturally in the environment in minute quantities, firms operating in the petrochemical industry produced the global supply of commercial methanol. In 2011, annual global demand for methanol was almost 50 million tonnes.

Methanol was created through a process of heating natural gas with steam to a temperature of 900°C to produce "syngas" (carbon oxides and hydrogen in gaseous form), cooling and condensing the resultant gas, then distilling the crude product with an additional catalyst into commercial-grade methanol (see Exhibit 1).

Demand

Methanol in its pure form is highly toxic and flammable and, therefore, has a very limited number of direct applications. Methanol was used primarily as a "feedstock" (a base ingredient) in the production of more stable chemicals. Approximately two-thirds of the global methanol supply was used in traditional applications, producing chemical derivatives such as formaldehyde and acetic acid. The remaining one-third was used in the energy sector for gasoline blending and in the production of dimethyl ether (DME) and methyl tertiary butyl ether (MTBE) (see Exhibits 2 and 3) and the conversion of methanol to olefins (MTO).

---

[1]All currencies are in US$ unless otherwise stated.

Roughly 34 per cent of the global methanol supply was used in the production of formaldehyde, a primary element in numerous building products, including wood adhesives (for plywood, particle board and fibreboard), polymers, paints, polyurethane and automotive parts. Demand for formaldehyde remained strong, although growing public concern surrounded the health risks associated with occupational exposure to the chemical. In May 2009, the U.S. National Cancer Institute (NCI) published a report on the health effects of occupational exposure to formaldehyde and a possible link to leukemia, multiple myeloma and Hodgkin's disease[2].

Acetic acid, accounting for 13 per cent of the global methanol demand, was primarily used in the production of vinyl acetate for later use in polymer adhesives such as wood glues. Acetic acid was additionally used as a base component for such products as photographic film, solvents, textiles and vinegar.

In the energy sector, demand for methanol had been increasing (see Exhibit 4). Eleven per cent of the global methanol supply was used in the production of MTBE. MTBE was primarily used as a source of octane and to oxygenate gasoline to reduce harmful automobile emissions. In response to environmental concerns in the late 1990s, demand for MTBE as a fuel additive in the United States rose to roughly two million tonnes annually by 2005, approximately 6 per cent of global demand. However, the presence of MTBE in some U.S. water supplies led to public concern regarding MTBE's safety, which led to the 2005 passing of the U.S. Energy Policy Act, which called for the replacement of MTBE with an alternative gasoline additive. MTBE was almost entirely phased out of U.S. gasoline by 2007. MTBE demand was also affected by some European and Latin American countries imposing taxes on fossil fuels, with the intention of encouraging the use of alternative fuels such as biofuel. However, MTBE demand globally remained relatively constant due to its use as a clean energy component in Europe and many developing economies.

Two relatively new uses of methanol, fuel blending and producing dimethyl ether (DME), had been increasing in demand annually. In 2010, approximately 10 per cent of the global methanol supply was used for fuel blending. To reduce reliance on crude oil for transportation fuel, methanol-blended fuels had been increasing in popularity as an alternative to gasoline. In 2009, China introduced national standards for the use of M85 and M100 (85 per cent and 100 per cent methanol blends) and, in the coming years, was expected to introduce M15 (a 15 per cent blend) as a national standard. Several countries, including Australia, Iran, Pakistan, Malaysia and Trinidad, were also researching methanol fuel blending as an alternative to pure fossil fuel.

Dimethyl ether comprised approximately 7 per cent of the global supply for methanol. The primary use of DME was as a fuel substitute for propane, used for residential heating and cooking needs. DME was an attractive alternative fuel because it was non-toxic and harmless to the ozone layer. As fossil fuel prices and concerns about emissions from carbon-based fuels rose globally, DME was quickly becoming an attractive alternative for domestic heating. The single largest market for residential DME was China, but other countries, such as Indonesia, Japan, Sweden, Iran, Egypt and India, were developing DME applications. DME also had applications as a propellant in aerosol containers, a solvent base and a refrigerant.

---

[2]L.E. Beane Freeman, A. Blair, J.H. Lubin, P.A. Stewart, R.B. Hayes, R.N. Hoover and M. Hauptmann, "Mortality from Lymphohematopoietic Malignancies Among Workers in Formaldehyde Industries,"
The National Cancer Institute Cohort, May 20, 2009, JNCI, Vol. 101, No. 10.

Annual global demand for methanol was 48 million tonnes. Due to regulations and restrictions around the uses of formaldehyde and MTBE, as well as rapid technological advancements in alternative energy sources, the North American market demanded only 14 per cent of the global supply, around seven million tonnes. China was the single largest consumer of methanol, in large part due to its fuel-blending policies and increasing reliance on DME. China demanded 37 per cent of the global supply, almost 18 million tonnes. The rest of the Asia-Pacific region (excluding China) accounted for 22 per cent of global demand, Europe for 23 per cent and Latin America the remaining 4 per cent (see Exhibit 5).

Supply

Supply to the methanol industry was largely dependent on the delivery of the primary feedstock, either natural gas or coal, to production facilities. Natural gas supply was subject to fluctuating prices, interruptions to supply lines and international policies and regulations governing imports and exports.

Methanol output supply could be greatly affected by planned and unplanned outages of methanol plants. The average annual output capacity of modern methanol production plants was between 1.3 million and 1.5 million tonnes, although most operated at approximately 85 per cent of total capacity to allow for output increases when economically beneficial. Considering the total market size, fluctuations in production from one large plant could have significant impacts on global supply and, therefore, on prices. In the long run, global methanol supply was largely dependent on industry growth and additions to global production capacity.

Since storage of methanol was costly and not directly related to revenue generation, most producers attempted to closely match their production output to customer demand. As such, input fluctuations and unforeseen plant outages dramatically reduced the available supplies of methanol, which caused methanol prices to fluctuate widely. As with most commodity markets, significant supply shortages caused spot prices to rise steeply, leading to increased production output from high-cost producers, which then caused spot prices to fall due to abundant supply. However, traditional demand for methanol was largely unaffected by changes in spot price for two reasons: methanol had few cost-effective substitutes for its traditional uses in the production of formaldehyde and acetic acid, and methanol costs accounted for relatively small percentages of the final products' downstream value. For methanol energy applications, demand was more elastic and impacted by the ratio of methanol and oil prices.

When spot prices of methanol rose above $340, the energy equivalent of $90 per barrel for oil, high-cost Chinese and Russian producers (who primarily produced methanol from coal, not from natural gas) displaced imported methanol and often began exporting methanol (see Exhibit 6). However, with growing demand for methanol in fuel blending and DME production, Chinese producers had a decreasing incentive to generate methanol for export.

The methanol market saw a compound annual growth rate (CAGR) of 4.7 per cent from 1997 through 2011 and was projected to have a future CAGR of up to 7.3 per cent, based on rising oil costs and increasing global demand for alternative fuel sources (see Exhibit 4). With the exception of 2009, methanol had traded above its energy value (i.e., its crude oil price equivalent) consistently for the past 15 years (see Exhibit 7).

METHANEX

Company History

Methanex was first known as Ocelot Industries, incorporated in 1968 in Canada as an oil and gas exploration company. In 1991, Ocelot Industries split into three entities, with the methanol and ammonia businesses forming Methanex Corporation. Originally only a North American enterprise, Methanex began international expansion by acquiring interests in methanol operations in the Caribbean and Europe in 1992, and in New Zealand and Chile in 1993. The international expansion was prompted by an expected (and subsequently realized) escalation in the price of methane in North America, as demand for natural gas escalated. The company continued to expand internationally by seeking remote locations where natural gas was "stranded." When high reserves of natural gas were identified, but local industry had limited use for the resource, Methanex was able to negotiate favourable long-term supply and pricing agreements.

By 2000, Methanex had become the world's largest producer of methanol, with production operations in Trinidad, New Zealand and Chile, and marketing offices in the Asia-Pacific region, North America, South America and Europe. The company had signed long-term contracts based on monthly volumes with numerous major multinational manufacturers, none of which represented more than 10 per cent of Methanex's revenues.

Trinidad. In 1992, Methanex acquired partial marketing rights to the 850,000 tonnes of methanol produced annually at the Titan facility owned by Metallgesellschaft of Germany.[3] In 2000, Methanex acquired exclusive marketing rights plus 10 per cent ownership of the plant and, in 2003, purchased the remaining 90 per cent from Metallgesellschaft. In 2004, its Atlas facility, a joint venture between BP (36.9 per cent) and Methanex (63.1 per cent), came online with a production capacity of 1.7 million tonnes per year, at the time, the largest methanol plant in the world. Trinidad was developed by Methanex as a low-cost production hub because of its convenient access to both North American and European markets (see Exhibit 8). The Trinidad operations generated 1.78 million tonnes of output annually. Contracts with the national natural gas suppliers for Methanex's two plants ran until 2014 and 2024. In 2010, Methanex initiated a pilot program to introduce methanol fuel blending in Trinidad.

New Zealand. By 1995, Methanex owned three methanol plants in New Zealand (two in Motunui and another in the Waitara Valley) with a total capacity of 2.23 million tonnes. Due to economics and resource extraction capabilities in the region, the local supply of natural gas was largely dependent on short-term contracts. In 2004 and 2005, unfavourable economic conditions led Methanex to idle its two larger plants, leaving only one smaller plant in Waitara operational. In 2007, sufficient supply contracts were secured to reopen one of the Motunui plants. By 2010, the company was producing 0.83 million tonnes annually from New Zealand facilities. With an additional 1.4 million tonnes of production capacity sitting idle, Methanex entered into a 50 per cent joint venture with Kea Exploration to develop oil and gas extraction facilities in the nearby Taranaki Basin.

---

[3]Metallgesellschaft owned two facilities in the Point Lisas Industrial Estate in Trinidad and had named them Titan and Atlas, respectively.

Chile. Although expansion into Chile in 1993 had been considered risky due to perceived political instability and relatively high capital investment costs, for Methanex, the move had delivered benefits as a result of low production costs and generally stable supplies. By 2005, Methanex had four fully operational plants and $1 billion invested in Chile. Largely dependent on natural gas inputs from Argentina, Chilean operations supplied 3.8 million tonnes of methanol, approximately 12 per cent of global supply. In June 2007, the Argentinian government decided to halt all exports of natural resources, almost instantaneously cutting off the primary supply of methane to Methanex's production facilities. Three of the four plants were shut down, and annual output from Chile dropped to 0.94 million tonnes. By 2010, Methanex was operating only one production facility in Chile, but was aggressively backing natural gas exploration and acquisition in the country. Investment opportunities had been pursued with several large energy companies, including GeoPark Chile Limited and state-owned Empresa Nacional del Petróleo.

Egypt. In early 2011, a 1.3 million tonne methanol production plant came online in Egypt. Located in Damietta on the Mediterranean Sea, the Egyptian plant was operated by EMethanex, a joint venture between Methanex (60 per cent) and the Egyptian government (40 per cent) that had been in place since late 2005. The capital cost of the facility was $870 million. The launch of the facility coincided with widespread anti-government protests and civil unrest in Egypt. For the safety and security of its assets and its largely Egyptian work-force, Methanex temporarily closed the plant and its Cairo offices until conditions stabilized. The plant, with capacity to generate more than $300 million in annual revenues, was brought online for a brief period in the spring of 2011 when peace was temporarily restored by Egyptian military control of the country. However, social unrest with the new regime began to swell in the following months, and the plant was again idled a few months later.

Canada. Methanex's original Canadian operations were serviced by short-term contracts, and thus were more sensitive to fluctuations in the supply and prices of natural gas. These fluctuations benefited the company in times of relatively low-cost North American pricing, but left it exposed when the price increased. Due to price volatility and high production costs, the original production facility in Kitimat, British Columbia, permanently ceased operations at the end of 2005 and was retained solely as a storage facility. Methanex's three facilities in Medicine Hat, Alberta, were idled and shut down between 1999 and 2002, due to the region's exceptionally high natural gas prices. However, in late 2010, the company decided to reopen its half-million tonne facility in Medicine Hat in response to rapidly declining prices in the North American natural gas market.

Production and Distribution

The roughly seven million tonnes of methanol sold annually by Methanex met 16 per cent of the global demand for methanol, 59 per cent of which was sold to the Asia-Pacific region, 23 per cent to Europe and 18 per cent to the Americas.

Since the mid-1990s, the company's strategy had been to become the industry cost leader in both the production and distribution of methanol. One of the company's stated objectives was to achieve the lowest delivered cost in each region it served

The production of methanol was reliant on two key processes: (1) the purchase and supply of natural gas to its production facilities and (2) the delivery of methanol to its customers. Energy and natural gas accounted for almost 80 per cent of Methanex's cash costs. Long-run contracts with low-cost suppliers of natural gas partially mitigated Methanex's risk from fluctuations in supply and prices.

For the global distribution of its methanol, Methanex required a fleet of tankers, barges, trains and trucks. In the early 1990s, the company hired ships on a spot basis, or short-term contract, to transport its methanol to customers. However, in 1995, the company developed the Waterfront Shipping Company, a stand-alone business created to manage a fleet of ocean-going vessels. The decision to develop its own distribution and logistics network resulted from the recognition that the methanol plants had life expectancies of more than 30 years and that delivery of its product to the customer was integral to the company's success. By 2007, Methanex's fleet had grown to more than 20 ships, including several of the world's largest chemical tankers. Waterfront Shipping offered transportation services on a contract basis to other companies on "backhauls," return trips to Methanex's storage and distribution terminals when the vessels were not being used to transport methanol.

Methanex attempted to reduce its vulnerability to market fluctuations in both price and supply by storing inventory. Unlike its industry competitors, Methanex owned storage and terminal facilities in key distribution hubs in Canada, Korea, China, the Netherlands and the United States. The company supplemented its own production with purchases of methanol from other producers when prices were favourable and kept approximately one-month's worth of methanol supply on hand. Despite the high costs associated with storage, Methanex viewed this product supplementation as integral to mitigating market risks and ensuring the company's ability to service clients consistently.

Because of its ability to deliver to all major methanol markets in the world through its extensive logistics network, irrespective of circumstance, Methanex was the preferred supplier for many of the world's major chemical customers, including Univar, Momentive, Lyondell, Evonik, Samsung, Taminco, Dow Chemical, and LG. Regional networks supported distribution and customer service through marketing offices in North America (Dallas and Vancouver), Europe (Brussels and Billingham, England), the Asia-Pacific region (Hong Kong, Shanghai, Tokyo and Seoul) and Latin America (Santiago, Chile).

COMPETITIVE LANDSCAPE

Competition

Methanex competed with many oil and gas companies for market share in the global methanol industry (see Exhibit 9). Most of its competitors did not consider methanol to be their core business, but produced methanol as one small portion of larger petrochemical production organizations. Many of Methanex's competitors, particularly in the Middle East, were state-owned and thus had differed in their objectives, cost structures and access to financial resources.

MHTL. Methanol Holdings Trinidad Limited (MHTL), headquartered in Trinidad, was the second largest producer of methanol in the world, with approximately 9.5 per cent global market share. MHTL was formed in 1999 with the consolidation of shareholding and management of three smaller companies and was a subsidiary of CL Financial Limited, created in 1993 to financially support government initiatives. CL Financial was a holding company that provided funding and management oversight to capital-intensive national projects, including subsidiary companies in financial services, property and real estate development, media and communications, forestry and agriculture, energy and petrochemicals, medical services and manufacturing.

MHTL owned five methanol plants in Trinidad, which had a combined production capacity of more than four million tonnes of methanol annually. MHTL was largely responsible for making Trinidad the world's leading exporter of methanol. In 2009, MHTL opened a new petrochemical complex of seven distinct but integrated plants for the production of urea, ammonia nitrate and melamine. The project represented a strategic diversification out of methanol into a broader range of petrochemicals for MHTL.

Sabic. Established by royal decree in 1976, the Saudi Basic Industries Corporation (Sabic) was the Middle East's largest non-oil company and the 13th largest in the world in terms of market capitalization. The company, a joint venture between the Saudi Arabian government (70 per cent) and the Gulf Cooperation Council (30 per cent), was created to make use of the natural gas associated with the production of crude oil for the production of chemicals, polymers and fertilizers. SABIC comprised six strategic business units: basic chemicals, intermediates, polyolefins, polyvinyl chloride (PVC)/polyester, fertilizers and metals. In 2010, Sabic was the third largest global methanol producer, with 8 per cent market share and approximately 3.5 million tonnes of output.

MGC. Mitsubishi Gas Chemical (MGC), founded in 1952, was the first methanol producer in Japan. By 2010, MGC had become the fourth largest supplier of methanol globally. MGC owned and operated joint ventures in Saudi Arabia, Venezuela and Brunei, producing methanol, ammonia and related derivatives. MGC, following Methanex's lead, operated two methanol storage facilities in the United States.

MSK. MSK (Mitsubishi Corporation) held equity positions and marketing rights in production facilities in Saudi Arabia and Venezuela, as well as off take positions in several diverse locations globally.

Petronas. Oil and gas producer Petronas, wholly owned by the Malaysian government, was ranked one of Fortune 500's largest companies in the world. A relatively small petrochemicals division of Petronas produced about two million tonnes of methanol in 2010, approximately one-quarter of its 2006 output of methanol.

Methanol Pricing

The contract price of methanol, which was posted monthly by trade newsletters, was driven by commodity spot prices. These unofficial prices were approximated using the average contract prices from several global suppliers.

Methanex's market-leader position enabled it, to some degree, to influence price fluctuations, but not price trends. For example, Methanex could absorb minor fluctuations in demand and supply through its global supply chain in an effort to remove volatility and set more consistent long-term supply prices for its customers.

Because of its size, market-leader position and ability to supply methanol consistently to customers around the globe, Methanex prices were regarded in the industry as the standard for contract price rates. In May 2001, Methanex began publishing the Methanex Non-Discounted Reference Price (MNDRP) on a monthly basis, which was quickly adopted by news outlets and industry reporting firms as the general benchmark price for methanol contract prices. The term *non-discounted* refers to the initial starting bid of a contract price; discounts were generally offered on the basis of contract size, length and service requirements.

Based on the success of the MNDRP, Methanex began posting European rates from its Rotterdam office in January 2002 as the Methanex European Posted Contract Price (MEPCP). In September of the same year, the company began posting the Methanex Asian Posted Contract Price (MAPCP).

PERFORMANCE

Since 1995, having divested its 51 per cent ownership in its only non-core business (an ammonia plant to commercialize the by-product of the methanol reaction process), Methanex had focused solely on producing methanol. As such, the company set itself apart from its competitors, who often integrated methanol production into a diversified portfolio of chemical offerings from a single production plant. Over the past 10 years, Methanex had outperformed the Dow Jones Chemical Index, which included many of its more diversified competitors.

In 2010, Methanex reported $267 million in EBITDA (earnings before interest, taxes, depreciation and amortization) and net income of $102 million on $1.97 billion in annual revenues (see Exhibits 10 and 11). The company's earnings peaked in 2006 at $482 million. Methanex was severely affected in 2009, when its revenues fell to half of its 2007 numbers and the company just barely broke even. In addition to the global financial crisis of 2008/09, which led to decreased production in many of Methanex's downstream methanol consumers, 2009 saw global methanol prices fall, as China restricted imports, which generated a surge in domestic production. It appeared in 2010 that Methanex's revenues were recovering with the global economy: total sales by volume (thousands of tonnes) grew by 16 per cent, outpacing the global industry demand growth of 13 per cent.

In 2010, Methanex remained the single largest methanol producer in the world for the 10th year in a row. Unlike its competitors with more than 10 times the infrastructure, Methanex employed just over 1,000 employees globally, including 200 at its corporate offices in Vancouver, Canada. Whenever possible, the company hired and trained local employees to work in its plants. Only a small number of employees were required at each production facility (compared with the hundreds required at similarly sized competing operations), due to the company's continual investments in technology and the high level of computerization and mechanization of its plants.

LOOKING TO THE FUTURE

While Floren was justifiably proud of the company's achievements, he knew that important strategic decisions would need to be made. Methanex faced immediate challenges associated with the political situation in Egypt, the idling of the company's newest production plant and the shared ownership of the joint venture with an unstable government.

In Chile, as a result of natural gas supply shortages, the company had been forced to close three of its primary production facilities and was sitting on more than two million tonnes of idle production capacity despite aggressive natural gas exploration efforts in the region. Floren was also concerned about MHTL's expansion in Trinidad and one of Methanex's long-term supply contracts that was up for renewal in a few short years.

One possible risk mitigation strategy would be to modify the strategy of seeking low-cost sources of natural gas in emerging markets. Floren had assembled an in-house development team to focus on potential locations for new production facilities where the political, economic and environmental conditions were favourable. For future methanol production plants, he required the team to locate natural gas that was accessible, transportable and available at secured low costs for 25 to 30 years. The company was also becoming involved in research into future uses of methanol and alternative sources of methane for the production of methanol.

Similar to those at many companies, Floren believed that China was critical to his company's future. In 2010, Methanex had the opportunity to participate in a dimethyl ether (DME) project in China. Methanex would be a 20 per cent shareholder and the sole supplier of methanol at a 200,000 tonne plant currently under construction near Shanghai. Methanex and China's XinAo Group would ideally enter into a long-term arrangement, under which Methanex would supply an initial quantity of approximately 300,000 tonnes per annum of methanol to XinAo. If successful, Methanex could potentially increase its investment in this venture and leverage it into future opportunities in China. Floren was aware that DME as an alternative residential fuel source was gaining traction not only in China but also in other countries such as Indonesia, Japan, Sweden, Iran and India. Pursuing this option would require an important modification to Methanex's focused and singular corporate strategy.

In addition, recent technological advances in China allowed for the conversion of methanol into olefins, piquing the interest of the development team. Olefins (ethylene and propylene) could be processed through a polymerization unit to create polypropylene, one of the world's most widely used plastic substances. Methanol-to-olefin (MTO) processes were being piloted as subunits of existing plants primarily in China; however, if demand for methanol as an input to this process increased significantly, producers would need to purchase additional merchant methanol for input supply. This opportunity could also divert the company from its focused strategy. Although the company had no experience or expertise with MTO technology or processes, expansion into the MTO industry represented a possible growth opportunity for Methanex and would help to secure long-term demand for methanol.

EXHIBIT 1: Methanol Production

Natural Gas
Steam [& Oxygen]
Reforming @ ~900°C
syngas
CO CO2 H2
Compression
Cooling
Synthesis
crude
CH3OH H2O
Distillation
chemical grade
CH3OH

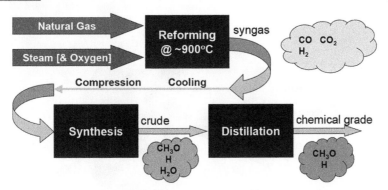

Source: Methanex.

EXHIBIT 2: Uses of Methanol

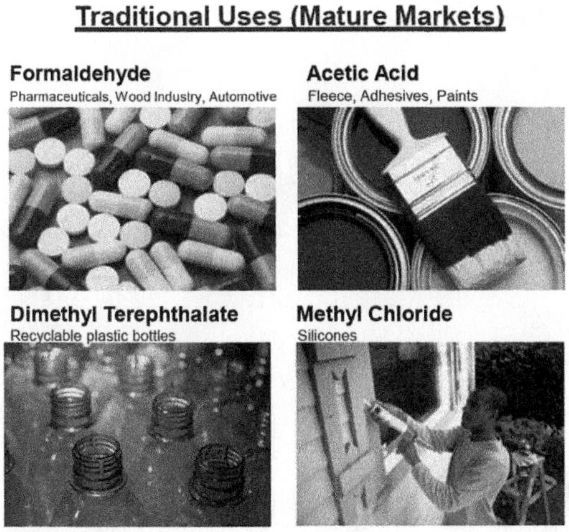

Traditional Uses (Mature Markets)
Formaldehyde
Pharmaceuticals, Wood Industry, Automotive
Acetic Acid
Fleece, Adhesives, Paints
Dimethyl Terephthalate
Recyclable plastic bottles
Methyl Chloride
Silicones

Energy & MTO (High Growth Potential Markets)
Methanol
Fuel Blending
DME
(dimethyl-ether)
BIODIESEL
MTO
Methanol-To-Olefins

Source: Methanex.

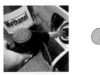

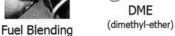

EXHIBIT 3: Methanol Usage by Derivative

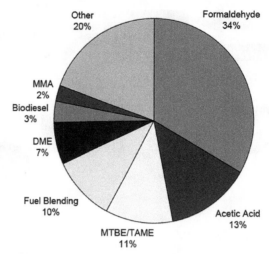

Note: MTBE = methyl tertiary butyl ether; TAME = tert-amyl methyl ether; DME = dimethyl ether; MMA = methyl methacrylate

Source: Methanex.

EXHIBIT 4: Global Demand for Methanol, 1997–2015

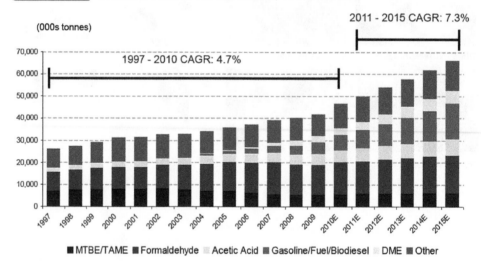

Note: CAGR = compound annual growth rate; MTBE = methyl tertiary butyl ether; TAME = tert-amyl methyl ether; DME = dimethyl ether

Source: Methanex.

EXHIBIT 5: Global Demand for Methanol by Region

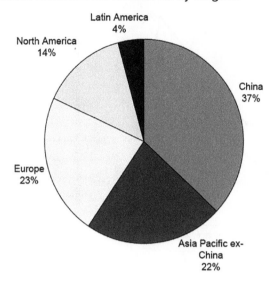

Source: Methanex.

EXHIBIT 6: Methanol Industry Cost Curve

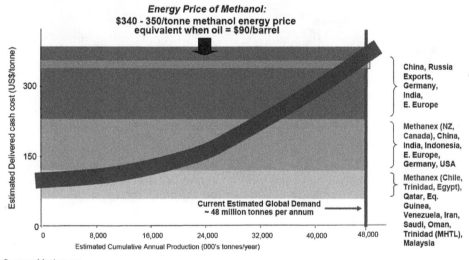

Source: Methanex.

EXHIBIT 7: Methanol Prices Versus Crude Oil Prices, 1996–2010

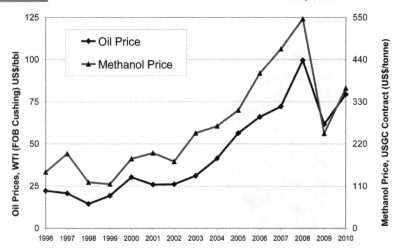

Source: Methanex.

EXHIBIT 8: Methanex's Production and Logistics Network

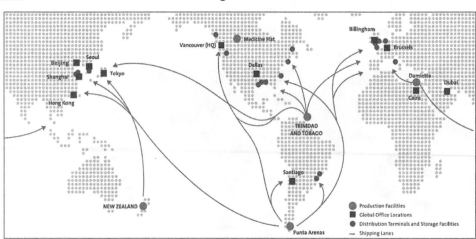

Source: Methanex.

EXHIBIT 9: Leading Methanol Producers (2011)

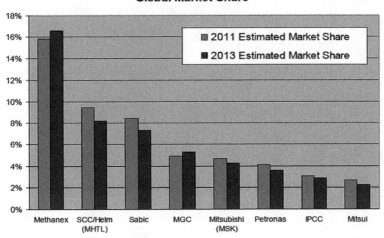

Global Market Share

Note: SCC = Southern Chemical Corporation; MHTL = Methanol Holdings Trinidad Limited; SABIC = Saudi Basic Industries Corporation; MGC = Mitzubishi Gas Chemical, IPCC = Iran Petrochemical Commercial Co.

Source: Methanex; Chemical Markets Associates, Inc. (CMAI).

EXHIBIT 10: Methanex's 10-Years' Financial Highlights

a) Consolidated Balance Sheets 2001–2010

(US$ millions)

	2010	2009	2008	2007	2006	2005	2004	2003	2002	2001
ASSETS										
Cash and cash equivalents	194	170	328	488	355	159	210	288	421	332
Receivables	320	257	213	402	366	296	293	221	201	135
Inventories	230	172	178	312	245	140	142	127	119	100
Prepaid expenses	27	24	17	21	24	14	17	15	12	9
Current assets	771	623	736	1,223	990	609	662	651	753	576
Property, plant and equipment	2,214	2,183	1,899	1,523	1,362	1,395	1,367	1,320	981	1,032
Other assets	85	117	164	116	101	101	96	111	86	85
TOTAL ASSETS	3,070	2,923	2,799	2,862	2,453	2,105	2,125	2,082	1,820	1,693
LIABILITIES AND SHAREHOLDERS' EQUITY										
Accounts payable and accrued liabilities	251	233	235	466	310	235	231	178	136	110
Current maturities on long-term debt	50	29	15	15	14	14	258	21	—	150
Current maturities on other long-term liabilities	13	9	8	17	17	10	10	12	6	5
Current liabilities	314	271	258	498	341	259	499	211	142	265
Long-term debt	897	885	767	582	473	487	351	756	547	250
Other long-term liabilities	129	97	97	74	69	80	60	69	50	79
Future income tax liabilities	308	301	299	339	352	331	266	261	173	164
Total liabilities	1,647	1,554	1,421	1,493	1,235	1,157	1,176	1,297	912	758
Non-controlling interest	146	133	89	36	9	—	—	—	—	—
Shareholders' equity	1,277	1,236	1,289	1,333	1,209	948	949	785	908	935
TOTAL LIABILITIES AND SHAREHOLDERS' EQUITY	3,070	2,923	2,799	2,862	2,453	2,105	2,125	2,082	1,820	1,693
Total capitalization	2,370	2,283	2,160	1,966	1,705	1,449	1,558	1,562	1,455	1,335

b) Income and Cash Flows 2001–2010

(US$ millions)

	2010	2009	2008	2007	2006	2005	2004	2003	2002	2001
Revenue	1,967	1,198	2,314	2,266	2,108	1,658	1,719	1,420	1,042	1,192
Cost of sales and operating expenses	(1,700)	(1,056)	(1,951)	(1,617)	(1,309)	(1,208)	(1,285)	(1,034)	(776)	(954)
Depreciation and amortization	(131)	(118)	(107)	(112)	(107)	(91)	(79)	(96)	(111)	(113)
Inventory write-down	—	—	(33)	—	—	—	—	—	—	—
Interest expense	(24)	(27)	(38)	(44)	(45)	(41)	(31)	(39)	(29)	(32)
Interest and other income	3	—	11	27	10	10	7	14	10	19
Unusual items, net[1]	22	—	—	—	26	(58)	—	(179)	(86)	(11)
Income tax recovery (expense)	(34)	4	(27)	(147)	(201)	(106)	(95)	(85)	(27)	(30)
NET INCOME	**102**	**1**	**169**	**373**	**482**	**164**	**236**	**1**	**23**	**71**
Add (deduct):										
Depreciation and amortization	131	118	107	112	107	91	79	96	111	113
Future income taxes	7	1	(39)	(13)	47	66	47	45	8	22
Non-cash unusual items[1]	(22)	—	—	—	(26)	—	—	170	88	—
Other, net[2]	33	9	(2)	19	12	7	7	16	15	13
CASH FLOWS FROM OPERATING ACTIVITIES BEFORE UNDERNOTED	252	129	235	491	622	328	369	328	245	219
Changes in non-cash working capital	(99)	(19)	78	33	(154)	29	(39)	31	(54)	157
CASH FLOWS FROM OPERATING ACTIVITIES	**153**	**110**	**313**	**524**	**468**	**357**	**330**	**359**	**191**	**376**
Increase (decrease) in cash position	24	(159)	(160)	133	196	(51)	(78)	(134)	89	106
Operating income	158	24	223	537	692	359	355	290	155	125
Income before unusual items (after-tax)	80	1	169	373	456	222	236	180	109	82
Adjusted EBITDA[3]	267	142	330	649	799	450	434	386	266	238

[1]Unusual items, net include gain on sale of Kitimat assets (2010), Kitimat closure costs (2005), adjustment to future income tax related to change in Trinidad tax legislation (2006/2005), asset restructuring charges (2005, 2003, 2002 and 2001), writedown of property, plant and equipment (2003) and site restoration expense (2002).

[2]Other, net includes stock-based compensation, other non-cash items and other cash payments related to operating activities.

[3]Adjusted EBITDA is a non-CAAP measure. Refer to page 45 of our 2010 Annual Report for a reconciliation to the most comparable CAAP measure.

EXHIBIT 10: (continued)

c) Financial Metrics 2001–2010

(all financial metrics are quoted in US$ terms)

	2010	2009	2008	2007	2006	2005	2004	2003	2002	2001
Year end share price (US$, NASDAQ)	30.40	19.49	11.24	27.60	27.37	18.74	18.26	11.23	8.38	5.54
Diluted net income per share	1.09	0.01	1.78	3.65	4.40	1.39	1.92	0.01	0.18	0.46
Diluted income before unusual items (after-tax) per share	0.85	0.01	1.78	3.65	4.17	1.88	1.92	1.88	1.40	0.70
Cash flow per share[1]	2.73	1.40	2.49	4.83	5.70	2.78	3.04	2.67	1.94	1.42
Adjusted EBITDA per share	2.89	1.54	3.49	6.38	7.32	3.82	3.57	3.14	2.10	1.54
Book value per share	13.78	13.42	14.01	13.56	11.43	8.35	7.91	6.54	7.23	7.13
Price to cash flow	11.14	13.93	4.52	5.72	4.80	6.73	6.01	4.21	4.33	4.73
Price to EBITDA	10.51	12.66	3.22	4.32	3.74	4.91	5.11	3.58	3.99	3.59
Price to book value per share	2.21	1.45	0.80	2.04	2.40	2.25	2.31	1.72	1.16	0.78
Dividends per share	0.62	0.62	0.61	0.55	0.49	0.41	0.28	0.47	0.10	—
Dividend yield (%)[2]	2.6%	4.5%	2.7%	2.1%	2.2%	2.4%	2.1%	4.8%	1.3%	—
Liquidity Ratios										
Quick ratio	1.72	1.66	2.16	1.83	2.18	1.81	1.04	2.48	4.46	1.80
Current ratio	2.45	2.30	2.85	2.46	7.90	2.35	1.33	3.09	5.30	2.17
Working capital (US$ millions)	457	352	478	725	649	350	163	440	611	311
Profitability Ratios										
Return on equity (ROE)	6.4%	0.1%	13.0%	29.5%	42.0%	24.0%	27.2%	21.3%	11.7%	8.3%
Debt Ratios										
Asset coverage	3.24	3.20	3.58	4.79	5.04	4.20	3.49	2.68	3.33	4.23
Adjusted EBITDA interest coverage	11.00	5.18	8.58	14.75	17.76	10.98	14.00	9.90	9.17	7.44
Debt to capitalization	40%	40%	36%	30%	29%	35%	39%	50%	38%	30%
Net debt to capatalization	35%	35%	25%	7%	10%	26%	30%	38%	12%	7%

Source: Methanex.

EXHIBIT 11: Methanex Financial Summary (2009/2010)

($ millions, except where noted)	Three Months Ended				Years Ended	
	Dec 31 2010	Sep 30 2010	Dec 31 2009		Dec 31 2010	Dec 31 2009
Production (thousands of tonnes)	913	895	955		3,540	3,543
Sales volumes (thousands of tonnes):						
Produced methanol	831	885	880		3,540	3,764
Purchased methanol	806	792	467		2,880	1,546
Commission sales[1]	151	101	152		509	638
Total sales volumes	1,788	1,778	1,499		6,929	5,948
Methanex average non-discounted posted price ($ per tonne)[2]	407	334	327		356	252
Average realized price ($ per tonne)[3]	348	286	282		306	225
Adjusted EBITDA[4]	71.3	57.3	72.9		266.7	141.8
Cash flows from operating activities	10.4	48.0	35.7		152.9	110.3
Cash flows from operating activities before changes in non-cash working capital[4]	77.0	53.1	74.2		251.6	128.5
Operating income[4]	41.2	45.9	40.9		157.6	24.2
Net income	27.9	32.8	25.7		101.7	0.7
Net income before unusual item[4]	27.9	10.6	25.7		79.5	0.7
Basic net income per common share	0.30	0.36	0.28		1.10	0.01
Basic net income per common share before unusual item[4]	0.30	0.11	0.28		0.86	0.01
Diluted net income per common share	0.30	0.35	0.28		1.09	0.01
Diluted net income per common share before unusual item[4]	0.30	0.11	0.28		0.85	0.01
Common share information (millions of shares):						
Weighted average number of common shares	92.3	92.2	92.1		92.2	92.1
Diluted weighted average number of common shares	94.0	93.3	93.1		93.5	92.7
Number of common shares outstanding, end of period	92.6	92.2	92.1		92.6	92.1

[1]Commission sales represent volumes marketed on a commission basis. Commission income is included in revenue when earned.

[2]Methanex average non-discounted posted price represents the average of our non-discounted posted prices in North America, Europe and Asia Pacific weighted by sales volume. Current and historical pricing information is available at www.methanex.com.

[3]Average realized price is calculated as revenue, net of commissions earned, divided by the total sales volumes of produced and purchased methanol.

[4]These items are non-GAAP measures that do not have any standardized meaning prescribed by Canadian generally accepted accounting principles (GAAP) and therefore are unlikely to be comparable to similar measures presented by other companies. Refer to *Additional information - Supplemental Non-GAAP Measures* for a description of each non-GAAP measure and a reconciliation to the most comparable GAAP measure.

Source: Methanex.

19

CASE 2

Vice Media: Competitive Advantage and Global Expansion

Under the brilliant blue skies of a summer's day in June 2013, Shane Smith and Suroosh Alvi boarded a plane from New York City to Banff, Alberta, where they would accept a media award at the Banff World Media Festival. Their company, Vice Media (Vice), was no stranger to winning awards (see Exhibit 1) and had received a great deal of public attention, both self-promoted and unsolicited.

The journey from "The Big Apple" to the Canadian wilderness was a fitting moment for Vice's founders to reflect on a corporate journey that had taken them in the opposite direction—Vice had gone from the wilderness of a media backwater in Canada to landing in New York and assiduously building a global youth brand. Alvi and Smith, two of three remaining founders, reflected with some satisfaction on Vice's meagre beginnings in Montreal, funded by a welfare-to-work program, to its position as a global media company headquartered in the Williamsburg neighbourhood of Brooklyn, New York, and now boasting a presence in 34 countries.

While Vice's ascendency as a global company defied easy description, the next steps were even less clear. Having secured a niche position among global media organizations, had Vice achieved the pinnacle of its powers, or was there an unwritten chapter in Vice's strategic journey? What might be the next step in Vice's strategic evolution? For Vice's management, the answer might lie in the nature and sources of the company's competitive advantage.

🛡 IVEY | Publishing

Professor Farzad H. Alvi wrote this case solely to provide material for class discussion. The author does not intend to illustrate either effective or ineffective handling of a managerial situation. The author may have disguised certain names and other identifying information to protect confidentiality.

This publication may not be transmitted, photocopied, digitized or otherwise reproduced in any form or by any means without the permission of the copyright holder. Reproduction of this material is not covered under authorization by any reproduction rights organization. To order copies or request permission to reproduce materials, contact Ivey Publishing, Ivey Business School, Western University, London, Ontario, Canada, N6G 0N1; (t) 519.661.3208; (e) cases@ivey.ca; www.iveycases.com.

Copyright © 2014, Richard Ivey School of Business Foundation   Version: 2014-04-11

One time permission to reproduce granted by Richard Ivey School of Business Foundation on April 22, 2014.

BACKGROUND

Vice flaunted a sarcastic, ribald, unconventional, thought-provoking and in-your-face ethos that spanned numerous business lines, including a print magazine; online initiatives with music, news and youth culture; unique collaborations with major brands such as Intel and YouTube; and even a London pub and a Williamsburg coffee shop (see Exhibit 2).

An earlier generation might have described the Vice ethos as "gonzo journalism,"[1] or what Vice itself self-referentially characterized as "immersionistic" and character-driven. Rather than purporting to offer an objective truth, which always varied in the eye of the beholder, Vice's program hosts and correspondents conveyed how they felt when reporting a story–the audience made an emotional connection, identifying with the correspondent and going along for the ride.

Reduced to its simplest form, Vice managed to do what Alvi described as "stupid things in a smart way, and smart things in a stupid way." Vice's cult-like admirers, 67 per cent of whom were males between the ages of 18 and 34, had a seemingly unquenchable thirst for Vice's brash and inimitable media style, while the mainstream media some-times responded with incredulity and criticism. For example, in 2013, Vice won plaudits from its followers and elicited disbelief in the mainstream media by sending one of its correspondents to chaperone former NBA star Dennis Rodman and members of the Harlem Globetrotters to play basketball in North Korea against the national team. The reporter played in the match, while Rodman accompanied reclusive North Korean leader Kim Jong-un courtside. The *New York Times*, although providing frequent and flattering coverage on Vice, in a moment of pique, described Vice's method as pursuing "soft-headed journalism."[2]

The Vice ethos reflected the personalities of its founders, neither of whom had formal business training. Alvi had been raised in Canada and the United States in a household of immigrant academics from Pakistan, where he was perpetually bridging the distance between the South Asian culture and Islamic religion of his parents and daily life in a North American context. He graduated from McGill University in Montreal with a B.A. in philoso-phy. His academic experiences included earning a failing grade in feminist literature and subsequently dropping out of graduate school–early indicators of his inability to embrace mainstream political correctness. He had also faced, and won, a personal battle in overcom-ing substance addiction. Alvi brought to Vice an edgy, hardened street credibility that, combined with his cerebral, philosophical view of freedom of expression and his editorial interests, produced a journalistic style that routinely pushed the boundaries of conven-tional sensibilities.

Smith was also the son of immigrants. Both his parents hailed from Ireland, and his father was an entrepreneur who founded and sold software companies. Smith graduated from Carleton University in Ottawa with a B.A. in political science. His anti-establishment tendencies had previously been expressed through music, fronting a punk rock band in

---

[1]Stefanie Stiles and Randy Harris, "Keeping Curious Company: Wayne C. Booth's Friendship Model of Criticism and the Work of Hunter S. Thompson," *College English*, 71(4), 2009, p. 315. "[Gonzo journalism] is . . . extreme journalism, influentially commingling fact, fiction, and overheated opinion and pushing the subjectivity envelope to its limits . . . erasing not only all pretense of objectivity, but also all distinctions between participant and observer."

Definition of *gonzo* from www.merriam-webster.com: 1. Idiosyncratically subjective but engagé; 2. Bizarre; 3. Freewheeling or unconventional especially to the point of outrageousness.

[2]Mike Hale, "They Bring You the World, in a Way: 'Vice,' a New Approach to News, on HBO," *The New York Times*, April 4, 2013.

Ottawa, and later, in Montreal, with the Ultraviolet Booze Catastrophe. When Smith joined Vice, he brought with him an exuberant in-your-face marketing sensibility that was prone to outlandish statements on Vice's plans for world domination. Smith's drive and naked ambition fuelled the growth of Vice.

Though unacquainted with one another at the time, as university students both Smith and Alvi had flirted briefly with revolution–joining, and subsequently leaving, the International Socialists movement. Both had also travelled to Eastern Europe for several years following graduation to teach English, Alvi to Slovakia and Smith to Hungary.

Vice began in Montreal in newsprint as the *Voice of Montreal,* a free monthly culture magazine distributed locally and funded by a government welfare-to-work program. Eventually, the magazine went glossy and moved to New York City, where its geographic and business line diversification continued. Vice's corporate journey was characterized by numerous experiments, misadventures and brazen stunts (see Exhibit 3).

Business Culture

Vice was known for its culture of hard work and free flow of ideas. Despite its success, Vice's senior management did not sit in swanky offices. Instead, Smith, Alvi and several other key executives shared a small office with a glass door, just off one of the reception areas.

> "The scale of what Vice does is large, but the approach to business decisions is flexible, nimble and entrepreneurial. Not bureaucratic–there is a hierarchy, but ideas flow from bottom-up and top-down."
>
> – Jonathan Lutzky, General Counsel

The Vice business culture was also a culture of being a family. During the economic crisis in 2008, when many smaller media companies were declaring bankruptcy, Vice senior management insisted on providing health care to all employees, at a time when the norm for American companies was to cut back on benefits. Further, the wild and crazy side of the Vice lifestyle could have casualties, and, when appropriate, Vice offered support to keep the family together. Employees who had issues with alcohol or drugs were sometimes helped personally by Alvi. As a result of what has been described by Smith and others as a "weird" and even "impenetrable"[3] company culture, employees that fit in at Vice tended to stay extremely loyal, even when offered higher salaries elsewhere.

BUSINESS MODEL

Vice created unique content that was free of charge to its audience and was disseminated through its print and online channels. Producing video content involved a producer, reporter and cameraperson documenting and commenting on an event, while sharing with the audience how it felt to be doing the story. Producers helped to stage and shoot the story. Then, in editing suites at Vice's offices in New York, Los Angeles, London, Berlin, Mexico City and Melbourne, the video content was edited into a high-quality and professional format for posting online. Editing suites were being built in Vice's offices around the world so that all the offices could one day contribute to the output of video content.

---

[3]Tim Bradshaw, "The Counterculture Club," *The Financial Times,* November 18, 2009.

Editorial Policy

Vice's content was often described as edgy. *Vice Magazine*'s editor-in-chief, Rocco Castoro, described what edgy meant for Vice News: "Our objective is not to intentionally make people uncomfortable, but if the content is true, raw, and honest and makes you uncomfortable, that's the barometer of a good story."

The immersionistic, emotionally transparent and character-driven Vice approach promoted a transparency that allowed the 18- to 34-year-old demographic to relate to the facts in a way that was not available in mainstream media. Vice's experiential approach was also well-suited for social media. Thus, many young people connected with Vice better than with the mainstream media. As Castoro noted, "Our reporting focuses on 'this is what happened–this is how it felt.' Unlike traditional news media, we lead the audience through the story without the reader knowing that's what we're doing. We're storytelling."

Vice's free-content model was serendipitously well-timed for digital media. Vice had never maintained a formal blog, but did have a space on the Internet where content was posted; the editorial content was engaged in storytelling, making sense of the world in a way that young people could understand. Vice's online strategy in 2013 had evolved from its online presence established more than five years before the mainstream media attempted similar initiatives. Viceland.com had been the home for Vice's online content until 2011, when Vice finally acquired the Vice.com URL to serve as the umbrella for all of its content channels.

Vice's business model was affected by its editorial policy. Editorially, Vice became multi-platform in a way that traditional media was not. The traditional view of multimedia was to reissue the same story across different media, such as print, television and online. But the development of Vice's multi-platform approach was different. Only 50 to 60 per cent of the story would overlap across different media, thereby "layering" the content as "show, don't tell storytelling": the audience read the story, watched the video and perhaps opened a related iPad info-graphic. Different elements of storytelling were layered so that the audience might feel, in the words of Castoro, "What the hell is this? I don't know, but I like it."

Revenue Streams

Vice had three principal revenue streams:

1. Monetizing video content online by selling advertising for online content,
2. Advertising revenue from the print magazine,
3. Advisory fees through Virtue and AdVice. Virtue was Vice's in-house agency that created customized initiatives for brands, everything from brand strategy and creative direction of their advertising campaigns to entire transmedia initiatives, including custom content, events and marketing. AdVice was a network of 200 sites whose ad inventory was represented by Vice; Vice controlled the banners that ran on the 200 sites and took a percentage of the revenues received by these sites. Not only did the AdVice network generate revenues but it also expanded Vice's reach beyond the core channels of Vice Media by creating access to the AdVice network sites' audience of 200 million persons.

In 2006, the magazine represented 94 per cent of Vice's revenues, but by 2013, it represented only 3 per cent of revenues.

Verticals

Vice had maintained an edgy appeal, reinforcing, with seeming effortlessness, a strong emotional connection with its audience, as a result of having extended its business model across content verticals or channels. Vice defined verticals as:

> Content channels built around a focused set of interests, defined by its original video offering, supported by text, photo and interactive content, then distributed across proprietary channels (e.g., vice.com, VICE on iOS), social channels (e.g., Facebook, Twitter, Instagram), video distribution channels (e.g., YouTube), and integrated into various digital communities (e.g., Reddit, Huffington Post, BuzzFeed, etc.).

After accessing the Vice network or ecosystem on vice.com, the audience could select from different content channels, similar to how one might change channels on television. In addition to posting *Vice Magazine* online, in 2013, Vice offered 10 additional channels, which covered news, music, fashion, photography, travel, sports, technology, food, not-safe-for-work, and do's and don'ts. The verticals at the end of 2013 were Noisey, Thump, Fightland, The Creators Project, Motherboard, Vice News and Vice Food.

Vice's approach to creating content and documentaries was to migrate to spaces where the audience wanted content in the Vice style (i.e., immersionistic, character-driven and created by people the audience could relate to), with each interest area potentially becoming a vertical. Alvi commented, "Vice does not try to guess at the interests of our audience, the audience leads us there and we build a vertical around it in the Vice style."

Evolution of the Business Model

Vice founders believed they did not have a business plan until 2008 or 2009.[4] Several key events had led to Vice developing its current business model. As the company diversified into creating video content for the Internet, the business model evolved concurrently. Several key events shaped Vice's strategic evolution:

1. *An understanding of the importance of market size and how to define the market.* As a newsprint "zine" in Montreal in 1994 and 1995, then known as *The Voice of Montreal*, the enterprise struggled to break even. Early in its existence, Vice management realized that to produce more revenue, they needed to find a geographically dispersed market. Financial solvency was more readily achieved by having a niche presence in numerous geographically dispersed markets rather than trying to win a greater share of a single market. Montreal could provide access to only a limited number of advertising dollars, and the company's expansion across Canada took place simply as a means of surviving. Thus, the business plan was to stay afloat and to engage in aggressive expansion in order to do so.

   The founders soon discovered that wooing advertisers was easier when the company had a national presence. In 1996, *The Voice of Montreal* (on the back of a publicity stunt falsely claiming that the *Village Voice* was going to sue them) dropped the "o" from Voice to become Vice and expanded to the United States. Expanding to larger markets was a strategic move to become an entrenched niche player. Vice found its audience in a sliver of numerous markets rather than aiming for a larger share concentrated in a single market.

---

[4]Ibid.

2. *Finding funding and a developing a strategic plan.* In 1998, at the height of the Internet bubble, the Vice founders noticed that not far from their ramshackle loft office in Old Montreal were the glistening premises of Discreet Logic, a NASDAQ-listed software company that produced "compositing technology for the film, television and advertising industries."[5] In an interview with the French newspaper *La Presse*, Vice told the reporter that Richard Szalwinski, the eccentric software millionaire founder of Discreet Logic, was interested in buying Vice. Life then imitated art, when, on the basis of the false rumour, Szalwinski read the article. With his curiosity piqued, he invited the Vice founders to lunch and eventually bought a minority stake at a seemingly arbitrary valuation of $4 million.[6] Vice then became part of Szalwinski's operations in New York, alongside *Shift* magazine and a high-end brand called Halo 46, all under the umbrella of Szalwinski's company BHVR, Inc. (Behaviour, later renamed Normal Network).

The move to New York was a radical change. Gone were Vice's hand-to-mouth existence and its modest offices in a Montreal loft. Szalwinski had a grand plan to create, grow and eventually take public an Internet TV enterprise with multiple channels, where Vice would be part of a stable of content-producing entities. Having taken start-ups public in the past, Szalwinski encouraged and facilitated taking on debt to accelerate the growth of Vice. The offices, the plans and the atmosphere were all in a league beyond anything the Vice founders had known. However, the grand plans for ecommerce and Internet-based television were interrupted by the bursting of the dot-com bubble. Szalwinski's operations were hit hard, and the overhanging debt threatened to bankrupt Vice. By borrowing money from family, Smith and Alvi bought Vice back from Szalwinski. Said Alvi:

> When Richard moved us to Manhattan, we felt like we were in the big leagues. We thought we were going to get rich. It was the first time we had seen a real business strategy. But something didn't feel right. As a business, we had always survived based on our cashflows and had zero debt. We were never in a position where we could lose money, but all of a sudden we were spending so much money and taking on debt. There were extremely limited revenues, which made us wonder how this model could possibly work. Richard was ahead of the curve in terms of multi-channel online content delivery, but the infrastructure wasn't there yet to get it into people's homes.

At the time, Smith commented: "[Richard had] a great idea [for Vice], [but] we're just going to do it completely differently. We believe in growing organically: finding the Vice people, making them our partners, teaching them how to do stuff and learning from them."[7]

3. *International expansion.* Having bought the company back, Vice moved to the lower-rent and then unfashionable neighbourhood of Williamsburg, Brooklyn, and stabilized its operations. By 2002, Vice began its international expansion to Australia, Japan and, most importantly, the United Kingdom, while at the same time launching a record label, Vice Music. It was through music and its failed fashion division that the Vice principals noticed a global youth audience for its ethos and brand. They saw

---

[5]As described on the LinkedIn profile of Richard Szalwinski.

[6]Tom Gierasimczuk, "Vice Age," *Marketing Advertising, Media and PR in Canada*, February 8, 2012. All currency amounts are shown in U.S. dollars unless otherwise noted.

[7]Dave Morris, "The Virtue of Vice," *The Globe and Mail*, August 24, 2012.

similarities in the musical tastes and fashion choices of youth from such seemingly unrelated locations as Tokyo, Melbourne, London, New York and Toronto.

After launching Vice Music, the magazine began global expansion. Using its British operations as a hub for European expansion, Vice entered into a series of partnerships in each market with individuals thought to share the Vice ethos.

4. *Learning a new skill set with the* Vice Guide to Travel–*how to make video content and tell stories through a different medium.* In 2006/07, Vice had its first experience in making video content with the *Vice Guide to Travel*, which led to a television show on MTV called *The Vice Guide to Everything*. Vice was inspired and encouraged by an MTV executive, Jeff Yapp, who was instrumental in this crucial phase of Vice's development. Alvi commented:

> The Vice Guide to Travel was very important for us. We were going to school, in public, in terms of making video content. The content wasn't very good, but its importance can't be understated–we learned how to make video content, and launched VBS [Internet TV, a precursor to the verticals ecosystem on vice.com], and saw how this content could travel through the Internet and be consumed by millions of people. Without this we would have stayed a small publishing outfit.

One of the advantages of Vice being headquartered in New York City was the opportunity to meet and work with leading creative people. Filmmaker Spike Jonze[8] was one such person. As a creative advisor to Vice, Jonze once queried the founders, "You guys are filming your content, right?" Jonze's comment prompted Vice to craft its own unique approach to making video content. Emboldened by the video-content producing experience of the *Vice Guide to Travel*, Vice launched VBS.TV with Jonze serving as creative director. Vice described VBS as an "experiment with online video content that worked."

5. *Advertising–Virtue and AdVice.* As Vice continued to grow, the founders learned much more about the advertisers they were working with and those they were trying to draw revenues from. The ads that Vice would run, whether in print or online, needed to fit with the content. For example, Vice would turn down ads from mainstream companies, such as shoe company Sketchers, in favour of edgier companies, such as American Apparel, which had a risqué, controversial aesthetic.[9] Vice began to guide its advertisers on the kind of ads that would work with its audience, with Alvi putting it as follows:

> The traditional advertising model for attracting 18-to 34-year-olds is broken. We realized that authentic content was the way to connect and engage with the audience. We created an in-house ad agency as a way to work with brands and make bespoke projects with them, brands who might otherwise have been cautious about working with Vice. We didn't realize it at the time, but it became a way for us to access large corporate budgets without compromising our edgy content.

6. *Improved organizational structure.* Through consolidation and acquisition, Vice aligned its organization structure with business strategy, thereby improving its business outcomes. Consolidating viceland.com and VBS.TV into vice.com, which included changes to the Williamsburg office layout, made the Vice brand whole, unified webplays,

---

[8]Spike Jonze's film credits include directing "Being John Malkovich," "Adaptation" and "Where the Wild Things Are."

[9]Tim Bradshaw, "The Counterculture Club," *The Financial Times*, November 18, 2009.

increased online traffic dramatically and improved cash flows and profitability. Additionally, Vice's traction with traditional ad agencies improved through a clearer structure for Virtue and AdVice. Agencies began sending RFPs (request for proposals) to Vice, which had never before happened, despite 10 years of effort.

7. *Growth through acquisitions.* With a strong brand and a strategy oriented to verticals, Vice began a growth-through-acquisitions strategy in 2012. Through joint ventures or acquisitions where Vice retained at least 51 per cent ownership, Vice's rationale was to acquire what Alvi described as a "landing strip" in different verticals where they had no expertise. For example, in 2012, Vice acquired the magazine *i-D*, a well-established British fashion title started by Terry Jones, a former art director at *Vogue*. Additionally, Vice established a joint venture with UFC (Ultimate Fighting Championship) for the Fightland vertical.

GLOBAL STRATEGY

As a "born-again global"[10] in a turbulent business sector, Vice's global strategy combined instinct, opportunism, perceptions of scale and personal networks. Whether it was finding or being approached by potential partners, Vice prioritized connections with individuals who could transmit the Vice ethos in another culture. Finding the right fit was paramount, as noted by Hosi Simon, general manager, head of international: "The Vice person on the ground is the key to making our global strategy happen–you know it when you see it. I see it when I meet potential partners abroad–are they taking me to a fancy "bottle service club," or to a punk show where cool stuff is happening."

Vice's global expansion had five distinct phases, but none of the five phases was preceded by formal market research.

Phase 1: United Kingdom, France Italy, Japan, Australia, 2001–2002. Vice's British operation was central to Vice's European expansion, while its U.S. office spearheaded efforts in Latin America, Australia and Asia. The most successful internationalizations were led by the British office, which had been a rich source of executive talent, promoting the global feel of the company. Vice's current president and chief operating officer (COO) were recruited to New York from the British office.

Phase 2: Rest of Europe, 2004–2007. Not all of the Phase 1 and 2 forays were successful. Smaller Eastern European markets, such as Bulgaria and Romania, proved to be too small to support the full range of Vice's business lines. Additionally, in Japan, Vice's partners were more fashion-oriented, and when Vice moved out of fashion, the Japan operations did not

---

[10]Pat H. Dickson, "Going Global," in *Entrepreneurship: The Engine of Growth*, Andrew Zacharakis and Stephen Spinelli (eds.), 2006, pp. 155–177. Dickson suggests that firms can choose from three types of firm internationalization: gradual globals, born globals and born-again globals. Gradual globals internationalize initially in culturally familiar markets, and later in places of greater "psychic distance." Over time, firms are exposed to an incremental process of knowledge development, increased resource commitment and integration. Born globals have an international vision from the outset, skipping the staged, orderly international development of the gradual globals. They typically experience complex interactions between the founders, the venture, the industry environment and the idiosyncrasies of the founders. For born-again globals, a triggering event causes internationalizing. This phenomenon can be described as punctuated equilibrium or leapfrogging. Vice was initially a gradual global as it internationalized its magazine. With the success of the VBS.TV experiment, however, Vice became a born-again global, characterized by its explosive global growth as a result of filming its content and using an online approach.

keep up with evolution of Vice. Japan subsequently re-launched in 2013, with greater success the second time around.

Phase 3: Brazil, Mexico, South Africa, 2008–2011. The attraction of these markets was the perception of scale and the prospect of potentially interesting content.

Phase 4: Consolidation and alternative entry mode, 2008–2013. Having learned from the company's first three phases of expansion, Vice principals felt they required better control over operations. Having too many minority partners in far-flung locations was unwieldy from an administrative point of view, and a new mode of expansion was deemed necessary. Thus, the Vice principals decided to pursue wholly owned subsidiaries, entering countries with the entire offering all at once, rather than starting with the magazine and then moving to other business lines, as had been done in Phases 1 to 3. Wholly owned subsidiaries were set up in Russia, Portugal and Greece. Simultaneously, Vice began a process of buying out all existing minority partners and licensees. By the end of 2013, almost all of Vice's operations globally were wholly owned.

Phase 5: China and India, 2013 onwards. Vice's strategy of attempting to find a common denominator in global youth culture was not extended to China and India. As noted by Simon: "In China and India, it's no longer about some 18-year-old being part of global youth culture. Culturally, China and India are just too different, and the Vice global youth culture approach is not exportable there."

In China, Vice's plan was to be a local company, with local staff creating content for local consumption. The approach was very different from finding the narrow sliver of common global youth culture that was shared across numerous countries. Instead, Vice hoped that from whatever content that was eventually created in China, some aspects of it might have global appeal—but globalizing Chinese content was an aspirational rather than a concrete, short-term strategic objective.

The China and India strategies represented what Hosi describes as:

> Tapping into a deep emotional need that young people have about expressing themselves, opening themselves up to the rest of the world. Basic human needs for self-expression are the same, but the vehicle is different. China is a big country with a small counterculture—so the self-expression may not be something familiar to us like skateboarding . . . we have to be broader in our outlook.

While the Internet was the enabling mechanism of the Vice strategy, Vice also faced political risks, and the founders realized that it needed to work within the constraints of Chinese expression. Themes of fashion and music would be emphasized, not politics and corruption. Elements of youth culture that invariably involved disenchantment with the mainstream, or otherwise might be seen as having the potential to stoke rebellion and strife, would be introduced slowly and Vice would recognize the limitations of the Chinese context.

Vice's India strategy was similar to its strategy in China, but with less overt restriction on content. Simon commented, "In India, there's an impending revolution of youth culture. You can just feel it's about to happen. We don't know what it will look like, but we aim to provide a voice to the youth of that revolution."

Building a Global Value Chain

The result of the five phases of Vice's global expansion was the creation and subsequent domination of a niche: the global youth culture segment. Vice had evolved into a global media player with little in the way of discernible, direct competition across all of its business lines. Alvi noted, "We are the voice of a global sub-culture–Vice provided an outlet that united global youth sub-culture. We create a singular editorial voice by tapping into local cultures that then speaks to a global audience."

Vice was conscious of the need to achieve an optimal balance between local and global content. By 2013, Vice estimated that 20 per cent of its magazine and online content was purely local, and 80 per cent was global, with the Williamsburg office deciding on the global content. At Vice headquarters, soliciting global input on editorial content occurred several times per week on global teleconferences, and there was also a weekly global call for sales–all calls during New York business hours.

Vice's global activities and operations also reflected its source of revenues. The vice. com ecosystem and its online content channels or verticals[11] supplanted the magazine as the main revenue sources. Producing video content globally, however, presented unique challenges for the business model.

Global shoots involved, more often than not, sending people from New York to the global shoot location. The idea was that a Vice person would travel to the location for several weeks and train local staff in the appropriate techniques for making Vice content. The content from global shoots would then be sent to editing suites before being posted online. As of 2013, the editing suites were located mostly in New York, but also in the United Kingdom, Germany, Mexico, Australia and Los Angeles. However, as noted by Simon, because "editing content is an art form, not a process . . . it's done mostly at our New York office."

Vice would have liked to have had content editing, production and activation capabilities in as many locations as possible. Instead of content ideas being dictated from New York, with the ideas then produced locally, Vice had preferred that more content ideas be developed and executed locally, with potential "franchising" of the content globally. For example, the food show *Munchies*, which focused on drunken chefs making great food, was developed in New York, but the idea was then exported for local production in Canada and the United Kingdom.

The need for greater local production capabilities was more acute for the important and influential Vice News vertical, where correspondents and producers needed to be dispatched quickly to a story. As a result, Vice planned to open dedicated news bureaus both to its current offices and in select cities.

Future Global Growth

Simon commented on Vice's plans for future global growth:

> There is no cultural imperialism–we think of local operations as local and distinct. Cool is what we used to sell, what others have called the "hipsters' bible." That's niche, but small. Vice is interested in becoming huge, so going "mainstream" is not a bad word for us, because it means being more influential. I think our content will not be compromised because we stay true to our approach–it's about the means of our journalism rather than the content itself. Our goal is to make authentic content and tell stories.

Having built global scale and possessing a large captive audience, Vice had changed the way it expanded. For example, expansion in such markets as Indonesia, India and Malaysia differed from previous growth because building up a large local presence was no longer the prerequisite

---

[11]Content channels built around a focused set of interests, defined by its original video offering, supported by text, photo, and interactive content, then distributed across proprietary channels (e.g., vice.com, VICE on iOS), social channels (e.g., Facebook, Twitter, Instagram), video distribution channels (e.g., YouTube) and integrated into various digital communities (e.g., Reddit, Huffington Post, BuzzFeed, etc.).

first step for growth. Since more than 90 per cent of Vice's activities were online, large global, regional or local companies could be partnered with in the pursuit of what Vice called "hyper growth." In other words, Vice began bypassing its historical route to growth taken in the early phases of global expansion. For example, in Mexico, Vice first licensed content to Sky Mexico, premiered its feature-length documentary *Heavy Metal In Baghdad*, organized events to raise awareness and only then launched its magazine.

Also important were increased connection and coordination between global operations, which helped to drive global expansion. Lucrative projects with brands such as Intel were global. Vice had the unique capability to execute in 20 countries at a very high quality—for youth culture, Vice claimed to be the only company that could do so. On the basis of vice.com and several very popular YouTube channels, where Vice content was streamed, major brands were aware of Vice's ability to connect with young people. Looking into the future, the challenge for Vice management was to transform a bricolage of international activities and adventures into a coherent global strategy.

INVESTORS IN VICE, STRATEGIC PLANNING

In 2009, Vice received its first taste of a financial investment from an undisclosed private equity fund. In April, 2011, a consortium of investors, including the advertising and marketing company WPP and the boutique investment bank Raine Group, invested more than $50 million in Vice.[12] At the time of the investment, Vice had gross assets of $34.3 million and had been profitable for several years, with 2009 revenues and earnings of $64 million and $16.7 million, respectively.[13]

In August 2013, 21st Century Fox invested $70 million for a 5 per cent stake in Vice, representing a $1.4 billion valuation of Vice.[14] Vice disclosed its 2012 revenues as approximately $175 million, citing the explosive growth of the company since 2008 as having been "fuelled by online video [including several of the most popular YouTube channels], particularly its gonzo-style films from world trouble spots."[15] For the sake of comparison, in mid-2013, the *New York Times* group of companies had a market valuation of $1.8 billion and the *Washington Post* was sold at what was considered to be a very rich valuation of $250 million.

Having investors required Vice to have a new financial and operational discipline that had not been a part of the company culture. Investors needed to see that Vice had systems in place to support its strategy. Additionally, the investment rounds enabled rapid growth. For example, Vice went from 100 full-time employees in 2008 to 350 in 2013. Crossing the 100-person threshold marked the establishment of a human resources department, and continued growth meant greater attention to labour standards, such as formalizing an internship program and providing employees with semi-annual performance reviews. In 2009, an organization chart with reporting lines was initiated, and the company established the positions of chief operating officer (COO) and chief technology officer (CTO). A general counsel was hired to standardize all licensing agreements and institute a process of reviewing all contracts.

Alvi commented that "before the investors came along, our operational approach was instinctive, organic, and reactive, but now we are operating like a real corporation while trying to maintain our culture at the same time." In terms of strategy, the investors

[12]Tim Bradshaw, "WPP Invests in Hipster Bible Vice," *The Financial Times*, April 5, 2011.
[13]Ibid.
[14]Matthew Garrahan, "21st Century Fox Takes Stake in 'Gonzo' Vice," *The Financial Times*, August 16, 2013.
[15]Ibid.

introduced a new strategic planning vernacular for Vice to address budgets, growth and return on investment. Vice's growth as a global media company was enabled by introductions to those at the highest levels, which were facilitated by having access to such well-connected individuals as Tom Freston (founder of MTV, former chief executive officer [CEO] of Viacom and current board member of Vice) and Ari Emmanuel (co-CEO of William Morris Endeavor Entertainment agency). One example was the genesis of its news program on HBO, *Vice: News from the Edge*, which was nominated for an Emmy Award in 2013, and renewed for a second season.

By the end of 2013, Vice's strategy was to become the largest youth media platform in the world, and the company had a plan to make it happen. All the years of diversification and launching territories internationally had come together, and Vice offered true scale. No longer just a niche player, Vice was very close to being considered mainstream. The global audience was growing steadily and consuming a type of content few organizations could create. It had taken 19 years of building on unique competitive advantages to establish a global youth media brand that was becoming an alternative to the mainstream media.

Farzad H. Alvi is an Associate Professor, Tecnológico de Monterrey, EGADE Business School (Mexico City).

EXHIBIT 1: Accolades and Awards

Webby Awards (Winner)
Vice News, 2013, news series
Mexican Mormon War, 2013, news episode
Creator's Project, 2013, website art
Vice Guide to Congo, 2012, travel
Vice Guide to Liberia, 2010, travel

Webby Awards (Honoree)
Creator's Project, 2013, branded ent. long form
Creator's Project, 2013, integrated ad campaign
Noisey "Meet Das Racist," 2012, music
Tattoo Age, 2012, documentary series
Swansea Love Story, 2011, documentary episode
VBS Meets BMX Legend Mat Hoffman, 2011, sports
Detroit Lives, 2011, branded entertainment
Space Shuttle Parking Lot, 2011, technology
Powder & Rails—Shawn Farmer, 2010, sports

Warsaw Film Festival
Heavy Metal in Baghdad, 2008, best documentary

Adweb 3.0 Excellence in Advertising
Virtue, Palladium Boots, 2010, best campaign

MIP Cube
Creator's Project, 2013, brand of the year

Ad Age's Media Vanguard
Best multimedia & experiential extravaganza, 2011
Best integration of video, editorial, experiential, 2010

People' Voice Awards (Winner)
Vice News, 2013, news series
Mexican Mormon War, 2013, news episode
Creator's Project, 2013, website art
Creator's Project, 2013, branded content
Vice Guide to Congo, 2012, travel
Gun Markets of Pakistan, 2010, news episode
Vice Guide to Liberia, 2010, travel
Epicly Later'd, 2009, sports

Tribeca Online Festival, Best Film
Lil Bub & Friendz, 2013

Award of Innovation
Vice Media, Inc., 2013

World Media Gold Award
All the wrong places, 2011, online ad

Fast Company's Most Innovative Companies
Vice Media, 2010, 3rd place

Cannes Lions
Branded content, 2012, silver
Best use of live events / stunts, 2012, finalist

Ad Age's Creativity 50
Vice Media, 2011

Source: Vice Media.

EXHIBIT 2: Business Lines

Magazine – 1994 to present
Vice Fashion – 1998 to 2002
Vice Music (record label) – 2002 to present
VBS.TV – 2007 to 2011, absorbed into Vice.com – 2011 to present
Virtue – 2008 to present
AdVice – 2010 to present

Source: Vice Media.

EXHIBIT 3: Timeline of Key Events

1994 – *Voice of Montreal* founded

1995 – *Voice of Montreal* distributed across Canada

1996 – *Voice of Montreal* renamed *Vice,* distribution in United States begins

1998 – Through Normal Networks (originally BHVR-Behaviour), software entrepreneur Richard Szalwinski acquires a minority stake in Vice, and moves operations to Manhattan

2000 – Following bursting of the tech bubble, Normal goes out of business, Vice founders reacquire all shares of the company, and move operations to Williamsburg, Brooklyn

2002 – Vice Music launched

2002 – International expansion begins to Europe, Japan and Australia

2007 – VBS.TV launched

2008 – Virtue founded

2009 – Private equity investment by an undisclosed fund

2010 – AdVice launched, a digital activation network delivering advertising and content to curated sites across vertical audiences

2011 – Consolidation of Vice's two main websites, viceland.com and VBS.TV, into a single site: vice.com

2011 – Private equity investment of $50 million by Raine Group / WPP

2012 – Vice partners with Google to launch original YouTube channels

2012 – Vice premieres news series on HBO, later nominated for an Emmy

2012 – Expansion to China and India begins

2013 – Investment of $70 million for 5 per cent stake by 21st Century Fox, values Vice at $1.4 billion

Source: Vice Media.

Bombardier Aerospace: The CSeries Dilemma[1]

"Bombardier Aerospace announced today the name of its new commercial aircraft family and revealed the aircraft's distinctive black and white livery. The CSeries, for competitive, continental and connector, would target airlines operating aircraft in the lower end of the 100- to 150-passenger market, a large segment that is not well served by any aircraft in production today."

Bombardier press release, July 19, 2004

"On March 15, 2005, Bombardier's board of directors granted Bombardier Aerospace authority to offer the new CSeries family of aircraft to customers. The authority to offer is an important step in the process that could lead to the aircraft program launch. Prior to launch, Bombardier will continue to seek firm commitments from potential customers and suppliers."

Bombardier press release, May 13, 2005

"Bombardier announced today that present market conditions do not justify the launch of the CSeries program at this time. The corporation will now reorient CSeries project efforts, team and resources to regional jet and turboprop aircraft opportunities to address regional airlines' future needs in the 80- to 100-seat aircraft market."

Bombardier press release, January 31, 2006

Ali Taleb and Louis Hébert wrote this case solely to provide material for class discussion. The authors do not intend to illustrate either effective or ineffective handling of a managerial situation. The authors may have disguised certain names and other identifying information to protect confidentiality.

This publication may not be transmitted, photocopied, digitized or otherwise reproduced in any form or by any means without the permission of the copyright holder. Reproduction of this material is not covered under authorization by any reproduction rights organization. To order copies or request permission to reproduce materials, contact Ivey Publishing, Ivey Business School, Western University, London, Ontario, Canada, N6G 0N1; (t) 519.661.3208; (e) cases@ivey.ca; www.iveycases.com.

Copyright © 2011, Richard Ivey School of Business Foundation   Version: 2013-04-30

One time permission to reproduce granted by Richard Ivey School of Business Foundation on April 22, 2014.

IVEY | Publishing

[1]This case has been written on the basis of published sources only. Consequently, the interpretation and perspectives presented in this case are not necessarily those of Bombardier Inc. or any of its employees.

In March 2005, the board of directors of Bombardier Inc. authorized its Aeronautics division, Bombardier Aerospace, to offer a new generation of aircraft named CSeries to its clients. The company postponed the actual launch of the project several times, prompting investors and analysts to question what the long-term strategy of the company was.

As the date of the company's annual meeting was imminent (scheduled for May 29, 2007) investors and industry analysts were expecting Pierre Beaudoin, president of Bombardier Aerospace, to clarify the company's plans for CSeries during this meeting.[2]

AEROSPACE: A CORE BUSINESS OF BOMBARDIER

Bombardier Inc., the parent company of Bombardier Aerospace, was headquartered in Montreal, Canada since its inception by Joseph-Armand Bombardier in 1942. As its original name–Auto-Neige Bombardier Ltd.[3]–implied, the company specialized initially in developing and trading snowmobiles in its home province of Quebec.

In May 2007, Bombardier's activities were structured into two relatively independent divisions: Bombardier Aerospace (BA) which was the global leader in business and regional aircraft manufacturing and Bombardier Transportation (BT) which was also a world leader in rail equipment. The strategic objective of Bombardier had always been to make both divisions global leaders in their respective markets. While BA was already the leading manufacturer of regional aircraft in 2001, Bombardier acquired the German DaimlerChrysler Rail Systems GmbH (ADtranz) and thus turned BT into the largest manufacturer of integrated rail equipment in the world.[4] However, Bombardier Inc. faced difficulties in late 2001, largely due to the crisis in the airline industry that followed the September 11 attacks on the World Trade Center. This led the company to rationalize its operations, lay off employees and divest its recreational line of business including snowmobile and jetski products. The sale of this division to a group of investors, which included members of the Bombardier family, helped reduce the debt of the company in 2003. Subsequent to this restructuring, the performance of Bombardier Inc. had improved over time. In April 2007, the company's overall revenues reached $4 billion on a quarterly basis and its gross margin was about 15 per cent. BA's contribution represented 57 per cent of revenues ($2.26 billion)[5] and 57.6 per cent of the gross margin ($344 million) (see Exhibit 1).

From an organizational perspective, each of the divisions had its own president–Pierre Beaudoin for the aerospace division and André Navarri for the transportation division. The structure of the group was highly decentralized in order to provide the divisions with a level of autonomy that was in line with their accountability in terms of growth and profitability.[6] The head office was involved only in providing shared services such as strategic planning,

---

[2]Pierre Sparaco, "Bombardier is hesitating," *Aero Morning*, March 30, 2007, www.aeromorning.com/en/chroniques.php?ch_id=178 (unless otherwise specified, all web resources have been accessed on August 1, 2011).

[3]Auto-neige is French for snowmobile.

[4]"Commission clears takeover of ADtranz by Bombardier, subject to commitments," *Europa*, April 3, 2001, http://europa.eu/rapid/pressReleasesAction.do?reference=IP/01/501.

[5]All figures are in USD unless otherwise noted.

[6]"Bombardier," *Canadian Business Resource*, www.cbr.ca/CompanyProfile.aspx?format=printable&CompanyID=2559.

human resources management, organizational development, public relations, finance and budgeting and legal affairs to the two divisions.

In addition to their divisional responsibilities, the two divisional presidents became executive vice-presidents (EVPs) of Bombardier Inc. in December 2004 and consequently formed the 'office of the president' along with corporate president and chief executive officer (CEO), Laurent Beaudoin. Industry analysts interpreted the nomination of Pierre Beaudoin as EVP of Bombardier Inc. as anticipatory of his future appointment to the head of the company as a replacement of his soon-to-retire father, Laurent Beaudoin.

Bombardier had essentially been a family-run business since its inception. The Bombardier and Beaudoin families had been leading the company for 58 years, thus providing leadership stability and strategic coherence during the company's successful diversification era between 1975 and 1999. Following this period, the company has been less stable as it changed leadership regularly (see Exhibit 2). Industry analysts suggested that frequent changes in leadership led the company to blurred vision and strategic uncertainty. This may explain why Bombardier had lagged behind its competition in the regional aircraft market since then.

AEROSPACE INDUSTRY: TEMPORARY TURBULENCE OR PERMANENT RESTRUCTURING?

The first powered flight in history took place in December 17, 1903 when Orville and Wilbur Wright flew briefly from Kitty Hawk, North Carolina. The aircraft they engineered is generally referred to as the Wright Flyer or the Kitty Hawk. Since then, air travel grew exponentially to become an integral part of people's everyday lives as trade globalized and individuals traveled more often due to decreasing airfares and increasing leisure time. Furthermore, competition intensified increasingly among rivals as the aircraft industry developed and the number of travelers increased.

Market Players

Airline companies. The direct clients of aircraft manufacturers were businesses (for private jets) and airline carriers (for commercial aircraft); however, the end-customers were passengers who travelled more often and became increasingly sensitive to ticket price. The expectations of the average traveler changed significantly with the democratization of air travel and their needs and preferences guided the buying decisions of airline companies when they acquired new aircraft.

The deregulation of the industry started in the United States in the late-1970s. Subsequently, it spread to the rest of the world and pressured airline companies to seek new means of reducing their costs. The preferences of travelers shifted from comfort in the 1980s and 1990s to low price (see Exhibit 3). This trend led to the proliferation of low-cost carrier (LCC) companies and to a significant drop in ticket price.

In addition, the passenger airplanes had to be reliable, comfortable and economical while those used in cargo[7] required modularity and flexibility in order to accommodate the varying needs of customers.

---

[7]Cargo involves the transportation of goods as opposed to the transportation of passengers.

Leasing companies. Starting in the mid-1990s, the industry experienced significant changes in the way new aircraft were acquired and financed. Airline carriers moved from the traditional model, which involved bank loans to acquire airplanes, to more flexible modes of ownership and financial arrangements. To adapt to changing technical requirements and fluctuating demand, they used a variety of financial mechanisms, two of which are most common.

First, lease financing allowed the carriers to own aircraft that were actually financed by manufacturers rather than banks. Indeed, financial solutions became critical to successful business development. For instance, Boeing Capital Corporation (BCC) was a division of Boeing whose mandate was to devise financial solutions for potential acquirers of Boeing airplanes. From Boeing's perspective, BCC's mission was to facilitate sales and support business development teams during the negotiation of new deals.

Second, equipment leasing was another financial mechanism that was used widely in the industry. Leasing companies bought and maintained airplanes that they subsequently lent to carriers on demand. This model allowed for the dynamic adaptation of an airline's fleet to fluctuating demand in terms of both number and size of airplanes. Moreover, rental companies were able to negotiate better deals with manufacturers thanks to the high volume of aircraft they acquired as brokers.

Outsourcing to suppliers and co-development with partners. The design and manufacturing of reliable and economical aircraft required high expertise in numerous areas. Consequently, aircraft manufacturers tended to leverage the know-how of external partners and subcontractors that had mastered very specific technologies and processes.

Like its competitors, Bombardier was primarily an integrator of technologies and components that were developed by select strategic partners in compliance with the company's specifications and requirements. An average airplane comprised about 55,000 parts, most of which were subcontracted to external partners. In 2007 alone, Bombardier paid nearly $6 billion in outsourcing costs to subcontractors. These were of three categories:[8] The first included manufacturers of major structural components such as wings, engines and landing gears (e.g., Allied Signals, Boeing Canada, GE Engines, McDonnel Douglas, Pratt & Whitney and Rolls-Royce Motors); the second type included suppliers of less complex but important parts (e.g., Parker Hannifin, Rockwell Collins, Honeywell, Goodrich and Hamilton Sundstrand); the third category consisted of repair and routine maintenance companies (e.g., Rolls-Royce, Field Aviation, CAE Aviation, Conair and Standard Aero).

Aircraft manufacturers typically sought strategic partnerships to access external expertise and competences they lacked internally. In terms of quality, the components provided by outside partners were expected to meet the highest standards set by industry regulators and fulfill the promises made to customers by the company, especially in terms of performance and operating costs.

Strategic partnerships were also used by some manufacturers to achieve economies of scale while focusing on their core competencies as well as to reduce time-to-market while developing and marketing new products. This was often achieved by joining research efforts and achieving synergies in terms of human and financial resources. Furthermore, partnerships

---

[8]"Québec Aeronautical Industry Development Strategy," Government of Quebec, 2006, www.mdeie.gouv.qc.ca/ministere/english/about-us/strategies/departmental-strategy/quebec-aeronautical-industry-development-strategy/.

allowed for the sharing of industrial and commercial risks that were inherent to high-tech and research-intensive ventures such as in aeronautics.

Governmental regulations and subsidies. Aeronautics had always been viewed as a highly strategic industry by governments. Companies like Bombardier were not only major job-creators but also symbols of pride and sovereignty. This may be explained by the possibility of technology transfer between the commercial and military streams of the industry.[9]

Accordingly, governments tended to support their national manufacturers and spend billions of dollars in direct or indirect subsidies to support their research and development efforts, promote their products and shield their local markets from foreign competition.

In Canada, for example, the provincial and federal governments initiated various programs to foster research and mitigate investment risks for local players. Three programs are particularly illustrative of the mechanisms they used to achieve this objective.

First, *Export Development Canada* (EDC) provided financial support and special warranty to all Canadian companies involved in the export of aerospace products and services.

Second, *Technology Partnerships Canada* (TPC) was set up to provide funding support for strategic research and development in areas including aeronautics.

Finally, *Program productivity of the industry of the material of defense* (PPIMD) provided generous credit lines to finance research and development projects that took place in Canada.

More specifically, the government of Canada granted loans to local airline companies when they acquired Bombardier's jets. While this program was clearly designed to support Bombardier against its main competitor (Brazilian Embraer) in the Canadian market, the government of Canada argued that the practice was common in the industry worldwide.[10]

Nevertheless, whenever a government intervened to support its national aircraft industry, foreign governments and competitors reacted vigorously and engaged in legal battles to prevent or delay them. They generally referred to the World Trade Organization's (WTO) trade framework and anti-dumping[11] policies that were ratified by their countries.

In particular, the WTO arbitrated several litigations between Canada and Brazil in relation to fair competition between Bombardier and Embraer. In August 2000, WTO authorized Canada to apply countermeasures of up to $2.1 billion in response to the government of Brazil's subsidies to Embraer through its PROEX program. However, Canada lost a battle to Brazil in December 2002 when the WTO granted Brazil the right to impose countermeasures of up to $385 million (instead of the $5.2 billion initially claimed by Brazil) against Canada. This conflict originated from a financing offer—with particularly low interest

---

[9]"Canada Aerospace," Industry Canada, 2008, www.ic.gc.ca/eic/site/ad-ad.nsf/vwapj/aero-brochure_eng. pdf/$file/aero-brochure_eng.pdf.

[10]"The Bombardier-Embraer Dispute and its Implications for Western Hemisphere Integration," Center for Strategic and International Studies, 2003, www.csis.org/files/media/csis/pubs/pp0312doh%5b1%5d.pdf.

[11]Dumping means "[t]he sale of goods of one nation in the markets of a second nation at less than the price charged within the first nation. Dumping can eliminate competitors by undercutting their prices," *American Heritage New Dictionary of Cultural Literacy*, 3rd Ed., Houghton Mifflin Company, 2005, dictionary.reference.com/browse/dumping, accessed on June 2, 2008.

rates—made by the government of Canada to Air Wisconsin in return for the acquisition of Bombardier's aircraft. It is important to note, however, that the WTO ruling allowed Brazil to increase its tariffs on Canadian exports temporarily but did not prevent the transaction between Bombardier and Air Wisconsin from materializing.

Another means by which governments intervened in the industry was through environmental regulations. As global warming debates intensified, several governments established laws and introduced incentives to mitigate the negative effects of air transportation on the environment.[12] For instance, the European Union (EU) ruled the application of its Emissions Trading Scheme (ETS) to air transportation beginning 2011. This trend resulted in a race for the development and acquisition of more environment-friendly aircraft, in increased demand for fuel-efficient jets and in early withdrawals of airplanes with high fuel consumption.[13] Accordingly, the new generations of airplanes were expected to be more energy-efficient and reduce noise pollution for the residential areas neighboring airports.

Evolution of Aircraft Market

The industry experienced major transformations as a result of several cyclical and random events, all of which had structuring and long-term effects on the dynamics of the industry as a whole.

Short-lived events but lasting effects. Overall, the market for commercial aircraft followed a growth trend since the 1970s in terms of both turnover and volume of sales. However, the period between 2001 and 2003 was particularly difficult for the industry as a whole for a variety of reasons.

Firstly, before 2001, the industry saw the emergence of a new category of carriers—generally referred to as LCC—initially in the United States and then globally. They were a natural response to the increasing sensitivity of travelers to pricing (see Exhibit 3). Oil crises also destabilized the industry in the 1970s and 1990s but their economic effects were quickly mitigated by airline carriers and manufacturers alike.

Secondly, between 2001 and 2003, the industry was confronted with a major crisis as a result of several unforeseeable events that occurred during a short period of time. The attacks on the World Trade Center in September 2001 had a devastating effect on many companies due to the immediate collapse of demand. Many carriers had to cancel or defer their orders to manufacturers.

Finally, as soon as the industry began to foresee its recovery from the effects of these events, an endemic disease appeared in Hong Kong and spread to the rest of the world. Between November 2002 and July 2003, the severe acute respiratory syndrome (SARS) affected 8,096 people and caused 774 deaths.[14] The impact on most airline companies was as quick as it was critical. A large number of flights were cancelled, which put airline companies in dire need. Several companies either sought hasty mergers with competitors or declared bankruptcy within the first few weeks of the outbreak.

---

[12]"Commercial Aircraft Market Forecast 2007-2026," Bombardier, 2007.

[13]"Emissions Trading System," International Civil Aviation Organization: Air Transport Bureau, www.icao.int/env/EmissionsTrading.htm.

[14]"Severe acute respiratory syndrome (SARS): Status of the outbreak and lessons for the immediate future," *World Health Organization*, 2003, www.who.int/csr/media/sars_wha.pdf.

For the companies that survived these events, industry activity began to recover in 2003. By 2006, this activity reached the level of 2001 (see Exhibit 4) and airline carriers became profitable again.[15]

A cyclical industry in structural mutation. The aircraft industry was cyclical by nature and the replacement of aging airplanes was an important driver of the demand. New airplanes were typically acquired to either increase capacity or replace aircraft that were not suitable for the transportation of passengers anymore. The retired airplanes were generally recycled and reassigned to the transportation of goods.

In the mid-1970s, airline carriers started to reconfigure their routes into networks (hub-and-spoke) instead of the traditional point-to-point configurations. Hub-and-spokes consisted of rings of small routes (spokes) used to consolidate traffic and feed regional airports (hubs) with larger numbers of passengers. This architecture led to a stunning development of regional carriers and subsequently to the commercial success of regional airplanes. This trend transformed the dynamics of the market in a profound way.

In 2007, the long-term forecasts of major airline manufacturers predicted an even faster development of regional hubs between 2010 and 2025. Consequently, they expected the demand for regional aircraft of fewer than 140 seats to increase dramatically during this period.

Buying Decision Criteria

The configuration of a carrier's network of routes was dependent upon the level of demand on each route, the pricing strategy of the company and the capacity of the fleet it operated. In addition to the acquisition costs of airplanes, their exploitation costs were critical to the profitability and performance of carriers; this was why high fuel prices continued to impede the profitability of airline companies despite a decrease in other operating costs and an increase in revenues.

The performance of airliner companies was essentially contingent on the effective control of their operating costs. The average consumption of commercial aircraft dropped by 37 per cent in just two decades. On average, modern aircraft consumed five per cent (or five litres of kerosene per 100 RPK[16]) in 2005 compared to eight per cent in 1985[17].

In addition, the technologies used in making engines played a major role in the level of performance of aircraft. Typically, manufacturers promised to improve the operating costs of a new aircraft by developing new technologies to save energy and reduce maintenance needs. For instance, turbo-reactors were generally considered less expensive to maintain than turbo-props. Conversely, turbo-props consumed less fuel, generated less pollution but provided a lower level of comfort for passengers than turbo-reactors. Accordingly, the number of turbo-props operated by regional carriers increased significantly as fuel prices increased.

---

[15]"Airline Financial Monitor", *International Air Transport Association*, 2011, www.iata.org/whatwedo/Documents/economics/AirlinesFinancialMonitorFeb11.pdf.

[16]RPK is an acronym for revenue per person-kilometre.

[17]"Airbus Global Market Forecast 2006–2025" report, Airbus, 2007.

Future Perspectives for the Industry[18]

Supported by a generally dynamic economy, the aircraft market grew by 30 per cent between 2000 and 2005. This was made possible by a combination of gains in productivity, increase in existing capacity and entry of new players in the market. Moreover, Airbus forecasted an annual growth of 4.8 per cent for passenger aircraft market over a period of twenty years, rising from 12,676 in 2005 to 27,307 in 2025.

Market trends by geographical area. The business model of LCCs has been viable since its inception in the early 1990s owing to tight control of operating costs. By the middle of the 1990s, regional carriers pushed to lower their costs and to specialize in short- to mid-range routes while seeking synergies with traditional carriers that operated longer distance transportation. This combination attempted to offer a viable and flexible alternative to LCCs. In 2007, the model was expected to develop further as regional traffic grew, especially in emerging markets.

Large emerging countries such as Brazil, China, India and Russia (BRIC) spanned wide geographic areas and their populations were growing quickly. Other smaller but fast-growing countries in Africa, Asia, Eastern Europe and Latin America were also expected to contribute to the growth of the industry in a significant way.[19] The orders by BRIC countries represented more than 35 per cent of the global demand in 2005. This was a major rebound from less than five per cent just a few years earlier (see Exhibit 5).

Market trends by category of aircraft. Airplanes were typically categorized according to their capacity and their range of reach. Most manufacturers and analysts made a distinction between three categories of aircraft or market segments.

First, commercial airplanes were designed to carry more than 100 passengers. The European Airbus and American Boeing were the two traditional manufacturers of commercial jets. Airlines were expected to acquire an average of 1,133 commercial airplanes every year between 2006 and 2025. The utilization of mid-size aircraft ranging from 100 to 140 seats had also increased steadily in both domestic and regional transportation segments. In North America, this category represented more than two-thirds of all aircraft sold between 2000 and 2006. Globally, this market segment was expected to grow by 56 per cent over twenty years, rising from 5,400 units in 2006 to 8,400 in 2026.

Second, the capacity of regional jets ranged between 30 and 100 seats. These crafts were primarily used by regional carriers to respond to two types of transportation needs: local point-to-point routes with high frequency and interconnections between regional hubs that were used by long-haul carriers. Regional transporters often operated turbo-reactors or turbo-props of fewer than 100 seats whereas large airline companies used larger airplanes on long-haul, continental and international routes. According to the General Aviation Manufacturers Association,[20] 245 regional aircraft were delivered worldwide in 2006. Bombardier also forecasted that the demand for regional jets of 30 to 100 seats was set to reach 5,400 units by 2026 (see Exhibit 6). Overall, the demand was increasingly shifting towards regional jets with a capacity of 100 to 150 seats.

Finally, business jets were designed to carry fewer than 20 passengers. They were intended for affluent individuals or large organizations seeking flexibility in travel arrangements for their executives.

---

[18]Bombardier Aerospace's Commercial Aircraft Market Forecast 2007-2026, Airbus's Global Market Forecast 2006–2025, Embraer's Market Outlook and Boeing's Current Market Outlook 2007.

[19]"Airbus Global Market Forecast 2006–2025," Airbus, 2007.

[20]"Annual Report: Global View (2006-2007)," Bombardier, 2007.

BOMBARDIER AEROSPACE: A LEADER IN THE REGIONAL JET MARKET

Bombardier specialized in the development and manufacturing of two types of airplanes: business jets and regional aircraft. To a much lower extent, they also manufactured amphibious airplanes that were used in firefighting, sold spare parts, provided maintenance and training services and offered multi-property Flexjet and Skyjet services (see Exhibit 7). In 2006, Bombardier delivered a total of 337 aircraft including 197 business jets, 138 regional jets and two amphibious aircraft.

Business Jets Segment

Bombardier had three major categories of businesses jets: the Learjet family, composed of narrow fuselage aircraft, and Challenger and Global Express families, which included larger fuselage airplanes. Compared to its competitors, Bombardier had a more diversified portfolio of products in this segment. In 2006, Bombardier had 27 per cent market share in this segment, which represented about 47 per cent of the total sales of the company.[21] In terms of volume, Bombardier made 213 units out of the 798 business jets delivered by the industry during the same year.

Regional Jets Segment

Bombardier also had two families of regional aircraft: CRJ and Q-Series. Both series were developed based on technologies from the 1970s that were fine-tuned over the following decades. The capacity of crafts in the CRJ family ranged from 40 to 100 seats. CRJ had the reputation of being energy-efficient and was the most popular regional airplane series in history[22] with 1,409 units sold as of January 2007.

The capacity of Q-Series crafts was relatively similar to that of CRJ as it ranged from 37 to 78 seats. However, Q-Series used turbo-propulsion technology whereas CRJ was based on turbo-reaction technology. Consequently, Q-Series required less maintenance and had considerable economic advantages, especially on short-distance routes; for example, Q-Series crafts allowed for 28 per cent reduction in fuel consumption, 83 per cent in engine maintenance costs and 14 per cent in personnel and crew costs.[23] They were, however, less comfortable for passengers compared to CRJ. This was due to their narrow body and much noisier engine, particularly during takeoff and landing.

In 2006, 245 regional aircraft of fewer than 100 seats were delivered by the industry worldwide, compared to 288 in 2005. Bombardier delivered 126 units in 2006, compared to 153 in 2005.

Competition in Regional Jets Market

Bombardier had two general competitors in the regional aircraft market: Embraer in the segment of turbo-reactors and ATR in the segment of turbo-props. However, Embraer was the only serious competitor in the segment of 90 to 149 seats. Embraer had two models

---

[21]"General Aviation Statistical Databook & Industry Outlook", General Aviation Manufacturers Association, 2009, http://ntl.bts.gov/lib/35000/35200/35288/GA_Statistical_Databook_and_Industry_Outlook_0.pdf

[22]"Annual Report 2007–2008", Bombardier, January 31, 2008, www2.bombardier.com/en/0_0/0_0_1/0_0_1_7/0_0_1_7_0.html

[23]Bombardier & Speed News public presentation, November 6, 2006.

(ERJ190 and ERJ195) that were specifically designed to satisfy the requirements of regional carriers in terms of both capacity and efficiency (see Exhibit 8). In addition, Boeing and Airbus had several models (B717 and B737-600 for Boeing and A318-100 for Airbus) with capacity of slightly above 100 seats but these aircraft were significantly more expensive to acquire and operate, especially on regional routes.

While Embraer and Bombardier were the leading manufacturers in the regional aircraft segment in 2007, several countries showed interest in entering this market. They were driven by their national needs as well as by the attractive opportunity of entering such a high-potential segment. For instance, the Chinese government expressed plans to build a modern aircraft industry and the state-owned AVIC-I (China Aviation Industry Corp.) announced its ARJ21-900 model (105 seats) for 2011. Japanese Mitsubishi Heavy Industries (MHI) also announced the development of a similar family of aircraft (MRJ) with two models: MRJ-70 (70 passengers) and MRJ-90 (90 passengers).[24] Interestingly, both AVIC-I and MHI were suppliers of parts used in Bombardier's Q-Series. Likewise, the Russian Sukhoi made public its intention to develop the RRJ (Russian Regional Jet)[25] family, also known as Superjet 100 Regional Jet with similar capacity. If the Chinese and Russian projects were carried forward, they could become serious competitors to Bombardier's CRJ1000 model (launched in February 19, 2007) and CSeries family.

BOMBARDIER AEROSPACE AND THE CSERIES DILEMMA

On February 19, 2007, Bombardier announced its decision to expand the CRJ family and offer a new model by 2010. The objective of the CRJ1000 model was to provide higher capacity (86 to 104 seats) and higher levels of comfort to passengers at lower operating costs in comparison to Bombardier's own models and those of competitors in the range of 90–100 seats. The program was launched with 38 conditional orders, including 15 conversions from existing CRJ900 orders.

Some analysts argued that the decision was tactical and short-lived because it merely extended an outdated family of products. It did not address Bombardier's fundamental issue of aging technologies within both the Q-Series and CRJ families. Other analysts suggested that the only way Bombardier could deal with the aging technology would be by developing a completely new generation of airplanes similar to those envisioned by the CSeries project.

CSeries: Bombardier's Response to Market Transformation?

Since July 2004, Bombardier was contemplating the development of the CSeries, a new family of aircraft capable of carrying between 100 and 135 passengers depending on models. It was intended for airliners who owned old generations of aircraft within the same capacity range. This included models such as DC9, Fokker 100, Boeing 737, BAE-146 and

---

[24]"Mitsubishi Spec to Rival Embraer, Bombardier RJs," *Aviation Week*, www.aviationweek.biz/aw/generic/story.generic.jsp?channel=awst&id=news/aw061807p3.xml&headline=Mitsubishi%20Spec%20To%20Rival%20Embraer,%20Bombardier%20RJs.

[25]"Annual Report 2008," Sukhoi Civil Aircraft Joint-Stock Company, 2009, http://ir.superjet100.com/assets/files/library/reports/annual_reports_en/annual%20report%202008.pdf.

MD80 which were aging and needed to be replaced with more comfortable and more effi-cient models.

For the airplanes available in 2007 (see Exhibit 8) to meet the capacity needs of regional carriers, they would have to be shortened (Airbus 318, Airbus 319, Boeing 737-200, Boeing 737-600) or lengthened (Embraer 190 and Embraer 195). Contrast-ingly, the CSeries family would be specifically optimized to operate on regional routes. Specifically, the C110 model was expected to consume 17 per cent less energy than the Airbus A318 while the C130 model would consume 11 per cent less than Airbus A319 (see Exhibit 9). In terms of operating costs, both Airbus and Boeing aircraft were signifi-cantly more expensive to operate than CSeries.

While Bombardier's C110 would have to face Embraer's 190 and 195 models as direct competition (see Exhibits 10 and 11), the C130 model did not have any serious challenger in the market. However, some analysts did not exclude the possibility that Embraer could work on a secretive project, especially given the potential of this market segment and the company's significant investments in research and development, which jumped from $92 million in 2005 to $113 million in 2006. Hence, the window of opportunity for Bombar-dier's CSeries seemed to narrow quickly as time passed and potential competitors loomed (see Exhibits 12 to 16).

The Genesis of the CSeries Initiative

In July 2004, at the Farnborough Aerospace Fair, Bombardier announced its intention to develop a new family of regional aircraft called CSeries. The company anticipated that the demand for airplanes in the capacity range of 100 to 150 seats would represent 13 per cent of the overall aircraft market by 2025. Accordingly, this segment would represent about 6,000 units and $25 billion in sales.

On March 15, 2005, Bombardier's board of directors approved the concept and gave Bombardier Aerospace permission to further investigate the feasibility of the project.

On May 13, 2005, the Canadian government announced its commitment to provide Bombardier with financial assistance conditional to development of the CSeries in Canada. The pledge consisted of an interest-free line of credit of $350 million dedicated to the development of new technologies for CSeries.

In 2005, the company conducted a feasibility study and released a mock-up of the aircraft at the Paris Air Show. During the same period, the company selected Bombardier's Montreal-Mirabel (Canada) site as the preferred location for the final assembly of the CSeries. They also announced an agreement with Pratt & Whitney Canada regarding the development of the engine for CSeries. Indeed, the company needed to secure a partner for the engine because, according to a spokesperson for Bombardier,[26] potential clients consistently asked them questions pertaining to the type and manufacturer of the CSeries' engine.

Notwithstanding these positive developments, on January 31, 2006, Bombardier announced their decision to put the project on hold because "market conditions (did) not justify the launch of the CSeries program at (that) time."[27] The project team was

---

[26]"Bombardier C-Series deal delayed by engine talks," *The Globe and Mail;* July 19, 2010; www.theglobeandmail.com/report-on-business/bombardier-c-series-deal-delayed-by-engine-talks/article1644486/.

[27]"Annual Report 2006–2007," *Bombardier,* 2007

subsequently reduced to about fifty people and the rest of the team was reassigned to other turbo-props regional jets within the range of 80 to 100 seats.

During a January 31, 2007 press conference, Bombardier announced that the company was still refining its plans and confirmed the tentative commercialization of CSeries by 2013, should the project be launched in 2008.

Two weeks later, on February 19, 2007, the company made public the launch of the CRJ1000 model targeting the 80-100 passengers range. This project was expected to proceed with the same resources that were released from the CSeries project in January 2006.

As of April 2007, the initial cost of the CSeries project reached $100 million, the ongoing monthly spend-rate was about $1 million and the total development cost was estimated at about $2 billion. To offset some of these costs, the governments of Canada, Quebec province and the United Kingdom were expected to finance about $700 million; specifically, Canada's federal government pledged about $260 million, Quebec's provincial government about $90 million and the U.K. government about $350 million. The conditional release of these funds required Bombardier to carry out some research and development and production activities in Montreal-Mirabel and Belfast (Northern Ireland).

THE DILEMMA

Questions remained about Bombardier's future strategy in the aerospace industry. Prospects for its existing regional jet product line were a concern for several analysts. In turn, the CSeries project involved important investments in a competitive market that provided both threats and opportunities. Still, with the upcoming shareholder annual meeting, both analysts and shareholders were expecting Pierre Beaudoin to clarify the future of the CSeries.

EXHIBIT 1:   Contribution of BA and BT to Bombardier Inc. Performance

	Revenue* ($)	Revenue (%)	Gross Margin* $ (%)	Contribution (%)
Bombardier Inc. (Corporate)	3.967	100	597 (15)	100
Bombardier Aerospace	2.260	57	344 (15.2)	57.6
Bombardier Transportation	1.707	43	253 (14.8)	42.4

All figures in US$ billions as of April 2007.

Source: Bombardier's annual reports, 2006–2007 and 2007–2008, compiled by the authors.

	2006	2005	2004	2003	2002	2001	2000	1999	1998
Currency (in million)	US$	US$	US$	US$	CA$	CA$	CA$	CA$	CA$
Bombardier Inc. revenue (BI)	$14,726	$15,546	$15,201	$13,277	$21,633	$15,944	$13,417	$11,286	$8,334
Aerospace revenue (BA)	$ 8,087	$ 7,980	$ 8,261	$ 7,271	$12,042	$10,562	$ 8,126	$ 6,444	$4,874
BA contribution ratio	55%	51%	54%	55%	56%	66%	61%	57%	58%
BA margin ($)	$ 266	$ 203	$ 438	$ 582	$ 1,206	$ 1,237	$ 904	$ 682	$ 480
BA margin (%)	3.3%	2.5%	5.3%	8.0%	10.0%	11.7%	11.1%	10.6%	9.8%

Source: Bombardier's annual reports, 2005–2006 and 2006–2007, compiled by the authors.

EXHIBIT 2: Evolution of Bombardier's Leadership

Year	Events
1942	Joseph-Armand Bombardier creates Auto-Neige Bombardier Ltd.
1964	Joseph-Armand Bombardier dies and Laurent Beaudoin is appointed general manager.
1966	Laurent Beaudoin becomes president of the company.
1969	Bombardier becomes a public company.
1979[a]	Laurent Beaudoin is named chairman and CEO of Bombardier Inc.
1990[a]	Pierre (son of Laurent) Beaudoin appointed vice-president of product development for the sea-doo/ski-doo division of Bombardier Inc.
1992[a]	Pierre Beaudoin is named executive vice-president of Sea-Doo/Ski-Doo.
1994[a]	Pierre Beaudoin serves as president of the sea-doo/ski-doo division.
1996[a]	Pierre Beaudoin is appointed president and chief operating officer (COO) of Bombardier Recreational Products. Robert E. Brown is promoted to president and COO of Bombardier Aerospace.
1999[a]	Laurent Beaudoin is named chairman of the board and of the executive committee. Robert E. Brown is appointed president and CEO of Bombardier Inc.
2001	Pierre Beaudoin is appointed president of Bombardier Aerospace, Business Aircraft in February, and president and COO in October.
2002[b]	In December, Robert E. Brown resigns.
2003[b]	In January, Paul Tellier is appointed president, CEO and director of Bombardier Inc.
2004[b]	In December, Paul Tellier resigns. Laurent Beaudoin is appointed CEO, Pierre Beaudoin is named EVP and a member of the board of directors of Bombardier Inc. in addition to his duties as president and COO of Bombardier Aerospace.

[a] Period of diversification; [b] Period of restructuring.
Source: Bombardier's annual reports, 2006–2007 and 2007–2008, compiled by the authors.

EXHIBIT 3: Passengers' Ticket Purchasing Decision Criteria

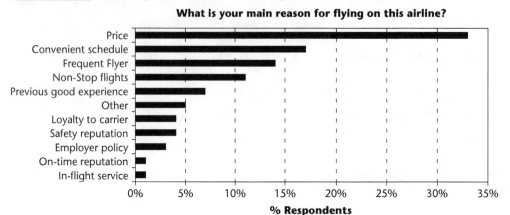

Source: "Survey of international air travel," U.S. Department of Commerce and Airbus, 2006, www.eads.com/dms/eads/int/en/investor-relations/documents/2005/presentations/Global-Investor-Forum/gif2005_airbus3_commercial_leahy.pdf, presentation by the authors.

EXHIBIT 4: New Aircraft Deliveries Between 1974 and 2006

Source: "Global Market Forecast 2006–2025: The Future of Flying," Airbus, 2006, presentation by the authors.

EXHIBIT 5: Global Demand Shifting Toward BRIC Countries

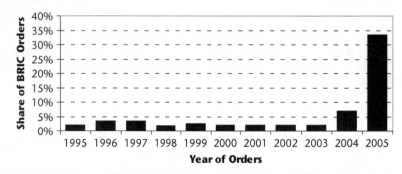

Source: "Global Market Forecast 2006–2025: The Future of Flying," Airbus, 2006, presentation by the authors.

EXHIBIT 6: New Regional Jet and Single-Aisle Demand for the 2006–2025 Period

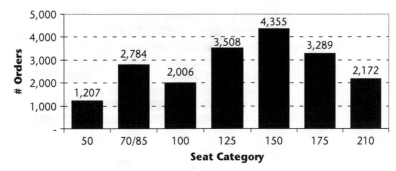

Source: "Global Market Forecast 2006–2025: The Future of Flying," Airbus, 2006, presentation by the authors.

EXHIBIT 7: Bombardier Products in 2007

Business aircraft	Regional aircraft	Service & new programs	Flexjet and Skyjet
Narrow-body models - Laserjet 40/40 XR - Laserjet 45/45 XR - Laserjet 60/60 XR Wide-body models - Challenger 300 - Challenger 604/605 - Global 5000 - Global Express XRS - Challenger 800 Series	Regional models - CRJ200 - CRJ700 - CRJ705 - CRJ900 - CRJ1000 (launched in February 2007) Turboprops models - Q200 - Q300 - Q400	- Parts logistics - Aircraft maintenance - Commercial training - Military aviation training - Amphibious aircraft - Specialized aircraft solution	- Fractional ownership - Hourly flight entitlement program

Source: Bombardier's annual reports, 2006–2007 and 2007–2008, compiled by the authors.

EXHIBIT 8: Categories and Capacity of Aircraft Available in the Market

Capacity	<100 Seats*	100–140 Seats*	>140 Seats*
Bombardier	CRJ700, 900 QSeries 200, 300, 400	CRJ1000 CSeries100, 130	
Embraer	ERJ 135, 140, 145 Embraer 170 (70), 175 (88), 190 (98)	Embraer 195 (108)	
Airbus		A318 (115), A319 (140)	A320 (160) , A321 (210)
Boeing		717–200 (110), 737–600, 737–700	737–800 (175), 737–900 (189)

* Figures between brackets refer to the number of seats in single-class configurations.

Source: Bombardier's annual reports, 2006–2007 and 2007–2008, compiled by the authors.

EXHIBIT 9: CSeries Fuel Consumption Advantage (500NM)

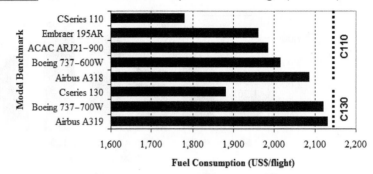

Source: Bombardier's annual report, 2006–2007, compiled by the authors.

EXHIBIT 10: Comparison of Bombardier and Embraer Product Activity

Year	Bombardier's product activity	Embraer's product activity
1991	Launch of Bombardier 415	
1992	Delivery of CRJ100	
1993		
1994	Delivery of Bombardier 415	
1995	Launch of Dash 8-200	Delivery of ERJ135
1996	Launch of CRJ200	
1997		
1998		
1999	Launch of Q400	Launch of Embraer 170
	Inaugural flight of CRJ700	Delivery of ERJ 135
2000	Delivery of Q400	Launch of Embraer 190
	Launch of CRJ900	
2001	Delivery of CRJ700	Delivery of ERJ140
	Inaugural flight of CRJ900	
2002		Launch of Embraer 175
		Launch of Embraer 195
2003	Delivery of CRJ900	Delivery of Embraer 170
	CSeries idea	
2004	CSeries announced	Delivery of Embraer 175
2005	Delivery of CRJ705	Delivery of Embraer 190
2006	CSeries on hold	Delivery of Embraer 195
2007	Launch of CRJ1000	

Source: Bombardier's annual reports, 2006–2007 and 2007–2008, compiled by the authors.

EXHIBIT 11: Bombardier and Embraer Sales Between 1998 and 2006 (Units Delivered)

Bombardier model	1998	1999	2000	2001	2002	2003	2004	2005	2006
CRJ100/200	77	81	103	136	140	152	100	44	36
CRJ 700	—	—	2	29	50	50	64	65	47
CRJ900	—	—	—	—	1	12	14	12	12
Q100/200	12	16	7	3	1	—	1	1	1
Q300	18	6	17	15	9	9	5	11	11
Q400	—	1	28	23	19	9	16	16	16
Embraer model	**1998**	**1999**	**2000**	**2001**	**2002**	**2003**	**2004**	**2005**	**2006**
EMB 120	13	7	—	2	—	—	—	—	—
ERJ135	—	16	45	27	3	14	—	2	—
ERJ140	—	—	—	22	36	16	—	—	—
ERJ145	80	80	112	104	82	57	87	46	12
EMBRAER 170	—	—	—	—	—	—	46	46	32
EMBRAER 175	—	—	—	—	—	—	—	14	11
EMBRAER 190	—	—	—	—	—	—	—	12	40
EMBRAER 195	—	—	—	—	—	—	—	—	3

Source: Bombardier and Embraer annual reports, 2006, 2007, 2008, compiled by the authors.

EXHIBIT 12: Evolution of Bombardier and Embraer Share Values (July 2001–July 2007)

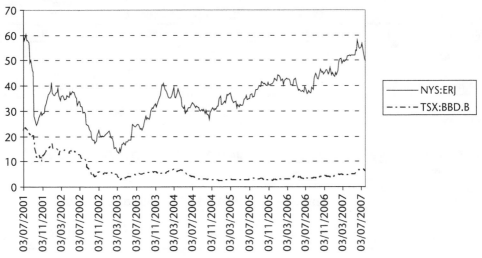

Source: Yahoo! Finance, http://finance.yahoo.com, presentation by the authors.

EXHIBIT 13: Simplified Income Statement of Bombardier Inc. (January 31, 2007)

In Millions of (except for per share items)	12 months Ending 2007-01-31	12 months Ending 2006-01-31	12 months Ending 2005-01-31	12 months Ending 2004-01-31	12 months Ending 2003-01-31
Revenue	13,250.00	13,245.00	13,912.00	19,953.40	19,773.93
Other Revenue, Total	1,632.00	1,481.00	1,634.00	1,186.85	1,235.44
Total Revenue	**14,882.00**	**14,726.00**	**15,546.00**	**21,140.25**	**21,009.37**
Cost of Revenie, Total	12,667.00	12,719.00	13,754.00	18,141.89	17,943.58
Gross Profit	**583.00**	**526.00**	**158.00**	**1,811.51**	**1,830.35**
Selling/General/Admin. Expenses, Total	929.00	842.00	859.00	1,356.40	1,485.30
Research & Development	173.00	175.00	148.00	186.41	189.38
Depreciation/Amortization	518.00	545.00	549.00	786.28	799.17
Interest Expense (Income)— Net Operating	30.00	—	—	—	—
Unusual Expense (Income)	8.00	88.00	172.00	425.36	1,299.89
Other Operating Expenses, Total	4.00	—	—	—	—
Total Operating Expense	**14,329.00**	**14,369.00**	**15,482.00**	**20,896.34**	**21,717.32**
Operating Income	**553.00**	**357.00**	**64.00**	**243.91**	**−707.95**
Interest Expense (Expenses), Net Non-Operating	−218.00	−207.00	−224.00	−234.00	−214.17
Gain (Loss) on Sale of Assets	—	—	—	—	—
Other, Net	—	—	—	—	—
Income Before Tax	**335.00**	**150.00**	**−160.00**	**9.92**	**−922.12**
Income After Tax	**243.00**	**135.00**	**−122.00**	**−193.35**	**−702.99**
Minority Interest	—	—	—	—	—
Equity In Affiliates	—	—	—	—	—
Net Income Before Extra. Items	**243.00**	**135.00**	**−122.00**	**−193.35**	−702.99
Accounting Change	—	—	—	—	—
Discount Operations	—	—	—	—	—
Extraordinary Item	—	—	—	—	—
Net Income Before Extra. Items	**268.00**	**249.00**	**−85.00**	**−88.25**	−609.79
Preferred Dividends	—	—	—	—	—
Income Available to Common Excl. Extra Item	**215.00**	**110.00**	**−145.00**	**−223.09**	**−731.74**
Income Available to Common Incl. Extra Item	**240.00**	**224.00**	**−108.00**	**−117.99**	**−638.54**

Source: Yahoo! Finance, http://finance.yahoo.com, presentation by the authors.

EXHIBIT 14: Simplified Income Statement of Embraer (December 31, 2006)

In Millions of (except for per share items)	12 months Ending 2006-12-31	12 months Ending 2005-12-31	12 months Ending 2004-12-31	12 months Ending 2003-12-31	12 months Ending 2002-12-31	12 months Ending 2001-12-31
Revenue	3,759.52	3,789.49	3,352.14	2,143.46	2,525.80	4,030.80
Other Revenue, Total	—	—	—	—	—	—
Total Revenue	**3,759.52**	**3,789.48**	**3,352.14**	**2,143.46**	**2,525.80**	**4,030.80**
Cost of Revenie, Total	2,806.80	2,738.91	2,336.74	1,335.03	1,531.72	2,355.02
Gross Profit	**952.72**	**1,050.59**	**1,015.41**	**808.43**	**994.08**	**1,675.79**
Selling/General/Admin. Expenses, Total	498.82	421.05	385.64	341.39	345.91	486.50
Research & Development	112.74	93.17	44.51	173.22	158.50	—
Depreciation/Amortization	—	—	—	—	—	—
Interest Expense (Income) - Net Operating	0.03	3.10	0.00	−0.05	−0.39	−0.42
Unusual Expense (Income)	—	—	—	—	—	—
Other Operating Expenses, Total	−1.68	26.08	41.27	29.06	20.50	62.02
Total Operating Expense	**3,416.72**	**3,282.30**	**2,808.16**	**1,878.64**	**2,056.24**	**2,903.11**
Operating Income	**342.80**	**507.19**	**543.99**	**264.81**	**469.56**	**1,127.69**
Interest Expense (Expenses), Net Non-Operating	105.43	-4.12	-38.00	-140.75	80.46	115.05
Gain (Loss) on Sale of Assets	—	—	—	—	—	—
Other, Net	−4.10	−6.17	−12.34	−15.79	−137.04	−311.39
Income Before Tax	**444.13**	**496.91**	**493.65**	**108.27**	**412.98**	**931.36**
Income After Tax	**399.72**	**455.34**	**381.51**	**136.26**	**224.47**	**646.98**
Minority Interest	−9.58	−9.62	−1.31	−0.22	−1.88	−2.78
Equity In Affiliates	—	—	—	—	—	—
Net Income Before Extra. Items	**390.14**	**445.72**	**380.21**	**136.04**	**222.59**	**643.98**
Accounting Change	—	—	—	—	—	—
Discount Operations	—	—	—	—	—	—
Extraordinary Item	—	—	—	—	—	—
Net Income Before Extra. Items	**399.43**	**441.09**	**385.38**	**136.04**	222.59	**643.98**
Preferred Dividends	—	—	—	—	—	—
Income Available to Common Excl. Extra Item	**390.14**	**445.72**	**380.21**	**136.04**	**222.59**	**643.98**
Income Available to Common Incl. Extra Item	**399.43**	**441.09**	**385.38**	**136.04**	**222.59**	**643.98**

Source: Yahoo! Finance, http://finance.yahoo.com, presentation by the authors.

EXHIBIT 15: Performance Ratios and Indicators (TSX:BBD B)

Profitability Ratios	1/31/2006	1/31/2005	1/31/2004	1/31/2003	1/31/2002	1/31/2001	1/31/2000	1/31/1999	1/31/1998
Return on Equity (%)	10.27	−3.7	−2.74	−22.44	9.56	25.58	19.9	15.88	14.54
Pre-Tax Margin	1.02	−0.64	0.05	−3.34	2.79	8.68	7.88	7.19	7.37
Net Profit Margin (%)	1.69	−0.54	−0.42	−2.6	1.81	6.06	5.28	4.82	4.94
Effective Tax Rate (%)	0.05	−0.05	0.49	−0.36	0.41	1.38	1.36	1.23	1.26
Liquidity Indicators	**1/31/2006**	**1/31/2005**	**1/31/2004**	**1/31/2003**	**1/31/2002**	**1/31/2001**	**1/31/2000**	**1/31/1999**	**1/31/1998**
Quick Ratio	0.29	0.22	0.11	0.07	0.03	0.15	0.21	0.22	0.21
Current Ratio	0.99	1.07	0.99	1.02	1.29	1.97	1.85	1.49	1.51
Working Capital/ Total Assets	0	0.04	−0.01	0.01	0.14	0.43	0.4	0.27	0.28
Debt Management	**1/31/2006**	**1/31/2005**	**1/31/2004**	**1/31/2003**	**1/31/2002**	**1/31/2001**	**1/31/2000**	**1/31/1999**	**1/31/1998**
Current Liabilities/ Equity	4.1	4.72	4.34	5.82	3.38	2.34	2.21	2.23	2
Total Debt to Equity	1.96	3.13	2.58	4.15	2.66	2.27	1.88	1.42	1.32
Long Term Debt to Assets	0.27	0.34	0.32	0.3	0.28	0.3	0.28	0.18	0.15
Asset Management	**1/31/2006**	**1/31/2005**	**1/31/2004**	**1/31/2003**	**1/31/2002**	**1/31/2001**	**1/31/2000**	**1/31/1999**	**1/31/1998**
Revenues/ Total Assets	0.84	0.79	0.83	0.82	0.78	0.79	0.8	0.81	0.8
Revenues/ Working Capital	−207.41	21.46	−146.03	86.84	5.48	1.86	2	3.01	2.91
Interest Coverage	—	0.34	1.04	—	—	—	—	—	—

Source: Mergent Online database, accessed August 1, 2011.

EXHIBIT 16: Embraer Performance Ratios and Indicators (NYS:ERJ)

Profitability Ratios	12/31/2006	12/31/2005	12/31/2004	12/31/2003	12/31/2002	12/31/2001	12/31/2000	12/31/1999	12/31/1998
Return on Equity (%)	12.33	14.97	28.43	15.75	35.44	44.81	41.93	59.12	31.6
Return on Assets (%)	3.82	4.17	8.85	4.58	10.49	14.25	12.65	11.91	6.42
Return on Investment	14.17	18.31	40.74	26.9	70.8	117.07	81.88	47.44	28.5
Gross Margin	0.025	0.024	0.033	0.036	0.045	0.042	0.031	0.029	0.028
Operating Margin (%)	6.23	4.97	9.9	10.49	16.67	22.49	16.05	11.6	10.65
Pre-Tax Margin	6.06	5.12	9.89	9.79	16.61	21.95	16.43	10.66	10.21
Net Profit Margin (%)	7.45	7.76	12.27	8.94	15.22	15.98	12.65	12.24	8.41
Effective Tax Rate (%)	0.98	1.06	1.88	2.25	3.54	4.37	2.32	-1.55	0.42

Liquidity Indicators	12/31/2006	12/31/2005	12/31/2004	12/31/2003	12/31/2002	12/31/2001	12/31/2000	12/31/1999	12/31/1998
Quick Ratio	0.59	0.72	0.66	0.6	0.42	0.44	0.87	0.26	0.25
Current Ratio	1.63	1.81	1.91	1.53	1.54	1.51	1.52	1.23	0.96
Working Capital/ Total Assets	0.25	0.3	0.35	0.25	0.27	0.26	0.27	0.14	-0.02

Debt Management	12/31/2006	12/31/2005	12/31/2004	12/31/2003	12/31/2002	12/31/2001	12/31/2000	12/31/1999	12/31/1998
Current Liabilities/ Equity	1.27	1.31	1.23	1.63	1.65	1.61	1.73	2.98	2.99
Total Debt to Equity	0.55	0.78	0.5	0.41	0.33	0.23	0.23	0.47	0.36
Long Term Debt to Assets	0.17	0.22	0.15	0.12	0.1	0.07	0.07	0.09	0.07

Asset Management	12/31/2006	12/31/2005	12/31/2004	12/31/2003	12/31/2002	12/31/2001	12/31/2000	12/31/1999	12/31/1998
Revenues/ Total Assets	0.51	0.54	0.72	0.51	0.69	0.89	1	0.97	0.76
Revenues/Working Capital	2.08	1.82	2.08	2.03	2.59	3.41	3.68	7.21	-33.84
Interest Coverage	3.33	2.68	3.22	5.17	5.77	9.95	9.91		—

Source: Mergent Online database, accessed August 1, 2011.

Movember:
More Mo Sistas

On January 18, 2012, at 9:30 a.m., Jesse Hayman, community development manager for Movember Canada, sat at his desk in the organization's downtown Toronto headquarters. Over the past few weeks, the Movember Canada team had been hard at work analyzing information from the organization's annual month-long November campaign. As a not-for-profit organization, Movember strived to raise both money and awareness for men's health, specifically prostate cancer.[1] Globally, in 2011, Movember had successfully raised over C$125.7 million,[2] with the Canadian campaign representing the top country worldwide, contributing a significant $42 million. However, more needed to be done to meet the challenge, as prostate cancer represented the number-one cancer threat to Canadian men, affecting one in six men during their lifetime.[3]

With the Movember Canada team already looking ahead to the 2012 campaign, Hayman contemplated how to continue to build upon the previous years of success. While men (called "Mo Bros") were engaging in Movember by gathering pledges and sporting Movember moustaches, Hayman wanted to encourage more women (referred

IVEY | Publishing

Michele Parkin, Paul Bigus and Shreya Tekriwal wrote this case solely to provide material for class discussion. The authors do not intend to illustrate either effective or ineffective handling of a managerial situation. The authors may have disguised certain names and other identifying information to protect confidentiality.

This publication may not be transmitted, photocopied, digitized or otherwise reproduced in any form or by any means without the permission of the copyright holder. Reproduction of this material is not covered under authorization by any reproduction rights organization. To order copies or request permission to reproduce materials, contact Ivey Publishing, Ivey Business School, Western University, London, Ontario, Canada, N6G 0N1; (t) 519.661.3208; (e) cases@ivey.ca;www.iveycases.com.

Copyright © 2013, Richard Ivey School of Business Foundation   Version: 2013-09-26

One time permission to reproduce granted by Richard Ivey School of Business Foundation on April 22, 2014.

[1]"About Movember," Movember, http://ca.movember.com/about, accessed January 7, 2013.

[2]All funds are given in Canadian dollars (C$), unless stated otherwise.

[3]"Canada Campaign Report 2009," Movember, http://ca.movember.com/uploads/files/Foundation/Canada_AR_2010.pdf, accessed January 7, 2013.

to as "Mo Sistas") to participate in and support the Movember campaign.[4] Although big steps had been taken towards changing the attitudes and habits relating to men's health around the world, there was still much to be done to catch up with the women's health movement. Many organizations relating to women's health were already well established and quite successful at reaching out each year for support and donations from the female demographic. Thinking ahead to the 2012 Movember campaign, Hayman needed to determine how the organization could attract and involve more women in battling a health issue that was not their own.

MOVEMBER HISTORY[5]

With humble beginnings in Melbourne, Australia, the Movember campaign first began as a bit of a joke in 2003 when two guys, sitting around in a bar having pints, decided to bring back the moustache and challenged each other to grow them for an entire month.[6] A year later, a small group of 30 followers realized that their month-long moustache challenge had the potential to make a difference.[7] In 2004, Movember was officially established as a not-for-profit organization with a campaign focused on raising awareness and funds for the number-one cancer affecting men—prostate cancer. With a campaign that focused on growing moustaches for the entire month of November, the seemingly appropriate portmanteau name of Movember was created. Each November 1, participating Mo Bros became walking, talking billboards for the month, raising awareness by prompting private and public conversation around the often ignored issues of men's health. Mo Bros raised funds by getting sponsorships for their moustache-growing efforts and were often supported in this by the women in their lives (who Movember dubbed Mo Sistas). In 2004, during the first year of the Movember campaign that involved fundraising, over 450 Mo Bros and Mo Sistas participated in Australia, raising more than $54,000 for the Prostate Cancer Foundation of Australia, representing the single largest donation the organization had ever received.[8]

The Movember campaign continued into a strong second year of operations in 2005, expanding across Australia, with 9,315 participants raising a total of $1.2 million. The organization officially received charitable status in Australia in 2006, as the Movember campaign raised $9.3 million from the efforts of over 56,000 participants in both Australia and New Zealand. Significant geographic expansion occurred in 2007, with the Movember campaign expanding to Canada, Spain, the United Kingdom and the United States, enabling other countries to raise awareness and funds to support programs for prostate cancer or other significant men's health issues. The growth and popularity of the Movember campaign could be seen with each passing November, as participation became an annual event in many workplaces, colleges and universities, and police and fire departments, as well as throughout the military and across professional sports teams. The campaign was furthered with giant moustaches appearing on buildings, boats and planes, and with media coverage of Movember-related events and stories.

---

[4]"About Movember," Movember, http://ca.movember.com/about, accessed November 22, 2012.

[5]"Movember Global Annual Report 2011," Movember, http://ca.movember.com/uploads/files/Annual%20 Reports/Movember_AR_2011.pdf, accessed January 7, 2013.

[6]http:ca.movember.com/about/history/, accessed January 7, 2013.

[7]Ibid.

[8]Ibid.

By 2011, Movember had expanded operations to include formal campaigns in 14 countries, with the additional participation of many other countries and cities around the world.[9] In total, the 2011 Movember global campaign inspired the involvement of over 854,000 Mo Bros and Mo Sistas to raise a total of $125.7 million (see Exhibit 1).[10]

JESSE HAYMAN

Hayman was raised in the community of Thornhill, north of Toronto, Ontario. His father owned a mechanic shop and his mother worked in automotive sales. After completing high school, Hayman pursued a post-secondary education at the University of Western Ontario (Western University), in London, Ontario. While at Western, he majored in philosophy and played for the men's varsity rugby team. It was during this time that Hayman first learned about the Movember campaign. Each fall, the Western men's rugby team had a tradition of growing moustaches during the playoffs. However, during Hayman's third year at Western, one of his teammates proposed the idea of participating in Movember, as both the playoffs and the campaign conveniently coincided. Hayman stated, "It was the first charity that really spoke to me. It reached out to an audience in a way other charities hadn't."

After graduating from Western in 2009, Hayman had no idea what he wanted to do next. He travelled for a year and eventually returned to England to start a sports charity organization. However, he realized the lengthy process it would take to obtain the necessary charitable status and so shifted his focus from starting a charitable organization to gaining experience in one. He thought back to his days at Western; his first and obvious choice was Movember. Hayman contacted Prostate Cancer Canada (PCC), Movember's men's health partner, and through a combination of motivation, timing and perhaps fate, he obtained the position of campus coordinator, responsible for facilitating the Movember campaign across Canadian campus locations. When Hayman officially joined the organization in June 2010, Movember was operating a small campus program with only 2,400 registrants from the previous November campaign. His mandate was to grow the campus program.

During Hayman's first year working with the Movember campaign, he was one of only three employees dedicated to Movember operations in Canada. Although his responsibility was to grow the campus program, he enjoyed the opportunity to become involved in many other campaign activities. Together, the small team was able to help increase the total number of registered Movember participants in Canada from 35,000 in 2009, to nearly 119,000 in 2010, with campus participation growing significantly to include over 12,000 students. Within the small Movember team, it was standard practice for people to "wear multiple hats" to make things work. As a result, Hayman often found himself involved with clubs, local committees, professional sports teams and various third-party events. In 2011, Movember Canada officially obtained charitable status in Canada, henceforth operating independently from PCC. With the growth and success of the Movember campaign in Canada, Hayman moved into the role of community development manager in 2011, to work strategically on the grassroots Movember in Canada.

---

[9]"About Movember," Movember, http://ca.movember.com/about, accessed January 7, 2013.
[10]Ibid.

MOVEMBER CANADA

In the short five years the Movember campaign had operated in Canada (2007–2012), the program had achieved significant growth (see Exhibit 2). Working with PCC as its official men's health partner since 2007, Movember remained PCC's largest donor each year, raising more donations and awareness than any other prostate cancer campaign in Canada.[11]

Operating around a simple but important set of strategic goals (see Exhibit 3), Movember coordinated activities with official committees located in cities across the country. It was difficult to enter into a new location, as it was a challenge to find the right people, select a chairperson and ensure that they were operating the campaign in the correct manner. As a result, the Movember Canada team did not attempt to add local committees where one had not already organically grown. An official Movember committee could only be established through an invitation from Movember Canada. Once an official local committee was established it did not receive monetary support from Movember, but instead obtained assistance in coordinating its various activities. They worked together to help support Movember's growth in those communities.

To participate in the month-long campaign, Mo Bros could register at Movember. com as part of a team or as an individual effort. While growing a moustache was a male-only activity, Mo Sistas could still get involved by registering online, recruiting a team, raising donations, organizing events, or simply showing support. Once a team or individual was registered, Movember provided all the necessary materials to fundraise, as well as outlined the rules to follow (see Exhibit 4). Participants could also order Movember posters, donation boxes, stickers and badges to support various events during the month-long campaign. Over the 30 days of Movember, participants would collect cash donations in person or have donations made to their registered account online. The Movember website also supported the spirit of healthy competition by providing a leaderboard to keep track of different fundraising totals and pictures of moustaches from around the world. At the end of the month, Mo Bros and Mo Sistas were encouraged to celebrate their moustaches and fundraising efforts by hosting their own Movember party or attending one of the Movember Gala parties in major cities across Canada (see Exhibit 5).

When asked to comment on what made Movember so unique, Steve Jones, former president and CEO of PCC, stated, "There is no other program like it. When companies participate, we are told that morale increases many times over–people simply have fun growing and comparing their Mo's all the while knowing that they are doing it for a good cause."[12] With the previous 2011 Movember campaign in Canada raising a record amount of $42 million, the small Movember Canada team, which had grown to comprise 10 full-time employees, prided itself on how lean and simple it was able to keep campaign operations. Although each staff member had a designated role and responsibilities, the flexibility and willingness of the staff to help in any area resulted in internal movement of staff between different functional areas at various times of the year.

Overall, efficient operations and a simple campaign allowed Movember Canada to allocate 86 per cent of all donations to cancer research programs and a further two per cent to men's health awareness and education in 2010. Only 10 per cent of all donations were

---

[11]"Canada Campaign Report 2009," Movember, http://ca.movember.com/uploads/files/Foundation/Canada_AR_2010.pdf, accessed January 7, 2013.

[12]"Canada Campaign Report 2009," Movember, http://ca.movember.com/uploads/files/Foundation/Canada_AR_2010.pdf, accessed January 7, 2013.

used to cover fundraising expenses and the remaining two per cent were used to cover all of Movember Canada's administration costs.[13] With only twelve cents of each dollar raised being used to cover administration and fundraising costs, Movember Canada remained well below the international standards best practice range of 15 to 25 per cent.[14] It was important that supporters knew this, as Movember Canada recognized that donor faith in not-for-profit efficiency was important.

NOT-FOR-PROFIT ORGANIZATIONS IN CANADA

Movember was operating in a challenging environment. When making a donation in Canada, a potential donor had many causes from which to choose, with over 85,000 not-for-profit organizations registered with Revenue Canada in 2012.[15] In Canada, not-for-profit organizations were spread across many different categories including healthcare, human rights, education, environment, religion, animal protection, international aid, arts and culture, sports and recreation, and social services. Some of the well-known not-for-profit organizations in Canada included the Heart and Stroke Foundation, Children's Wish Foundation, Canadian Cancer Society, Terry Fox Foundation, SickKids Foundation, Canadian Red Cross, and The United Way. In addition, many other smaller not-for-profit organizations also existed across the country, providing essential services in communities, such as food banks, shelters and counseling.

In return for making a monetary donation, a not-for-profit organization often provided donors with a tax receipt. A donor could then claim the tax receipt on their year-end tax return to help reduce the amount of tax they owed based on their income. In 2010, over 5.7 million Canadians filed tax returns that reported making a charitable donation, with an average donation amount of $260.[16] Overall, the total value of all charitable donations in 2010 for which a tax receipt was issued in Canada was just under $8.3 billion, representing a 6.5 per cent increase from 2009.[17]

However, with so many not-for-profit organizations, competition was fierce. Some organizations created large marketing and advertising campaigns each year in order to increase awareness, placing costly advertisements in mainstream media, on television and radio, and in magazines, alongside consumer products and services. Some larger not-for-profit organizations also ran lotteries offering cash prizes, dream homes, cars and trips. There was a brewing controversy regarding how some Canadian not-for-profit organizations were operated. An investigation by the *Toronto Star* newspaper in 2002 revealed that almost one in six Canadian charities spent more money on running the organization than on actual charitable work.[18] This claim would be further validated in 2011, when the Canadian Broadcasting Corporation (CBC) released a report analyzing the financial operations of the Canadian Cancer Society (CCS).[19] The detailed report

---

[13]"About Movember," Movember, http://ca.movember.com/about, accessed January 7, 2013.

[14]Ibid.

[15]Canadian Registered Charities, Canada Revenue Agency, 2012, www.cra-arc.gc.ca/ebci/haip/srch/basicsearchresult-eng.action?s=registered&k=&p=1&b=true, accessed January 7, 2013.

[16]"Charitable Donors," Statistics Canada, December 5, 2011, www.statcan.gc.ca/daily-quotidien/111205/dq111205a-eng.htm, accessed January 7, 2013.

[17]Ibid.

[18]Sarah Efron, "The 2010 Charity 100: Where Is Your Money Going?" *Money Sense*, June 17, 2010, www.moneysense.ca/2010/06/17/the-charity-100-where-is-your-money-going, accessed January 7, 2013.

[19]Erica Johnson, "Cancer Society Spends More on Fundraising Than Research," *CBC News*, July 6, 2011, www.cbc.ca/news/canada/story/2011/07/04/cancer-society-funding.html, accessed January 7, 2013.

revealed that as the amount of money the CCS obtained in donations increased each year, the proportion of money being spent on cancer research decreased, from over 40 per cent in 2000, to below 22 per cent in 2011.[20] The CBC's analysis of the financial reports of the CCS also showed that the greatest amount of money was being allocated to fundraising, representing 42.7 per cent of all donations in 2011.[21] With various reports in the media questioning how not-for-profit organizations were operated, many Canadians were left speculating on what percentage of their donations actually went to a program, research or cause.

DONOR DIFFERENCES

Various research studies indicated that significant differences existed in how men and women donated their time and money to not-for-profit organizations. According to a report released by Statistics Canada in 2010, women were overall more likely than men to donate to charitable and not-for-profit organizations.[22] The Statistics Canada report also specified that women were more likely to donate to hospitals and organizations involved in social services, while men were more inclined to contribute to sports and recreation organizations and to those involved in grant-making, fundraising and volunteerism promotion.[23]

The Statistics Canada report further identified that people who did more volunteer work each year donated substantially more, regardless of gender. Among people who had performed 60 or more hours of volunteer work, 91 per cent made financial donations, contributing on average $784 to charities and not-for-profit organizations, compared to an average of $288 by individuals who had not participated in any volunteer activities during the year.[24] On the issue of volunteerism, an economic news release by the United States Department of Labor indicated that in 2011, women volunteered more than men across all age groups, educational levels and other major demographic characteristics.[25]

The Women's Philanthropy Institute at The Center on Philanthropy at Indiana University released a report in 2010 that analyzed the giving habits of single women compared to single men. The study identified factors contributing to the growth in women's giving, which included a higher percentage of women in the workforce with a post-secondary education; women earning more than ever before (although imbalances still existed); and marriage becoming a less dominant lifestyle.[26] The implications of the study were that women were often an overlooked and untapped resource for philanthropy, stating the important point, "Savvy nonprofit organizations and fundraisers will change the way they approach donors, will include more women in their fundraising strategies, and reach out to 'half the sky' to fulfill their mission."[27]

[20]Ibid.

[21]Ibid.

[22]Statistics Canada, "Charitable Giving by Canadians," April 16, 2012, www.statcan.gc.ca/pub/11-008-x/2012001/article/11637-eng.htm#a12, accessed January 7, 2013.

[23]Ibid.

[24]Ibid.

[25]"Volunteering in the United States, 2011," Bureau of Labor Statistics, February 22, 2012, www.bls.gov/news.release/volun.nr0.htm, accessed January 7, 2013.

[26]Debra J. Mesch, "Women Give 2010," Center on Philanthropy at Indiana University, October 2010, www.philanthropy.iupui.edu/files/research/women_give_2010_report.pdf, accessed January 7, 2013.

[27]Ibid.

Regardless of statistics and gender habits, many female-focused not-for-profit causes unarguably remained much further ahead of men's causes in terms of public exposure and popularity. The Breast Cancer Society of Canada was a not-for-profit, charitable organization dedicated to funding Canadian breast cancer research with a focus on detection, prevention and treatment.[28] Around the globe, the month of October each year had become designated as Breast Cancer Awareness Month, with various fundraising and awareness activities. In Canada, The Canadian Breast Cancer Foundation CIBC Run for the Cure represented the largest single-day, volunteer-led fundraising event, with over 170,000 volunteers running and walking to raise over $30 million in 2011.[29]

Breast Cancer Awareness Month had also become well known for advocates wearing a wide variety of pink attire in order to show support and help raise money and awareness for breast cancer initiatives. An indication of the success of the breast cancer awareness campaign was the support received each year from many professional sports leagues, which allowed male athletes to wear pink uniforms or equipment during games in the month of October, thus allowing men to actively participate in a "women's issues campaign." The success of women's health initiatives such as Breast Cancer Awareness Month provided a good example from which men's health initiatives could learn. It also raised a significant question: could women be encouraged to embrace male-focused causes such as prostate cancer as successfully as men had embraced female-focused causes?

IN SEARCH OF MO SISTAS

With Movember Canada's small team and determination to keep administrative costs low, it was a challenge to reach out to new donors and supporters. Hayman realized that one "untapped market" was developing the numbers of Mo Sistas.

Obtaining the involvement of more Mo Sistas represented an opportunity to make a larger impact, not just on donations and awareness, but on prevention. According to research, up to half of all male cases of cancer could be prevented by making healthier diet and lifestyle choices.[30] One of the major issues was the way men thought about their health, with preventative health measures being something that often just did not occur to them. One of Movember's goals was to get men to take responsibility for their health, to encourage them to prevent illness by leading a healthy lifestyle, and to assist them in understanding the symptoms and signs of illness in both themselves and others so they could appreciate when and how to seek help if needed.[31] Therefore, a positive role for Mo Sistas was asking the men in their lives (husbands, fathers, grandfathers, brothers, sons, boyfriends, etc.) to live a healthier lifestyle and encouraging them to get their annual health check. Raising money for men's health research and organizations such as PCC represented an important and noble cause, but it was equally important to change the attitudes and actions of men.

---

[28]"About Us," Breast Cancer Society of Canada, www.bcsc.ca/p/77/l/43/t/Breast-Cancer-Society-of-Canada–About-Us, accessed January 7, 2013.

[29]"About Us," Canadian Breast Cancer Foundation CIBC Run for the Cure, www.runforthecure.com/site/PageServer?pagename=2012_About_Us, accessed January 7, 2013.

[30]"Awareness and Education," Movember, http://ca.movember.com/about/awareness, accessed January 7, 2013.
[31]Ibid.

As the size and popularity of the Movember campaign increased over the years, the Movember Canada team received a frequent number of e-mails and phone calls with inquiries asking how women could become more involved in Movember. Different proposals from the public included women wearing fake moustaches, not shaving their legs, or possibly dying their hair. However, as Movember was a male-centric campaign, the team needed to ensure it was staying true to the moustache and men's health, while trying to support and engage new audiences.

DECISION

With the 2012 Movember campaign fast approaching, Hayman and the team needed to devise a strategy to more effectively communicate how Mo Sistas get involved with Movember. Not only did the participation of more women play a very important role in helping change attitudes towards men's health and raise significant awareness but it could also impact monetary fundraising. It was a "hairy situation," as Movember Canada operated a very simple campaign and did not want to add complexity or risks that might jeopardize the momentum built over the previous few years. With Canada representing the largest fundraising country in Movember operations globally, Hayman knew that any successful measures developed within Canada had the potential to help benefit other Movember campaigns around the world.

EXHIBIT 1: Movember Annual Global Registrants and Funds Raised Globally

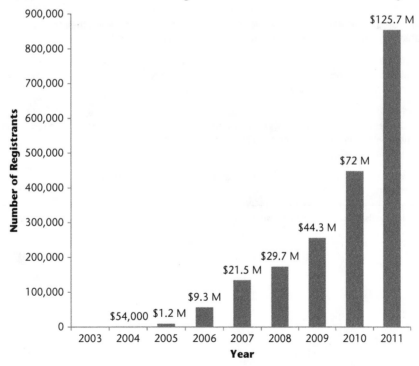

Source: "About Movember," Movember, http://ca.movember.com/about/about-campaign, accessed January 7, 2013.

EXHIBIT 2: Movember Canada Number of Registered Participants and Annual Donations Raised

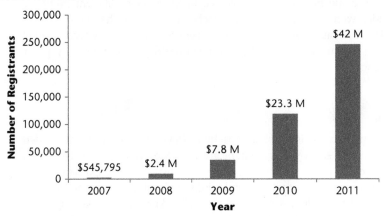

Source: "Annual Reports," Movember, http://ca.movember.com/about/annual-reports, accessed January 7, 2013.

EXHIBIT 3: Movember "OUR GOALS"

Campaign strategic goal:
We will get men to grow moustaches by creating an innovative, fun and engaging annual Movember campaign that raises funds and awareness globally.

Strategic goals from the funds raised:

Survivorship
We will fund survivorship initiatives that provide information and support for men and their families affected by prostate cancer that helps them make informed decisions and improves their quality of life.

Awareness and education
Through our annual campaign and funded programs we will significantly increase the understanding of the health risk that men face and encourage men to act on that knowledge.

Prostate cancer research
We will fund catalytic research and clinical trials infrastructure that leads to significantly improved diagnostic and prognostic tests and treatments to reduce the burden of prostate cancer.

Influencing change in men's health
We will fund research that helps to inform health policy and knowledge translation that accelerates improved health outcomes for men.

Source: "Vision, Values and Goals," Movember, http://ca.movember.com/about/vision-goals, accessed January 7, 2013.

EXHIBIT 4: Movember Rules of Participation

ONE

Once registered at Movember.com each Mo Bro must begin the 1st of Movember with a clean shaven face.

TWO

For the entire month of Movember each Mo Bro must grow and groom a moustache.

THREE

There is to be no joining of the mo to your side burns. (That's considered a beard)

FOUR

There is to be no joining of the handlebars to your chin. (That's considered a goatee)

FIVE

Each Mo Bro must conduct himself like a true country gentleman.

Source: "Moustache Season Rules for the Great Outdoors," Movember, http://ca.movember.com/uploads/files/Downloads/Movember%20Rules.pdf, accessed January 7, 2013.

EXHIBIT 5: Movember Campaign Pictures

Source: 2011 Movember Photos, www.flickr.com/photos/movemberphoto/sets/72157631185243726/?page=18, accessed January 7, 2013. Used with permission.

CASE 5

Swimming in the Virtual Community Pool with PlentyofFish

On a Monday morning in January of 2008, Markus Frind, chief executive officer (CEO) and founder of PlentyofFish.com, was undoubtedly the topic of many conversations as people grabbed their morning coffees from a local vendor. The *New York Times* had just published an article about the Vancouverite's free, online dating site, PlentyofFish (PoF). Now that the world was watching and salivating at the $10 million per year that the site was generating, one had to question whether its business model could be sustained. Could Frind maintain his strong foothold in the virtual world of social networking sites? Could PlentyofFish continue to maintain its financial success with advertising as its only source of revenue?

If the concept of offering a free, online dating site was so fatally flawed, PoF would not have experienced the success that it had. Frind did not spend the $10 million a month on marketing that some of his competitors like Match.com, eHarmony and Lavalife did. What he was doing was working just fine–for now, and continued to generate a substantial annual profit.

Frind had proudly announced, on many occasions, that his company consisted of just one employee–himself. While he had hired another employee in late 2007, it was only to assist in providing customer service. As the sole operator of the site, Frind had been able to handle massive amounts of traffic. In fact, for the week of April 28, 2007, PlentyofFish was ranked by HitWise as the 96th-busiest website in the United States. To put this into perspective, PoF outranked Apple.com in terms of traffic! How then, was he able to do all

IVEY | Publishing

Wilfred Cheung, Chris Ellison, Prarthana Kumar, Jeremy Kyle and Stacey Morrison wrote this case under the supervision of Professor Michael Parent solely to provide material for class discussion. The authors do not intend to illustrate either effective or ineffective handling of a managerial situation. The authors may have disguised certain names and other identifying information to protect confidentiality.

Richard Ivey School of Business Foundation prohibits any form of reproduction, storage or transmission without its written permission. Reproduction of this material is not covered under authorization by any reproduction rights organization. To order copies or request permission to reproduce materials, contact Ivey Publishing, Richard Ivey School of Business Foundation, The University of Western Ontario, London, Ontario, Canada, N6A 3K7; phone (519) 661-3208; fax (519) 661-3882; e-mail *cases@ivey.uwo.ca*.

Copyright © 2008, Richard Ivey School of Business Foundation   Version: 2011-09-21

One time permission to reproduce granted by Richard Ivey School of Business Foundation on April 22, 2014.

of this alone? Did his success lie in his web design philosophy that allowed users to take part in running the site? Was it the automation the processing? Could he chalk it all up to efficiency? Other concerns included whether this model could be easily replicated, and should PlentyofFish be concerned about others entering the market with better technology and fancier sites?

As people milled around the corner, some on bikes, and others on rollerblades, several couples casually walked along the street, holding hands. With millions having surfed websites looking for that special someone, one had to wonder how many of these people met through PlentyofFish and how much longer others would continue to do so.

THE CONCEPT

Social Networking

The term "social network" was coined by J.A. Barnes who defined it as a group of 100 to 150 people drawn together by family, work or a hobby. In 2008, thanks mainly to the Internet, social networking had expanded to hundreds of millions of people around the world, creating a virtual community for people to interact with one another about anything and everything. Members created their own online "profiles" with biographical data, pictures, likes, dislikes and any other information they chose to post and share. They communicated with each other by voice, instant messaging, videoconference and blogs. In many cases, these sites also served as a vehicle for meeting in person. One could find dating sites, friendship sites, and sites with a business networking purpose or hybrids that offered a combination of these applications.

Looking for Mr. or Ms. Right or looking at your neighbour's pictures from vacation while checking your e-mail at the same time seemed to define the growing industry of social networking websites. The genius of these sites lay in their ability to capture the essence of informal exchanges while expanding the matrix of searchable, linked pages. Social networking on the Internet was a growing phenomenon which could be broadly categorized into three segments—virtual communities like Facebook; classified listing sites such as Craigslist; and the growing plethora of dating sites like PlentyofFish.

As participants in a social network started to become more entrenched in the social aspect of their network they often became members of that particular virtual community. A virtual community described "People who use computers to communicate, form friendships that sometimes form the basis of communities, but you have to be careful to not mistake the tool for the task and think that just writing words on a screen is the same thing as real community."[1] Much like a real community, a virtual social networking community was based on the idea that once one joined, they needed to actively participate. There was a reciprocal nature to being part of a virtual community; they depended upon social interaction and exchange among users. A person in a virtual community was motivated to contribute valuable information to the group, starting with a valid profile or an honest response with the expectation that they would receive the same in return.

The lifecycle of a membership in a virtual community went through the same stages as that of any other community. Members of virtual communities began their lifecycle first as visitors, clicking through and around a site to determine whether they could connect with other users and fit into the group. After deciding to break into the community and set up

---

[1]Howard Rheingold, *The Virtual Community*, http://www.rheingold.com/vc/book/intro.html, accessed January 27, 2008.

a profile or username, they began participating in the virtual community. Those who contributed for a sustained period of time became regulars. If they took the initiative to recruit others to join the community, they became leaders.

Another category of social networking sites were ones that focused on classified listings and operated as a hub aggregating buyers and sellers. Buyers listed a variety of goods ranging from private planes to services such as housekeeping. Craigslist was one of the most popular sites of this kind.

Dating websites allowed individuals to post their profile, view others' and perhaps develop a romantic or intimate relationship. The market was dominated by several large commercial websites such as Lavalife, eHarmony, and Match.com as well as the newer PlentyofFish. These sites targeted teens to retirees, with a number of new sites targeting niche markets based on religion, race, and occupation. They were based on a shift in thinking about web applications, built on interactivity between developer and users called Web 2.0.

Web 2.0

Web 2.0 was a term first coined in 2004 at a Web conference whose theme was "The Web has become a platform,[2] a foundation upon which thousands of new forms of business would emerge."[3] According to Tim O'Reilly, one of the conference's moderators,

> Web 2.0 is the business revolution in the computer industry caused by the move to the Internet as platform, and an attempt to understand the rules for success on that new platform. Chief among those rules is this: Build applications that harness network effects to get better the more people use them. (This is what I've elsewhere called "harnessing collective intelligence.")

Web 2.0 systems were theoretically unconstrained as they would harness "the power of user contribution, collective intelligence, and network effects."[4] PlentyofFish was able to take advantage of this new business model by encouraging user contributions and their collective intelligence, while also capitalizing on the network effects it had built with these very users.

PLENTYOFFISH.COM

Business Model

Founded in 2003, PlentyofFish was free to users, a feature that differentiated it from other online dating sites. This was reinforced in the site's slogan: "100% Free. Put away your credit card." However, this came at a cost to users. While other online dating sites provided customer support as part of their service, PlentyofFish did not have that same support structure. It only responded to fraudulent identity notifications and subpoena requests. For example, instead of providing customer service, ". . .users rely on fellow

---

[2]Tim O'Reilly, "Web 2.0. Compact Definition: Trying Again," O'Reilly *Radar: O'Reilly Media Inc.*, December 10, 2006, http://radar.oreilly.com/archives/2006/12/web_20_compact.html, accessed January 27, 2008.

[3]Web 2.0 SUMMIT, *About Web Summit 2.0*, http://conferences.oreillynet.com/pub/w/62/about.html, accessed January 27, 2008.

[4]Ibid

members, whose advice is found in online forums. The Dating & Advice category listed more than 320,000 posts, making up in sheer quantity what it lacked in a soothing live presence available by phone."[5] However, this also meant that users had to be willing to comb through the wide array of content before finding the information they needed. Therefore, while the growth of Web 2.0 aided Frind in achieving his goal of allowing users to drive the website, this setup raised questions about the quality of content being provided.

Despite it, the site had proven popular, with more than three million members in January 2008–double the membership in the past year, and despite an attrition rate of 30 per cent of members per month who were purged from the site for inactivity. These members generated traffic volume of more than 600,000 unique logins per day, and more than 1.5 billion page views per month (an average of roughly 50 million page views per day!). PlentyofFish had managed to grow its membership not only in number, but in terms of active members, despite the growing number of alternative online dating services. This was especially appealing to advertisers.

With the overwhelming supply of online dating sites in the market, one had to marvel at what set PlentyofFish apart: PlentyofFish had built an engaged, passionate community of users who felt emotionally attached to the site. This created high switching costs for users as well as allowing PlentyofFish to benefit from network effects.

PlentyofFish was sustained by revenue from companies advertising on the site. The advertising mix currently returned an estimated $10 million per year through banner ads, Google ads (AdSense), and affiliated dating sites. Ads sent users to other sites, even other dating sites, which in turn generated revenue for PlentyofFish. For example, when a user clicked on a banner ad for a dating and relationship book, PlentyofFish might receive the full revenue from the sale of the book as the advertiser gained another customer who might become profitable. In this way, the other site cheaply outsourced customer acquisition to PlentyofFish.

The Technology Behind PlentyofFish—ASP.NET

While Frind originally created the site to learn the ASP.NET web application framework, it was still being used for PlentyofFish in 2008. Frind claimed that he had stuck with using ASP.NET "because it's trivial and easy and gets the job done."[6] Additionally, Frind believed that he had "gotten really, really good at it" pointing out that, "(what he had) done is about 10 to 20 times more efficient than what anybody else has done with ASP.NET."[7] In fact, PlentyofFish had grown to the scale where "nothing can be brought off the shelf and everything must be built from the ground up."[8] Therefore, while there was no one software package that could accommodate PlentyofFish's needs, Frind believed that he could adapt ASP.NET to meet its needs

In June 2006, when PlentyofFish was receiving approximately "500 million pageviews a month," Frind believed that he would have "no problem running it (by himself) even if it

---

[5]Randall Stross, "From 10 hours a Week, $10 million a Year," *NY Times [US]*, January 13, 2008, http://www.nytimes.com/2008/01/13/business/13digi.html?_r=2&scp=1&sq=plenty+of+fish&st=nyt&oref=slogin&oref=slogin, accessed January 22, 2008.

[6]Plentyoffish.com, "Changing the Online Dating Industry," *Plentyoffish Media Inc.* http://www.PlentyofFish.com/about_team.aspx, accessed January 27, 2008.

[7]Ibid

[8]Markus Frind, "The Paradigm Shift–Adapt or Die," *Plentyoffish Media Inc.* http://PlentyofFish.wordpress.com/2007/08/08/looking-for-3-senior-software-developers, accessed January 27, 2008.

gets to three times its current size."[9] This stemmed from his belief that he could be successful in automating more and more as the site grew. In early 2008, PlentyofFish was serving 1.2 billion pageviews.

ASP.NET coding enabled the site to maintain itself through automated recognition of spam on its forums and the allowance of user-screening for the thousands of photos uploaded daily. This combination of site automation and user engagement made it possible for only one person to operate the site. For example, the "Love and Dating" forum had 320,000+ posts in January, 2008, all of which had to be monitored for unwanted postings and spam. Frind had been able to effectively rid his site of spam by refining "a formula for analysing customer feedback and arriving at a determination of whether a given forum post is spam and should automatically be deleted."[10] Posted photos were checked by users to ensure they did not contain nudity and were of a person. In fact, some 120 "member volunteers"–unpaid members dedicated to monitoring photographs posted to the site–reportedly checked 100,000 photos each year. The founder explained this behaviour as a means of giving back to the free site: "Lots of people feel they want to give back to the site because it is free."[11] Frind likened this automation to putting his website on autopilot, with users supporting themselves through online forums, while receiving minimal support from the site administrator.

Servers

PoF was able to minimize the amount of servers it employed by being more efficient. Frind stated that he used "one web server, one mail server, two database servers now and a couple of little web servers to run the Userplane instant messenger. So under 10 but I've started to scale up."[12] To bring this into perspective, similar social networking sites such as Friendster and AmericanSingles.com (with less traffic) used 200 servers each. Having fewer servers meant that there was less or, in Frind's case, no need to employ technicians to ensure that the servers were kept up and running. This translated to significantly lower operating costs.

PoF's servers ran on SQL Server 2005. The growth of the website meant that they would need to add new servers. On February 27, 2008, Microsoft released a number of upgrades–Windows Server 2008, Visual Studio 2008, and SQL Server 2008. Frind's need to add additional servers in the near future meant that he would likely have to make a decision on which servers–SQL server 2005 or 2008–to employ. With Frind's heavy reliance on creating efficiencies for his website, could he afford to wait to employ SQL Server 2008? Conversely, if he did switch to SQL Server 2008, could he afford to work out the kinks which might ultimately cause problems for the site?

---

[9]Richard Macmanus, "Plenty of Cash for one-man band," ReadWriteWeb.com, June 10, 2006 http://www.readwriteweb.com/archives/plenty_of_cash.php, accessed January 27, 2008.

[10]Randall Stross, "From 10 hours a Week, $10 million a Year," *NY Times [US]*, January 13, 2008, http://www.nytimes.com/2008/01/13/business/13digi.html?_r=2&scp=1&sq=plenty+of+fish&st=nyt&oref=slogin&oref=slogin, accessed January 22, 2008.

[11]Randall Stross, "From 10 hours a Week, $10 million a Year," *NY Times [US]*, January 13, 2008, http://www.nytimes.com/2008/01/13/business/13digi.html?_r=2&scp=1&sq=plenty+of+fish&st=nyt&oref=slogin&oref=slogin, accessed January 22, 2008.

[12]Plentyoffish.com, "Changing the Online Dating Industry," Plentyoffish Media Inc. http://www.PlentyofFish.com/about_team.aspx, accessed January 27, 2008.

Scalability

At the heart of most database applications was a database management system (DBMS). For most mid-to-large scale databases this was either Oracle or Microsoft SQL Server. Understanding the nuanced differences between the two products could be difficult for even the most seasoned database professional. One very important difference between the two was that SQL Server ran only on the Windows platform, while Oracle ran on a variety of platforms like UNIX or Linux.

Frind's choice for a DBMS was SQL Server 2005, but other popular sites, such as Craigslist, had chosen Oracle to manage their databases. Craigslist received over nine billion page views per month. This was six times the number of page views that PoF received.

On the issue of scalability, there were two basic concepts–scaling up and scaling out. Scaling up meant adding additional expensive hardware to handle higher loads, while scaling out meant distributing the load using low cost multiple servers. Frind needed to consider what route he wanted to take if he continued to grow. Would he be able to achieve the scale that Oracle allowed for Craigslist, with SQL Server 2005 as PlentyofFish's DBMS?

The PlentyofFish User Experience

From the moment that you entered the website, until the moment you left, you were bombarded by pictures of users of the site. Intrigued by the fuzzy and distorted photos, one click and you were viewing a user's profile page. Simplistic in design, the profile page offered information such as height, age, body type and ethnicity. You read the brief description and curiously continued to scroll down the page. More pictures of your "fish" appeared and as you ran your cursor over each one, they expanded to give a much larger, clearer view. Hooked, you might have thought "How can I meet this attractive and witty individual?"

In order to contact any of the 600,000 "fish," a user first had to become a member. This was easily done by moving through the registration screens–two very simple and user-friendly pages. The entire process took only a couple of minutes to complete and the majority of information requested (aside from secure information such as a password) was presented on a profile page. By accurately representing themselves with respect to age, location and preferences, the user was instantly given the opportunity to connect with potential matches in the immediate area that were similar. The prospect of meeting new people immediately was one of the most important driving factors for the website's popularity.

This ability to connect with others so readily had been leveraged by PlentyofFish to create the company's successful online dating community. The longer the user was active, the greater the chance of building a network and finding the "right" match. This idea was reinforced by PlentyofFish's design, which matched users that would be most interested in each other based on their past messaging and searches. Moreover, new users were constantly adding themselves to the website's profile database, creating a new source of people to meet. Thus, how deep a "fish" chose to swim in the virtual community pool was user-determined.

Catching a Fish

Once the user had initiated contact or been contacted, the process of communication was quite simple. Assuming that the parties involved fulfilled the requirements outlined by the other individual such as age range or more specifically, "must not be looking for an intimate encounter," the user could openly send and receive messages. These messages were placed directly in the inbox and easily accessible as the system was similar in design to many other email platforms. Frind had also recently added a VoIP (voice-over-Internet protocol) which allowed users to send voice messages to other members as well.[13] This ease of use allowed members to immediately "jump into the pool," establishing online conversations with whomever they chose. The type of message sent–voice, email or instant message–was entirely up to the user.

However, not every match that a user made was going to be positive. Even the most optimistic user might have run into individuals that were rude, creepy or downright shocking. Thus, the user had to wade through the pools looking for "fish" that met their needs. If the user did establish contact with a disreputable individual they could block that other user. However, if someone was bent on creating havoc, a new user profile could always be created. There were no user services available to help deal with these types of issues, which made it difficult to fix any problems that did occur. In this sense, PlentyofFish could be thought of as the Wild West of online dating, whereby users policed themselves.

What was Lurking in the Sea?

There were several forces that posed serious threats to PlentyofFish. A significant force that PlentyofFish had to contend with was the threat of new entry. The capital, or rather lack of capital, required to start a dating site similar to that of PlentyofFish was minimal. All that one needed was the purchase of a domain name and servers to hold information. This meant that there were numerous potential competitors, ranging from major corporations such as Google to minor ones such as freelance web designers. Also, despite the scale that PlentyofFish had been able to achieve, there were no cost disadvantages for any new competitors. A second threat to PlentyofFish was from other, unrelated sites. While sites such as Craigslist and Facebook were not seen as dating sites, they had each branched into that area to attract more users. Craigslist had a personals section while Facebook added dating applications to its site. Dating sites, such as PlentyofFish, also had to contend with fierce rivalry from their current competitors. Whether they were first movers such as Lavalife or niche players such as HonestyOnline, the market for dating sites was becoming increasingly saturated. With spectacular success stories such as PlentyofFish, one could only expect firm rivalries to become more intense.

OTHER VIRTUAL COMMUNITIES

Friendster

With more than 58 million members worldwide, Friendster was the pioneer in the field of social networking. Driven by simplicity, Friendster prided itself on delivering a clean, user-friendly and interactive environment where users could easily connect with anyone around the world. Friendster targeted the 25-and-under market with no professional or group affiliation. Friendster set itself apart by being the first at introducing innovative features such as a network graph server, as well as launching a choice of languages to navigate the site,

---

[13]Matt Harley, "Money and relationships: It's Love 3.0," *The Globe and Mail*, February 14, 2008, pp. B1 & B6.

thus expanding its ability to tap non-English markets. Friendster continued to innovate and recently expanded its targeted demographic to include older adults.

LinkedIn

LinkedIn was an online network of more than 17 million professionals from around the world, representing over 150 industries. LinkedIn prided itself on claiming that it was not networking–it was what networking should be. The mission of the website was to help the user be more effective in their work and open doors to opportunities using the professional relationships they already had.

The registration process for LinkedIn closely resembled completing a professional resume. LinkedIn focused on information such as current or most recent job position, job industry,. past experience, and professional overview. Firms used this site to keep internal and remote employees connected with each other, search out potential employees and as a knowledge management site where they could compare their job postings to their competitors'.

Members could join LinkedIn through invitations or by starting a network of their own. LinkedIn was not purely a free service, but rather offered levels of service ranging from free membership to premium accounts that charged users anywhere from $19.95 to $200 a month. In 2007, LinkedIn was the fourth most popular networking website, behind Yahoo 360, MySpace and Facebook.

Facebook

Facebook was a social utility that connected people through its website, requiring only a valid email address to register. To connect with coworkers or classmates, members used their school or work email addresses to join a network. Since its launch in February 2004, Facebook enrolled over 63 million users worldwide.

Facebook was completely free, and like PoF supported by ads. In August 2006 Facebook signed a three year deal with Microsoft to provide and sell ads on their site in return for a revenue split. The deal followed an announcement from Facebook's direct competitor, MySpace, who signed a similar deal with Google. The youthful demographic that both services attracted was highly prized amongst advertisers and a number of companies were eager to jump on the bandwagon. In July of 2006, Apple signed an agreement with Facebook to give away 10 million free iTunes samplers to Facebook members. There was even rumor of a Facebook credit card.

MySpace

MySpace was an online community that encouraged its members to create their "own" space online reflecting their personality in music, movies, photos, journal entries and interests that they might share with their growing network of friends. MySpace was for everyone–from friends to family, from singles to colleagues and from classmates to those looking for long lost friends. Although MySpace called itself a private community it gained great popularity through the increasing number of bands using this site to get their music heard and to connect with fans. Even Presidential candidates, such as Hillary Clinton, used MySpace as a means to journal their days on the campaign trail. MySpace was constantly expanding rapidly all over the world with the latest addition being China in 2007.

LISTING SITES

Craigslist

Craigslist was much like other social networking sites in its structure and revenue generation, operating as a hub that aggregated buyers and sellers. One of the top 10 busiest English
language sites in the world, Craigslist was a free website which offered very little customer
support. Since it only employed 25 staff, they only fixed problems sporadically, requiring
users to serve themselves or request other members' assistance. Craigslist served buyers and
sellers in 50 countries and 450 localities. Their sites generated 10 billion total pageviews
and six million unique visitors a month, more than any other site of its kind. Craigslist, like
other listing sites, charged fees for a few of its listings but did not contain commercial listings other than postings.

DATING SITES

Match.com

Launched in 1995, Match.com was an online dating site that charged for its service. It
brought people together by creating the opportunity for them to post their profiles and
pictures for others to view. With more than 15 million members worldwide, members of
the site had the ability to interact with an enormous group of potential matches. Match.
com was available on six different continents, in 30 different countries, and 18 different
languages. This large scale approach increased members' chances of finding the person and
relationship they were searching for. Match.com estimated 200,000 people entered into
relationships because of the site. If, however, a member was finding it hard to find a match
then he or she could browse through Match.com's free online magazine, Happen. This
magazine contained helpful articles about romance, sex and relationships. Although communication between members required a fee, Match.com allowed visitors to browse the
extensive library of profiles and pictures. This gave prospective users a sneak peak at the
types of matches available to them if they joined. The site provided secure and anonymous
interactions between members whether they communicated via email, instant messaging
or audio and video. In addition to the traditional online communications, the company
also offered a wireless dating experience whereby members could match via their cellular
phones.

SINK OR SWIM?

There were several challenges that PlentyofFish might have to face, the most obvious of
which was competition. The PlentyofFish website was also replete with unfinished patches
and quirks that made the site visually unappealing.

Should Frind expand PlentyofFish globally? Should he follow the likes of Friendster
and MySpace and develop sites in Korean, Japanese, Chinese and other languages? Should
he increase the number of applications available on the site? If he did so, should he imitate
Facebook and invite third-party developers to provide applications suited to his target
market?

To increase or protect revenues, Frind could change the membership structure of the
site to have members pay for basic access and optional services. If he chose to add these

functions or features would ASP.NET be sufficient? If PlentyofFish continued to grow at its current rate would SQL Server 2005 or 2008 handle the load? To what extent did the business need to invest in new technology?

As commuters scrambled to get to work during the Monday morning rush hour, some of them might have thought of what it was like to be Markus Frind—not having to work 9 to 5. Frind had nicely summed up the situation he had created for himself, stating: "Most of the time I don't have to do anything."[14] Would this continue to be the case, or did he need to invest substantial time, money and effort in protecting his business? After five successful years of operation, had PlentyofFish run its course?

[14]Randall Stross, "From 10 hours a Week, $10 million a Year," *NY Times [US]*, January 13, 2008, http://www. nytimes.com/2008/01/13/business/13digi.html?_r=2&scp=1&sq=plenty+of+fish&st=nyt&oref=slogin&oref=slo gin, accessed January 22, 2008.

CASE
6

The Chinese Fireworks Industry

In February 2009, Jerry Yu was spending the Chinese New Year holidays in Liuyang (lee-ou-yang), a city known as "the home of firecrackers and fireworks," located in Hunan Province in China. Jerry was an ABC (America-Born-Chinese). With an MBA, he was running a small family-owned chain of gift stores in Brooklyn, New York. Liuyang was his mother's hometown. During his visit, his relatives invited him to invest in a fireworks factory that was owned by a village. Mr. Yu had been impressed by the extravagant fireworks shows he had seen during the festival; however, he wanted to assess how attractive the Chinese fireworks industry was before he even looked at the financial details of the factory.

HISTORY OF FIREWORKS AND FIRECRACKERS

Fireworks referred to any devices designed to produce visual or audible effects through combustion or explosion. The art of making fireworks was formally known as pyrotechnics. Firecrackers were a specific kind of fireworks, usually in the form of a noisemaking cylinder. Firecrackers were often strung together and fused consecutively, a staple of Chinese New Year celebrations, weddings, grand openings, births, deaths and other ceremonial occasions.

The main ingredients of fireworks had remained almost the same over the past thousand years: 75 parts-by-weight potassium nitrate, 15 parts charcoal and 10 parts sulfur.

IVEY | Publishing

Ruihua Jiang wrote this case under the supervision of Professor Paul W. Beamish solely to provide material for class discussion. The authors do not intend to illustrate either effective or ineffective handling of a managerial situation. The authors may have disguised certain names and other identifying information to protect confidentiality.

Richard Ivey School of Business Foundation prohibits any form of reproduction, storage or transmission without its written permission. Reproduction of this material is not covered under authorization by any reproduction rights organization. To order copies or request permission to reproduce materials, contact Ivey Publishing, Richard Ivey School of Business Foundation, The University of Western Ontario, London, Ontario, Canada, N6A 3K7; phone (519) 661-3208; fax (519) 661-3882; e-mail cases@ivey.uwo.ca.

Copyright © 2011, Richard Ivey School of Business Foundation   Version: 2011-09-21

One time permission to reproduce granted by Richard Ivey School of Business Foundation on April 22, 2014.

It burned briskly when lighted, but did not erupt or make any noise. When it was found that a projectile could be thrust out of a barrel by keeping the powder at one end and igniting it, black powder became known as gunpowder. Today, smokeless powder has replaced black powder as the propellant in modern weaponry, but black powder remains a main ingredient in fireworks, both as a propellant and as a bursting charge.

It was generally believed that the Chinese were the first makers of fireworks. The Chinese made war rockets and explosives as early as the sixth century. One legend said that a Chinese cook, while toiling in a field kitchen, happened to mix together sulfur, charcoal and saltpetre, and noticed that the pile burned with a combustible force when ignited. He further discovered that when these ingredients were enclosed in a length of bamboo sealed at both ends, it would explode rather than burn, producing a loud crack. This was the origin of firecrackers. In fact, the Chinese word for firecrackers–*bao-zhu*–literally means "exploded bamboo."

The loud reports and burning fires of firecrackers and fireworks were found to be perfect for frightening off evil spirits and celebrating good news at various occasions. For more than a thousand years, the Chinese had been seeing off past years and welcoming in new ones by firing firecrackers.

Fireworks made their way first to Arabia in the seventh century, then to Europe sometime in the middle of the 13th century. By the 15th century, fireworks were widely used for religious festivals and public entertainment. Most of the early pyrotechnicians in Europe were Italians. Even today, the best-known names in the European and American fireworks industry were Italian in origin. From the 16th to the 18th century, Italy and Germany were the two best known areas in the European continent for fireworks displays.

In 1777, the United States used fireworks in its first Independence Day celebration, and fireworks have become closely associated with July Fourth celebrations ever since.

Up until the 1830s, the colors of the early fireworks were limited, but by 2009, there were six basic colors used in fireworks.

LIUYANG—THE HOMETOWN OF FIRECRACKERS AND FIREWORKS

According to historical records in China, firecrackers and fireworks "emerged during the Tang dynasty (618-907 AD), flourished during the Song Dynasty (960-1279 AD), and originated in Liuyang." For more than 1,000 years, Liuyang had been known as the "hometown of firecrackers and fireworks of China," a title that was officially conferred to Liuyang by the State Council of China in 1995. As early as 1723, Liuyang fireworks were chosen as official tributes to the imperial family and were sold all over the country. Exports started early: by 1875, firecrackers and fireworks were being shipped to Japan, Korea, India, Iran, Russia, Australia, England, the U.S., and other countries. In China, the name Liuyang had become almost synonymous with firecrackers and fireworks. Liuyang-made firecrackers and fireworks won numerous awards over its long history of fireworks making.

The long history and tradition had made fireworks more than just a livelihood for the Liuyang people. Almost every native person in the area knew something about fireworks making, or had actually made firecrackers or fireworks in their lifetime. As a result, Liuyang claimed an impressive pool of skilled labor. Firecrackers and fireworks had become the pillar industry of Liuyang, accounting for nearly 50 per cent of all jobs or about one-third of the total population in the Liuyang District (including Liuyang City and the surrounding counties). In 2008, Liuyang claimed 2,702 fireworks manufacturers with an additional 2,144 in the surrounding area. In total, there were 6,458 fireworks producers in China. While there has been some trend towards consolidation in the industry, most factories were still owned either by villages or families. Among them, about a dozen or so were medium to large factories with employment between 100 to 500 workers. The rest were small workshops employing anywhere from 10 to 50 people, depending on market demand.

Liuyang was the top fireworks exporter in the world, making up 60 per cent of global production. The trademarked brand "Red Lantern" had become well known to fireworks-lovers around the world. China now accounted for 89 per cent of worldwide fireworks exports with the vast majority of that coming from Liuyang. In addition, over the past ten years, China had become the largest market for fireworks. The ratio of domestic use to exports was 6:4, and Chinese imports of fireworks were negligible.

The increase in demand in the Chinese market had only intensified the competition. All new demand was more than met by the Chinese fireworks industry. Thus, instead of seeing increased margins, the profit margins for many small manufacturers had shrunk over the past decade. In order to make up the difference, manufacturers were cutting corners. However, some of these cost cutting efforts came at the expense of safety. A 2007 factory explosion that left 11 workers dead was blamed primarily on decreased safety standards, which were blamed on a lack of money due to cut throat competition. In response, the government and company officials from Luiyang and surrounding areas agreed to regulate the price of fireworks with the hope of increasing profit margins. With higher profit margins, company officials vowed to increase workers safety.

The Product

Fireworks could be classified into two categories: display fireworks and consumer fireworks. The display fireworks, such as aerial shells, maroons, and large Roman candles, were meant for professional (usually licensed) pyrotechnicians to fire during large public display shows. They were devices that were designed to produce certain visual or audio effect at a greater height above the ground than the consumer fireworks, which the general public could purchase in convenience stores and enjoy in their own backyards. Display fireworks were known as Explosives 1.3 (Class B prior to 1991) in the U.S. The consumer fireworks belonged to Explosives 1.4 (Class C prior to 1991). The difference lay mainly in the amount of explosive components contained in the product. Canada had a similar classification system. In the U.K., it was more carefully divided into four categories: indoor fireworks; garden fireworks; display fireworks; and display fireworks for professionals only.

There were many varieties of fireworks. Liuyang made 13 different types with more than 3,000 varieties. The major types included fountains, rockets, hand-held novelties, nail and hanging wheels, ground-spinning novelties, jumping novelties, floral shells, parachutes and firecrackers.

Historically, firecrackers made up 90 per cent of the total production and sales. Over the past 50 or so, however, there had been a shift away from firecrackers to fireworks. In 2009, firecrackers made up less than 20 per cent of the total sales. The skill levels of fireworks-making had been greatly improved. For instance, the old-day fireworks could reach no more than 20 metres into the sky, while the new ones could go as high as 400 metres.

Not much had changed in fireworks-making. Over the last few decades, numer-ous novelties were added to the fireworks family. However, innovation had never reached beyond product variations. The ingredients had remained more or less the same.

The process technology had not changed much either, although some manual processes, such as cutting the paper, rolling the cylinders, mixing powder, and stringing the cylinders could now be done by machines.

Safety Issues

The fact that fireworks were made with gunpowder and listed under explosives brought about the issue of safety. Numerous accidents related with fireworks had resulted in tragic human injuries and considerable property damages. As a result, fireworks had become heavily regulated in most countries.

According to the manufacturers, fireworks were the most dangerous during the production process. Powder mixing and powder filling, in turn, were the two most dangerous procedures. The workers had to abide by strict safety measures. Even a tiny spark caused by the dropping of a tool on the floor or the dragging of a chair could start a major explosion. The quality of the ingredients was also of significant importance. Impure ingredients could greatly increase the possibility of accidents. In Liuyang, almost every year, there would be one or more accidents that resulted in deaths and damages. With an ever increasing number of firms entering the industry, safety was an ongoing concern.

Once the fireworks were made, they were relatively safe to transport and store. Even in firing, good quality fireworks rarely caused any problems if everything was done properly. Most of the fireworks-related accidents occurred during private parties or street displays, and quite often involved children playing with fireworks that needed to be handled by adults, or adults firing shells that required professional expertise. Most accidents were linked to consumer backyard events rather than to public displays.

According to the United States Consumer Products Safety Commission's (CPSC) data, injuries related to fireworks had declined substantially, even though their use had increased (see Exhibit 2). For 2009, there were an estimated 5,244 fireworks-related injuries, 30 per cent of which were caused by firecrackers and bottle rockets. Of all the injuries related to firecrackers and fireworks, most were treated in the emergency department. Eight per cent of patients had to be admitted to hospital, and 7 people died due to sustained injuries.

Children from ages five to 14 were the most frequently involved in fireworks-related injuries. However, fireworks were not the only consumer product that might cause injuries to this age group. According to a 2008 CPSC Injury Surveillance Report, fireworks were actually safer than swing sets and baseballs. However, fireworks-related injuries were usually the most dramatic and the most widely publicized accidents, which partly explained the fact that fireworks was the only category among the products listed in Exhibit 3, for which prohibition, instead of education and adult supervision, was often urged.

In the United States, multiple government agencies were involved in regulating fireworks. The Bureau of Alcohol Tobacco and Firearms (BATF) controlled the manufacture, storage, sales and distribution of explosives, i.e., Class B fireworks. The CPSC regulated Class C consumer fireworks, and the Department of Transportation dealt with the transportation of fireworks. Although at the federal level, fireworks and firecrackers were allowed as long as the safety features were up to the standard, local governments would have their own different regulations regarding fireworks consumption. Out of the 50 states, one would allow only novelty fireworks, 5 had banned all consumer fireworks but allowed professional pyrotechnics, and 4 allowed customers only wire or wood stick sparklers and other novelty items. However, the remaining 40 would allow essentially all consumer fireworks. For display fireworks, permits would have to be obtained from federal and local authorities and fire departments.

All legal consumer fireworks offered for sale in the United States had been tested for stability by the Bureau of Explosives and approved for transportation by the U.S. Department of Transportation. Because of the limited amount of pyrotechnic composition permitted in each individual unit, consumer fireworks would not ignite spontaneously during storage, nor would they mass-explode during a fire. Therefore, no special storage was required.

In most of Europe, similar regulations were in place for safety considerations, only the requirements were regarded as less stringent. In Canada, however, regulations were extremely restrictive. However, over the past decade Chinese fireworks companies had made great strides in the Canadian market. In 1999, there were no Chinese companies allowed to sell fireworks in Canada. By 2009, over 75% of all fireworks imports to Canada were from China.

THE FIRECRACKERS AND FIREWORKS INDUSTRY IN CHINA

The firecrackers and fireworks industry in China was dominated by small family-owned-and-operated workshops. It was essentially a low-tech, highly labor-intensive industry. After 1949, government-run factories replaced the family-owned workshops. The increased scale and government funds made possible the automation of some processes. However, the key processes like installing powder, mixing color ingredients, and putting in fuses, were still manually done by skilled workers.

The factories themselves were made up of small workshops that stood away from each other, so that in case of an accident the whole factory would not explode. For the same safety consideration, the workshops were usually located near a water source and in sparsely populated rural areas, to reduce the noise and explosion hazard.

After the reform towards a market economy started in 1979, most of the factories were broken up and became family-run units of production again. It was hoped that this privatization might help to motivate people to increase their productivity and raise output. However, this move also served to restrict further technological innovations. There were hardly any research and development (R&D) facilities, nor human and capital resources allocated to R&D in most fireworks companies. The few resources that were available were all spent on product varieties. Even in Liuyang, out of the 400,000 or so people working in the industry, very few were engineers with advanced professional training.

In response, the Hunan and other local governments began initiatives aimed at upgrading the traditional fireworks industry. Substantial amounts of money were spent on R&D. The Liuyang Firecrackers and Fireworks Authority reported that they had spent RMB 2,000 million in projects with the Beijing University of Technology and the Nanjing University of Science. Among these initiatives were environmentally friendly fireworks, which used cold flame fireworks technology.

The majority of the manufacturing workers were regular farmers who had learned how to make fireworks just by watching and following their elders. They would come to work in fireworks workshops when there were jobs to be done, and return to till their fields if there were none. In Liuyang, for instance, few factories operated year-round. Most workshops would operate as orders came in. Since the fireworks-making communities were very concentrated geographically and had lasted for generations, only a few places (like Liuyang) could claim a large pool of skilled fireworks-makers.

Although Liuyang was by far the most well-known place for making fireworks in China, it faced increasing competition within the country. Also located in Hunan Province,

Liling was another major manufacturing community of fireworks. Liling fireworks did not enjoy the same reputation and variety as Liuyang products, but they were fierce in price competition. In the neighboring Jiangxi Province, Pingxiang and Wanzai fireworks had become strong competitors both in price and quality, especially on the low- and medium-priced market. In the high-end product market, especially in large-type display fireworks and export market, Dongguan in Guangdong Province, had taken advantage of its closeness to Hong Kong and more sophisticated management and marketing practices, and snatched market share from Liuyang. By 2009, however, more than one third of all firms and 60 per cent of Chinese production remained in Luiyang.

The initial capital requirement for starting a fireworks-manufacturing facility was relatively low. To set up a factory with the necessary equipment for making large display shells would require around RMB1,250,000.[1] However, setting up a small family workshop making consumer firecrackers and fireworks would require less than RMB125,000. Consequently, the number of small manufacturers mushroomed after the government started to encourage private business ventures.

While labor costs in the area were still low, they were steadily increasing. As a result of Chinese economic growth, wages had almost doubled over the past 5 years. This was in part because many workers were moving into less dangerous occupations. Skilled workers engaged in major processes would earn an average of RMB1,200 to RMB1,800 per month. A non-skilled worker would be paid only RMB500 to RMB700 every month. In larger factories, labor costs were between 20 and 30 per cent of total costs.

The main raw materials for fireworks were gunpowder, color ingredients, paper, fuse and clay soil. None would be difficult to procure. However, because of the growth in the Chinese domestic fireworks market, costs of raw materials were steadily rising. Another possible problem in supply was quality. Major manufacturers would usually establish long-term relationships with their suppliers to guarantee the quality of the materials. The small workshops would often go with the lowest prices, sometimes at the cost of quality, which could lead to fatal results.

The number of small companies intensified competition. The private workshops were flexible and quick in responding to market demand. They did not entail much administrative cost. Compared to government-owned or some collectively-owned factories, they did incur the costs of providing health care, retirement benefits and housing. They usually did not do any product research or design. Oblivious to intellectual property protection, they would copy any popular product design and sell it for much less. The resulting price drop had become a serious problem for the whole industry. As the profit margin kept shrinking, some workshops would hire cheap unskilled workers, and use cheap equipment and raw materials to cut down on cost. The results could be disastrous.

THE DOMESTIC MARKET

Firecrackers and fireworks had long been an integral part of any ceremonies held in China. Until recently, demand had been stable, but had risen in the past three decades because of increased economic development and living standards. Economically, market reform and unprecedented growth had given rise to the daily appearance of multitudes of new companies and new stores. As people's income level and living standards kept rising, fancier and pricier fireworks and firecrackers were desired over the cheap simple firecrackers, thereby creating more profit opportunities for fireworks manufacturers. Almost every household

---

[1] In 2009, the exchange rate was around 6.60 yuan per US$1.00.

would spend at least a couple of hundred RMB on firecrackers and fireworks during the Spring Festival.

However, during the 1990s, increased concerns over environmental pollution and safety of human life and property led more and more cities to regulate the consumption of fireworks and firecrackers. Every year, high profile fireworks-related accidents were reported and emphasized on mass media before and after the traditional Spring Festival. Some articles even condemned firecrackers and fireworks as an old, uncivilized convention that created only noise, pollution and accidents. In a wave of regulations, city after city passed administrative laws regarding the use of fireworks. By 1998, one-third of the cities in China had completely banned the use of firecrackers and fireworks. Another one-third only allowed fireworks in designated places. This led to a decline in domestic market demand.

However, all this began to change in the mid 2000s. Demand began to soar when Beijing lifted a 12-year ban on fireworks in 2005. Other cities followed suit. In 2005, 106 cities eased restrictions on fireworks; in 2006 another 54 cities eased restrictions. This was followed by 40 cities in 2007 and another 79 cities in 2009. All this lead to an explosion in the Chinese domestic fireworks market.

In the meantime, domestic competition grew intensely. The reform towards a market economy made it possible for numerous family-run workshops to appear. They competed mainly on price. Almost every province had some fireworks-making workshops or factories, many set up and run with the help of skilled workers who had migrated from Liuyang. These small establishments usually were located in rural, underdeveloped areas where labor cost was low. The manufacturing was done manually, sometimes without safety measures, using cheap raw materials and simplified techniques. The products were sold locally at low prices, making it difficult for Liuyang fireworks to sell in those areas. To make things worse, these products would often copy any new or popular product designs coming out of Liuyang or other traditional fireworks communities, even using their very brand names.

In the past, fireworks were sold through the government-run general merchandise companies. Eventually, private dealers took over a large part of the business. Overall, the distribution system was rather fragmented. The old government-run channels were not very effective, especially for general merchandise. In the new distribution channels, wholesale dealers would get shipments directly from the manufacturers, and then resell to street peddlers and convenience stores.

In the countryside, wholesale markets would appear in focal townships, with wholesale dealers and agents of the manufacturers setting up booths promoting their products. Small peddlers in the surrounding areas would get supplies from the market and then sell them in small towns or villages. The wholesale markets in China were important outlets for distributing general merchandise like fireworks.

In the display fireworks market, the buyers were often central and local governments, who would purchase the product for public shows on national holidays or special celebrations. Obviously, a local company would have advantages in supplying to local government in its area. Large fireworks shows usually would use invited bidding to decide on suppliers. The amount of fireworks used could range from RMB100,000 to several million yuan, depending on the scale of a fireworks show.

Account receivables and bad debt control was a problem not just for fireworks manufacturers, but for all businesses in China. Bad debts and lack of respect for business contracts had created a credit crisis in China. The bad debt problem greatly increased transaction costs, slowed down the cash turnover, and had become a headache for fireworks manufacturers. Some had chosen to withdraw from selling in the domestic market, although the profit margin was higher than in the export market.

Legal restrictions, local protectionism, cutthroat price competition, hard-to-penetrate distribution channels and bad debt were impacting negatively on the domestic sales of Liuyang fireworks. In 1997, seeing the decline of its fireworks sales, Liuyang Firecrackers and Fireworks Industry Department, the government agency in charge of the overall development of the pillar industry, decided to start an offensive strategy. First, it opened local offices in most of the 29 provinces, major cities and regions to promote Liuyang fireworks. Second, it regulated the prices that Liuyang fireworks companies could quote and sell in export sales. Third, it resorted to a government-to-government relationship in order to secure contracts for large public fireworks displays in each province. One year after introducing the offensive strategy, Liuyang fireworks sales had increased. By 2009, they controlled an estimated 60 per cent of the global market.

Over the next ten years, many legal restrictions were lifted. One of the most notable legal restrictions to be eased was foreign direct investment. With huge growth in both the Chinese domestic market and with China nearing a virtual lock on the export market, the Chinese Fireworks industry had become a magnet for foreign investors. Liuyang remained the center of the Chinese fireworks industry and an attractive region for foreigners and foreign firms looking at controlling the entire fireworks value chain.

THE EXPORT MARKET

Since the opening of the Chinese economy in 1979, exporting had become a major market for the Chinese fireworks industry. As one of the most celebrated products out of China, export sales of fireworks had risen dramatically between 1978 and 2009. According to independent research, the recorded exports of firecrackers and fireworks reached US$675 million in 2009. This was up from an estimated US$143 million in 1994.

The products from China were rich in variety and low in price, but also had a lower reputation in quality control, packaging and timing control, compared to the products made in Japan and Korea. China-made fireworks also would wholesale for much lower prices, usually 80 per cent lower than similar products made in Japan or Korea.

There had been little overall co-ordination of export sales. As more and more companies were allowed to export directly, competition kept intensifying and the profit margins on export sales kept slipping. As a result, underpricing each other became a common practice. Therefore, despite its dominant share of the world market, the Chinese fireworks export industry enjoyed limited profitability. The export price of Chinese fireworks was between one-fifth and one-third the wholesale price in the United States.

The importers enjoyed a high markup even after paying the 2.4 per cent U.S. import duty. Of course, the importers had to absorb the cost of getting permits, shipping, storing and carrying the inventory for three to four months before making the sales. This gap pushed both domestic and foreign companies to find ways to control more of the value chain from production to retail.

Besides suffering from low profit margin, the Chinese fireworks makers were also risking losing their brand identities. Given the low cost and reasonably good quality of the Chinese fireworks, many large fireworks manufacturers and dealers in the West started to outsource the making of their brand-name fireworks. Failing to see the importance of brand equity, the Chinese fireworks manufacturers were sometimes reduced to mere manufacturing outfits for foreign companies, gradually losing their own brands. There were also fireworks merchants in Korea, Japan or Spain, who would buy the products from China, and then repackage them, or replace the fuses with better quality ones, then resell them for much higher prices.

The export market was usually divided into five blocks: Southeast Asia, North America, Europe, South America and the rest of the world. The most popular market had been Europe, where the regulations on fireworks were less stringent, and orders were of larger quantities and better prices. The United States was considered a tough market because of complex regulations and high competition, nevertheless a necessary one if a company wanted to remain a viable world-player. While in the past, the Canadian market was virtually closed to the Chinese fireworks due to its regulations, by 2009 Chinese imports dominated the entire Canadian market.

The foreign importers were powerful buyers for several reasons. First, they were very well informed, both through past dealings with China and the Internet. Second, they were able to hire agents who were very familiar with the industry in China. Third, they could deal directly with the factories that were willing to offer lower prices. Fourth, there were basically no switching costs, so they could play the suppliers against each other.

The diversity of the cultures in the destination countries greatly reduced the seasonality of the fireworks production and sales. As a result, orders evened out throughout the year. However, the peak season was still towards the end of the year. For the U.S., it was before July 4. Usually, the importers would receive the shipment two or three months beforehand. While the U.S. was still China's major export market for fireworks, other countries were also importing large quantities of Chinese made fireworks (see Exhibit 4).

The Internet had become a marketing outlet for Chinese fireworks. 20 per cent to 25 per cent of the worldwide sales were through the Internet. However, export sales were still made mainly through foreign trade companies or agents.

In recent years, foreign investments were also funneled into the fireworks industry. In Liuyang, four of the large fireworks factories had foreign investments, made mainly by the fireworks trading companies in Hong Kong. In 2009, the Liuyang Fireworks Company was listed on the Toronto Stock Exchange (TSE), a first for a Chinese fireworks manufacturer.

The Future of the Fireworks Industry in China

The managers of the Chinese fireworks companies that Jerry talked to expressed mixed feelings towards the future outlook of their industry. One pessimistic view was that fierce competition and more stringent safety regulations were killing the industry. As the Chinese economy advanced, the government was forcing more manufacturing regulations onto firms that were driving up costs. Moreover, as people became more environmentally-conscious and more distracted by the endless diversities of modern entertainment, traditional celebrations using firecrackers and fireworks would die a gradual death. As to the function of attracting public attention for promotional purposes, fireworks also faced challenges from new technologies, such as laser beams combined with sound effects.

In fact, "make-believe firecrackers" already appeared as substitutes in China. These were made of red plastic tubes strung together like firecrackers with electric bulbs installed inside the tubes. When the power was turned on, the lights would emit sparks, accompanied by crackling reports that sounded like firecrackers. These were being used at weddings and grand openings in cities where firecrackers and fireworks were banned. More interesting substitutes were spotted at some weddings in Beijing, where people paved the road with little red balloons, and made the limousine carrying the bride and groom run over the balloons to make explosive cracking sounds as well as leave behind red bits and pieces of debris. Also, more and more young couples were getting married in western styles, in a church or a scenic green meadow outdoors, where serene and quiet happiness prevailed over the traditional noisy way of celebrating. Therefore, some managers believed that firecrackers and fireworks were doomed to fade off into history.

The more optimistic view, however, was that the industry would not die at all. If the right moves were made by the industry, it could even grow. Some said that tradition would not die so easily. It was in their national character for the Chinese to celebrate with an atmosphere of noisy happiness. Moreover, even in the West, the popularity of fireworks was not suffering from all the regulations. No real substitutes could replace fireworks, which combined the sensual pleasures of visual, audio and emotional stimuli. For instance, the U.S. Congressional resolution in 1963 to use bells to replace fireworks in celebrating Independence Day never really caught on.

Fireworks were also being combined with modern technologies like laser beams, computerized firing and musical accompaniment to make the appeal of fireworks more irresistible. The safety problem was not really as serious as people were made to believe, and would only improve with new technological innovations like smokeless fireworks. With the success of the fireworks displays at the Beijing Olympics, China's brand as a world class fireworks producer was on the rise. With better management practices, perhaps margins could be increased.

However, both sides agreed that the Chinese fireworks industry would have to change its strategy, especially in international competition, to stay a viable and profitable player.

THE DECISION

While the Liuyang fireworks industry dominated the worldwide industry, Jerry had to decide whether he should invest in the industry. If he did invest, what was the best way to capitalize on the potential that remained unexploited in this industry? He wondered whether he could apply the industry analysis framework he had studied in his MBA program.

EXHIBIT 1: China & Liuyang Firecrackers and Fireworks: Total Revenue (US$000)

	2007	2009
Total Revenue Domestic (estimated)		
All China	742,395	1,009,757
Liuyang	450,000	757,500
Total Revenue Exports		
All China	494,930	673,171
Liuyang	300,000	505,000
Total Revenue (estimated)		
All China	1,237,325	1,682,928
Liuyang	750,000	1,262,500

Sources: International Fireworks Association; ICON Group Ltd "The World Market for Fireworks: A 2009 Global Trade Perspective.

Notes:

1. Domestic Revenue estimate based on a 6:4 domestic to export ratio as reported by http://www.articlesbase.com.

2. Alternative sources put the Chinese domestic market much higher.

3. 2009 data and 2007 data are from different sources. Caution should be used when making comparisons. Growth rates of 15 to 18 per cent per year have been reported by other news sources (especially: http://www.newsreelnetwork.com).

EXHIBIT 2: Total Fireworks Consumption and Estimated Fireworks-Related Injuries in U.S.: 2000 to 2008

Year	Fireworks Consumption, Millions of Pounds	Estimated Fireworks-Related Injuries	Injuries per 100,000 Pounds
2000	152.6	11,000	7.2
2001	161.6	9,500	5.8
2002	190.1	8,800	4.6
2003	220.8	9,700	4.4
2004	236.2	9,600	4.1
2005	281.5	10,800	3.8
2006	278.2	9,200	3.3
2007	265.5	9,800	3.7
2008	213.2	7,000	3.3

Source: American Pyrotechnics Association.

EXHIBIT 3: Estimated Emergency Room Treatment Per 100,000 Youths (Ages 5 to 14) from Outdoor Activities (June 22 to July 22, 2008)

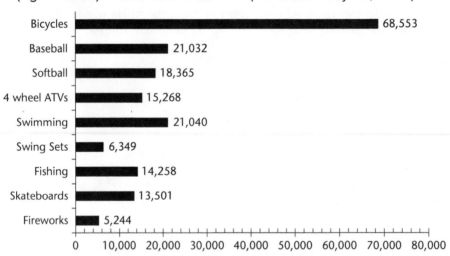

Bicycles	68,553
Baseball	21,032
Softball	18,365
4 wheel ATVs	15,268
Swimming	21,040
Swing Sets	6,349
Fishing	14,258
Skateboards	13,501
Fireworks	5,244

Source: American Pyrotechnics Association As cited from the CPSC National Injury Information Clearinghouse.

EXHIBIT 4: Fireworks Exports from China, 2009

Country of Destination	Rank	Value (000 US$)	% Share	Cumulative %
United States	1	301,500	44.8	44.8
Germany	2	83,553	12.4	57.2
United Kingdom	3	33,645	5.0	62.2
The Netherlands	4	32,586	4.8	67.0
Japan	5	26,764	4.0	71.0
Russia	6	16,157	2.4	73.4
Italy	7	15,967	2.4	75.8
France	8	13,574	2.0	77.8
Spain	9	13,009	1.9	79.7
Denmark	10	9,935	1.5	81.2
Canada	11	9,817	1.5	82.7
Poland	12	9,580	1.4	84.1
Taiwan	13	8,130	1.2	85.3
Finland	14	6,002	0.9	86.2
South Africa	15	5,623	0.8	87.0
Austria	16	5,488	0.8	87.8
Ukraine	17	5,445	0.8	88.7
Sweden	18	4,868	0.7	89.4
Albania	19	4,835	0.7	90.1
Argentina	20	4,793	0.7	90.8
Turkey	21	4,592	0.7	91.5
Belgium	22	4,583	0.7	92.2
Norway	23	4,336	0.6	92.8
Czech Republic	24	4,312	0.6	93.5
Venezuela	25	4,257	0.6	94.1
New Zealand	26	4,024	0.6	94.7
Switzerland	27	3,316	0.5	95.2
South Korea	28	3,104	0.5	95.6
Thailand	29	2,720	0.4	96.0
Indonesia	30	1,925	0.3	96.3
Other	31	24,731	3.7	100.0
Total		**673,171**	**100.00**	**100.00**

Source: Professor Philip M. Parker, INSEAD, copyright © 2009, www.icongrouponline.com.

CASE
7

Sher-Wood Hockey Sticks: Global Sourcing

In early 2011, the senior executives of Sher-Wood Hockey (Sher-Wood), the venerable Canadian hockey stick manufacturer, were pondering whether to move the remaining high-end composite hockey and goalie stick production to its suppliers in China. Sher-Wood had been losing market share for its high-priced, high-end, one-piece composite sticks as retail prices continued to fall. Would outsourcing the production of the iconic Canadian-made hockey sticks to China help Sher-Wood to boost demand significantly? Was there any other choice?

THE HISTORY OF ICE HOCKEY[1]

From the time of early civilization in places as diverse as Rome, Scotland, Egypt and South America, the "ball and stick" game has been played. The game has had different names, but its basic idea has been the same; the Irish, for instance, used the word "hockie" to refer to the sport. Some reports trace the origins of the game to 4,000 years ago, but it has survived to the present.

The modern version of ice hockey emerged from the rules laid down by two Canadians, James Creighton and Henry Joseph, when they studied at McGill University in the late nineteenth century. Their rules were used in the first modern game, which was played in

IVEY | Publishing

Megan (Min) Zhang wrote this case under the supervision of Professor Paul W. Beamish solely to provide material for class discussion. The authors do not intend to illustrate either effective or ineffective handling of a managerial situation. The authors may have disguised certain names and other identifying information to protect confidentiality.

Richard Ivey School of Business Foundation prohibits any form of reproduction, storage or transmission without its written permission. Reproduction of this material is not covered under authorization by any reproduction rights organization. To order copies or request permission to reproduce materials, contact Ivey Publishing, Richard Ivey School of Business Foundation, The University of Western Ontario, London, Ontario, Canada, N6A 3K7; phone (519) 661-3208; fax (519) 661-3882; e-mail cases@ivey.uwo.ca.

Copyright © 2012, Richard Ivey School of Business Foundation   Version: 2013-03-25

One time permission to reproduce granted by Richard Ivey School of Business Foundation on April 22, 2014.

[1]Summarized from Jacqueline L. Longe, *How Products Are Made (Volume 4)* (Farmington Hills: Gale Research,1998); http://www.historyhockey.net, accessed on July 18, 2011; http://www.mcgilltribune.com, accessed on July 18, 2011; and http://www.madehow.com, accessed on July 18, 2011.

Montreal, Quebec in 1875. In 1892, Canada's governor general, Lord Stanley, introduced the game's first national title, the "Lord Stanley's Dominion Challenge Trophy," later simply referred to as the Stanley Cup. In 1917, the National Hockey League (NHL) was founded in Montreal.

Ice hockey found its way to the United States in 1893. By the early 1900s, it had also become prevalent in Europe. Ice hockey was played as a part of the Olympic Summer Games for the first time in April 1920 in Antwerp, Belgium.

By the late twentieth century, ice hockey represented an important source of national pride to Canadians, and it had become popular in other countries in the northern hemisphere, especially the United States, Czech Republic, Finland, Russia and Sweden.

ICE HOCKEY STICK[2]

In ice hockey, players use specialized equipment both to facilitate their participation in the game and for protection from injuries. The equipment can be classified into five categories: goalie, head/face (helmet, neck guard), protective (shoulder pads, shin pads, elbow pads, hockey pants and gloves), sticks and skates. "Head-to-toe equipment suppliers" typically offered all equipment except for goalie equipment. Among the five categories of equipment, sticks and skates drove the industry, accounting for almost two-thirds of global equipment sales.[3]

A hockey stick is a piece of equipment used in ice hockey to shoot, pass and carry the puck. It is composed of a long, slender shaft with a flat extension at one end called the blade. The goaltender (goalie) has a slightly modified shaft with a wider paddle. Hockey stick dimensions can vary to suit a player's comfort, size, usage and stickhandling skills.

Hockey sticks are manufactured either as one-piece sticks with the blade permanently fused to the shaft or as two-piece sticks, where the blade and shaft are made as separate pieces that are joined later in the manufacturing process. One-piece hockey sticks emerged more recently with the advent of new component materials.

The three qualities that players seek in a hockey stick are lightness, responsiveness and "the feel." There were three characteristics which professional players looked for: lie, flex and blade pattern. The lie of a stick refers to the angle between the shaft and the blade. Players usually seek a lie that will put the blade flat on the ice when they are in their skating stance. Hockey stick shafts are highly flexible, and this flexibility is a key component in their performance. Flex, bend, stiffness and whip are all terms used to describe the amount of force required to bend a given length of stick shaft.

Until the late 1950s, hockey stick blades were rarely curved. However, in the 1960s, players began asking their stick manufacturers to create sticks with pre-curved blades for better performance. Soon after, many NHL players became proponents of the "banana blade." In 2011, the legal limit for hockey blade curves in the NHL was 19 mm, or 3/4 of an inch. In addition, players generally expected a hockey stick to be light enough to use easily and flexibly.

To satisfy these qualities, the greatest change came in the materials used to make a hockey stick. One consequence of employing more advanced (composite) materials was that the manufacturing process became more complicated and required more innovations. Custom designs were prevalent among professional players who wanted their sticks to fit their own physical features (i.e., height and strength) and skills.

---

[2]Summarized from J.L. Longe, *How Products Are Made*,1999, http://www.prohockeystuff.com, accessed on July 18, 2011; and http://www.nhlhockeyice.com, accessed on July 18, 2011.

[3]http://www.thehockeysource.tv, accessed on July 18, 2011.

The three primary materials for manufacturing hockey sticks were wood, aluminum and composite. The earliest hockey sticks were made with solid wood. These sticks were not very durable and were inconsistent in length and shape. In the 1940s, laminated sticks were created with layers of wood glued together to create a more flexible and durable design. In the 1960s, manufacturers began adding additional fibreglass lamination or other synthetic coatings, which further enhanced the durability of the sticks.

In the early 1980s, Easton Hockey introduced single piece, all-aluminum sticks that were much lighter than wooden sticks. Because the stiff aluminum did not have the proper "feel" to players, manufacturers then developed a light aluminum shaft with a replaceable wooden blade. The design became popular in the late 1980s and early 1990s.

In the mid-1990s, advanced composite sticks were developed. Composites were comprised of reinforcing fibres, such as graphite (carbon) and Kevlar, and binders such as polyester, epoxy or other polymeric resins that held the fibres together. In the following decade, graphite had become by far the most popular material for sticks used in the NHL, and it was growing rapidly in popularity for amateur and recreational players. Although graphite sticks were originally sold as shafts alone while a separate blade was purchased by the hockey player, one-piece sticks that included both the shaft and the blade eventually predominated. Some manufacturers also used titanium to produce composite sticks. Moreover, Sher-Wood used foam materials, such as polyurethane, to fill blades and paddles of goalie sticks for shock absorption and stiffness.

New, lighter and more durable composites were always being developed. Ice hockey sticks, roller hockey sticks, lacrosse sticks, baseball bats, softball bats and hockey skates required similar technologies to manufacture because almost all of these athletic products incorporated composite materials. R&D, manufacturing and quality control processes continued to advance in the industry. Increasingly, precise technologies were employed throughout the production process.

For most composite and aluminum sticks, the stick's flex characteristic was expressed numerically. This number, which ranged from 50 through 120, was printed on the stick and corresponded to the amount of force (in pounds-force) that it took to deflect or bend the shaft one inch. By contrast, the flex characteristic of their wooden counterparts could not be derived precisely, because the sticks were produced using a high-volume production process that yielded sticks with variable flex properties.

BASICS OF HOCKEY EQUIPMENT INDUSTRY[4]

According to most industry analysts, the global hockey equipment market was showing signs of maturity, growing at just 1 to 2 per cent per annum.[5] The global hockey equipment market in 2010 was $555 million, with skates and sticks accounting for an estimated 62 per cent of industry sales.

Ice hockey equipment sales were driven primarily by global ice hockey participation rates (registered and unregistered). There were about 600,000 hockey players in Canada in 2010. The number of registered hockey players in Canada between the ages of 5 and 25 was

[4]Summarized from Preliminary Prospectus of Bauer Performance Sports Ltd. (January 27, 2011), http://www. secure.globeadvisor.com/servlet/articlenews/story/gam/20110614/GIVOXBAUERMILSTEADATL, accessed on July 18, 2011; http://www.sgma.com/press/93_sanctioned-team-sports-play-in-the-us-remains-strong,-but, accessed on July 18, 2011; and http://www.ehow.com/way_5191903_ice-hockey-equipment-guide.html, accessed on July 18, 2011.

[5]Source: https://secure.globeadvisor.com/servlet/ArticleNews/story/gam/20110614/GIVOXBAUERMILSTEADATL, accessed on July 18, 2011.

expected to shrink by 30,000 players, or 5 per cent, over the next five years. Nevertheless, some industry analysts believed that growth rates of casual and unregistered hockey participation, especially in the United States, as well as growth rates in Eastern Europe (particularly Russia) and women's hockey had exceeded that of the registered segment as a whole. Other drivers of equipment sales included demand creation efforts, the introduction of innovative products, a shorter product replacement cycle, general macroeconomic conditions and the level of consumer discretionary spending.

Relative to European football (soccer) or American baseball, all of the equipment required to participate in organized hockey was more expensive to purchase. Outfitting a teenager or an adult to play recreational hockey cost approximately $600. The equipment for younger players was less expensive. However, nearly 40 per cent of all ice hockey players lived in homes where the annual household income was more than $100,000 per year.

The hockey sticks endorsed by professional hockey players enjoyed a strong position in the hockey stick market. Children and amateur players liked to have sticks embossed with specific players' names. Hockey stick manufacturers typically paid NHL players to use their sticks and provided the players with custom designed sticks.

Competitor Brands and Strategies[6]

Before a Montreal company began manufacturing ice hockey sticks in the late 1880s, most players made their own. By the early twenty-first century, more than 20 brands of ice hockey sticks existed in North America and Europe, and many of the smaller equipment manufacturers had failed or been purchased by larger competitors. The main brands were Easton (Easton-Bell Sports), Bauer (Bauer Performance Sports), CCM (Reebok-CCM Hockey), Warrior (Warrior Sports), Sher-Wood (Sher-Wood Hockey), Mission ITECH (acquired by Bauer) and Louisville/TPS (acquired by Sher-Wood). Bauer, CCM and Sher-Wood originated in Canada, and Easton and Warrior originated in the United States.

Over 80 per cent of the ice hockey equipment market was shared by three major competitors: Bauer, Reebok (which owned both the Reebok and CCM brands) and Easton, each of which was a head-to-toe supplier offering players a full range of products (skates, sticks and full protective equipment). Moreover, Bauer and Reebok also provided goalie equipment. The balance of the equipment market was highly fragmented with many smaller equipment manufacturers, such as Warrior and Sher-Wood, offering specific products and catering to niche segments within the broader market. Exhibit 1 lists the proportion of NHL players using sticks made by the five major suppliers. Each of the five major companies sought new growth in diverse categories.

Easton-Bell Sports operated divisions dedicated to hockey, baseball, lacrosse and softball. Easton established itself as a worldwide leader in designing, developing and marketing performance sports equipment, as well as a broad spectrum of accessories for athletic and recreational activities. Easton Hockey's technical prowess made its stick the number one choice among NHL players and amateurs alike and kept its gloves, skates and helmets at the forefront of technological advance. For years, Easton Hockey had signed head-to-toe contract extensions with NHL players. Easton's innovation processes followed a unique

---

[6]Summarized from Preliminary Prospectus of Bauer Performance Sports Ltd., http://www.fundinguniverse.com, accessed on July 18, 2011; http://www.eastonbellsports.com, accessed on July 18, 2011; http://www.bauer.com, accessed on July 18, 2011; http://www.sher-wood.com, accessed on July 18, 2011; http://www.adidas-group.corporate-publication.com, accessed on July 18, 2011; http://www.warrior.com, accessed on July 18, 2011; http://www.stickshack.com, accessed on July 18, 2011; and http://www.hockeystickexpert.com, accessed on July 18, 2011.

routine—developing new technologies for composite ice hockey sticks first and then apply-ing the advances in materials to skates, baseball bats and softball bats. In 2011, Easton-Bell offered 48 types of player and goalie sticks in its Synergy and Stealth lines. Easton-Bell's net sales for 2006 were $639 million compared to $379.9 million in 2005, an increase of 68 per cent. Gross profit for 2006 was $212.9 million or 33.3 per cent of net sales, as compared to $134.9 million or 35.5 per cent of net sales for 2005.

Bauer Performance Sports manufactured ice hockey, roller hockey and lacrosse equipment as well as related apparel. Bauer was focused on building a leadership posi-tion and growing its market share in all ice hockey and roller hockey equipment products through continued innovation at all performance levels. It produced products at competi-tive prices using alternative materials, sourcing arrangements and supply-chain efficiencies. It also targeted emerging and underdeveloped consumer segments, including Russian play-ers and female players. In 2008, Bauer Performance implemented several strategic acquisi-tions to enter new industries and to enhance its market leadership in its chosen categories. In 2011, Bauer offered 20 types of player and goalie sticks in its Supreme and Vapor lines. Bauer was the number one manufacturer of skates, helmets, protective gear and goalie equipment, and a close number two to Easton of sticks in 2010. It enjoyed a 45 per cent share of the global hockey equipment market. Bauer's profit margin as a percentage of net revenues was 37 per cent.

Reebok-CCM Hockey concentrated on providing hockey equipment and apparel. The company leveraged its multi-brand approach to target different consumer segments. In particular, it developed innovative technologies that appealed to image-conscious con-sumers. Its products were best suited to the physical side of the game and were frequently purchased by consumers seeking performance and quality. In 2011, they offered 32 types of player and goalie sticks. Reebok-CCM's net sales in 2010 were $280 million, and its key markets were Canada, the United States, Scandinavia and Russia.

Warrior Sports concentrated on providing lacrosse and ice hockey equipment, apparel and footwear. The company was dedicated to a core set of philosophies and strengths: tech-nical superiority, grassroots marketing, original and creative youthful expression, and strong partnerships with retailers and suppliers. In 2011, Warrior offered 15 types of player and goalie sticks.

Generally, hockey companies provided one type of hockey stick at three different price points—junior, intermediate and senior. The reference retail prices of the five competi-tors' best senior composite sticks varied. The Bauer Supreme TotalOne Composite, Easton Stealth S19 Composite and Warrior Widow Composite Senior were all priced at $229.99. The CCM U+ Crazy Light Composite and Reebok 11K Sickkick III Composite came in at $209.99, while the Sher-Wood T90 Pro Composite was priced at $139.99.[7]

Global Sourcing in the Hockey Equipment Industry

Similar to other industries, the hockey industry eventually entered the global sourcing era. Global sourcing is the process by which the work is contracted or delegated to a company that may be situated anywhere in the world.[8] Sourcing activities can be categorized along both organizational and locational dimensions (Exhibit 2 lists several types of global

---

[7]Source for all, http://www.amazon.com, accessed on May 29, 2011.

[8]This paragraph is summarized from Ilan Oshri, Julia Kotlarsky, and Leslie P. Willcocks, *The Handbook of Global Outsourcing and Offshoring* (Hampshire: Macmillan, 2009); and Marc J. Schniederjans, Ashlyn M. Schniederjans, and Dara G. Schniederjans, *Outsourcing and Insourcing In An International Context* (New York: M.E. Sharpe, 2005).

sourcing). From an organizational perspective, the choice between insourcing and outsourcing involves deciding whether to keep the work within the firm or contract it out to an independent service provider. From a locational perspective, three choices are available–onshoring (within the nation), nearshoring (to a neighbouring country) and offshoring (to a geographically distant country). To optimize the overall benefits and hedge risks, companies often seek to balance their global outsourcing and insourcing activities. Exhibit 3 lists several of the factors typically considered by manufacturers faced with the decision of whether to onshore insource or offshore outsource.

As early as the 1980s, western sports equipment manufacturers, such as Nike and Reebok, started to outsource the manufacture of sporting goods, such as running shoes, to Asia. Nevertheless, before the year 2000, hockey companies preferred insourcing over outsourcing and executed this strategic focus through organic growth, strategic acquisitions and establishing company-owned factories in other countries; for example, Easton and Warrior had factories in Tijuana, Mexico. During the past decade, the hockey industry began to outsource. In 2004, Bauer Nike Hockey shut down or downsized three plants in Ontario and Quebec, eliminating 321 manufacturing jobs. The company outsourced about 90 per cent of its production to other makers in Canada and the rest to international suppliers. From 2002 to 2008, Reebok-CCM closed five plants in Ontario and Quebec and outsourced manufacturing to other countries, eliminating about 600 manufacturing jobs. Easton and Warrior also outsourced part of their manufacturing to Asia but still kept their factories in Mexico. The capacity of Warrior's Mexican factory was estimated to be 4,000 composite sticks per week produced by 250 employees in 2008. (Exhibit 1 lists the manufacturing sites associated with several of the leading hockey stick brands.)

Global manufacturing outsourcing was characterized by some drawbacks. It separated manufacturing activities from R&D and marketing activities and challenged a company's ability to coordinate initiatives between these functions, such as product innovation, designing for manufacturability, supply chain efficiency and quality control. Especially in offshore outsourcing, cultural differences caused miscommunication, technology distance necessitated extra training, and geographic distance resulted in extra lead time or cycle time.[9] In March 2010, Bauer Hockey recalled 13 models of junior hockey sticks, manufactured outside of Canada, due to excessive lead levels in the sticks' paint that was detected by public health officials in random testing.

Offshore outsourcing also threatened to negatively impact a company's public image if it reduced domestic employment. In November 2008, UNITE HERE[10] launched a national campaign to persuade Reebok to repatriate the production of its hockey equipment and jerseys.[11]

Additionally, global economic dynamics, such as changing labour costs, raw material costs and exchange rates, introduced new uncertainties into global sourcing. Exhibit 4 lists a sample of comparative labour rates prevailing in Canada, the United States, Mexico and China. In 2011, the Boston Consulting Group (BCG) concluded that with Chinese wages rising and the value of the Yuan continuing to increase, the gap between U.S. and Chinese wages was narrowing rapidly.

Industries other than sporting goods had already begun to practice repatriating manufacturing, also known as reshoring or backshoring. In fact, reshoring had been an alternative

---

[9]This paragraph is summarized from Masaaki Kotabe, Global *Sourcing Strategy: R&D, Manufacturing, and Marketing Interfaces* (New York: Quorum Books, 1992.)

[10]UNITE HERE: a union representing 50,000 food service, apparel, textile, hotel and distribution workers across Canada.

[11]http://www.cbc.ca/news/story/2010/03/18/nike-hockeystick-recall.html, accessed on July 18, 2011.

in global sourcing planning from the beginning. For German manufacturing companies in the period 1999 to 2006, every fourth to sixth offshoring activity was followed by a reshoring activity within the following four years, mainly due to lack of flexibility and quality problems at the foreign location. This served as a short-term correction of the prior location misjudgement rather than a long-term reaction to slowly emerging economic trends.[12]

SHER-WOOD HOCKEY INC.: COMPANY TIMELINE[13]

Sher-Wood Hockey Inc. manufactured and distributed hockey sticks and equipment in Canada. Based in Sherbrooke, Quebec, it was founded in 1949 and was formerly known as Sherwood-Drolet, Ltd. For more than 60 years, it had been one of Canada's best-known hockey equipment manufacturers. In 1976, Sherwood-Drolet introduced its flagship wooden stick, the PMP 5030, which was described as "the best stick in the world" by NHL legend Guy Lafleur. By 2007, the company had made more than 6 million PMP 5030s.

In 2006, Sherwood-Drolet sold about one million wooden and 350,000 composite sticks. The company anticipated that the composite stick business would continue to grow in terms of volume and profitability. Earlier, Sherwood-Drolet had started contracting out the production of its lower end wooden models to producers in the Ukraine. In 2007, it outsourced the production of PMP 5030 (mid to high end wooden) sticks to a local provider in Victoriaville, Quebec. Meanwhile, the company concentrated on making composite sticks fashioned from graphite, Kevlar and other synthetics. Notwithstanding the company's efforts to move its wooden stick production offshore, it claimed that it would continue to make custom wooden models for professional hockey players, such as Jason Spezza of the Ottawa Senators.

However, when Spezza learned that Sherwood-Drolet would no longer be manufacturing his favourite wooden sticks in Canada, he decided to move to another company. "They [local manufacturers] can get sticks to me in a week now. If it's over there [China], the process will probably be just too much," said Spezza.[14] Ultimately, Montreal-based Reebok designed and produced a stick for him that had a graphite shaft and wooden blade, but the look of a one-piece. In November 2008, Reebok issued a press release announcing that Spezza would start using their sticks, ". . .we are excited to work with Jason, not only on marketing initiatives, but also on the research, design and development of future Reebok Hockey equipment."[15]

By May 2008, Sherwood-Drolet had filed a proposal to its creditors under the Bankruptcy and Insolvency Act. CBC News reported, "It has been hurt in recent years by shift from

---

[12]Source: S. Kinkel and S. Maloca. "Drivers and Antecedents of Manufacturing Offshoring and Backshoring: A German Perspective," *Journal of Purchasing and Supply Management* 15.3 (2009): 154–65.

[13]summarized from http://www.sher-wood.com, accessed on July 18, 2011; http://hockeystickexpert.com, accessed on July 18, 2011; http://www.canada.com/topics/sports/story.html?id=87c5d6b3-8872-496a-8d4f-01f5f4e36342, accessed on July 18, 2011; and http://www.thestar.com/news/canada/article/273561, accessed on July 18, 2011.

[14]http://www.canada.com/topics/sports/story.html?id=87c5d6b3-8872-496a-8d4f-01f5f4e36342, accessed on July 18, 2011

[15]http://www.reebokhockey.com/labs/labs-blog/entries/2008/Nov/25/entry/jason-spezza-reebok-hockey-family/, accessed on July 18, 2011.

wooden hockey sticks to composite sticks."[16] Richmond Hill, Ontario-based Carpe Diem Growth Capital bought the company and changed its name to Sher-Wood Hockey Inc.

In September 2008, Sher-Wood purchased the hockey novelty and licensed assets of Inglasco. In December that same year, it purchased TPS Sports Group, a leading manufacturer and distributor of hockey sticks and protective equipment. Sher-Wood transported TPS's assets from Wallaceburg and Strathroy, Ontario to Quebec, consolidated three companies and invested an additional $1.5 million to set up the new factory.

Production

As of March 2011,[17] Sher-Wood produced sticks (sticks, shafts, blades), protective equipment (gloves, pants, shoulder pads, elbow pads, shin pads), goalie gear (goalie pads, catcher, blocker, knee protector, arm and body protector, pants) and other accessories (pucks, bags, puck holders, mini sticks, bottles, carry cases) for ice hockey. The company also sold some equipment and accessories for street hockey (goalie kit, sticks, pucks, balls), as well as sports novelties for hockey fans.

The company introduced new sticks twice a year–in May/June and at the end of October. The life cycle of a product line in the market was about 18 to 24 months. By the end of 2010, Sher-Wood provided 27 types of player and goalie sticks. Thirteen of them were wooden.

Although Sher-Wood had targeted various NHL players in order to support the credibility of the brand, the company mostly targeted junior teams, AAA teams and a couple of senior leagues. Sher-Wood only conducted a low volume of custom design for high-end players and mainly provided custom products from a cosmetic standpoint. For example, personalizing the graphic or colour of the sticks. Sher-Wood used to need two to three weeks to produce customized sticks for an NHL player.

In 2010, Sher-Wood sales volume for sticks produced in Sherbrooke dropped almost 50 per cent compared to 2009. Its Chinese partners manufactured most of their composite hockey sticks. Sher-Wood's plant manufactured the remaining high-end, one-piece composite sticks and goalie foam sticks, about 100,000 units annually, with 33 workers in the factory and seven staff in the office. The return on investment of the fixed cost in Canada was low.

Executives believed that they needed to provide a competitive retail price to boost the demand. To do so, they also needed to afford retailers a higher margin than their competitors did, so that retailers would help with product presentations in stores and marketing efforts. These approaches called for low cost production as well as decent quality. To reduce the cost and fully utilize the facilities, they could outsource the remaining production to the partner based in Victoriaville and move facilities there. However, according to regulations in Quebec, Sher-Wood did not have enough latitude to move or sell the equipment to their subcontractor in Quebec. They also considered backshoring the manufacturing out of China. They concluded that it would be more advantageous to stay in China from both cost reduction and R&D standpoints.

Chinese Partners' Condition and Collaboration

Sher-Wood's suppliers were located in Shanghai, Shenzhen and Zhongshan City near Hong Kong. They were producing tennis and badminton rackets, developing the expertise in composite technology and relevant sporting goods production. Sher-Wood began to cooperate

---

[16]http://www.cbc.ca/news/business/story/2008/05/05/sherwood-filing.html?ref=rss, accessed on July 18, 2011.
[17]Summarized from http://www.sher-wood.com, accessed on May 29, 2011.

with them about 10 years ago when it started selling composite sticks. For years, these suppliers manufactured one-piece and two-piece composite hockey sticks for hockey companies around the world. Gradually, they accumulated manufacturing capacity and R&D capability. Sher-Wood's main supplier in Zhongshan City operated two shifts for 10 hours a day, six days a week. Their annual capacity was more than 1 million units. Moreover, they possessed an R&D team with 10 to 15 engineers, which was able to produce a prototype within one day with full information. On the contrary, it would cost Sher-Wood four to five months with a team of two to three engineers to produce a similar prototype. More importantly, as a consequence of their long-term cooperation, the main supplier had developed a certain feeling about hockey so that language and cultural barriers were not problems any more. "They were becoming a partner rather than one section within the supply chain," said Eric Rodrigue, Sher-Wood's marketing vice president.

Sher-Wood and its Chinese supplier partner needed to collaborate closely. On one hand, Sher-Wood had to send their experts to China to coach the partner about how to produce sticks according to their specifications. On the other hand, although Sher-Wood and the partner had similar on-site labs to conduct product tests, Sher-Wood mainly focused on the feeling of the stick, that is, the reproduction of how the slap shot, passes, reception, etc., would feel when a player placed his or her hands a certain way on the stick. Sher-Wood also conducted tests on ice with professional players, something their supplier could not do.

Moreover, with young, passionate and knowledgeable new managers in management and marketing, company executives thought they were ready to meet the extra cost and effort in market collaboration between Sher-Wood, the partner in China and retailers.

Company executives were concerned with rising labour costs, material costs and the currency exchange rate in China. Nevertheless, the overall cost of manufacturing in China was still lower than the cost in Quebec. They estimated that cost reduction was 0 to 15 per cent per unit depending on the model, with good quality and fast turnaround time. Moreover, some industries such as textiles had started to relocate their manufacturing to new emerging countries, such as Vietnam and Cambodia, for low labour and equipment costs; however, there was no R&D advantage in composite materials in these alternative locales.

Executives were also concerned with other issues. First, although the main supplier was able to produce customized sticks for an NHL player within 24 hours, the shipping was quite expensive from China to Quebec. Second, the main supplier used to produce huge volumes fast but without product personalization. Third, the game of hockey was perceived as a Western cultural heritage sport, so anything relevant to hockey which was made in China had the potential to negatively influence the market perception. However, all their competitors had outsourced manufacturing to China for years.

THE CHALLENGE

In early 2011, the question for Sher-Wood senior executives was how to boost their hockey stick sales. They believed that they should cope with this challenge by providing sticks with better quality, better retail price and better margin for retailers. They wondered whether they should move the manufacturing of the remaining high-end composite sticks to their suppliers in China or whether there was any alternative.

If they decided to shift their remaining manufacturing outside of the company, they needed to deal with a variety of issues. To fully utilize the facilities in Sherbrooke, they needed to move equipment to China, which was difficult and time-consuming because of export regulations. To set up the manufacturing machines and guide the manufacturing team, they would need to send experts there. To complete the coming hockey season between September and

April but still implement the decision, they needed to plan every phase precisely. They also needed to figure out what to say and do about the 40 affected employees. Many had worked for Sher-Wood for more than 30 years, and their average age was 56. How could this be communicated to the public? They needed to make a final decision soon.

EXHIBIT 1: NHL Share of Hockey Stick Brands and Their Manufacturing Sites

Company	NHL Share	Manufacturing Sites
Easton	45.1%	Tijuana, Mexico and China
Bauer	15.7%	Composite sticks made in China and Thailand
RBK/CCM	13.7%	Composites sticks in China, wooden sticks in Canada and Finland
Warrior	11.8%	Tijuana, Mexico (insourcing), China (outsourcing)
Sher-Wood	2.3%	Composite, high-end wood goalie sticks in Canada and China, most wood stick production in Eastern Europe
Louisville TPS, Mission, and others	11.4%	N/A

Source: http://www.usatoday.com/, January 2008, accessed on May 29, 2011.

EXHIBIT 2: Types of Global Sourcing

	Insourcing	Outsourcing
Offshoring	Keeping work in a wholly owned subsidiary in a distant country.	Contracting work with a service provider in a distant country.
Near-shoring	Keeping work in a wholly owned subsidiary in a neighbouring country.	Contracting work with a service provider in a neighbouring country
On-shoring	Keeping work in a wholly owned subsidiary in the home country.	Contracting work with a service provider in the home country.

Source: Derived from Oshri, Korlarksy, and Willcocks, *The Handbook of Global Outsourcing and Offshoring,* 2009; Macmillan Publishers.

EXHIBIT 3: Evaluation of Global Sourcing

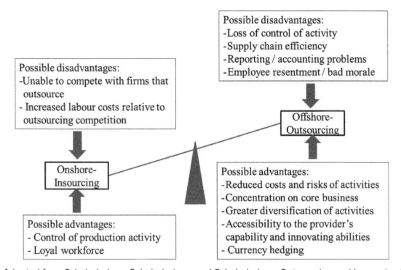

Source: Adapted from Schniederjans, Schniederjans, and Schniederjans, *Outsourcing and Insourcing in an International Context;* 2005; M.E. Sharpe.

EXHIBIT 4: Hourly Compensation Costs in Manufacturing (US$)

Year	China (urban)	China[1]	Canada	USA	Mexico	Estonia	Finland
2002	0.95	0.41	18.05	27.36	5.59	3.11	22.62
2003	1.07	0.44	21.08	28.57	5.31	4.11	28.12
2004	1.19	0.45	23.67	29.31	5.26	4.86	32.47
2005	1.30	0.49	26.26	30.14	5.61	5.52	33.64
2006	1.47	0.53	28.58	30.48	5.88	6.58	35.23
2007	1.83	0.64	31.27	32.07	6.17	8.73	39.17
2008	2.38	0.82	32.06	32.78	6.47	10.56	43.85
2009	2.69	N/A	29.59	34.19	5.70	9.83	43.47
2010	3.16	N/A	34.60	34.81	6.14	9.42	41.10

Source: http://www.bls.gov, accessed on July 18, 2011.

[1]The data is for town or village.

Charles Chocolates

In March, 2012, Steve Parkland started his new job as president of Charles Chocolates (Charles), a privately held premium chocolate producer based in Portland, Maine. The board of directors had asked him to double or triple the size of the company within 10 years. Each member of the board and the management team had a different idea about what Charles needed to do. Parkland needed to devise a strategy that would fit the company's culture, and then gain the support of the board, the management team and the employees.

THE PREMIUM CHOCOLATE MARKET

The U.S. market for chocolates was US$19.3 billion[1] in 2011, and had been growing at about 6 per cent annually. The premium chocolate market ($2.7 billion), which had higher margins, was growing at 10 per cent annually, and imports of ethically produced cocoa grew by 156 per cent[2] as aging baby boomers emphasized quality and ethics in their purchases. Incumbents such as Hershey's and Cadburys had moved into the premium chocolate market through acquisitions or upmarket launches.

About one-quarter of annual chocolate sales typically occur in the eight weeks prior to Christmas. Twenty per cent of "heavy users" account for more than half of these pre-Christmas sales. These heavy users tend to be established families, middle aged childless

Professor Charlene Zietsma wrote this case solely to provide material for class discussion. The author does not intend to illustrate either effective or ineffective handling of a managerial situation. The author may have disguised certain names and other identifying information to protect confidentiality.

This publication may not be transmitted, photocopied, digitized or otherwise reproduced in any form or by any means without the permission of the copyright holder. Reproduction of this material is not covered under authorization by any reproduction rights organization. To order copies or request permission to reproduce materials, contact Ivey Publishing, Ivey Business School, Western University, London, Ontario, Canada, N6G 0N1; (t) 519.661.3208; (e) cases@ivey.ca; www.iveycases.com.

Copyright © 2013, Richard Ivey School of Business Foundation   Version: 2013-09-05

One time permission to reproduce granted by Richard Ivey School of Business Foundation on April 22, 2014.

IVEY | Publishing

---

[1]All currency in U.S. dollars unless specified otherwise.

[2]http://www.vreelandassociates.com/us-chocolate-sales-up-6-while-premium-jumps-10/, accessed August 14, 2013.

couples and empty nesters with high incomes. They purchase more high quality boxed chocolate than bars or lower quality chocolate.[3]

In line with social trends, demand was growing for organic chocolate and dark chocolate due to its heart-healthy anti-oxidant properties. At the same time, however, large chocolate manufacturers wanted the United States Food and Drug Administration to redefine the term "chocolate" to allow them to produce cheaper versions (with less chocolate content) and still call it chocolate. Consumers and employees also increasingly demanded corporate social responsibility. Chocolate companies were targeted because forced labor and child labor was still sometimes used in cocoa bean production in West Africa. Environmental concerns influenced packaging, procurement and operational decisions.

COMPETITORS

Chocolate competitors in the premium chocolate segment in the United States featured strong regional brands and large international players. Godiva, backed by Nestle, had taken the business by storm with glitzy packaging, high price points, and widespread distribution among gift retailers. Godiva's quality was not as high as Charles, but it obtained about 15 per cent higher price points for standard products on the strength of its sleek and modern packaging, variations in chocolate molding and coloring, advertising and distribution. Godiva's high-end products sold for 200 per cent to 300 per cent of Charles prices. Lindt, a large Swiss firm, sold mid-quality chocolate bars and truffles broadly in mass merchandisers, drug and grocery retailers, and their pricing was about 90 per cent of Charles.

Strong regional players included Delice Chocolates and Cardon's. Delice, based in Providence, Rhode Island, had 32 retail stores, mostly in tourist and downtown locations in northeastern states, with four stores in California. The company's quality was high and it excelled at frequent flavour introductions. Delice's copper boxes could be customized at the store. Pricing was similar to Godiva. Cardon's was a 120 year-old Boston firm with 50 locations nationally, nearly all in malls. Cardon's was most successful in New England. It had tried to launch in Chicago, but had not done well there. Cardon's price point was about 35 per cent lower than Charles, and it had moderate product quality level. Cardon's did a strong business in corporate gifts and group purchases, offering 20 per cent to 25 per cent discounts for high volume orders.

Other premium chocolate companies included extremely high end custom chocolatiers, Belgian producers that sold through American retailers or online and niche wholesalers of single varietal bean or organic chocolates. Other companies commanded price premiums over their quality level because of their distribution and/or store concept. For example, Dolce Via, which emphasized mall stores, and The Great American Candy Company, which sold more candy than chocolate and used a franchise model, had higher price points than Cardon's but lesser quality.

CHARLES CHOCOLATES COMPANY HISTORY

Founded in 1885, Charles Chocolates was New England's oldest chocolate company. For the last two decades (during which time sales had grown by more than 900 per cent), the company had been owned by a private group comprised principally of two financial executives, an art dealer, and a former owner of a bus company. These four plus a past

---

[3]Company insider citing a presentation by Neilson at the Confectionary Manufacturer's Association conference, 2007.

president of Charles comprised the board of directors. Charles' head office was located above its flagship store in Portland's Old Port area, a tourist area known for its cobblestone streets, 19th century buildings, and active nightlife.

Charles produced high-quality, hand-wrapped chocolates including its premier line, Portland Creams, along with truffles, nuts and chews, almond bark, chocolate-covered ginger, caramels, brittles, and orange peel in various assortments, bars, nutcorn and premium ice cream novelties. Charles chocolates were of the highest quality, and the company had many loyal customers around the world. In 2009, the company won a prestigious Superior Taste Award from Belgium's Institute for Taste, which described the product as "classy, refined and elegant," and "top-of-the-range," with "rich chocolate aromas."

PRODUCTION

Charles chocolates were made in a 24,000-square-foot factory owned by Charles on the outskirts of Portland. There were 75 retail and 35 production employees, all non-unionized, and 20 employees in management, administration and sales (see Exhibit 1). Production took place from 7 a.m. to 4 p.m. each day. With so many different products, batch processing and hand packing were used, and set-up times were a significant component of costs. Employees learned multiple job functions and enjoyed a variety of work and tasks. There were no measures of productivity or efficiency in the plant, and thus no way of telling on a day to day basis if the plant was doing a good job.

Demand forecasting was difficult due to the seasonality of sales, but product shelf life was long (up to a year), and significant inventories were kept. Nevertheless, there were significant problems with out-of-stocks each week. The Christmas season was particularly chaotic. The wholesale business required early seasonal production, whereas the online and retail business required late production. Production planning was complicated by data distortions arising from out-of-stocks and over stocks. When an item was produced after being out of stock for a month, filling back orders would unnaturally spike sales, yet these spikes would be used for production planning the following year. Similarly, when there was too much stock, the retail stores would push or discount the items, creating distortions in the sales data, which would be used for production planning the following year. Because out-of-stocks in the wholesale channel created problems with customers, short supplies were diverted from the company's own stores and delivered to wholesalers. Furthermore, when a special order arrived in wholesale, it was not uncommon for the plant to put production plans on hold to focus on the special order.

The company's heritage, commitment to quality and strong family values were cherished by employees, some of whom were third-generation Charles employees. New ideas were often resisted by employees over fears that the company was compromising its values and heritage. Turnover was low, and wages were competitive. Permanent employees were on a first-name basis with all of the senior leaders, including the president.

BUSINESS LINES

Charles earned revenues in four major areas: retailing chocolate products through company-owned stores, wholesaling, online/phone sales and sales from Sandwich Heaven, a well-known eatery in Portland, which Charles had purchased in 2009.

Retail. Charles' 11 wholly owned retail stores produced 50 per cent of sales. The stores' theme was heritage, and the flagship store had been designated a heritage site. Sales staff offered chocolate samples to customers, and the aromas and images in the store contributed to an excellent retail experience. In 2005, Charles had won America's Innovative Retailer of the Year award in the small business category. Most stores were in tourist locations, such as Bar Harbor, and Boston's Back Bay and Beacon Hill areas. Most were leased, though the flagship store was owned. Stores were about 500 square feet in size, with the exception of the Bar Harbor and cruise ship terminal locations, which were booths. Although other retailers sold Charles Chocolates, they purchased the products wholesale through direct sales from Charles. Exhibit 2 shows the store locations and their approximate annual sales. The two newest stores, Back Bay and Beacon Hill in Boston, were showing steady sales growth in their first two years of operations, but significantly shy of expectations. The Portland stores benefited from Charles iconic brand image in Maine.

Wholesale. Approximately 30 per cent of sales came from wholesale accounts in five categories: 1) independent gift/souvenir shops, 2) large retail chains, 3) tourist retailers, such as duty-free stores, airport or train station stores and hotel gift shops, 4) corporate accounts that purchased Charles products for gifts for customers or employees and 5) specialty high-end food retailers. Some large accounts, including department stores, gift chains and coffee chains, had been significant Charles customers, but had recently changed their purchasing to focus either on their own products or on less expensive lines. A salaried national sales manager based in Boston oversaw eight sales agents across the United States, and a salaried rep located in Maine. Sales agents had exclusive rights to sell Charles products within their territory but also carried non-competing giftware lines. Many had been with the company as long as the previous president, who had established the wholesale division nearly two decades earlier, but contractually, they could be terminated with 90 days' notice. Marketing Vice-President Mary Bird said:

> Some [reps] perform very well. They cite many challenges with our brand–niche market, high prices, inadequate shelf life, old fashioned ("not glitzy or fashionable enough") packaging, and an unknown brand in many areas. Some reps have stronger lines and just carry Charles as an add-on. The salaried rep in Maine receives constant requests for our products, as it is our "home turf" and we do extensive advertising locally for our own stores. In Portland, some accounts will say they are honored to carry Charles. In other parts of the United States, they have not heard of us and are dismissive of the products and their price points as they do not understand the brand and the value of the product. If the remote reps are not well trained, they just cannot present the brand adequately and sell it.

Retailers typically marked items up by 100 per cent. Charles earned about half the gross margins on wholesale sales as it did on retail and online sales and the company paid its sales agents approximately 10 per cent commission. There were 585 active wholesale customers in 2011. Of these, 221 purchased less than $1,000 per year, and another 125 purchased between $1,000 and $2,000 per year. There had been problems in the past with smaller accounts selling stock past its expiration date. Some wholesale accounts ordered custom products, such as logo bars for special events. In the past, some regular customers had ordered with too little lead time, so the plant typically kept some logo bars in inventory for customers in anticipation of their orders.

Online and Phone. Charles' online business generated four per cent of sales and its phone business generated 6 per cent of sales. Sixty per cent of all orders were from regular customers. Average sales were $138 by phone and $91 from the website. The proportion of people who shopped online in the United States had grown considerably in the last decade, with about 59 per cent of respondents in a 2012 Neilsen poll saying they prefer to shop online because of its convenience.[4] Charles' online business had not gone up with the trends. Orders received by phone, mail or online were processed within three to four days, then shipped via FedEx. Shipping was free for orders over $500. Orders went to the United States (60 per cent), Canada (35 per cent) and 50 countries internationally (5 per cent). They were delivered to the far North, sometimes via dogsled, to lighthouses on both coasts and to Antarctica. Online and phone orders were given priority for inventory allocation, and stock would be transferred back to the factory from the retail stores if necessary.

Sandwich Heaven. Ten per cent of sales came from Sandwich Heaven, which featured made-to-order sandwiches, soups and salads, desserts (including Charles ice cream) and wine and beer. At lunch in the summer, the lineup regularly extended out the door. Since Charles had purchased Sandwich Heaven, most of the long term staff had turned over, and recruiting new employees was difficult in Portland's tight labor market. Sandwich Heaven had had to curtail its evening hours due to staff recruiting problems. Although Sandwich Heaven had a liquor license, the volume of alcohol sold was very small.

MARKETING

Since Charles' chocolates were fairly expensive, the company targeted affluent customers for themselves or for gifts. Cruise ship visitor and other tourists visited the store then often became phone or online customers. Locals were frequent and loyal purchasers. Local businesses also saw Charles as their corporate gift of choice. According to Bird:

> Our most loyal clients have an emotional connection to Charles. For example, they were in the Portland store on a holiday, or it was a traditional gift in their family. Many then give Charles as a gift and some of those recipients then become loyal customers. Other customers are affluent people who want something unique. They see us as an obscure but classic gift. But how do you reach these people to promote to them? They are scattered across the United States and of course they are courted by every advertiser. We cannot make mistakes or disappoint them in any way. If we do, we apologize and replace the product immediately–good old-fashioned service.

The Charles brand emphasized heritage, with traditional packaging, including pink or brown gingham-wrapped squares, packed in a burgundy box or tins. Some tins featured old-fashioned scenes such as English roses, cornucopias or floral arrangements, while others featured American art. Chocolate bars came in a variety of packaging.

The brand had a very loyal following. Parkland described the brand perception:

> When I first began investigating Charles, I asked everyone I knew what they thought of the brand. Most people had never heard of it. Others said "Oooooh, Charles! That's the best chocolate I've ever had." The retail experience is key in creating memories that lead to repeat sales. Through store décor, sampling, aromas, taste and service, I think Charles delivers "chocolate orgasms" to its customers.

The growth challenge would be to increase awareness without diluting the brand. The premium price scared some consumers and wholesalers. Discounting, or making cheaper products to piggyback on the brand, would risk brand integrity. The brand's heritage image

---

[4]http://www.medialifemagazine.com/nielsen-59-percent-prefer-to-shop-online/, posted June 7, 2012.

was an issue. As Charles' loyal customers aged, would younger buyers appreciate the traditional image? Bird cited brands such as Chanel and Lancôme, which had developed classic images and refused to compromise, and brands such as Jaguar, Cadillac, BMW and Volvo, which had developed a younger, sexier image while maintaining core design elements to maintain brand integrity.

Charles advertised in tourist publications, seasonal print media and radio spots. Charles also donated product extensively to charitable events. Direct mail and solid search engine rankings promoted the online business. Charles' website was kept basic to make it load easily. It had an ordering facility, a reminder service that emailed customers about their upcoming special occasions and optimized search engine placement. The website also had links to resellers, however, the sales agents had not been good about providing links for their top accounts, as they did not seem to understand the value provided by such links.

FINANCIALS[5]

Charles was in a strong financial position. Although Charles had gone through a period of significant growth just after the current shareholders acquired the company, growth had slowed considerably in the past few years. In part, this decline had resulted from the slowdown in tourism since the financial crisis. In fact, chocolate sales had declined since 2008, though the company's revenues had grown slightly due to the contributions of Sandwich Heaven. Margins remained strong, however, at about 50 per cent of sales on average. Financial statements are shown in Exhibits 3 to 6.

LEADERSHIP

Jim Bell had been president of Charles from 1989 until 2012. When he announced his intention to retire in 2010, the controlling shareholders (and board of directors) considered selling Charles. It was a healthy company with significant assets, great cash flow and good margins. Yet the board felt that Charles had significant potential to grow and sought a new leader (see Exhibit 7). In the two years during the search, managers knew that Bell was retiring, and decisions were put off until a new leader could be found.

Steve Parkland was vice-president of operations for a meat processing company, in charge of six plants and approximately 2,300 employees, when he saw the ad. Previously, Parkland had been president of a seafood company and general manager of a meat processing subsidiary. His career had involved stints in marketing and sales in addition to operations, and he had an MBA from Duke University. Parkland had an empowering style and a strong commitment to values and integrity. Charles appealed to Parkland because he enjoyed the strategy aspect of general management, and wanted to move to New England. He was offered the job with the provision that he purchase a significant number of shares in the company each year for the first three years.

The senior management team included three others. Mary Bird, vice-president of sales and marketing, a Charles employee since 1999, managed the retail stores, developed marketing plans and oversaw the online and wholesale businesses, Sandwich Heaven, and the ice cream business. She supervised the wholesale sales manager, the retail operations manager, a communications manager, and the order desk staff. The product development person and purchasing and sales planner reported indirectly to Bird, though they worked

---

[5] All financial figures in the case are disguised.

more directly with Ray Wong. Bird worked long hours at the office and often helped at Sandwich Heaven when staff didn't show, or drove product to stores on the weekends when they were short-shipped. Bird was a shareholder.

Ray Wong, vice-president of production, oversaw production at the factory. Wong earned a bachelor of food science in 1983, and later took courses in material requirements planning, candy-making, ice-cream making and management. He had worked in progressively responsible operations positions in a variety of food and beverage companies prior to joining Charles in 1995. Wong did not own shares in the company. Wong was especially interested in computer programming, and he had developed all of Charles internal production planning systems himself.

Sven Amundsen, vice-president of finance and chief financial officer, had retired as chief financial officer of a bus company in 1996, but joined Charles in 2002 at the urging of his former partner, who was on Charles' board. Previously, Amundsen had worked in financial management in manufacturing and retail after articling as a chartered accountant with Price Waterhouse. Amundsen's expertise was in reorganizations, acquisitions and dispositions. He maintained Charles books by hand, as he had never learned accounting or spreadsheet software programs. Amundsen owned shares in the company.

Bird and Amundsen were a cohesive team, but conflict between Bird and Wong had escalated to the board level during the past two years, as Bird sought to reduce out of stocks and launch new products, while Wong sought to retain control of scheduling and production. Furthermore, because the wholesale division was favored by the past president, the wholesale manager in Boston had regularly gone over Bird's head to have the president overturn her decisions.

GROWTH OPPORTUNITIES

During the recruitment process, Parkland had been probing the managers and board members to get their perspectives on growth options. There was a dizzying array.

The idea of franchising Charles stores or Sandwich Heaven had been discussed but not truly investigated. The online business also appeared exciting, with its low costs of sales, lack of intermediaries, and high reorder rate. The corporate gift market also seemed promising. Offering discounts of 25 per cent to corporate purchasers enabled Charles to still earn stronger margins than wholesale, without the costs of retail. One board member said Charles approach to cruise ship traffic needed to be reconsidered as many of the passengers were bypassing Charles' location to visit attractions in other parts of town that were promoting themselves aggressively on the ships.

There were many other possibilities. Should Charles open more stores in Boston? Or should Charles extend its product line to take advantage of its strong brand awareness in Maine? Although ice cream had not been the runaway success the company had hoped, its sales were still building. Another option might be for Charles to concentrate its efforts outside of Maine. If tourists had stopped coming to Portland, should Charles go to them? Should Charles increase its wholesale or retail penetration outside of New England? Would the current sales agency structure be appropriate for increased wholesale penetration? Should Charles consider an acquisition of another niche chocolate company or a joint venture with another firm to increase its geographical reach? Were there opportunities to pair Charles chocolates with other high end brands for mutual benefit?

Charles traditional brand image was also a concern: while it was treasured by loyal customers and employees alike, it didn't seem to play well outside of Portland. The packaging had been described as homey or dowdy by some, yet others were adamant that it should not be changed. Parkland had spoken to a brand image consultant that had won numerous awards in the wine industry. The consultant had suggested that the only dangerous thing in today's market was to play it safe – consumers loved edgy brands. Should Charles throw off tradition and try to reinvent itself?

Of course, if sales were to be increased, Charles would need more internal capacity to produce products and fill orders. Should more capacity be added in Portland, with its expensive real estate and significant shipping costs to reach large markets, or should it be placed somewhere with lower costs and easier access to markets?

As Parkland pondered all these options, he also knew that he had to take into consideration the culture of the organization and the desires of the board of directors and owners. Would the current managers and employees be willing and able to grow the organization? Would the board endorse a growth strategy that would increase the risk profile of the company? And with all these options, what should Parkland do first?

EXHIBIT 1: Organization Chart

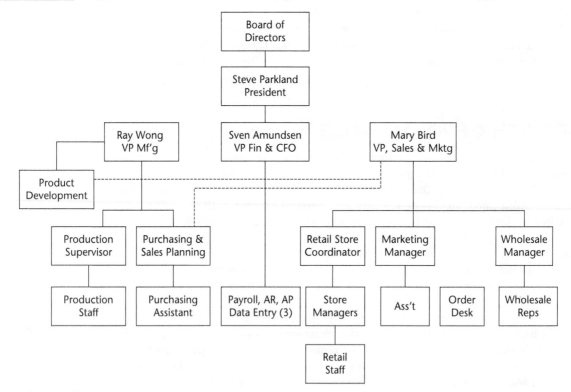

Source: Company files.

EXHIBIT 2: Retail Stores Sales in Fiscal 2007 (Rounded to Nearest Thousand)

Store	Date Acquired	Approximate Annual Sales	Contribution Margin
Portland Old Port	1885	$2,775,000	45.3%
Sandwich Heaven	2009	$1,598,000	8.9%*
Factory Store	1990	$726,000	36.7%
Boston Beacon Hill	Dec. 2010	$686,000	(11.5%)
Portsmouth	2000	$639,000	8.2%
Portland Arts District	1988	$517,000	22.86%
Portland Fore Street	2008	$401,000	29.1%
Boston Back Bay	April 2011	$138,000	(22.3%)
Portland Cruise Ship Terminal	2005	$60,000 (Mostly ice cream)	15.5%
Bar Harbor downtown	2011	$42,000 (All ice cream; summer only)	18.2%
Bar Harbor Cruise Ship Terminal	2010	$35,000 (All ice cream; summer only)	21.1%

*Reflects full costs of expenses to refurbish the store.
Source: Company files.

EXHIBIT 3: Consolidated Statement of Earnings and Retained Earnings

Year Ended March 31	2011	2010
Sales	$ 11,850,480	$11,991,558
Cost of sales		
Amortization of property and equipment	135,385	108,759
Direct labour	1,545,794	1,677,247
Direct materials	1,770,603	2,745,995
Overhead	1,933,306	846,186
	5,385,088	5,378,187
Gross profit	6,465,392	6,613,371
Interest income	664	1,610
	6,466,056	6,614,981
Expenses		
Interest on long term debt	91,465	86,943
Selling and administrative	5,221,520	5,007,145
	5,312,985	5,094,088
Earnings before income taxes	1,153,071	1,520,893
Income taxes	261,989	451,567
Net earnings	$ 891,082	$1,069,326
Retained earnings, beginning of year	$ 4,748,611	4,381,155
Net earnings	891,081	1,069,326
Dividends	—	(701,870)
Retained earnings, end of year	$ 5,639,692	$ 4,748,611

Source: Company files.

EXHIBIT 4: Schedule of Selling and Administrative Expenses

Year ended March 31		2011	2010
Selling	Advertising & Promotion	$ 489,345	$ 536,886
	Bad debts	23,000	12,796
	Credit card charges	125,198	125,544
	Mail order	118,606	133,081
	Office & Telephone	29,975	27,274
	Postage and freight	483,003	476,724
Stores:	Factory Store	112,885	122,897
	Sandwich Heaven	572,495	323,995
	Portland Fore Street	75,854	84,047
	Cruise Ship Terminals	42,709	38,592
	Dept. Store Boston (closed in 2006)	3,938	4,058
	Dept. Store Portland (closed in 2006)	4,236	2,759
	Bar Harbour downtown	—	24,179
	Portland Arts District	87,103	119,058
	Portsmouth	168,157	182,939
	Royalties	29,862	31,099
	Salaries & benefits	812,269	715,325
	Travel	68,364	46,830
	Total	3,246,999	3,013,658
	Less: postage and freight recoveries	343,116	369,823
		2,903,883	2,638,260
Admin	Amortization	196,970	135,267
	Automotive	28,658	24,404
	Bank charges and interest	22,533	20,882
	Consulting	102,241	107,379
	Foreign exchange	−6,272	
	Insurance	80,704	78,777
	Management fees	191,226	183,627
	Office supplies and postage	134,159	118,582
	Professional fees	42,872	67,952
	Rent, property taxes and utilities	61,211	56,815
	Repairs and maintenance	18,378	21,105
Stores:	Sandwich Heaven	326,901	179,834
	Portland Fore Street	26,559	28,159
	Cruise Ship Terminals	22,038	26,927
	Dept. Store Boston	10,082	18,251
	Dept. Store Portland	32,123	37,939
	Bar Harbor Downtown		14,647
	Portland Arts District	49,849	45,002
	Portsmouth	112,450	105,720
	Salaries and benefits	810,049	1,030,336
	Telecommunications	27,824	32,588
	Travel and promotion	27,082	34,692
Total Admin Expenses		$ 2,317,637	$2,368,885
TOTAL S, G & A Expenses		$5,221,520	$ 5,007,145

EXHIBIT 5: Consolidated Balance Sheet

March 31	2011	2010
Assets		
Current		
Cash	$ 112,185	$ 750,948
Receivables	358,969	461,874
Inventories		
Packaging materials	620,452	576,287
Raw materials	169,235	179,119
Work in progress	89,146	66,467
Manufactured finished goods	643,105	692,517
Finished goods for resale	21,878	36,241
	1,543,816	1,550,631
Investments	103,136	76,822
Income taxes receivable	127,515	—
Prepaids	84,620	56,566
	2,330,241	2,896,842
Property and equipment (see Note 1)	4,364,527	3,922,183
Intangible assets		
Goodwill	916,999	916,999
Trademarks	783,596	783,596
Total Intangible Assets	1,700,595	1,700,595
TOTAL ASSETS	**$8,395,363**	**$8,519,620**
Liabilities		
Current		
Bank indebtedness	$ 186,929	$ 599,146
Payables and accruals	1,098,232	1,226,570
Income taxes payable	—	127,845
Current portion of long term debt	419,971	373,405
	1,705,132	2,326,966
Long term debt	1,017,679	1,411,184
TOTAL LIABILITIES	**2,722,811**	**3,738,150**
Shareholders' Equity		
Capital stock	32,860	32,860
Retained earnings	5,639,691	4,748,611
TOTAL EQUITY	**5,672,551**	**4,781,471**
TOTAL LIABILITIES & EQUITY	**$8,395,362**	**$ 8,519,621**

EXHIBIT 5: (Continued)

Note 1				
Property and equipment			**2011**	**2010**
	Cost	**Accumulated Amortization**	**Net Book Value**	**Net Book Value**
Land	1,219,819.20	—	1,219,819.20	1,219,819.20
Buildings	2,799,181.35	1,099,926.90	1,699,254.45	1,770,056.19
Manufacturing equipment	1,693,140.69	1,375,596.00	317,544.69	231,858.99
Furniture and fixtures	749,496.78	385,684.35	363,812.43	249,376.83
Office equipment	108,352.86	90,299.22	18,053.64	24,020.76
Computer equipment	250,683.90	225,157.26	25,526.64	53,214.81
Leasehold improvements	914,332.83	193,817.19	720,515.64	373,836.12
	7,735,007.61	3,370,480.92	4,364,526.69	3,922,182.90

Source: Company files.

EXHIBIT 6: Consolidated Statements of Cash Flows

Year Ended March 31	2011	2010
Increase (decrease) in cash and cash equivalents		
Operating		
Net earnings	$ 891,081	$1,069,326
Amortization	332,355	244,026
	1,223,436	1,313,352
Change in non-cash oper. working capital	(328,344)	350,045
	895,092	1,663,397
Financing		
(Repayments of) advances from LT debt	(349,168)	661,806
Dividends paid	—	(701,870)
	(349,168)	(40,064)
Investing		
Purchase of assets of Sandwich Heaven	—	(1,198,500)
Purchase of property and equipment	(772,470)	(419,307)
	(772,470)	(1,617,807)
Net (decrease) increase in cash and cash equivalents	(226,546)	5,526
Cash and cash equivalents, beginning of year	151,802	146,276
Cash and cash equivalents, end of year	$ 74,744	$ 151,802
Comprised of:		
Cash	$ 112,185	$ 750,948
Bank indebtedness	(186,929)	(599,146)
	$ 74,744	$ 151,802

Source: Company files.

EXHIBIT 7: JOB AD

A unique company..... a unique location..... a unique opportunity.

Our client, one of New England's oldest and respected confectionery companies, is seeking a **PRESIDENT** to oversee the entire business on a day-to-day basis, and provide the vision and guidance for long-term success and profitable growth.

Reporting to the Board of Directors, the President will:

- Deliver superior results and guide the organization to improve.
- Develop formal planning systems and ongoing personnel development.
- Oversee the development of business and marketing strategies to maintain market leadership.
- Provide the necessary leadership to motivate and transform the organization to meet growth expectations.
- Leads, protects and reinforces the positive corporate culture, and is the overseer of the ethics and values in the organization.

   An executive level compensation plan commensurate with the importance of this role is offered.

An opportunity that blends an executive level position with the lifestyle only Portland can offer.

CANDIDATE PROFILE:

Given the high levels of autonomy and accountability, the President must display considerable maturity and business experience.

From a personal perspective, the ideal candidate will be:

- A strong non-authoritative team builder.
- A highly motivated and results oriented self-starter.
- Extremely, customer, quality and safety oriented.
- People oriented with the innate ability to establish a high degree of credibility.
- Capable of providing objective insight in a non-confrontational manner.

The successful candidate will likely be or have been in one of the following positions in a manufacturing environment:

- President or General Manager
- At a VP level in operations/finance/marketing looking to rise to the next level

While food manufacturing experience would be a clear asset, it is not a pre-requisite.

CASE

9

The Prince Edward Island Preserve Company: Turnaround

In April 2008, Bruce MacNaughton, president of Prince Edward Island Preserve Co. Ltd. (P.E.I. Preserves), was focused on turnaround. The company he had founded in 1985 had gone into receivership in May 2007. Although this had resulted in losses for various mortgage holders and unsecured creditors, MacNaughton had been able to buy back his New Glasgow shop/café, the adjacent garden property and inventory, and restart the business. He now needed a viable product-market strategy.

BACKGROUND

Prince Edward Island Preserve Co. was a manufacturing and retail company located in New Glasgow, P.E.I. which produced and marketed specialty food products. The company founder and majority shareholder, Bruce MacNaughton, had realized that an opportunity existed to present P.E.I. strawberries as a world-class food product and to introduce the finished product to an "up-scale" specialty market. MacNaughton had made good on the opportunity he had perceived years earlier. It had not been easy, however.

MacNaughton arrived in Prince Edward Island from Moncton, New Brunswick, in 1978. Without a job, he slept on the beach for much of that first summer. Over the next few years he worked in commission sales, waited tables in restaurants, and then moved to Toronto. There he studied to become a chef at George Brown College. After working in the restaurant trade for several years, he found a job with "Preserves by Amelia" in Toronto.

🛡 IVEY | Publishing

Nathaniel C. Lupton wrote this case under the supervision of Professor Paul W. Beamish solely to provide material for class discussion. The authors do not intend to illustrate either effective or ineffective handling of a managerial situation. The authors may have disguised certain names and other identifying information to protect confidentiality.

Ivey Management Services prohibits any form of reproduction, storage or transmittal without its written permission. Reproduction of this material is not covered under authorization by any reproduction rights organization. To order copies or request permission to reproduce materials, contact Ivey Publishing, Ivey Management Services, c/o Richard Ivey School of Business, The University of Western Ontario, London, Ontario, Canada, N6A 3K7; phone (519) 661-3208; fax (519) 661-3882; e-mail cases@ivey.uwo.ca.

Copyright © 2008, Ivey Management Services   Version: (A) 2008-09-05

One time permission to reproduce granted by Richard Ivey School of Business Foundation on April 22, 2014.

After six months, he returned to Prince Edward Island where he opened a restaurant. The restaurant was not successful and MacNaughton lost the $30,000 stake he had accumulated. With nothing left but 100 kilograms of strawberries, MacNaughton decided to make these into preserves in order to have gifts for Christmas 1984. Early the following year, P.E.I. Preserves was founded.

The products produced by the company were priced and packaged for the gift/gourmet and specialty food markets. The primary purchasers of these products were conscious of quality and were seeking a product which they considered tasteful and natural. P.E.I. Preserves felt its product met the highest standard of quality at a price that made it attractive to all segments of the marketplace.

Over the next few years as the business grew, improvements were made to the building in New Glasgow. The sense of style which was characteristic of the company was evident from the beginning in its attractive layout and design.

In 1989, the company diversified and opened "The Perfect Cup," a small restaurant in Prince Edward Island's capital city of Charlottetown. This restaurant continued the theme of quality, specializing in wholesome, home-made food featuring the products manufactured by the company. The success of this operation led to the opening in 1990 of a small tea room at the New Glasgow location. Both of these locations showcased the products manufactured by P.E.I. Preserves.

In 1989, the company also opened a small (22-square-metre) retail branch in the CP Prince Edward Hotel. MacNaughton hoped this locale would expand visibility in the local and national marketplace, and serve as an off-season sales office. P.E.I. Preserves had been given very favourable lease arrangements and the location would require minimal financial investment. Two years later, the CP hotel location was closed and the company opened the Piece of Cake restaurant and a retail location a short distance away in the Confederation Court Mall. As Table 1 suggests, various forms of diversification had occurred over the years.

TABLE 1:

Operation (Year Opened–Closed)
Charlottetown—Manufacturing and Retail (1985–1987)
New Glasgow—Manufacturing and Retail (1988–Present)
Charlottetown—Restaurant (Perfect Cup) (1989–1990)
Charlottetown—Retail (CP Hotel) (1989–1991)
New Glasgow—Restaurant (Tea Room) (1990–Present)
Charlottetown—Restaurant (Piece of Cake) (1991–1992)
Charlottetown—Retail (1991–1993)
Moncton, N.B.—Retail Franchise (1992–1994)
New Glasgow—Garden (bought 1994, opened 2003)
New Glasgow—Theatre (2003–Present)
Charlottetown—Sweater Shop (2006–2006)

MARKETPLACE

Prince Edward Island was Canada's smallest province, both in size and population. Located in the Gulf of St. Lawrence, it was separated from Nova Scotia and New Brunswick by the Northumberland Strait. The major employer in Prince Edward Island was the various levels of government. Many people in Prince Edward Island worked seasonally in farming (especially potato), fishing, or tourism. During the peak tourist months of July and August, the island population would swell dramatically from its base of 138,000. Prince Edward Island's one million annual visitors came "home" to enjoy the long sandy beaches, picturesque scenery, lobster dinners, arguably the best tasting strawberries in the world, and slower pace of life. Prince Edward Island was best known in Canada and elsewhere for the books, movies and television series about Lucy Maud Montgomery's turn-of-the-century literary creation, Anne of Green Gables. 2008 was a special year for many tourists as it marked the 100th anniversary of the publication of Anne of Green Gables.

P.E.I. Preserves felt it was competing in a global market. Its visitors were from all over the world, and in 2008, it expected the numbers to exceed 150,000 in the New Glasgow location alone. New Glasgow (population 100) was located in a rural setting equidistant (15 kilometres) from Charlottetown and Prince Edward Island's best-known north shore beaches. In its mailings, it planned to continue to promote Prince Edward Island as "Canada's Garden Province" and the "little jewel that was in everyone's heart!" It had benefitted, and would continue to benefit, from that image.

MARKETING

Products

The company had developed numerous products since its inception. These included many original varieties of preserves as well as honey, vinegar, mustard and repackaged tea (Exhibit 1 contains a 2008 price list, order form and a page from the mail order catalogue). The company had also added to the appeal of these products by offering gift packs composed of different products and packaging. With over 80 items, MacNaughton felt that a diverse product line had been achieved, and efforts in developing new product lines were expected to decrease in the future. Approximately three-quarters of total retail sales (including wholesale and mail order) came from the products the company made itself. Of these, three quarters were jam preserves.

With the success of P.E.I. Preserves, imitation was inevitable. Several other small firms in Prince Edward Island also retailed specialty preserves. Another company which produced preserves in Ontario emphasized the Green Gables tie-in on its labels.

Price

P.E.I. Preserves was not competing with "low-end" products, and felt its price reinforced its customers' perception of quality. The 13 types of jam preserves retailed for $6.95 for a 250-millilitre jar, significantly more than any grocery store product. However, grocery stores did not offer jam products made with such a high fruit content and with champagne, liqueur or whisky. The food products were not subject to the five per cent national goods and services tax or Prince Edward Island's 10 per cent provincial sales tax, an advantage over other gift products which the company would be stressing.

Promotion

Product promotion had been focused in two areas—personal contact with the consumer and catalogue distribution. Visitors to the New Glasgow location (approximately 125,000 in 2007) were enthusiastic upon meeting MacNaughton "resplendent in the family kilt," reciting history and generally providing live entertainment. MacNaughton and the other staff members realized the value of this "island touch" and strove to ensure that all visitors to New Glasgow left with both a positive feeling and purchased products.

Visitors were also encouraged to visit the New Glasgow location through a cooperative scheme whereby other specialty retailers provided a coupon for a free cup of coffee or tea at P.E.I. Preserves. In 2007, roughly 2,000 of these coupons were redeemed.

Approximately 25,000 people received their mail order catalogue annually. They had experienced an order rate of 7.5 per cent with the average order being $66. They hoped to devote more time and effort to their mail order business in an effort to extend their marketing and production period.

In addition to mail order, the company operated with an ad hoc group of wholesale distributors. These wholesalers were divided between Nova Scotia, Ontario and other locations. For orders as small as $150, buyers could purchase from the wholesalers' price list. Wholesale prices were on average 60 per cent of the retail/mail order price. Total wholesale trade for the coming year was projected at $211,000, under the assumption of a three per cent increase over the previous year.

Over the past few years, the company had received numerous enquiries for quotations on large-scale shipments. Mitsubishi had asked for a price on a container load of preserves. Airlines and hotels were interested in obtaining preserves in 28- or 30-gram single-service bottles. One hotel chain, for example, had expressed interest in purchasing three million bottles if the cost could be kept under $0.40 per unit. (MacNaughton had not proceeded due to the need to purchase $65,000 worth of bottling equipment, and uncertainty about his production costs.) This same hotel chain had more recently been assessing the ecological implications of the packaging waste which would be created with the use of so many small bottles. It was now weighing the hygiene implications of serving jam out of larger, multi-customer use containers in their restaurants.

FINANCIAL

Growth, although indicative of the success of the company's products, had also created its share of problems. Typical of many small businesses, the company had not secured financing suitable to its needs. This, coupled with the seasonal nature of the manufacturing operation, had caused numerous periods of severe cash shortages.

Recent years, however, had been especially difficult for the company. The company had lost over $313,000 to start 2007, and this deficit grew to over $365,000 by the end of March. After going through four different bookkeepers, an unsuccessful attempted acquisition of an unrelated store in Charlottetown which proved costly, and general "distractions" with his garden and other projects, MacNaughton realized his company was not going to be able to manage payments to creditors any longer. The company officially went into receivership on May 10, 2007, after the bank reduced its line of credit to zero. Exhibit 2 presents the balance sheet of the P.E.I. Preserve Co. Ltd. The new company, Prince Edward Island Preserve Co., with a fiscal year end of April 30, opened shortly thereafter.

Sales of the new company up to the end of March 2008 were a little over $1,570,000. These sales were made up of $1,065,000 from retail and wholesale (including mail order) of what they manufactured and/or distributed, $494,000 from the café and dairy bar, and $13,000 in sales and donations from visitors to the garden. Exhibit 3 provides a departmental income statement from these operations, while Exhibit 4 contains a consolidated balance sheet.

At this time, MacNaughton was attempting to provide a sound financial base for the continued operation of the company. Projected sales for the period from May 1, 2008, to April 30, 2009, are summarized in Table 2 (see Exhibit 5 for details).

TABLE 2:

New Glasgow Restaurant	$ 565,000
Retail (New Glasgow)	$ 708,000
Wholesale (New Glasgow)	$ 211,000
Mail Order (New Glasgow)	$ 163,000
Kiosk (Charlottetown Mall)	$ 140,000
Garden Donations	$ 24,600
Gallery and Tea Room	$ 15,000
Shipping	$ 50,230
Total	$1,876,830

OPERATIONS

Preserve production took place on site, in an area visible through glass windows from the retail floor. Many visitors, in fact, would videotape operations during their visit to the New Glasgow store, or would watch the process while tasting the broad selection of sample products freely available.

Production took place on a batch basis. Ample production capacity existed for the $30,000 main kettle used to cook the preserves. Preserves were made five months a year, on a single shift, five day per week basis. Even then, the main kettle was in use only 50 per cent of the time.

Only top quality fruit was purchased. As much as possible, P.E.I. raw materials were used. For a short period the fruit could be frozen until it was time for processing.

The production process was labour intensive. MacNaughton was considering the feasibility of moving to an incentive-based salary system to increase productivity and control costs. While there were some minor differences due to ingredients, the variable costs for the 250-ml size are shown in Table 3 for both the traditional line of products and a new certified organic line developed for export to Japan (discussed later). The Japanese retailer required a unique style of jar and shrink-wrapping for the lid which increased the overall cost in addition to the premium price for organically grown fruit.

TABLE 3:

	Traditional Line	**Certified Organic**
Ingredients	$ 1.24	$2.37
Labour	$0.47	$0.47
Packaging	$0.40	$0.90
Total	$2.11	$3.74

Café, Gallery and Tea Room

Restaurant operations were the source of many of MacNaughton's headaches. The New Glasgow Restaurant had evolved over time from offering dessert and coffee/tea to its present status where it was also open for meals all day from late May until mid-October. McNaughton spent about 40 per cent of his time on restaurant-related activities.

Retail and Mail Order

Retail accounted for the greatest portion of both sales and income for the company (see Exhibit 3). Most retail took place in the New Glasgow store as visitors stopped in individually or on bus tours. Although road travel vacations were on a steady decline due to record high gas prices, cruise ship travel received a major boost after the opening of a new pier in 2008, as shown in Table 4. With major expansions to the port still under way in Charlottetown, the number of visiting cruise ships was expected to rise to about 80 within two years. In the past, cruise ships would stay in Prince Edward Island for about half a day before heading off to other ports. However, due to the popularity of the location they began staying for a full day in 2007. MacNaughton estimated that about 30 per cent of the ship's passengers would stop in New Glasgow in the morning, and another 30 per cent in the afternoon. Based on this, he forecast that the number of visitors would increase from about 125,000 to 150,000.

TABLE 4:

Year	Cruise Ships	Passengers
2004	28	23,118
2005	23	23,894
2006	25	28,830
2007	16	21,360
2008	40	69,380

Source: http://historiccharlottetownseaport.com/cruiseships/

About 85 per cent of the passengers of these ships were American with the majority of the remaining 15 per cent divided evenly between Canadians and Germans. MacNaughton noted that the European consumers were not interested in purchasing products to take back with them but preferred items they could consume on the premises. American consumers were also beginning to shy away from purchases of preserves and other products as new air travel regulations disallowed liquids and gels in containers with volumes greater than 100-ml in carry-on luggage. When MacNaughton suggested these customers place the bottles in their checked luggage, customers expressed fears about the bottles breaking. For these customers, MacNaughton agreed to ship the products to their homes for the same fee used for mail orders (see Exhibit 1). The goal of P.E.I. Preserves was to operate shipping on a breakeven basis but in actuality it was proving to be an expense (see Exhibit 3).

Some of the customers who purchased products while visiting the New Glasgow location would become repeat customers who would order using the P.E.I. Preserve mail order catalogue or through the company's website (www.preservecompany.com). Shipping to the United States had become difficult over the last few years. The Food and Drug Administration's (FDA) bioterrorism act required that any shipment of food products be announced well in advance of the shipment date. In addition, the FDA notified P.E.I. Preserves early in 2008 that their labels were not compliant with new regulations in terms of the print location and presentation of the size of the container and the ingredients. As a result, the 40,000 labels the company had printed were now useless and mail order was halted for a period of two months while new labels were designed and printed.

In addition to the retail location in New Glasgow and mail order, P.E.I. Preserves Co. opened a small kiosk in the Charlottetown Mall to gain access to the estimated $150,000 local market. MacNaughton felt the kiosk was an efficient way of educating customers about his products. The kiosk operated during the summer months only in 2007, but MacNaughton decided to keep it in operation from July 1 to December 25 in 2008 in order to increase sales during the holiday season.

Wholesale

The company's wholesale operation largely resulted from market pull forces. Prior visitors to the New Glasgow location who did not want the inconvenience and added cost of purchasing products through mail order requested that their local high-end food distributors import P.E.I. Preserves products. The company established several relationships with these distributors in locations from Eastern Ontario to the Maritimes, and a few in Alberta and British Columbia. In general, however, MacNaughton was always worried about how his products were marketed in these stores and how that might affect his brand. He strongly believed customers needed to sample the products, as they regularly did in the New Glasgow shop, in order to be convinced that the premium price was justified. He felt he should visit locations that wished to sell his products, but he did not have the time to do so, given the demands of managing his business.

The Country Garden

P.E.I. Preserves purchased 12 acres of land adjacent to the New Glasgow location in 1994 and committed substantial time, energy and money in landscaping and adding new structures beginning in 2003. One structure was an old church which was donated to the company and was to serve as a gallery for local artists in 2008. Another was a pavilion where local classical musicians were paid to perform on occasion during the summer. The third building was a butterfly observatory which was popular with visitors to the location.

After the first year of operation for the garden, MacNaughton discovered that while visitors truly enjoyed the scenery, most were not willing to pay for the experience. From that point on, the garden was operated on a breakeven basis funded through donations and staffed by local volunteers. In 2007, the garden managed a very slight profit and the company planned to hire back a caretaker on a part time basis in 2008.

The long term plan for the gardens was to build a respite for chronically ill patients and their caretakers. As the land was now designated by the provincial government as a hospice and wildlife park, property taxes were negligible.

Japanese Exports

In 2005, Kosaku Morita visited Prince Edward Island from Japan to meet with MacNaughton and Raymond Loo, a local organic farmer and president of P.E.I. Certified Organic Producers Co-op. Morita was specifically interested in the organic black currants grown by Loo, which Japanese consumers appreciated for their health benefits, most notably their high levels of antioxidants. Morita was so impressed with the quality of P.E.I. Preserves' products he invited both Loo and MacNaughton to Foodex in Japan in March of the following year.

Foodex was an annual event held in Japan in which 2,000 food and beverage producers showcased their wares to roughly 100,000 restauranteurs, caterers, distributors and wholesalers. MacNaughton was impressed with the interest in his preserves, so he decided to extend his line of organics and return the following year in 2007.

P.E.I. Preserves made an initial shipment of 90,000 125-ml and 250-ml bottles of their new organic line of products to a Japanese distributor in 2007. The bottles retailed for ¥1,000 (about $10) and ¥1,800 (about $18), respectively, of which the distributor and retailer took the majority of the margin. P.E.I. Preserves' wholesale price for these organic products was $3.00 for the 125-ml and $4.92 for the 250-ml bottle, both priced to obtain a margin of about $1.00 per bottle. The freight cost of about $0.30 per bottle was paid by the importer. In 2008, the company's Japanese partners were running a two week trial of the organic products during which time they expected to place two orders of 90,000 bottles each.

Together, P.E.I. Preserves, local organic farmers and their Japanese business associates marketed products under the name "Anne's P.E.I. Farm" and created a new Japanese language website (www.annespeifarm.com) which contained information about the products and their health benefits. The website also provided information about the province of Prince Edward Island, including sustainable energy projects, organic farming, photographs capturing the natural beauty of the land and, of course, Anne of Green Gables. In addition, the site recounted the "stories" of the individuals involved in the production and delivery of the end product including the farmers, MacNaughton and P.E.I. Preserves, and the Japanese business associates.

Management

During the peak summer period, P.E.I. Preserves employed 65 people among the restaurants, manufacturing area and retail locations. Of these, five were managerial positions. The company was considered a good place to work, with high morale and limited turnover. Nonetheless, most employees (including some management) were with the company on a seasonal basis. This was a concern to MacNaughton who felt that if he could provide year-round employment, he would be able to attract and keep the best quality staff.

MacNaughton felt that the company had survived on the basis of word-of-mouth. Few follow-up calls on mail order had ever been done, although MacNaughton read every e-mail sent to the customer service address. MacNaughton did not enjoy participating in trade shows—even though he received regular solicitations for them from across North America. He participated in one retail show in 2007 and four in 2008, all of them in or close to Prince Edward Island. He hoped to be able to eventually hire a sales/marketing manager.

The key manager continued to be MacNaughton. He described himself as "a frugal but fair person to deal with when it comes to purchasing. However, I like to spend enough money to ensure that what we do—we do right." Financial and managerial constraints meant that MacNaughton felt stretched ("I haven't had a vacation in years") and unable to pursue all of the ideas he had for developing the business. Other key members of the administrative staff included Lynn Whitlock in charge of production and purchasing, Sian Morris in charge of bookkeeping and administration, retail and human resources manager, Judy Clark, and Don Croiter, chef and product development manager.

THE JAPANESE CONSUMER

Japan was one of Canada's most important sources of foreign tourists. In 2006, there were 364,000 Japanese visitors to Canada. The number of visits by Japanese tourists to each province is shown in Table 5. Most Japanese visitors entered through the Vancouver or Toronto airports. Within Canada, the most popular destination was the Rocky Mountains (in Banff, Alberta, numerous stores catered specifically to Japanese consumers). Excluding airfare, these visitors to Canada spent an estimated $500 million in 2006, making it the third largest international market for tourism. These figures were expected to decline slightly for 2007, and rebound in 2008.

The Japanese fascination with Prince Edward Island could be traced to the popularity of Anne of Green Gables. The Japanese translation of this and other books in the same series had been available for many years. However, the adoption of the book as required reading in the Japanese school system since the 1950s had resulted in widespread awareness and affection for "Anne with red hair" and Prince Edward Island.

TABLE 5:

Province	Japanese Visitors, 2006
Newfoundland	200
Prince Edward Island	4,100
Nova Scotia	5,400
New Brunswick	2,000
Quebec	36,900
Ontario	168,800
Manitoba	7,300
Saskatchewan	1,100
Alberta	87,900
British Columbia	183,000
Yukon	3,000
Northwest Territories	2,300

Source: 2006 facts & figures: Canada Tourism Commission *www.canada.travel/research*.

The Japanese Jam Market

Japanese annual consumption of jam was approximately 80,000 tons. Imports made up six to nine per cent of consumption, with higher-grade products (¥470 or more per kilo wholesale CIF) making up a third of this total. Several dozen firms imported jam, and utilized a mix of distribution channels. Prices varied, in part, according to the type of channel structure used. Exhibit 6 provides a common structure.

Future Directions

P.E.I. Preserves needed a viable product-market strategy. Many options existed to expand manufacturing and serve a larger market size in order to grow. The factory in New Glasgow was adequate for existing business but too small to meet the demands of a larger market.

One option MacNaughton considered was setting up a manufacturing operation independent of P.E.I. Preserves in which he would be a minority shareholder and would manage initially. Once the operation was up and running, P.E.I. Preserves could continue to license its brand name to the products, provided strict quality standards were maintained. This would allow MacNaughton the freedom to devote his time to the existing New Glasgow operations.

Before expanding production, however, MacNaughton had to decide what product market should be targeted, and to establish what the demand from that market would be. He could attempt to expand one or more of his retail, wholesale, mail order or Japanese export operations. There were also decisions to be made around pursuing his established product lines and the new organic line. He wondered if there were other potential opportunities he had not considered as well.

MacNaughton was the first to acknowledge that, while the business had been "built on gut and emotion, rather than analysis," this was insufficient for the future. The challenge was to determine the direction and timing of the desired change.

EXHIBIT 1: Prince Edward Island Preserve Co. Mail Order Catalogue

Order Date_____

PRESERVES

Description	250ml	Price	Qty.	250ml	Price	Qty.
Blackcurrant	997	$6.95		9944	$4.95	
Blueberry Raspberry	993	$6.95		9942	$4.95	
Blueberry Lemon	996	$6.95		9949	$4.95	
Cabernet/Sauvignon/Jelly	9918	$6.95		9954	$4.95	
Lemon Ginger/Marmalade	9911	$6.95		9946	$4.95	
Lime Marmalade	9912	$6.95		N/A	$4.95	
Orange Marmalade	9910	$6.95		9945	$4.95	
Raspberry Champagne	992	$6.95		9941	$4.95	
Raspberry Jelly	9919	$6.95		9952	$4.95	
Raspberry Peach	995	$6.95		9943	$4.95	
Sour Cherry Marmalade	999	$6.95		9951	$4.95	
Strawberry Rhubarb	994	$6.95		9947	$4.95	
Strawberry Grand Mariner	991	$6.95		9940	$4.95	
Very Berry	9914	$6.95		9948	$4.95	

Preserves 375ml	375ml	Price	Qty.
Strawberry Grand Mariner	9930	$9.95	
Raspberry Champagne	9931	$9.95	
Blue Raspberry Champagne	9932	$9.95	
Very Berry	9933	$9.95	
Strawberry Rhubarb	9934	$9.95	
Blueberry Lemon	9935	$9.95	

Gift Boxes	125ml	Price	Qty
2 x 125ml	99171	$10.95	
3 x 125ml	99172	$15.95	
6 x 125ml	99173	$29.95	
2 x 250ml	99174	$15.95	
3 x 250ml	99175	$22.95	
6 x 250ml	99170	$43.95	
9 x 250ml	99176	$66.95	
2 x 375ml	99177	$23.50	
3 x 375ml	99178	$34.95	

BBQ Sauce 375ml	375ml	Price	Qty
Tomato & Herb	99140	$6.95	
Smoked Hickory & Maple	99141	$6.95	
Habanero & Mango	99142	$6.95	

Salsa	250ml	Price	Qty
Peach Salsa 250ml	9923	$6.95	
Cherry Salsa 250ml	9924	$6.95	
Cherry Salsa 375ml	9937	$8.95	
Peach Salsa 375ml	9936	$8.95	

Miscellaneous Items

_____

_____

_____

_____

SOLD TO INFO Telephone:

Name:

Address:

City:

State/Province: ZIP/Postal Code:

☐ same as ship to

SHIP TO INFO Telephone:

Name:

Address:

City:

State/Province: ZIP/Postal Code:

Gift Message:

METHOD OF PAYMENT

☐ Visa ☐ Mastercard ☐ American Express
☐ JCB ☐ Cheque/Money Order ☐ Diners Club

Exp. Date MM/YY 3 Digit Security Code

Name on Card

Shipping Cost

STANDARD RATES FOR CANADA AND USA*

For delivery please allow up to 15 business days.

Value or Order	Shipping Cost
$25 - $40.99	$12.00
$41 - $55.99	$13.00
$56 - $65.99	$14.00
$66 - $75.99	$15.00
$76 - $100.99	$16.00
$101 & over	20% of order

*Surcharge of 20% for Northern Canada, Newfoundland Labrador, Alaska and Hawaii.

FREE * SHIPPING with a minimum order per address of 24 jars valued @ $3.50 or more.

Subtotal	$
Shipping IF ASSISTANCE NEEDED CALL 1-800-565-5267	$
GST/HST NO TAX CHARGED TO U.S. DESTINATIONS *Amount paid is set by the province to which the order is being shipped. NF, NB and NS is HST (14%) The rest of Canada is GST (6%)	$
TOTAL ORDER	$

EXHIBIT 1: (Continued)

PRESERVES·JELLY·MARMALADE

Strawberry & Grand Marnier — *our most popular flavour!*

Using only the finest and freshest fruits possible, we produce a wonderful low sugar, high fruit content preserve. Our ingredients are only the highest quality and for flavour enhancement we use freshly squeezed orange and lemon juices. No added preservatives! See complete listings at www.preservecompany.com

Strawberry & Grand Marnier
991 250ml   9940 125ml   9930 375ml
Using only Prince Edward Island Strawberries we have created a high in Strawberry flavour product complemented by the addition of Grand Marnier Liqueur. You can taste summer! *Texture: Smooth*

Wild Blueberry and Lemon
996 250ml   9949 125ml   9915 375ml
This recipe has the least amount of sugar and the freshest taste. The fresh lemon and the fresh mint work to enhance the flavour of Wild Blueberries. *Texture: Loose/Smooth*

Raspberries and Champagne
992 250ml   9941 125ml   9931 375ml
This one bursts of fresh raspberry flavour only to be enhanced further by the addition of Champagne. *Texture: Loose/Smooth*

Very Berry
9914 250ml   9948 125ml   9933 375ml
The staff's favourite. Combining Strawberries, Raspberries, Cherries and Wild Blueberries we have created a flavour that is delicious and unique. Great topping as well as preserve. *Texture: Loose/Smooth*

Wild Blueberry and Raspberry w/Champagne
993 250ml   9942 125ml   9932 375ml
My personal favourite. Adding two of the world's most favourite flavours together and adding Champagne to complement is ambrosia in a jar. *Texture: Smooth*

Strawberry and Rhubarb
994 250ml   9947 125ml   9934 375ml
A flavour trip back in time. This combination of flavours is a memory of time past for many people. Delicious! *Texture: Smooth/Loose*

Raspberry and Peach
995 250ml   9943 125ml
This preserve is looser than most and suitable for desserts or ice cream. *Texture: Loose*

Black Currant
997 250ml   9944 125ml
Good morning sunshine! This very flavorful berry and the use of little sugar are sure to wake your mouth up any time of day. Oude tart! *Texture: Smooth*

Lime Marmalade
9912 250ml
Wow! If you like lime and you like marmalade, you will have thought you reached the nirvana of flavour when you taste this marmalade. *Texture: Chunky*

Sour Cherry Marmalade
999 250ml   9951 125ml
Unique, colourful, flavourful are a few words that describe this marmalade. *Texture: Smooth/Chunky*

Lemon and Ginger Marmalade with Amaretto
9911 250ml   9946 125ml
A very unique combination. One of our best selling marmalades. We use fresh lemons, fresh ginger and real Italian Amaretto. *Texture: Smooth/Chunky*

Orange Marmalade with Chivas Regal
9910 250ml   9945 125ml
One way to their hearts. Sweet oranges, a little sugar, lime and Chivas Regal is a combination of flavours certain to be enjoyed by anyone who enjoys marmalade. *Texture: Smooth/Chunky/Loose*

Cabernet Sauvignon Wine Jelly
9918 250ml   9954 125ml
This is a full bodied wine jelly loaded with flavour. *Texture: Smooth*

$4.95   125ml/4.4oz.

$6.95   250ml/8.8oz.

$9.95   375ml/13.5oz.

2

3

EXHIBIT 2: P.E.I. Preserve Co. Ltd.Balance Sheet as at March 31, 2007

	$
Assets	
Current assets	
Accounts receivable	14,927
Accounts receivable - related parties	127,224
Prepaid expenses	6,312
Inventory	358,204
	506,667
Investment tax credits receivable	19,048
Property and equipment	1,642,265
Due from related parties	602,387
Intangible assets	29,787
Funds held on deposit	200,000
	3,000,154
Liabilities	
Current liabilities	
Bank advances	4,704
Accounts payable and accrued liabilities	248,595
Accounts payable - related parties	86,472
Current portion of capital lease	1,229
Current portion of long-term debt	1,652,814
	1,993,814
Advances from shareholders	155,468
Long-term debt, less current portion	126,748
Deferred government assistance	76,681
Preferred shares	200,000
	2,552,711
Shareholders' Equity	800,000
Capital stock	13,300
Contributed surplus	(365,857)
Deficit	447,443
	3,000,154

EXHIBIT 3: Prince Edward Island Preserve Co. (New Company) Departmental Income Statement May 11, 2007, to March 31, 2008

	Cafe/ Dairy Bar	Retail	Wholesale	Mail Order	Garden	Preserves Production	Admin.
Revenue							
Sales	505,369	735,087	180,784	132,409	1,225	0	0
Freight revenue	0	6,325	3,362	27,178	0	0	0
Discounts	(11,209)	(17,266)	(1,976)	(269)	0	0	0
Donations	0	0	0	0	11,830	0	0
Interest/Tax/Other	0	0	0	0	0	0	548
Total Revenue	494,160	724,146	182,169	159,318	13,055	0	548
Direct Costs							
Materials	132,894	0	0	0	0	243,567	0
Supplies	25,952	143,268	0	30,708	0	17,423	0
Wages	186,363	44,125	0	0	0	88,870	0
Repair & maint.	6,991	0	0	0	12,739	2,281	0
Cash over/short	(333)	62	0	(28)	0	0	0
Freight expense	0	6,826	13,017	33,538	0	17,523	0
Opening inventory	0	0	0	0	0	166,172	0
Ending inventory	0	0	0	0	0	(197,610)	0
R & D expense	0	0	0	0	0	4,308	0
Total Direct Costs	351,868	194,280	13,017	64,218	12,739	342,533	0
Admin. Expenses							
Adv. & promotion	0	0	0	0	0	0	29,005
Land & equipment	0	0	0	0	0	0	77,261
Interest expense	0	0	0	709	0	0	58,624
Admin. wages	0	0	0	0	0	0	142,253
Wage & empl. exp.	0	0	0	0	0	0	80,591
Office	0	0	0	0	0	0	57,928
Repairs & maint.	0	0	0	0	0	0	24,074
Other	0	0	0	0	0	0	9,511
Foreign exchange	0	0	0	0	0	0	(447)
TOTAL EXPENSE	351,868	194,280	13,017	64,927	12,739	342,533	478,799
NET INCOME	142,292	529,866	169,152	94,391	317	(342,533)	(478,250)

EXHIBIT 4: Prince Edward Island Preserve Co. (New Company)
Balance Sheet As at March 31, 2008

ASSETS

Current Assets

Cash	7,108
Accounts receivable	5,318
Prepaid expenses	49,525
Inventory	197,610
Total Current Assets	259,560

Long Term Assets

Land	143,840
Building	367,743
Equipment	34,588
Automotive Equipment	2,555
Computer Hardware	2,244
Total Long Term Assets	550,970

TOTAL ASSETS	810,530

LIABILITIES

Current Liabilities

Accounts payable	12,500
Receiver General payable	−290
PST Payable	5
Total Current Liabilities	12,215

Other Liabilities

Advances from shareholder	−1,918
Loan and Mortgage	685,000
Total Other Liabilities	683,082

TOTAL LIABILITIES	695,297

EQUITY

Capital Stock	0
Retained Earnings	115,234
TOTAL EQUITY	115,234

LIABILITIES AND EQUITY	810,530

EXHIBIT 5: Prince Edward Island Preserve Co. (New Company) Cash Flow Budget for the Year May 1, 2008–April 30, 2009

Sales	$
Café	565,000
Retail	708,000
Wholesale	211,000
Mail order	163,000
Garden donations	24,600
Gallery & Tea room sales	15,000
Charlottetown Mall Location	140,000
Freight (retail—1% sales)	7,080
Freight (wholesale—5% sales)	10,550
Freight (mail order—20% sales)	32,600
TOTAL SALES	**1,876,830**
Wages & Benefits	
Wages—Management gross	143,000
Wages—Café	184,928
Wages—Retail	69,548
Wages—Mail Order	22,920
Wages—Production	77,358
Wages—Garden Maintenance Gross	6,760
Wages—Maintenance Gross	10,920
CPP, EI, Workers Compensation	40,438
Total Wages & Benefits	**555,872**
Cost of Sales	
Café (28% sales)	158,200
Retail (22% sales + 15% mall)	176,760
Mail order	6,460
Production - preserves	260,800
Freight - production (5% of above)	13,040
Freight - retail (1% sales)	7,080
Freight - wholesale (8% sales)	16,880
Freight - mail order (25% sales)	40,750
Total Cost of Sales	**679,970**
Total Professional Fees	**18,000**
Repairs & Maintenance	**32,000**
Utilities	**61,320**
Insurance	**21,909**
Office	**53,475**
Leases	**16,726**
Advertising & Promotion	**41,200**
Vehicle & Travel	**18,000**
Supplies & Miscellaneous	**75,243**

EXHIBIT 5: (Continued)

Interest & Bank Charges	
Interest on operating loan—150k	2,367
Interest on long-term debt + principle	73,707
Bank interest and back charges	16,400
Credit card fees	2,650
Total Banking Charges	**95,124**
Rent	**21,000**
Commission Paid	**5,000**
TOTAL EXPENSES	**1,694,839**
CASH IN (OUT)	**181,991**
Corporate income taxes, 2008	−15,300
Corporate income tax installments, 2009	−15,300
Cash out to pay creditors	−60,000
Cash from operating line	−55,000
Cash balance—beginning	**0**
Cash balance—ending	**36,391**

EXHIBIT 6: The Japanese Jam Market

To expand sales of imported jam or enter the Japanese market for the first time, it is necessary to develop products after a precise study of the market's needs. Importers who are making efforts to tailor their products to the Japanese market have been successfully expanding their sales by 10 per cent each year. Based on the analysis of successful cases of imported jam, the following factors may be considered very important.

Diversification of consumer preferences: Strawberry jam occupies about 50 per cent of the total demand for jam and its share is continuing to rise. Simultaneously, more and more varieties of jam are being introduced.

Low sugar content: European exporters have successfully exported low sugar jam that meets the needs of the Japanese market. Jam with a sugar content of less than 65 per cent occupies a share of 65 to 70 per cent of the market on a volume basis.

Smaller containers: Foreign manufacturers who stick to packaging products in large-sized containers (650 grams, 440 grams, 250 grams), even though their products are designed for household use, have been failing to expand their sales. On the other hand, foreign manufacturers who have developed products in smaller containers (14 grams, 30 grams, 42 grams) specifically for the Japanese market have achieved successful results.

Fashionable items: Contents and quantity are not the only important aspects of jam. The shape and material quality of the containers and their caps, label design and product name can also influence sales. It is also important that the label not be damaged in any way.

Development of gift items: Sets of various types of imported jams are popular as gift items. For example, there are sets of 10 kinds of jam in 40-gram mini-jars (retail price ¥2,000) sold as gift sets.

Selection of distribution channel: Since general trading companies, specialty importers and jam manufacturers each have their own established distribution channels, the selection of the most appropriate channel is of the utmost importance.

Pricing Structure: An importer of products typically pays about 50 per cent of the final retail price for the goods and adds about 10–15 per cent when selling to primary and secondary wholesalers. Wholesalers in turn add about 10 per cent of the final cost of the good when selling to retailers, who add the final mark-up of about 30–35 per cent of the retail price to consumers.

Source: Access to Japan's Import Market, *Tradescope*, June 1989.

The Entrepreneurs at Twitter: Building A Brand, A Social Tool or A Tech Powerhouse?[1]

INTRODUCTION

In mid-April 2014, a technology analyst working for a large North American investment bank was scrutinizing Twitter as part of her analysis for an industry note on the company. Twitter, a micro blogging service that allows subscribers to send "tweets" of 140 characters or less to their "followers", had launched a successful initial public offering (IPO) on the New York Stock Exchange in November 2013, which valued the company at $24.46 billion. By the end of March 2014, Twitter's market capitalization had risen to $26.63 billion. Yet despite posting revenues of $242 million in the final quarter of 2013, according to Twitter's first publicly disclosed accounts, the company made a net loss of $511 million in the same quarter.[2]

The analyst leant back in her chair and pondered. Starting from nothing in 2007, Twitter had more than 500 million users by the start of 2014, of which over 200 million

Ken Mark wrote this case under the supervision of Professor Simon Parker solely to provide material for class discussion. The authors do not intend to illustrate either effective or ineffective handling of a managerial situation. The authors may have disguised certain names and other identifying information to protect confidentiality.

This publication may not be transmitted, photocopied, digitized or otherwise reproduced in any form or by any means without the permission of the copyright holder. Reproduction of this material is not covered under authorization by any reproduction rights organization. To order copies or request permission to reproduce materials, contact Ivey Publishing, Ivey Business School, Western University, London, Ontario, Canada, N6G 0N1; (t) 519.661.3208; (e) cases@ivey.ca; www.iveycases.com.

Copyright © 2010, Richard Ivey School of Business Foundation   Version: 2014-04-07

One time permission to reproduce granted by Richard Ivey School of Business Foundation on April 22, 2014.

[1]This case has been written on the basis of published sources only. Consequently, the interpretation and perspectives presented in this case are not necessarily those of Twitter or any of its employees.

[2]Dominic Rushe, "Twitter posts revenues of $242m but share price plummets as growth stalls," *The Guardian*, February 5, 2014, accessed March 29, 2014.

were active users who post a total of 340 million tweets per day (see Exhibit 1). Twitter was widely regarded as one of the hottest technology companies after Google and Facebook, often being referred to as the "SMS of the Internet". Given the scale of Twitter's user base, the analyst reasoned, wasn't it inevitable that the company would eventually monetize and realize supernormal returns? On the other hand, she worried that Twitter's stock might be overvalued, and time series commercial promise exaggerated–a charge that had been repeatedly made against the company ever since its inception. The fact was that Twitter's business model and strategy remained opaque, and the gulf between its revenue aspirations and financial performance seemed to be wider than ever.

As the analyst weighed the competing arguments for and against the commercial future of Twitter, she was drawn back to the origins of the company, its early growth path, and the role of the founding entrepreneurs in the creation of the profoundly enigmatic value proposition known as Twitter. Might the idiosyncratic nature of Twitter's founders have imprinted itself on the company in a way which makes it no more than a shiny brand, resistant to the single-minded pursuit of a commercial purpose? Or is the Twitter service no more than a useful social tool with few, if any, ways of convincing its users to pay for the service? If, however, Twitter really was a tech powerhouse in the making, how exactly would it monetize and justify the faith its numerous deep-pocketed investors had in it?

COMPANY—ORIGINS

Twitter founder's Evan Williams' early background hinted at the entrepreneurial path he would take. As a teenager growing up in Nebraska, he preferred the mental challenge of coming up with great business ideas to the physical demands of hunting or farming. Bored with university, he did not focus on a major and dropped out without completing his degree. He moved from job to job, pursuing entrepreneurial ideas on the side, but he struggled to follow through on any of his early projects, discarding them as soon as a more alluring idea emerged. "It was turning into a constant pattern," recalled Williams.[3]

Looking to restart his career in 1996, Williams took a marketing job in Marin County before progressing to writing software code for large companies such as Intel and Hewlett-Packard. "For the first time, I learned what it was like to work in an office and have a normal career. To be in real meetings. I also learned that I did not want to do that," added Williams.[4]

In August 1999, several years before Twitter was founded, Williams and his friends were working as IT contractors on web projects during the day and thinking about their own Internet startup on the side. While in the midst of creating what they believed would be a much-sought after technology, they veered off-course on a whim, and ended up creating a landmark service that allowed Internet users to disseminate information to others, in real-time. With just a handful of employees, the company raised a small amount of venture capital and started releasing new versions of technology for free in order to build traction with users. As they reached a million users, competitors started to emerge. Less than four years after it started, the company had not yet generated any significant revenue and was not close to turning a profit. Even so, Google offered to buy it in exchange for stock, and Williams accepted the offer.

That company was Pyra Labs, the firm behind the blog creation tool Blogger.com, which was started in August 1999 and sold to Google in 2003. One of the business partners

---

[3]http://online.wsj.com/article/SB124000817787330413.html, accessed March 2, 2010.
[4]Ibid.

working on Blogger.com was Christopher Isaac "Biz" Stone, a fellow programmer whom Williams had met online. Stone had dropped out of college, lured by the prospect of designing book covers at Little, Brown Book Group. Soon after, he learned to write software code and design websites.[5]

Despite the fact that Pyra Labs had a willing buyer in Google, some observers were skeptical of the deal. Danny Sullivan of Search Engine Watch, for example, in an article entitled "Google Buys Blogging Company–But Why?" speculated that "one chief reason Google has done this is for ad distribution reasons,"[6] which implied that Blogger.com, on its own, would not be profitable.

Williams stayed with Google until October 2004, and then launched a podcasting firm named Odeo, Inc. Podcasting–a play on the words "iPod" and "broadcasting"–i.e., the practice of recording and releasing digital media files via the web.

With just five people working from a walk-up apartment in San Francisco, Odeo's objective was to build a profitable company by building an "all-in-one system that makes it possible for someone with no more equipment than a telephone to produce podcasts," and "for users to assemble custom playlists of audio files and copy them directly onto MP3 audio players."[7] Williams commented: "Odeo aims to enable this new distribution channel and medium by creating the best one-source solution for finding, subscribing to, and publishing audio content."[8]

Once again, many observers were skeptical. A journalist commented in The New York Times:

> The question for Odeo, and for the many other entrepreneurial efforts almost certain to come, is whether there is any money to be made from podcasting. Recall that the dot-com boom was full of start-ups betting on one or another notion of the Web's potential. But for every felicitous pairing like Google and keyword searching, there were dozens of broken marriages like Pets.com and online dog food sales.[9]

Williams was undeterred as he saw huge potential in the podcasting industry. His excitement about the Odeo project and his belief that podcasting would become the next great technological medium convinced him to stay put on this particular path.[10]

Soon after Odeo shipped its major product, Odeo Studio, deep-pocketed competitors such as Apple, Inc. started to enter the market. In early 2006, faced with poor prospects for the company's future, Odeo's board of directors requested that Odeo revamp its strategy. It was during this period that one of Odeo's employees, an engineer called Jack Dorsey, presented an idea to the team that was based around a service that would enable users carrying standard cellular phones to update small groups of people on their current situation by pressing a few buttons and tapping out a message. The key insight was that users would not need to enter the address of each recipient separately, every single time a message was to be sent. All the user had to do was enter a short numerical code before beginning the message. Odeo decided to adopt Dorsey's idea, initially for internal usage. At first, Odeo's team members kept the testing of the service close–no one affiliated with a large firm was allowed to participate in the test. By the spring of 2006, "Twttr Beta" was launched.

---

[5]Ibid.

[6]http://searchenginewatch.com/2165221, accessed October 15, 2009 and www.blogger.com/about, accessed October 15, 2009.

[7]www.nytimes.com/2005/02/25/technology/25podcast.html?r=1, accessed July 15, 2009.

[8]http://evhead.com/2005/02/how-odeo-happened.asp, accessed July 15, 2009.

[9]www.nytimes.com/2005/02/25/technology/25podcast.html?r=1, accessed July15, 2009.

[10]http://evhead.com/2005/02/how-odeo-happened.asp, accessed July 15, 2009.

The original product name or codename for the service of "twttr"was inspired by Flickr and the fact that American SMS short codes were five characters.

But Odeo's board was hard pressed to see the relevance of Twttr Beta and chose to conserve cash by trimming headcount. Six employees had their contracts terminated. Even so, on the midst of this turmoil, Twttr.com was made available to the public. In an attempt to put more focus on this new project, Stone, Williams, Dorsey and their team set up Obvious Corp. in October 2006 to acquire the Twttr project. The URL www.twitter.com was acquired and the team rebranded the service. Dorsey explained why the name "twitter" was chosen:

> The working name was just "Stat us" for a while. It actually didn't have a name. We were trying to name it, and mobile was a big aspect of the product early on . . . We liked the SMS aspect, and how you could update from anywhere and receive from anywhere.
>
> We wanted to capture that in the name—we wanted to capture that feeling: the physical sensation that you're buzzing your friend's pocket. It's like buzzing all over the world. So we did a bunch of name-storming, and we came up with the word "twitch," because the phone kind of vibrates when it moves. But twitch is not a good product name because it doesn't bring up the right imagery. So we looked in the dictionary for words around it, and we came across the word "twitter" and it was just perfect. The definition was "a short burst of inconsequential information," and "chirps from birds." And that's exactly what the product was.[11]

A nagging question was whether the nascent Twitter would be just another short-lived fad, which might attract users but not a revenue stream. It was not clear at this early stage what potential, if any, the new service might have. Another nagging question was whether Twitter's founders were serious innovators who could see a project through to fruition, or were just dilettantes who, magpie-like, would quickly move on to another shiny attractive idea once they tired of this one.

TWITTER: HOW IT WORKS

Twitter can be described as an easy-to-use, micro-blogging application, instant messenger or social presence notifier.[12] It is essentially a broadcasting system that allows users to transmit short bursts of information to lots of strangers as well as to friends. Twitter is built on open source software and allows users to send and receive messages to a mailing list of recipients ("followers") in real-time. Followers log on to Twitter and add themselves to an author's list of followers. To send a message to their list of followers, authors type in 140-character messages ("Tweets") via Twitter's website, by SMS (short message service) from cell phones, through an IM (instant messaging) client, through an RSS (really simple syndication) feed, or through third-party web tools. Authors can restrict their subscription lists to selected subscribers, or they can leave it open, which allows anyone to sign up to read their Tweets.

Twitter can be accessed through its website, SMS or mobile device app. Twitter is not a proprietary technology, being based on open-source software. It offers the option of

---

[11]David Sano, "Twitter creator Jack Dorsey illuminates the site's founding document," *Los Angeles Times,* February 18, 2009, http://latimesblogs.latimes.com/technology/2009/02/twitter-creator.html, accessed September 15, 2009.

[12]http://dev.aol.com/article/2007/04/definitive-guide-to-twitter, accessed November 15, 2009.

integrating other applications or web services with Twitter via an application programming interface (API).[13] APIs, which allow third-party software developers to build programs to interface with Twitter's data, were introduced by Twitter in September 2006. Twitter has continually updated its search stack, databases and message handling technology, shifting from its initial choice of Ruby on Rails to Java and Scala, in order to handle increasing levels of traffic,

An observer described how Twitter differs from online chat forums:

> We've all chatted online before—reserved our handle, entered a chatroom, and started messaging away. Well, there are two problems with chat in that form. First, the chatroom is (usually) filled with strangers, and second, you must be logged into the chatroom to have access to messages. Twitter is essentially a net-based chatroom filled with your friends.[14]

Twitter also differs from Facebook, which has rapidly become the world's largest social networking site, counting over 1.23 billion monthly active users worldwide by the end of 2013.[15] Facebook users can communicate with each other only by mutual consent, whereas anyone can log into Twitter and sign up to view any public tweets they like. Another difference between the two tools is that Facebook allows people to exchange videos and photos, whereas (despite the acquisition of Vine in October 2012) Twitter remains essentially text-based. For this reason, Stone has said that he sees a greater affinity between Twitter and Google than with Facebook, describing his business as an "information company."

Promoting the Service

For the first six months of Twitter's existence, the company relied on its original users to become "personal evangelists" for the service.

By April 2007, Twitter.com was spun out of Obvious Corp. as its own company. A big break for the new Twitter came in March 2007, in Austin TX, at the South by Southwest festival. There, participants were able to see their tweets flash across television screens in real time. The number of tweets tripled to 60,000 per day, as participants talked about the service and the bloggers in attendance wrote about it.

Williams and his team were pleasantly surprised that their service was a hit. Referring to Twitter, he stated: "It took us a while to figure that it was a big deal."

Stone added: "I found myself watching groups of people twittering each other to co-ordinate their actions—which bar to go to, which speech to attend—and it was like seeing a flock of birds in motion."[16]

Building on the success at South by Southwest, Twitter added new features to its product such as RSS feeds and integration with IM. Each feature that was added boosted the number of users and usage per user.[17]

Over the next year and a half, Twitter's service was mentioned numerous times in the media. Journalists in particular turned out to be enthusiastic adopters of the service, since

---

[13]http://apiwiki.twitter.com/Things-Every-Developer-Should-Know, accessed November 15, 2009.

[14]http://dev.aol.com/article/2007/04/definitive-guide-to-twitter, accessed November 15, 2009.

[15]www.theguardian.com/news/datablog/2014/feb/04/facebook-in-numbers-statistics, accessed March 26, 2014.

[16]http://online.wsj.com/article/SB124000817787330413.html, accessed March 2, 2010.

[17]www.140characters.com/2009/01/30/how-twitter-was-born/, accessed Mary 2, 2010.

its "instantaneous" quality enables them to access and spread news faster than ever. More generally, adoption of the service by new users came as a result of word-of-mouth promotion. As Twitter added employees, its founders marveled at the growing complexity of the organization. Stone stated: "We've never had a company that grew past 15 to 20 people. We're kind of excited about that."[18] The rapid growth of Twitter brought its own problems, however, with several server crashes raising questions about the reliability of the service. More recently, these problems have been largely ironed out, though outages continue to occur, most recently on March 2, 2014 during the 86th Academy Awards ceremony when host Ellen DeGeneres posted a selfie of herself and other celebrities which crashed Twitter for more than 20 minutes.

Organizations began to take note of Twitter's potential to reach out to a more technologically savvy audience. The service is especially valuable to small companies, with limited budgets, looking to gain recognition in the marketplace. With Twitter, these small firms can reach out and provide updates to a growing list of followers. Within larger organizations, there was the potential for managers to update and co-ordinate groups of employees. However, managers were aware of the downside as well–employees could be spending unnecessary amounts of time on the service.

Twitter gained in usage during the 2008 U.S. presidential campaign and was cited as a key tool during the 2008 attacks in Mumbai, India. During the Iranian presidential election, the popularity of Twitter as a tool used by protesters grew; participants relied on the service to co-ordinate their movements and to send messages to the world outside Iran. Reliance on the service grew to such a point that Twitter delayed a 90-minute maintenance shutdown following a request from the U.S. State Department to keep the service available for the Iranian protesters.[19] Since 2009, Twitter has constantly been in the news, recording spikes in usage during the 2010 World Cup tournament, the start of the New Year in 2013, and the Academy Awards in March 2014, hosted by Ellen De Generes. Twitter has also played an important role politically, being used to organize protests, sometimes referred to as "Twitter Revolutions." These include the 2011 Egyptian revolution, the Tunisian protests of 2010-2011, and the 2009–2010 Iranian election protests. The governments of Iran and Egypt have retaliated by blocking the service.

Twitter's user growth has followed the same "hockey-stick" trajectory as that of Facebook and other successful social networks (see Exhibit 2). The growth in user numbers has been a factor behind the ability of Twitter's entrepreneurs to attract venture capital, culminating in the company's successful IPO in November 2013.

Venture Capital Invests in Twitter; Twitter's IPO

Seeking to capitalize on what seemed to be the next Google or Facebook, investors injected a total of $155 million into Twitter in 2009, valuing the company at US$1 billion. In August 2010, Twitter announced $800 million of investment by Digital Sky Technologies, reported to be the largest venture round in history.[20] Following on from this, in December 2011, the Saudi Prince Alwaleed bin Talal invested $300 million in Twitter, valuing the company at about $8.4 billion.

---

[18]http://online.wsj.com/article/SB124000817787330413.html, accessed March 2, 2010.

[19]Andrew LaVallee, "Web Users in Iran Reach Overseas for Proxies," *The Wall Street Journal*, June 15, 2009, http://blogs.wsj.com/digits/2009/06/15/web-users-in-iran-reach-overseas-for-proxies/, accessed June 16, 2009; and Mike Musgrove, "Twitter Is a Player In Iran's Drama," *The Washington Post*, Fun 17, 2009, www.washingtonpost.com/wp-dyn/content/article/2009/06/16/AR2009061603391.html?hpid=topnews, accessed July 09, 2009.

[20]www.timeslive.co.za/scitech/2011/08/02/twitter-gets-800m-investment, accessed March 28, 2014.

Twitter's founders wanted to ensure that they had enough funds to continue building the company and supporting the millions of users who were using the service. Williams stated: "It was important to us that we find investment partners who share our vision for building a company of enduring value. Twitter's journey has just begun, and we are committed to building the best product, technology and company possible."[21]

David Garrity, principal of GVA Research LLC, stated: "It's interesting to see, almost 10 years since we had the first Internet bubble, that we've now got billion-dollar valuations on companies that haven't defined how they're going to monetize their traffic. It would be nice to see how the company is going to, one, generate revenues, and two, generate profits."[22] Ellen Siminoff, a former Yahoo! Inc. executive who co-founded the education website Shmoop University Inc., disagreed, saying: "Where you have audiences, you will make money."[23]

These disparate views are still unresolved, even after Twitter's successful IPO on the New York Stock Exchange in November 2013. On November 6, 2013, 70 million shares were priced at $26 each: the share price increased after the first day of trading on November 7, 2013, to $44.90. At the close of trading on Friday March 28, 2014, they were trading at $47.30, valuing the company at $26.63 billion.[24] In the aftermath of the IPO, Williams was worth $2.56 billion, Dorsey $1.05 billion, and Costolo $345 million.[25]

Acquisitions

Twitter's growth in user numbers has been partly organic, and partly driven by acquisitions. Twitter has opened several offices to supplement the activities of its headquarters in San Francisco, in New York City, Boston, San Antonio, Detroit and Dublin. It has also made many acquisitions; several of the most prominent are listed in Exhibit 2. Most acquisitions were made for undisclosed sums, though the values of some of its 2013 purchases have leaked out. These include Crashlytics, rumored to have been bought for more than $100 million in cash and stock;[26] and Bluefin Labs, for around the same sum.[27]

The number and cost of Twitter's acquisitions seem to be growing. The companies that have been acquired are diverse: many of them are very recent start-ups themselves, and they span a wide range of product categories, including search, app platforms, database and analytics, advertising, privacy and security, large scale computing and Big Data tools.

The analyst paused and tried to make sense of the disparate nature of these acquisitions. While it seemed clear that Twitter was using some of these acquisitions to help diversify itself from a simple communications platform to a full-featured multi-media hub, what was less clear was whether any of these acquisitions contained the key to how Twitter could make money in the future. Mapping revenue streams from the expanded set of services Twitter was a key part of answering this question; but the task of answering it was complicated by the uncertain nature of Twitter's business model.

---

[21]http://blog.twitter.com/2009/09/new-twitter-funding.html

[22]www.bloomberg.com/apps/news?pid=20601087&sid=aPAHFu.jBrhM

[23]www.bloomberg.com/apps/news?pid=20601087&sid=aPAHFu.jBrhM

[24]http://ca.finance.yahoo.com/q?s=TWTR, accessed March 29, 2014.

[25]http://mashable.com/2013/11/07/twitter-ipo-who-got-rich/, retrieved March 30, 2014.

[26]www.xconomy.com/boston/2013/02/05/twitters-boston-acquisitions-crashlytics-tops-100m-bluefin-labs-close-behind/, accessed March 30, 2014

[27]Ibid.

Twitter's Business Model—Still in Question

Documents uncovered by hackers and posted on TechCrunch in 2010, with Twitter's (reluctant) approval, revealed, among other things, that Twitter was aiming to be more than just a micro-blogging service. It was aiming at one billion active users by 2013–an "active user" being "a unique individual having a conscious twitter experience in a given week."[28] The types of revenue models being talked about were still very broad: business-to-business services; e-commerce, especially retailing recommended products; and advertising. Twitter also expected to employ 5,200 people by 2013 (from 450 people by March 2011) and earn profits of $62 million by the end of 2010 (see Exhibit 3).

These expectations have turned out to be over-optimistic. Instead of one billion active users by 2013, it had only 200 million. Instead of employing 5,200 people by 2013, it employed just over half that number, 2,700.[29] And instead of becoming profitable by the end of 2010, Twitter was making a net loss in the final quarter of 2013.[30]

The technology analyst wondered how the company planned to ramp up revenues and profits to justify its stock market valuation. Given all the publicity around the over-pricing of Facebook–a much larger social networking site than Twitter–could stock analysts the world over really be making a big mistake about Twitter's potential?

Todd Chaffee, a Twitter board member and general partner at Institutional Venture Partners, one of Twitter's investors, suggested that e-commerce was an avenue the company could explore:

> Commerce-based search businesses monetize extremely well, and if someone says, "What treadmill should I buy?" then you, as the treadmill company, want to be there. As people use Twitter to get trusted recommendations from friends and followers on what to buy, e-commerce navigation and payments will certainly play a role in Twitter monetization. Over time, Twitter will develop filters to help users manage and classify their tweet streams into useful categories, such as tweets from friends, family, celebrities, news organizations, charities.[31]

Twitter refers to any word, phrase or topic that users tag at a greater rate than others as a 'trending topic'. Users can make concerted efforts to create trending topics, for example, self-promotion by celebrities; and trending topics can also reflect the popularity of events in the news or sports. Trending topics help Twitter and their users understand what is currently going on in the world. That can also be of benefit to companies using Twitter, especially as Twitter also collects personally identifiable information about its users which can be shared with third parties. While Twitter displays no advertising on its site, advertisers can target users based on their history of tweets and may quote tweets in ads directed specifically to given users. In addition, Twitter offers companies the possibility of purchasing "promoted tweets," a new service launched in 2010 and extended to mobile devices in 2012. Promoted tweets allow advertisers to insert themselves in the stream of real-time conversations on Twitter, based on their relevance to the subject matter being discussed. Several companies quickly signed up to advertise in this way, including Best Buy, Virgin America, Starbucks and Bravo.

---

[28]www.techcrunch.com/2009/07/16/twitters-internal-strategy-laid-bare-to-be-the-pulse-of-the-planet/, March 2, 2010.

[29]https://about.twitter.com/company, accessed March 29, 2014.

[30]Dominic Rushe, "Twitter posts revenues of $242m but share price plummets as growth stalls" The Guardian, February 5, 2014, accessed March 29, 2014.

[31]http://bits.blogs.nytimes.com/2009/06/19/twitter-plans-to-offer-shopping-advice-and-easy-purchasing/

The organization eMarketer has estimated advertising revenues at Twitter to be $139.5 million in 2011 and $259.9 million in 2012, rising to $540 million in 2014.[32] The implied growth rates for 2011 through 2014 are 213 per cent, declining to 86 per cent, 53 per cent and finally 35 per cent in 2014. An open question is whether these growth rates will be enough to justify Twitter's stock market valuation. If not, it remains to be seen how the company's business model needs to adjust to cope with limited advertising revenues. Whatever the company has in mind, it continues to be a closely guarded secret.

Other opportunities certainly beckon for Twitter. A role model might be Skype, an Internet telephone service that offers users "free and great value" calls. Skype has gained in popularity by offering users free Internet calls, and has now started to charge fees for certain connections while retaining free Skype-to-Skype calls. Skype quickly gained a critical mass of users and sold itself to eBay in 2005 for US$2.6 billion in up-front cash and eBay stock, and performance-based options.[33] By 2009, Skype was thought to be generating approximately US$600 million a year in revenues. That year, eBay changed its strategy, selling a controlling stake in Skype in a deal that valued the service at US$2.75 billion in 2009.

WHAT WILL TWITTER'S FUTURE LOOK LIKE?

Despite the continuing growth in the number of users, not all has been well at Twitter. First, Twitter is still losing money and facing challenges attracting new users and advertisers. Operating expenses have grown far more than revenues. Twitter's user growth is slowing, and prices for advertisements, which make up the bulk of the company's revenue, are falling. It has fewer users, and generates less revenue per user, than Facebook. Like Facebook, Twitter makes money mostly by selling advertising based on users' posts. Twitter's second business, of licensing its data to companies that analyze user tweets for insights about news events and social trends, is less well entrenched.

Second, there has been organizational turbulence. For example, Jack Dorsey was replaced as CEO in 2008 by Evan Williams, with Dorsey becoming chairman. Two years later, Williams was replaced by former COO Dick Costolo, with Williams focusing on product strategy. In March, 2011 Dorsey returned to Twitter to lead product development; his time is split with another start-up, Square, where he is CEO. Rumors abound about the working relationships between Dorsey and Williams.

Third, competitors had started to emerge, offering functionality that was unavailable from Twitter. For example, Friendfeed allowed users to send text messages as well as import information from their blogs, Flickr photos, and YouTube videos. Facebook has also introduced several Twitter-like changes to its service, including updating users' home pages to allow them to provide real-time updates to friends. Facebook also gave more visibility to its pages for celebrities and other high-profile figures and lifted the ceiling on the maximum number of online fans they could have on the site.

The technology analyst sat down at her desk and pondered the future of Twitter. She revolved the following questions in her mind. Can Twitter retain the attention of its user base, continue to grow that user base, and somehow generate profits at the same time as maintaining the service free to users? If so, how? Could Twitter transform itself into a multi-purpose, fully-fledged social media and information giant, or would it be destined to

---

[32]www.emarketer.com/newsroom/index.php/strong-2011-twitter-ad-revenues-grow-86-259-million-2012/, accessed March 30, 2014.

[33]http://about.skype.com/2005/09/ebay_to_acquire_skype.html, accessed March 2, 2010.

perpetually over-promise and under-deliver, ending up as a monument to the folly of investors and the over-optimism of its entrepreneurial founders? The analyst tried to put herself in the shoes of CEO Dick Cotolo, as she began to think about high-value strategic choices for the company.

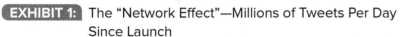

EXHIBIT 1: The "Network Effect"—Millions of Tweets Per Day Since Launch

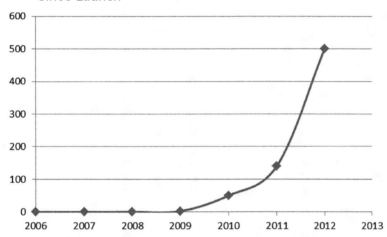

EXHIBIT 2: Some Major Acqusitions made by Twitter

Date	Name of Company Acquired	Product or Service
April 2010	Atebits	Twitter client "Tweetie" for the Mac and iPhone. This free app is now called "Twitter" and is the official Twitter client for Apple devices
May 2011	TweetDeck	Web and desktop client for Twitter
October 2012	Vine	App which allows users to create and share six-second looping video clips. Vine videos are now visible in users' Twitter feeds
January 2013	Crashlytics	Software enabling app developers to identify errors and bugs that make their apps crash
May 2013	Lucky Sort	Big Data Visualization tool
August 2013	Trendrr	A digital and social media business intelligence platform, allowing users to gather information from social media around their product and brand, and display trends to evaluate social media's impact on advertising performance
February 2013	Bluefin Labs	Data mining analytics tool identifying the brands, companies and TV shows most chatted about in social media
September 2013	MoPub	A platform enabling mobile app publishers to manage their inventory of advertising channels

EXHIBIT 3: Twitter's Forecast Financials as Posted on Techcrunch

	2009				2010			
	Q1	Q2	Q3	Q4	Q1	Q2	Q3	Q4
Users in millions	8	12	16	25	35	48	72	100
Revenue	$ 0	$ 0	400,000	$ 4,000,000	$ 8,000,000	$17,000,000	$53,000,000	$ 62,000,000
Total Yearly				$ 4,400,000				$140,000,000
Number of Employees	30	45	60	78	120	197	275	345
People Costs	$ 1,050,000	$ 1,575,000	$ 2,100,000	Target: 65 $ 2,730,000	$ 4,200,000	$ 6,895,000	$ 9,625,000	Target: 500 $ 12,075,000
Organization Costs	$ 2,030,000	$ 3,045,000	$ 4,060,000	$ 6,343,750	$ 8,881,250	$ 12,180,000	$ 18,270,000	$ 25,375,000
Gross Margin	$43,950,000	$39,330,000	$33,570,000	$28,496,250	$23,415,000	$21,340,000	$46,445,000	$ 70,995,000
Net Earnings	$28,567,500	$25,564,500	$21,820,500	$18,522,563	$15,219,750	$13,871,000	$30,189,250	$ 46,146,750

Source: www.techcrunch.com/2009/07/16/twitters-internal-strategy-laid-bare-to-be-the-pulse-of-the-planet/, accessed March 2, 2010.

Time Warner Inc. and the ORC Patents

In early July 1992, John Adamson, president of Optical Recording Corporation (ORC), sat depressed and second-guessed his company's decision to sue Time Warner Inc. for patent infringement. An in-house patent counsel from the U.S. Philips Corporation, whose parent firm developed and licensed the compact disc (CD) technology in partnership with Sony Corporation, had just finished his testimony in the Wilmington, Delaware, courtroom.

The Philips attorney had just advised the court that Philips International N.V. had indeed signed a license agreement with ORC but only to "get rid of ORC with a modest nuisance payment." He had gone on to say that in spite of their decision to accept a license from ORC, the Philips engineers and attorneys had never believed that the Russell patents owned by ORC were valid nor that any compact disc products infringed these patents. Adamson watched in shock as the Philips man made his way out of the courtroom.

Given that Time Warner had mounted a very credible defense and that ORC's entire licensing program might be at risk, Adamson needed to decide whether he should make a modest settlement with Time Warner, in order to save the licensing program.

BACKGROUND

Optical Recording Corporation (ORC) was incorporated in 1984 to exploit a technology invented by James T. Russell, an American inventor, then working in laboratories in Salt Lake City, Utah. Due to the desperate financial straits of SLC[1], his employer, Russell had

John Adamson prepared this case under the supervision of Professor Paul Beamish solely to provide material for class discussion. The authors do not intend to illustrate either effective or ineffective handling of a managerial situation. The authors may have disguised certain names and other identifying information to protect confidentiality.

Ivey Management Services prohibits any form of reproduction, storage or transmittal without its written permission. Reproduction of this material is not covered under authorization by any reproduction rights organization. To order copies or request permission to reproduce materials, contact Ivey Publishing, Ivey Management Services, c/o Richard Ivey School of Business, The University of Western Ontario, London, Ontario, Canada, N6A 3K7; phone (519) 661-3208; fax (519) 661-3882; e-mail cases@ivey.uwo.ca.

Copyright © 2001, Ivey Management Services   Version: (A) 2009-08-28

One time permission to reproduce granted by Richard Ivey School of Business Foundation on April 22, 2014.

IVEY | Publishing

[1]Due to a series of commercial lawsuits lasting 10 years with Russell's former employer, the author prefers to omit any real name reference to this company that had been a party to the technology transfer agreements with ORC. It is referred to here as "SLC." In all other references herein to persons, places or businesses, the actual names are used.

made little progress in the previous two years and both he and SLC were anxious to secure a buyer for the technology.

Through Wayne White, a fellow MBA 1972 graduate from the University of Western Ontario, then working with Dominion Securities in Toronto, John Adamson was put in contact with Dr. R. Moses and Dr. A. Stein. These two Toronto businessmen had been working for close to a year to buy Russell's technology. By happenstance, Adamson had contacted White looking for business opportunities to start his next business, preferably in electronics or software, just days after Moses and Stein had advised White that they were going to throw in the towel on their Russell project. In spite of the considerable time that they had spent, it appeared unlikely that they would be successful in securing the necessary finances to proceed.

Adamson negotiated an option with these gentlemen to assume their "interests" in the Russell project, on the condition that he secure the necessary funding for a technology transfer by April 1, 1985, a propitious date as it would turn out. In return, Adamson agreed to reimburse their expenses to date and to give to each, a five per cent equity interest in the incorporation formed to exploit the Russell project in Toronto.

After completing a "due diligence" investigation of the Russell technology, with the assistance of Warner Sharkey, an alumnus and friend from the Royal Military College of Canada and a senior technology consultant who operated from offices in New York and Toronto, Adamson began planning in earnest. He wanted to transfer the Russell technology to Toronto, where he expected a well qualified team of scientists and engineers could be assembled to pursue a cost-effective development of a pocket-portable digital storage device.

For the next nine excruciating months, he worked to find investors for an issue of special debentures from his Toronto start-up. These debentures also offered a very attractive cash-back feature under a research tax credit program of the Canadian government. Funding was secured and the technology transfer agreements were signed on March 28, 1985, only three days before the option agreement with Moses and Stein would have expired. Adamson had resisted the temptation to request an extension of time on his option agreement with Moses and Stein. He feared that, better informed, they might rekindle their interest in the Russell technology and work to obstruct what little chance he still had to find funding prior to the option expiry on the first of April.

With the debenture funding and the transfer agreements signed, the new Toronto company, soon to be called Optical Recording Corporation (ORC), was now ready to hire Russell and transfer SLC's technology to Toronto.

JIM RUSSELL

By 1984, Jim Russell had worked for close to 20 years toward an improvement in recorded music beyond what was possible with the analog magnetic tape technology. This quest was motivated in part by his love of opera and a desire to listen to more accurate playbacks of recorded performances. When Adamson first visited Russell's lab in Salt Lake City, he was treated to the playback of a recording of Richard Wagner's "Ride of the Valkyries" (or "Die Walkure" in the original German). It was a most rousing introduction to a technology!

Russell had accomplished this playback by shining an argon ion laser beam onto a pre-recorded glass plate, the size of an index card. This was the latest of his laboratory prototypes designed to demonstrate his patented techniques. These techniques were claimed in his extensive portfolio of 26 U.S. patents with corresponding foreign issues in seven other countries.

In Russell's way of recording music, the acoustic signal of the music was first pre-processed into a single *digital* bit stream from a series of time-coincident frequency samples. A laser, an *optical* device, was then used as the energy source to mark the music, as digital bits, onto a glass plate in the recording step and then used to read the music, as digital bits, in the playback step. This technology was known as *digital optical* audio recording.

Adamson was not the first to visit Russell's lab, far from it. Over the course of the previous 10 years, both at SLC in Salt Lake City, and at Battelle Northwest Laboratories in Richland, Washington, electronics manufacturers around the world beat a path to Russell's laboratory door and at his invitation. SLC had been trying to sell technology licenses to the Russell technology but with virtually no success. Prominent among the visitors to SLC's labs were representatives from Philips International N.V., the multinational electric/electronics giant headquartered in Eindhoven, the Netherlands. They had made three separate visits over that 10-year period.

Prior to the commercial availability of the diode laser in the early 1980s, Russell's recording and playback devices were operated with the use of a gas ion laser and as such could be made no smaller than the dimensions of an office desk. Gas ion lasers were too bulky, complicated and expensive to be used in consumer products. This may explain SLC's lack of success in licensing and their resultant financial distress. With the advent of the diode laser, essentially a powerful light source on a silicon chip, a light, compact and economical consumer product such as the compact disc was possible. Although never well funded, SLC's money troubles really began in 1981, just as the mass commercialization of a digital optical audio recording device became feasible.

From Adamson's viewpoint, Russell's greatest achievement was not any one of his inventions, but his success in demonstrating the technical feasibility of recording a digital audio signal optically. Before Russell had successfully demonstrated this technical feat in 1975, no one else had even attempted it. By early 1984, however, the electronics trade papers were reporting that Sony and Philips were developing a so-called compact disc player. SLC and Russell must have felt that they were being left on the sidelines in Salt Lake City, a bitter fate for the inventor and his investors who had all contributed so much.

In bringing Russell and his technology to Toronto, Adamson had decided that there was little point in continuing audio research toward a digital optical tape recorder. The opportunity to develop a massive random access data storage device using credit card-sized media was seen a less ambitious technical challenge and possibly of greater commercial value than a music device like the CD. With the insight of Russell, Adamson envisioned books, medical records, equipment schematics, maintenance instructions and records on this type of device–and all pocket-portable.

In order to determine what protection the existing Russell patents would provide to the new research focus, Adamson employed the services of John Orange, a patent agent, then with the Toronto law firm of McCarthy & McCarthy. (Orange was recommended by Daniel Cooper, a corporate attorney with the same law firm, who earlier had prepared all of the financing and technology transfer agreements for ORC.)

After working with Russell for several months, Orange advised Adamson in early 1986 that the Russell patents may not provide much protection to the new company's research focus, as the most relevant patents appeared to be limited in their claims to audio applications. Adamson had already understood that it was the precise language of the claims within a patent that determined the patent's intellectual property rights.

DISCOVERING A TREASURE

In completing his study of ORC's patents with the assistance of Russell, Orange also concluded that the newly released compact disc players and discs might infringe one or more of the claims in the Russell patents. What a finding!

Russell had mentioned this possibility to Adamson during their first meeting in the Salt Lake City lab; however, Adamson had put little faith in Russell's remark at the time, as no consumer electronics firm had bothered to license the technology, in spite of SLC's efforts. Furthermore there were no CD products on the market then and its commercial success could not be anticipated.

Encouraged by the report from Orange and the early market success of the compact disc by the spring of 1986, Adamson retained the services of Adrian Horne, an established patent licensing professional of Dolby acoustic research fame. With Horne's assistance, ORC set out to advise every electronics firm likely to market a compact disc player anywhere in the world that "they may infringe the Russell patents" by doing so. Horne was most clear on the point that ORC must not appear to threaten legal action in their notice, as it may give grounds to the recipients to file a preemptive request for Declaratory Judgment and thereby force ORC into premature legal proceedings that ORC could ill afford.

In conjunction with the initial contact of alleged infringers, Adamson prepared cost estimates for the licensing effort and started to gain some early information on what it would cost to sue for patent infringement. He knew that once launched, any investment in the licensing program was certain to be incurred, whereas the return by way of royalty revenues would be anything but certain. He also made early estimates of the royalty potential for the licensing program, but these royalty estimates carried an enormous emotional impact.

Simple arithmetic established that if 100 million CD players were sold in ORC's patent-protected territories at an average manufacturer's selling price of US$100 and if ORC licensed their patent rights for this product at two per cent of revenues, ORC's projected royalties would total US$200 million. And this figure ignored the royalties to be earned on the manufacture and sale of the compact disc media itself! It was clear that a successful licensing program could be mounted given these simple estimates. Adamson chose not to dwell on these figures, however, as his typical reaction oscillated between a measured excitement and a raw fear of the business of licensing beyond what little he knew.

ORC's first meeting with a suspected infringer took place in the early summer of 1986 in Tarrytown, New York, in the offices of N.A. Philips Corporation. Legal representatives for both N.A. Philips and their Philips parent in Eindhoven, the Netherlands, and for the DuPont Corporation of Wilmington, Delaware, were in attendance. For ORC there were Cooper, Orange, and Adamson and a lawyer from Battelle Laboratories of Columbus, Ohio, Jim Russell's first employer, and the original owner and assignor of the Russell patents, first to SLC and then to ORC.

This first meeting with the Philips and DuPont people ended three and one-half hours later, after a full exchange of views and some acrimony, but no progress toward a licensing agreement. The attorneys representing both Philips and DuPont were of the view that no patents were infringed and further that there was some question about the validity of the Russell patents in the first place. There seemed little point in a further meeting and it seemed very likely that ORC might get no further without filing a patent infringement suit.

In August 1986, Adamson made a first trip to Tokyo on behalf of ORC, with Horne and Russell. A week-long series of company presentations had been arranged by Horne, with the assistance of Far East Associates, a technology licensing agency based in Tokyo, with whom Mr. Horne had collaborated in his Dolby days. Only one prominent manufacturer was invited to each meeting.

On Horne's advice, ORC had booked conference room space at the prestigious Okura Hotel, located directly across from the American Embassy in Minato-ku, a district of central Tokyo. Adamson choked on the daily expense of US$2,000 per day for a meeting room that comfortably held only six people. Horne, however, had stressed the importance of the location to ensure that the status-sensitive Japanese gained the best initial impression of ORC and its business offering.

The ORC team was overwhelmed by the turnout to their presentations. Each firm sent at least four executives and engineers; and in two instances, a group of over 10 people arrived, forcing the ORC team to scramble for a larger meeting room. Many guests recognized Horne from his previous Dolby research licensing days and more than a few appeared quite knowledgeable of Russell's research and patents. In fact, three firms clearly had comprehensive files on Russell's work and appeared very familiar with the technology.

The ORC presentations were made in English. Horne had advised that the executives in the international departments of all Japanese companies were invariably fluent in English. The younger members, however, tended to be more at ease in English, while some of the more experienced guests appeared to be there simply to witness the process and tone of the meeting and to gage the visitors as adversaries. Adamson concluded that some of the groups had arrived en masse, ready to take notes, in order to do a team translation, once they returned to their corporate offices. This would explain the large numbers of guests from some companies.

Nonetheless, this initial series of meetings convinced the ORC team that their patent infringement claims were being taken seriously by the Japanese firms. Apart from Philips, only the Japanese had announced CD player products by the fall of 1986.

During this initial trip by the ORC team to Tokyo, Yoshihide (Josh) Nakamura, then senior general manager, Intellectual Property, Sony Corporation invited the ORC team to Sony's headquarters for another meeting on their next visit to Japan.

Adamson returned to Tokyo with Orange and Horne in November 1986, for another series of presentations and meetings, but this time at each company's offices as prearranged again by Far East Associates. The most important of these meetings was with Sony Corporation, as the ORC team felt certain that Sony's decision on whether to license the Russell patents, would predetermine ORC's success with all other firms in Japan. (It was a Philips-Sony partnership that had launched the compact disc and taught an industry how to make them.)

On a schedule of two and even three meetings each day, including shuttles between companies located around Tokyo and Osaka, the ORC team made 12 more presentations. All discussions were held in English, again with only a perfunctory objection from the Japanese hosts. Everyone appreciated that the United States represented the largest domestic market for the compact disc industry and as Jim Russell had first filed his patents in the United States, it was also likely to be the site of ORC's most comprehensive patent protection.

In fact, ORC's patents were most comprehensive in the United States, Britain and Canada, but appeared to provide a weaker protection in Germany, France and the Netherlands. The prosecution of ORC's patents before the Japanese Patent Office had been stalled for many years, partly due to SLC's lack of funds. As such, while virtually all of the CD players were being manufactured in Japan, apart from those made by Philips, the greatest exposure of these Japanese manufacturers to ORC's claims of infringement lay in their export shipments to North America and Europe. Their shipments within Japan and to the rest of the world would only be exposed if ORC succeeded in getting the Japanese Patent Office to issue a key patent. (ORC never succeeded at having their Japanese patent issued.)

Some firms, including Sony, had gone to the expense of having a U.S. patent attorney present at all meetings with ORC, but Sony appeared the most ready to enter into substantive discussions. In this second round of discussions, Sony's team of six or seven engineers and executives presented ORC with a package of over 25 U.S. patents, all cited as Prior Art against the Russell patents.

PUBLISHING THE "BLUE BOOK"

Adamson had been warned by both Horne and Orange to expect such a patent defense from Sony. He understood that if the techniques that Russell had claimed in his patents as inventions could be found in any reference that had been published or made public prior to the filing of his patents (i.e. Prior Art), Russell's patents would be found "invalid" and unenforceable. In spite of the warnings, Adamson was highly alarmed and wondered whether ORC was in for a challenge.

On returning to Toronto and on the suggestion of Orange, Adamson tasked him to collaborate with Russell in a review of documents that Sony had provided. Orange prepared a technical response for each reference and compiled these results in a bound booklet for distribution to each prospective licensee. Thus, the so-called "Blue Book" was born. It was thought that by making a general distribution of the "Blue Book," any duplication of effort from one set of technical discussions to another could be minimized, while hopefully speeding all talks toward the signing of licenses.

Adamson had no sense whether one or other of the Prior Art references might hold a "golden arrow" that would pierce the assumed validity for the Russell patents. He knew that a patent was generally assumed to be valid as issued, and therefore enforceable before the courts, but any unanswered Prior Art reference could quickly dispose of ORC's credibility and their licensing prospects.

DISTRACTIONS ALONG THE WAY

Adamson had another more urgent reason to wish the licensing talks to progress quickly. As a research firm, ORC was funding its operations from its initial financing, gained through a tax credit program of the Canadian government. With an initial net investment of just Cdn$6.5 million and a monthly "burn-rate" approaching Cdn$250,000 for the research program, Adamson knew that ORC would likely run out of cash by the end of 1987, at the latest. (Luckily for ORC, the mid-1980s were a period of rampant inflation and ORC was earning 10 per cent, and 12 per cent per annum on its cash hoard.)

To add to the general instability of the situation, the Canadian government, SLC (the firm that had transferred the Russell technology to ORC) and the inventor himself, Russell, were now all objecting to the terms of the agreements that had brought the technology to Toronto. The Canadian government wished to rescind their tax credits and were demanding an immediate cash reimbursement while SLC and Jim Russell were both interpreting their respective agreements in their favor, to secure some respective right to ORC's potential licensing windfall from the compact disc industry.

Adamson remained of the view that all claimants were incorrect in their positions and vowed privately to resist their claims even into bankruptcy. Despite all of these distractions, he also knew that ORC had to maintain the appearance of complete stability, control and competence, in order to avoid "losing face" before their Japanese prospective licensees. Many hours of sleep were lost during this desperate period.

THE SONY PROTOCOL

By their second meeting with ORC, the Sony team were stating that they wished to deal directly with ORC and not through Far East Associates, as Sony reportedly had for their patent licence with the Dolby firm. They also indicated that if Sony agreed to a licence, they would want the right to act as ORC's exclusive agent to license all other manufacturers based in Japan, for their CD player production. As only Japanese manufacturers were then making CD players, apart from Philips in the Netherlands, this was difficult to agree to, given that ORC had resisted a similar proposal from Far East Associates.

Both the services of Horne and Far East Associates had been contracted on a fee-for-service basis, with ORC retaining all licensing rights to the Russell patents. Both could be terminated without cause in the normal course of business. As consultants, their services were required only as long as the client thought they were adding value. Far East Associates had indicated a desire to assume a full agency role on behalf of ORC with the full authority to license ORC's patents on behalf of ORC, but Adamson had resisted this overture, convinced that ORC would be better served by dealing with each manufacturer directly.

Now Sony was asking ORC to terminate Far East Associates and to make presentations directly to Japanese manufacturers, in anticipation of Sony agreeing to a patent licence. This licence, however, would only apply to CD players, with Sony assuming the role of exclusive agent, possibly for all of Asia. Adamson accepted this protocol with Sony, but he had to trust that Sony was in earnest in their desire to be the exclusive agent and not just leading ORC toward a dead end.

Further, as with Far East Associates, he had no idea how ORC was to monitor the work and licensing progress of an exclusive agent based in the Far East, directly licensing Asian manufacturers. How was one to know when a licence signed and royalties collected, if not by the exclusive agent? In any case, as co-licencer with Philips of the CD technology, Sony's support was clearly paramount to ORC.

So a pattern developed. Every four to eight weeks, Adamson and Orange traveled to Tokyo, Osaka and other cities in Japan to hold patent infringement and licensing discussions with the major Japanese consumer electronics firms such as Matsushita (Panasonic), Toshiba, Hitachi, Sanyo, Pioneer, Sharp and particularly Sony.

With each visit, new Prior Art references were put forward by one or other of the manufacturers, and ORC, in the person of Orange, would respond "on the fly" if an obvious separation from the art could be discerned. If not, ORC would fax a response to all participants upon returning to Toronto.

As the months passed, it was becoming increasingly clear to all that the Russell patents as presented by the ORC team, could withstand the invalidity challenges from the Prior Art. Equally important, the compact disc technical standard that ensured manufactured compatibility across all compliant CD products included techniques claimed in the Russell patents. To comply with this CD standard was to infringe the Russell patents! In short it appeared that the Russell patents were valid and infringed by all CD products!

To balance this rosy picture, however, it was equally clear that, month by month, ORC's cash was disappearing into its research program. The company had lost any of the financial strength with which to mount a credible court challenge against even one of the established manufacturers: Sony, Philips or any of the twenty other firms of similar bulk.

THE END GAME?

Finally in the fall of 1987, Adamson realized that neither Sony nor any other firm was likely to accept a license without more pressure being applied and more pressure than ORC could bring to the negotiating table. With nothing left to lose, Adamson flew to Tokyo in mid-January 1988 for a final meeting with Sony Corporation. No other firm was as advanced in discussions with ORC as Sony and Adamson reasoned that Sony had become fairly certain of the profit potential as ORC's master licensee for Japan. Sony would also have something to lose if the talks with ORC failed.

To add to this pressure, he could advise Sony that ORC was close to bankruptcy and, if ORC went into bankruptcy, the Russell patents would revert to their former owner, SLC, a firm that, in his direct experience, proved to be very litigious. The Sony team requested a lunch break.

Over lunch Josh Nakamura asked Adamson whether he would continue to be involved with the Russell patent licensing if ORC went bankrupt. Adamson replied that while his ownership of the patents would be lost, he could no doubt strike a deal with SLC such that the licensing program would not "skip a beat." However the program would then be well financed by a very litigious American backer and, under the circumstances, Adamson would have little interest in favoring Sony in any way. Given his rocky relations with SLC, Adamson painted a most optimistic view of his future.

Returning to the Sony offices after lunch, the Sony team requested a further break and Adamson and Cooper sat quietly for an hour and a half in the meeting room at the Sony corporate head offices in Kita-Shinagawa; Adamson pondering his fate.

ORC'S FIRST LICENSE

Back in the meeting, Nakamura advised that Sony would be ready to sign a license with ORC. The license, however, would only cover CD players, not compact disc media. Further, ORC had to significantly reduce their royalty demands, accept Sony as the exclusive agent with full authority to license all CD player manufacturers based in Asia and pay Sony an administrative fee for their exclusive agency representation out of the royalties to be received. The proposal also required that ORC transfer the right to sue Asian CD player manufacturers for patent infringement to Sony as their exclusive agent. Adamson felt he had no choice but to accept this proposal if he wished to maintain his control of the Russell patents.

It was then agreed that the outline of the license and agency agreements be developed that very afternoon with a final negotiation of royalty rates to occur by telephone in the following week. Cooper took on the task of drafting the required changes to ORC's standard patent license agreement. Negotiations were then completed by telephone the following week and the Sony CD player agreement was signed in early February 1988.

From this shaky last-minute effort, Adamson had managed to retain his full ownership of the Russell patents through ORC. By licensing Sony, ORC now had a royalty cash flow with which to maintain the research program underway in Toronto, as well as the resources to fend off the law suits from the Government of Canada and SLC. For the first time in its existence, ORC was cash flow positive and in that sense, time was now on ORC's side;

however, when measured against industry norms, the license with Sony cost ORC plenty. Nakamura and the Sony team had done their job well.

Apart from Sony's hard bargain, they were always gracious but now as business partners, Nakamura and Sony's negotiating team seemed to relish this role even more.

Adamson came to look forward to an invitation to dine at one restaurant in particular. High above Akasaka in central Tokyo, directly overlooking the Diet, Japan's national parliament, there was a restaurant laid out in a series of private dining rooms, each in a unique Western décor of a particular color and at least one Monet or similar Old Master painting dominating the room. Their chefs were trained at the Paul Bocuse culinary school in France and the wine list read like a vintners' award booklet.

Adamson also came to realize that the superb ambiance and staff service of the Hotel Okura was very habit-forming and in spite of the expense, he opted to stay there whenever he was in Tokyo. Horne had been right. Being invited to lunch or dinner at the Hotel Okura, was also a great treat for ORC's licensing prospects and other business associates in Tokyo.

ONWARD

Among the more difficult challenges that ORC faced in mounting the licensing program was the determination of the size of the infringing production unit volumes and sales revenues. A prospective licensee is not about to divulge this data, as it would impair their negotiating position and possibly increase their chances of being sued before one of their competitors. Nevertheless in the case of CD media, it was pretty obvious that the five sisters of sound; Philips (Deutsche Grammophon), Sony (Columbia), Time-Warner (Warner), EMI (London and Angel) and Bertelsmann (RCA) were the largest manufacturers of CD media. After Philips and Sony, Time-Warner was likely to be the largest compact disc maker in the United States.

Government agencies and industry trade associations publish trade statistics, but this data is usually on an industry-wide basis (not by company) and for broad product categories, not for individual products, such as a CD player. Beyond these sources, there are industry consultants of varying usefulness and reliability. Nevertheless the licenser must develop estimates of the production and sales volumes for the infringing product by manufacturer and for each year from the start of the infringement to the expiry of the patent or the end of the infringement, whichever comes first.

Without such numbers it is not possible to decide which companies are the more lucrative licensing prospects and more importantly whether a licensing program is even feasible. Without this data the licenser cannot know which infringer to sue or in which jurisdiction to bring the suit, to ensure the most favorable cost-benefit ratio for such an action.

In the ensuing 12 months, Sony sub-licensed over 50 per cent of the remaining Japanese production for CD players and ORC began to develop a substantial "war-chest." Still unresolved were ORC's equivalent infringement claims against the manufacturers of the discs, the compact disc media. Sony had refused to include this item in the initial license as they advised that they needed more time to study the matter. They also stated the view that the Russell patents were less likely to be infringed by the discs.

In the summer of 1988, however, ORC succeeded in licensing the Philips Corporation for both CD players and media and with this success, somewhat confirming Sony's earlier license commitment, Sony agreed to sign a license for CD media in November 1988. By the end of 1988, ORC had a cash position well in excess of US$10 million and the licensing program was on a roll.

The next largest manufacturer of CD media in the United States, by production volume, after American subsidiaries of Sony and Philips-Dupont, was known to be WEA Manufacturing, a subsidiary of Time Warner Inc. Commencing in 1987, Adamson held several discussions, by mail, telephone and face-to-face meetings, with TimeWarner's in-house counsel. These discussions lead nowhere however as Time Warner's often-repeated view was the standard "non-infringement and invalid patents" position of an alleged infringer.

ENFORCING ORC'S PATENT RIGHTS

In early 1990, ORC had retained Davis Hoxie Faithfull & Hapgood, a patent law firm just next door to Time Warner's corporate head office in the Rockefeller Centre in New York City. Charles Bradley, a senior patent litigating attorney with Davis Hoxie had been recommended to Adamson on a chance encounter, while in Tokyo, with an American attorney who had the misfortune of opposing Bradley in a previous patent case. Bradley and Lawrence Goodwin, his partner, were engaged to pursue ORC's interests with the respect to the alleged infringement by WEA Manufacturing, a subsidiary of Time Warner Inc. Goodwin became the "lead" attorney on the ORC file with Bradley providing oversight, senior counsel and strategic advice to Goodwin.

On ORC's behalf, the Davis Hoxie firm filed a patent infringement complaint against WEA Manufacturing in the Federal District Court in Wilmington, Delaware, in June 1990. Like many other major American corporations, Time Warner and its subsidiary, WEA Manufacturing, were incorporated in the State of Delaware.

Not the least of Adamson's concerns in deciding to sue Time Warner in early 1991, was a looming patent expiry date in July 1992, for a U.S. patent, the key to ORC's infringement claims against CD media manufacturers.

The greatest threat that a patent-holder has against a recalcitrant infringer is a court injunction to stop the infringer's production lines. By 1991, this threat was all but lost to ORC as the July 1992 expiry date of ORC's key U.S. patent was likely to pass before any court could rule on the matter.

Without the threat of a court order to stop an infringing production, the patent-holder's leverage is reduced to the probability of a favorable court award being considerably more arduous for the infringer than the royalty payable if a license had been accepted. Even this leverage is diminished by the reality that, at any time prior to an appeal court ruling on a lower court award, the infringer is free to negotiate a settlement with the licenser, even well past a court decision which declares them to be infringing. The infringer can also hope that the patent-holder will capitulate before the end of a full trial, for lack of sufficient funds.

These considerations were very much on Adamson's mind in March 1992 as he drafted a letter (see Exhibit 1) to be sent directly to Time Warner's in-house counsel with a copy to Goodwin. Goodwin had advised against sending the letter, given that ORC had filed their patent infringement suit against Time Warner almost two years earlier. However, Adamson felt certain that Time Warner should be willing to settle for the modest sum of US$3 million, just to avoid the patent infringement trial now scheduled for June 1992, with all of its costs and disruption. Of no surprise to Goodwin, Time Warner politely declined ORC's settlement proposal, perhaps thinking that the letter was a clear indication that ORC was about to capitulate, if they had not already, with their modest US$3 million settlement offer.

WILL THEY LIKE US IN WILMINGTON?

Now faced with the certainty of a trial in the United States, Adamson had to deal with a personal overriding concern. Could an American jury be prejudiced against a Canadian company such as ORC? Goodwin had told him not to worry about it, but Adamson was concerned that Goodwin simply did not know.

Too embarrassed to advise Goodwin of his continuing concern with a potential American prejudice toward a Canadian company, Adamson hired the New York office of Goldfarb Consultants, a Canadian market survey firm. Their assignment was to conduct an opinion survey on attitudes, toward Canadian companies, of people drawn from the "jury-pool" population around Wilmington, Delaware. The Goldfarb team suggested that they conduct this survey with focus group interviews based on a set of questions pre-cleared by ORC.

In April 1992, Adamson traveled to Wilmington to witness the interviews firsthand by watching the proceedings on a video monitor in an adjacent room. There were three sessions comprising a total of 35 participants, who gave up a part of their evening for the survey in return for dinner and a modest stipend.

The interviews were conducted in two parts. The first part was designed to solicit an unprompted reference to Canada, in its role as a trading partner of the United States. The second part was designed to solicit directly any opinions that they may hold toward Canadian companies and then specifically a Canadian company's right to protect their American rights by suing an American company in Delaware.

The survey was of great benefit to Adamson as it quickly became clear that he should not be concerned about an American prejudice toward Canadian companies. If a prejudice did exist, it could only be positive because the survey, in every focus group, turned into a love-fest for Canada and Canadians.

Each focus group became frustrated with the first part of the survey. In trying to find the trading partner that they might be concerned about, Canada was never mentioned, even in their desperate attempts to finally yell out the "correct answer." This desperation was then followed by groans when Canada was finally noted by the session moderator at the beginning of the second part of the survey. Very few of those surveyed knew that Canada was indeed the largest trading partner of the United States.

With Canada now on the table and not hiding as in a trick question, many positive views were openly expressed. In fact more than a few had vacationed in Canada, some had close Canadian relatives and one woman was so effusive as to simply say, "I love Canadians," quickly adding that she and her husband vacationed regularly in the Montreal area.

A little sheepishly, Adamson returned to Toronto and phoned Goodwin to advise him that "the ball was now in his court" and that ORC would see the Time Warner case through to appeal, if necessary. He did not mention the survey.

THE RUBBER MEETS THE ROAD

Led by Goodwin, the Davis Hoxie team was comprised of one other full-time attorney, Robert Cote, and a support staff of three, all of whom stayed in Wilmington for the duration of the trial (with some weekends at home in New York). This Delaware team worked from the offices of a Wilmington law firm. This law firm in turn provided its own legal and support staff to ORC's team on an as-required basis. At Davis Hoxie in New York, at least one additional full-time attorney, Peter Bucci, and various other support staff were employed in research and document preparation for the duration of the trial. This entire trial effort was monitored and when appropriate, coached by Charles Bradley.

The trial began in the last days of May 1992, and it was to run for five and one-half weeks. Throughout the trial period, the Davis Hoxie team worked a daily double shift, one in courtroom and then a second in their law offices and hotel rooms, debriefing the day's events and preparing for the next day's court sessions. This preparation included a review of salient facts, prior affidavits, deposition testimony and then general court procedures with each individual witness, in preparation for the court appearance.

It also included a daily review of defendant witness testimony for discrepancies. The review of the court plan for the following day might include witness questioning, preparing motions that pulled together now-important facts and revising presentation materials imperiled by the day's events.

Adamson had decided to remain in Wilmington and attend every court session, given the importance of its outcome for ORC. Having watched the jury selection a few days before, he was highly stressed on the morning of the first day of the trial. He took some comfort in the size and evident competence of the Davis Hoxie team until the Time Warner team appeared.

Either by chance or design, 20 minutes prior to the official court start-time, opposing attorneys began to file into the courtroom. First they filled to overflowing the small defendant's bench in front of the commons rail, and then gradually they occupied the entire commons observer section on the defendant side of the courtroom, spacing themselves comfortably. Adamson sat as a lone observer for ORC directly behind the Davis Hoxie team of five on the plaintiff's side until three more groups of attorneys whom he had never met, filed in to sit behind him, also on the plaintiff's side.

Possibly the entire recording industry, including a few Japanese firms with still unlicensed CD plants in the United States, had sent attorneys, some 30 in all, to observe the start of the trial. The contrast between the sizes of the defendant and plaintiff legal teams was so evident that, prior to the jury entrance, lead counsel for Time Warner told the attorneys behind him to scatter into the plaintiff's observer benches.

Apparently unfazed by the obvious imbalance, a few minutes later, Goodwin stood up to address judge, jury and courtroom on behalf of ORC in a calm, humble but masterful tone. He was to continue as he had started through five and one-half weeks of trial, through surprise, setback, equipment failure, client panic and one or two staff confusions.

ORC's case was further strengthened by the skill of a superb expert witness, Leonard Laub. Laub was responsible for explaining ORC's highly technical infringement case, to a jury with no technical training except for one retired man with an engineering degree dating back to the 1930s. This was accomplished with Laub's testimony guided by questioning from Goodwin and with the use of circuit diagram blow-ups and point summaries on white three feet by five feet storyboards. Adamson was satisfied that if there were a chance that the jury could come to understand ORC's case, it would be solely through the ample teaching skills of Goodwin and Laub.

ORC asked the court and jury for an award in lieu of royalty of six cents per disc against Time Warner and their American subsidiaries and a tripling of that award in punitive damages for willful infringement. The decision to ask for six cents per disc was partly based on ORC's initial licensing request of three cents per disc. Legally, licensers are able to change their royalty demands at any point in a negotiation, before or after the filing of a suit, just as infringers are free to agree to previously unacceptable terms.

(In normal licensing practice, it is simply wise to give active infringers, some substantial incentive to sign a license prior to the filing of a suit. This is usually accomplished by increasing the royalty rate by some multiple of the original, say two, three, five or even 10 times. The practical upper limit of a royalty rate is, of course, at that point where the manufacturer can make little profit after paying the royalty, as it is unlikely that any judge or jury would endorse a more onerous royalty request.)

Hearing Goodwin make this request for six cents per disc in open court was a thrilling moment early in the trial. Weeks later the Time Warner attorney was obliged to produce for the court, the unit volumes of their subsidiary's infringing production of compact discs. Their infringement for the period covering the start of production in 1986 through July 1992, the month of the expiry of ORC's patent, totalled over 450 million discs and, at six cents per disc, represented a potential court award for ORC of over US$27 million. The addition of pre-judgment interest and a possible tripling of those damages were more than Adamson could fathom or entertain.

In spite of the good efforts of the Davis Hoxie team with Laub and several other strong witnesses, including Russell, the inventor, and the prospect of an enormous court award, all was not well. After the court appearance by the Philips attorney, Adamson believed that ORC's decision to sue Time Warner might have been taken too lightly.

Goodwin had warned that corporate litigation in the United States was a very expensive enterprise. It was also very demanding of management time, given the need to find, assemble and organize relevant business records, to educate the attorneys in the minutiae of events that usually had happened long ago and to attend court hearings as observers and witnesses. He had also noted that, in the normal course of a robust cross-examination, the combatants and their witnesses could expect personal insults and general verbal abuse. Adamson observed somewhat ruefully that Goodwin had been correct on all counts.

Preliminary motions, production and review of plaintiff and defendant business records and correspondence files, witness depositions, private investigators and trial preparations for the attorneys, company personnel and expert witnesses had already consumed close to US$750,000 of ORC's hard won royalties all before the actual trial had begun. Adamson had budgeted an additional US$1.5 million for fees and expenses to be incurred from the trial itself; however, after the first three weeks of the trial, Adamson saw no end in sight to the trial or its expense.

As was its right as the plaintiff, ORC had chosen to have its case against Time Warner heard before a jury. Even this decision seemed to backfire as it was clear that the jury was putting a good deal of attention and apparent credence into what the defendant's attorneys had to say. The Time Warner litigating team had mounted a very credible defense. They seemed to cloud the technical issues of patent validity and product infringement as these related to the Russell patent claims and the compact disc technology, so that even Adamson found himself confused with ORC's claims from time to time. He had little hope left that the jury would be able to sort through the haze.

With this technical complexity and possible jury confusion, Adamson worried that the direct and damning statements of the Philips attorney toward the Russell patents and ORC's infringement claims could be disastrous for ORC, as these arguments gave the jury, a reasonable and easy "out," from all the confusing technical jargon. Perhaps he was simply someone who knew better about these matters than they could ever hope to know.

Adamson also reflected on the fact that he had been forced to curtail the on-going licensing program for the other CD manufacturers. He had been concerned that some event within ORC's licensing program, such as an agreement with a royalty rate for CD discs below the six cents per disc demanded in the court case, might affect the outcome of the case; however this concern was made mute by the simple fact that the other CD manufacturers had displayed little interest in signing a license with ORC as long as a major record company such as Time Warner was challenging ORC's infringement claims in court.

Should the court case result in anything less than a complete endorsement of ORC's infringement claims, ORC's entire licensing program could collapse including the all important quarterly payments from Sony. The CD player license with Sony may have been a "done deal." As a matter of practicality, Adamson wondered whether ORC would be prudent to take Sony to court, should Sony simply stop paying royalties to ORC after a jury verdict had cleared Time Warner of ORC's patent infringement claims.

Over the course of the six years from 1986 to 1992, Adamson had been drawn away from ORC's research effort and future prospects and ever deeper into patent licensing and then this litigation struggle. As he had testified in the Time Warner trial, "there seems little point in investing in the creation and development of new intellectual property rights if major industrial firms are prepared to ignore and infringe existing patent rights that you already own." Playing somewhat to the jury, he knew that he had purposefully overstated his predicament but the basic truth of his simple observation resonated in the momentary silence of the court that day.

Adamson had made the very difficult decision early in 1991, to temporarily shelve ORC's research program and to reduce the Company's technology development team to a skeleton staff of five team leaders. This move had been made for reasons other than the need to focus the Company's resources on the Time Warner litigation. Nonetheless as he sat in that Delaware courtroom, watching the door close after the hasty exit of the Philips attorney, Adamson felt that he had bet ORC's entire future on the outcome of the court case against Time Warner.

The Richard Ivey School of Business gratefully acknowledges the generous support of John Adamson (MBA '72) in the development of this case as part of THE JOHN ADAMSON JAPAN CASE SERIES.

EXHIBIT 1: Draft Letter to Time Warner's In-House Counsel

~~CONFIRMATION ONLY~~

FACSIMILE MESSAGE OF TWO PAGES TO: 1 (212) 522-1252

March 4, 1992

<u>WITHOUT PREJUDICE</u>

Dear

<u>RE:</u>   <u>ORC vs Time Warner Inc.</u>

Over the past week, we have prepared estimates on the costs and probable outcome of this case. We share this information with you now, in the hope of developing a common understanding from which a mutually satisfactory settlement might result. Our New York counsel is aware of this communication but, the views expressed here may not necessarily coincide with theirs.

Assuming that your costs to date equal ours, Time Warner has spent US$1,000,000. in out-of-pocket expenses alone,. Assuming that we will each spend another US$1,000,000. to the end of trial and then another US$200,000. on an appeal, we will each have spent another US$1,200,000. for a total of US$2,200,000 on this case. Give or take a few $100,000., these costs have a 100% probability of being incurred, if we proceed.

As to the outcome, it is our view that ORC has a significantly stronger case, as Justice Farnan's recent rulings might suggest. Further, we have substantial confidence in our representation. Nevertheless, we accept that the trial process is highly unpredictable. Therefore, we would attach a conservative estimate of perhaps 50% to the probability of ORC winning at both, trial and appeal.

Our licensing program had been based on the royalty rate of US$0.015 per disk and against the estimated and actual production totals for WEA and Allied of 400 million disks, a royalty amount of US$6,000,000. can be estimated. The size of award by the court could vary up or down from this royalty estimate but, it is our view that US$6,000,000 is a good average to assume of all possible court awards. If we assume a 50% probability that ORC will win, then it follows that there is a 50% probability that Time Warner will be required to pay the average award of US$6,000,000.

.../...

OPTICAL RECORDING CORPORATION

141 JOHN STREET, TORONTO, CANADA M5V 2E4 • TELEPHONE (416) 596-6862 • FAX (416) 596-0452

EXHIBIT 1: (continued)

OPTICAL RECORDING CORPORATION

- 2 -

To summarize, at this point in time, Time Warner has a 50% probability of paying out $6,000,000 in award and a 100% probability of paying $1,200,000 in continuing litigation costs, if we proceed.

We believe that a final attempt at settlement is in the interest of both companies at this time. Therefore, we now propose a patent license to Time Warner for their manufacture of Compact Disc in the United States, for $3,000,000.; that is, for 50% of the $6,000,000. which we contend that Time Warner has at least a 50% probability of incurring as a court award.

This offer will remain open until 5:00pm, Friday, March 6, 1992, after which, this and all previous offers will be withdrawn.

We would appreciate your comments on the logic presented here, particularly if you have a significantly divergent view on any point. Please feel free to call me directly if you wish to discuss any point in this letter.

Yours very truly,

G. John Adamson
President

GJA/gj

Source: Company files.

Immunovaccine (IMV): Preparing to Cross the "Valley of Death"

In 2008, Immunovaccine (IMV) was a small biotechnology company in Halifax, Canada, developing a technology that could have the potential to improve future vaccines. There were attractive external opportunities due to the changing nature of the relationship between the pharmaceutical and biotechnology industries. Nonetheless, IMV had to deal with several internal issues, such as getting the right management and scientific staff, setting the strategic direction and developing the means to raise more finances. The company had undergone a recent change of management with Dr. Randal Chase taking over as president and CEO. Chase was a veteran of the vaccine industry and hoped to take IMV's technology from a research project to a successful commercial product.

THE PHARMACEUTICAL INDUSTRY: THE BIG PHARMA

The pharmaceutical industry consisted of a handful of large multinational companies (MNCs), such as Pfizer Inc., GlaxoSmithKline, Sanofi-Aventis, Novartis, Merck Inc. and AstraZeneca, along with a few medium-size competitors, such as Wyeth (see Exhibit 1). These large MNCs had operations around the world. At any time, they had hundreds of technologies and products in development and undergoing clinical trials. In 2006, the total revenue for the pharmaceutical industry was more than $555 billion, a 4.9 per cent growth

Ella Korets-Smith and Suhaib Riaz wrote this case solely to provide material for class discussion. The authors do not intend to illustrate either effective or ineffective handling of a managerial situation. The authors may have disguised certain names and other identifying information to protect confidentiality.

Richard Ivey School of Business Foundation prohibits any form of reproduction, storage or transmission without its written permission. Reproduction of this material is not covered under authorization by any reproduction rights organization. To order copies or request permission to reproduce materials, contact Ivey Publishing, Richard Ivey School of Business Foundation, The University of Western Ontario, London, Ontario, Canada, N6A 3K7; phone (519) 661-3208; fax (519) 661-3882; e-mail cases@ivey.uwo.ca.

Copyright © 2010, Richard Ivey School of Business Foundation   Version: 2011-09-21

One time permission to reproduce granted by Richard Ivey School of Business Foundation on April 22, 2014.

IVEY | Publishing

since 2005. The four largest pharmaceutical companies represented 25.6 per cent of the total market share with Pfizer leading the group at 8.7 per cent market share.[1]

The small number of competitors in the industry was due to very high barriers to entry. Companies had to be able to finance long-term product development programs that involved high risks. The average cost of bringing a medication from research to market was estimated to be anywhere from $200 million to $2 billion, with an average cost of about $800 million[2] (see Exhibit 2). The timeline of product development from research to introduction in the market was about 10 years per product. The success rate for developing medications, starting from a research project to a marketed product, was about six per cent. This meant that the companies had to be able to absorb development costs associated with a 94 per cent failure rate. Few other industries had to sustain such losses. In 2006, the pharmaceutical industry spent more than $70 billion on drug development but only 24 new drugs were approved. The rising costs and timelines of development led to increasing consolidation among pharmaceutical companies, with the few large ones buying out the products and human assets of the smaller companies.

The costs, timelines and success rate of bringing medications to the market had been seriously affected by the increasingly stringent and risk-averse regulatory environment. In order to be approved for use in humans, a new medication had to go through a long and expensive process of clinical trials. For example, a novel breast cancer treatment had to first show positive results in animal models and undergo extensive safety testing in animals before it was allowed for clinical trials in humans. The medication then went through at least three different phases of clinical trials, starting with very small trials to show safety in humans, then slightly larger trials to show effectiveness and lock in the dosing, and finally large sample trials to show statistically significant effectiveness before approval. Any of these steps might have to be repeated several times. Detailed documents had to be submitted and approved at every step. The trial might be stopped at any point if safety concerns arose or no efficacy was seen. Companies incurred most of the expenses in the later stages of the trials. If a medication was not approved after the final stages of clinical trials, companies could often lose around $1 billion in development costs.

However, successful products could reap major rewards. A truly novel medicine could even capture one hundred per cent of the market share for a specific treatment. A medication that was truly effective and the only option for treatment could be sold in large quantities and at a huge profit. Market forces in other industries that typically led to a decrease in price with the passage of time and an increase in volume, often did not apply in the pharmaceutical industry. Niche monopolies were created and sustained for long periods of time. For example, Herceptin, an anti-cancer drug, was the first effective drug of its kind to receive FDA (United States Food and Drug Administration) approval and come on the market in 1998.[3] Though other types of cancer drugs became available by 2008, Herceptin remained the most effective and therefore the most used therapy for breast cancer. The costs of manufacturing an approved product were relatively minor compared to the price of that product. The majority of the costs were incurred in the earlier development phase of around 10 years.

---

[1]Datamonitor Industry Profile: Global Pharmaceuticals, reference code 0199-0372, December 2006.

[2]C. Adams and V. Brantner, "Estimating the cost of new drug development: is it really 802 million dollars?" *Health Aff (Millwood)*, 25:2, pp. 420-428.

[3]"Medsafe grants Herceptin approval," *TVNZ*, March 23, 2006; "Genentech wins approval for new Herceptin indications," *FierceBiotech*, November 16, 2006.

In the investment community, pharmaceutical and biotechnology companies had to compete with more traditional businesses for investment dollars. The differential pattern of returns across industries created a tension when companies in different industries competed for the same investors to raise capital. Investors in the pharmaceutical and biotechnology industries often had to forgo short-term returns for the potential of significantly higher long-term returns.

Traditionally, the major players in the pharmaceutical industry had been very profitable and confident about their future profitability. The large pharmaceutical companies invested relatively little money into truly novel research projects since their business model of strong intellectual property protection and incremental improvements was deemed sufficient to sustain profitability.

BIOTECHNOLOGY INDUSTRY AND THE CONNECTION TO BIG PHARMA

Unlike the pharmaceutical industry, the biotechnology industry consisted of a few larger players, e.g., Amgen, Biogen Idec and Genentech, and also hundreds of significant but small technology-driven, innovative companies. Since most biotechnology companies were small, they could not compete head-on with the pharmaceutical industry to develop products. Very few biotechnology companies had enough funding to take a novel drug from inception to the market. For this reason, licensing, mergers and acquisitions were very common. Typically a biotechnology company would be built around one central platform technology that it would apply to a variety of opportunities. The typical strategy for small biotech companies was to innovate, develop and patent a technology or product and then license or sell to large pharma or large biotech companies. For example, Coley Therapeutics, a biotechnology company that developed vaccines and cancer therapeutics, worked on its products up to Phase 2 of development, partnered with Pfizer for Phase 3 development, and was then eventually bought by Pfizer.[4]

The key to success in the biotechnology industry was innovation, driven by science and protected by intellectual property. The patent regulatory system had been created in order to encourage innovation. Patents were filed to protect novel ideas. The basic principle was that in exchange for disclosing the invention in significant detail, the inventor was given a period of exclusivity for 20 years during which no one else was allowed to use the invention. In the pharmaceutical and biotechnology industries, patents on inventions allowed companies to commercialize their inventions and protect their discoveries from use by other companies. However, patents in these industries were often similar in content, and the companies were forced to try novel things to gain competitive advantage.

Large pharmaceutical companies held patents for many of the commonly used medications. The traditional model for Big Pharma was to look inward for new products to continue to fill their pipelines. However, over the years, Big Pharma had become slow and innovation was increasingly difficult in large companies with well-established ways of doing things. Big Pharma were often over-focused in their areas of expertise and did not do enough to invest in and support exploratory research internally. In contrast, small and nimble biotechnology companies were known for their creativity. They allowed employees to explore peripheral opportunities and invested research and development dollars in new, unexplored ideas.

4"Pfizer buys Coley for $164M," *FierceBiotech*, November 16, 2007.

In 2008, the pharmaceutical and biotechnology industries were more interrelated then ever. Big Pharma had recognized the benefits of looking outward for innovation in order to stay competitive. Biotechnology firms were seen as potential sources of competitive advantage in an environment where many pharma companies were suffering from dwindling patent coverage and fewer product pipelines. Many patents for the most common and most profitable medications were expiring and companies stood to lose billions of dollars in revenues. For example, Pfizer's major product, Lipitor, would come off patent in 2010, followed by Viagra and Geodon by 2014.[5] With the loss of these three products, Pfizer was projected to lose close to $19 billion in revenues through loss of sales to generic medications that were expected to enter the market. Generic medications were copies of the brand name medications and therefore had the same effect and the same safety profile. These medications were often much cheaper because the companies manufacturing generics did not have to take these medications through the costly development process. Though availability of generics was potentially good for consumers in the immediate term, sales of generics resulted in large losses for the pharmaceutical industry.

The year 2008 was both a good and a bad time to be in the biotechnology industry. The growing dependence of Big Pharma on products from the biotechnology industry was providing exciting merger and acquisition (M&A) and partnership opportunities for small technology-driven companies. However, in order to sell a technology, it had to be first developed to a point where Big Pharma could see value in it. For this reason, a significant upfront investment was required. The global financial crisis that started in 2007 and the overall negative outlook for the U.S. economy made it difficult for biotechnology companies to raise capital. As investors tried to reduce their risk exposure, high-risk industries such as biotechnology could be hit hard. Many companies could fall into "the valley of death." This industry phrase referred to the investment period when the technology had to be developed for use on a larger scale and undergo clinical trials. If companies were unable to find financing for this essential development stage, they often did not survive. Such companies had to either give up their technology or make unfavourable deals that did not yield reasonable returns and often cost founders and researchers their jobs and savings. In the harsh world of small biotech companies, a fight for resources in this critical period could truly mean life or death for a new technology.

IMMUNOVACCINE (IMV)

In the 1980s, the fishing industry on the east coast of Canada faced a crisis of declining fish stocks attributed to an infestation of fish with seal worms. An increase in the seal population was held responsible for the increased seal worm infestation. An alternative view on the declining fish stocks was that large populations of seals were consuming too many fish. The focus on the seal population resulted in calls to increase seal hunting, while there was also public pressure to cease the practices of harvesting seals for human consumption. The chair of the biology department at Dalhousie University and a team of three other senior scientists put together a proposal to develop a single-dose birth-control vaccine for seals. A birth-control vaccine was considered a humane way to reduce the seal population. The vaccine could reduce the fertility of seals by more than 90 per cent and sustain the desired immune response for at least 10 years.[6] The single-dose vaccine was

---

[5]Maureen Martino, "Pfizer's future rests with biotech," *FierceBiotech*, September 13, 2007.

thus ideally suited to the situation as finding and monitoring the seals for multiple doses was practically impossible.

The team filed and obtained patents for the composition and use of the new technology. The scientists wanted to develop the technology further because they saw great potential in the success of the single-dose vaccine in seals. They began evaluating the usefulness of the technology in other areas of animal health. They sought the help of a local businessperson, who used his influence and contacts in the region to secure financing from local angel investors, to the order of a million dollars. This allowed Immunovaccine (IMV) to be incorporated and to purchase the patents for its technology from Dalhousie University in the year 2000.

IMV's technology, later called the VacciMax platform, was able to enhance vaccine performance. IMV thus started looking for new problems to solve with its technology. The founders were not sure where the fit was most lucrative, so the technology was initially developed on a "try and see" principle and everything was a bit of an experiment. Since the company started with animal vaccines, this was where the technology was first applied. It soon became apparent that the technology could also be applicable in the human vaccine field. In 2003, IMV hired a cancer biologist to begin experimentation with the VacciMax platform in the area of cancer prevention and treatment in humans.

MANAGEMENT

Out of the four original founders, three remained involved with the company in the roles of president and chief executive officer (CEO), chief science officer, and vice-president of business development. They played key roles in the development of the technology and the creation of the company outside the walls of Dalhousie University. During his years as the dean of science, the founder-CEO had seen the problems of a business remaining within a university and believed that IMV was doing the right thing for the technology by taking it out of the academic environment. However, due to the involvement of prominent Dalhousie researchers, the company maintained a relationship with the university and was able to use some university facilities and expertise when required. The founders had a very strong belief in the technology and held an attitude that "they will all come to us soon because we have the answer." This optimistic view made them believe that a major deal with a pharmaceutical company was not very far off and would be easily forthcoming.

IMV had started out small, with almost everyone having a scientific educational background and working in the laboratory facilities. The founder-CEO handled all issues, large and small, strategic and operational. As the company became more involved in a variety of collaborative projects, another person was hired to take care of business development. This individual had prior experience in the biotechnology industry, but little understanding of the IMV technology. Since the company's strategy at this time was to experiment with all possible uses of its technology, his role and contribution was difficult to assess. Though IMV formed a few new collaborations, it did not succeed in attracting Big Pharma and joining the big league.

---

[6]R.G. Brown, W.C. Kimmins, M. Mezei, J. Parsons, B. Pohajdak and W.D. Bowen, "Birth control for grey seals," *Nature*, 379, 1996, pp. 30–31; R.G. Brown, W.D. Bowen, W.C. Kimmins, M. Mezei, J.L. Parsons and B. Pohajdak, "Evidence for a long-lasting, single-administration contraceptive vaccine in wild grey seals," *J. Reprod. Immun.*, 35, 1997, pp. 43–51; R.G. Brown, W.D. Bowen, W.D. Eddington, W.C. Kimmins, M. Mezei, J.L. Parsons and B. Pohajdak, "Temporal trends in antibody production in captive grey, harp, and hooded seals to a single administration immunocontraceptive vaccine," *J. Reprod. Immun.*, 35, 1997, pp. 53–64.

IMV's organizational structure at this time was simple (see Exhibit 3). The three founders and the local businessperson held the top executive positions in the company. The remaining staff comprised scientific researchers working under the direction of two head scientists.

FINANCING

The local businessperson's involvement made it possible for IMV to acquire more than one round of seed financing by angel investors and government agencies. IMV's technology and the involvement of a respected businessperson generated a lot of local support in the community and sustained the company in the early stages.

As the company's requirement for capital increased, funding from venture-capital (VC) firms had to be sought as the follow-up to initial angel investment. In comparison to angel investors, VC firms often invested with an eye on returns in a relatively short period of time. They often imposed stringent terms, which could include veto rights, low company valuations, and seats on the board of directors. However, VCs were a source of credibility and professional advice for the companies in which they invested. At a certain stage in a company's development, if angel investors had been the only type of financing that the company had received, the investment community began to question the value of the company. Financing was a continuous struggle not just for IMV, but for every small biotech company. Much of management's time was taken up by issues of identifying sources of money, raising the money, allocating money and then repeating this cycle almost every year.

STRATEGIC DIRECTION

Since IMV's beginnings were in the field of animal vaccines, the company had started developing a proof of concept for an animal health business. IMV started a few collaborations in animal health, including one with CSL in Australia. Reflecting the continual consolidation in the industry, CSL was later bought by Pfizer Animal Health. This was a favorable turn of events for IMV, since it now had a collaboration with one of the largest animal health companies in the world. Over time, IMV also started seeing the potential of its technology for human health and decided to invest time and money towards developing proof of concept for this field.

Companies that tried to participate in both the animal and human health fields often faced difficulties due to the differences between the two businesses. In the past few years, the majority of pharmaceutical companies had developed or acquired animal health capabilities. For example, Pfizer acquired CSL to add to its Pfizer Animal Health division. Merck Inc. and Sanofi Pasteur started a very successful joint venture called Merial. Bayer Inc. bought Schering Plough, which had just recently acquired InterVet. Though both animal and human health businesses seemingly existed under one umbrella, they were generally distinct and autonomous. Very little communication went on between the two groups. Even though synergies existed, they were often overlooked.

Timelines for product development in the animal business were shorter, since regulatory barriers were much lower. Though products still had to go through trials approved by USDA (United States Department of Agriculture), these trials were conducted on smaller samples of animals, were shorter in duration, and had higher risk tolerance (e.g. some product reactions in a cow could be considered within tolerable limits, whereas almost any product reactions in humans were considered unacceptable). Once the product was on the market, the profits from such products were also lower. The price of most live-stock products was very low and was determined largely by what the market was willing to pay. Better but more expensive products were rarely introduced unless an unmet need was identified. However, this was not strictly true in the companion animal market. Pet owners would often purchase premium-priced products for their pets.

On average, profitability from developing an animal health product was lower, and therefore deals made with Big Pharma in the animal health field were not as highly valued as deals for human health products. For this reason, relatively few biotechnology companies were working towards developing technologies for animal health and the competition for getting a partnership with Big Pharma in this area was low.

In contrast to animal health, the human health business was based on high risk and high reward. The timelines for product development were longer, mainly because there were more regulatory barriers due to lower risk tolerance by the regulatory agencies. Though the industry had a few large players, there were thousands of small biotechnology firms vying for a piece of the Big Pharma budget to be spent on their technology. This competition allowed Big Pharma players to be choosy with the technologies they would support. It allowed the large players to use a "wait and see" approach, which involved watching a small player develop a technology, show its effectiveness and safety, and only then decide to purchase or partner to get access to that technology. This reduced the risk for the large companies but significantly increased the risk for the small biotech companies that had to bear the costs of the initial risky development. However, the value of the deals made in the human health field was also considerably higher than in the animal health field. Upfront payments to biotech companies in human health could be in hundreds of millions of dollars for a single technology program. Royalty rates paid to biotech companies for their technology were also relatively higher in human health.

The broad potential of IMV's technology in the animal and human health fields, as identified by the management, led to an unfocused partnering strategy. The approach essentially boiled down to work with "whoever comes first to use IMV's technology" and efforts were made to appeal to multiple groups simultaneously. The business development function was based in Toronto while the research and development function was based in Halifax. This resulted in weak communication between these functional areas and added to the confusion. One example of this was that the information presented to potential partners was not updated regularly.

The company as a whole had very little experience in taking projects past the laboratory stage. There was little expertise in chemistry and manufacturing, which was required to make the products for human trials. No regulatory or medical expertise was available in-house that could anticipate these types of challenges. A longer-term strategic plan was not a priority since the management team believed that the technology was good enough to be picked up by large pharma or large biotech companies at a very early stage (even without trials in humans).

By 2006, it became increasingly clear that IMV was not going to get the attention of Big Pharma with the technology that had not yet left the laboratory area. Big Pharma had a lot of choice when it came to vaccine enhancement. Competing groups were working on technologies that were not like the VacciMax platform but could accomplish the same goal in different ways. This was exactly the type of innovation encouraged by the system of intellectual property protection. For example, instead of liposomes that were used by IMV, some competing groups used what were called "virus-like particles" to achieve the delivery of antigens to the immune system in an effective way.

A major possible application of the IMV technology platform was delivering cancer vaccines. However, Big Pharma was more risk averse when it came to the area of cancer vaccines. Though a major need for new cancer treatments existed, no cancer vaccine had yet been approved for use in humans. The approval of Gardacil, a preventative cancer vaccine, by Merck Inc. in 2007 had opened the doors to the possibility of an effective therapeutic cancer vaccine. IMV's pre-clinical data for cancer vaccines in animals was extremely strong. The company was able to achieve 100 per cent tumor elimination with a single dose of vaccine in three different tests at the pre-clinical stage. Though most found this interesting and impressive, this was not enough to sign a licensing deal.

It seemed that IMV had to develop its technologies and products further before major partnerships or financial exits could materialize. One approach would be for the company to focus on the technology side of the business and license the technology to multiple partners. However, this meant reduced control over the destiny of its products and its own future. Also, returns from such licensing would always be limited to single-digit royalties.

CHANGE IN MANAGEMENT

In 2006, the company learned that the founder-CEO was not well and some sort of leader succession planning was required. IMV thus began the search for a new president and CEO, a difficult undertaking considering that very few individuals with the right experience were available and even fewer would be looking to relocate to Nova Scotia.

Dr. Randal Chase was an ideal candidate for the position. Chase was a vaccine industry veteran. He had spent his entire career of more than 30 years in the biotechnology and pharmaceutical industries. He held a Ph.D. from the University of British Columbia and had attended the executive program of the London Business School. His past positions included president of Shire Biologics, senior vice-president–vaccines operations of Biochem Pharma, president and CEO of North American Vaccine, president and CEO of Pasteur Merieux Connaught, president and CEO of Quadra Logic Technologies Inc. and senior vice-president of Glaxo Canada Inc. Dr. Chase was an active board member of four biotechnology companies and was known in the industry for having turned around several organizations. At one point, Jacque Lapointe, president of Glaxo Canada, had introduced Chase to Francesco Belini, another veteran in the industry, by saying "he fixes companies."

Chase was impressed by the data on IMV's technology. He took on the job as interim president and CEO in 2007 and later dropped the "interim" because it looked non-committal on his part. He continued living in the Toronto area and began commuting to Halifax regularly. Shortly after Chase joined IMV, the founder-CEO passed away.

Under Chase, IMV started on the path to take its technology out of the laboratory and into the clinic, the first step towards making a vaccine product. Chase set out to develop a viable strategy for the company. He said:

> The most important thing was to build a strategic backbone for the company and develop a plan with everyone to execute to achieve that purpose. The first goal is to identify the NORTH STAR, the place where you want to end up as a company. One can't start at the bottom and then wonder where to go. You have to fix the star and identify how to get there, derive a strategy to get there and then derive an execution plan to implement the strategy. In a small technology driven company, it is important to put into place the strategy and you also HAVE to be a little bit flexible as well as allowing opportunities to arise. You should be ready for things, as if standing by the door waiting to run in. If the door is opened, you run, seize the opportunity and act.

Unlike the founder CEO, Chase had no desire to deal with all issues, big and small. He had observed how much ended up on the desk of the president and CEO at IMV and had made it clear that continuing this practice was not his intention. After Chase joined the company, the management team began to hold a series of brainstorming sessions to identify all the issues related to IMV's technology that needed to be addressed. During these meetings, Chase remained an observer, pointing out those issues that he felt were more pressing than others. His contributions were limited to arranging the issues in order of priority for the group. He allowed the team to propose what the issues were, who the best person was to deal with them, and what a reasonable time in which the issue would be resolved was. He stressed that the team would be held to the deadlines they set for themselves.

Chase commented:

> In small companies, everyone's jobs seem to overlap. It is the leader's major role to give people specific, identifiable responsibilities. One of my most important roles is to assess people. Right from the start, I need to decide who is competent and who are the stars of the organization. These people will play a key role in the organization's success.

Under Chase, IMV was starting on its way towards what is considered the most difficult time in a company's development. IMV had to start thinking about how to take its technology out of the laboratory and into the clinic. This would be the first step towards making a vaccine product. It could mean making IMV a different organization compared to what it had been under the founder-CEO. It could also require large funds to enable the company to commercialize its technology.

NEW STRATEGIC DIRECTION

Chase quickly identified that being a technology platform company and licensing the technology to multiple partners was not a viable strategy. IMV would not be in control of its destiny, would be limited to single-digit royalties and would always be dependant on Big Pharma for revenues. Chase decided that IMV needed to focus exclusively on the human health field and also work towards development of its own vaccine products. IMV would therefore try to divest all of its animal health business. To this end, IMV signed two licensing deals and an agreement with Pfizer Animal Health in January 2008 for use of IMV's technology in future livestock vaccines. IMV also began working to divest the rest of its animal health technology to qualified partners.

Chase started to implement the new strategic direction. He commented:

> It was most important for IMV to become credible to its potential partners and investors. This credibility is built through the science and the strong pre-clinical data, which IMV has, but also through taking all the right steps towards commercialization. In particular, IMV needed to show that we could manufacture the VacciMax platform at a large scale and that it would produce consistent results. Many liposome technology companies have failed to do so in the past, so the manufacturing issue is a real show-stopper for potential partners. We needed to show that we are in control of our product to become credible.

IMV faced a choice between developing its own manufacturing capabilities and outsourcing the manufacturing function to a contract manufacturer. Building a manufacturing capability in-house was difficult since material made for human use needed to be manufactured under GMP guidelines (Good Manufacturing Practices).[7] All GMP manufacturing facilities needed to go through multiple steps of qualification and inspection, which were both time consuming and extremely costly.

Chase focused on ensuring that IMV's core team was in place. IMV's co-founder and chief science officer had recently retired and a young and energetic scientist, who had been with the company since its inception in 2000, was promoted to that position. IMV had a strong biological science team but had a marked lack of expertise in most other areas required to take a product from the laboratory to clinical trials. Chase hired a scientist to head the biology group and consolidate its strengths. He also pushed for the creation of an analytical chemistry team to further test the VacciMax platform. Two research associates with chemistry backgrounds were hired as part of the chemistry team and a scientist from GlaxoSmithKline was hired as head of the team (see Exhibit 4).

The newly formed analytical chemistry team spent several months developing a method for manufacturing VacciMax vaccines. When this was accomplished, IMV transferred the method to a manufacturing facility, Dalton Pharma, in Toronto. Using IMV-dedicated equipment and under the direction of IMV's scientists, Dalton manufactured commercial-size batches of the VacciMax platform (50 liters or 200,000 doses). One year after initiation of the project, this was considered a major success for IMV. IMV continued to optimize and implement changes to the methods as necessary.

PRODUCT PIPELINE

To ensure long-term success, IMV needed to have a pipeline of vaccine products that it could move closer to the market over time. IMV's own technology, the VacciMax platform, was just one part of a vaccine product. Under the guidance of Chase, the business development team set off to identify complementary technologies and companies that would be compatible with the VacciMax platform and would provide the pieces of the puzzle for IMV to take its products into the clinic.

In 2008, IMV identified and started the process of acquiring Immunotope Inc., a clinical-stage biotechnology company based in Pennsylvania. Immunotope's technology and intellectual property comprised a large selection of active components for vaccines—the pieces that were missing from the IMV portfolio. The acquisition of Immunotope would allow IMV to start developing its own proprietary vaccine products. Immunotope would bring with it a team of scientists who would continue the discovery of other vaccines, which would then be fed into IMV's vaccine pipeline.

IMV's first product into the clinic was likely to be a small cancer vaccine product. This type of product would be directed towards a niche market and would considerably speed up IMV's progress through clinical trials. After the first clinical trials in cancer patients, IMV planned to initiate further trials for other products with broader market appeal, such as an influenza vaccine.

REGULATORY EXPERTISE

In order to advance the newly formulated vaccine products into the clinic, IMV would need to meet and file documentation with regulatory agencies in the United States and Canada. This required very specific regulatory expertise. Individuals with relevant regulatory

---

[7]Drug and Health products: Guidance documents, Health Canada, www.hc-sc.gc.ca.

experience were difficult to find and expensive to have on staff. Since IMV was a small company, Chase used his extensive network to hire an expert as a part-time consultant. Under the consultant's guidance, IMV began working with regulatory agencies to understand and plan the most efficient way forward for IMV's products.

INTELLECTUAL PROPERTY

Since intellectual property was the key to success for biotechnology companies, Chase pushed for an R&D strategy that would lead to more intellectual property creation and better protection. Several provisional applications were filed for new applications of IMV's technology. It was hoped that this type of focused research would serve to increase the value of the company in the eyes of Big Pharma. Considering the potential of the technologies, a decision was made (contrary to the previous management's decision) to protect the company's intellectual property not just in North America, but also in Europe, Asia and Australia.

COMPANY IMAGE

Besides becoming more credible, IMV needed to become more visible in the industry. Chase felt that regardless of how good a company's science and product were, if few people knew about the company, it would not succeed in the industry. IMV thus hired a public relations (PR) firm, a small and dedicated group located close to IMV's head office in Halifax. In line with the company's new strategy, the PR firm was given a number of tasks: redesign the IMV logo, move IMV's image away from animal health into human health and get IMV on the radar of potential partners and investors. IMV thus changed to a new logo and a new slogan that positioned it as a vaccine developer, not a technology provider (see Exhibit 5).

EMPLOYEE MORALE

Chase understood that employee empowerment was crucial for a small and innovative company like IMV. In order to motivate the scientific team, Chase initiated an employee personal development program. All employees were interviewed to discuss their future goals and aspirations. Employees were encouraged to identify what they wanted to learn or courses they would like to take. The company made sure they were able to attend such courses for personal development.

Prior to Chase's involvement, the laboratory and the management office of IMV were two separate entities. Employees were rarely told of major company policies, strategic direction or successes. The founders, though very enthusiastic about IMV, often were not able to share this enthusiasm with other employees.

Chase initiated company gatherings and events, which included the monthly Lunch and Learn program. For this program, the company invited various speakers to talk to the entire group on a topic of interest. Regular updates to employees were also initiated, which became a forum for the CEO to share the latest developments, future goals and challenges. Chase emphasized that all accomplishments, even incremental ones, must be celebrated. This was the best way to motivate the scientific staff–the people on whose creativity and hard work the future of the company rested.

BUSINESS DEVELOPMENT

Chase revamped the business development function. It was co-headed by an internal person with a scientific background and experience in the company's R&D function, and an experienced external consultant who would bring a wealth of negotiation experience and an extensive list of personal contacts inside Big Pharma.

Several types of partnerships could be important for IMV. Partnerships with small, science-based organizations or academics could provide access to novel technologies and research skills not currently present in the company. This was valuable for validating the technology and creating the product pipeline. Big Pharma partners could provide funding to advance products that the company might not otherwise be able to fund. They could also provide expertise in areas that IMV might not be strong in, such as conducting large clinical trials, marketing and sales. In such partnerships, a small company like IMV would usually get upfront payments for licenses, milestone payments based on progress, and royalties when the product was licensed and sold by the large partner.

IMV's strategy involved finding partners for various research programs, which would all be at different stages of product development. IMV would partner for a few programs early on, in order to fund the company's development of more products. For certain programs, IMV would handle the development alone in the initial stages, typically until Phase 2, to show the value of the product through more data. This would lower the risk for partners and also increase the premiums that they would be willing to pay to IMV. Chase understood that the further IMV was able to develop its products, the more a partner would value the product. However, value maximization involved a balancing act between the money IMV was able to invest in development and the value that a potential partnership deal would place on the product.

MORE FINANCING

IMV was entering the difficult valley of death period. Large amounts of capital were required for clinical trials, but not enough data was available to show the value proposition. This was the time when it was most difficult for companies to raise the required funds. IMV needed a significantly larger round of investment than the local angel investors could provide.

Chase felt that several sources of funding would have to be considered. IMV could try to partner with Big Pharma in order to get upfront payments and fund the development of products. This had proven to be difficult so far. Other types of funding available to IMV included VC firms or the public markets accessed through an initial public offering (IPO).

The VC firm route was considered desirable since VCs could bring both money and expertise to the organization. They would also lend credibility to the company through their investment. IMV had been searching for a VC firm that would take the lead on doing due diligence and set the valuation for the financing round. This would create the conditions for others to invest in the company. Going down the VC route could potentially mean a move to the United States, since many VCs were located in the United States. Other Canadian companies were known to have resorted to this approach. IMV's acquisition of Immunotope gave the company a U.S. presence but it remained to be seen whether this would be enough to attract U.S.-based investors. Chase was hopeful that relocation would not be required since many in IMV preferred that it remain in Canada.

Chase did not prefer the IPO route because he believed it carried many downsides. A company in IMV's position was quite far away from having products on the market. The public markets typically did not value companies in such early stages of development very highly, so even if IMV was able to get a significant amount of funding through the IPO, follow-on financing would be difficult. Investors might become reluctant to invest in a devalued, illiquid company that IMV had the potential of becoming. Several examples of post-IPO negative outcomes were available in the biotech sector and a number of IPOs had been withdrawn in the last year.

IMV's attempts to raise finances became more challenging in the recessionary environment engendered by the global financial crisis of 2008. Investors typically opted for safe havens in such environments. Given their limited cash flows, many biotechnology companies were expected to struggle for survival through the recession. In this environment, IMV could not get VC funding and, in June 2009, the company announced that it would go public through a reverse-takeover. A reverse-takeover involved acquiring an existing public company that would act as a "shell" to enable IMV to be publicly listed on the TSX Venture (TSX-V) Exchange. The TSX-V Exchange allowed companies that had not yet reached the stringent reporting standards required for the TSX to become publicly listed. The company's financial situation until the end of 2009 is presented in Exhibits 6 through 9.

Chase commented: "All of the strategic changes and directions are currently a work in progress. The next six months will determine in what shape IMV goes forward."

EXHIBIT 1: Pharmaceutical Industry Concentration

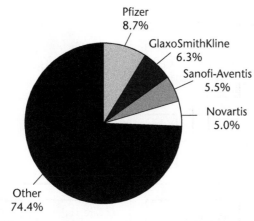

- Pfizer 8.7%
- GlaxoSmithKline 6.3%
- Sanofi-Aventis 5.5%
- Novartis 5.0%
- Other 74.4%

Source: Datamonitor, 2006.

EXHIBIT 2: Drug Development Costs

Stage	Description	Approximate Cost
Pre-clinical	In test tubes and on animals; use wide-ranging doses to assess efficacy, toxicity, etc.	Variable
Phase 1	Small sample (20–100) of healthy humans; assess safety and dosage	$0.25–1.5 million
Phase 2	Medium sample (100–500) of healthy and patient humans; assess effectiveness, safety and dose-response	$2–20 million
Phase 3	Randomized, large sample (1,000–5,000) trials on humans; definitive assessment of effectiveness compared to existing treatments, confirm safety	$20–100 million
Phase 4 (optional)	Post-marketing safety surveillance	Variable

Note: Figures shown are approximate, actual values might differ. Costs shown are per trial—standard practice involves multiple trials per phase.
Source: MaRS Discovery District presentation (2007) on "Clinical Trials Strategy."

EXHIBIT 3: Organization Chart

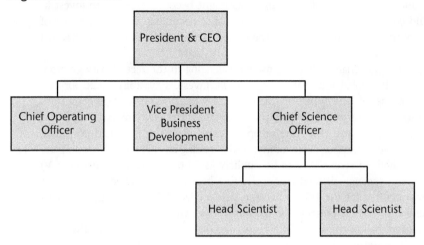

Source: Company files.

EXHIBIT 4: New Organization Chart Under Randal Chase

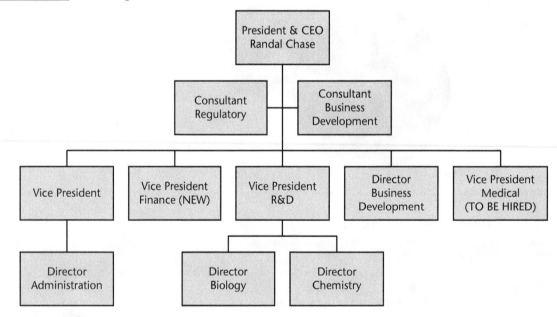

Source: Company files.

EXHIBIT 5: IMV's Logo and Image Re-Design Outcome

This combination of logo, slogan and image appears on all IMV documentation (the logo shows the company's acronym at that time, IVT).

Source: Company files.

EXHIBIT 6: Overview of Immunovaccine Financing Up to December 31, 2009

Funds Raised	
Equity Invested 2000–2009	$ 11.0 M
Government Grants & Loans	$ 9.0 M
Equity Private Placement September 2009	$ 8.8 M (24% Institutional)
License Fees Collected—Animal Health	$ 1.8 M
Total	**$30.6 M**
Funds Remaining	
Cash & Equivalents	$ 7.8 M
Access to Government Loans	$ 2.4 M
Total Working Capital	**$ 10.2 M**

Use of Private Placement Proceeds

- Completion of Phase 1 clinical trial
- Move an infectious disease vaccine towards the clinical stage
- Working Capital to Quarter 1—Quarter 2, 2011

Notes: All figures are in Canadian dollars. Conversion rates (Bank of Canada) for all financial Exhibits 6 to 9: Cdn$1=US$0.96 (Dec. 31, 2009), US$0.79 (Mar. 31, 2009) and US$0.97 (Mar. 31, 2008).

M stands for million.

Source: Company files.

EXHIBIT 7: Consolidated Balance Sheets

	At December 31, 2009 $	At March 31, 2009 $
Assets		
Current assets		
Cash and cash equivalents	7,777,303	713,872
Amounts receivable	595,436	24,423
Share subscription receivable	28,877	—
Prepaid expenses	183,441	47,073
Investment tax credits receivable	553,448	895,113
	9,138,505	1,680,481
Intangible asset	430,460	—
Property and equipment	322,356	345,749
	9,891,321	2,026,230
Liabilities		
Current liabilities		
Accounts payable and accrued liabilities	720,861	550,625
Current portion of long-term debt	67,821	40,829
Deferred revenues	24,000	—
	812,682	591,454
Long-term debt	5,782,959	4,716,521
	6,595,641	5,307,975
Shareholders' equity (deficiency)		
Capital stock	18,730,299	10,770,437
Contributed surplus and other	633,970	489,400
Warrants	136,672	—
Deficit	(16,205,261)	(14,541,582)
	3,295,680	(3,281,745)
	9,891,321	2,026,230

Note: All figures in Canadian dollars (see conversion rates in Exhibit 6 notes).
Source: Company financial statements.

EXHIBIT 8: Consolidated Statements of Loss, Comprehensive Loss and Deficit

	9 months to December 31, 2009 $	12 months to March 31, 2009 $
Revenue	1,420,412	105,830
Expenses		
General and administrative	942,341	1,134,890
Research and development	1,801,982	2,422,189
Business development	365,134	320,795
Stock-based compensation	154,634	259,200
	3,264,091	4,137,074
Loss from operations	(1,843,679)	(4,031,244)
Investment tax credits	180,000	299,000
Net loss and comprehensive loss for the period	(1,663,679)	(3,732,244)
Deficit—Beginning of period	(14,541,582)	(10,809,338)
Deficit—End of period	(16,205,261)	(14,541,582)
Basic and diluted loss per share	(0.05)	(0.12)
Weighted-average shares outstanding	35,473,757	30,288,44

Note: All figures in Canadian dollars (see conversion rates in Exhibit 6 notes).

Revenue figures for 12 months to March 31, 2008 are $244,815.

Source: Company financial statements.

EXHIBIT 9: Consolidated Statements of Cash Flows

	9 months to December 31, 2009 $	12 months to March 31, 2009 $
Cash provided by (used in)		
Operating activities		
Net loss for the period	(1,663,679)	(3,732,244)
Charges to operations not involving cash		
Amortization of intangible asset	16,305	—
Amortization of property and equipment	55,050	95,692
Stock-based compensation	154,634	259,200
Shares issued for professional services	—	34,281
	(1,437,690)	(3,343,071)
Net change in non-cash working capital balances related to operations		
Decrease (increase) in amounts receivable	(281,533)	29,127
Increase in share subscriptions receivable	(28,877)	—
Decrease (increase) in prepaid expenses	(136,368)	125,205
Decrease (increase) in investment tax credits receivable	341,665	(94,988)
Increase in accounts payable and accrued liabilities	170,236	216,992
Increase in deferred revenues	24,000	—
	(1,348,567)	(3,066,735)
Financing activities		
Shares issued for net assets on the reverse take-over	127,511	—
Repayment of employee loan	37,500	—
Proceeds from issuance of capital stock, net of issuance costs	7,747,184	1,482,309
Proceeds from long-term debt	835,101	1,454,475
Repayment of long-term debt	(31,151)	—
Repayment of obligation under capital lease	—	(4,082)
Proceeds from exercise of stock options	174,275	—
	8,890,420	2,932,702
Investing activities		
Acquisition of intangible asset	(446,765)	—
Acquisition of property and equipment	(31,657)	(29,694)
	(478,422)	(29,694)
Net change in cash and cash equivalents during the period	7,063,431	(163,727)
Cash and cash equivalents - Beginning of period	713,872	877,599
Cash and cash equivalents - End of period	7,777,303	713,872
Cash and cash equivalents are comprised of the following:		
Cash on hand and balances (overdrafts) with banks	1,269,506	(86,128)
Short-term investments	6,507,797	800,000
	7,777,303	713,872
Supplementary cash flow information		
Income taxes paid	—	—
Interest paid	3,836	2,737

Note: All figures in Canadian dollars (see conversion rates in Exhibit 6 notes).

Source: Company financial statements.

car2go: Individual Urban Mobility and the Sharing Economy

On December 17, 2012, Nicholas Cole, chief operating officer (CEO) of car2go North America, and Katie Stafford, communications manager for car2go North America, reviewed the latest performance data (see Exhibit 1) of the company's car sharing business in Vancouver. It had been more than 18 months since car2go had launched in Canada. Much had changed since car2go decided to venture into Canada. There was a noticeable presence of car2go cars spread across the greater Vancouver area now, with 325 'smarts,' the German built two-seater micro car (see Exhibit 2). The results had exceeded expectations and were among the best of all of car2go's 18 markets in Europe and North America. The number of new members in Vancouver had reached 15,000. Encouraged by the results, Cole approved the expansion to other Canadian cities including Calgary with its compact downtown but far reaching urban sprawl, and the Toronto metropolitan area, characterized by more than 14 urban sub-centres that merged along their boundaries and included more than 6.2 million inhabitants. Other Canadian cities also offered attractive opportunities for launching car2go service; but the question would now remain—which Canadian city would be the next best fit for car2go? Cole wondered how he and his team should strategically plan for future growth in the Canadian market. Would the company have to modify its operating model to address the different location characteristics? Would the marketing and communications tactics used in Vancouver, Calgary and Toronto be easily replicated in other Canadian markets or would the strategies need to be adapted? Would the existing locations continue to grow and if so, what would be the true market potential?

Dmitry Alenuskin and Andreas Schotter wrote this case solely to provide material for class discussion. The authors do not intend to illustrate either effective or ineffective handling of a managerial situation.

This publication may not be transmitted, photocopied, digitized or otherwise reproduced in any form or by any means without the permission of the copyright holder. Reproduction of this material is not covered under authorization by any reproduction rights organization. To order copies or request permission to reproduce materials, contact Ivey Publishing, Ivey Business School, Western University, London, Ontario, Canada, N6G 0N1; (t) 519.661.3208; (e) cases@ivey.ca; www.iveycases.com.

Copyright © 2014, Richard Ivey School of Business Foundation   Version: 2014-02-11

One time permission to reproduce granted by Richard Ivey School of Business Foundation on April 22, 2014.

IVEY | Publishing

CAR SHARING

Car sharing, also known as car clubs or car co-ops, was introduced as an alternative to full car ownership. After a driving record check, one had first to become a member. Memberships were approved and canceled based on official driving records and good standings in payment of membership fees. For instance, car2go annually reviewed the driving records of its members and could suspend services for members with more than three traffic violations in 24 months.

Members had 24/7 access to the system. Access to cars was usually organized through communities or in collaboration with transit operators, employers or dedicated car sharing facilities.[1] The car sharing model allowed members to enjoy the benefits of a personal vehicle without paying the costs associated with purchasing, maintaining and operating it. Operators charged pay-by-use rates based on the driving time or mileage. Usually, car sharing vehicles had to be returned to designated parking stalls but car2go employed a slightly different system–car2go members could pick any available vehicle using their membership card as an access key, drive it without time constraints and park it anywhere within the service zone (see 'Using car2go' section for more details).

Unlike the traditional car rental business, car sharing did not restrict users to the physical locations of rental car companies as vehicle pick-up and drop off spots. Neither were members restricted by office hours. Exhibit 3 provides an overview of the main differences between car2go and traditional car sharing and car rental services.

Individuals drawn to car sharing tended to be relatively affluent, young (between 25 and 35 years of age) and educated urban residents of densely populated areas with many alternative transportation options. The well-developed infrastructure of such areas did not require this demographic to own cars in the first place in order to go about their daily lives. In fact, low vehicle ownership rates were one of the best predictors of the economic viability of car sharing programs. Key location choice criteria were based on demographics, assessments of the level and characteristics of environmental and social consciousness, and local societal consumer preference changes evidenced by declining social prestige attached to car possession.

Car sharing began in Europe in 1948 when the first car cooperative was organized in Zurich, Switzerland. In 2010, Germany, the United Kingdom and Switzerland held 75 per cent of all 500,000 European car sharing members. In total, Europe had over 200 car sharing organizations with approximately 12,000 vehicles available to members. The largest European car sharing organizations, such as StadMobil and StadtAuto in Germany, Autolib in France, and Mobility in Switzerland, operated as for-profit companies, often in partnership with national railways public transit providers.

Members of traditional car sharing organizations acted as operators, who were in charge of the individual reservations based on Internet or social media friendly mobile applications. Members also had to take care of fueling, cleaning, pick up and returning of vehicles to pre-defined parking stalls or designated zones within the service area. In 2012, Zipcar operated 160 parking locations in Vancouver compared to only eight locations that Enterprise Car Rental company operated. However, Enterprise offered its customers a free pick-up and drop off service to their rental offices. Traditional car sharing models offered various selections of cars and membership terms. The greatest differences were parking locations, model variety, advanced notice for bookings and per usage charges. Membership

---

[1]"Some Carshare Basics," The Commons: Open Society Sustainability Initiative, www.ecoplan.org/carshare/general/basics.htm, accessed July 8, 2012.

terms also varied—some companies asked for a refundable deposit or a registration fee, and some companies had no charges for new members and even offered free driving time.

Although Daimler was the first automotive manufacturer worldwide to offer a car sharing service with car2go, over the past few years, several large car manufacturers have also entered the car sharing business. In 2010, Peugeot launched its "Mu by Peugeot" service in 12 French cities. In 2011, BMW, together with the Sixt Car Rental company, launched a "DriveNow" program in the German cities of Munich, Berlin and Düsseldorf employing a total of 950 Mini Coopers, BMW 1 Series compact cars and X1 Series small utility vehicles at a flat rate of 38 cents a minute. In 2012, BMW launched the same service with 70 electric Active-E vehicles in San Francisco. Volkswagen teamed up with Streetcar, the biggest U.K.-based car sharing company, and supplied the Polo and Golf compact cars, Touran small mini-vans and the larger Transporter van models in 10 cities. In 2009, as a part of Europcar Car Rental company's Zero Emission program, French car manufacturer Renault signed a partnership agreement with the goal to provide a fleet of electric cars to 2,500 European locations for short-term rentals by 2011, but the project was still in the works in 2012 because of the logistic complexities of the car sharing business.

Car manufacturers did not consider car sharing as a threat to their core business of selling cars. Ian Robertson, an executive board member of Bayrische Motoren Werke Corporation (BMW) responsible for sales and marketing, commented:

> As a mobility provider, the BMW Group is not simply an automobile manufacturer. There is a growing demand for flexible mobility products in urban areas. Our DriveNow premium car sharing services are aimed precisely at this gap in the market. We are intending to launch a profitable new line of business while at the same time introducing potential new customers to our brands.[2]

CAR SHARING IN CANADA

Modern car sharing in Canada took off in Quebec in 1994 and then spread to the United States. Due to the lack of existing models, car sharing in Canada during the early years did not receive much governmental support. Moreover, pioneers of Canadian car sharing faced criticism from local transit operators who believed that car sharing might discourage rather than attract riders. As a result, member-to-vehicle ratios, an important metric in the car sharing business, had been growing at a slow pace in Canada as compared to the United States, which is characterized by one of the highest member-vehicle ratios in the world (approximately 49:1). The Canadian member-to-vehicle ratio stood at only 26:1 on average.[3]

car2go in Vancouver was doing much better. For example, it reached ratios of more than 46:1, although this number could be misleading, experts said. Karen New, information systems director of Modo, a car sharing co-operative from Vancouver, said:

> The difficulty with this measure is defining the word 'member'. If you define it as people who have access to your cars, you can drive this ratio as high as you like by

[2]BMW Group and Sixt AG establish DriveNow Joint Venture for premium car sharing, press release, https://www.press.bmwgroup.com/pressclub/p/pcgl/pressDetail.html?outputChannelId=6&id=T0100973EN&left_menu_item=node_2201, accessed July 8, 2012.

[3]S.A. Shaheen, A.P. Cohen and M.S. Chung, "North American Carsharing: A Ten-Year Retrospective," Institute of Transportation Studies, www.escholarship.org/uc/item/8jg510td#page-1, accessed July 8, 2012.

reducing barriers to entry, including very low membership fees. Or you could simply give away memberships and then drive up the ratio with people who have no intentions of using your service regularly. But if you define a 'member' as someone using your vehicles actively, the ratio would be different. It is these active members that you are after.[4]

In 2012, Canada's 17 car sharing operators had more than 60,000 members in total. Eleven of these organizations were member-owned cooperatives. During the prior three years, car sharing memberships had risen by 117 per cent and this growth was expected to continue over the next five to 10 years.

Many Canadian car sharing companies offered roaming memberships, which allowed members of one company to use services from that same company in different cities without incurring additional application or membership fees. Members could use their home key fob to get access to vehicles in other cities, albeit at the specific rates of the respective roaming partners. In 2012, six Canadian, nine American, one Australian and one Brazilian car sharing company had joint roaming agreements. car2go also provided roaming services in Canada, but only within its own local system and, at the time, offered no official roaming membership across borders from Canada to the United States or Europe. Zipcar had no geographic restrictions and offered roaming access for its cars at the same rates in the United States, Canada and the United Kingdom.

AutoShare pioneered car sharing in the Greater Toronto Area (GTA) in 1998. The company had a strong environmental stand and by operating the largest and the greenest fleet of hybrid and electric cars in Ontario, AutoShare strived to provide a shared vehicle within a five minute walk of anywhere in the city, at every Toronto Transit Commission (TTC) station. AutoShare claimed that each of its vehicles eliminated as many as ten privately owned cars on Toronto's roads. According to the company survey, its customers used personal cars only for four per cent of travel needs, and most often members chose alternative transportation or public transit. AutoShare established partnerships with major real estate developers and provided commuting vehicles to residents of 31 apartment complexes and five commercial centers in Toronto. The company was an officially recognized partner of the transportation system of the City of Toronto.[5]

The top five Canadian car sharing companies in 2012 were car2go, Communeauto from Quebec, AutoShare Inc. from Toronto, Modo cooperative from Vancouver, and Zipcar, a U.S. based company with operations in Vancouver and Toronto (see Exhibits 4, 5 and 6).

In June 2010, the rental car company Hertz launched, as an effort to enter the car sharing market with only five cars, a trial hourly rental business in Calgary and Edmonton in collaboration with the University of Alberta and the University of Calgary. Later, Hertz announced plans to equip its entire North American 357,000 vehicle fleet with the technology for short-term rentals by the summer of 2013. Enterprise, the largest U.S. rental car company with 140 locations across Canada, announced plans to enter the now fast growing car sharing market in 2012.

According to autoshare.com, the top 10 car sharing uses in Canada in 2012 were: 1. Business meeting; 2. Grocery shopping; 3. Private meeting; 4. Large items shopping (kitchen appliances, furniture); 5. Personal trips; 6. School drop off/pickup; 7. Driving to the gym; 8. Hockey practice; 9. Rehearsal; and 10. Family visit.

---

[4]Author interview with Karen New.

[5]"The Smart Alternative to Owning a Car," www.autoshare.com/about.html, accessed July 8, 2012.

CAR SHARING BUSINESS MODEL

Car sharing was a hugely data-driven business. Making a booking, driving the car and changing the booking–all these activities generated large amounts of data that needed to be managed. Because it was a self-service business, many touch points with members were automated. Car sharing operators also wanted to ensure that members would have a streamlined and intuitive user experience with as little hassle as possible. The key to success in this business of low margins (most companies operated in the negative 10 per cent to positive 10 per cent gross margin range) depended on the variety of different vehicle options, the availability of designated parking spots and an efficient billing system. An efficient billing system meant that usage prices needed to be as low as possible to encourage frequent usage but at the same time prices needed to be high enough to make most of the individual drives profitable. Calculating the sweet spot was very complex and depended heavily on the urban characteristics of the individual locations. For example, if there was a homogeneous neighborhood where the majority of residents had similar demographics, lifestyles and schedules, they would all need cars at the same time and not spread out evenly over a 24 hour day. Meanwhile, in heterogeneous neighborhoods with different demographics, members would likely have different schedules with different needs for cars, which would help ensure a more even utilization of the service and more billable minutes per day. This would then reduce per drive charges and in turn attract more members.

Per city economics heavily drove the number of employed vehicles and their placement. Operations in densely populated urban areas involved high parking rates and similar use patterns among the target group. Therefore, car sharing operators were most successful in smaller cities, where the average commute time was shorter and vast geography offered various parking opportunities. Strategic placement of available vehicles was another important consideration. An executive of Modo commented:

> Other companies denote the neighborhood, place their cars and then try to create demand for those cars by driving up membership. We place our cars in response to pre-existing demand. Our members join us to use the fleet as it exists, and then, based on where those members live, we can add cars in their neighborhoods to better serve an area. This means that instead of defining a particular neighborhood where we want to be in, we let members define this for us.[6]

Industry per vehicle utilization rates varied widely, ranging between 20 per cent and 60 per cent. Costs were driven by the financing associated with the purchase of the vehicle, parking charges, fuel expenses, repairs and maintenance, administration and general marketing expenses, and insurance premiums.

Per member economics were driven by member acquisition costs, average revenue per user (ARPU), mileage, hours used and collected subscription fees. Many companies had additional surcharges that ranged from paid telephone services for car bookings (Communeauto), fines for late car returns (Zipcar), additional mileage charges (car2go) or upfront deposits, which were used to support vehicle financing (charged at most co-ops). For more detailed information on car sharing costs and revenues see Exhibit 7.

CAR2GO BACKGROUND

The car2go concept was developed, financed and brought to market by Germany's Daimler AG, the parent company of Mercedes-Benz. The idea behind the concept was first

---

[6]Author interview with Phil Baudin, Executive Director, Modo.

introduced in 2007 by Daimler's Business Innovation Department in order to provide on-demand urban mobility solutions based on a citywide free-floating, not rental station-based fleet of vehicles, which members could access at pay-per-minute rates. In 2012, car2go was integrated into Daimler Financial Services, the largest provider of financial services for commercial vehicles worldwide.

Before the first customer roll-out, the concept was tested among employees of the Daimler Research Center in the southern German city of Ulm. The pilot stage launched in October 2008 with 50 cars that were available to 500 employees of Daimler and 200 family members. After six months of gathering data on user acceptance and behaviour, and testing the technical systems, the service was launched to all 120,000 residents of Ulm in March 2009. During the same time period, a U.S. pilot project was launched in Austin, Texas, a city of 750,000 (at the time), where car2go's North American headquarters were established in 2009. Full service to the public in Austin was launched in May 2010.[7]

car2go was well perceived and within three years it had branched out to 18 cities worldwide (see Exhibit 8). In 2012, Daimler announced that it now had more than 300,000 members who had taken advantage of automatic rentals more than three million times. Daimler had plans to expand the program to 50 more European and North American cities through 2017. In every new city, car2go usually employed 250–300 cars.

Vehicle of Choice

car2go initially started with a clear one-vehicle type/one-model strategy, utilizing the smart fortwo, a two-seater micro car–Daimler's smallest vehicle. The smart, an acronym for Swatch Mercedes ART, was the result of a joint venture formed in 1994 between Daimler and the Swiss watchmaker Swatch. Daimler AG began building smarts in Northern France in 1997. The annual capacity of Smartville, the name given to the manufacturing plant for the smart fortwo, was 200,000 cars but it had never reached full production capacity. In 2006, Smart GmbH was restructured and its operations were absorbed within Daimler and partner Swatch was paid out. Altogether, Daimler accumulated U.S.$5 billion[8] in losses on this model between 2003 and 2007.

While initially selling 24,622 units during its U.S. launch in 2008, sales had been declining steadily to only 5,208 for 2011. As in the United States, the Canadian market also did not embrace the Cdn$14,400 sub-compact car. For example, from February to March 2012, Canadians purchased fewer than 100 smarts.[9] Globally, sales dropped from 145,000 units in 2005 to 102,000 units in 2011. Daimler identified the main problem as a distribution issue; hence, in 2012, the company took control of the distribution. From that point on, sales once again grew steadily.

Convinced of the potential of the smart car, Daimler explored alternative business models including its usability for fleet services in urban areas. The smart car was the perfect size for car2go, and the car2go edition was the first factory pre-configured car sharing vehicle in the world. The cars were fitted with intelligent stop-start functions, newly developed telematics and a computerized telecommunications unit that allowed a fully automated rental processes. A solar roof supplied the electrical system

---

[7]A. Osterwalder and Y. Pigneur, *Business Model Generation: A Handbook for Visionaries, Game Changers, and Challengers,* John Wiley & Sons, 2010.

[8]All currencies are in US$ unless otherwise stated.

[9]Smart Fortwo Sales Figures, "Good Car, Bad Car," www.goodcarbadcar.net/2011/01/smart-fortwo-sales-figures.html, accessed July 8, 2012.

with 100 watts of power, which reduced fuel consumption by around 10 per cent. All car2go vehicles were equipped with a touch screen radio and a navigation screen. In addition, the smart fortwo was the perfect size for most trips that were taken in urban areas.

CAR2GO MARKETING AND PROMOTION

car2go used different marketing communication strategies for each city. Depending on the media preferences of the target audience, the location of the popular destination and other specific city attributes, car2go adjusted its press campaigns and launch events. Promotion teams would appear in central venues of the city, grocery stores and on popular street corners to demonstrate the vehicle, to explain the principle of the car sharing service and to encourage people to join on the spot based on free ride minutes and waived joining fees.

For example, for its Washington D.C. launch, in March 2012, car2go chose a catchy advertising campaign "A better way to car share is coming to D.C." placed in Washington newspapers and on "DCist," a popular local Internet blog. The advertisement included the promo code *capital* that waived the $35 application fee and offered 30 free minutes of driving time. car2go organized two launch "Ride and Drive" parties at one of Washington's hippest restaurants. It was announced with the tagline "Join us for free food, promos and swag as we celebrate the launch of a better way to car share."

Successful co-branding was another critical element for car2go promotion. For example, in Vancouver, car2go partnered with IKEA for a member appreciation event. The advertisement featured a picture of a smart packed with furniture from two different IKEA rooms and promised to demonstrate how this fitting worked during the event and to reward new members with shopping sprees and gift cards.

Unlike other car sharing companies, car2go did not invest in extensive continuous marketing campaigns. The print ads and local promotions generated enough interest to match rival Zipcar's popularity. Zipcar was widely regarded as an industry benchmark, with its innovative community-oriented social media campaigns, by giving each individual car a unique name that would create a personality.

car2go was also different in many other ways compared to the competition. Katie Stafford explained:

> We see ourselves as complementary rather than direct competitors to traditional car sharing companies. Our model is very unique in that we focus on bringing the simplest, most convenient and most flexible personal transportation system to entire communities–our model uses exclusively smart fortwo cars–each 'up-fitted' with the most advanced car sharing technology. Members can use the cars on demand without first making a reservation, and they can use the car for a few minutes or a few hours. The vast majority of trips taken in a car2go are one way (meaning members start their trips in one location and end their trips somewhere else), and they last approximately 30 minutes. That said, we are one piece of the larger urban mobility landscape–which typically includes a combination of car2go, public transit, traditional car sharing, peer-to-peer car sharing, bike-sharing and walkable areas. This is the ideal setting for car2go.

car2go focused on making car2go as simple as using one's own car, with the added benefit of universal parking space availability and a walk-up and drive rental model instead of the need for pre-booking like the competition would require. Stafford added:

City authorities appreciate that we only use a very small footprint for our cars. The smart fortwo takes up less space than most other cars, and in some cases, two car2gos can fit into parking spaces that typically host one full size car. Overall, we provide simple, cost-efficient individual transportation for one to two people in and around metropolitan areas. If a customer needs to transport larger goods, or if a person wants to take his or her family out for a long weekend trip or to tour around town, then they may need to rent a car or use a peer-to-peer car sharing service that offers larger vehicles. We embrace this. We know that as cities continue to develop and grow, there must be a healthy mix of transportation options, and we know that we are one very important piece of that mix. We are proud to be part of a generational shift, where technology and economic factors give people instant access to many different methods of sharing. It is a really exciting time.

For example, when I have a special event to go to, I may think about purchasing a new dress. But now, instantaneously, I can browse through thousands of designer dresses at www.renttherunway.com, choose the one that suits my occasion the best, and they'll deliver it to me within a few days. Then, it's mine to wear for that evening, at a very small fraction of the original price, and I just return it within a few days, and suddenly it becomes available for the next person to wear. Or, if my family is visiting Austin, Texas and I don't have enough space for them to stay with me in my small city flat, but I still want my family to feel like they're living like a local, I can rent someone's home for a few days or a week through HomeAway or Air BnB. This is new consumer behaviour, not just a phenomenon. And technology makes sharing–anything–easier today than ever before.

"CUSTOMER–OPERATOR" CONCEPT

In 2012, the "customer–operator" concept was widely used by service and retail companies as a way to improve operational excellence and save costs since customers would not require salaries, benefits or office allocations. For example, by installing self-service terminals, grocery stores put the labour of scanning, packaging, searching for codes for weighted items and processing the payment on the shoulders of customers rather than salaried employees. Banks strongly encouraged customers to pay bills and make transfers online rather than in branches. Under this model, the customer played an active operating role in delivering an integrated service through co-creation. However, customers were not very motivated to participate in a do-it-yourself service if there was no specific financial, experiential or time-saving benefit attached to it.

The car sharing business relied heavily on this concept since it would not be able to match the economies of scale that the big car rental companies had achieved. In the car rental world, economies of scale were critical in order to have sufficient buyer power for purchasing or leasing cars. Among car sharing companies Zipcar operated a model where customer compliance–refueling, cleaning and returning vehicles at specified time–was a critical element of the business system. In cases where customers did not comply with the requirements (i.e., if they returned vehicles later than promised), Zipcar would charge a $35 penalty. To add to the customer compliance element, Zipcar constantly reminded its members that violating the communal obligations of the service would harm other members and would ultimately undermine the overall system. The company often hosted events and introduced customers, whom they empathetically called *zipsters,* to each other. Zipcar's market research showed that from a psychological perspective it was much easier to ruin the experience for some anonymous user than to ruin that of another zipster that the misbehaving customer may have met at the last event.

Although car2go made many efforts to create community involvement among its members, the ability to leave cars wherever a customer liked, plus a standard vehicle and automated check-in process, provided much more individual freedom for car2go users.

CAR2GO RATES

Use of the car2go system cost 38 cents per minute plus applicable local taxes. Cars were also available on an hourly basis for $13.99, which was more economical for rentals that exceeded 38 minutes. A daily rate was available for $72.99. All prices included fuel, insurance and free parking in "residents only" areas or designated car2go parking spots in downtown areas (see Exhibit 9 for a sample invoice).

car2go rates, depending upon how the service would be used by an individual, were comparable to national consumer reports on car ownership expenses. According to the Canadian Automobile Association, the total ownership cost (including fuel, insurance, taxes and financing) per kilometre in 2010 for a Chevrolet Cobalt was 47 cents, for a Dodge Grand Caravan 69 cents and 54 cents for a Toyota Prius. This estimation was based on a four-year ownership period and 18,000 kilometres driven per year.

In the case of an at-fault accident, car2go had a $1,000 deductible, making members financially responsible for minor damage. car2go charged a one-time registration fee of $35, plus taxes, but when entering a new city, the company often waived the registration fee as an incentive to attract new customers. During launches in a new city, car2go also offered 30 free minutes of driving time to new members. In addition, social media sites like Facebook were utilized for marketing purposes that included special contests that frequently awarded free minutes of driving time to winners—ranging from 15 minutes to 500 minutes.

New members could enroll online or at local offices. The minimum age requirement was 18 (with a student ID), and members were required to have three years driving experience and a valid credit card. Members were also responsible for providing car2go with an official driving record from the local licensing authorities. After successfully signing up, each member would receive a membership card and a PIN by mail within five business days.

USING CAR2GO

Operating instructions were simple. A member could use a car2go vehicle either as an instant rental by taking the first available car in the street or by placing a 15-minute advance booking. Available vehicles could be located and booked online (up to 30 minutes in advance) on a computer or through a smart phone application. If the member was late or did not show up for the booking, there would be no penalty. To access a vehicle, a customer had to hold a valid membership RFID (Radio Frequency Identification) card against a reader, which was installed in the windshield area, and after entering the individual membership PIN the member could drive off. A touchscreen inside the car provided a navigation system (which displayed points of interest such as fuel stations and designated car2go parking areas), eight pre-selected radio stations, an EcoScore App to show how efficiently the member was driving and an SOS button that could be used to reach the car2go customer service team 24 hours a day. Extra options were limited. There were no iPod or USB connectors for drivers to use, and at the time, there was no option to scroll through radio stations.

Before starting the engine, the system would ask the driver to assess the cleanliness of the vehicle inside and outside, and report damage. During the ride, the electronic system evaluated on a scale from 0 to 100 how environmentally friendly the driving style was and displayed messages for how to adjust to a more calm and relaxed driving style if the driver's EcoScore was low. car2go encouraged and rewarded safe—and gas-saving—driving among its members. For example, a Facebook contest launched in Vancouver in June 2012 offered 30 minutes of free driving time for posting a picture with the highest EcoScore.

Members could drive car2go vehicles as long as they liked and to whatever location they liked, except for cross-country border destinations. When members wanted to return their car2go, they would park the vehicle in any public parking space or at a car2go designated parking spot located within the designated home area—a city zone covered by car2go service. Otherwise, the rental would simply continue. Usually, the home area included only downtown areas and close-by residential neighborhoods. For example, in Vancouver, car2go served only the central city zone, but not nearby Burnaby, Richmond, or North and West Vancouver.

With the free float system, cars naturally gravitated to where car2go members lived, worked and played. This natural ebb and flow of the cars meant that, at times, there would be a concentration of cars in certain neighborhoods; for example, those that were popular for dining and entertainment. In Vancouver and in all car2go cities, the company employed a fleet team who would monitor the use of the 300+ car fleet. The car2go fleet team would ensure that cars were not staying in one area for too long (after 24 hours, if a car had not moved, the company would relocate the car to popular areas for car2go members).

As the volume of members increased and as usage of the service increased, car2go worked to expand the home area when needed and eventually added additional cars to accommodate growth and demand. This was a careful balancing act, since more cars meant higher fixed costs but also greater revenue potential, while a greater number of fleet team employees would mean higher variable costs but a more flexible buffering per vehicle utilization.

Availability was critical, as a loyal member explained when she canceled her car2go membership after nine months:

> In general, car2go was a good experience—cheap to use and cheap to join. But then I noticed that too many people in my home area used car2go, and there were not enough cars available in the morning. When I wear a business outfit for a meeting and sometimes have to walk ten blocks for the nearest car—forget it, I'll take a cab. [10]

Although she enjoyed the bean-shaped smart and its parking ease, this former member decided to buy a pre-owned compact car instead. She explained:

> For me, a car is just a convenience, a commodity, so I go with the more practical option although, averaging only $20 per month, car2go was much cheaper for me than owning a car, which costs me now about $140 after everything is accounted for. I still take public transportation frequently.[11]

DECISION

Cole spent a few days reviewing the results of the Vancouver operations. Everything pleased him including: high utilization rates, great reserved parking arrangements, and a monitoring and communication system that worked without any glitches. Cole's main dilemma was to

---

[10]Author interview with Sohee Lim, former car2go member.
[11]Ibid.

decide which city to choose next for the company's Canadian expansion. Montreal had an established car sharing business with Communeauto's fleet of 1,150 cars. Edmonton and Winnipeg offered low competition, along with attractive income levels. Victoria, with its large student population, limited public transportation and long distances between island cities, had good growth potential but might require some adjustments to rates and home area definition. Ottawa was another interesting destination to consider. Along with the location decision, Cole had to decide what kind of marketing strategies car2go should deploy to ensure the launch of the program would be a success in the next Canadian city. Cole knew that he had to move quickly since rental giants Hertz and Enterprise were looking actively into joining the growing car sharing business. In early 2013, Avis acquired Zipcar. car2go was on a mission to change modern urban transportation and Cole and his team were prepared to lead the way (see Exhibit 10).

EXHIBIT 1: car2go Operations in Vancouver. 2012 Results

Number of members (growing constantly)	21,000 +
Number of vehicles (growing with membership growth)	400
Utilization rate	21%
Number of parking pads (and recently expanded home zone)	52 (+ free floating)
Average trip duration in minutes	30
Total revenue (case writer estimation)	$4,500,000
Fee revenue (case writer estimation)	15%
Vehicle usage revenue (case writer estimation)	85%

Source: Case writers and company data.

EXHIBIT 2: Smart Fortwo Coupé

The smart fortwo started production in 2006 as the second generation of the rear-engine two-passenger car first introduced by Smart GMBH in 1998. The inception of smart created a new group in car classification—city microcars.

The smart suited urban environments: with a width of 1.5 metres, a height of 1.5 metres and a length of only 2.5 metres, this car had a remarkably small turning circle of 8.5 metres (compared to 10.6 metres for MINI and 10 metres for Toyota Yaris). The European Union rated the smart mileage as one of the best: at 4.7 litres/100 kilometres (60 miles per imperial gallon; 50 miles per U.S. gallon) for the gasoline model and 3.4 litres/100 kilometres (83 miles per imperial gallon; 69 miles per U.S. gallon) for the diesel version. Recently, an all-electric version was introduced.

The smart fortwo was one of the lightest cars on the market, with a weight of only 730 kilograms, and its rigid steel frame, marketed as the 'Tridion safety cell,' surrounded and protected the riders. However, according to ADAC crash test reports, smart fortwo (3 Stars Rating) was behind Fiat 500, Honda Jazz and Toyota Yaris (5 Stars Rating for all three models) in terms of safety.

The Canadian manufacturer's suggested retail price (MSRP) for smart fortwo was $14,400 for the coupe version and $20,500 for the cabriolet. The high performance Brabus versions of the fortwo sold for $20,900 and $23,900 respectively. In 2012, Vancouver retailers offered two years of free gas with the purchase of the fortwo model.

Source: Daimler Global Media; Daimler AG spells the 'smart' model name in lowercase.

EXHIBIT 3: Car Sharing Vs. Car Rental

	Car Sharing	Car Rental
Basic proposition	Alternative to car ownership for people who don't use cars often	Cars for business trips, vacations or insurance replacement
Customers	Urban dwellers and commuters; campus students and faculty	Business and leisure travelers; owners getting their cars repaired; some local residents
Usage model	Membership/community based	Transactional
Car locations	Dispersed throughout urban centers, neighborhoods and campuses	Central depots at airports and other geographic hubs
Access to vehicles	Online, mobile apps; car doors opened using smartcards or smartphones; 24/7	Counters, keys, contracts, store hours
Pricing	All-inclusive pricing with parking, insurance and gas included for first 180 miles	Gas and insurance options sold separately
Reservation duration	By the minute, hour or by the day; majority of reservations are hourly, not daily	By the day, multi-day or week

Source: Zipcar presentation by Scott Griffith, Zipcar's Chairman & Chief Executive Officer at Jefferies Global TMT Conference, May 7, 2012; http://files.shareholder.com/downloads/ABEA-48TM4M/0x0x566810/8c39190c-285d-480c-8176-c1d778fa9e39/Jefferies_May_7_2012_FINAL.pdf&sa=U&ei=qfGZUt6tLeWu4QSmz4HACw&ved=0CCcQFjAC&sig2=n4BKoWW85pNAYu61eakkyg&usg=AFQjCNEyPmRX9M1OnDKbFoxvmLM3_vK6bw, accessed December 15, 2012.

EXHIBIT 4: Top 3 Car Sharing Operators (CSO) In Canada

Auto-Com	Modo	Zipcar
• The first Canadian co-op car sharing service established in Quebec City in August 1994. In September 1995, the same owners established Communeauto Inc. in Montreal.	• Previously known as the Cooperative Auto Network (CAN), Modo was founded in Vancouver, British Columbia in 1997 with just two cars and 16 members. Modo was the second oldest car sharing organization in North America and the first that started using online booking.	• Established in 2000 in Cambridge, Massachusetts, Zipcar is the membership leader in the North American car sharing industry with over 200,000 members.
• Communeauto was started as a for-profit business, and in June 1997, it merged with Auto-Com. As a result of the deal, the merged company serviced Montreal and Quebec City, had 44 vehicles and 596 members.	• Operated as a local not-for-profit member-owned co-operative, in 2012, Modo had over 9,000 members sharing more than 275 vehicles at 200 locations throughout Vancouver. TransLink, Vancouver's regional transportation authority, supported Modo through the provision of designated parking pads at select stations along Vancouver's rapid transit line.	• Zipcar launched in Toronto in September 2006 and in Vancouver in April 2007. By 2012, the company operated 131 vehicles in Vancouver and 450 in Toronto and had over 15,000 members in Canada. Zipcar offered more than 25 different cars, including high-end vehicles such as MINI Coopers and BMW's 3 Series.
• In December 2011, Communeauto had a fleet of 1,154 vehicles and 24,684 members in four cities (Montreal, Sherbrooke, Quebec and Gatineau). The company reported that the vehicles had utilization rate of 50% (i.e., 12 hours per day).[2]	• The City of Vancouver also provided special "Modo-car only" parking stalls in densely populated neighborhoods. Like Communeauto, Modo paid fees to the city for parking permits for all of its vehicles.[13] Parking expenses varied depending on the location of the parking pod. Phil Baudin, Modo's executive director, explained: "In neighborhoods like downtown Yaletown, which has very little parking space because of the design of existing buildings, we can pay upwards of $500 per month. Outside of the core areas of Vancouver, though, parking can be available at $30 a month."	• Zipcar used a gender-neutral term 'zipster' to describe its members as those who believe in cost-efficient transportation solutions that are "good for the planet and easy on the wallet."
• Zipcar went public in 2011 although the business had only one profitable quarter since it began operating. Zipcar had never had a profitable quarter prior to its $100 million worth IPO last spring.[14] In 2011, Zipcar posted a net loss of $7.2 million, down from $14.1 million in 2010[15]. So far, the company has accumulated losses of $65.4 million[16], and reported another loss of $3 million in the first quarter of 2012. Since the IPO in April 2011, the company stock price has dropped from $31 to less than $10 in May 2012.

Source: Case writers' summary based on company information from www.modo.coop, accessed January 1, 2013; www.zipcar.ca, accessed January 15, 2013; www.communauto .com, December 15, 2012.

EXHIBIT 5: Car Sharing Operators in Canada as of Early 2013

Firm	Established	Cities	Ownership	Number of Members	Number of Vehicles	Parking Stalls
1. Communeauto	1994	Quebec, QB Montreal, QB Sherbrooke, QB Gatineau, QB	For-profit	24,684	1,154	94 Quebec 333 Montreal 13 Sherbrooke 15 Gatineau
2. Zipcar	2007	Vancouver, BC Toronto, ON	For-profit	4,000 Vancouver 11,000 Toronto	131 Vancouver 450 Toronto	160 Vancouver 200 Toronto
3. AutoShare	1998	Toronto, ON	For-profit	12,000	300	150
4. car2go	2011	Vancouver, BC	For-profit	20,000+ Vancouver	325	52 (+free floating)
	2012	Toronto, ON		12,000+	325	167
	2012	Calgary, AB		Toronto18,000+ Calgary	300	39
5. Modo	1997	Vancouver, BC	Co-op	9,000	275	200
6. Vrtucar	2000	Ottawa, ON Gatineau, QB	For-profit	1,800	100	72
7. Victoria Car Share	1996	Victoria, BC	Co-op	575	22	20
8. Green Earth Coop	1998	Kingston, ON	Co-op	550	20	N/A
9. Kootenay Carshare	2001	Kootenay area, BC	Co-op	220	20	0
10. Grand River Carshare & Hamilton Carshare	1998	Kitchener, ON Cambridge, ON Hamilton, ON	Co-op	225	5 Waterloo 9 Kitchener 4 Hamilton	N/A
11. Nanaimo Carshare	2010	Nanaimo, BC	Co-op	N/A	2	0
12. Options for Cars	2009	Toronto, ON	Co-op	230	11	8
13. PegCity Car Co-op	2011	Winnipeg, MB	Co-op	103	4	4
14. Regina Car Share	2008	Regina, SK	Co-op	30	1	1
15. Hertz on Demand	2010	Edmonton, AB Calgary, AB	For-profit	N/A	3 Edmonton 2 Calgary	5
16. Calgary Carshare		Calgary, AB	Co-op	270	8	N/A
17. Carshare HFX	2008	Halifax, NS	Co-op	N/A	20	17

Source: Case writers' summary based on information from company websites.

EXHIBIT 6: Membership Terms of Top Three Canadian Car Sharing Operators (Prices in Cdn$, Not Including Local Taxes) as of January 2013

	car2go	Zipcar	Modo
Sign-up fee	$35 + $2 insurance annual fee	$65 annual fee $25 application fee	$20
Deposit	None	None	$500 (refundable purchase of co-op shares)
Rates	$0.38/minute $13.99/hour $72.99/day	$8–$15.50/hour (Mo-Fri) $8.75–$16.75/hour (weekend) $72–$102/day (Mo-Fri) $88–$118/day (weekend) • Lowest rate is for hybrid vehicles, highest for a BMW. • Lower rates available for prepaid plans	$0.40/kilometre for the first 35kilometre $0.25/kilometre for each additional kilometre up to 150kilometre $0.15/kilometre after that $7.50/hour or $60/day rate applies for Casual Membership plan (no deposit, $50 annual fee)
Extras	• $0.45/kilometre after 200 kilometres per rental • No fee for late/no-show for reservations • $1,500 unauthorized drivers fee • $25—$50 unauthorized parking • $50 cleaning charge (i.e., pet hair) • $50 unlocked car • $25 drained battery • $25 declined credit card • $400 lost key	• $0.30/kilometre after 200 kilometres per rental ($0.40 for BMW) • $55 for additional driver to the account • $750 accident fee • $35/hour for late returns • $30 gas left below ¼ tank • $3.50 agent reservation charge • $165 any violation fee	• $2 administration fee for the first three bookings • $20 referral credit • Extra gas surcharge, once gas is over $1.10/litre • $25 for late returns • $6—$15 cancelations/no show for booking fee • $35 unlocked car • $500 if the car is stolen • $10 gas left below ¼ tank • Smoking in vehicle = membership termination • $25 insufficient funds fee • $50 if vehicle is taken without reservation
Typical trip cost (3 hours, 38 kilometres)	• $40 (the average rental for car2go was just 30 minutes due to the flexibility that the free-floating system allowed for).	• $46	• $36
Fleet	smart fortwo	Hybrid, SUVs, premium (25 models)	Compact cars, electric vehicles, trucks, minivans

Note: The fee structure for other coops and for-profit companies is similar, with minor differences in rates and extra charges.

Source: Company information, www.carsharingtoronto.com, December 15, 2012.

EXHIBIT 7: Vehicle Unit Economics (Per Vehicle)

Average Capital Cost	$20,000
Revenue/Month	$ 2,000
Cost/Month (Ex. depreciation)	$ 1,000
Proceeds on Sale	$ 10,000
Marketing Cost (50 members/Vehicle)	$ 2.200
Internal Rate of Return (no financing)	39%
Internal Rate of Return (financing 65% at 5% borrowing rate)	81%

Source: Zipcar presentation by Scott Griffith, Zipcar's Chairman & Chief Executive Officer at Jefferies Global TMT Conference, May 7, 2012.; http://files.shareholder.com/downloads/ABEA-48TM4M/0x0x566810/8c39190c-285d-480c-8176-c1d778fa9e39/Jefferies_May_7_2012_FINAL.pdf&sa=U&ei=qfGZUt6tLeWu4QSmz4HACw&ved=0CCcQFjAC&sig2=n4BKoWW85pNAYu61eakkyg&usg=AFQjCNEyPmRX9M1OnDKbFoxvmLM3_vK6bw, accessed December 15, 2012.

EXHIBIT 8: car2go Locations

Location	Number of Members	Number of Vehicles	Launch Date
1. Vancouver, Canada	21,000	400	June 2011
2. Calgary, Canada	15,000	300	July 2012
3. Toronto, Canada	10,000	325	June 2012
4. Austin, U.S.A.	20,000	300	May 2010
5. Miami, U.S.A.	7,000	240	July 2012
6. Portland, U.S.A.	3,000	250	March 2012
7. San Diego, U.S.A.	6,000	300 (electric drive)	November 2011
8. Seattle, U.S.A.	8,000	350	December 2012
9. Washington D.C., U.S.A.	1,800	200	March 2012
10. Birmingham, U.K.	Not launched yet	250	Fall 2012
11. London, U.K.	5,000	500	December 2012
12. Amsterdam, Netherlands	2,500	300	November 2011
13. Lyon, France	Service suspended	200	February 2012
14. Berlin, Germany	8,000	1,200	April 2012
15. Dusseldorf, Germany	4,000	300	February 2012
16. Hamburg, Germany	10,000	300	February 2011
17. Ulm, Germany	21,000	300	October 2008
18. Cologne, Germany	5,000	350	September 2012
19. Vienna, Austria	7,000	500	December 2011

Notes: car2go service in Lyon, France was suspended due to a trademark dispute. car2go offers electric vehicles in San Diego. All information retrieved December 15, 2012.

Source: Company information, case writer's estimate.

EXHIBIT 9: car2go Sample Invoice

car2go	Trip Start	Destination	Distance (KM)	Time d:h:m	Net (C$)	HST (C$)	Total (C$)
854WDR	W 10th Ave 24, V5Y Vancouver 11.18.2012 4:46 PM	Nelson St 1177, V6E Vancouver	4.00	00:00:20	7.60	0.91	8.51
Total Amount					7.60	0.91	8.51

Source: Casewriter's own material.

EXHIBIT 10: Canada: Large Cities Comparison

	Calgary	Toronto	Montreal	Edmonton	Ottawa	Winnipeg
Population (metropolitan area)	1.2 million	6.2 million	3.5 million	1.15 million	0.93 million	0.61 million
Urban density	1,554.8 per square kilometre	4,149 per square kilometre	4,438 per square kilometre	1,186 per square kilometre	1,724 per square kilometre	1,365 per square kilometre
Area	726 square kilometres	630 square kilometres	365 square kilometres	684 square kilometres	512 square kilometres	464 square kilometres
Share of population age 15–64	72%	70%	68%	70%	68%	65%
Median family income	$89,490	$68,110	$67,010	$87,930	$81,040	$72,050
Registered vehicles per 1,000 people	780	470	380	560	410	510
Universities	3	5	4	5	2	3

Source: Statistics Canada, www.statcan.gc.ca, accessed December 15, 2012.

Sawchyn Guitars: Can an Old Business Learn New Tricks?

"So . . . this is it. What do you think?" Peter Sawchyn hesitantly asked his family as they surveyed the vacant commercial space available for rent in the warehouse district of downtown Regina, Saskatchewan. It was December 24, 2011, and his children were all home for Christmas. As the sole proprietor of Sawchyn Guitars, makers of fine handmade guitars and mandolins, Sawchyn had decided to ask for his family's input regarding the move he and his wife were considering, which would uproot his 40-year-old business from its home on the second floor of their backyard garage to this spacious, open and sunny new location on one of the city's main streets. Although Sawchyn had been quietly contemplating such a move for several years, this space was the first he had seen that had the right combination of a great location, a welcoming feel, just the right size and an affordable price. Finding the space had made him aware that it might actually be possible to realize his vision of his business as a full-service haven for the local guitar and mandolin musical community. Knowing how unexpected such a move would be for the 57-year-old lifelong entrepreneur, he was anxious to hear what his family thought of such a surprising–and risky–idea. If Sawchyn was really serious about this opportunity, he knew he would need to act quickly to lease the space and update his business model.

SAWCHYN GUITARS

Looking over the empty warehouse space with his family, Sawchyn reflected on the unplanned route he had taken to arrive at this point. With an interest and aptitude for woodworking but no formal training in instrument-making, Sawchyn had begun by

IVEY | Publishing

Meredith Woodwark and Matthew Wong wrote this case solely to provide material for class discussion. The authors do not intend to illustrate either effective or ineffective handling of a managerial situation. The authors may have disguised certain names and other identifying information to protect confidentiality.

This publication may not be transmitted, photocopied, digitized or otherwise reproduced in any form or by any means without the permission of the copyright holder. Reproduction of this material is not covered under authorization by any reproduction rights organization. To order copies or request permission to reproduce materials, contact Ivey Publishing, Ivey Business School, Western University, London, Ontario, Canada, N6G 0N1; (t) 519.661.3208; (e) cases@ivey.ca; www.iveycases.com.

Copyright © 2013, Richard Ivey School of Business Foundation   Version: 2013-08-23

One time permission to reproduce granted by Richard Ivey School of Business Foundation on April 22, 2014.

repairing instruments when he was a teenager and had built his first instrument from scratch, a dulcimer, more than 40 years earlier. He had spent many years studying the design and construction of great instruments to learn about the construction characteristics that resulted in particular acoustic qualities. Today, he was the proud maker of instruments for many of Regina's most recognized musicians who played his instruments all over the world, including Canadian Music Hall of Famer and six-time Juno Award-winner Colin James and two of Canada's most acclaimed finger-style guitarists, Joel Fafard and Bob Evans, winner of the U.S. National Fingerstyle Guitar Championship. His custom instruments had been in demand internationally for the better part of three decades due to his focus on sound quality and craftsmanship. Not bad, he thought, for a business built from raw talent, perseverance and a keen interest in folk music and operated out of his backyard shop. Dedicating one's life to being a luthier (makers of stringed instruments) in a small city like Regina was a modest living, but between the two of them, he and his wife, Kendra, a retail manager, had been able to provide for themselves and their two children while Peter had pursued his passion for instrument-making.

In the modern disposable consumer culture, the business of handmade instruments harkened back to an age of true craftsmanship. As Sawchyn explained on his original website:

> Instrument making is an exacting process that involves a clear understanding of structure and acoustics in relation to the physical properties of wood. With this in mind, I personally carry out each step of a Sawchyn instrument construction, from selecting the wood, carving and voicing the top, to polishing out the finish and setting the action. This personal attention ensures a high degree of detail is present in each instrument I build.[1]

Although some luthiers had incorporated computerized machinery into their production in an effort to increase efficiency, Sawchyn had elected to keep his instruments free from computerized numerical control machining, or "CNC-free," opting instead to make all of the wooden components of his instruments entirely by hand. See Exhibit 1 for examples of the various stages of guitar production.

Rather than focus on producing more instruments, his strategy was to keep his production small and to focus on producing exceptionally high quality. Whereas some luthiers emphasized the external décor and finish of an instrument, Sawchyn elected to place particular emphasis on the internal construction of the instrument while still providing a beautiful finish. Consequently, his instruments particularly appealed to serious musicians for whom the unique sound of a particular instrument was of paramount importance. Over the years, Sawchyn had developed the rare ability to listen to musicians' description of the distinctive sound they were seeking in an instrument, and then be able design and construct an instrument that delivered that sound quality. Depending on the requirements of the customer, each instrument took between 60 and 80 hours of painstakingly detailed work to complete. The effusive testimonials on Sawchyn's website attested to his customers' delight with the products of his efforts. The result of his approach to instrument-making was clearly evident in the final instruments: "Guitars that respond to a subtle touch or a heavy attach, yet keep clarity and definition in their tonal character, and mandolins that respond quickly and evenly with power and grace."[2] The excellent playability and responsiveness

---

[1]Sawchyn Guitars, "About Sawchyn Guitars," www.sawchyn.com/index.php/about, accessed January 11, 2012.

[2]Ibid.

of his instruments had attracted the attention of many true musicians, both amateur and professional, who sought out and appreciated the attention to detail in Sawchyn guitars.

PRODUCT OFFERINGS

The Sawchyn product offering consisted of two main product lines: acoustic guitars and mandolins. Acoustic guitars were either classical, flamenco, standard or signature models, all of which could be custom ordered with a range of upgrades and accessories. Altogether, Sawchyn had a total of 23 guitar models that could be ordered, including 12 standard models, four signature models (including 1 twelve-string guitar and the SSD-83CJ "Colin James" model), three classical models and four flamenco models. Base guitar prices ranged from $2,920[3] for two standard models–the SD-83 designed after the famous dreadnought guitar and the SW-83 in the Hawaiian guitar style–to $8,150 for the JA-84, a classic jazz archtop guitar. See Exhibit 2 for Sawchyn's posted price list.

Although handmade guitar makers were rare, Sawchyn had also cultivated his skills in mandolin making. Though the mandolin was not as popular as the guitar, it had enjoyed a resurgence in the late 1990s and early 2000s during the rise of the Celtic Tiger when the Irish economy was booming, as Celtic music used mandolins extensively. During that period, instrument makers had experienced some difficulty keeping up with demand. Sawchyn Guitar's product offerings included an unusually broad collection of mandolin models, including traditional mandolins, mandolas, octave mandolins, mando-cellos, Irish bouzoukis and Beaver Tail mandolins, Sawchyn's own brand of entry-level handmade mandolins. See Exhibit 3 for the Beaver Tail brand logo and tagline "Best by a Dam Site." Like the guitars, mandolins could be custom ordered and upgraded to the customer's specifications. Mandolin prices ranged from $899 for the AN-83 Beaver Tail to $5,980 for an S-5 scroll-style traditional mandolin.

All of Sawchyn's instruments were numbered and sold under the name Sawchyn Guitars, with the exception of the flamenco-style guitars, which were sold under the guitar maker's full name, Peter Allan Sawchyn, in accordance with the Spanish guitar-making tradition. Despite being far from the regions of the world with strong traditions in handmade guitar design and construction, Sawchyn had developed the expertise to build instruments that were praised as being "as good" as the famous but rare classic vintage Martin and Gibson guitars.[4]

Sawchyn Guitars was one of approximately half a dozen custom guitar makers in the province of Saskatchewan, although some were not direct competitors, as they produced bass guitars or electric guitars.[5] The province did not have another handmade mandolin maker. Canada had approximately two dozen custom acoustic guitar makers, with most located in Ontario.[6] The country had far fewer mandolin makers–likely fewer than half a dozen, although an exact number was difficult to obtain. With the advent of Internet shopping, however, geographic borders had become less of a constraint to finding the perfect guitar maker when commissioning an instrument. Sawchyn had shipped many instruments internationally, particularly to the United States, Ireland and the United Kingdom. Internationally,

---

[3]All currencies are shown in Canadian dollars unless otherwise noted.

[4]Brian Bowman, "World Class Instruments Hand-made on Dewdney Avenue," *BuzzCity Magazine*, http://www. buzzcity.ca/SawchynGuitars.html, accessed February 3, 2013.

[5]Hotfrog, "Businesses for Guitar in SK," http://www.hotfrog.ca/Products/Guitars/SK, accessed February 3, 2013.

[6]Harmony Central, Acoustic Guitar Forum, http://www.harmonycentral.com/t5/Acoustic-Guitars/bd-p/ acapella-42, accessed February 3, 2013.

there were roughly 130 handmade guitar manufacturers worldwide, including the custom-build departments of international guitar giants Gibson and Martin.[7] Once again, mandolin makers were far fewer internationally than guitar makers.

In Regina, three music stores in the city sold instruments. Long & McQuade, a national chain of music stores, provided a broad selection of entry to mid-range instruments. In cities where Long & McQuade located a store, it typically set the market price, and other stores generally followed. Long & McQuade was the big-box store of the music industry, the superstore of music stores. Regina also had two small independent music stores, B-Sharp Music, which specialized in electric guitars and instrument rentals, and St. John's Music, which specialized in band instruments.

CHANGES OVER 40 YEARS

Over the 40 years that Sawchyn Guitars had been in business, Peter Sawchyn had witnessed a dramatic shift in terms of customers' awareness of their instrumental options. In the 1970s, when he had started, few people except professional musicians were aware of the option to purchase a handmade guitar, let alone recognized the difference in quality between a handmade guitar and a factory-produced guitar. Over time, customer awareness of the handmade option had grown to the point where even the large factory producers had launched their own handmade options to meet the demand for these unique instruments. As in other industries, the guitar manufacturing business had seen several trends since the 1970s, in terms of the popularity of models, sizes and characteristics, and in the rise of new products to meet changes in artistic styles, such as the rise of the fingerstyle guitar.

In addition to stylistic changes, Sawchyn had seen dramatic economic and environmental changes that had affected his business. During the early years, when the Canadian dollar was well below the American dollar, sales from the United States had been a large part of his business because the exchange rate offered American customers a 20 to 35 per cent discount. Now, with the Canadian dollar at or above par for several years, that advantage had been lost; consequently, his American sales of guitars and mandolins had fallen sharply. Further, those instruments he did ship to the United States were now subject to more stringent import rules for exotic woods and décor materials, thereby limiting both the types of materials available for those instruments and the desirability of purchasing those instruments outside of the United States.

Almost coincident with the decline of American economic fortunes around 2008, the fortunes of the province of Saskatchewan rose significantly, driven by the demand for natural resources such as potash and natural gas. By 2011, Saskatchewan boasted the lowest unemployment rate in Canada at 4.5 per cent, while Regina tied with Guelph, Ontario, for the lowest unemployment rate in the country at 4.7 per cent, and another Saskatchewan city, Saskatoon, was in fourth place at 5.1 per cent.[8] According to the Saskatchewan government, the strong employment trend in the province meant that in the fall of 2011 there were "more people working full time than ever before in the province's history."[9] The province's Advanced Education, Employment and Immigration Minister, Rob Norris, declared in 2011:

---

[7]Electric Guitar King, "Other Handmade Guitar Manufacturers," http://www.electricguitarking.com/Handmade-Guitar-Manufacturers.asp, accessed February 3, 2013.

[8]Government of Saskatchewan, "Saskatchewan Unemployment Rate Drops to 4.5 Per Cent–Lowest in Canada," news release, September 9, 2011, http://www.gov.sk.ca/news?newsId=a25a6047-e928-4fe2-92fc-435f16e6ab3f, accessed February 10, 2013.

[9]Ibid.

Saskatchewan is probably the best place to be in North America right now. . . . Saskatchewan leads all provinces in several economic indicators including housing starts, value of building permits, retail and wholesale trade and manufacturing shipments. No wonder Saskatchewan business owners are among the most optimistic in the country.[10]

The strong economic standing of the local area was a far cry from the 1980s, when Saskatchewan was considered a "have-not" province, and few in the local community other than professional musicians would have paid a premium for a custom, handmade instrument. Today, people both in Regina and more broadly in Saskatchewan had money to spend, and they were seeking interesting, unique luxury items to spend it on.

THE CHALLENGES

Although things were looking rosy in the local consumer market, Sawchyn didn't feel well positioned to take advantage of the region's good fortunes. Because the vast majority of his business was from online orders for customers outside of the city, he had continued to run his business out of the two-storey garage in his backyard since he hadn't had a need for a public face to Sawchyn Guitars. Although his local customers would come to his shop on the second floor where he constructed all his instruments, most customers relied on his website and on word of mouth as their sources of information about his business. Consequently, Sawchyn had continued to operate out of his small garage.

Because of the space constraints in the garage, Sawchyn's production was spread across two storeys, which meant frequent trips up and down the stairs for materials and equipment. The space was dark and crowded with instruments in various stages of construction, and others that had been purchased for refurbishment or consignment stored wherever room was available. As a result, Sawchyn was unable to accommodate frequent requests for instrument repairs since he had little extra space to store any additional instruments. Early on in his business, Sawchyn had operated a healthy repair business but had stopped the repair work so he could focus his time and space on custom orders. He also had nowhere to store instrument accessories that customers needed for their new instruments, such as extra strings, straps and cases, so he sent customers to other stores for these products. The layout of production necessitated by the space constraints limited any production innovation because he had insufficient room to develop new models to add to his range of products. As he continued to master his instruments, Sawchyn felt the need to grow as an instrument maker by continuing to pursue new challenges, but felt unable to do so because of the current space restrictions.

His shop had served him well for many decades but Sawchyn was beginning to realize how his lack of workspace was limiting his business's growth and new opportunities in the vibrant economic climate. He was aware of greater demand for repairs, accessories and the consignment of vintage guitars. He also suspected that his custom-order business would benefit from providing a more customer-friendly public face to the people of the city and, more widely, people across the province who were quickly becoming the base of his clientele. He also knew that, as a craftsman, he needed to continue to grow and develop, even after four decades of mastering his craft.

----

[10]Ibid.

THE POTENTIAL OPTIONS

The Sawchyns had periodically discussed the idea of acquiring a new space for the workshop to take advantage of some of these opportunities. They had even gone so far as to view several rental spaces over the years, but had never found a space that they liked enough to seriously consider. Their indecision in part reflected their uncertainty about what kind of space they were looking for: just a new workshop or a retail store location. In many ways, a bigger workshop space with a more efficient layout and more storage capacity would be sufficient to meet most of Sawchyn's immediate needs. This option would also resolve his production issues and allow him to again take on repairs and pursue challenging new projects.

Although he had seriously considered the new workshop route, he had never acted on it, in part because, despite a new space resolving his production challenges, he had a lingering feeling that such a move would leave many other opportunities on the table. Sawchyn had long been attracted to the idea of having a proper music store where he could sell his instruments and provide related products such as instrument accessories and related services such as repairs. Due to his connections in the music industry, he often found himself with great opportunities to either consign rare vintage instruments or to buy and restore them. He felt he might one day have an opportunity to combine all of these products and services into one fantastic music store. Sawchyn had given much thought to what the right store space would look like and how he would adapt his business to develop the full suite of product and service offerings that his customers wanted: custom-ordered handmade instruments, retail instrument accessories, consignment of vintage instruments and instrument repairs. His personal dream for the final decade of Sawchyn Guitars was to be able to provide all those products and services in a welcoming, community-friendly environment where musicians could have all their instrument needs met under one roof.

But Sawchyn's expertise was instruments not business management, and he was unsure what would be the best option for him. Perhaps he should consider putting more effort into marketing his custom work through more promotion online. He maintained a decent website and tried to keep an online presence, but he hadn't devoted much time to developing an online marketing strategy. If he increased his orders enough, he might be able to offset the extra cost of a new workshop that would help him produce more efficiently. Also, maybe the time had come to realize that his stance on CNC-free instruments was overly limiting his throughput. On the other hand, perhaps instead of increasing capacity and sales, he should consider increasing his prices. He had always been careful to keep his prices lower than those of comparable-quality products as he built up his brand in the industry. Perhaps it was time to start reaping credit for superior quality and 40 years of expertise by reflecting those qualities in his prices. If he could get away with lower volume sales at higher prices maybe he didn't need a new workshop after all. With all these possibilities on his mind and no clear winning strategy, Sawchyn had simply continued managing with the status quo set-up.

THE OPPORTUNITY

One night in late 2011, Sawchyn and his wife learned through a friend about a retail space on Dewdney Avenue that might be attractive to them. It was on the main floor of an old warehouse building that had been renovated and converted into condominiums. The martial arts school that had previously operated on the site had been closed for about a year, and the space was just sitting empty. They heard that the landlord was not actively looking for a renter but might be interested in a stable tenant that would not attract heavy customer traffic, thereby not adding to the location's current parking and noise problems.

As life would have it, earlier that year, Sawchyn's wife, Kendra, had been laid off from her job at the RCMP Heritage Centre. Since then, she had been working several part-time jobs but was finding it difficult to secure full-time work appropriate for her skills and experience. She had experience in several retail management jobs over the past few decades, including at Superstore and Eddie Bauer. She had also tried her hand at running a small gift shop business in the 1980s. Kendra had been thinking about new business opportunities for herself, including opening a restaurant, but had recognized that she would be facing a very steep learning curve on such a venture. While she pursued more rewarding work, it had occurred to them that maybe they should invest in developing Sawchyn Guitars by combining Peter's existing business with Kendra's retail and managerial experience. Perhaps with their combined concerted attention and the investment of time and money, they could work on realizing Peter's vision of a full-service music store.

As they peered in the window of the empty rental space, the location appeared to meet all their criteria. It was on a busy, well-known street and had an attractive entrance that faced the street with parking on the side. At 2,400 square feet, it was roughly the size they had imagined. Even better, it was within three to four blocks of the major music store competition, Long &McQuade, and was surrounded by the popular bars and restaurants frequented by local musicians.

Driving home that night, they discussed the idea and decided to try to view the inside of the space as soon as possible. If they liked the interior, it could be just the place to transform Sawchyn Guitars into a full-service music store. Such a move would accomplish two things: it would resolve many of Sawchyn's production challenges and it would allow them to take advantage of the opportunities they were currently missing. Plus, they realized they knew the building owner and were confident they could get a good deal on rent. As they thought about the possibility, they grew more and more excited that perhaps at last things were coming together for realizing the vision for Sawchyn Guitars. With Peter managing production and repairs, and Kendra managing retail and consignment, they felt they could offer a music store for customers who disliked the big-box model and instead sought personalized attention and expertise. As long as the interior of the shop could be renovated into a high-class space that fit the image of Sawchyn's products, his new store could really become a hotspot for the local musical community. Having a bricks-and-mortar store for the first time could even increase the legitimacy of his business and help boost sales of commissioned instruments through higher consumer confidence.

CONCERNS AND DELIBERATIONS

A quick tour of the space a few days later and a discussion with the landlord confirmed that it was about as perfect a spot as they would ever find. It was available immediately, the price was right[11] and the room had a warm, welcoming feel and flexible layout. Faced with a realistic opportunity for the first time, the Sawchyns now had to stop and consider: Were they serious about this idea? Were they willing to put in all the work to effectively start what would appear to be a brand new business?

---

[11]Annual lease rates for industrial office space in Regina were $12 per square foot. Source: NAI Commercial, Saskatchewan, "Market Surveys, Projections 2012" http://www.naisask.com/market-surveys.html, accessed June 30, 2013.

As they took stock of the work required to make their plan a reality, they quickly realized that they were considering not simply moving the shop to Dewdney Avenue but a complete reinvention of Sawchyn Guitars. They would need to renovate and decorate the space, which, as handy people, they would do themselves to save money. They would also need to invest in retail inventory, such as string, picks, cases and straps and to purchase vintage and other retail instruments. They estimated the upfront cost for the renovations and increased inventory would be in the range of $20,000 to $25,000 since all the manufacturing equipment was already owned. That was a substantial amount of money that they didn't want to waste, but they knew they could finance those costs using their secured line of credit. Plus, they would also have the additional monthly operating costs of running the shop, including rent. Although they hoped the extra monthly costs would be almost offset by taking on the repair work currently being turned down, it was difficult to know for sure; and, if their calculations weren't correct, they didn't want to find themselves out of pocket each month.

The Sawchyns had prepared estimates of the new costs and revenues they expected as a result of running the new store (see Exhibit 4).[12] With a little digging, most of the additional expenses were easy to estimate, such as rent, utilities, insurance and telecommunications. Because they knew a store would require more advertising than just the current website, they assumed they would need to run a regular classified ad for repair and consignment services in the local newspaper. Additionally, they would need to advertise each in-house concert as well as at each of the city's two major annual music festivals. Although they would have loved to have more part-time help available to cover the retail counter when they were busy, they knew it would cost them at least $15 per hour and so budgeted for a bare minimum of three hours per week. They were unsure whether they could afford that luxury until the store was more established, especially because they knew that running the store was sure to involve unanticipated expenses as well, which they needed to consider. Finally, because the Sawchyns would now have to drive to work each day, the business would have automobile expenses for the first time, which they estimated at $250 per month.

The new revenue side was much more difficult to estimate. Sawchyn thought he could get a minimum of 35 hours of repair work each month at a rate of $55 per hour (materials charged separately). This estimate was conservative because it was roughly based on the amount of work he was currently turning down; the demand for high-quality repairs could be much higher but how much higher was difficult to estimate. Kendra estimated they could sell approximately $100 of accessories per day (Monday to Saturday) at a markup of 30 per cent. She also estimated she could sell 30 tickets to each of the concerts every other month and net $20 each. The biggest unknowns were how many more consigned instruments and new instruments they would sell each month at the store. They charged a 25 per cent commission fee on each consigned instrument sale and 50 per cent of the price of each new instrument sold was profit. They weren't sure how many instruments would sell at the store each month but estimated that initially it would be at least one and maybe even two of each kind. As news about the store spread, they hoped that instruments sales would reach one of each type per week. Although they had compiled all this information, the Sawchyns were unsure how to calculate whether they would break even on the store, and if so, how long it would take to repay their line of credit.

Looking at the list of things they would need to do, they felt exhausted just thinking about it. Did they really want to take on such a huge time commitment? Reinventing Sawchyn Guitars would be a seven-day a week commitment with long hours for many

---

[12]All estimates provided by the authors.

months–maybe even for many years. They considered the prospect that in their excitement they were taking on more work than they could handle. It was a distinct possibility that this venture could simply unravel everything they had worked for and that pursuing the dream for Sawchyn Guitars at this late stage would only lead to its demise.

TIME FOR A CHANGE?

With the family tour of the rental building over, Sawchyn closed the door behind him, wondering whether opening such a store was the craziest move he had ever contemplated. While most 57-year-olds were busy planning a relaxing retirement, he was contemplating completely reinventing the business he'd been running since he was a teenager. He considered himself lucky that with the two of them working they had been able to earn a comfortable living while dedicating his entire adult life to his passion for instrument-making, but the prospect of opening a store was an altogether different league of risk and commitment. It was one thing to take that kind of risk at age 20 and quite another at his current age. He reminded himself that neither he nor Kendra had pensions to fall back on if his business failed. Sure, he knew how to make guitars and mandolins like the back of his hand, but what did he know about running a store, managing inventory and employees, marketing and all the other new tasks that would be required to realize his vision for a full-service musical instrument store? He knew wood and instruments, and he knew how to make his customers happy, but the rest would all be completely new to him. Even with Kendra's help, he wasn't sure it would be manageable, let alone financially viable. They still needed a decent income stream from this business for many more years; and, if Kendra dedicated herself to running the store, then she would be giving up the potential for a steady employment income when a new job opportunity came along. Was it crazy to take this level of risk now when there was really no need to? After all, his old business model wasn't really that broken since he continued to have sufficient custom orders to keep his business afloat, so why unnecessarily change it?

On the other hand, in some ways, the convergence of a great space and the local economic boom could be just the opportunity he had been waiting for to truly fulfill his vision for the business to which he had devoted his entire adult life. A new challenge could provide him with his most satisfying working years after many decades of devotion and sacrifice. Plus, both the Sawchyns felt the new store could lead to more options for an eventual exit strategy when the time came that they wanted to be less involved in the daily running of the business. Still, he couldn't help but wonder how long the boom in the local economy would last, and whether the city would support a new luxury-goods store at all let alone for several more years. Regina and Saskatchewan had seen tough times before–and not that long ago either. Although there was no slowing of the Saskatchewan economic engine in sight, the boom couldn't last forever. Was the timing right for this new venture, or had they already missed their chance to transform Sawchyn Guitars? Were they making the right choice between all the alternatives available to them? As he turned the key in the lock, he knew he needed to decide soon whether to open the door on a new life for Sawchyn Guitars, or whether to close that door for good.

ONE YEAR LATER—MANAGING GROWING PAINS

Since the grand opening of the new store in April 2012, Sawchyn Guitars looked and felt like an entirely new business. Gone was the cramped workshop in Sawchyn's backyard, now replaced by the bright and spacious workshop at the back of the renovated shop on

Dewdney Street. The new workshop was approximately three times the size of the old one and already it was brimming with equipment, materials and instruments. The main display room was right off the main entrance and featured Sawchyn's guitars and mandolins and select instruments by other manufacturers. Sawchyn's handmade instruments remained the highlight of the store and were prominently displayed. The till display case featured picks and other accessories, and the selection of strings was hung behind the counter. The side display room featured vintage Gibson and Martin guitars. The shop had a warm, welcoming feel and was playfully decorated with a variety of beaver-themed decorations—gifts in honour of their Beaver Tail mandolins.

The Sawchyns had decided to seize the opportunity and jump in with both feet, signing a five-year lease for the space. To prepare for the new store, Sawchyn changed Sawchyn Guitars from a sole proprietorship to a limited company. They rented the space in January 2012 and renovated until April when they opened for business. They did all the renovations and decorating themselves with the help of friends and family. The renovation and inventory were financed by a secured line of credit from their local credit union.

In an effort to draw traffic to the store and start building a sense of musical community, the Sawchyns had started a series of in-house concerts in the front retail area. The concerts were held every second month or so and featured local musicians from a range of musical styles. With only 30 seats, tickets were always in demand and sold out quickly. Although the in-house concerts were a lot of work to put together, they brought customers and media exposure to the store. Kendra also promoted the store using classified ads in the local paper and a few ads in specialized outlets like the Regina Folk Festival program (see Exhibit 5). Several local media outlets had covered the opening of the new store, which had also helped with promotion. The Sawchyns also started more actively networking with the local music industry and using social media.

Production-wise, Sawchyn was now able to arrange his workshop more efficiently—no more going up and down stairs for materials and equipment. He also had much more storage capacity for instruments in various states of production and for repairs, while still having plenty of space to work. As he had hoped, the demand for instrument repairs was strong and accounted for approximately one-third of the store's revenue. Sawchyn quickly felt he was more productive due to the better set-up of his workspace. For efficiency, he was planning to start building Beaver Tails in larger batches so he could sell them wholesale to other stores.

The response from customers and the city had been complimentary and supportive. Local musicians appreciated a store where all the services and products they needed were available in one place, a feature that made the store "pretty much unique to Western Canada."[13] The media coverage of the store's opening also praised the shop's one-stop format. Customers, in particular, loved that Sawchyn could repair both acoustic and electric guitars and other stringed instruments. The focal point of the store, however, remained Sawchyn's handmade instruments, which were praised by the local media as world-class instruments available at affordable prices.[14]

Strong early sales at the store had been a pleasant surprise. In fact, the Sawchyns had been a bit surprised by how quickly his own instruments had sold within the first months of opening. That was great news, of course, but it had left them short on showcase instruments for display in the store. Being accustomed to mostly custom orders, they had underestimated the need for a stockpile of Sawchyn's instruments to put on display as the

---

[13]Brian Bowman, "World Class Instruments Hand-made on Dewdney Avenue," *BuzzCity Magazine*, http://www.buzzcity.ca/SawchynGuitars.html, accessed February 10, 2013.

[14]Ibid.

retail items sold. As the economic indicators had suggested they would, people were spending money in Regina. Even farmers had been buying expensive instruments! Consequently, in the eight months since they opened, they had already used their cash flow to start paying down their line of credit.

NEW CHALLENGES—CHRISTMAS 2012

With strong demand for repairs, retail instruments and custom orders, Sawchyn had limited capacity to keep producing new instruments for display in the shop. He was able to be more efficient in production than in his old shop, but the improved efficiency wasn't enough to offset the demands on his time from repairs and other new responsibilities. Even with Kendra taking over responsibility for managing the website, inventory, promotion and bookkeeping, Peter still had many more demands on his time than before. Customers dropped by and wanted to talk, they wanted someone to demonstrate a guitar, they brought in repairs, they asked about accessories and they enquired about vintage instruments. All these interactions, while fun and interesting, consumed time that Sawchyn needed to devote to instrument-making.

Consequently, they were both still spending long hours at the shop before and after retail hours. Nonetheless, the new spray room that they had planned to finish installing soon after they opened was no further ahead in late December than it had been in April. Though they were both careful about being organized, their days just never seemed to have enough hours to finish what needed to be done. And since neither of them had anticipated the constraint to be on the production rather than the sales side, they hadn't planned for this scenario.

When one of Sawchyn's musician customers, Ben, expressed an interest in working part-time at the store, they gladly accepted. Ben worked the front desk about 50 hours per month on days when they expected higher traffic. While he was a great asset on the retail side since he knew the products well and could demonstrate them to customers, Sawchyn still found it difficult to produce enough instruments. Ben was not experienced with woodworking so was unable to help in the workshop when the front area wasn't busy. So although Ben's help was an improvement, it wasn't a complete solution to the production capacity problem. Sawchyn knew he needed a solution fairly quickly because experience told him that custom orders dropped off when the wait times increased. Finding local people with the right skills who were willing to work part-time with little job security, however, was a challenge in the city's competitive labour market.

Despite these growing pains, the Sawchyns were both having far more fun at work than either of them had experienced in many years. They enjoyed getting to know new customers and had gained a tremendous sense of accomplishment. If things kept going well and they could maintain a stable income, their goal was to run the shop for at least another five years. Sawchyn wondered how he could build the business into something that he could sell when he decided to retire and what he needed to do to make that possible.

Although they were enjoying running the new business, it was definitely all-consuming and constantly stressful. While they were pleased with their progress so far, the lingering concerns about limited production capacity and questions about how they should be prioritizing the work kept them awake at night over this year's Christmas season.

EXHIBIT 1: Various Stages of Acoustic Guitar Production

Source: Sawchyn Guitars, "About Sawchyn Guitars," http://www.sawchyn.com/index.php/about, accessed January 29, 2013.

EXHIBIT 2: Sawchyn Guitars Price List

Models	Price Range
Acoustic Six String	
Standard models	$2,920–$8,150
Signature models	$2,920–$3,440
Acoustic Twelve String	$4,530
Classical	$4,900
Flamenco	$2,495–4,490
Mandolins	
Beaver Tail models	$899–1,099
Traditional models	$3,230–$5,980
Mandola	$3,880
Octave Mandolin	$4,490
Mando-Cello	$5,120
Irish Bouzouki	$2,450

Note: All prices include a hardshell case. For top bound in abalone add $450. For abalone rosette only add $125. Pickup system at cost, no installation charges. Other models available, inquire. All prices are subject to change.

Source: Sawchyn Guitars, "Pricing," http://www.sawchyn.com/index.php/pricing, accessed January 29, 2013.

EXHIBIT 3: Sawchyn Guitars' Beaver Tail Brand Handmade Mandolins

Source: Peter Sawchyn.

EXHIBIT 4: Estimated Additional Monthly Costs and Revenues From the Store Model

Monthly Expenses		
	Rent	$ 2,400
	Utilities	300
	Insurance	200
	Telecom	150
	Advertising	250
	Personal automobile usage	250
12 hours @ $15/hour	Part-time staff	180
	Miscellaneous/unexpected expenses	200
	Total	$ 3,930
One-Time Expenses (on Line of Credit)		
	Renovations	$20,000
	Extra stock	5,000
	Total	$25,000
Monthly Revenues		
	Instrument repairs – labour @ $55/hour (35 hours)	$ 1,925
	Accessory sales (net) @ 30% markup	720
	Bi-monthly concert tickets (net) 30 @ $20	300
Based on 1 extra per month	Consignment commission fee @ 25%	375
Based on 1 extra per month	In-store instrument sales (net) @ 50% margin	1,000
	Total	$ 4,320

Note: All estimates provided by the authors.

EXHIBIT 5: Sawchyn Guitars Advertisement in Regina Folk Festival Program 2012

Source: Peter Sawchyn.

Ganong Bros. Limited

On March 30, 1995, David Ganong, president of Ganong Bros. Limited (GBL), walked out of the annual board meeting gravely concerned. Ganong Bros. Limited was a small, private family confectionery firm in St. Stephen, New Brunswick, with a wide variety of sugar confectionery and chocolate product lines. The board of directors had just reviewed the year-end financial statements, which essentially showed two consecutive years of financial losses. The board had pressed Ganong hard for a solution and had given him six weeks to return with a recommendation that would restore the company to profitability. The board had also challenged Ganong to develop a growth plan that would increase company revenues by 50 per cent. Furthermore, this growth was required to take place above and beyond changes that were made to the main business lines, and was to be driven by business models, products or services that were not currently considered to be part of the core business.

THE CONFECTIONERY INDUSTRY IN CANADA[1]

The confectionery industry was divided into sugar confectionery, chocolates and other cocoa-based products, and chewing gum. The major products in Canada consisted of chocolate bars (34 per cent), boxed and bulk chocolates (28 per cent), hard and soft candies (18 per cent), gum (15 per cent), and other products (five per cent). Most Canadian

Vanessa M. Strike prepared this case under the supervision of Professor Eric Morse solely to provide material for class discussion. The authors do not intend to illustrate either effective or ineffective handling of a managerial situation. The authors may have disguised certain names and other identifying information to protect confidentiality.

Richard Ivey School of Business Foundation prohibits any form of reproduction, storage or transmission without its written permission. Reproduction of this material is not covered under authorization by any reproduction rights organization. To order copies or request permission to reproduce materials, contact Ivey Publishing, Richard Ivey School of Business Foundation, The University of Western Ontario, London, Ontario, Canada, N6A 3K7; phone (519) 661-3208; fax (519) 661-3882; e-mail cases@ivey.uwo.ca.

Copyright © 2004, Richard Ivey School of Business Foundation   Version: 2011-09-21

One time permission to reproduce granted by Richard Ivey School of Business Foundation on April 22, 2014.

IVEY | Publishing

[1]Industry, Science and Technology Canada; Agriculture and Agri-Food Canada.

confectionery goods were produced in Ontario, accounting for 67 per cent of industry employment and 65 per cent of shipments; Quebec followed closely behind.

Profits tended to be higher in the sugar confectionery industry than in the chocolate industry. Furthermore, return on sales in the chocolate bar industry was less in Canada than in the United States. Canada was the only country in which the four major multinational chocolate bar companies, all essentially equal in size, co-existed in the same market. The intensely competitive market conditions caused by this unique situation kept profits low. In addition, the demand for many domestic confectionery products had decreased recently, due to a lower proportion of children in Canada and to a growing number of health-conscious Canadians; conversely, exports showed a slight increase.

Production facilities ranged in size from small one- and two-person operations to several plants with more than 1,000 employees at each plant. Operations with fewer than 20 employees accounted for 70 per cent of total establishments, but only five per cent of the industry's employment and three per cent of shipments. About 52 per cent of total industry employment was shared among 15 per cent of the firms that contributed 85 per cent of total shipments. Approximately 44 per cent of all products sold at retail made their way from the manufacturers to the final outlets through wholesale distributors. Most of the rest was sold directly to retail stores.

It was estimated that the industry operated at about 75 per cent of production capacity, in large part because specialized equipment was used only for seasonal product lines. Managing production, full-time employees, inventory, marketing and cash flow could thus be particularly challenging for smaller firms.

THE CHANGING CANADIAN ENVIRONMENT

The industry in Canada originally consisted mainly of independents, but in the late 1980s, consolidation led to greater concentration of market shares, resulting in the increased plant efficiencies necessary to compete internationally. There were still several large independent firms but their numbers were dwindling. Many brand-name acquisitions were also being made by American parent firms. These acquisitions were not meant to build international distribution or gain market share, but they provided a way for multinationals to prevent the erosion of their domestic market share.

There were two additional main issues facing confectionery firms in the late 1980s. The first one was free trade. Prior to free trade the industry was protected behind a tariff wall. Canadian firms had protection from confectioneries coming into the country. Some of the product lines had tariffs as high as 15 per cent and Canadian firms going into the United States faced tariffs as low as five per cent to 7.5 per cent; with free trade the Canadian industry lost this tariff differential.

The second issue was the belief that Canadian firms would find it difficult to penetrate the U.S. market. Canadian plants typically faced scale disadvantages compared with U.S. and European firms; they were smaller, had less capacity and served smaller markets. As a result, their unit costs of production were higher. Even if Canadian firms were able to penetrate the U.S. market, they often did not have the capacity to cope with orders of the magnitude that the market dictated.

In the late 1980s, the growth of retail gourmet candy shops, such as Laura Secord, pointed to a consumer trend toward purchasing high-quality, specialty products at premium prices. While many shops sold imported merchandise, they would also sell high-quality domestic products. The industry began to adapt to the more open global trading environment through a series of rationalizations that resulted in more efficient and specialized operations.

By 1994, there were 87 confectionery plants in Canada that employed almost 9,500 people and manufactured products worth more than $1.5 billion. Approximately $400 million of these were exported outside of Canada, and $540 million worth of confectionery products were imported into Canada, mainly from the United States and Europe. Foreign ownership of the industry was high, as multinationals had a major position in the industry. Approximately 60 per cent of industry shipments were accounted for by foreign-controlled enterprises located in Canada, and the number was growing.

THE CHOCOLATE GANONGS

Ganong Bros. Limited was founded in 1873 by two brothers in St. Stephen, New Brunswick (Exhibit 1). The town, situated on the U.S. border, had a population of approximately 5,000 people and was officially named "Canada's Chocolate Town."

GBL was Canada's oldest confectionery company. It had invented the widely imitated chicken bone–a cinnamon-flavored, pink, hard candy jacket over a chocolate centre–and was the first company in Canada to make lollipops using butchers' wooden skewers. It had invented the first five-cent chocolate nut bar in North America (originally made to take along on fishing trips), and it was the first in Canada to sell Valentine heart boxes. All GBL products were made with great professional care using only the finest ingredients.

GBL was a small company compared to the international giants, but it had done a good job of becoming "Canadian competitive." It had built a name for itself in boxed chocolates, competing with similar Canadian firms such as Moirs, Laura Secord, Smiles and Chuckles, Neilson and Lowney. GBL maintained its traditional regional markets through local allegiances and seasonal products; for example, the firm enjoyed a 30 per cent market share for its Valentine's Day chocolates in heart-shaped boxes. Yet, although GBL was a strong player in boxed chocolates in Atlantic Canada, it was a fringe player in other product lines.

PRIVATE OWNERSHIP

GBL had survived four generations remaining a private, family firm. Private ownership was important to GBL as it ensured that they could remain committed to their community and employees, it provided them with the ability to make long-term decisions, and it avoided the time investment of a public company. The firm's success in large part was due to its unique business ethic, where the commitment to both the community and to its workers ranked above all else, including, on occasion, profitability.

As with many family firms in Atlantic Canada, GBL's strong commitment to the community played a significant role in the firm's business decisions over the years. For example, there were several opportunities to sell the firm, but the commitment to the community and to the employees who worked in the company came first. Historically, in other small towns in Atlantic Canada, when the ownership left the community, the firm eventually left as well, and those from the town employed with the company lost their jobs. The economic benefit to Atlantic Canada provided through the location of head offices in that region could not be overstated.

While GBL was "Canadian competitive," it was not North American competitive. Several years earlier, Nicholas Highfield had expressed concerns for the future of GBL. Highfield was the president of the leading manufacturer and marketer of boxed chocolates and chocolate bars in Canada; he was also the president of the Confectionery Manufacturers Association of Canada and knew the industry well. Highfield had said that GBL was an "anachronism," having lived beyond its time. It was dated, the world had changed, and GBL was too small. He asserted that due to its lack of critical mass, research and development capabilities, financial capacity and managerial capabilities, GBL was not big enough to compete in the world of global giants.

THE GBL BOARD OF DIRECTORS

For a family firm, GBL had a robust governance process. The board of directors was a strong diverse board consisting of six external members and two family members. Ganong was the only person from the management team on the board, and he reported directly to the board's non-executive chairman. The board approved all business plans, financial statements and compensation. The philosophy for having such a disciplined governance structure came from Arthur Ganong two generations earlier, who said "when ownership and management are the same, you need a board of directors to protect you against yourself; it is important to not get carried away with your own ideas, and the board fills the essential role of providing a sobering second thought." Several of the board members had been selected because they owned and led firms of their own; as a result they were able to provide valuable insights based on their own successes.

DISTRIBUTION

GBL used both its own sales force and independent brokers to sell its chocolate across Canada (see Exhibit 2). In Western Canada, Ontario and the Atlantic Provinces, GBL had its own sales operation with a sales force of 29 personnel. The company employed 10 sales people and two managers in the west, nine sales people and a manager in Ontario, and 10 sales personnel and two managers in Atlantic Canada. Having its own sales force resulted in fixed costs that would be incurred whether sales were doing well or not; these fixed costs averaged about 10 per cent of sales.

In Quebec, GBL used a broker, which resulted in variable costs of approximately five per cent of sales. Typically, brokers, who carried hundreds of lines of products, were most successful with grocery goods. Brokers were less successful, however, with drug-related goods, a category in which chocolates were usually sold. As a result, despite the lower cost of using brokers, there was sometimes hesitancy to use them for confectionery products.

GANONG'S RESPONSE TO CHANGES IN THE ENVIRONMENT

St. Stephen Factory

The series of rationalizations within the industry in the late 1980s resulted in more efficient operations for most large and mid-sized firms. The modernization of competing plants and the establishment of free trade were the key determinants to build a new factory in St. Stephen. GBL felt it needed to make a quantum change and had initially looked at dramatic expansion to the old facility, but it didn't have the long-term growth prospects. In the modern world, the original factory could not compete effectively. The firm required more automation, more buying leverage for supplies and more volume to cover fixed costs.

In 1988, GBL began building the new St. Stephen plant, and it moved into the facility in 1990. GBL now had a facility with the potential for expansion and growth and the ability to reduce unit costs so it could compete with the onslaught of U.S. confectioners that would come with free trade.

The near term results of the expansion were modest. GBL had had very solid boxed chocolate performance in the 1980s, and felt that it could capture more of the Canadian market based on extrapolating the success of boxed chocolates. While variable costs fell, fixed costs from the new facility were higher, and the company did not build sales as quickly as projected. GBL had also thought there would be an opportunity to capture some of the U.S. market as a result of changes that were taking place in the U.S. confectionery industry. The U.S. market offered potential for specialty products, particularly in large border markets. Unfortunately, GBL was not successful in extracting the customer support it anticipated and it experienced a direct profit loss from the U.S. drive.

Overseas Market

The domestic market exhibited very little real growth in the late 1980s. As a result, GBL realized it needed to become more aggressive in the export market. The company decided to go into partnership with a firm in Thailand that would provide an opening into the growing Asian market. On Halloween in 1989, GBL opened the new Bangkok factory, which coincided with the building of the St. Stephen plant.

The Thailand factory produced several products that were brought back to Canada. It also produced chocolates that were exported to the Middle East and Japan, where chocolate imports were increasing and there was a strong demand for Western consumer products. The Thailand operation did well; while it did not create purchasing synergies, it made money. It provided a small amount of royalties and dividends, and accounted for approximately seven per cent of total sales with a four per cent total cost of goods sold.

In conducting business in Asia, the relationship with the partner was critical, and it took time to maintain. Ganong was the primary contact, and he spent significant time traveling to and from Bangkok to nurture the relationship.

Ganong in the 1990s

As GBL entered the mid-1990s, the competitive environment intensified across all lines of business from both U.S. and Canadian producers. GBL employed 207 in the factory and 15 staff. The factory was operating at 50 per cent of capacity, and not one of the individual product lines was pushing its capacity limits. As a result, GBL had to apply twice the amount of fixed cost to its products. Overhead costs were making GBL uncompetitive in various markets. For example, jelly beans were only made for part of the year, but the fixed costs associated with maintaining the floor space (depreciation, interest and taxes) still had to be paid for the entire year, resulting in slim margins and fixed costs that were high, relative to the competitors. David Ganong wondered if the firm should cut selling prices to try to increase volume or increase prices to try to cover fixed costs.

In total, GBL had 400 lines of product in seven product categories (see Exhibit 3). The firm wanted to use its labor force, equipment and capacity to build volume; consequently it ended up with very broad and diverse product lines. Not all of the lines were profitable, and some were more profitable than others (Exhibit 4). With so many independent lines it was difficult to achieve economies of scale. In addition to its own brands, GBL also made products for private labels. GBL was fairly reactive in this market, providing its services occasionally and only when asked.

ALTERNATIVES

As David Ganong walked out of the meeting, he tried to figure out what his options were, given the board mandate; he recalled some of the strategies board members had previously shared with him, ones that they had used for their own firms. He wasn't sure which ones, if any, made sense for GBL.

Alternative Financing

As a private firm, GBL had limited financial flexibility; the past two years of losses had tapped the financial resources that it required to take the business where it needed to go, and obtaining additional funds was a challenge. In addition, GBL had a covenant with the bank where all of its assets were secured, thus it was difficult to pursue other lines of financing. The firm had hit a crisis point (see Exhibits 5, 6 and 7).

Recently, GBL had been approached by an international chocolate firm who was interested in becoming a partner with a minority position. To accept such an offer was a defensive strategy, a "rear guard action," but Ganong felt they had their back in the corner. He thought this option may be feasible as the company could keep the business in St. Stephen and build the firm, while establishing an umbilical cord for the resources it lacked. Ganong's one concern was whether the partner would continue to be satisfied with a minority position. He had seen too often the detrimental results on the community when a family firm was purchased by an outsider, and he was wary of such offers.

Contract Packs

One of the board members had explained how he had built his business by focusing on contractual business lines. These contract packs were with firms who required a reliable source of supply that would meet certain specifications for a particular product. In return for adhering to such specific terms, these firms would sign a long-term contract that allowed the supplying firm to obtain the financing required to purchase the necessary specialized manufacturing equipment and raw materials. Such arrangements were very common in the auto industry. For example, Ford would sign a long-term contract with a car-part supplier to have that firm manufacture parts that met Ford's specific requirements.

Private Labels

The management team had also explored the possibility of becoming more proactive in the private label sector as they felt the private label trend would grow in Canada. Private label products, also known as in-house or store brands, were products that carried a store's name as its brand or another name owned by the store, where the selling prices were relatively lower. For example, Loblaw's private label, President's Choice, produced by George Weston Ltd., accounted for 80 per cent ($23 billion) of Weston's sales.

Private labels offered wide product lines, including budget, value and premium products. The market for private-label foods was driven both by a desire on the part of retailers to increase their profit margins and by consumer demand for good quality foods at prices lower than those of brand-name products. Retailers retained a greater portion of the margin for private-label products than for brand-name products. This increased gross margin allowed them to pass on savings to their customers, who typically saved from 10 per cent to 25 per cent.

For the manufacturer, private labels provided an opportunity for increased volume and limited competition. This ability to deliver high-quality products at a reduced price was due to lower marketing, lower overhead and lower logistical costs. To keep up with private labels, brand names had to make greater marketing efforts and keep introducing new, value-added products.

Moving the Factory

Another option Ganong considered was to move the GBL operations. As the majority of the Canadian population and a large portion of the company's market were located in Ontario, it could move the enterprise and build a new factory in a more central location. Ganong wondered if such a move would help to increase the firm's presence and thereby increase sales.

Consolidation of Manufacturing and Shared Ownership

The previous year, GBL, along with two other confectionery firms, had hired an outside consultant to complete an extensive study on the prospect of consolidating the operations of the three firms. The purpose of the study was to determine which of the firms were the lowest cost producers for their shared product lines, and then to explore the possibility of having the lowest cost producer complete the production runs for all three firms for that particular product. Once produced, the product would be marketed under each separate company name.

A variation of this idea was to go a step further and share the ownership of the confectionery assets that each firm had in common. The three firms would consolidate their candy production and form a new independent company that each would have stake in. While each firm shared product lines with the other firms, they also had their own unique lines. One company, for example, produced biscuits, which the other two did not, and GBL produced chocolate, while the other two did not. The companies would continue with their own independent product lines under their original firm. GBL, for example, would continue to produce chocolate on its own premises and under the Ganong name.

MARCH 30, 1995

Ganong realized he had to convince the board of a solid plan going forward to solve these issues. At the end of the first year of losses, the management team had convinced the board they did not need to change the business model, that they would do a better job of executing the current strategy. The board was losing patience with its ability to pull out of the red. Ganong realized they had to make fundamental changes to the business model to bring the firm back to profitability and to develop a new $10 million block of business. It was already several months into the new fiscal year, and Ganong was unsure of where to go next. The gravity of the results was apparent, and he had committed to get back to the board within six weeks. The leadership of Ganong Bros. Limited in chocolate making went back four generations, and David Ganong wanted to preserve and perpetuate the firm's rich heritage.

As he left the board meeting, Ganong thought back to his conversation with Nicholas Highfield. Highfield's comment about GBL being an "anachronism" had stuck with Ganong over the years. This comment had challenged his fundamental belief system and pushed him to succeed. Until this time, he had proven Highfield wrong, but now the words came back to haunt him as he wondered how their small independent firm, based in the middle of nowhere, could possibly compete among the international giants.

EXHIBIT 1:   ST. Stephen, New Brunswick Head Office Location

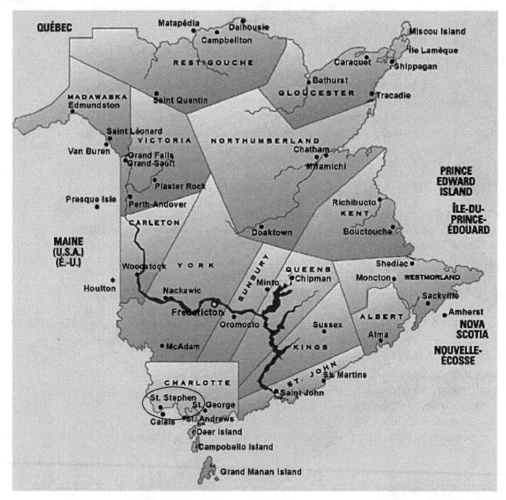

Source: National Geographic Maps, www.nationalgeographic.com/xpeditions/atlas/index.html.

EXHIBIT 2: Sales Analysis For 1994 (in $000s)

	1994
Ganong Brand Sales	
Atlantic	$ 7,082
Quebec	1,798
Ontario	4,485
Prairies	2,013
British Columbia	980
National Accounts	3,855
Private Label	1,450
Domestic Ganong Sales	$ 21,663
Export	950
United States	577
Total Ganong Sales	$ 23,190
Distributor Line Sales	
Atlantic	$ 40
Quebec	3
Ontario	50
Prairies	93
British Columbia	42
Special	39
Private Label	15
Domestic Distributor Line Sales	$ 282
Export	—
United States	—
Total Distributor Line Sales	$ 282
Total Sales	$23,472

Source: Company Records.

EXHIBIT 3: Description of Product Categories

Packaged Chocolates	Boxed or packaged chocolates; sold as gifts for birthdays, Christmas, Valentine's Day, etc.
Portable Confections	Non-chocolate sugar confection bars sold for less than $1; e.g., mint rolls.
Chocolate Bars	Chocolate pre-packed snack that sold for less than $1.
Cellos	Sugar confectionery such as jelly beans, jujubes, mints packaged in flexible packaging.
Staples	Bulk product.
Fruit Snacks	Portable nutritional snack with real fruit content, generally marketed in the cereal section of grocery stores.
Distributor Lines	Products purchased and resold by Ganong Bros. Limited under another firm's name; these helped to reduce sales cost and allowed the company to employ more sales people.
National Accounts	Accounts with centralized warehousing where the product was shipped to a customer who redistributed it (e.g. Wal-Mart).

EXHIBIT 4: Partial Income Statement For 1994 (in $000s)

	1994
Sales–Packaged Chocolates	$11,817
COGS	7,326
Gross Margin $	4,491
Gross Margin %	38.0%
Sales–Portable Confections	447
COGS	286
Gross Margin $	161
Gross Margin %	36.0%
Sales–Chocolate Bars	1,056
COGS	542
Gross Margin $	514
Gross Margin %	48.7%
Sales–Cellos	4,804
COGS	3,167
Gross Margin $	1,637
Gross Margin %	34.1%
Sales–Staples	2,485
COGS	1,731
Gross Margin $	754
Gross Margin %	30.3%
Sales–Fruit Snacks	2,580
COGS	1,624
Gross Margin $	956
Gross Margin %	37.1%
Sales–Distributor Lines	283
COGS	249
Gross Margin $	34
Gross Margin %	12.0%
Total Sales	23,472
Total COGS	14,925
Pre-Discount Gross Margin $	8,547
Pre-Discount Gross Margin %	36.4%
Discounts	796
Net Gross Margin $	7,751
Net Gross Margin %	33.0%

Source: Company Records.

EXHIBIT 5: Partial Balance Sheet (in $000s)

	1994	1993	1992
Current Assets			
Cash	$ 48	$ 21	$ 15
Accounts Receivables	4,263	5,049	4,155
Inventories:			
Raw Materials	2,590	2,254	2,399
Work in Process	245	215	260
Finished Goods	1,581	1,727	1,708
Prepaid Expenses	446	370	477
Total Current Assets	**9,173**	**9,636**	**9,014**
Long-Term Assets			
Land & Building—Net	8,583	8,953	9,464
Machinery & Equipment—Net	3,517	3,818	4,065
Notes & Misc. Receivables	71	70	68
Investments In/Due from Affiliates	16	16	16
Other Investments	199	189	189
Deferred Charges (Pension, Startup)	496	513	470
Total Assets	**22,055**	**23,195**	**23,286**
Current Liabilities			
Notes Payable—Bank	1,479	1,478	1,238
Accounts Payable	3,821	3,620	3,920
Income Taxes	203	225	146
Current Portion—LTD	399	422	311
Current Liabilities	**5,902**	**5,745**	**5,615**
Long-term Liabilities			
Long-term Debt	6,236	6,593	7,029
Deferred Government Grants	5,027	5,372	5,663
Deferred Taxes	1,135	1,317	1,097
Total Liabilities	**18,300**	**19,027**	**19,404**
Capital Stock	83	83	83
Retained Earnings	1,463	1,864	1,569
Subordinated Debt	2,209	2,221	2,230
Net Worth	**3,755**	**4,168**	**3,882**
Total Liabilities & Net Worth	**$22,055**	**$23,195**	**$23,286**

Source: Company Records.

EXHIBIT 6: Key Operating Ratios

Key Operating Ratios	1994	1993	1992	Industry Medians*
Liquidity				
Current Ratio	1.6	1.7	1.6	2.5
Quick Ratio	0.7	0.9	0.7	1.1
Days' Receivables	61 days	71 days	59 days	21 days
Inventory Turnover	3.2	3.3	3.0	4.2
Coverage				
EBIT/Interest	(0.0)	1.2	1.5	9.5
Leverage				
Fixed assets/net worth	3.2	3.1	3.5	0.5
Total debt/net worth	4.9	4.6	5.0	0.6
Operating				
Profit before taxes/net worth	−14.9%	13.3%	9.7%	13.3%
Profit before taxes/total assets	−2.5%	2.4%	1.6%	7.7%
Net sales/fixed assets	1.8	1.9	1.7	5.4
Net sales/total assets	1.0	1.0	1.0	1.6

* For firms $10 million to $50 million in assets.
Source: Robert Morris Associates Annual Statements.

EXHIBIT 7: Statement of Operations 1992 to 1994 (in $000s)

	1994	1993	1992
Net Sales	22,346	23,803	23,554
Cost of Sales	14,075	13,706	13,182
Gross Profit $	8,271	10,097	10,372
Gross Profit %	37.0%	42.4%	44.0%
Admininstration and Selling Expenses	8,279	9,368	9,239
Operating Profit $	(8)	729	1,133
Operating Profit %	0.0%	3.1%	4.8%
Interest Expense	651	625	770
Other (Income) Expenses—Net*	(98)	(452)	(15)
Net Profit (Loss) Before Taxes	(561)	556	378
Income Taxes	(159)	261	167
Net Profit After Taxes $	(402)	295	211
Net Profit After Taxes %	−1.8%	1.2%	0.9%

* Includes sale of old factory in 1993.
Source: Company Records.

Phase Separation Solutions (PS2): The China Question

In early 2008, Paul Antle, president and chief executive officer (CEO) of Phase Separation Solutions (PS2), received a call from the State Environmental Protection Agency of China, expressing interest in PS2's Thermal Phase Separation (TPS) technology. PS2 was a small, Saskatchewan-based environmental solutions company that had grown, under Antle's entrepreneurial direction, to become a North American leader in the treatment of soil, sludge and debris impacted with various organic contaminants. The company specialized in the cleanup of two waste streams using its TPS technology. The first was the remediation of soil contaminated with persistent organic pollutants (POPs), such as pesticides and polychlorinated biphenyls (PCBs). The second was recovering usable oil from industrial sludge generated in various industries, such as the oil and gas industry.

Despite Antle's initial concerns that the call had been a scam, he soon visited China to learn more about the market in China and to build relationships. The Chinese inquiries were sincere. By mid-2010, nearly one-and-a-half years after Antle's first visit, potential cooperative opportunities had emerged with two separate Chinese organizations: one in soil remediation, and the other in oil recovery from oil sludge. The two potential opportunities were attractive to PS2. The international geographic diversification would transform PS2 from a domestic player to an international player, and in so doing, would significantly improve its growth potential.

The PS2 management team was no stranger to international markets. The TPS technology had been successfully employed in 14 countries in the past 15 years.

George Z. Peng and Paul W. Beamish wrote this case solely to provide material for class discussion. The authors do not intend to illustrate either effective or ineffective handling of a managerial situation. The authors may have disguised certain names and other identifying information to protect confidentiality.

Richard Ivey School of Business Foundation prohibits any form of reproduction, storage or transmission without its written permission. Reproduction of this material is not covered under authorization by any reproduction rights organization. To order copies or request permission to reproduce materials, contact Ivey Publishing, Richard Ivey School of Business Foundation, The University of Western Ontario, London, Ontario, Canada, N6A 3K7; phone (519) 661-3208; fax (519) 661-3882; e-mail cases@ivey.uwo.ca.

Copyright © 2012, Richard Ivey School of Business Foundation   Version: 2012-03-30

One time permission to reproduce granted by Richard Ivey School of Business Foundation on April 22, 2014.

IVEY | Publishing

Hill Paul J. Hill
School of Business

However, the modes of international involvement had been on a non-equity basis, in the forms of equipment exporting, licensing and service contracts. Although the cooperative opportunities in China would bring PS2 to a higher level of internationalization, the decision was not to be taken lightly. A series of questions needed to be answered. Should PS2 enter the Chinese market? Which of the two opportunities should it pursue? Would it be feasible to pursue both? Did PS2 possess the required resources and capabilities to pursue an equity-based entry? What ownership levels should PS2 assume for each option? How would PS2 staff its Chinese operation(s) if PS2 decided to pursue the opportunities in China?

COMPANY OVERVIEW[1]

PS2 was founded in 2004 by a group of Canadian entrepreneurs who believed that the key to the safe management of environmental liability was the proper application of advanced clean technology, such as their TPS technology. By combining their extensive experience in the fields of hazardous waste management, remedial technology development and environmental engineering, they created PS2 to take advantage of the new opportunities in the Canadian environmental market. In the Government of Canada's 2004 budget, it had pledged $3.5 billion[2] over the following 10 years for environmental cleanup.

In 2005, after securing an investment of $3 million from Golden Opportunities Fund Inc.[3] in the form of senior secured debentures, the company constructed a fixed soil reclamation facility in Wolseley, Saskatchewan. This facility was capable of treating a wide variety of soil contaminated with POPs, industrial sludge and waste pharmaceuticals. The location was chosen so that PS2 could target the markets in both Eastern and Western Canada, and in the United States. The facility, which had a capacity of 20,000 tons per year, was permitted to treat a wide variety of pollutants. It was one of only three fixed facilities in Canada permitted to treat PCB and dioxin/furan-impacted soil. In late 2005, the facility became operational and started generating revenue. It was fully commissioned in early 2006.

PS2 generated revenue by securing service "contracts" for the treatment of contaminated soil or on a "fee-for-service basis," wherein small quantities of contaminated soil were accepted from customers. Its customer base comprised environmental service companies, utility companies and general industry. The number and size of contracts obtained each year

---

[1]Summarized from: Phase Separation Solutions Inc., http://www.phaseparation.com/index.html; Fundamental Research Corp., "West Mountain Capital Corp. (TSXV: WMT)–Initiating Coverage–Thermal Treatment of Soil, Sludge and Other Waste Streams," March 23, 2010, http://www.baystreet.ca/articles/research_reports/fundamental_research/WestMountainCapital040110.pdf; "Investment Fund Sees Gold in Clean Dirt," *Daily Commercial News and Construction Record*, December 19, 2005, http://dcnonl.com/article/20051219300. All web links in this case were accessed in February and March 2012

[2]All currency amounts shown in Canadian dollars unless otherwise specified.

[3]Golden Opportunities is a labour-sponsored investment fund (LSIF) corporation under Saskatchewan's Labour-sponsored Venture Capital Corporations Act. An LSIF, or simply retail venture capital (RVC), is a fund managed by investment professionals that invests in small to mid-sized Canadian companies.
The Canadian federal government and some provincial governments offer tax credits to labour-sponsored venture capital corporation (LSVCC) investors to promote the growth of such companies. Golden Opportunities is the largest provincial RVC fund in Saskatchewan.

for contaminated soil varied and depended on the funding that customers had budgeted for remedial projects.

PS2 went public in 2007 through a reverse merger with West Mountain Capital Corporation (WMT), a capital pool company (see more information in a later section). The reverse merger brought PS2 to an advanced level of growth by introducing more funds and professional management expertise.

In early 2008, PS2 diversified into pharmaceutical waste management by acquiring an Ontario firm. Later that year, however, PS2 decided to divest it to focus its resources on the Wolseley facility, in response to the contaminated soil market that had opened up significantly since the acquisition. The soil treatment market in Canada received a big boost in late 2008, when the federal government introduced new regulations that established deadlines for ending the use and long-term storage of both PCBs and products containing PCBs. The new regulations also required that these products be sent for destruction by the end of 2009 (later extended to 2011). Such a policy change resulted in a strong demand for PS2's TPS technology: subsequent to this announcement, PS2 secured contracts for 2009 and into 2010, utilizing 80 per cent of its capacity at its Wolseley facility.

As a result of the new regulations in 2008, PS2 posted record revenues of $5.88 million and net profits of $2.51 million in 2009 (see Exhibits 1, 2 and 3 for PS2's financial statements). In 2010, PS2 was expected to fulfill the contracts it had secured in 2008 and 2009. However, PS2's ability to secure new contracts and source new business for its unused treatment capacity in 2010 and future years could be affected by the economic climate of the day. For example, if the economy was poor, potential customers might need to suspend their remedial projects, which could lead to delays in securing revenue.[4] In addition, recent regulatory changes with regard to PCBs would provide PS2 with only a short-term momentum as PCB treatment was a declining market.

By mid 2010, the management team comprised Antle, Stephen Clarke as vice-president of Business Development and Paul Coombs as chief financial officer (see Exhibit 4 for a biography of Antle). The company had 15 employees.

THE THERMAL PHASE SEPARATION (TPS) TECHNOLOGY[5]

The TPS technology is an indirectly heated thermal desorption process that adopts a closed-loop system using non-incineration engineering principles. The mechanism of the technology is akin to a household clothes dryer, which is indirectly heated, vaporizing the water from laundry. In a TPS unit, the contaminated soil is indirectly heated

---

[4]"Management's Discussion and Analysis of Financial Position and Results of Operations for West Mountain Capital Corp.for the Three Months and Year Ended December 31, 2009," http://ca.hotstocked.com/docs/west_mountain_capital_corp/management_s_discussion_analysis/20091231mda.pdf.

[5]Summarized from Phase Separation Solutions Inc., "Patented Thermal Phase Separation (TPS) Technology," http://www.phaseparation.com/links/techt.html; Fundamental Research Corp., "West Mountain Capital Corp. (TSXV: WMT)–Initiating Coverage–Thermal Treatment of Soil, Sludge and Other Waste Streams," March 23, 2010, http://www.baystreet.ca/articles/research_reports/fundamental_research/WestMountainCapital040110 .pdf; http://www.sunrisepublish.com/common/pdfs/publications/SaskBusiness_Magazine/SB_JanFeb2012_web. pdf; West Mountain Capital Corp., "Phase Separation Solutions Expands License to Cover China," news release, August 10, 2009, http://www.phaseparation.com/images/pdf/aug10.pdf

to boil off the hazardous contaminants, which are subsequently captured as a vapour. The vapour is then re-condensed into a liquid so the contaminants don't escape to the environment. The TPS technology was the only technology capable of extracting up to 90 per cent of oil (by volume) from industrial sludge. It was also capable of separating hydrocarbons with boiling points up to 550°C. The technology had been internationally proven and was recognized as being world-class for its performance, lack of harmful air emissions, mobility and reliability. The technology had been used to treat hundreds of thousands of tons of contaminated material worldwide at many high-profile projects, such as the Sydney, Australia's 2000 Olympic Games Site Restoration Project. The technology had been used or was permitted to be used in more than 10 countries.

TPS technology was originally developed as a mobile, onsite remedial technology. However, because of its modular design, it could be easily deployed at a fixed facility if required due to cost considerations (e.g., to take advantage of economies of scale or to avoid prohibitive transportation costs). Compared with the traditional means of treating contaminated soil and industrial sludge, such as incineration or land filling, TPS technology had a series of advantages. First, the TPS process produced safe soil with an 85 per cent decrease in volume that could be returned to the environment. This process was a better alternative to burying contaminated soil in landfills, which was only a temporary solution, as it did not destroy or remove contaminants. Second, the TPS process not only enabled the recovery of oil and other hydrocarbons for reuse or resale but also generated its own fuel source to fire the system. Third, compared with incineration and land filling, TPS technology produced no harmful air emissions and no land and water pollutants. Fourth, compared with incineration, the TPS process produced significantly fewer greenhouse gas emissions.

Although the TPS technology had significant advantages over the traditional technologies, the TPS technology could compete only in applications and regions where it was cost-competitive compared with the traditional technology, or where government regulations required the proper treatment of waste.

The PS2 management team launched the Thermal Phase Separation (TPS) technology in 1994 from the firm they had founded. The technology and company were sold to Stratos Global Corp. in 1996 and bought back again in 1998, only to be resold to MI Drilling Fluids of Houston, Texas, in 1999. Since the acquisition, MI Drilling Fluids had used the TPS technology exclusively for the treatment of drilling mud and cuttings generated by the oil and gas industry.

In 2002, the founders of PS2 licensed the technology from MI Drilling Fluids, wherein PS2 received exclusive rights to use the technology, in Canada and the United States, for the decontamination treatment of all types of hazardous waste streams, until 2012. In return, PS2 paid an initial licensing fee of $61,460 and agreed to start paying a royalty of US$10 per ton of material processed, after the first 15,000 tons. PS2 also agreed to pay US$0.10 million for each TPS unit installed subsequent to the first unit. Although the company had yet to reach its first 15,000 tons of production, PS2 had started paying royalties in October 2008, after the licence was renegotiated to extend the expiry date to 2019. In 2009, MI Drilling Fluids granted PS2 the exclusive rights to use the technology in China.

All the patents associated with the TPS technology were set to expire in 2019, after which the company would not need to renew its licence. This patent deadline implied that competition would increase after 2019, when potential competitors would be able to more easily adopt the TPS technology.

THE MARKET FOR PERSISTENT ORGANIC POLLUTANTS AND INDUSTRIAL SLUDGE IN CANADA[6]

PCB Market

Due to their fire resistance and chemical stability, PCBs had been primarily used as insulating fluids and coolants in electrical equipment and machinery since the early 1900s.[7] However, PCB production had been banned in North America since the 1970s, due to their harmful effects on humans and the environment. Despite the ban on production, PCBs still persist in the environment due to their resistance to environmental degradation. According to the United Nation's 2001 Stockholm Convention on Persistent Organic Pollutants (POPs), PCBs were considered one of the 12 most persistent organic pollutants.

Even though the TPS technology could be used to treat oil sludge and a variety of POPs and other organic contaminants, the main focus of PS2 was the PCB-contaminated soil treatment market in Canada. The PCB market was believed to have high entry barriers due to high start-up costs, difficulty in sourcing and securing friendly locations for facilities and a minimum of two to three years of environmental assessment and regulatory evaluation.[8] In addition, this market was a niche market that needed special expertise that could only be developed through many years of immersion in the industry. PCB soil remediation in North America was a declining market because PCB production had been banned since the 1970s. PS2's Wolseley facility was one of only three plants in Canada with the environmental certification to service the PCB market.

Although PS2 also had the exclusive rights to use the technology in the United States, it was banned from transporting PCB contaminated soil from the United States to Canada. All other types of contaminated soil, however, were allowed to be transported to Canada for treatment. Because the U.S. market for contaminated soil was highly competitive, PS2 did not have any immediate plans to establish a fixed facility there. However, an entry through licensing by granting the use of the TPS technology to an American company might be considered.

Market Size In 2008, the known amount of PCB-contaminated soil in Canada was only approximately 200,000 tons. Even though many believed that several additional sites potentially contained unknown amounts of PCB-contaminated soil, the future prospects for the industry were not good. In addition to limited sustainable future revenue, past revenues for the industry in Canada had been highly volatile.

Competitors and Strategies The Canadian PCB market was an oligopoly, with PS2 and Bennett Environmental (BEV) as the main competitors. BEV provided solutions for soil contamination problems throughout Canada and the United States, using a technology called

---

[6]Based on Fundamental Research Corp., "West Mountain Capital Corp. (TSXV: WMT)–Initiating Coverage–Thermal Treatment of Soil, Sludge and Other Waste Streams," March 23, 2010, http://www.baystreet.ca/articles/research_reports/fundamental_research/WestMountainCapital040110.pdf and Other sources as specified.

[7]"The History of PCBs," http://www.foxriverwatch.com/monsanto2a_pcb_pcbs.html.

[8]Phase Separation Solutions Inc., "Elevating the Thinking in Waste Management," http://www.phaseparation.com/images/pdf/Golden%20Opportunities%20Presentation.pdf.

thermal oxidation, essentially an incineration technology.[9] BEV had a market capitalization of $81 million. Compared with PS2, BEV was the major player with a capacity of 80,000 tons, four times the capacity of PS2's 20,000 tons. Because both PS2 and BEV had similar cost structures, they competed on the basis of the locations of their facilities relative to project sites because transportation costs played a significant role in the economics of such projects. PS2's facility was located in Saskatchewan, whereas BEV's facility was located in Quebec. As such, BEV had an advantage in Quebec, and in most of Ontario, whereas PS2 clearly had an advantage in Western Canada. The majority of PCB contaminated soil was located in Ontario and Quebec, with British Columbia a distant third.

Although BEV had recently entered into a contract to remove and treat approximately 10,500 tons of PCB-contaminated soil located in southern Ontario (which was estimated to be worth $7 million to $9 million), the remaining amount of PCB-contaminated soil available for removal and treatment was in decline.[10]

Due to limited growth potential in the PCB treatment market (i.e., the "known" amounts of PCB-contaminated soil in Canada was only approximately 200,000 tons, or approximately two years of production at PS2 and BEV's combined capacity), BEV had been seeking opportunities for geographical diversification and product diversification to reduce volatility in revenues and improve efficiency through continuous operations. It had diversified into the treatment of contaminated construction debris.

Industrial Sludge Market in Canada

Industrial sludge referred to the residual, semi-solid waste generated as a result of an industrial production process. Although industrial sludge could be of different types, PS2's target was hydrocarbon-based sludge with more than 50 per cent hydrocarbons. Conventionally, such sludge either ended up in man-made lagoons or landfills, or was incinerated. Landfills and incineration were much less expensive than PS2's TPS technology; however, such methods created environmental liabilities due to their potential impacts on subsoil, groundwater and air.

As a result of the general public's ever-increasing environmental awareness, the conventional disposal method of using landfills was under siege. For example, in September 2008, the Ontario government had initiated regulatory changes to its Land Disposal Restrictions (LDR), which required proper pre-release treatment of industrial sludge. Under the new regulations, land disposal of untreated hazardous wastes was prohibited, and treated wastes were required to meet specific treatment standards before being disposed of. Such treatment requirements were specified as either concentration-based numerical levels or as specified treatment methods.

Such regulatory changes created demand for technologies that could meet the environmental regulation, such as PS2's TPS technology. One potential target identified by PS2 in the industrial sludge sector was paint sludge. According to data from Stewardship Ontario,[11] the collection target of Ontario for paint and coatings contents and containers was 10,573 tons per year, or 47 per cent of available for collection. Based on PS2 management's

---

[9]Bennett Environmental Inc., www.bennettenv.com.

[10]Fundamental Research Corp., "West Mountain Capital Corp. (TSXV: WMT)–Two Joint Ventures to Be Established in the Chinese Waste Management Market," August 11, 2010, http://www.phaseparation.com/images/pdf/WMT%20-%20Aug%202010%20Master.pdf.

[11]Stewardship Ontario, *Final Consolidated Municipal Hazardous or Special Waste Program Plan*, Volume 1, July 20, 2009, https://ozone.scholarsportal.info/bitstream/1873/15214/1/295182.pdf.

estimation that the paint sludge market represented about 7 per cent to 10 per cent of the industrial sludge market, the 2009 industrial sludge market in Ontario was, at most, approximately 150,000 tons . Assuming that Ontario's GDP was 40 per cent of Canada's GDP, and that paint waste generation would be proportional to GDP, the total industrial sludge in Canada was estimated to be at 375,000 tons in 2009.

Despite the potential size of this market appearing to be of a decent size for small firms such as PS2, the market was still at an emerging stage. The prohibition against dumping sludge into landfills might simply create more opportunities for other conventional disposal methods, such as incineration. The real market potential for firms such as PS2 would largely depend on their comparative cost advantages over other conventional disposal methods, and on future regulatory evolution, which was a slow process. The potential of this market for PS2 was also limited due to the distance between Ontario and PS2's facility in Saskatchewan. PS2 had yet to break into the industrial sludge market in Canada.

PS2 STRATEGIC MOVES

The vision of PS2 was to become a fully integrated environmental service company.[12] As such, the company was always seeking opportunities to expand both organically and through acquisition for the purpose of transforming itself into a more integrated and more diversified waste management company. On the domestic front, PS2 had gone through the following strategic moves.

Diversification into Pharmaceutical Waste Management[13]

Given the limited growth potential in soil remediation and oil recovery from industrial sludge, PS2 was searching for growth opportunities. It ventured into the pharmaceutical waste treatment market by acquiring a pharmaceutical waste-processing firm, Pharma Processing, on March 17, 2008. Pharma Processing was a well-known pharmaceutical waste management service provider that processed hazardous and non-hazardous pharmaceutical waste at its facility in Brampton, Ontario. Pharma Processing had been in operation since 1994. The acquisition was completed on July 23, 2008. The rationale behind the acquisition included geographic diversification, product diversification and scope economies.[14]

---

[12]Jordan Luy, "TSX Venture 50 Spotlight: West Mountain Capital Corp.," http://www.tmxmoney.com/en/news/interviews/Apr6-2011_WMT.html.

[13]Summarized from: Westcap Mgt. Ltd., "Golden Opportunities Fund's Investee Company–Phase Separation Solutions Inc. Enters into Agreement to Acquire Pharma Processing," news release, March 17, 2008, http://www.westcapmgt.ca/news/news_details.php?news_id=33; "West Mountain Completes Pharma Processing Acquisition," news release, July 23, 2008, http://www.stockwatch.com/swnet/newsit/newsit_newsit.aspx?bid=Z-C:WMT-1514767&symbol=WMT&news_region=C; http://www.neia.org/file/d569e488-b451-4310-b444-ff0eaf728d39.pdf; Phase Separation Solutions Inc., "Elevating the Thinking in Waste Management," http://www.westmountaincapital.com/pdf/Golden%20Opportunities%20Presentation.pdf; West Mountain Capital Corp,, "Consolidated Financial Statements, June 30, 2010 and 2009," http://ca.hotstocked.com/docs/show/west_mountain_capital_corp/financial_statements/q22010fs.pdf.

[14]Westcap Mgt. Ltd., "Golden Opportunities Fund's Investee Company–Phase Separation Solutions Inc. Enters into Agreement to Acquire Pharma Processing," news release, March 17, 2008, http://www.westcapmgt.ca/news/news_details.php?news_id=33.

The pharmaceutical waste stream was 49.6 per cent plastic packaging comingled with pharmaceuticals. Because of the co-mingling, the plastic in this waste stream was not readily recyclable. Thus, pharmaceutical wastes were typically incinerated. Using a modified version of its TPS technology, PS2 patented a process to depolymerize the plastic and deactivate the pharmaceutical ingredients. Using this process, PS2 was able to generate up to 44 litres of No. 2 fuel oil and up to 20 cubic metres of "synthetic" natural gas from 1cubic metre of pharmaceutical waste, while producing only 60 kilograms (kg) of carbon dioxide per metric tonne (CO_2/mT). In comparison, incineration not only cost more but also produced more than 300 kg CO_2/mT of waste without offering any recovery value.

Despite PS2 having succeeded in developing and commercializing its pharmaceutical waste business unit, the company decided, in October 2008, to exit this business to free capacity at the Wolseley facility for the soil market, which had increased since the acquisition. The decision was made as a result of the slower than projected growth rates and the higher per-unit transportation costs of pharmaceutical waste, which typically had a much lower density than contaminated soil. On December 12, 2008, the unit was acquired by an undisclosed firm. The pharmaceutical waste unit was sold at a profit, and the patent resulting from this business remained the property of PS2. Thus, the door was left open for PS2 to enter the business in the future.

Going Public through Reverse Acquisition of West Mountain Capital Corp.

Because PS2 was a small growth company, it needed to raise money to fund the various growth strategies required to realize its vision. In the absence of further venture capital financing, going public was a necessary strategy. However, an initial public offering (IPO) in its own name might not be appropriate for several reasons. First, the IPO market was not strong enough during a time of recession. Second, the company was at too early a stage for a broadly distributed regular IPO. Third, and most importantly, a traditional IPO might not allow the company founders to retain higher ownership levels, whereas at the company's current stage of development, the technical expertise of the strong founder–manager team was critical.

PS2 resorted to TSX Venture Exchange (TSXV), the public venture capital marketplace in Canada, which provided growth companies with access to capital and offered investors a venture investment market. TSXV offered a unique listing vehicle, the Capital Pool Company® (CPC)[15] program, which provided an alternative, two-step introduction to the capital markets that would meet PS2's requirements. The CPC program identified entrepreneurs whose development and growth-stage companies required capital and public company management expertise and introduced them to investors who had financial market experience. Unlike a traditional IPO, the CPC program enabled seasoned directors and officers to form a CPC with no assets other than cash and no significant commercial operations. They could then list the CPC on TSXV and raise a pool of capital. The CPC then used these funds to seek out an investment opportunity in a growing business. Once the CPC had completed its "qualifying transaction" and acquired an operating company that met TSXV's listing requirements, its shares continued trading

---

[15]Refer to [TSX Inc., "Capital Pool Company Program," http://www.tmx.com/en/pdf/CPCBrochure.pdf] for a description of the Capital Pool Company® program, a two-step introduction to the Canadian capital market at TSX Venture Exchange.

as a regular listing on the TSX Venture Exchange. Alternatively, an existing operating company could reverse acquire the CPC. The use of CPCs not only provided a going-public process that had more certainty, greater flexibility and allowed for greater control by the operating company but also removed the company's risk from the going-public process.

PS2 reverse acquired West Mountain Capital (TSXV: WMT), a CPC that was incorporated in 2005 with its headquarters in Calgary, Canada.[16] As a CPC, it did not have commercial operations. It intended to identify and evaluate entrepreneurial companies with a view to completing a "qualifying transaction" to become integrated with an existing company satisfactory to its evaluation. In December 2007, based on the strength of PS2's technology and the recognized expertise of its executive team, WMT decided to be taken over by PS2 in a reverse takeover. In so doing, PS2 went public on the TSXV and, by April 2010, had grown to a market capitalization of $12.67 million. In the newly integrated corporate structure, PS2 became the only wholly owned subsidiary of WMT, the parent firm. The new vision and mandate of West Mountain Capital was to evaluate and seek complementary acquisition in the environmental services industry with a view to building a fully integrated environmental services firm focused in Western Canada.[17]

Other Potential Future Moves

Consistent with its vision of building a fully integrated and diversified environmental services firm, WMT also had plans for geographical diversification. Its Wolseley facility had an annual treatment capacity of 20,000 tons (which could be expanded to 60,000 tons, subject to regulatory approval, at a relatively low capital expenditure of $2 million). However, because the Wolseley facility was a fixed facility, and all the contaminated material needed to be transported there, transportation costs played a huge role in the viability of the company's business model. The company could establish a second facility in Ontario (the largest market in Canada) if and when demand exceeded the current plant capacity of 20,000 tons.

THE CHINESE MARKET

China has seen rapid economic development since its opening up to the outside world three decades earlier. Real GDP per capita rose from $220 in 1980 to $2,883 in 2010,[18] or an annual growth rate of approximately 9 per cent from 1980 to 2010. However, this economic achievement had been made at the cost of the environment. Residents in big cities rarely saw a clear sky due to ubiquitous smog resulting from industrial pollution, coal-based power generation, and transportation exhaust.

Environmental pollution was becoming a big issue in China due to its many negative consequences. Smog affected worker attendance and productivity rates in many cities. Various types of pollution also placed a big burden on the country's medical system. An

---

[16]"Company Overview of West Mountain Capital Corp,, Prior to Reverse Merger with Phase Separation Solutions, Inc., *Bloomberg Businessweek,* http://investing.businessweek.com/research/stocks/private/snapshot. asp?privcapId=26000232.

[17]West Mountain Capital, "Portfolio," http://www.westmountaincapital.com/links/portfolio.html.

[18]"Real Historical Gross Domestic Product (GDP) Per Capita and Growth Rates of GDP Per Capita for Baseline Countries/Regions (in 2005 Dollars) 1969-2011," www.ers.usda.gov/Data/Macroeconomics/Data/Historical RealPerCapitaIncomeValues.xls.

estimated 410,000 Chinese people died each year as a result of pollution.[19] Environmental pollution had also become a social issue. For example, in recent years, the number of mass protests caused by environmental issues had grown by an annual rate of 29 per cent.

The social pressure became even more urgent after the 2008 Beijing Olympics. To prepare for the games, the Chinese government had taken a series of measures to reduce pollution in the participating Chinese cities, including restricting vehicle use, reducing coal combustion and closing some pollution-emitting factories. As a result of these measures, city dwellers saw a clear sky for the first time in decades. The 2008 Beijing Olympic Games not only provided China with an opportunity to showcase its beauty, history and power but also presented the Chinese people with a new perspective on the relationship between economic development and environmental protection. A consensus emerged in China that environmental protection needed to become a priority in the country's agenda. The Chinese government now regarded environmental protection as a "basic state policy."

Since 2008, the Chinese government had stepped up its involvement and commitment in environmental protection. In 2009, the environmental expenditure by the Chinese State Environmental Protection Agency was at $162.5 billion, up from $75 billion in 2005.[20] The government had also sped up its implementation of the Stockholm Convention on Persistent Organic Pollutants (POPs), an international environmental treaty that aimed to eliminate or restrict the production and use of POPs for their damage to human health and the environment.

POPs Market in China

PCB Market Size PCB production had been banned in China since the 1980s. Prior to the ban, approximately 10,000 tons of PCBs had been produced, some of which were released into the environment. The total amount of high-density PCB waste (>500 parts per million [ppm]) in China was estimated to be 50,000 tons, and the total amount of low-density wastes (50–500 ppm) was estimated to be 500,000 tons.[21] This amount was three times the Canadian PCB market size. Assuming a treatment cost of ¥3,000,[22] the Chinese PCB market was ¥1.65 billion, or approximately $255 million.

The PCB contaminated soil was spread in numerous PCB-contaminated sites, which were difficult to identify. Zhejiang and Liaoning provinces alone had 83 sealed PCB contaminated sites. Based on the distribution of PCB use in China, China might have as many as 800 PCB-contaminated sites.[23]

POPs Market Size in General In addition to the 550,000 tons of soil contaminated with PCBs (which was one of many POPs), an additional 1 million tons of soil was contaminated

[19]The Common Language Project, "China Fact Sheet," http://clpmag.org/article.php?article=China-Fact-Sheet_4.

[20]West Mountain Capital Corp., "Phase Separation Solutions Expands License to Cover China," news release, August 10, 2009, www.phaseparation.com/images/pdf/aug10.pdf.

[21]The People's Republic of China, "National Implementation Plan for the Stockholm Convention on Persistent Organic Pollutants," April 2007, http://www.pops.int/documents/implementation/nips/submissions/China_NIP_En.pdf.

[22]http://www.infzm.com/content/64914; http://nf.nfdaily.cn/nfzm/content/2011-11/18/content_33440330.htm.

[23]Authors' estimates based on the project document for "Building the Capacity of the People's Republic of China to Implement the Stockholm Convention on POPs and Develop a National Implementation Plan," 2004, http://www.thegef.org/gef/sites/thegef.org/files/repository/China_-_POPs.pdf.

with other POPs.[24] Assuming a similar treatment cost to that of PCBs, of ¥3,000,[25] the POPs market size was estimated to be ¥3.00 billion, equivalent to approximately $470 million. Experts estimated that China might have as many as 300,000 to 600,000 sites contaminated with POPs.[26]

Because PS2's technology could be applied regardless of the types of POPs to be treated, it would compete in a market of $725 million. Even this number may have been conservative and would probably rise as the Chinese government improved its environmental protection measures. Furthermore, the ongoing rapid industrialization and urbanization in the country would probably continue to generate POP wastes.

Current Market Situation The Chinese government was strongly committed to the Stockholm Convention on Persistent Organic Pollutants. It also had a strong resolve to tackle the issue of POP contamination. In 2010, the Chinese government announced that it would invest more than US$3 billion in soil investigation and soil remediation over the next five years, beginning in 2011.

Compared with developed countries, the management of POP-contaminated soil in China was still at an early stage. China lagged behind with respect to research capabilities, policies, procedures and techniques for safely managing and disposing of its enormous POPs contamination. As such, in 2006, the Chinese government embarked on the China PCBs Management and Disposal Demonstration Project, which was jointly funded by the Global Environment Facility Trust Fund (through the World Bank). The project was to be implemented in Jiangsu and Liaoning provinces, with the specific objective to help China establish and strengthen its policies, regulations and standards for PCB management and disposal. It also aimed to establish and enhance China's capability in PCB waste monitoring, treatment and disposal.[27] The successful PCB management and disposal experience from this project would then be disseminated across the country.[28] Launched in 2006, the project had been progressing well. In 2009, a successful trial run was conducted on the Shenyang PCBs High Temperature Incineration Facility in Liaoning Province.

Under the same demonstration project, an indirect Thermal Desorption Unit (TDU) was to be procured to dispose of PCB-contaminated soil and to carry out the cleanup, treatment and disposal of PCB equipment storage sites in the two demonstration provinces. After following the World Bank's international competitive bidding procedures, the consortium of Beaudin Consulting (U.S.), BRISEA Group, Inc. (U.S.) and Beijing Construction Engineering Group won the bid in early 2009 at the price of $3,732,453. The TDU would take up an area of about 5,000 square metres and would have a daily capacity of treating 70 tons of soil contaminated with PCBs up to 20,000 ppm. Contaminated soil would be transported to the TDU facility for treatment. After treatment, the PCB level in treated soil would be less than 1.0 ppm. The TDU unit had been delivered to Jiangsu Province in China after its fabrication

---

[24]http://www.cenews.com.cn/xwzx/hq/qt/200802/t20080214_220144.html. This number may be extremely conservative.

[25]This number may be conservative. See Ralph S. Baker et al., "In-pile Thermal Desorption of Soil and Sediment," 2006, http://www.terratherm.com/pdf/white%20papers/paper7-11-6-09.pdf.

[26]"Soil Pollution Poisons More than Farmland," *China Daily*, March 10, 2011, http://www.china.org.cn/environment/2011-03/10/content_22098214.htm.

[27]"Project Progress," *POPs Action in Canada*, September/October 2009, pp. 2-3, http://en.mepfeco.org.cn/Resources/Periodicals/PAIC/201009/P020100908629022960445.pdf.

[28]"Project Document on a Proposed Grant from the Global Environment Facility Trust Fund in the Amount of USD 18.34 Million to the People's Republic of China for a PCB Management and Disposal Demonstration Project," April 25, 2005, http://www.thegef.org/gef/sites/thegef.org/files/repository/China_-_PCB_Mgmt_Disposal_Demo.pdf.

in the United States. However, no information was available about whether the TDU unit worked to specification and expectations.

PS2's Advantage Even though a TDU unit had been procured from another contractor for the PCB demonstration project, PS2 and its TPS technology would provide the Chinese market with a competitive alternative for the Chinese market for several reasons. First, the TPS technology had originally been developed as a mobile, onsite remedial technology. This attribute would prove to be attractive to the Chinese market, which had numerous small contaminated sites. PS2's TPS-PS model had a handling capacity of 50 kg per hour, whereas the smallest model from Beaudin Consulting, which had been used in the demonstration project, was in the range of 2 to 3 tons per hour.[29] Although the TDU unit also claimed to be capable of being easily installed and dismantled,[30] the TPS technology had higher mobility. Second, PS2 had been seriously considering China, as was demonstrated by its involvement with the Chinese market in the past one-and-a-half years of relationship building and market research. Many other environmental firms were still locked in the mentality of creating an entry mode through equipment export and service contracts.

PS2's TPS technology was likely to be embraced in a market such as China, where hundreds of thousands of contaminated sites were widely dispersed across the country. In the demonstration project, the contaminated soil would need to be transported to the TDU for treatment, and the desorbed POPs would need to be further transported to a high-temperature incineration facility. This approach might not be sustainable in the longer run for several reasons. First, soils contaminated with POPs could not be easily transported because of their bulk. Second, new laws and regulations were expected to ban the importation of waste containing POPs from province to province, in response to public pressure.

Oil Sludge Market in China

Three to five per cent of crude oil becomes sludge, which is unusable if not further treated.[31] When sludge is transported in oil tankers or stored in storage tanks, it settles to the container bottom, where it cannot be drained but must be removed and hauled away at considerable expense. Oil sludge is caused by oil solidifying or gelling in a storage tank, often as a result of an excess of water in the oil.[32] Sludge can cause major problems in oil storage tanks if not cleaned regularly. Typical crude oil tank bottoms contain more than 50 per cent by weight oil, 30 to 45 per cent water and 5 to 20 per cent solids.[33]

The Chinese petrochemical industry generated approximately 5.67 million tons of oil sludge each year, based on its processing of domestic production.[34] China's oil import

---

[29]http://www.ygnfilcore.com/content.asp?id=44&menuId=72|6; Beaudin Consulting webpage, http://www.beaudins.com/.

[30]Hangzhou DADI Environmental Protection Engineering Co., Ltd., "Thermal Desorption System," http://www.dadi-ep.com/en/jishu.aspx?id=8.

[31]"Oil-sludge-processing Industry Overview," *Russian-American Business*, October 19, 2010, http://russianamericanbusiness.org/web_CURRENT/articles/654/1/Oil-sludge-processing-industry-overview.

[32]LianDi Clean Technology Inc., "LianDi Clean Technology Inc. Announces Landmark Strategic Alliance with Leading Japanese Oil Sludge Company," news release, September 13, 2010, http://www.china-liandi.com/September%2013%20-%20Liandi%20Landmark%20Agreement%20with%20SKK.html.

[33]Dee Ann Sanders, "Pollution Prevention and Reuse Alternatives for Crude Oil Tank-Bottom Sludges," ipec.utulsa.edu/Conf2001/sanders_123.pdf.

[34]Authors' calculation is based on China's crude oil production in 2009 of 3.79 million barrels per day and the assumptions later in the paragraph.

dependence ratio surpassed 55 per cent in early 2010 and was forecasted to reach 60 per cent in 2015. Thus, more sludge would likely be generated from oil imports. China imported 4.08 million barrels of crude oil per day (BPD), or 1.49 billion barrels on a yearly basis in 2009.[35] Based on a BPD to tons per year conversion ratio of 49.8,[36] China imported 203.2 million tons of oil in 2009. Assuming a conservative ratio of 3 per cent of oil sludge to oil, China would need to treat 6.1 million or more tons of oil sludge as a result of its annual oil imports. Much of the huge amount of oil sludge would need to be treated at facilities close to coastal oil terminals or oil reserve bases in China.

Traditionally, oil sludge in China had been dumped directly into the environment (e.g., into unlined, earthen pits), buried without treatment or incinerated. This situation would not be able to be continued as new regulations in some provinces enforced proper treatment, in response to the environmental awareness of the general public. As such, an emerging industry was oil sludge treatment. However, the industry was still in its infancy, and the market was very fragmented. This fragmentation was in part because of the spread of oil sludge generation in many oil fields and port facilities.

Pharmaceutical Waste Market

In 2006, China produced 570,000 tons of pharmaceutical waste, most of which were incinerated, generating up to 1176.3 grams of toxic equivalents (g TEQ) of dioxins, or 11 per cent of total dioxin release in China.[37] The amount of pharmaceutical waste would continue to increase because of an aging Chinese population that would lead to greater future spending on health care. The Chinese government had decided to offer basic medical care to farmers in rural areas. Although the pharmaceutical waste market was not a priority for PS2, compared with the other two waste streams of POP-contaminated soil and oil sludge, PS2 could still consider it as a market to diversify into in the future, especially when considering the absolute size of the pharmaceutical waste market and PS2's past experience in pharmaceutical waste management in Canada.

THE OPTIONS IN CHINA FOR PS2

Option 1: Remediation of POP-Contaminated Soil

The first option required the cooperation of the Nanjing Institute of Environmental Sciences (NIES) of the State Environmental Protection Agency, Ministry of Environmental Protection for the People's Republic of China. Located in Nanjing, the capital city of Jiangsu Province, NIES was a key technical provider for policies, legislation, action plans and technical guidelines on biodiversity conservation in China. Its research areas included rural environmental protection, nature conservation and biodiversity protection. NIES employed more than 200 scientific and technical staff, who carried out research on rural ecology, nature conservation, pollution prevention of township and village enterprises, and agriculture chemicals. NIES undertook key national research programs and scientific research projects on the rural

---

[35]Reuters Africa, "UPDATE 2-China 2010 Crude Oil Imports up 17.5 pct to Record High," January 10, 2011, http://af.reuters.com/article/energyOilNews/idAFTOE70607320110110.

[36]"How Many Barrels of Crude Oil in One MT?" http://www.onlineconversion.com/forum/forum_1058197476.htm.

[37]Ministry of Environmental Protection of the People's Republic of China, Foreign Economic Cooperation Office, *POPs Action in China*, July 2009, http://en.mepfeco.org.cn/Resources/Publications/201009/P020100908621278591698.pdf.

environment. It also provided the scientific basis and technical support for the management of rural environments and nature and of ecological conservation while assisting in the formulation and implementation of relevant action plans.

In the NIES option, a joint venture (JV) would be established between PS2 and NIES on a mutually beneficial date. In addition, NIES would act as an agent for PS2's TPS technology in China. The JV would construct a mobile TPS unit in China and use it in a demonstration project for the treatment of 2,000 to 3,000 tons of POP-contaminated soil. (The TPS unit had a capacity to treat approximately 30,000 tons of soil per year). This task would cause no concern to PS2 because its TPS technology had originally been a mobile, onsite remedial technology. PS2 also had extensive experience in applying its mobile technology on numerous contaminated sites around the world.

After the success of the demonstration project, the JV would subsequently use its TPS technology to design, plan, launch, bid for, operate and participate in various remediation projects throughout China. To use its technology in this way, the JV would need to design, engineer, manufacture and market TPS units in China for use in various parts of China. The JV was also proposed to provide solutions and consulting services for environmental remediation issues.

The JV would need an investment of approximately $3.0 million. This option offered several attractive advantages. First, NIES was a government agency, which significantly reduced the risk of the project. Second, NIES had extensive remedial experience and expertise. Third, NIES had identified and inventoried more than 300 sites in just three provinces. The sites ranged in size from 3,000 tons to 2,000,000 tons of contaminated soil. Fourth, the project was a demonstration project, which not only had a lower risk level but also acted as a free advertising campaign for PS2's technology. Being involved in a demonstration project also implied that PS2 was an early entrant into the emerging environmental market in China and would most likely enjoy certain first-mover advantages.

Option 2: Oil Recovery from Oil Sludge

The second option was to cooperate with Zhoushan Nahai Solid Waste Central Disposal Co. Ltd. (Nahai) in Zhejiang Province. Established in September 2009, Nahai was a private company and was the largest and only solid waste management company in the Zhoushan area of Zhejiang. It covered a land area of 33,700 square metres, and the investment was ¥62.35 million (approximately Cdn$9.8 million).[38] Despite Nahai's short history, it had become a leader in the management of hazardous waste and oil sludge in the Zhoushan area. The company had an excellent infrastructure, including an oil storage facility (capacity of 2,500,000 tons), a waste oil recovery facility (capacity of 1,000,000 tons per year), bilge water treatment process (capacity of 20,000 tons per day) and a solid waste destruction facility (capacity of 20 tons per day). Nahai possessed the only waste management processing permit in Zhoushan.

Zhoushan comprised a group of islands located at the opening of the Yangtze River, just south of Shanghai. It was in the centre of the world's largest four fisheries and had been ranked as the ninth biggest harbour among Chinese coastal harbors and the biggest commercial petroleum transit base in China. Many oil storage facilities were located in this region due to its accessibility to the traditional shipping lanes. For example, Zhoushan was

---

[38]"Environmental Impact Assessment," http://app.zjepb.gov.cn/UpLoad/xzxksb/201081290007.doc.

home to the Aoshan Oil Terminal, China's largest oil transshipment base, and Zhoushan National Oil Reserve Base Co., Ltd. (one of China's 12 state strategic crude oil reserve bases).

The cooperation with Nahai would be in the form of a JV. The JV was proposed to establish a fixed facility in Zhoushan, which would be capable of processing 10,000 tons of oily sludge per year and expandable to 100,000 tons per year. The facility would process and recover oil from the oily sludge waste generated from oil storage operations and oil tanker cleaning activities in the region. PS2's management team was well suited for this task due to their global experience. The JV would also further define and develop other technologies to complement the oily sludge treatment process, provide solutions and consulting services with respect to oil recovery issues, and explore opportunities of applying the oily sludge treatment technology to other parts of China.

The JV would need an investment of approximately $3.0 million. This option was attractive for several reasons. First, Nahai's owner was an accomplished entrepreneur, similar to Paul Antle. The two entrepreneurs had identified with each other from the beginning. Throughout their interactions, a solid trust had been developed. Second, Nahai had solid assets and had obtained a wide range of permits. Third, Nahai was located in a region that generated approximately 180,000 tons of oily sludge waste per year.[39] This amount was about 3 per cent of the total amount of oil sludge China generated in 2009 (6.1 million tons as previously shown) from its oil imports.

THE DECISION

The environmental market in China presented PS2 with both challenges and opportunities. For a small entrepreneurial firm such as PS2, the cooperative opportunities with NIES and Nahai in such a large market would not only affect the metrics of the company but would also strain corporate resources and the organizational structure. The China entry would also mark an important stage along its internationalization path. Although the entrepreneurial leadership at PS2 had been successful in the past and was eager to achieve even higher goals, this situation differed from its past projects in the international market, which had been based on the export of equipment and service contracts.

After careful deliberation, PS2 had arrived a point where a series of decisions needed to be made. Any delay might open opportunities for competitors. Should PS2 enter the Chinese market? Should PS2 pursue the NIES option or the Nahai option? Would it be feasible to pursue both? What ownership levels should PS2 assume for each option? How would PS2 staff its Chinese operation(s)? Antle needed to use a thorough analysis of market situation and PS2's resources and technical and organizational capabilities to arrive at some answers.

> This case was written with generous financial assistance from the Hill-Ivey Case-Writing Fund.

---

[39]Fundamental Research Corp., "West Mountain Capital Corp. (TSXV: WMT)–Two Joint Ventures to Be Established in the Chinese Waste Management Market," August 11, 2010, http://www.phaseparation.com/images/pdf/WMT%20-%20Aug%202010%20Master.pdf.

EXHIBIT 1: Phase Separation Solutions Income Statements (In Canadian Dollars)

	2007	2008	2009	2010E	2011E
Revenue	**255,633**	**—**	**5,884,361**	**4,900,000**	**7,233,333**
Cost of goods sold	257,473	103,323	2,009,746	1,760,000	2,893,333
Gross profit	**(1,840)**	**(103,323)**	**3,874,615**	**3,140,000**	**4,340,000**
Expenses					
General & administrative	415,567	608,493	886,620	822,312	904,543
Stock-based compensation	19,488	91,555	71,244	98,000	144,667
EBITDA	**(436,895)**	**(803,371)**	**2,916,751**	**2,219,688**	**3,290,790**
Amortization	335,609	393,091	420,941	407,448	361,331
EBIT	**(772,504)**	**(1,196,462)**	**2,495,810**	**1,812,240**	**2,929,459**
Interest & Bank Charges	31,783	17,682	9,745	8,980	3,417
Earnings from operations	**(804,287)**	**(1,214,144)**	**2,486,065**	**1,803,259**	**2,926,042**
Interest income	5,661	21,386	—	—	—
Interest on long-term debt	(368,161)	(44,484)	(106,948)	—	—
EBT	**(1,166,787)**	**(1,237,242)**	**2,379,117**	**1,803,259**	**2,926,042**
Discontinued operations, net of income taxes	(345,983)	(193,516)	129,030	—	—
Taxes	—	—	—	—	907,073
Net earnings for the Period	**(1,512,770)**	**(1,430,758)**	**2,508,147**	**1,803,259**	**2,018,969**

Source: Fundamental Research Corp., "West Mountain Capital Corp. (TSXV: WMT)—Initiating Coverage—Thermal Treatment of Soil, Sludge and Other Waste Streams," March 23, 2010, http://www.baystreet.ca/articles/research_reports/fundamental_research/West-MountainCapital040110.pdf.

EXHIBIT 2: Phase Separation Solutions Balance Sheets (In Canadian Dollars)

	2007	2008	2009	2010E	2011E
Assets					
Cash and cash equivalents	1,253,446	783,993	3,255,003	5,072,250	7,432,087
Accounts receivable	117,725	155,344	681,075	696,499	1,028,166
Income tax receivable	—	177,861	—	—	—
Assets related to discontinued operations	—	141,988	—	—	—
Prepaid expenses and deposits	2,750	12,094	9,144	8,843	13,053
Current assets	**1,373,921**	**1,271,280**	**3,945,222**	**5,777,592**	**8,473,306**
Restricted cash	145,301	167,383	217,394	217,394	217,394
Capital assets	2,970,732	2,982,937	2,716,322	2,408,874	2,147,543
Other assets	51,216	46,096	41,904	41,904	41,904
Total assets	**4,541,170**	**4,467,696**	**6,920,842**	**8,445,763**	**10,880,146**
Liabilities & shareholders' equity					
Bank loan	—	107,000	—	—	—
Accounts payable & accrued liabilities	296,207	299,658	864,972	509,952	838,331
Deferred revenue	184,409	393,798	—	—	—
Convertible debentures	—	—	474,203	—	—
Liabilities related to discontinued operations	—	184,903	38,732	38,732	38,732
Current portion of obligations under capital lease	5,570	56,412	61,318	97,631	—
Current liabilities	**486,186**	**1,041,771**	**1,439,225**	**646,315**	**877,063**
Obligations under capital lease	—	158,652	97,631	—	—
Convertible debentures	—	464,274	—	—	—
Shareholders' loans	—	—	—	—	—
Long-term debt	—	—	—	—	—
Asset retirement obligations	93,431	102,775	113,052	153,052	193,052
Shareholder's equity					
Share capital	6,915,817	6,935,817	6,935,817	7,459,213	7,459,213
Contributed surplus	90,141	181,696	252,940	350,940	495,607
Equity component of convertible debentures	—	57,874	49,193	—	—
Deficit	(3,044,405)	(4,475,163)	(1,967,016)	(163,757)	1,855,212
Total liabilities & shareholders' equity	**4,541,170**	**4,467,696**	**6,920,842**	**8,445,763**	**10,880,146**

Source: Fundamental Research Corp., "West Mountain Capital Corp. (TSXV: WMT)—Initiating Coverage—Thermal Treatment of Soil, Sludge and Other Waste Streams," March 23, 2010, http://www.baystreet.ca/articles/research_reports/fundamental_research/West-MountainCapital040110.pdf.

EXHIBIT 3: Phase Separation Solutions Statements of Cash Flows (In Canadian Dollars)

	2008	2009	2010E	2011E
Operating activities				
Net earnings for the period	(1,430,758)	2,508,147	1,803,259	2,018,969
Discontinued operations, net of income taxes	193,516	(129,030)	—	—
Items not involving cash				
Asset retirement obligations	18,992	48,868	40,000	40,000
Amortization	390,017	410,664	407,448	361,331
Gain on settlement of debentures	—	(5,621)	—	—
Stock-based compensation	91,555	71,244	98,000	144,667
	(736,678)	2,904,272	2,348,708	2,564,967
Changes in non-cash operating working capital	168,894	(173,404)	(370,143)	(7,499)
Cash from (used in) operating activities—discontinued operations	(630,629)	24,847	—	—
Cash from (used in) operations	**(1,198,413)**	**2,755,715**	**1,978,565**	**2,557,468**
Financing activities				
Cash acquired on reverse takeover	—	—	—	—
Repayment of long-term debt	—	—	—	—
Proceeds from bank loan	107,000	—	—	—
Repayment of bank load	—	(107,000)	—	—
Payment of capital lease obligations	(48,483)	(56,115)	—	—
Proceeds (repayment) of debentures—net	500,000	(31,722)	—	—
Proceeds from issuance of common share & exercise of stock options	20,000	—	—	—
Cash provided by (used in) financing activities	**578,517**	**(194,837)**	**—**	**—**
Investing activities				
Increase in restricted cash	(22,082)	(50,011)	—	—
Purchase of capital assets	(322,076)	(139,857)	(61,318)	(97,631)
Capital expenditures	—	—	(100,000)	(100,000)
Cash provided by investing activities—discontinued operations	494,601	100,000	—	—
Cash provided by (used in) investing activities	**150,443**	**(89,868)**	**(161,318)**	**(197,631)**
Increase (decrease) in cash	(469,453)	2,471,010	1,817,247	2,359,837
Cash beginning of period	1,253,446	783,993	3,255,003	5,072,250
Cash end of period	**783,993**	**3,255,003**	**5,072,250**	**7,432,087**

Source: Fundamental Research Corp., "West Mountain Capital Corp. (TSXV: WMT)–Initiating Coverage—Thermal Treatment of Soil, Sludge and Other Waste Streams," March 23, 2010, http://www.baystreet.ca/articles/research_reports/fundamental_research/West-MountainCapital040110.pdf.

Paul Antle, The Serial Entrepreneur: A Biography

Paul G. Antle, B.Sc., M.Eng., CCEP, was the president and chief executive officer of Phase Separation Solutions, Inc. A recognized leader in the Canadian environmental and waste management industries, he had over 25 years of experience and had started, operated, grown and sold numerous businesses.

Antle was born in St. John's, Newfoundland and Labrador. He graduated from Memorial University in 1985 with a B.Sc. degree in Chemistry. With no desire to do research or teach, he went on to the University of New Brunswick (UNB) to pursue a master's degree in Chemical Engineering, with an aim to apply his chemistry background in a practical application. Antle graduated from UNB with a master's degree at the age of 22 in 1987. With résumés in hand and an eagerness for work, he journeyed to Toronto, Ontario. However, he was not successful in landing a job he wanted. Antle returned to Newfoundland, empty handed but not discouraged.

Two months later, Antle was hired to kick-start a newly opened waste management division for a local construction company that had encountered PCBs at its construction site. After working for the company for nine months and achieving all his goals, Antle determined that it was time for a new challenge. Armed with a bank loan and helped by some friends, he hung out his own shingle as an entrepreneur on July 14, 1988, when he founded the SCC Environmental Group (SCC) in Newfoundland and Labrador.

From its meager beginnings, SCC grew during the first half of the 1990s to become known for its advanced site remediation and integrated hazardous waste management. The company employed 150 Newfoundlanders and worked on four continents. In 1994, SCC launched the TPS Technology. The reputation of SCC grew to such a point that Stratos Global Corp., a satellite communications company, purchased SCC in September 1996 for $3.2 million.

Stratos Global invested in the TPS technology and financed the promotion of it to the international oil and gas sector. SCC soon started dealing in international contracts. During 1997/98, however, Stratos Global refocused its business and decided to divest any interests that were not related to telecommunications. Antle decided to buy the company back, and the transaction was completed on July 13, 1998. He then sold it to MI Drilling Fluids of Houston, Texas, on December 14, 1999, for $10.0 million. MI Drilling Fluids used the TPS technology for the treatment of drilling mud and cuttings generated by the oil and gas industry. Antle served as the president and CEO of SCC from 1988 to 1999, as vice president of Stratos Global Corporation from 1996 to 1998, and as vice president of Thermal Operations at MI Drilling Fluids from 1999 to 2001.

In 1995, Antle founded Island Waste Management Inc., which he sold for $5.6 million in August 2006. He joined PS2's management/ownership team in 2005 to oversee its growth into a public company and its diversification into pharmaceutical waste management. Antle holds a majority equity interest in PS2 and runs it as president and CEO.

Antle was inducted into the Academy of Entrepreneurs in September 1995; was a finalist for Atlantic Canada's Entrepreneur of the Year Award in 1995; received a World Young Business Achiever Award in 1997; was recognized for his contribution to the Newfoundland and Labrador Environmental Industry in 2002; in August 2002 was part of Canada's official delegation to the United Nations World Summit on Sustainable Development held in Johannesburg, South Africa; in May 2003 was named one of Canada's Top 40 Under 40™; and in November 2003 was named Alumnus of the Year for Gonzaga High School.

CASE
17

Cervus Equipment Corporation: Harvesting A New Future

Looking out his office window at the growing skyline surrounding the Calgary Airport, Graham Drake thought about the recent growth of Cervus Equipment Corporation (Cervus Equipment). The company had realized several significant accomplishments over the previous five years–Drake had never dreamed that Cervus Equipment would be approaching $1 billion in revenue!

Why, then, was he cautious about the future?

The company had accomplished so much over the previous nine years, growing from $56 million (in 2003) to $734 million. Profits had grown even faster than revenue. It was a good news story in the face of a global economic slowdown and a contribution to a proud legacy that had begun with the company's founder, Peter Lacey. Customers were experiencing unprecedented growth amid a dynamic business environment. Shareholders were happy with the growth in their shares and dividends. Original equipment manufacturer (OEM) partnerships with John Deere, Bobcat, JCB, Clark, Peterbilt and others were stronger than ever. And Cervus Equipment had recently topped 1,200 employees.

However, Drake knew that to reach his board's goal of $2.5 billion in revenue by 2020[1]–three times the current run rate–they would have to stretch both their business model and organization well beyond anything they had experienced to date. This would likely take them into new markets and new product and service categories and would require a much more focused innovation effort than they had experienced in the past. Could they achieve this growth and maintain the corporate values their employees had

⬥IVEY | Publishing

Daniel J. Doiron and Davis Schryer wrote this case solely to provide material for class discussion. The authors do not intend to illustrate either effective or ineffective handling of a managerial situation. The authors may have disguised certain names and other identifying information to protect confidentiality.

This publication may not be transmitted, photocopied, digitized or otherwise reproduced in any form or by any means without the permission of the copyright holder. Reproduction of this material is not covered under authorization by any reproduction rights organization. To order copies or request permission to reproduce materials, contact Ivey Publishing, Ivey Business School, Western University, London, Ontario, Canada, N6G 0N1; (t) 519.661.3208; (e) cases@ivey.ca; www.iveycases.com.

Copyright © 2013, Richard Ivey School of Business Foundation   Version: 2013-09-27

One time permission to reproduce granted by Richard Ivey School of Business Foundation on April 22, 2014.

---

[1]This does not necessarily reflect the actual target, forecast or goal for the company at the time of publication; it is designed to complement the teaching goals associated with this case study.

grown to embrace–the *principles over policy* approach and the practice of letting employees make critical decisions about customer needs and requirements. Could they continue to be seen as "local" by their customers, yet achieve the economies of scale in their operations they knew were needed to effectively grow their business? Could they continue to have close, meaningful partnerships with OEMs in an industry that was beginning to see a number of arguably revolutionary changes? Were they diversified enough, given the cyclical nature of the farming and construction industries and the relatively small geographic footprint they served in western Canada and New Zealand? Could they foster the leadership talent throughout the organization needed to achieve this level of growth? Could they continue to successfully acquire small equipment retailers at reasonable valuations that would enable acceptable payback periods?

These questions would all have to be carefully considered before Drake met with his board in April to prepare for the 2013 annual shareholder meeting. Board members expected him to present a new growth strategy for Cervus Equipment.

THE EARLY YEARS

The foundation for Cervus Equipment was a simple notion: that owners of John Deere farm equipment dealerships were nearing retirement and looking for viable succession opportunities. Second-generation owners had difficulty accessing the large amount of capital required to purchase dealerships and/or were not able to provide the level of leadership and management necessary to run the growing operations; given this, some dealerships were not performing at optimal levels. It became apparent that these types of owners were becoming interested in divesting their dealerships but not to just anyone. They cared not only about achieving a fair value for their businesses but also about selling to a reputable operator who would continue to dutifully service and respect the rural communities where they lived with their customers and employees. These factors amounted to a real opportunity for Cervus Equipment to execute its business plan by establishing a reputation built upon integrity and goodwill.

Cervus Equipment began as a partnership between Peter Lacey, Graham Drake and other owners of a few John Deere dealerships in the 1990s. At the time, they had no intention of managing these dealerships from a central organization. Rather, they believed that entrepreneurs with a material ownership position in the stores were in the best position to operate and grow these businesses. The model had no integration challenges, as no integration was required–until 1999, that is, when the business partners pooled their remaining dealership assets into the company, took it public[2] and embarked on an aggressive consolidation-based growth strategy.

The second important element of their approach was the relationship with the OEM John Deere. They knew OEMs were usually treated as "suppliers" by dealers, and this could result in a business relationship that might become confrontational or contentious. Cervus Equipment recognized that a more positive "partnership" approach with OEMs would provide, among other things, opportunities to purchase dealerships with growth potential. After all, John Deere was knowledgeable about the relative market performance of all their dealers, was aware of opportunities for potential acquisitions and had final approval of all ownership transactions within their dealer network.

Lastly, Lacey and Drake knew that they wanted to represent premium brands in the markets they served. John Deere was by far *the* premium leading brand in the North American farming equipment industry, with industry leading technology and market share.

---

[2]As of 1999, Cervus Equipment trades on the Toronto Stock Exchange under the ticker symbol CVL.

These three factors, when put together, provided a great foundation for Cervus Equipment's business and growth strategy. Over the next 13 years, the company amassed 55 wholly or partially owned (via partnerships) equipment dealerships, with 36 representing John Deere in the agricultural industry. The remaining 19 stores represented construction equipment brands Bobcat and JCB, material handling equipment OEMs Sellick, Clark, Nissan Forklift and Doosan (forklifts, mulching, etc.) and, recently, long haul trucking manufacturer, Peterbilt (refer to Exhibit 1 for a timeline depicting Cervus Equipments' growth path). Interestingly, Cervus Equipment was the only public company representing multiple stores in the John Deere dealer network.

Further consolidation of John Deere dealerships was, however, going to be more difficult for a number of reasons. First, historically, manufacturers were uncomfortable having one organization amass a large amount of scale over its dealer network in Canada, as this afforded dealership owners too much bargaining power. For OEMs, the market risk of having too many of their dealerships in one basket was a legitimate concern, because OEMs expect proper coverage of assigned trade areas, and bigger territory equals higher risk. Secondly, Cervus Equipment had already acquired the majority of the low hanging fruit–the smaller, independently run dealerships. Remaining dealerships had already been consolidated into groups of five to nine stores. These more savvy organizations would likely cost more to purchase. Cal Johnson, vice-president Agriculture, dubbed this "round two of consolidation," suggesting that "these would be more difficult to integrate from a cultural and leadership perspective." Third, John Deere, at this point in time, was not entertaining Cervus Equipment expansion in the U.S. market, although this had not been ruled out for the future.

MAKING ACQUISITIONS WORK

Conventional wisdom suggests that up to 80 per cent of acquisitions fail.[3] Consolidation via acquisition of small, independently owned businesses often fail to meet the required synergy targets crucial to realizing a reasonable return on the investment premium. Cervus Equipment leaders knew this, so they focused on the practical problems of achieving realistic synergies and avoiding integration failure.

They did this in a few ways. First, they built the organization around an employee- and customer-centric model using a value over policy approach that entailed decentralized decision making, that is, keeping key decisions as close to the customer as possible. These factors, coupled with a strong ethos of accountability applied to store managers (and employees), represented a unique approach in the industry. The traditional, smaller mom-and-pop dealerships, more often than not, were built on command-and-control management. Employees of newly acquired companies often experienced the Cervus Equipment approach first as frightening, then as enlightened.

Using this model to build positive change through new acquisitions was the primary focus. (Exhibit 2 illustrates the acquisition integration approach developed and successfully implemented by Cervus.) Within three months of an acquisition, the new store management team would present a growth strategy for the store, which they were then empowered to execute. This was wildly successful, with most stores achieving a significant growth in sales in their first year under the Cervus Equipment banner. As Randall Muth, the company's chief financial officer, said:

---

[3]Rick Johnson, "Why 80% of all Acquisitions Fail," Supply House Times, 49.2, April 2006, pp. 90–91.

We brought our acquisition integration timeline down from three years to eight months, including operational and cultural integration. This is an extraordinary achievement that has, among other things, enabled us to exceed our synergy targets with our recent acquisitions.

Second, Cervus Equipment was very patient in purchasing new dealerships (although the growth numbers would suggest otherwise). It would only purchase dealerships that were not performing to their current market potential (from John Deere's perspective), or were located in a strong regional growth market, or both. This led to fair valuations at acquisition, followed by exceptional payback in 12 to 18 months.[4]

An abundance of investment opportunities at reasonable prices, combined with this successful integration model, helped Cervus Equipment to invest in more than 55 dealerships with $734 million in sales.

AGRICULTURE: A GROWTH INDUSTRY

The global agricultural machinery market was forecasted for accelerated growth, reaching over $102 billion by 2016 (up from $61.7 billion in 2011), with a compound annual growth rate (CAGR) of 10.7 per cent, according to MarketLine Analyst. Key markets would grow robustly, with Europe growing at 12.1 per cent, the Americas 8.7 per cent and Asia-Pacific 12.1 per cent. This would lead to Europe being the largest regional market, with a value of more than $41.9 billion. The Americas would be a close second, valued at $41.1 billion.[5]

In 2012, the farming industry in western Canada achieved unprecedented growth. Commodity prices for wheat, corn and soybean were at or near historic highs,[6] and farming technology enabled increases greater than 20 per cent in crop yields. The future, it would seem, was full of potential. World population was predicted to grow 23 per cent by 2025, while arable farmland remained relatively constant. Global food production was expected to increase by 50 per cent over this same time, driven in part by significant increases in yield productivity enabled by new equipment technology, such as Site Specific Farming. While drought had been on the rise in arid regions of the world, its impact had not reached water-rich Alberta and Saskatchewan. Even in the United States, which had experienced a near record year of drought, farm income was expected to grow 3.7 per cent in 2012 to an unprecedented US$122 billion (the highest level since 1873 when adjusted for inflation).[7] Overall U.S. farm cash receipts and balance sheets were at historically high levels, expected to reach US$400 billion in 2013, with debt-to-asset ratios of just 10 per cent.[8] This drove the farm and garden equipment wholesale industry in the United States to a record high of US$55 billion, with farm-related equipment representing 75 per cent of this spend.

---

[4]The valuations were relative to the immediate growth opportunity in the market or in some cases the performance of the business relative to its current potential.

[5]www.marketline.com/blog/the-global-agricultural-machinery-market-reached-a-value-of-61-7-billion-in-2011, accessed December 12, 2102.

[6]Index mundi, www.indexmundi.com/commodities/?commodity=wheat&months=120, accessed December 20, 2012.

[7]http://online.wsj.com/article/SB10000872396390444230504577617720338696432.html, accessed December 12, 2012.

[8]"John Deere Committed to Those Linked to the Land," Deere & Company, December 2012/January 2013, www.deere.com/en_US/docs/Corporate/investor_relations/pdf/presentationswebcasts/2012/roadshow_deck .pdf, accessed January 12, 2013.

Regulatory changes were also having an impact on the industry. Recent changes to the Canada Wheat Board regulations now enabled (larger) farmers to market their product directly, essentially eliminating a wholesaler in the supply chain. Also, the legislated requirement for higher levels of bio-fuel in gasoline[9] was driving a higher demand for corn acreage, with a high level of certainty for continued growth well into the future.

Additionally, interest rates were at an all-time low. This was important as a large portion of farmers preferred to acquire new equipment using loans or leases. U.S. farm equipment loans grew 3 per cent to US$7.1 billion in 2012. While leasing provided an opportunity to turn over farm equipment more often, thus increasing sales, it also presented a challenge to the dealerships, as they were tasked with profitably selling off used equipment.

Farming was also consolidating, with many industry insiders predicting "the death of the small farmer." Crop yield increases, driven by scale and advanced farming technology, were making consolidation more attractive and viable for larger farms, advantages not available to smaller farms. The number of farms in Canada actually decreased 10 per cent to 205,000 farms in 2011, while the average size of farms grew 7 per cent to 778 acres. At the same time, the number of farms with sales greater than $1 million grew 31.2 per cent from 2006.[10] These farms accounted for 49.1 per cent of farm sales. This was driving important changes and opportunities in the farm equipment business; large combine sales grew 7.3 per cent in 2011 to 2,899 units, while tractor sales only grew by approximately 2.0 per cent. Younger farmers, with bigger farms and more of a business mindset, were an important factor in this trend. These farmers preferred to purchase new combines every one or two years in order to access new, enhanced farming technology. Close to 3,000 new combines were being sold in Canada each year with a price tag from $250,000 to $400,000. This also presented a challenge, as the used equipment inventories were growing and now represented a significant financial risk to equipment dealerships. Year over year, the values of used combines diminished by 1.5 per cent.[11] According to Lacey:

> There's been a bit of overzealousness by the manufacturers to get new product out the door. So there are lots of very, very competitive, multi-unit discounts and strong financial incentives to encourage new sales. We're seeing a definite trend toward multi-unit deals, lots of trades and flips done every year. We don't think flipping every year is a good strategy. The industry can't absorb that much used, so you're really stealing sales from the future and it's going to come in one big crash if the industry doesn't sort it out. Unfortunately, we all can talk about it and agree that it's not sustainable, but it still happens.

> Our preference would be for farmers to trade every two or three years where the owners make full use of the warranty period and get some hours on the equipment, especially combines. By rotating equipment every two or three years, the industry can absorb that; there are enough buyers of used for that.[12]

Refer to Exhibit 3 for further information related to changing trends in the agricultural sector.

---

[9]Particularly in the United States.

[10]Statistics Canada 2011 Census of Agriculture, www.statcan.gc.ca/ca-ra2011/, accessed December 10, 2012.

[11]Ag Equipment Intelligence & Cleveland Research, www.farm-equipment.com/pages/Spre/Forecast-&-Trends-Used-Equipment-Pricing-Slips-As-Inventories-Climb-August-6,-2013.php, accessed December 8, 2012.

[12]Dave Kanicki, "The New World of Used Equipment," June 2012, www.farm-equipment.com/pages/In-this-Issue-June-2012-Showcase-The-New-World-of-Used-Equipment.php, accessed December 8, 2012.

John Deere was by far *the* premium producer in the North American market. Such a strong brand made running a John Deere equipment dealership easier from a sales and marketing perspective. Very little marketing and advertising was required on the local level, as many customers sought out the brand and had personal relationships with the dealers. As one senior executive put it: "Failure to run a successful [John] Deere dealership was a difficult task. You had to try hard to fail with this brand!" Also, the rural location of these dealerships meant local competition was not as strong, which ultimately drove gross margins on equipment sales and service to 17 per cent on average.

These factors positioned the industry for continued strong growth that was projected to exceed 5 per cent annually over the next five to eight years.

COMMERCIAL AND INDUSTRIAL EQUIPMENT

More recently, Cervus Equipment had focused on executing a diversification growth strategy in the construction and industrial equipment markets. The company purchased and operated a number of construction and materials handling equipment dealerships that sold globally recognized brands such as Bobcat, JCB, Clark, Nissan Forklift, Doosan, Sellick and, most recently, Peterbilt trucks. With the continued aggressive growth in the oil and gas industry in western Canada, these dealerships were exceptionally well-positioned. Construction investment for non-residential construction and machinery and equipment had grown from $55.3 billion in 2009 to $84.1 billion in 2012 in Alberta alone.[13] (Refer to Exhibit 4 for information related to growth in Alberta's construction industry.) In the United States, the rental and leasing of equipment represented combined annual revenue of US$45 billion in 2012, with 50 companies accounting for more than half of the revenue.[14] Residential construction in Alberta also continued to boom, with 19.4 per cent increase in housing starts in 2012. These dealerships were clearly positioned for strong continued annual organic growth in the 5 to 10 per cent range.[15]

The global construction and equipment market was expected to reach US$192.3 billion by 2017, up from US$143.6 billion in 2012, growing at 6.0 per cent CAGR.[16] China was forecast to represent the majority of global construction equipment consumption. India was also expected to grow through multi-billion dollar expenditures in building power plants, telecommunications, ports and roads, with 21 per cent annual growth expected through 2015.[17] Material handling equipment was forecast to grow to US$100 billion by 2015.

Much like the agricultural dealership network, the remaining dealerships available in this sector tended to be larger multi-store operations that had already been through a round

---

[13]2009 is actual investment, while 2012 represents intended investment. "Q4 2012 Investor Presentation Rocky Mountain Dealerships," p. 27, http://files.shareholder.com/downloads/RMD/2671480266x0x616170/2BA5C25E-00AC-4475-A4D3-4FDA3487D262/Q4_2012_RMDI_Investor_Presentation.pdf, accessed March 1, 2013.

[14]First Research–Commercial & Industrial Equipment Rental & Leasing. October 22, 2012. www.mergent.firstresearch-learn.com/industry_full.aspx?pid=297, accessed December 12, 2012.

[15]Six of the Best, ConstrucionWeekOnline.com, www.constructionweekonline.com/article-24031-six-of-the-best/1/print/, accessed September 9, 2013.

[16]Associated Equipment Distributors, www.prnewswire.com/news-releases/construction-equipment-market-will-reach-usd-1923-billion-globally-by-2017-transparency-market-research-183321381.html, accessed December 12, 2012.

[17]RNCOS Industry Research Solutions, www.rncos.com, accessed February 10, 2013.

of regional consolidation. These would be more difficult to purchase, likely demand a larger premium and thus require a stronger effort to achieve synergies and a more focused integration process to realize the payback period Cervus Equipment shareholders expected. On the positive side, there was much more room to grow within these sectors, especially with Peterbilt, whose managers had expressed an interest in having Cervus Equipment grow within their dealer network, with potential for future expansion in the northwestern region of the United States.[18]

INTERNAL CHALLENGES

Cervus Equipment had seen its organization grow from 176 employees in 2003 to more than 1,200 in 2012. The company wanted to maintain its value-based employee model, but the new opportunities drove a need to build in centralized services for the dealerships in order to drive efficiencies in areas of the business such as parts sourcing, finance and human resource management. Cervus Equipment leaders also did not want to forego the strong entrepreneurial philosophy that ensured that decisions were made as close to the customer as possible, which had proven a very effective approach; now, however, it was proving difficult as they purchased dealerships run with a completely different management philosophy, that is, command-and-control by the owner. On top of this, they were finding it progressively more difficult to find leadership candidates in sales, service, parts and dealership management positions. They required leadership at the dealership level that, among other things, came from the farming community, people who understood the challenges customers were facing. These kinds of employees were becoming increasingly difficult to find. To address this problem, they created Cervus Leadership University (CLU), an internal leadership development initiative.[19] Although very promising, CLU could not immediately address the significant current leadership gaps within dealerships. A large number of positions were currently unfilled, with a number of them at the dealership management level. Because of this, the Cervus Equipment leadership team was cautious about seeking out large new acquisitions before CLU was able to grow a strong foundation of new leadership talent. The general manager of the Agriculture division, Sheldon Gellner, stated, "when you stretch an elastic, you can see where it begins to fray along the edges before it breaks. Cervus's edges are fraying like this and if we stretch it too much further, it may just break!

Since the company followed a decentralized management model, it was perhaps not surprising that they had not finely tuned centralized processes, functions or information technology (IT) systems. This became an issue as the organization grew. Supporting the dealerships were multiple IT systems of varying vintages with related and formidable maintenance and evolution requirements. Only recently had the company leaders integrated some aspects of the parts supply chain. While opportunities for continued centralization of services within the organization were abundant, the efforts to seize these opportunities played second fiddle to the primary focus on integrating new acquisitions.

---

[18]OEMs in this market had traditionally been resistant to cross-border dealer ownership among dealership consolidators.

[19]Currently more than 100 Cervus Equipment employees were participating in this leadership development program; Cervus Equipment 2012 Annual Report.

OPERATIONAL PERFORMANCE

Cervus Equipment was performing near, or slightly above, industry levels. Gross margins in the agricultural industry stood at approximately 17 per cent. In the forklift and materials handling industry, gross margins averaged 34.6 per cent, while in the construction industry they came in around 22.5 per cent. However, given the size and potential for achieving economies of scale (in a fragmented industry), analysts continued to expect better than average results from Cervus Equipment; performance at the industry standard was considered below its potential given the strength of its business model and management team. (Refer to Exhibits 5, 6 and 7 for financial results and performance across business segments.)

Cervus Equipment had yet to implement the sales competencies its leaders believed were needed to achieve future growth success in the construction and industrial side of the business. This was clearly a more competitive business segment. Cross selling across brands in this segment represented a strong growth opportunity, yet it was somewhat elusive. John Higgins, vice-president of the Commercial & Industrial department, said:

> We are committed to build best-in-class sales management and market penetration competencies within the construction and industrial segments of our business. This will enable us to more deeply penetrate the oil and gas sector with a broader range of solutions, from construction through to materials handling. Our vision for this is clear; however, we are a long way from achieving this goal.

INTERNATIONAL EXPANSION

In 2009, the leadership team was invited by John Deere to visit a number of dealerships in New Zealand to explore possible partnership opportunities. Cervus Equipment's founder and CEO at the time, Peter Lacey, went to New Zealand to investigate. He saw these dealerships as a great opportunity for immediate consolidation under the Cervus Equipment model and concluded deals to purchase them on the spot.[20] Thereafter, Cervus Equipment moved to consolidate 10 John Deere dealerships in New Zealand, becoming an international company in the process. However, the transition from regional player in Canada to international firm proved challenging. The company did not fully understand the complexity and difficulties of running dealerships halfway around the world and the complexity related to achieving integration synergies associated with the New Zealand investments. Implementing Cervus Equipment's decentralized management philosophy in New Zealand was accomplished by working closely with stores to find key synergies the company could implement to improve store performance; senior managers were eventually moved to New Zealand full time to lead this integration process. In addition, there are significant differences in the agricultural market in New Zealand versus western Canada. For example, the majority of farms in New Zealand are smaller and tend to buy smaller, higher margin tractors and equipment that is not replaced as often. Thus, overall margins are higher but volume is lower, resulting in used equipment sales representing a bigger challenge. Moreover, the centralized services Cervus Equipment built for western Canada just didn't translate well to New Zealand. By collaborating closely with the New Zealand store level management team to pick and choose the best practices to support their operations, Cervus Equipment progressed with

---

[20]This is representative of Cervus Equipment's acquisition strategy: it was rarely planned and very opportunistic. When opportunities presented themselves, the company was prepared to embrace them and move quickly when required.

the New Zealand stores but admitted that it had work to do before these would contribute in a material way to the company's overall growth targets. These investments in New Zealand ultimately provided Cervus Equipment with an opportunity to develop a greater understanding of the differences in international markets and new cultures.

Undaunted, the company embarked on a less risky partnership in 2012 through Windmill AG as a minority investor in five John Deere dealerships in Australia. Although Cervus Equipment was a non-controlling stakeholder in these dealerships,[21] its leaders viewed this as an opportunity to stick a toe in the Australian market, which many thought ripe for consolidation. Australia represented a market growth opportunity equal in size to that of Cervus Equipments' Canadian market. That being said, Cervus Equipment managers were not so naïve as to believe they could jump into the Australian market and achieve instant success with their Canadian business model–a lesson the New Zealand experience had painfully taught them. The experience in New Zealand made the board and senior management somewhat cautious about expansion in Australia.

More recently, John Deere had invited Cervus Equipment to Russia as a prelude to having it purchase some underperforming dealerships in Eastern Europe. Titan Machinery, a competitor, had begun to expand in this fashion in the Balkans, exploiting a close relationship with Case Construction, a primary supplier of construction and farming equipment. While these represented opportunities for potential expansion and growth, Cervus Equipment quickly concluded that the political and legal environment in these countries had yet to mature to the point where acquiring businesses would be considered a reasonable risk. The experience in "safe" New Zealand had not been satisfactory, and the challenges in Eastern Europe would likely be tougher.

John Deere was also very focused on building a market in Brazil, one of the largest growing economies in the world. Once again, it invited Cervus Equipment to join it on a visit. This was indeed an interesting opportunity, but John Deere was rightfully pursuing a slow and methodical approach to brand building in this market that would take years to unfold. Jumping in now would ensure great growth opportunities for Cervus Equipment in five to 10 years time, but it offered few immediate returns.

COMPETITORS

Cervus Equipment had two primary competitors who were executing similar growth strategies: Rocky Mountain Equipment (RME) in western Canada and Titan Machinery (Titan) in the United States. Both companies had strong ties with the OEM Case Construction.

RME was, in fact, bigger than Cervus Equipment and represented reputable international brands such as Case Construction and Case IH (New Holland) in agriculture. With more than $1 billion in revenue across 39 locations in western Canada, RME amounted to a formidable competitor. The company had grown very quickly from 12 dealerships in 2007. Its range of products in the construction industry was better positioned to take advantage of the oil and gas boom in Alberta and Saskatchewan. Because its growth, which occurred much more quickly than Cervus Equipment's, resulted in lower margins and bigger consolidation challenges, market analysts were hesitant to support it and seemed to be waiting for the company to rationalize its dealerships and operations. This resulted in a market valuation much lower than Cervus Equipment's (on 25 per cent higher revenues), which spoke well of that company's business model, leadership and execution capabilities.

---

[21]Cervus Equipment owned 35 per cent of Windmill AG Pty Ltd.

Titan represented a diversified mix of agricultural, construction and consumer product dealerships across the U.S. upper Midwest. Headquartered in Fargo, North Dakota, the company had 104 North American dealerships and 12 European dealerships in 2012. It also represented Case IH, Case Construction, New Holland and New Holland Construction. Titan went public in 2007 and had since grown to an estimated FY2013 revenue of US$2.0 billion to US$2.15 billion.[22] This represented a greater than 35 per cent increase over FY2012. Some store sales were growing 19.2 per cent with gross profit margins at 14.8 per cent.[23] Titan had no intentions of venturing into Canada, but it was a force to be reckoned with in the U.S. Midwest. However, its current inventory of used equipment was at an all-time high of US$1.05 billion and represented its toughest business challenge. With inventory turn ratios at historic lows of 1.5 times annually,[24] this issue had the potential to ruin the company. Titan was buoyed by the growing energy sector in North Dakota and the related construction industry growth. It had also turned its attention to growing its business in Eastern Europe.

Refer to Exhibit 8 for a basic financial comparison of these organizations.

THE DEALERSHIP OF THE FUTURE

The farm equipment business was not what it used to be, having been truly revolutionized in the last 10 years. The industry was being driven by the requirement to continue to increase crop yield productivity to feed a growing world population with little new arable land. To meet this demand, the industry evolved farming technology in the direction of Site Specific or Precision Farming, which was:

> a system to better manage farm resources. Precision farming is an information and technology based management system now possible because of several technologies currently available to agriculture. These include global positioning systems, geographic information systems, yield monitoring devices, soil, plant and pest sensors, remote sensing, and variable rate technologies for application of inputs.[25]

This change was described as a revolution in farming techniques and technology. For example, the application of fertilizer or seed could be manipulated to the centimeter with enhanced GPS-controlled information systems linked, in real time, to tractor technology. With this revolution, there was pressure to change the fundamental services provided through farm equipment dealerships and their OEM suppliers. For example, dealerships would be expected to have some expertise in agronomy, data management and analytics. IT had moved to the forefront of farming, with all the complexities that came with it.

To better position itself in this space, Cervus Equipment invested in a small company called Prairie Precision Networks, which had a real time kinetics (RTK) product that enabled

---

[22]FY 2013 ends March 31, 2013, Titan Machinery Fiscal Third Quarter 2012 Earnings Conference Call, December 6, 2012, http://phx.corporate-ir.net/phoenix.zhtml?c=214897&p=irol-calendarPast, accessed December 12, 2012.

[23]Titan was rated #66 in Fortune's Fastest-Growing Companies (September 2012). www.farm-equipment.com/pages/Industry-News-Titan-Machinery-Ranks-66-on-Fortunes-100-Fastest-Growing-Companies-List.php, accessed December 12, 2012.

[24]Down from 3 per cent in January 2011 (Seeking Alpha). More Downside For Titan Machinery; October 31, 2012, www.seekingalpha.com/article/965261-more-downside-for-titan-machinery, accessed December 12, 2012.

[25]University of Georgia College of Agricultural and Environmental Sciences, Tifton GA. www.nespal.cpes.peachnet.edu, accessed December 12, 2012.

GPS devices to build accuracy to one centimeter.[26] Cervus Equipment also partnered with Agri-Trend, a farming data analytics and consultancy company, through a joint venture investment.

This growing technological change also introduced new business challenges to and added pressures on farmers. They would spend less time in their fields and more time managing crop yields, capital investments, human resources and bottom lines. By default, this moved the focus in dealerships from traditional sales and service to account management and solution-based selling. The conversation with farmers evolved from how many tractors and related implements they needed to what equipment and services they required to produce a target crop yield (and margin) across current acreage. Dealer services now had to include operator training, optimization, yield data management systems (and benchmarking), human resource management, analytics and information management. Their business model was also changing. How do you make money in this new world? Clearly it would not be on the backs of equipment and parts sales alone.

In fact, when faced with the question of what a dealership of the future should look like, the answers were equally diverse and vague. This was not an easy question to answer. One thing that was certain was that Cervus Equipment was going to need to build and execute an innovation strategy both within and outside its OEM partners. John Deere was a leader in farm equipment technology, but it wasn't necessarily leading the way in introducing site-specific farming technology. It tended to be more conservative when it came to releasing new products and services under the Deere banner. Cervus Equipment understood this and thus would pursue its desire to move forward in site-specific farming through separate investments and partnerships. Investing in this new level of knowledge and service delivery at its dealerships while growing the number of dealers was a tall order. There was only so much time and capital available within the firm. Gellner discussed this notion:

> We can utilize our limited resources to grow our product and service capability to our clients and optimize our operational requirements (like investing in IT systems for just-in-time parts management or used equipment sales solutions) OR we can fund and integrate new acquisitions. Clearly we have chosen in the past to fund growth through acquisitions, but we cannot continue to do this to the detriment of the services available to our customers or our back end systems and processes.

The senior team realized that the dealership of the future would be quite different from those they were running today. How to get there was a deeper, more perplexing question that could not be ignored and would certainly tie up valuable resources in the very near future.

THE NEXT PHASE OF GROWTH

Drake knew one thing for certain: the next phase of growth for Cervus Equipment would make the last few years look easy. On the one hand, he had concerns about which direction the company should choose to grow and how it was going to muster the resources to execute such an ambitious plan while maintaining strong financial performance. He knew that the current approach, while previously successful, would not get the company to its future revenue goal. He also knew the company would need to begin investing

---

[26]Regular GPS is usually only accurate within a metre or so and thus is not good enough for site specific farming applications.

more aggressively in its current dealerships to support them as they evolved into the dealerships of the future. On the other hand, he knew that Cervus Equipment was fortunate to be in such a strong financial position in such a robust market and had the solid and reliable relationships it had built with its OEM partners, like John Deere and Peterbilt. Graham also had great confidence in his current senior leadership team to execute a new growth strategy.

This would be the plan that would define his era of leading Cervus Equipment.

EXHIBIT 1: Cervus Equipment Growth Timeline

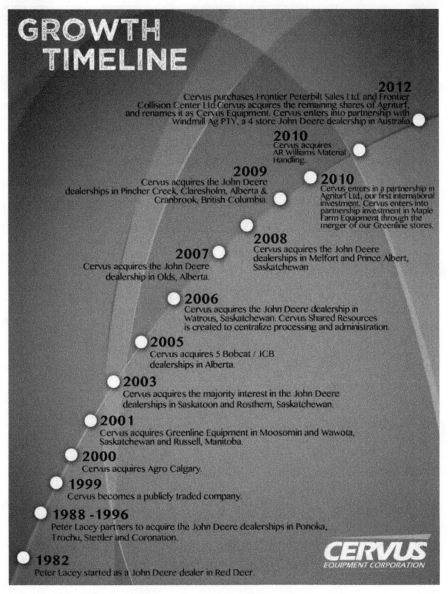

Source: Company files.

EXHIBIT 2: Acquisition Integration Model at Cervus Equipment Corporation: Acquisition, Integration, Strategy and Culture Best Practice

	Pre-Close										
Process Step	Identify Potential Partner	Sign Confidentially Agreement	OEM Consultation and Approval	Build Financial Models to Price	Letter of Intent Start Due Diligence	HR Audit	Vision Tour & Integration Process Review - Senior Team	Vision Tour Dealerships	Finalize Negotiations Draft Legal Documents	Complete Due Diligence	Mentor Program Launch
Time Line (Days)					-90	-60	-40	-30	-15	-10	-5

	Post-Close												
Deal Close	Launch Communication Plan	Launch Tactical Plan	Launch NPS & Employee Satisfaction Surveys	Strategy & Culture Senior Team (SWOT)	Strategy & Culture Mid-Level Team (SWOT)	Build Out Strategy Action Items Each Dealership	Consolidate & Finalize Division Strategy	Complete Competency Assessments	Cervus Leadership University Launch	Acquired Team Presents Strategy	Implement Performance Management / KPIs / Join Performance Group	Launch Cervus Brand Strategy	Team Presents Strategy Progress
0	+1	+5	+5	+15	+30	+45	+60	+60	+65	+70	+70	+90	Quarterly

SWOT—Strengths, Weaknesses, Opportunities & Threats
KPI—Key Performance Indicators
NPS—Net Promoter Score
Source: Company files.

EXHIBIT 3: Farming Industry

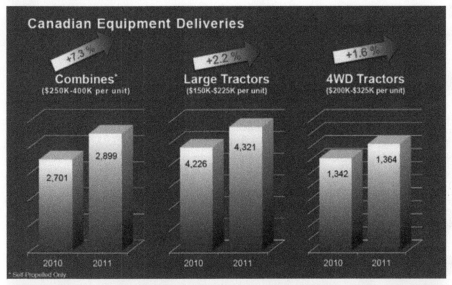

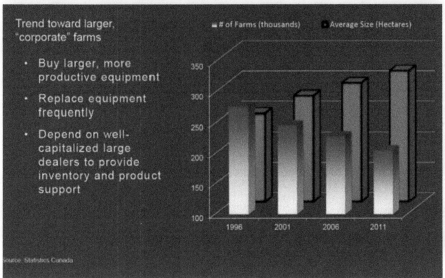

Source: Rocky Mountain Equipment 2012 Q4 Investor Presentation, pp. 9-10, http://files.shareholder.com/downloads/RMD/2671480266x0x616170/2BA5C25E-00AC-4475-A4D3-4FDA3487D262/Q4_2012_RMDI_Investor_Presentation.pdf, accessed September 9, 2013.

EXHIBIT 4: Alberta Construction Industry

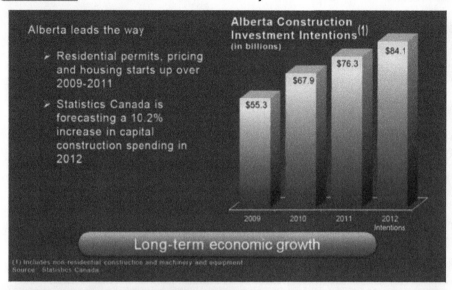

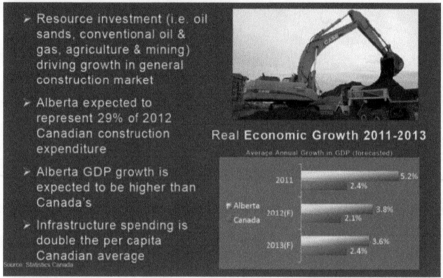

Source: Rocky Mountain Equipment 2012 Q4 Investor Presentation, pp. 27, 14, http://files.shareholder.com/downloads/RMD/2671480266x0x616170/2BA5C25E-00AC-4475-A4D3-4FDA3487D262/Q4_2012_RMDI_Investor_Presentation.pdf, accessed September 9, 2013.

EXHIBIT 5: Cervus Equipment Financial Summary

Consolidated Statement of Financial Position (as of December 31, 2012 & 2011)		
($ thousands)	2012	2011
Assets		
Current Assets		
Cash & Equivalents	8,156	6,536
Accounts Receivable	38,810	50,189
Inventory	172,857	106,776
Other		3,447
Total Current Assets	**219,823**	**166,948**
Non-Current Assets		
Property & Equipment	92,091	29,185
Deferred Tax Asset	44,197	53,546
Intangible Assets	26,717	19,905
Goodwill	5,812	5,154
Other	13,317	6,717
Total Non-Current Assets	**182,134**	**114,507**
Total Assets	**401,957**	**281,455**
Liabilities		
Current Liabilities		
Trade & Other Accrued Liabilities	37,655	22,514
Floor Plan Payments	73,626	51,944
Other	18,329	13,350
Total Current Liabilities	**129,610**	**87,808**
Non-Current Liabilities		
Term Debt	39,028	7,276
Notes Payable	—	2,652
Debenture Payable	30,534	—
Total Non-Current Liabilities	**69,562**	**9,928**
Total Liabilities	**199,172**	**97,736**
Equity		
Shareholder Capital	76,503	72,925
Other	10,490	6,971
Retained Earnings	115,792	102,084
Total Equity attributable to equity holders	**202,785**	**181,980**
Non-Controlling Interest	—	1,739
Total Equity	**202,785**	**183,719**
Total Liabilities & Equity	**401,957**	**281,455**

Consolidated Statement of Comprehensive Income (for the year ended December 31, 2012 & 2013)

($ thousands)	2012	2011
Revenue		
Equipment Sales	554,349	429,442
Parts	104,225	73,172
Service	62,824	45,852
Rentals	12,847	11,132
Total Revenue	**734,245**	**559,598**
Cost of Sales	(594,067)	(453,263)
Gross Profit	**140,178**	**106,335**
Other Income	2,984	1,839
SG&A Expense	(108,667)	(82,601)
Results from Operating Activities	**34,495**	**25,573**
Net Financing Costs	(3,265)	(893)
Share of profit of equity accounted Investees	2,457	1,346
Income Tax Expense	(9,105)	(7,900)
Profit for the year	**24,582**	**18,126**
Foreign Currency Translation	71	213
Total Comprehensive Income	**24,653**	**18,339**

Consolidated Statement of Cash Flows (for the year ended December 31, 2012 & 2013)

($ thousands)	2012	2011
Cash Flows from Operating Activities		
Profit for the Year	24,582	18,126
Depreciation	7,253	5,505
Amortization of Intangibles	2,677	2,447
Net Finance Costs	3,524	1,292
Income Tax Expense	9,105	7,900
Change in non-cash working capital	(21,720)	(7,437)
Other	(1,726)	(319)
	23,695	27,514
Interest Paid	(4,744)	(1,665)
Net Cash from Operating Activities	**18,951**	**25,849**
Cash Flows from Investing Activities		
Business Acquisitions	(22,260)	(2,000)
Advances to Related Party	15,354	(14,684)
Purchase of Property & Equipment	(42,832)	(11,455)
Other	5,579	1,697
Net Cash used in Investing Activities	**(44,159)**	**(26,442)**
Cash Flows from Financing Activities		
Proceeds from (repayment of) Term Debt	6,680	(121)
Advance from Debenture Offering, net of costs	33,159	—
Dividends Paid	(9,902)	(9,797)
Other	(3,109)	(2,558)
Net Cash Used in Financing Activities	**26,828**	**(12,476)**
Net Decrease in Cash & Cash Equivalents	1,620	(13,069)
Cash & Cash Equivalents Beginning of year	**6,536**	**19,605**
Cash & Cash Equivalents End of Year	**8,156**	**6,536**

Source: Cervus Equipment Corporation Annual Report 2012.

EXHIBIT 6: Summary Financial Performance Information

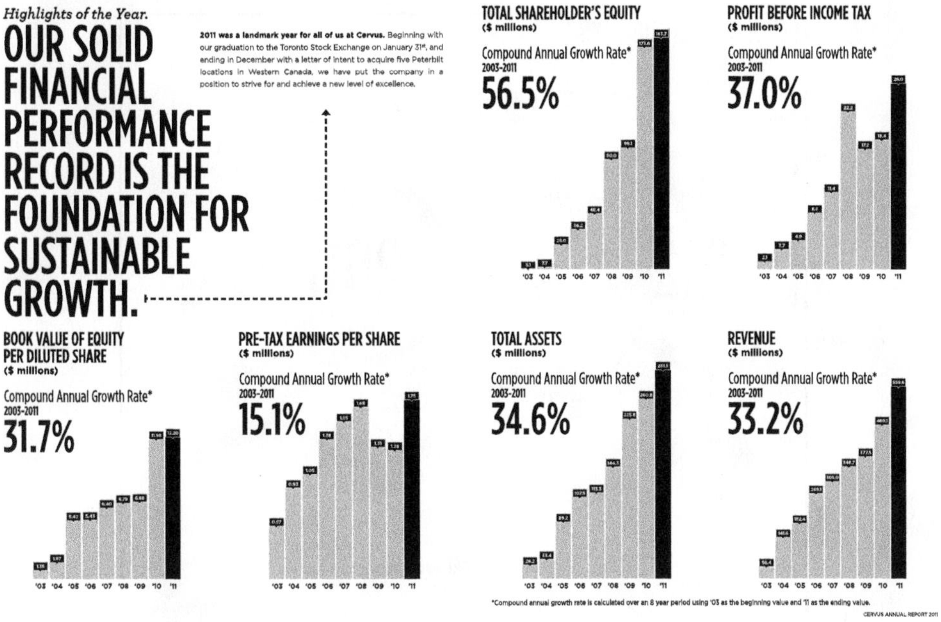
Highlights of the Year.
OUR SOLID FINANCIAL PERFORMANCE RECORD IS THE FOUNDATION FOR SUSTAINABLE GROWTH.
2011 was a landmark year for all of us at Cervus. Beginning with our graduation to the Toronto Stock Exchange on January 31st, and ending in December with a letter of intent to acquire five Peterbilt locations in Western Canada, we have put the company in a position to strive for and achieve a new level of excellence.
TOTAL SHAREHOLDER'S EQUITY
($ millions)
Compound Annual Growth Rate*
2003-2011
56.5%
PROFIT BEFORE INCOME TAX
($ millions)
Compound Annual Growth Rate*
2003-2011
37.0%
BOOK VALUE OF EQUITY PER DILUTED SHARE
($ millions)
Compound Annual Growth Rate*
2003-2011
31.7%
PRE-TAX EARNINGS PER SHARE
($ millions)
Compound Annual Growth Rate*
2003-2011
15.1%
TOTAL ASSETS
($ millions)
Compound Annual Growth Rate*
2003-2011
34.6%
REVENUE
($ millions)
Compound Annual Growth Rate*
2003-2011
33.2%
'03 '04 '05 '06 '07 '08 '09 '10 '11
*Compound annual growth rate is calculated over an 8 year period using '03 as the beginning value and '11 as the ending value.
CERVUS ANNUAL REPORT 2011

Source: Cervus Equipment Corporation annual Report 2012.

EXHIBIT 7: Cervus Equipment Revenue Breakdown

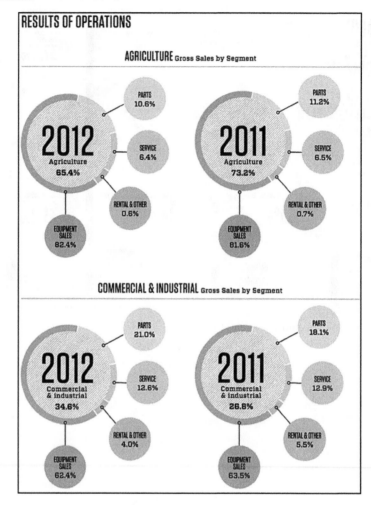

Source: Cervus Equipment Corporation Annual Report 2012.

EXHIBIT 8: Competitor Comparables

Company	Share Price	Market Cap	Price/Earnings		Dividend Yield	2012 Revenue
	Jan 31, 2012	($mm)	2012 E	2013 E	2012	($B)
Cervus	$ 19.07	$ 281	12.9x	11.2x	3.91%	$0.74
Titan	$28.88	$ 608	13.7x	9.2x	n/a	$2.00–$2.15
Rocky Mountain	$ 12.10	$ 228	9.30x	7.1x	2.23%	~$0.91
John Deere	$94.17	$36,500	12.33x	n/a	2.00%	$36.16

Clearly Cervus Equipment price to earnings (P/E) ratio reflects a higher confidence from the Canadian market in their business strategy and approach. Cervus Equipment senior leadership believes this is tied to their *principles* over policy management philosophy, among other things.

Vincor and the New World of Wine

On September 16, 2002, Donald Triggs, chief executive officer (CEO) of Vincor International Inc. (Vincor) was preparing for the board meeting to discuss the possible acquisition of Goundrey Wines, Australia. Vincor had embarked upon a strategic internationalization plan in 2000, acquiring R.H Phillips and Hogue in the United States. Although Vincor was the largest wine company in Canada and the fourth largest in North America, Triggs felt that to be a major player, Vincor had to look beyond the region. The acquisition of Goundrey Wines in Australia would be the first step. Convincing the board would be difficult, as the United States was a close and attractive market where Vincor had already spent more than US$100 million on acquisitions. In contrast, Australia was very far away.

THE GLOBAL WINE INDUSTRY

Wine-producing countries were classified as either New World producers or Old World producers. Some of the largest New World producers were the United States, Australia, Chile and Argentina. The largest of the Old World producers were France, Italy and Spain (see Exhibit 1). The world's top 10 wine exporters accounted for more than 90 per cent of the value of international wine trade. Of those top 10, half were in western Europe, and the other half were New World suppliers, led by Australia (see Exhibit 2).

Nikhil Celly prepared this case under the supervision of Professor Paul W. Beamish solely to provide material for class discussion. The authors do not intend to illustrate either effective or ineffective handling of a managerial situation. The authors may have disguised certain names and other identifying information to protect confidentiality.

IVEY | Publishing

Ivey Management Services prohibits any form of reproduction, storage or transmittal without its written permission. Reproduction of this material is not covered under authorization by any reproduction rights organization. To order copies or request permission to reproduce materials, contact Ivey Publishing, Ivey Management Services, c/o Richard Ivey School of Business, The University of Western Ontario, London, Ontario, Canada, N6A 3K7; phone (519) 661-3208; fax (519) 661-3882; e-mail cases@ivey.uwo.ca.

Copyright © 2003, Ivey Management Services   Version: (A) 2009-10-08

One time permission to reproduce granted by Richard Ivey School of Business Foundation on April 22, 2014.

France

France had been a longtime world leader in the production of wine, due to historical and cultural factors. France was the top producer of wine in the world (see Exhibit 1). The French had developed the vins d'appellation d'origine contrôlée (AOC) system centuries ago to ensure that the quality of wine stayed high. There were many regions in which quality grapes could be grown in France. Some of their better known appellations were Bordeaux, Burgundy and Champagne. France was the second largest exporter of wine (see Exhibit 2).

Italy

Italy, like France, also had a very old and established wine industry that relied on the appellation method to control the quality. Italy was the second largest producer of wine in the world (see Exhibit 1) and the largest exporter (see Exhibit 2).

Australia

Grape vines were first introduced to Australia in 1788. The wine "industry" was born in the 1860s when European immigrants added the skilled workforce necessary to develop the commercial infrastructure. The Australian wine industry grew after 1960 with the development of innovative techniques to make higher quality wine while keeping costs down. Australia was the sixth largest producer of wine in the world (see Exhibit 1). Australia had 5.5 per cent of the total export market and was ranked fourth in the world for its export volume (see Exhibit 2).

Chile

The first vines were introduced to Chile in the 16th century. Due to political and economic instability, the wine industry was not able to develop and take on a global perspective until 1979 when Chile began to focus on the exporting of natural resources to strengthen its economy. Despite being only the 10th largest producer, Chile had 4.5 per cent of the total export market and was ranked fifth in the world (see Exhibit 2).

Argentina

Argentina had a long history of making wine. However, the quality of the wine from Argentina was never as high, due to the small area of land that was capable of producing high quality grapes. Argentina was the fifth largest producer of wine in the world (see Exhibit 1), but did not feature in the top 10 exporters of wine.

All of the countries, with the exception of Argentina, were capable of shipping brands that could compete at a wide range of price points. The French wines typically were capable of competing in the higher price classes, and could retail for more than US$100 per bottle.

MAJOR WORLD MARKETS

After a 2.2 per cent gain in 2001, the global wine market was estimated to have increased another 1.2 per cent in 2002 to 2.55 billion cases, according to *The Global Drinks Market: Impact Databank Review and Forecast 2001 Report*. Wine consumption was projected to expand by 120 million cases by 2010. Most of the growth was expected to come from major wine-consuming nations, such as the United States, United Kingdom, Australia and South Africa, as well from less developed wine markets, such as China and Russia.

Wine imports were highly concentrated. The 10 top importing countries accounted for all but 14 per cent of the value of global imports in the late-1980s. In 2001, half the value of all imports were purchased by the three biggest importers: the United Kingdom (19 per cent), the United States (16 per cent) and Germany (14 per cent).

France and Italy were the number one and two countries in the world for per capita consumption (see Exhibit 3). However, the consumption rate in France was relatively stagnant, while Italy was showing a decrease. Italy, unlike France, had a very small market for imported wines. The import market sizes for France and Italy were respectively 13.4 per cent and 2.8 per cent in 2001, based on volume.

The United Kingdom's wine market was considered to be the "crucible" for the global wine market (Wine Market Report, May 2000). The United Kingdom had very small domestic wine production and good relationships with many of the wine-producing countries in the world. This, coupled with the long history of wine consumption, resulted in an open and competitive market. The United Kingdom was ranked number seven for consumption in 2001 with a trend of increasing consumption. The United Kingdom wine market was dominated by Old World country imports, however New World imports had grown as Australian wines replaced French wines as the number one import (see Figure 1).

FIGURE 1: United Kingdom Wine Market Share

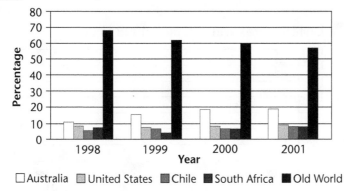

Source: Company files.

Other Countries

In 2001, Canada was ranked number 30 in the world for per capita consumption with an increasing trend. Japan had seen a steady increase in the size of its imported wine market. Asia presented a great opportunity for wine producers around the world because it had populous markets that had yet to be tapped.

THE U.S. WINE INDUSTRY

The international image of the U.S. wine industry until the mid 1970s was that of a low quality jug wine producer. This changed in 1976 during a blind wine-tasting contest in France where California wines from Napa Valley beat out several well- established European wines for the top honors. From that time forward, there has been a focus on developing high quality wines that could compete in the international market from the northern California appellations, such as Napa Valley and Sonoma County. The United States was the fourth largest producer of wine (1.98 billion litres) in 2001 (see Exhibit 1), with California wines accounting for 90 per cent of production volume. There were more than 3,000 wineries in all 50 states. The nation's top wine-producing states were California, New York, Washington and Oregon.

The United States saw huge gains in the total volume and value of its wine exports, increasing from US$85 million in 1988 to US$548 million in 2002. The major markets for U.S wines included the United Kingdom, Canada and Japan. Together they represented 66 per cent of the total export market value for the United States (see Exhibit 4).

The United States was the third largest wine market in the world, consuming 2.13 billion litres a year in 2001. It was also one of the biggest untapped wine markets in the world; seven per cent of the U.S. population accounted for 86 per cent of the country's wine consumption. The total wine market in the United States in 2001 was $21.1 billion with an average growth rate of six per cent since 1994. Of this, approximately $10 billion were sales of New World wines.

While California wines dominated the domestic market (67 per cent market share) due to the ideal growing conditions and favorable marketing and branding actions taken by some of California's larger wineries, imports were on the rise. The United States had one of the most open markets in the world for wine, with low barriers to entry for imports. Imports represented 530 million litres for a 25 per cent share of the market. By 2002, wine imports grew by 18 per cent (see Figures 2 and 3).

FIGURE 2: United States Wine Markets 1998 to 2001

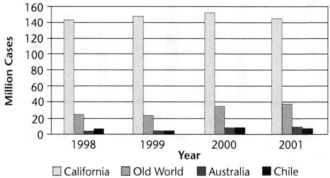

Source: Company files.

FIGURE 3: United States Wine Market Growth Rates

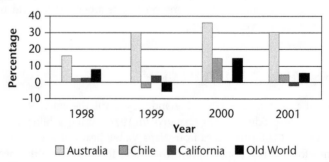

Source: Company files.

Wine was the most popular alcoholic beverage in the United States after beer, which accounted for 67 per cent of all alcohol consumed. The table wine category represented 90 per cent of all wine by volume, dessert wine was six per cent and sparkling wine accounted for four per cent. U.S.-produced table wine held an 83 per cent share of the volume and 78 per cent of the value. Premium wine ($7 and more per 750 ml bottle) sales increased eight per cent over 2001, accounting for 30 per cent of the volume but a sizeable 62 per cent of winery revenues. Everyday value-priced wines selling for less than $7 per bottle grew about 1.5 per cent by volume. This segment represented 70 per cent of all California table wine shipments and 38 per cent of the value.

The United States wine industry was fragmented with the largest producer, E. & J. Gallo, supplying 30 per cent and no other producer supplying more than 15 per cent by volume in 2002.

In the United States, a law mandated the implementation of a three-tier distribution system. The wine producers were required to sell to a wholesaler, who then sold to an established customer base of grocery stores, liquor stores, hotels and restaurants. Wineries were capable of using a two-tier distribution system, which allowed wineries to sell directly to the customers through gift shops located at the winery. The role of the distribution channel was growing and taking on greater strategic importance as the trend towards international and domestic consolidation grew.

THE CANADIAN WINE INDUSTRY

Canadians had been making wine for more than two centuries, but Canada's modern day success in the production of high quality vinifera-based wines went back only a quarter century. The signing of the North American Free Trade Agreement in 1988, together with a ruling under the General Agreement on Tariffs and Trade (GATT), required Canada to abandon the protection it offered its wine industry. While many producers felt threatened, many more responded by reaffirming their belief in their capacity to produce premium wines, and redoubled their efforts to prove it. New vineyards were planted with only the finest varieties of grapes: Chardonnay, Riesling, Sauvignon Blanc, Pinot Gris, Gewürztraminer, Pinot Noir, Cabernet Sauvignon, Merlot and others.

During 1988, the Vintners Quality Alliance (VQA) was launched in Ontario, culminating six years of voluntary initiatives by the leaders of Ontario's wine industry. This group set the standards, to which they agreed to comply, to elevate the quality of Canadian wines and provide quality assurances to the consumer. British Columbia adopted similar high standards in 1990, under the VQA mark.

The 1990s was a decade of rapid growth. The number of commercial wineries grew from about 30 in 1990 to more than 100 by the end of the decade, and consumers began to recognize the value represented by wines bearing the VQA medallion. Canadian vintners continued to demonstrate that fine grape varieties in cooler growing conditions could possess complex flavors, delicate yet persistent aromas, tightly focused structure and longer aging potential than their counterparts in warmer growing regions of the world.

In Canada, despite increasing import competition, sales of Canadian quality wines were increasing as consumers moved up the quality and price scale (see Figure 4).

Canadian quality wines began to capture both domestic and international recognition not only in sales but also by garnering an impressive list of significant wine awards, beginning in 1991 when Inniskillin won the Grand Prix d'Honneur for its 1989 icewine at the prestigious VinExpo, in Bordeaux, France. New access for Canadian wines, especially icewine, in the European market, and expanding market opportunities in the United States and Asia were giving Canadian wines greater market exposure.

FIGURE 4: The Canadian Wine Market

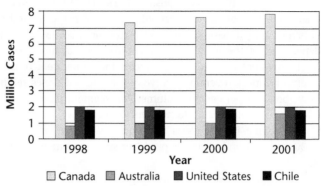

Source: Company files.

THE AUSTRALIAN WINE INDUSTRY

The Australian wine industry was structured to be able to deliver large quantities of high quality branded wine to the world's major markets, at costs less than many of their Old World and New World competitors. Since Australia had a very limited domestic market (population of only 17 million), the wineries realized that if the industry was to continue to grow it would have to do so internationally.

As a result, Australian wineries had gained, and were expected to continue to gain, market share. Growth had been in exports as well as domestic sales (see Exhibits 5 and 6). Australia had recently overtaken France as the largest exporter to the United Kingdom, where seven of the top 10 wine brands were Australian. Exports to North America had grown at 27 per cent by volume in 2001. Consumption of Australian wine in Canada was up 24 per cent and in the United States consumption was up 35 per cent. The growth trends were expected to continue. Export growth had been driven by sales of premium red wine which accounted for 53 per cent of Australia's wine exports.

Domestic wine consumption had grown from 296 million litres in 1991 to 398 million litres in 2001, an annual growth rate of four per cent. The Australian domestic market was relatively unregulated compared to North America, although alcohol taxes were high (42 per cent). Wineries were allowed to have their own retail outlets and sell directly to retailers or on-premise customers. The 7,500 licensed liquor retail outlets accounted for 56 per cent of wine sales, while the 28,000 licensed on-premise outlets accounted for 44 per cent of wine sales.

Although there were 1,300 wineries in Australia, the industry was the most concentrated of any major wine region, with 80 per cent of production being accounted for by four players: Southcorp Wine, Beringer Blass, BRL Hardy and Orlando Wyndham. The large wineries had their own sales forces, as well as warehouses in the major markets.

Southcorp Wines was Australia's largest winery and vineyard owner, with sales of AUD$1.5 billion. Beringer Blass was owned by the Fosters Group and had wine revenues of approximately AUD$800 million (seven million cases). The purchase of Beringer (for AUD$2.6 billion) provided the company with significant growth and U.S. market access.

BRL Hardy had revenues of more than AUD$700 million. The company had several top brands and a very strong U.K. market position. A recent joint venture in the United States with Constellation brands had improved their United States market access. Orlando Wyndham was owned by Pernod Ricard, a French publicly traded spirits company.

TRENDS IN THE GLOBAL WINE INDUSTRY

Wine was unique among alcoholic beverages in that its top 25 brands represented only seven per cent of the global market. In 2002, Martini vermouth was the world's most widely distributed wine, while Gallo's E. & J. Wine Cellars was the largest-selling brand, at 25 million cases annually, with most of those sales in the United States.

Globally, vermouth and other fortified wines were projected to continue their long-term decline, but this would be more than offset by expected growth in table wines, which accounted for more than 90 per cent of total wine consumption. The hottest sales category was Australian wines, with brands such as Rosemount Estate, Jacob's Creek and Lindemans showing double-digit growth rates.

The North American market was expected to exhibit annual growth rates of three per cent. There were positive demographics with the 20 to 39 age group having a per capita consumption at 7.9 litres and the 40+ age group having a per capita of 14.0 litres. The ongoing trends were a shift in consumer preference to red wines and premium wines (see Exhibit 7, 8).

The global wine market was consolidating in terms of its retail, wholesale and production operations. One key to success seemed to be distribution and marketing. Globalization was also altering the structure of firms both within the wine industry and among those distributing and retailing wine. Rapid growth in supermarkets and in concentration among distributors was driving wine companies into mergers and acquisitions to better meet the needs of those buyers and their customers. Since information about the various niches and the distribution networks in foreign markets was expensive to acquire, new alliances between wine companies were being explored with a view to capitalizing on their complementarities in such knowledge.

Recent examples of such alliances included the purchase by the owner of Mildara Blass (Fosters Brewing Group) of Napa Valley-based Beringer, the alliance between Southcorp/Rosemount and California's Mondavi, BRL Hardy's joint venture with the second largest U.S. wine company, Constellation Brands (to operate as Pacific West Partners) and the purchase by New Zealand's biggest wine firm (Montana) of the country's second largest winery (Corbans). See Exhibit 9 for the 10 largest wine companies worldwide.

VINCOR INTERNATIONAL INC.

Vincor International Inc. (Vincor) was formed as a combination of a number of Canadian wineries: Barnes Wines, Brights Wines, Cartier Wines, Inniskillin Wines and Dumont over the period from 1989 to 1996. Vincor began operations in 1989 with a management buy-out of Ridout Wines (Ridout) from John Labatt Ltd. The Ridout management team, led by Allan Jackson, Peter Graigner and John Hall, sought out Donald Triggs to lead the purchase and become CEO. They raised more than Cdn$2 million in equity, largely from personal finances, and borrowed $25 million to buy out Ridout. The new company was renamed Cartier Wines and Beverages.

Vincor had grown in three stages to become Canada's largest wine company in 2002. The first stage of growth had been a leveraged buyout (LBO) in turbulent times (1989 to 1995), followed by a period of consolidation and rationalization-Building Canada's Wine Company (1990 to 2000). The third stage of growth was Building an International Wine Company (2000 onwards).

The first stage had seen the formation of Vincor and wine company acquisitions. From 1995 to 2000, Vincor acquired eight wineries, integrated its sales, marketing, production and accounting and merged two wine kit companies. This lead to economies of scale and a 21 per cent market share in 2000.

During this period, Vincor developed Canada's first premium wine brands: Jackson-Triggs, Inniskillin and Sawmill Creek. The Canadian wine market had seen a shift from popular (less than $7 retail price) to premium ($7 to $10 retail price), leading Vincor to start focusing on the premium and super premium ($10 to $15 retail price) segments. They developed vineyards and re-capitalized wineries to support premium growth. Product coverage was also achieved in the growing ultra premium ($15 to $20 retail price) and specialty (more than $20 retail price) segments. The year 2000 saw Vincor at a strategic crossroad. Triggs recalled:

> We were faced with three options. We could choose to be a cash cow by further developing our dominant Canadian position. A second option was to develop a diversified Canadian beverage conglomerate. A third option was to expand to the United States and perhaps beyond.

> We went for option 3. The move was driven by opportunities as well as threats. In terms of opportunities, the global trend was one of strong growth and premiumisation. There was an industry consolidation favoring global brands. The market was fragmented with the largest player only having one per cent market share. The markets for New World wine were growing. The dynamics in the U.S. market were highly profitable with very high profit margins. We were already #5 in North America and #22 globally.

> On the risk side, wine was an agricultural industry and as such susceptible to changing weather conditions. A diversified portfolio in terms of production and markets would only be an asset.

Triggs and Vincor decided to go international. The company's mission statement was drafted to reflect the new strategic plan:

> To become one of the world's top-10 wine companies, producing Vincor-owned New World, premium branded wines, which are marketed and sold through Vincor-controlled sales and distribution systems in all major premium wine consuming regions.

Where Were the Big Markets?

According to Triggs:

> The United States was the largest market with New World wine sales of $10 billion followed by the United Kingdom and Australia at $3.7 billion each. Canada and the rest of Europe were next at $700 million. Japan was the sixth largest with sales of about $500 million. To be a New World market player, Vincor needed to be in five to six markets.

In 2002, the company's strategy was formulated for each region. In Canada, the aim was to build share in premium segments, to develop export capability and to generate cash and improve return on capital employed. In the United States, Vincor decided to focus on portfolio migration to high-end super-premium, enhancement of sales capability, product innovation and a shift to consumer marketing. Vincor's international strategy was to develop new geographic markets for core brands, specifically for icewine, a signature product for Canada that had attained world recognition. It was a luxury product in terms of pricing and margins and one of the top-five wine brands in select Asian duty-free stores. The U.S. launch was in F'01 in 1,850 high-end restaurants. By 2002, Inniskillin was being sold in 3,300 premium restaurants across the United States. The European launch of Inniskillin was slated for F'02.

U.S. ACQUISITIONS

R.H. Phillips

On October 5, 2000, Vincor acquired R.H. Phillips, a leading California estate winery, which produced a range of super premium wines. The aggregate purchase price, including acquisition costs, was US$56.7 million. In addition, R.H. Phillips' debt of US$33.8 million was assumed and refinanced by the company. The Phillips acquisition and the refinancing of the assumed debt were funded entirely through borrowing from the company's senior lender.

R.H. Phillips was established in 1981 by John and Karl Giguiere. It was located in the Dunnigan Hills Viticultural Region near the wine regions of Napa and Sonoma. R.H. Phillips specialized in the production of super premium wines, marketing its products under the brands R.H. Phillips, Toasted Head, EXP and Kempton Clark. Its wines were sold throughout the United States and in several other countries, including Canada. In 2001, its brands generated sales revenues of approximately US$25 million for Vincor. Its wines were distributed across the United States by a network of 13 sales executives, distributors and brokers.

The Phillips acquisition established a presence for Vincor in the U.S. wine market, in addition to adding strong brands, which were well-positioned in the super premium category, one of the fastest growing segments of the wine market. With its national network of distributors and sales professionals, R.H. Phillips provided a platform for future acquisitions in the United States (such as the Hogue acquisition), while also facilitating the marketing of Vincor's products in the United States.

The Hogue Cellars

On September 1, 2001, Vincor acquired Hogue Cellars for US$36.3 million. Hogue was the second largest wine producer in Washington state, well-known for its super premium wine. Hogue was a family controlled and family operated winery founded in 1982 by Mike and Gary Hogue.

The Washington state wine industry had emerged as the second largest producer of premium wines in the United States, after California. Hogue produced red varietals, including Cabernet Sauvignon, Merlot and Syrah, as well as white varietals, including Chardonnay, Sauvignon Blanc, Riesling and Pinot Gris. In 2001, sales of Hogue-produced premium wine were 415,400 cases. In addition to its owned brands, Hogue was the U.S. agent for Kim Crawford wines of New Zealand and Heritage Road wines from Brian McGuigan wines of Australia.

The Hogue acquisition added 11 sales people nationally and immediately increased Vincor's annual U.S. sales volume to more than one million cases and its annual U.S. revenues to more than US$60 million.

INTEGRATION WITH R.H. PHILLIPS

Vincor's management believed that Hogue was an excellent complement to the R.H. Phillips portfolio, as Hogue was primarily a super premium brand, with approximately 88 per cent of its volume in the super premium category. The strength of the Hogue product range lay in different varietals from the R.H. Phillips range. Different appellations greatly reduced portfolio overlap, as the character and taste of the wines were clearly distinct.

Given the price and quality positioning of both businesses, customers were similar and opportunity existed to improve the efficiency and effectiveness of the sales force, while simultaneously developing incremental sales for all brands in the combined portfolio. Vincor incurred expenses of US$4 million from the integration of Hogue and R.H. Phillips and from transaction costs related to the Hogue acquisition. It was management's objective that the integration of Hogue and R.H. Phillips would result in the realization of annual synergies of US$2.8 million.

VINCOR IN 2002

In 2002, Vincor was Canada's largest producer and marketer of wines with leading brands in all segments of the market in Canada. Vincor had a 22 per cent market share and sales of Cdn$376.6 million (see Exhibit 11 for Financials). Andrés Wines Ltd., the second largest winery in Canada, had approximately an 11 per cent market share. Vincor was North America's fourth largest wine producer in terms of volume and the world's 22nd largest wine producer in terms of revenue.

The company had wineries in British Columbia, Ontario, Quebec, New Brunswick, California and Washington state, marketing wines produced from grapes grown in the Niagara Peninsula of Ontario, the Okanagan Valley of British Columbia, the Dunnigan Hills of California, the Columbia Valley of Washington state and other countries. The company's California and Washington wines were available throughout the United States and in parts of Canada. (see Exhibit 10 for Corporate Structure).

Canada's government liquor distribution systems and the company's 165-store Wine Rack chain of retail stores sold Vincor's well-known and industry-leading brands: Inniskillin, Jackson-Triggs, Sumac Ridge, Hawthorne Mountain, R.H. Phillips, Toasted Head, Hogue, Sawmill Creek, Notre Vin Maison, Entre-Lacs, L'Ambiance, Caballero de Chile, Bellini, Spumante Bambino, President Canadian Champagne, Okanagan Vineyards, Salmon Harbor and other table, sparkling and fortified wines, Vex and the Canada Cooler brands of coolers, and the Growers and Vibe brands of cider.

In the United States, R.H. Phillips, Toasted Head, EXP, Kempton Clark and Hogue wine brands were distributed through a national network of more than 127 distributors, supported by eight brokers and 40 sales managers. The company's icewines were sold in the United States through a dedicated team of sales managers and internationally, primarily through the duty-free distribution channel. The company had seven employees outside of Canada engaged full-time in the sale of icewine.

Vincor's portfolio had evolved as per Table 1.

The company's objectives in 2002 were to obtain a top quartile return on capital employed (ROCE) of 16 per cent to 20 per cent and to achieve sales of Cdn$1 billion and an earnings per share (EPS) increase of more than 15 per cent. At the time these objectives were to be met as per Table 2.

TABLE 1:   Evolution of Vincor's Portfolio—Table Wine

	F'95		F'02	
	% By Vol	% by $	% By Vol	% by $
Popular	83	80	47	28
Premium	17	20	53	72

Source: Company files.

TABLE 2:   Company Sales Objectives (Cdn$ millions)

	Current	5 Years
Canada	300	400
United States	100	200
Icewine	15	50
Acquisitions	0	350
Total	415	1,000

Source: Company files.

GOUNDREY WINES PTY. LTD.

Goundrey Wines was one of the pioneer winery operations in Western Australia. The Goundrey family had established the vineyard in 1972, and the first vintage was produced in 1976. By 1995, the business had grown to approximately 17,000 cases in annual sales and was sold to Perth businessman Jack Bendat. Bendat expanded both the vineyards and the winery to reach 2002 sales levels of 250,000 cases annually and revenues of AUD$25 million. Goundrey was one of the largest wineries in Western Australia selling under two labels, Goundrey and Fox River (see Exhibit 12 for Financials).

Bendat was 77 years old, and health and family concerns had resulted in his recent decision to sell the business. Vincor believed it would be able to purchase the assets of Goundrey for AUD$46 million plus working capital at close (estimated at AUD$16.5 million) plus transaction costs of AUD$2 million for an enterprise value of AUD$64.5 million.

The majority of the Goundrey brand volume (85 per cent) was sold in the AUD$15 to AUD$30 super premium segment of the Australian market. The ultra premium segment ($30 to $50) accounted for seven per cent of sales and the premium ($10 to $15) for the remaining eight per cent. The company's sales were almost entirely in the domestic market with three per cent export sales. When asked what was Goundrey's export strategy, Bendat said, "I answer the phone."

Goundrey employed its own sales force in Queensland and New South Wales, with a total of 13 sales reps and four sales managers in two states. In other states, Goundrey had appointed distributors. In all regions, Goundrey was the most important winery for the distributor. Goundrey had tighter control of its distribution capability in Australia than most of its competitors. Goundrey consumption was running at more than 26 per cent year over year growth versus 2001.

Located 350 km south of Perth, the winery could process 3,500 tonnes of grapes. The winery also had its own bottling capability, enabling it to support an export business where each export market has different labeling requirements.

Triggs felt the Goundrey acquisition would be an important strategic move for Vincor. He saw several major advantages. First, the acquisition would be a significant step in achieving Vincor's strategy of converting from a North American to a global player. The Australian wine industry had captured market share in the world's new wine markets and was poised to continue to do so. Second, the Western Australia region had an established reputation for super and ultra-premium wines. Although the grape harvest was a mere four per cent of the Australian total, more than 25 per cent of Australia's super-premium wines were sourced from that state. Third, the company had developed its own sales force in Queensland and New South Wales. Triggs wanted the proposal to go through.

EXHIBIT 1: Top 10 Producers of Wine in The World 2001

Country	Wine Production* (million litres)	Share of World Production (%)
France	5,330	19.9
Italy	5,090	19.0
Spain	3,050	11.4
United States	1,980	7.4
Argentina	1,580	5.9
Australia	1,020	3.8
Germany	900	3.4
Portugal	770	2.9
South Africa	650	2.4
Chile	570	2.1
World	27,491	

*Does not include juice and musts (the expressed juice of fruit and especially grapes before and during fermentation; also the pulp and skins of the crushed grapes).

Note: 1 litre = 0.26 gallons; each case contains 12,750 mil bottles = 9 litres.

Source: G. Dutruc-Rosset, Extract of the Report on World Vitiviniculture, June 24, 2002.

EXHIBIT 2: Top 10 Exporters of Wine in The World 2001

Country	Wine Production* (million litres)	Share of World Exports (%)
Italy	1,830	26.5
France	1,580	22.9
Spain	990	14.4
Australia	380	5.5
Chile	310	4.5
United States	300	4.3
Germany	240	3.5
Portugal	200	2.9
South Africa	180	2.6
Moldavia	160	2.3
World	6,897	

Source: G. Dutruc-Rosset, Extract of the Report on World Vitiviniculture, June 24, 2002.

EXHIBIT 3: Top 10 Wine Consuming Nations 2001

Country	Wine Consumption (millions litres)	Share of World Consumption (%)
France	3,370	15.4
Italy	3,050	13.9
United States	2,133	9.7
Germany	1,966	9.0
Spain	1,400	6.4
Argentina	1,204	5.5
United Kingdom	1,010	4.6
China	580	2.6
Russia	550	2.5
Romania	470	2.1
World	21,892	

Source: G. Dutruc-Rosset, Extract of the Report on World Vitiviniculture, June 24, 2002.

EXHIBIT 4: U.S. Wine Exports Top Countries (By Dollar Value in 2002)

Country Ranking by 2002 Dollar Value	Value ($000)	Volume (litres 000)
United Kingdom	188,895	95,446
Canada	92,571	50,348
Japan	81,199	32,342
Netherlands	53,201	26,388
Belgium	18,791	10,884
France	13,326	5,943
Germany	11,818	8,634
Ireland	10,153	5,380
Switzerland	7,199	3,914
Denmark	5,710	3,933
Mexico	5,001	3,705
Taiwan	4,868	2,736
South Korea	3,865	2,439
China	3,370	2,537
Singapore	3,002	1,822
Sweden	2,782	1,145
Hong Kong	2,393	1,140

Source: Wine Institute and Ivie International using data from U. S. Dept. of Commerce, USA Trade Online. History revised. Numbers may not total exactly due to rounding.

EXHIBIT 5: Australia Wineries

	1998 to 1999	2000 to 2001
Wineries (number)	1,150	1,318
Hectares under vine	122,915	148,275
Wine grape production	793	1,035
Wine consumption	373	398
Wine exports million litres	216	339
AUD$ million	$991	$1,614
Wine imports million litres	24	13
AUD$ million	$114	$92

Source: Company files.

EXHIBIT 6: Australia—Top Export Markets 2001

	Million Litres	AUD$ Million
United Kingdom	183	762
United States	78	457
Canada	17	106
New Zealand	23	83
Germany	13	55
Other	61	301
All Markets	375	1,764

Source: Company files.

EXHIBIT 7: The Wine Market—Canada Fiscal 2002

	Retail Price	% By Volume	Trend	% By Sales
Popular	<$7	33%	−5%	20%
Premium	$7–$10	35%	5%	30%
Super Premium	$10–$15	24%	19%	33%
Ultra Premium	$15–$20	6%	31%	15%
Specialty	>$20	2%	45%	6%

Source: Company files.

EXHIBIT 8: The U.S. Market For California Wine Fiscal 2002

	Retail Price	% By Volume	F'02 Trend*	% By Sales
Jug	<$3	36%	−4%	12%
Premium	$3–$7	36%	−2%	27%
Super Premium	$7–$15	18%	8%	28%
Ultra Premium	>$15	10%	3%	33%

* Total U.S. table wine market +1%; imports +9%; states other than California +4%
Source: Company files.

EXHIBIT 9: Top 10 Wine Companies and Sales in 2002 (US$)

Company	Country	Wine sales ($ million)
E. & J. Gallo Winery	United States	1,500
Foster's Group	Australia	818
Seagram	Canada	800
Constellation Brands	United States	712
Southcorp	Australia	662
Castel Freres	France	625
Diageo	Britain	590
Henkell & Sonlein	Germany	528
Robert Mondavi	United States	506

Note: Excludes France's LVMH, which earned more than 75 per cent of its $1.6 billion in wine sales from champagne.
Source: Direction des Etudes/Centre Français du Commerce Exterieur.

EXHIBIT 10: Vincor's Significant Legal Subsidiaries 2001
(all wholly owned)

Subsidiary	Jurisdiction of Incorporation
Hawthorne Mountain Vineyards (2000) Ltd	Canada
The Hogue Cellars, Ltd	Washington
Inniskillin Wines Inc.	Ontario
Inniskillin Okanagan Vineyards Inc	British Columbia
R.H. Phillips, Inc	California
Spagnol's Wine & Beer Making Supplies Ltd	Canada
Sumac Ridge Estate Winery (2000) Ltd.	Canada
Vincor (Quebec) Inc	Quebec

Source: Company files.

EXHIBIT 11: Vincor Consolidated Financials (1998 to 2002) (Cdn$ millions)

	F'98	F'99	F'00	F'01	F'02	Average Annual Growth	
						F'01–02	F'98–02
Revenue	206.4	253.2	268.2	294.9	376.6	27.7%	17.7%
EBITDA	28.1	35.0	37.9	49.5	70.5	42.4%	26.1%
% Revenue	13.6%	13.8%	14.1%	16.8%	18.7%		
Net Income	10.8	11.7	13.3	14.3	26.9	40.1%	25.6%
Avg.Capital Empl'd	145.5	191.6	222.1	310.4	468.2		
ROCE (EBIT)	14.5%	13.8%	12.7%	13.1%	12.5%		
Funds Employed							
Receivables	30.4	33.3	35.7	37.4	55.1		
Inventory	65.1	83.1	70.7	125.9	175.6		
Working Capital	57.8	73.3	67.9	111.9	184.9		
Net Fixed Assets	45.2	60.0	73.3	165.9	178.8		
Other Assets	59.8	87.1	82.7	133.4	161.5		
Funds Employed	162.8	220.4	223.9	411.2	525.2		
Turnover	1.2x	1.1x	1.2x	.7x	.7x		
Financing							
Debt (net)	50.9	92.5	80.5	254.5	110.1		
Deferred Tax	9.6	12.1	14.1	11.4	18.3		
Equity*	102.3	115.8	129.3	145.3	396.8		
Financing	162.8	220.4	223.9	411.2	525.2		

Note: EBITDA—Earnings Before Interest, Taxes, Depreciation and Amortization
*Increased in 2002 due to the fact two equity issues were completed that year.
Source: Company files.

EXHIBIT 12: Goundrey Financials (for years ending June 30) AUD$ (000s)

	1999	2000	2001
Sales (000)	16,280	21,509	20,942
EBITDA	3,102	6,014	3,548
EBITDA%Sales	19.1%	28.0%	16.9%

Source: Company files.

CASE 19

CIBC Mellon: Managing A Cross-Border Joint Venture

Thomas MacMillan leaned back in his chair and glanced out of his office window down onto Bay Street, the epicenter of the Canadian financial industry. During his 10-year tenure as president and CEO of CIBC Mellon, MacMillan had presided over the dramatic growth of the jointly owned, Toronto-based asset servicing business of CIBC and The Bank of New York Mellon Corporation (BNY Mellon). However, now it was an overcast day in mid-September 2008 and MacMillan had a front-row seat to witness the onset of the worst financial crisis since the Great Depression.

CIBC Mellon was facing this oncoming global financial storm with a solid balance sheet and was secure in the knowledge that both of its parents were also well capitalized. However, the well-publicized impending collapse of several long-standing financial titans threatened to impact all players in the financial services industry worldwide. Despite the fact that joint ventures (JVs) were uncommon in the financial sector, MacMillan believed that the CIBC Mellon JV was uniquely positioned to withstand the fallout associated with the financial crisis and that it would be able to weather the most significant risks facing the JV—execution risk and the potential exodus of assets and clients who were panicked by the wider financial pandemonium. MacMillan and his team recognized that it would be critical for the JV to continue to deliver a high level of client service and to avoid any major operational missteps.

MacMillan's moment of introspection was interrupted by a knock on the door. He was scheduled to meet with three members of the company's executive management committee, Paul Marchand, Mark Hemingway and James Slater, to discuss two pressing issues

IVEY | Publishing

Professor Paul Beamish wrote this case with the assistance of Michael Sartor solely to provide material for class discussion. The authors do not intend to illustrate either effective or ineffective handling of a managerial situation. The authors may have disguised certain names and other identifying information to protect confidentiality.

Richard Ivey School of Business Foundation prohibits any form of reproduction, storage or transmission without its written permission. Reproduction of this material is not covered under authorization by any reproduction rights organization. To order copies or request permission to reproduce materials, contact Ivey Publishing, Richard Ivey School of Business Foundation, The University of Western Ontario, London, Ontario, Canada, N6A 3K7; phone (519) 661-3208; fax (519) 661-3882; e-mail cases@ivey.uwo.ca.

Copyright © 2010, Richard Ivey School of Business Foundation   Version: 2012-05-24

One time permission to reproduce granted by Richard Ivey School of Business Foundation on April 22, 2014.

facing the JV. First, they needed to discuss how to best manage any risks confronting the JV as a consequence of the financial crisis. Given the massive size and global reach of the largest financial service giants, and the likelihood that some of these behemoths might now be teetering on the edge of bankruptcy, CIBC Mellon, like other players in the financial services industry, would be forced to move adeptly to protect its operations from any potential exposure to the larger players' fates. While the systems, structure and culture that prevailed at CIBC Mellon served as evidence of MacMillan and his team's diligent efforts over the past 10 years to focus on risk management and to foster a culture of synergistic cooperation, the question remained—how could the policies and practices developed during the past decade be leveraged to sustain the JV through the broader financial crisis? Second, the four men were scheduled to continue discussions regarding options for refining CIBC Mellon's strategic focus, so that the JV could emerge from the financial meltdown on even stronger footing. Notwithstanding the immediate urgency of the financial crisis, the JV's management team recognized the need to continue to manage the business with a view towards future growth.

BACKGROUND

The Asset Servicing/Global Custody Business

When the JV was conceived in 1996, its principal emphasis was on asset servicing—the global custody business—which was generally viewed as "a dull business, with dull services, in a dull little corner of the financial services sector." Asset servicing delivers securities-related administrative services to support the investment processes and goals of clients. Such services include global custody, securities lending, cash management, multicurrency accounting and reporting, global performance measurement and analytics, transition management, commission recapture and foreign exchange. Clients include pension plans, investment managers, mutual funds, insurance companies, and global financial institutions. The fees charged to provide such administrative services would typically be much less than one half of one per cent of the value of the asset being supported.

In 1996, CIBC was one of the big five Schedule 1 (domestic) banks in Canada. At that time, it had an average custodial operation, with approximately 14 competitors, principally trust companies and the security departments of the major banks. CIBC had $100 billion in custody assets and a handful of clients. Its technology platform was poor and needed significant investment. It had three choices to make:

1. Invest—the problem there was that it would have had to invest a lot of money ($300–$500 million)—to come up with a world-class custodial system. It was concerned that the revenue potential from the Canadian market would not result in it receiving adequate returns for its investment.

2. Exit the business—as a lot of companies in Canada subsequently did.

3. Form a joint venture if it could find the right partner. CIBC believed there was the potential of creating a good, viable Canadian-based business, but it needed a partner.

In 1996, Pittsburgh-based Mellon Bank had a Schedule II (Canadian bank which was a subsidiary of a foreign bank) banking operation in Canada, which MacMillan ran. Its Canadian custody market share was about one per cent—specifically one client, Cdn$8 billion in assets under administration, which was being administered out of Boston. However, Mellon had a world-class technology platform, had scale (in a scale business) and was committed to growing its market share but was having difficulty breaking into the Canadian marketplace.

It knew it would be a difficult and slow process to get established in Canada by setting up a greenfield operation.

CIBC approached several potential partners, but it was Mellon's technology and people that impressed it the most. CIBC had a Canadian presence and a client base, but no technology and its service was average. Mellon had great technology, products and services, but no presence and few clients in Canada. And it was receptive to CIBC's overtures. It seemed the ideal circumstance for the birth of a joint venture—a great fit. Both parties needed each other and there was very little overlap. The opportunity to create a world-class Canadian asset servicing company—when not many existed in Canada at the time—was too enticing to pass up for both organizations. CIBC Mellon was the first significant JV for either parent.

Given the relative rarity of JVs in the financial services sector, the two sole shareholders in the proposed JV (CIBC and BNY Mellon) devoted a considerable amount of thought and planning during 1996 to the design and structure of the entity. A significant volume of legal agreements was negotiated to establish the parameters that would govern the relationship between the two shareholders. Buried within the reams of legal documents were provisions drafted to prohibit each of the shareholder parents from competing against the JV; to detail the limitations surrounding the JV's use of the parent shareholders' trademarks and other intellectual property; to outline the basis upon which each parent would provide services to the JV, including, in the case of BNY Mellon, the basis upon which it would provide and "Canadianize" its technology for the JV; and to require each of the shareholders to utilize the JV as a supplier of asset servicing and global custody services.

One of the most critical governance clauses pertained to voting rights. Under the JV's shareholder agreement, each of the parties would enjoy a 50 per cent vote on every issue. In effect, this eliminated the need to vote on any issue—only consensus could yield a decision and the JV managers needed to secure the approval of both shareholders before taking any major issues to the board. Accordingly, at the outset MacMillan and his team recognized that in order for the JV to execute on its mission both strategically and operationally, it would be critical for the two shareholders, their employees and the JV's employees to develop an acute understanding and respect for the unique capabilities that each shareholder brought to the JV. MacMillan acknowledged that "the governance processes developed for this JV effectively facilitated our ability to leverage the expertise of each shareholder." While both parties were strong players in the credit markets, BNY Mellon had a strong understanding of credit in the global custody market and enjoyed a strong reputation with federal regulators in the United States. CIBC, on the other hand, had a strong understanding of credit in the Canadian marketplace and was known for its strong global trading platform (CIBC World Markets).

Equally important were provisions pertaining to risk management. The shareholders agreed to the formation and to the membership on the JV's Asset & Liability Committee (ALCO). ALCO was tasked with the responsibility of overseeing the formulation of risk management policies and asset investment policies associated with the JV's treasury and securities lending activities—principal activities under which financial services firms could become exposed to credit risk and market risk. This pivotal committee was populated by senior management from CIBC, BNY Mellon and the JV itself. MacMillan acknowledged that both shareholders had sought to structure the JV to develop a discrete, low-risk business and that risk tolerance would be maintained in the parents' businesses. As such, the JV only engaged in very conservative transactions and did not engage in proprietary trading. Appropriately managing risk necessitated clear and constant communication in order to ensure that the JV was aligned with its shareholders. It also effectively positioned the JV's management team to tap into the knowledge assets and accumulated experience of two major financial institutions.

When formed at the end of 1996, the JV had fewer than 200 employees, $110 billion in assets under administration, a market share of less than 10 per cent and revenues of about $25 million. However, over the next decade, the business grew dramatically. In 1997, it acquired the Canada Trust custody business. In 1999, it acquired the Bank of Montreal custody business, in 2002, the TD Bank third-party custody business, and in 2006, it was awarded the IG/Mackenzie custody business. By 2006, there were 1,400 employees and 1,140 custody clients. At this point, the asset servicing business offered a wide and integrated range of products and services from custody to risk management which could be grouped into two broad categories—core asset servicing functions and capital markets functions (see Exhibit 1). Historically, each of these two categories of business functions contributed approximately 50 per cent of the profits generated by the JV's asset servicing business. While the core asset servicing business functions supplied a stream of recurring-fee revenue to the JV, the income stream generated by the capital markets functions could be more volatile, depending upon the state of the capital markets. The global securities lending component of the capital markets functions involved acting as an agent in facilitating the lending of debt and equities from the JV's clients to other clients, who were typically brokers. While they did not disclose to CIBC Mellon why they were undertaking any particular loan, it could be expected that the brokers that borrowed the assets from CIBC Mellon would utilize the assets both for their own proprietary trading and to loan to the brokers' clients, sometimes including hedge funds that pursued short positions in equities. Short positions were established by traders who sold equities that they did not currently own. In essence, short sales involved selling borrowed equity assets. Consistent with regulatory requirements and its low-risk culture, CIBC Mellon routinely secured the loans that it extended to its broker clients by requiring the borrowers to pledge high-quality assets in excess of the value of the underlying loans as collateral. Exhibit 2 illustrates the interactions that occurred between external parties and CIBC Mellon's securities lending service.

By 2007, assets under administration for the JV's asset servicing business exceeded $800 billion, and were growing. The JV had become the second-largest asset servicing business in Canada, with a market share over 30 per cent. It was settling 15,000 transactions each day. Total revenues for CIBC Mellon exceeded $350 million, and healthy quarterly dividends were being paid to each partner.

The Stock Transfer and Corporate Trust Businesses

In 1997, the JV entered the trust services business through CIBC's purchase of a 50 per cent interest in Mellon's R-M Trust Company. The purchase was undertaken because the JV required a trust company as a deposit-taker for its asset servicing business and because R-M also had established stock transfer and corporate trust businesses. Through this business, Canadian companies that issued securities that traded on major stock exchanges relied on CIBC Mellon to manage administrative duties like security holder record keeping, securities transfers, investor communication, dividend payments and employee plan administration. The JV also acted as a corporate trustee for its trust clients' assets. In its corporate trustee role, the JV acted as indenture trustee for a number of series of asset-backed commercial paper (ABCP). ABCPs were typically short-term commercial paper investments that were collateralized by other financial assets which were characterized by very low risk. As of 2006, the JV had 1,200 trust clients. CIBC Mellon did not borrow or lend any securities in connection with this line of business.

In a November 2006 speech to the Financial Services Institute, MacMillan was asked to reflect on both the reasons he felt many joint ventures failed (see Exhibit 3) and the reasons why CIBC Mellon had been so successful.

Let me start with the one main reason that towers over all of them: our people. They are amazing and we have together somehow created an atmosphere where we can all thrive. Our people are our big differentiator. This can happen in any company. It has happened in our JV. We have succeeded because:

- **The original business plan made sense.**   CIBC Mellon is profitable, growing, with good returns because the original business rationale was solid. It wasn't two "lousy" businesses coming together. Outstanding Mellon technology and service was introduced into Canada relatively quickly through a JV that had CIBC in its name and made an immediate positive market impact.

- **The parents receive benefit from the JV itself in the form of dividends but also from outside of the JV.**   Both parents make significant FX revenues for their own books from JV clients. We help Mellon win global custody bids, we help CIBC win additional banking business that is often tied to asset servicing, for example cash management. We contribute to the building of strong client relationships for both parents. Mellon gets to appropriately allocate costs to the joint venture connected with their technology spend—and this spend is significantly larger than what they could otherwise afford because of the JV.

- **Both parents cooperate.**   I see it at every board meeting—they respect and appreciate the contribution of the others; work collaboratively to make the JV a success. Despite the historical, jurisdictional and managerial differences, we've managed to put these differences to the side to make the JV work. And when there are differences of opinion (and frankly there's not that many) they work it out; and both organizations complement each other: CIBC defers to Mellon's expertise in the global custody business; Mellon defers to CIBC's knowledge/expertise relative to Canadian business and banking. I think it helps that both banks had a good solid friendship for many decades prior to the formation of the JV. They were (and are) comfortable with each other. They don't really compete against each other in any major business lines. Canadians are generally comfortable working with Americans and vice versa. Both parents' head offices are in the same time zone.

- **Commitment of the parents.**   They have from the very beginning wanted to see the JV succeed and grow and they spent time making this happen. When more capital was required for acquisitions (the asset servicing business of Canada Trust, BMO, TD)—both parents were there. Early on in our history we had teething pains (our level of client service was not what it is today)—the parents didn't waiver and constructively helped us overcome issues and push on.

- **The JV has effectively leveraged the strength of both parents.**   Mellon has 50 per cent ownership, but we benefit 100 per cent from their ongoing technology spend—over US$200 million a year. On a stand-alone basis, we couldn't afford US$200 million each year for technology in support of asset servicing business. This is an enormous plus for us.

  From CIBC, we consistently leverage their client banking relationships to win new business for CIBC Mellon. We also leverage governance standards and risk management practices from both partners.

- **And finally—our company is well managed.**   We have a strong board composed of mature, competent executives who can speak for their organizations. There has been minimal board turnover and when it has happened the transitions have been smooth. My lead board members from both organizations have been there since day one.

But equally important, I am blessed with an extremely strong executive management team. This team gets direction from the board and we run with it. They are also very skillful at working with both shareholders to ensure that all interests are balanced and satisfied and the strengths of both parents are fully realized. This is a skill requirement unique to joint ventures. For example:

- Leveraging technology development at Mellon and sales development at both parents.
- Working with both parents' risk, audit and compliance.
- It is a skill to unleash the power of our parents without being overwhelmed by them.

And while we are proactive in leveraging the strengths of our shareholders, we never forget we are a stand-alone organization that needs to be managed effectively. We have developed a strong internal culture quite independent of our parents, including our own strategy, brand, vision and core values. And we've shown enormous skills in initiating and successfully concluding major acquisitions at critical times.

- **We have also been a little bit lucky.** The markets have been generally favourable the last 10 years. There has been tremendous growth in the mutual fund industry, a major sector for us. There has been an accelerating trend to globalization of the capital markets, including increased complexity of financial instruments, and heightened requirements for reporting and transparency and real time information. These all play to our strengths. Not all of this was anticipated back in 1996. Over the past 10 years, we've had a good tailwind. You are better to be lucky than good, but we have been good.

2007–2008: FROM TAILWIND TO HEADWIND

The growth that had characterized the global financial sector up until 2006 began to materially change in 2007. A rapid series of problems began to either emerge or become more widely acknowledged. Fundamental differences that existed between the Canadian and U.S. banking sectors posed a unique set of concerns for financial institutions with operations on both sides of the border. Discrepancies in consumer debt and equity levels, divergent banking regulations and differences in the structure of each country's mortgage security industry comprised some of the most significant concerns.

The Canadian Financial Sector[1]

Canada as a whole was entering the crisis with a strong balance sheet and economic position. Consumers had lower debt and more savings than in the United States.

Mortgages were originated and held by Canadian banks, not packaged up and sold as securities. Canadian mortgages were generally five years or less, and mortgage interest was not tax deductible in Canada, so homebuyers were not encouraged to buy beyond their means. There were no 40-year terms, and buyers had to be able to have a down payment. Canadian Banks could not lend more than 80 per cent of the value of a house without mortgage insurance from the Canada Mortgage and Housing Corporation.

Canadian banks were large, stable and sophisticated national entities (an oligopoly). With branches across the country and often in other countries, Canadian bank risk was dispersed. Canadian bankers tended to be more risk-averse than their U.S. and international

---

[1]This section is from "You Can Take It to the Bank," *Ivey inTouch Magazine*, Fall 2009, p. 14.

counterparts. Canadian banks were required to maintain a tier one capital ratio of seven per cent and generally exceeded it. They had to cap overall leverage at 20X capital.

Canadian banks were regulated by a single piece of legislation, the Bank Act, which was reviewed every five years, and one national body, the Office of the Superintendant of Financial Institutions (OSFI). OSFI had broad oversight–there was no "shadow banking system" that fell outside the regulations. Canada also had strong monetary policy set by the Bank of Canada and the Department of Finance.

In Canada, most investment banks were owned by commercial banks, providing them with access to capital during a crisis.

The U.S. Financial Sector

Despite the close geographic proximity, the nature of the United States banking and mortgage industry differed significantly from the system that prevailed in Canada. Decades ago, the U.S. government launched two agencies to promote home ownership in the United States–the Federal National Mortgage Association ("Fannie Mae") and the Federal Home Loan Mortgage Corporation ("Freddie Mac"). These agencies were designed to increase the availability of funds for originating mortgages and to encourage the emergence of a secondary market for mortgages. Subsequently, mortgages could be traded without the involvement of either the original borrower or the original lender.

In the 1990s, to further encourage home ownership in the United States, policymakers lowered the amount of equity that homebuyers were required to invest in the purchase of a home. As a consequence of this policy shift, borrowers who were previously unable to secure a mortgage were able to enter the housing market. Further, the overall degree of leverage in the U.S. housing market increased substantially and a housing bubble emerged as homeowners began to speculate by moving into more expensive homes.

The coincident emergence of three financial innovations in the United States–interest-only mortgages, asset securitizations and credit default swaps–ultimately set the stage for the perfect storm that had converged over the U.S. financial system by 2007. Unlike self-amortizing mortgages in which the mortgage principal was retired through regular payments of principal and interest over the life of a mortgage, interest-only mortgages were mortgages in which the borrower was given the opportunity to pay only the interest portion of a regularly scheduled mortgage payment. Interest-only mortgages were designed to open home ownership to low-income earners who demonstrated enhanced future earning potential, at which point their mortgage would be converted into a self-amortizing mortgage. Interest-only mortgages benefitted these low-income homeowners by facilitating their entry into the housing market through payments which were lower than the payments under a self-amortizing mortgage. However, the emergence of interest-only mortgages also contributed to speculation in the housing market, as some investors purchased homes, made the interest payments while waiting for the value of their homes to increase and then sold the homes, paying back the mortgage principal with the proceeds from the home sale and pocketing the surplus.

Asset securitization involved aggregating a series of future cash flows into a security which was then sold to investors. Mortgage-backed securities (MBSs) were a type of asset securitization in which the underlying asset backing the security was a mortgage which generated cash flows from the interest payments. A securitization was a structured finance product that was originally designed to distribute risk. In fact, when conceived, MBSs were regarded as low-risk investments because they were backed by mortgages and mortgage defaults were relatively rare occurrences.

Credit default swaps (CDSs) resembled insurance policies in the sense that one party paid a series of cash flows to a counter-party in exchange for the promise that the counter-party would reimburse the payer if the underlying asset defaulted. A significant portion of the market for CDSs was built around MBSs. Investors in asset-backed securities such as MBSs regularly insured their investments by purchasing CDSs. The premium revenue stream associated with a CDS on an MBS was considered particularly attractive due to the low level of perceived risk, again due to the relatively rare occurrence of mortgage defaults. Despite their resemblance to insurance policies, CDSs were traded as contracts in the derivatives markets and were free from insurance industry regulations. Consequently, the relative ease with which CDSs could be issued, coupled with the fact that it was not necessary to own the underlying asset in order to purchase a CDS, effectively fueled speculative behaviour in the CDS market.

Two phenomena associated with these three financial innovations further compromised the precarious foundation upon which the U.S. banking and mortgage industry was perched–subprime mortgages and individual compensation systems prevailing in the financial sector. While mortgages issued to creditworthy borrowers were known as prime mortgages, subprime mortgages were issued to borrowers with poor credit. MBSs based on subprime mortgages became particularly attractive investment vehicles due to their high returns and low levels of perceived risk (due to the assumption that widespread mortgage defaults were highly unlikely). At the same time, mortgage originators and derivative traders were being compensated on the volume of mortgages originated and derivatives sold (MBSs and CDSs). Increased trading volumes in these assets were fueled by the fact that compensation was rarely adjusted to the riskiness of either the borrower or the underlying asset.

By 2007, the robust growth in U.S. home prices slowed dramatically. As home prices began to decline, the value of mortgages began to exceed the market value of many homes. A flood of mortgage defaults ensued to the point that mortgage-backed securities began to decline in value. The complex nature of these securities further undermined their value. Given that it was not possible to link an MBS to specific properties, investors could not evaluate the risk of default on specific MBSs and, therefore, were unable to ascertain market values for these MBSs. The secondary market for mortgages was near collapse.

The difficulty associated with valuing these securities proved to be particularly problematic for financial institutions that owned the devalued MBSs and for financial institutions facing insurance-like claims on the CDSs they had written on the bet that widespread mortgage defaults would never occur. Consequently, these financial institutions were required to raise more capital to shore up their capital ratios. However, the increasing pervasiveness of uncertainty effectively turned off the taps in both credit and capital markets, making the task of raising capital almost impossible.

As the cost of capital skyrocketed and credit stopped flowing in the United States, financial institutions began to fail. Several "runs on the bank" were triggered in which customers lined up to fully withdraw their deposits. In June 2008, panicked customers of IndyMac Bank in the United States withdrew $1.5 billion in deposits (approximately 7.5 per cent of total bank deposits). Similarly, over the course of ten days in September 2008, customers withdrew more than $16 billion from Washington Mutual Bank (totaling nine per cent of total bank deposits). The uncertainty spilled over U.S. borders, triggering bank runs and failures overseas as well. Most notable was the bank run and subsequent failure of the U.K.-based Northern Rock bank, which was subsequently nationalized, in part, to subdue the panic.

CONCLUSION

The Challenge of Refining the Future Direction of the Joint Venture

As early as the summer of 2007, credit spreads for certain financial companies and instruments widened dramatically. In Canada, the marketplace for ABCP began to show signs of stress. The JV's ALCO Committee, on the recommendation of CIBC Mellon's risk management group, and leveraging the respective credit market specialties of both shareholders, directed the JV to refrain from using any of CIBC Mellon's treasury or client funds (the latter in the form of cash collateral for securities lending transactions) to purchase non-bank-owned ABCP. Eventually, in August 2007, the $30 billion market for non-bank-owned ABCP essentially froze. The looming financial crisis did not portend a quick or strong recovery in the credit markets, particularly in the ABCP market.

MacMillan and his team suspected that the future growth potential for the stock transfer and corporate trust business segments was more limited than it was for the asset servicing business. Notwithstanding the onset of the financial crisis, MacMillan debated whether the JV should retain or divest these business lines in order to focus more intensely on the asset servicing business for which the JV was formed.

The Challenge of Avoiding Major Operational Missteps

The brewing financial storm became fodder for the media and it started to rattle financial markets. Despite the fact that there were reasons to believe that the impending financial crisis might not be as bad in Canada as it was likely to be in the United States and elsewhere, numerous challenges remained. Not least of these was the fact that the crisis would likely bring out the worst in many long-term business relationships. As liquidity was tightening, many financial sector lenders, borrowers and partners alike were putting aside years, even decades, of cooperation in order to ensure their own survival. This was in contrast to the approach adopted by CIBC Mellon in the months leading up to and during the crisis. It retained its long-standing practice of emphasizing very extensive communication with its clients and its shareholders, ensuring shared understanding of issues, including having representatives from both parents on ALCO and maintaining transparency.

By mid-September 2008, the most significant risks facing CIBC Mellon were credit risk, operational risk and market risk, as well as the potential exodus of assets and clients who were panicked by the wider financial chaos. MacMillan and his team recognized that it would be critical for the JV to continue to deliver a high level of client service and to avoid any major operational missteps. A key challenge facing the JV pertained to efforts to remain loyal to both long-time and newer business clients, while not exposing the JV to excessive risk in the context of an increasingly volatile market. While CIBC Mellon's global securities lending operations had extended considerable credit to some of the now more precariously perched financial giants, the JV was comfortable that these loans were adequately collateralized. Nevertheless, in order to ensure that the loaned assets were not subsumed into any debtors' possible bankruptcy proceedings, the JV would need to execute against legal agreements with rigour, to preserve its legal rights, including, if necessary, taking possession of collateral assets and then liquidating these assets in an increasingly turbulent market. Critical decisions were faced by MacMillan, Marchand, Hemingway and Slater, ranging from short-run decisions such as how to determine when to call in credit extended to some of the JV's global securities lending clients and how to liquidate any collateral that the JV was forced to take into possession, to longer-run decisions surrounding how to manage the JV's relationships with its solvent clients, so as to stem any risk of client or asset flight.

MacMillan closed the door to his office. Notwithstanding the 110 years of collective experience between MacMillan, Marchand, Hemingway and Slater, the four men recognized that the markets were headed for uncharted waters. MacMillan opened the meeting, reminding the group, "Gentlemen, now more than ever, we need to leverage our JV's administrative heritage, the guidance of our shareholders and the respective strengths of the parents to move through these unprecedented times. . ."

EXHIBIT 1: CIBC Mellon Asset Servicing Business Functions

CORE ASSET SERVICING BUSINESS FUNCTIONS:

The following eight functions constituted the core asset servicing business functions:

CUSTODY   The CIBC Mellon custody system is a real-time, multicurrency processor of security and currency movement for the institutional trust/custody business. It maintains automated interfaces to/from depositories and subcustodians, supporting trade affirms/confirmation, trade instructions, settlement confirmations, cash instructions and cash and security position status.

TRADE PROCESSING & SETTLEMENT   Trades entering the custody system are auto-matched and confirmed to CDS (*Canadian Depository for Securities*) and its U.S. equivalent, DTC (*Depository Trust Company*). Discrepancies are flagged, reported to the client and updated with fail codes. If matched, trades automatically settle on the settlement date and the clients' securities and cash positions are updated. Each day, the service team validates the CDS Daily Settled Trades Report against the settled transactions in the system. CIBC Mellon offers contractual settlement of buys, sells and maturities for issues publicly traded on recognized exchanges in 47 countries. All other markets across all asset classes and registration locations, including physical delivery of securities, settle on the actual settlement date.

ACCOUNTING   The CIBC Mellon accounting system integrates both Canadian and international securities on a single platform. This trade date, multicurrency system reflects cash movements on the actual settlement date and security transactions on the trade date. Integrated with its custody system, the accounting system manages derivative investments and accommodates both pending trades and income accruals.

SAFEKEEPING   CIBC Mellon provides a secure facility for the safekeeping of stocks, bonds, notes and other securities—in both physical and book-based environments. It ensures assets are held securely and recorded accurately in its custody system. These two objectives are accomplished by performing an annual depository risk assessment along with regular reconciliation of physical vault and depository positions.

CORPORATE ACTIONS   CIBC Mellon has a Corporate Actions Security Capture and Delivery Engine (Cascade) to keep it informed on all relevant announcements, while providing clients and their investment managers with instant access to information. It provides notification within hours of receipt of notice, with immediate encumbrance of position on receipt of response, and instant settlement on receipt of payment. Its online, real-time mandatory and voluntary corporate action and class action notifications enable clients to respond to events quickly. The most comprehensive sources of corporate action information for Canadian, U.S. and international markets are used, comparing vendor data to ensure accuracy and timely notification is provided to clients.

EXHIBIT 1: (Continued)

CORE ASSET SERVICING BUSINESS FUNCTIONS:

INCOME COLLECTION   The system automatically accrues for all interest and dividend income for each security, providing the amount in local currency prior to the payable date. A contractual income policy for dividends, interest and maturities is offered in which CIBC Mellon guarantees to pay income on the day it is due; amounts are credited to client accounts regardless of receipt of payment. In non-contractual markets, income is credited upon actual receipt of funds. Assets must be held in the depository or registered in CIBC Mellon's name or its agent's nominee name. The funds are credited in local currency on the pay-date, unless otherwise specified.

ONLINE REPORTING   Workbench offers a wide array of browser-based information capabilities allowing customers to effectively manage, evaluate and report on their individual or consolidated portfolios. The key features range from access to market news and analysis to a fully-secured virtual meeting place to performance analytics and monthly statements. Workbench cash availability and forecast reports are updated in real-time during business hours and also include custody share reports, pending trades, transaction settlements, corporate action notifications and cash balance projections of portfolios. The reporting feature, Workbench Express, facilitates the automatic distribution of reports to a designated printer, a local network drive, an e-mail account or an FTP server, all without manual intervention.

PERFORMANCE & RISK ANALYTICS (P&RA)   This unit provides performance measurement, attribution, and investment analysis services to over 1,800 institutional investors in 50 countries and is responsible for US$8.2 trillion in assets under measurement. In Canada, it has 151 clients using performance measurement services and products. Its suite of value-added products and services includes tools for performance measurement, portfolio analytics and universe comparison. Its performance measurement systems are fully integrated with CIBC Mellon's systems.

CAPITAL MARKETS FUNCTIONS:

The following two functions constituted the asset servicing business's capital markets functions:

FOREIGN EXCHANGE   CIBC Mellon executes foreign exchange (FX) transactions through the trading desk of one of its corporate parents. From the perspective of the counterparty to the transaction, CIBC or BNY Mellon deals as principal directly with its clients. Only one step is required to execute a trade and instruct for settlement, reducing operational risks and duplication of tasks. CIBC Mellon has neither a principal nor broker role in the transaction but acts simply as a service provider. It facilitates the transactions required to support clients' global trading activity, providing a complex FX trading solution from initiation and execution to settlement and reporting.

GLOBAL SECURITIES LENDING   The company delivers client-tailored solutions to the 120 institutional clients participating in its in-house program. Beneficial owners for whom securities are lent include pension funds, government agencies, insurance companies, mutual funds, asset managers and pooled funds. The focus is on the strategic development of new products and services to enhance client revenue performance, with a commitment to product collateral and risk management. Global One is used—the lending system of choice for more than 70 financial institutions in over 20 countries—designed by top market participants.

Source: Company materials.

EXHIBIT 2: The Interactions Between External Parties and CIBC Mellon's Global Securities Service

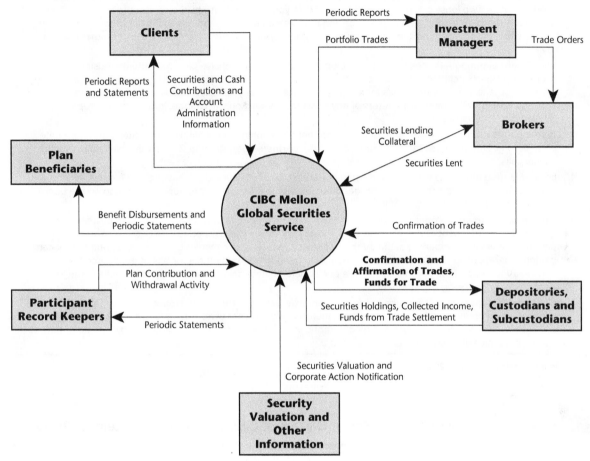

Source: CICA 5970 Report, CIBC Mellon, 2009.

EXHIBIT 3: Top General Reasons for Joint Venture Failures

1. **The rationale for setting up the JV wasn't a good one** —Two lousy businesses put together will not make one good business. Two lousy businesses put together give you one big lousy business. Double the fun! At the core there has to be a good business proposition that creates adequate returns to the shareholding partners. It helps when the founding partners each bring something special to the joint venture that the other doesn't have.

2. **Insufficient planning** —Parties need to agree up front to a comprehensive plan outlining the business transaction, which includes governance, dispute resolution, ownership of intellectual property, how each party will contribute to the JV (whether it's money, expertise, technology, etc.). It's also very important to identify and agree on exit arrangements. Parameters of any business transaction will change. You need to agree to how the exit occurs, up front.

3. **Inadequate capitalization** —Starting out, each partner must commit a set amount of capital that is adequate enough to get the business off the ground. Also, both partners need to agree on how they will fund additional capital calls.

4. **Lack of leadership** —This may be the most important factor of all. If you don't have strong leadership, you are going to fail. In any business, you always need outstanding leadership, but never more so than on the board of a joint venture and within the JV itself.

5. **Lack of commitment** —Poor performance by the JV can result in one or both parties getting disinterested quickly. Results do count. But even if the JV is successful, things can happen to one of the parents quite unrelated to what is happening at the JV that will lead to a lack of commitment. For example, one parent can get into operational difficulties which will cause them to take their eye off the JV ball or even force them to exit the JV. Or, one of the parents can have a perfectly legitimate change in strategy that results in the joint venture no longer being core to them.

6. **Cultural differences and differences of opinion emerge between the two partners.** There is definitely a JV mindset—it's different working with another partner than just on your own. You have to sometimes temper your own culture to accommodate a quite different culture or approval of your partner to the benefit of the JV. Some companies are good at it, and some aren't.

Source: Tom MacMillan, November 2006.

EXHIBIT 4: Organization Chart of Senior Officers of CIBC Mellon as of September 2008

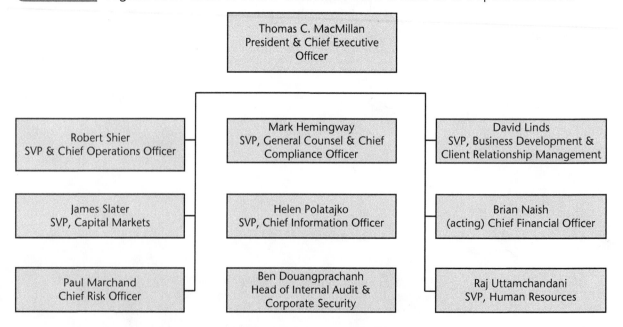

EXHIBIT 5: Brief Bios of Select Senior Officers

Thomas C. MacMillan was president and chief executive officer of CIBC Mellon. He had 35 years of extensive experience in the financial services industry in both Canada and the United States. From 1994-1998, he was chairman, president and chief executive officer of Mellon Bank Canada. Mr. MacMillan was instrumental in the formation of the CIBC Mellon joint venture, and previously held various senior positions with the Bank of Montreal, Chase Manhattan Bank of Canada and Montreal Trust. A native of Toronto, Mr. MacMillan received a bachelor's degree from Princeton University and a master's degree from the London School of Economics and Political Science. He also had significant board experience in both the private and not-for-profit sectors.

Mark R. Hemingway was senior vice president, general counsel and chief compliance officer, and a member of the company's executive management committee. He was responsible for the legal, compliance, corporate secretarial and privacy functions at CIBC Mellon. Mr. Hemingway had 20 years of experience in the legal profession. Prior to joining CIBC Mellon, he held general counsel and corporate secretary positions in a number of large Canadian companies, and was previously a litigation lawyer at Torys. He received his law degree from Queen's University and his master of laws degree from Cambridge University. He articled at the Supreme Court of Canada.

James E. R. Slater was senior vice president, capital markets, and a member of the company's executive management committee. Mr. Slater had overall leadership responsibility for CIBC Mellon's capital markets function, which included global securities lending, treasury and cash management. Mr. Slater's accountabilities also included providing strategic client service engagement in relation to his trading and financial markets responsibilities. He also chaired the company's asset liability committee. Mr. Slater had 20 years of experience in the financial services industry with CIBC World Markets and CIBC Mellon. While at CIBC World Markets, he was part of the team charged with the formation of CIBC Mellon.

C. Paul Marchand was the head of risk management. He joined CIBC Mellon in 2002, after 35 years with a major Canadian bank. At CIBC Mellon, he was responsible for designing and overseeing the company's Risk Management frameworks and programs for both CIBC Mellon Trust Company and CIBC Mellon Global Securities Services Company. His mandate included bringing together comprehensive oversight and reporting of all risk issues affecting CIBC Mellon including credit, market and operational risks up to and including the boards of directors and joint venture partners. He also served as the enterprises' chief compliance officer and chief anti-money laundering officer from 2002 to 2006. Marchand held a bachelor of commerce degree from McGill University.

David S. Linds was senior vice president, business development and client relationship management, and a member of the company's executive management committee. Mr. Linds also oversaw the company's product management and client integration solutions group, which was responsible for ensuring existing and future development of products and services as well as client reporting needs of institutional clients for asset servicing and ancillary services. Mr. Linds had more than 25 years of experience in the financial services industry, including 18 years with CIBC World Markets and CIBC Mellon. While at CIBC World Markets, he was part of the team charged with the formation of CIBC Mellon.

Robert M. Shier was senior vice president and chief operations officer, and a member of the company's executive management committee. Mr. Shier was responsible for CIBC Mellon's operational divisions, including client and investment management services, asset servicing, investment fund accounting for the CIBC Mellon Global Securities Services Company and investor services, stock transfer and employee plan administration for CIBC Mellon Trust Company. He joined CIBC Mellon in 1997, and had more than 25 years of operational experience in financial services including brokerage, banking, asset servicing and transfer agency services.

Where Have You Been? An Exercise to Assess Your Exposure to the Rest of the World's Peoples

A key requirement to assess a potential international market opportunity is an understanding of basic demographics. At its most fundamental level, the overall size of a national population provides a starting point.

There are literally hundreds of potential national markets. These vary greatly in terms of population level, income levels, etc... As firms (and managers) consider which markets to enter, a major consideration is experience in the market: "Where They Have Been."

INSTRUCTION

1. On each of the attached worksheets, note the total number and names of those countries you have visited, and the corresponding percentage of world population which each country represents. Sum the relevant regional totals on p. 287.

2. If used as part of a group or class analysis, estimate the grand total for the entire group. Then consider the following questions:

🎓Ivey | Publishing

Professor Paul Beamish wrote this case solely to provide material for class discussion. The author does not intend to illustrate either effective or ineffective handling of a managerial situation. The author may have disguised certain names and other identifying information to protect confidentiality.

This publication may not be transmitted, photocopied, digitized or otherwise reproduced in any form or by any means without the permission of the copyright holder. Reproduction of this material is not covered under authorization by any reproduction rights organization. To order copies or request permission to reproduce materials, contact Ivey Publishing, Ivey Business School, Western University, London, Ontario, Canada, N6G 0N1; (t) 519.661.3208; (e) cases@ivey.ca; www.iveycases.com.

Copyright © 2013, Richard Ivey School of Business Foundation   Version: 2014-03-26

One time permission to reproduce granted by Richard Ivey School of Business Foundation on April 22, 2014.

3. Why is there such a high variability in individual profiles (i.e., high exposure vs. low exposure)?
4. What are the implications of each profile for one's career?
5. What would it take to get you to personally change your profile?

Region: Africa

Country	2013 (July) Population (in millions)	% of World Total
1) NIGERIA	174.5	2.5
2) ETHIOPIA	93.9	1.3
3) EGYPT	85.3	1.2
4) CONGO (DEM. REP)	75.5	1.1
5) SOUTH AFRICA	48.6	0.7
6) TANZANIA	48.3	0.7
7) KENYA	44.0	0.6
8) ALGERIA	38.1	0.5
9) SUDAN	34.8	0.5
10) UGANDA	34.8	0.5
11) MOROCCO	32.6	0.5
12) GHANA	25.2	0.4
13) MOZAMBIQUE	24.1	0.3
14) MADAGASCAR	22.6	0.3
15) CÔTE d'IVOIRE	22.4	0.3
16) CAMEROON	20.5	0.3
17) ANGOLA	18.6	0.3
18) BURKINA FASO	17.8	0.3
19) NIGER	16.9	0.2
20) MALAWI	16.8	0.2
21) MALI	16.0	0.2
22) ZAMBIA	14.2	0.2
23) SENEGAL	13.3	0.2
24) ZIMBABWE	13.2	0.2
25) RWANDA	12.0	0.2
26) CHAD	11.2	0.2
27) GUINEA	11.2	0.2
28) SOUTH SUDAN	11.1	0.2
29) TUNISIA	10.8	0.2
30) BURUNDI	10.9	0.2
31) SOMALIA	10.3	0.1
32) BENIN	9.9	0.1
33) TOGO	7.2	0.1
34) ERITREA	6.2	0.1
35) LIBYA	6.0	0.1
36) SIERRA LEONE	5.6	0.1
37) CENTRAL AFRICAN REPUBLIC	5.2	0.1

Region: Africa (Continued)

38) CONGO, REP.	4.5	0.1
39) LIBERIA	4.0	0.1
40) MAURITANIA	3.4	0.0
41) NAMIBIA	2.2	0.0
42) BOTSWANA	2.1	0.0
43) LESOTHO	1.9	0.0
44) GAMBIA, THE	1.8	0.0
45) GUINEA-BISSAU	1.6	0.0
46) GABON	1.6	0.0
47) SWAZILAND	1.4	0.0
48) MAURITIUS	1.3	0.0
49) COMOROS	0.8	0.0
50) DJIBOUTI	0.8	0.0
51) EQUATORIAL GUINEA	0.7	0.0
52) CAPE VERDE	0.5	0.0
53) WESTERN SAHARA	0.5	0.0
54) MAYOTTE (FR)	0.2	0.0
55) SÁO TOMÉ and PRINCIPE	0.2	0.0
56) SEYCHELLES	0.1	0.0
Total Africa	1,099.2	15.5

Region: North America and Caribbean

Country	2013 (July) Population (in millions)	% of World Total
1) USA	316.7	4.5
2) MEXICO	116.2	1.6
3) CANADA	34.6	0.5
4) GUATEMALA	14.4	0.2
5) CUBA	11.1	0.2
6) DOMINICAN REPUBLIC	10.2	0.1
7) HAITI	9.9	0.1
8) HONDURAS	8.4	0.1
9) EL SALVADOR	6.1	0.1
10) NICARAGUA	5.8	0.1
11) COSTA RICA	4.7	0.1
12) PUERTO RICO (U.S.)	3.7	0.1
13) PANAMA	3.6	0.1
14) JAMAICA	2.9	0.0
15) TRINIDAD AND TOBAGO	1.2	0.0
16) BELIZE	0.3	0.0
17) BAHAMAS, THE	0.3	0.0
18) BARBADOS	0.3	0.0
19) ST. LUCIA	0.2	0.0
20) CURACAO	0.1	0.0

Region: North America and Caribbean (Continued)

21) VIRGIN ISLANDS (U.S.)	0.1	0.0
22) GRENADA	0.1	0.0
23) ARUBA (NETH.)	0.1	0.0
24) ST. VINCENT & THE GRENADINES	0.1	0.0
25) ANTIGUA AND BARBUDA	0.1	0.0
26) DOMINICA	0.1	0.0
27) BERMUDA (UK)	0.1	0.0
28) CAYMAN ISLANDS	0.1	0.0
29) ST. KITTS AND NEVIS	0.1	0.0
Total North America and Caribbean	551.6	7.8

Region: South America

Country	2013 (July) Population (in millions)	% of World Total
1) BRAZIL	201.0	2.8
2) COLOMBIA	45.7	0.6
3) ARGENTINA	42.6	0.6
4) PERU	29.8	0.4
5) VENEZUELA	28.5	0.4
6) CHILE	17.2	0.2
7) ECUADOR	15.4	0.2
8) BOLIVIA	10.5	0.1
9) PARAGUAY	6.6	0.1
10) URUGUAY	3.3	0.0
11) GUYANA	0.7	0.0
12) SURINAME	0.6	0.0
Total South America	401.9	5.7

Region: Western Europe

Country	2013 (July) Population (in millions)	% of World Total
1) GERMANY	81.1	1.1
2) FRANCE	66.0	0.9
3) UNITED KINGDOM	63.4	0.9
4) ITALY	61.5	0.9
5) SPAIN	47.4	0.7
6) NETHERLANDS	16.8	0.2
7) PORTUGAL	10.8	0.2
8) GREECE	10.8	0.2
9) BELGIUM	10.4	0.1
10) SWEDEN	9.1	0.1
11) AUSTRIA	8.2	0.1

Region: Western Europe (Continued)

12) SWITZERLAND	8.0	0.1
13) DENMARK	5.6	0.1
14) FINLAND	5.3	0.1
15) IRELAND	4.8	0.1
16) NORWAY	4.7	0.1
17) LUXEMBOURG	0.5	0.0
18) MALTA	0.4	0.0
19) ICELAND	0.3	0.0
20) JERSEY	0.1	0.0
21) ISLE OF MAN	0.1	0.0
22) ANDORRA	0.1	0.0
23) GUERNSEY	0.1	0.0
24) GREENLAND (DEN.)	0.1	0.0
25) FAROE ISLANDS (DEN.)	0.1	0.0
26) LIECHTENSTEIN	—	—
27) SAN MARINO	—	—
28) MONACO	—	—
Total Western Europe	415.7	5.8

Region: Eastern Europe

Country	2013 (July) Population (in millions)	% of World Total
1) RUSSIA	142.5	2.0
2) UKRAINE	44.6	0.6
3) POLAND	38.4	0.5
4) ROMANIA	21.8	0.3
5) CZECH REPUBLIC	10.2	0.1
6) HUNGARY	9.9	0.1
7) BELARUS	9.6	0.1
8) SERBIA	7.2	0.1
9) BULGARIA	7.0	0.1
10) SLOVAKIA	5.5	0.1
11) CROATIA	4.5	0.1
12) BOSNIA and HERZEGOVINA	3.9	0.1
13) MOLDOVA	3.6	0.1
14) LITHUANIA	3.5	0.0
15) ALBANIA	3.0	0.0
16) LATVIA	2.2	0.0
17) MACEDONIA	2.1	0.0
18) SLOVENIA	2.0	0.0
19) KOSOVO	1.8	0.0
20) ESTONIA	1.3	0.0
21) MONTENEGRO	0.7	0.0
Total Eastern Europe	325.3	4.6

Region: Central Asia and Indian Subcontinent

Country	2013 (July) Population (in millions)	% of World Total
1) INDIA	1,220.8	17.2
2) PAKISTAN	193.2	2.7
3) BANGLADESH	163.7	2.3
4) AFGHANISTAN	31.1	0.4
5) NEPAL	30.4	0.4
6) UZBEKISTAN	28.7	0.4
7) SRI LANKA	21.7	0.3
8) KAZAKHSTAN	17.7	0.2
9) AZERBAIJAN	9.6	0.1
10) TAJIKISTAN	7.9	0.1
11) KYRGYZSTAN	5.5	0.1
12) TURKMENISTAN	5.1	0.1
13) GEORGIA	4.6	0.1
14) MONGOLIA	3.2	0.0
15) ARMENIA	3.0	0.0
16) BHUTAN	0.7	0.0
17) MALDIVES	0.4	0.0
Total Central Asia and Indian Subcontinent	1,747.3	24.6

Region: Middle East

Country	2013 (July) Population (in millions)	% of World Total
1) TURKEY	80.7	1.1
2) IRAN	79.9	1.1
3) IRAQ	31.9	0.4
4) SAUDI ARABIA	26.9	0.4
5) YEMEN	25.4	0.4
6) SYRIA	22.5	0.3
7) ISRAEL	7.7	0.1
8) JORDAN	6.5	0.1
9) UNITED ARAB EMIRATES	5.4	0.1
10) WEST BANK AND GAZA	4.5	0.1
11) LEBANON	4.1	0.1
12) OMAN	3.2	0.0
13) KUWAIT	2.7	0.0
14) QATAR	2.0	0.0
15) BAHRAIN	1.3	0.0
16) CYPRUS	1.2	0.0
Total Middle East	305.9	4.3

Region: Asia Pacific

Country	2013 (July) Population (in millions)	% of World Total
1) CHINA (EXCL. HK & MACAU)	1,349.6	19.0
2) INDONESIA	251.2	3.5
3) JAPAN	127.3	1.8
4) PHILIPPINES	105.7	1.5
5) VIETNAM	92.5	1.3
6) THAILAND	67.4	0.9
7) BURMA	55.2	0.8
8) SOUTH KOREA	49.0	0.7
9) MALAYSIA	29.6	0.4
10) NORTH KOREA	24.7	0.3
11) TAIWAN	23.3	0.3
12) AUSTRALIA	22.3	0.3
13) CAMBODIA	15.2	0.2
14) HONG KONG (SAR—CHINA)	7.2	0.1
15) LAOS	6.7	0.1
16) PAPUA NEW GUINEA	6.4	0.1
17) SINGAPORE	5.5	0.1
18) NEW ZEALAND	4.4	0.1
19) TIMOR—LESTE	1.2	0.0
20) FIJI	0.9	0.0
21) SOLOMON ISLANDS	0.6	0.0
22) MACAU (SAR—CHINA)	0.6	0.0
23) BRUNEI	0.4	0.0
24) FRENCH POLYNESIA (FR.)	0.3	0.0
25) NEW CALEDONIA (FR.)	0.3	0.0
26) VANUATU	0.3	0.0
27) SAMOA	0.2	0.0
28) GUAM (U.S.)	0.2	0.0
29) MICRONESIA, FED. STS	0.1	0.0
30) TONGA	0.1	0.0
31) KIRIBATI	0.1	0.0
32) MARSHALL ISLANDS	0.1	0.0
33) AMERICAN SAMOA (U.S.)	0.1	0.0
34) NORTHERN MARIANA ISLANDS	0.1	0.0
35) PALAU	—	—
Total Asia Pacific	2,248.8	31.7

SUMMARY

Region	# of Countries	Which You Have Visited	2013 (July) Population (millions)	Region's % of World Population	% of Population You Have Been Exposed To
AFRICA	56	_____	1,099.2	15.5	_____
NORTH AMERICA and CARIBBEAN	29	_____	551.6	7.8	_____
SOUTH AMERICA	12	_____	401.9	5.7	_____
WESTERN EUROPE	28	_____	415.7	5.8	_____
EASTERN EUROPE	21	_____	325.3	4.6	_____
CENTRAL ASIA and INDIAN SUBCONTINENT	17	_____	1,747.3	24.6	_____
MIDDLE EAST	16	_____	305.9	4.3	_____
ASIA PACIFIC	35	_____	2,248.8	31.7	_____
GRAND TOTAL	212	_____	7,095.7	100.0	_____

CASE
21

Developing an International Growth Strategy at New York Fries

It was May 2011 at the head office of 122164 Canada Ltd. (the Company) in uptown Toronto. The Company was the parent company of New York Fries (NYF) and South St. Burger Co. (SSBC). The mood at the head office was subdued, disguising the hectic pace that came with being one of the few companies that had managed to escape the recent global economic turmoil. In fact, business at the Company had been on an upward trajectory ever since it was founded in 1983. As the eight-person management team shuffled out of the boardroom, Jay Gould, the Company's president and founder, asked Warren Price to stay behind. Price, the Company's executive vice-president, had been Gould's sounding board since Price joined the privately-held company 22 years before (see Exhibit 1).

In three days, the Canadian franchisees were scheduled to meet along with the international franchisees from South Korea, Hong Kong and the United Arab Emirates in Toronto. The biannual meeting was a chance for the head office to update the franchisees on all upcoming corporate strategies and plans (e.g. domestic and international operations, marketing and purchasing) for the next 12 months and to provide an opportunity for the franchisees to interact with one another. The meeting also offered the opportunity for Gould and Price to reveal a new international growth strategy, in terms of both identifying new prospective territories and offering strategies to increase same-store sales.

There was a lot to discuss at the Company this year. New opportunities had been identified in China and India and growth of the newer brand, SSBC, was underway. Although the international franchisees had been asking for permission to take the SSBC brand to new territories, Gould and Price were wary. They had had some negative experiences with international expansion, particularly in expanding NYF to Australia and South Korea.

IVEY | Publishing

Sharda Prashad wrote this case under the supervision of Christopher Williams and W. Glenn Rowe to provide material for class discussion. The authors do not intend to illustrate either effective or ineffective handling of a managerial situation. The authors may have disguised certain names and other identifying information to protect confidentiality.

Richard Ivey School of Business Foundation prohibits any form of reproduction, storage or transmission without its written permission. Reproduction of this material is not covered under authorization by any reproduction rights organization. To order copies or request permission to reproduce materials, contact Ivey Publishing, Richard Ivey School of Business Foundation, The University of Western Ontario, London, Ontario, Canada, N6A 3K7; phone (519) 661-3208; fax (519) 661-3882; e-mail cases@ivey.uwo.ca.

Copyright © 2011, Richard Ivey School of Business Foundation   Version: 2011-08-18

One time permission to reproduce granted by Richard Ivey School of Business Foundation on April 22, 2014.

However, Gould and Price felt that they had learned how to uncover opportunities, take risks and learn from poor performance in overseas markets. "We have a great product," Gould said. "All of the franchisees understand that we make quality French fries but what we have to understand is how to keep our brand intact while we bring our premium fries to the world."

How could Gould and Price pursue new opportunities while maintaining their premium brands of French fries and hamburgers?

COMPANY BACKGROUND

The Company was founded in 1983 when Jay Gould and his brother Hal discovered the South Street Seaport restaurant (South Street). The brothers first heard about South Street after reading about it in the *New York Times*. After tasting the restaurant's French fries, Gould bought the Canadian rights for the company based on the strength of the product and the single item concept. At the time of Gould's purchase, South Street was just four months old. One year later, the first Canadian location of NYF was opened in Scarborough Town Centre. In 1987, Gould bought the assets (i. e., trademarks, systems, design and operations manuals) from the U.S. company (see Exhibits 2 and 3).

NYF fries were made from real–i.e., not reconstituted–potatoes. They were hand-cut and fried in non-hydrogenated, trans fat-free, sunflower oil. Since the company was committed to using the "best available" oil, the oil used was open to change. NYF had limited product offerings at its outlets: 1) French fries; 2) fry meals, such as poutine–French fries with toppings, such as beef, gravy and cheese; 3) hot dogs; 4) soda; 5) toppings and dips (gravy, cheese sauce); and 6) free seasonings, such as its signature California and Cajun seasonings and different varieties of vinegar, ketchup and salt. NYF and SSBC were quick-service restaurants.

In 2011, there were more than 190 NYF stores in six countries (Canada, Hong Kong, Macau, United Arab Emirates, Bahrain and South Korea), with sales in excess of $64 million (see Exhibit 4). Profit margin hovered around 22 per cent for company-owned stores. The highest-margin items were the a la carte fries and soda. Fifteen of the NYF stores were owned by the Company, the rest by franchisees. All of the wholly-owned stores were located in Canada.

The Company had been recognized with several awards over the years. For example, in 2011 SSBC was the recipient of the Special Recognition Award for Innovation in Energy by the A.R.E. Sustainability Awards,[1] in 2009 NYF received two gold Frankie awards by the Canadian Franchise Association for its "Real Fries in a Fake World campaign"[2] and in 2008 NYF won the award for Franchise Excellence presented by *Foodservice and Hospitality* magazine.[3]

Jay and Hal Gould were not new to the industry when they started the Company. In 1977, the pair founded Cultures, a popular salad chain. When the brothers decided to cash out in 1987, there were 58 stores. Hal was a silent partner in the Company. He had his own business which he ran from the same building as NYF's headquarters.

---

[1]"South St. Burger Co. Wins 2011 A.R.E. Sustainable Design Award," South St. Burger Co.," March 10, 2011, www.southstburger.com/theword/, accessed on April 16, 2011

[2]"NYF Wins 2 GOLD Frankie Awards with Real Fries in a Fake World Campaign," NYF, www.newyorkfries.com/about_nyf/news/view/30, accessed on April 16, 2011

[3]"New York Fries awarded Franchise Excellence at 2008 Pinnacle Awards," NYF, www.newyorkfries.com/about_nyf/news/view/18, accessed on April 16, 2011

Jay Gould received several honours and accolades for his business success and acumen and had also been invited to speak to Canadian Parliament for his decision in 2004 to eliminate trans fats from NYF's menu; NYF was the first Canadian quick-service restaurant to make that decision.

EXPANSION INTO HAMBURGERS

In 2004, Jay Gould founded the premier hamburger concept, SSBC. SSBC allowed him to offer the top two quick-service foods eaten outside the home (French fries and hamburgers) under one roof. Similar to NYF, SSBC promoted high-quality, fresh, natural ingredients. The beef hamburgers were hormone-and antibiotic-free and were prepared in front of the customer. Gould believed that "if you are going to indulge, then do it with the best-quality and best-tasting products." SSBC, like NYF, had very limited offerings at its stores.

Five years after it was founded, SSBC had 11 company-owned stores, all in Ontario. In 2009, the first franchise store was opened in Calgary. When Gould came up with the concept for SSBC, he planned to focus on Ontario in the first five years, Alberta and British Columbia growth in the next two and then expand into Hong Kong and Dubai in the subsequent five years.

Gould did not believe the brands would cannibalize each other: NYF and SSBC were complimentary brands occupying different real estate. NYF occupied shopping mall real estate, which skewed toward female, teenager and family demographics. SSBC was predominantly located in big box centres[4] with anchors such as Home Depot, Best Buy and the provincially-regulated Liquor Control Board of Ontario, which tended to draw more male consumers.

SSBC and NYF operated as distinct units within the Company. Due to the strength of the Company's balance sheet, SSBC was financed with credit facilities. Because NYF was a mature brand with demonstrated success in growing same store sales each year, the Company was able to secure capital for its SSBC expansion.

FRANCHISE STRUCTURE

NYF was operated as a franchise. Franchise owners bought the rights to operate NYF in different locations. In return for a franchise fee, NYF offered assistance with equipment, branding and purchasing. The franchise fee varied by location; in Hong Kong, for example, the fee was $300,000, with $25,000 refunded for each of the next five stores opened. In this way, the franchisee needed to secure substantial funding upfront to purchase NYF. The refund structure acted as an incentive for the franchisee to grow the business.

In addition to the upfront fee, franchisees paid head office a monthly royalty based on 6 per cent of gross sales for domestic franchisees and 3 per cent for international franchisees. These rates were consistent with the industry. The lower international fee was due to lower administrative support being offered abroad. This regular inflow of royalties ensured that NYF's financial statements were always cash-flow positive.

A general rule for profitability was that the franchisees needed to operate five to seven outlets to enjoy a good return on their investment, while head office needed three outlets in each territory to break even. International franchisees required five units to break even and with 10 units a territory was considered very successful. The average franchisee owned three stores.

---

[4]A large retail establishment.

Products consumed by the franchisee were charged at cost. Head office were responsible for purchasing/sourcing consumables, locating sites, negotiating leases, marketing, branding, purchasing, etc. The franchisees offered recommendations, but the ultimate decision lay with Gould.

Gould believed that all franchise arrangements needed to be governed by a franchise agreement to protect both parties; however, he also believed that if the franchisee and franchisor were constantly referring to the agreement to determine how the operation would run, then the relationship was likely doomed. Gould and Price therefore believed that trust was necessary for the franchise relationship to work. "The defining characteristic for franchisees has been, 'They get it,'" noted Price. "New York Fries is an unusual restaurant brand. The narrow menu is often difficult for potential franchisees to grasp. Those that acquire an NYF franchise do so because they grasp the advantages in marketing, purchasing, training and operations."

JAY GOULD'S APPROACH

Jay Gould believed in the value of slow and steady progress. He did not want NYF to be in every shopping mall in Canada–just the top-tier malls. With the exception of Quebec, NYF occupied real estate in all of the country's top-tier malls. As a result, growth opportunities were running out in Canada.

Gould believed there were three main growth areas for the company. First, the new SSBC concept could offer growth opportunities in Canada since it was a brand designed to work in big box centres and on the street front. SSBC offered growth because, unlike NYF, it was not designed for shopping malls. Second, as emerging markets developed a greater affinity for Western culture and food, NYF had an opportunity to capture emerging market consumers. Third, poutine was proving to be a popular product in Canada and around the world. In Canada, poutine was ranked as the "national dish" in a reader survey by a leading national newspaper[5] (as voted by 53 per cent of respondents) and "poutineries" were opening around the world. Gould believed the Company could make poutine as commonplace as the hamburger. Since NYF had already removed the meat ingredients from its gravy, the product was 100 per cent vegetarian, which widened the potential consumer base considerably. Poutine offered a similar profit margin to French fries (35 per cent).

Among the reasons that NYF was not affected by the global recession beginning in 2008 was its ability to rely on mall traffic and its product placement as an "affordable treat." Gould believed these were critical success factors.

While the Company had articulated its goals (see Exhibit 3), Jay Gould learned early in his career at Cultures that too much bureaucracy could get in the way of an efficient, productive business. While at Cultures, he employed 40 head office staff to oversee 75 franchise locations; by the time he exited Cultures, Gould felt that these staff were getting in the way of an efficient business. Consequently, Gould and the 18 employees who worked with him at the Company adopted a business culture that was not reliant on process and hierarchy.

THE MIDDLE EAST INITIATIVE

In 2002, the Company partnered with the Afifi brothers (Seirous, Sievash, and Suroosh) after receiving an unsolicited request to take the franchise to the United Arab Emirates. The Afifi brothers owned the master franchise for the Middle East territory, meaning that no one else could open a NYF location in the region.

---

[5]Ibid.

Gould and Price felt that the Afifi brothers had done an outstanding job in bringing the NYF brand into the region as both parties had intended. There was now a loyal customer base for the brand in the Middle East.

The Afifi brothers had 14 NYF locations in premier shopping malls in Dubai and Abu Dhabi. In 2009, the brothers opened the first NYF in Bahrain, marking the first location outside the United Arab Emirates. The newly opened Bahrain location was also in a premier shopping mall.

The recent recession had impacted business in the region. The NYF stores in Abu Dhabi and Dubai experienced less traffic because of lower levels of tourism to the region and the fact that locals were not going out as often. The United Arab Emirates' NYF locations were not near conflict zones but in Bahrain, NYF had to stay closed for days at a time because of political unrest. Together, these factors meant that these locations did not perform as well as they had in the past. It also meant two new franchise developments were being postponed.

The Afifi brothers believed that there was great potential to open NYF in India. They had some specific locations in mind, but unlike the expansion in the Middle East, the Indian locations would be on storefronts instead of in shopping malls. Gould had never been to India and was worried about moving away from the tried and tested formula of appealing to impulse shoppers in shopping malls. However, the Afifi brothers believed that the time was right to enter the Indian market, as locals began to develop favourite Western quick-service restaurants based on other chains that had already infiltrated the area.

Gould and Price had been very impressed by the brothers' ability to execute but were still not convinced about taking NYF to India. One concern was that NYF would have to build new relationships with suppliers in the region. Looking ahead to the eventual expansion of SSBC, Gould also wondered whether it made sense to expand to a country that was not a large consumer of beef.

The Afifi brothers also wanted to start opening SSBC in their existing franchise territories in the United Arab Emirates. They believed NYF had enough brand recognition that the local marketplace was ready for the premier hamburger concept. However, because the Middle East imported the vast majority of its food, it could be difficult to build relationships with suppliers for the raw materials needed to make premier hamburgers and buns. Gould and Price also worried that SSBC was too young to be taken internationally. SSBC's only franchised unit was less than two years old and SSBC had only one location outside Ontario: a location in Calgary, a market very similar to where the SSBC concept has been developed. Furthermore, exporting the necessary products to the Middle East would be a new challenge for head office.

EXPANSION INTO ASIA

NYF entered Hong Kong in 2009 after Gould received two different unsolicited requests to buy the rights for Hong Kong in 2008. At the time of the requests, Gould had never been to Hong Kong; his first visit was to select the new Hong Kong partners and scout locations for the franchise. Gould and Price settled on a group of franchise owners, Next Step Limited, which was led by two recent graduates from the University of British Columbia (Ricky Takasu and Thomas Lau). These young men were raised in Hong Kong and Canada and went to school in Canada, returning to Hong Kong after graduation. Besides having an appreciation for both cultures, they also had the necessary contacts for securing prime real estate in Hong Kong.

When the first Hong Kong franchise opened in 2009, the franchisees hoped to open 10 locations in Hong Kong and Macau within the first five years and then expand to China since the group had the rights to expand into Macau, China and Taiwan; however, two years into the Asia expansion, there were just three locations in Hong Kong and one in Macau: two were in shopping malls, one was at a tourist destination and the Macau NYF was operated by a sub-franchisee in a theatre/casino complex. All four locations were posting good financial results but the growth had been slower than expected; part of the reason for this, was the demanding amount of management needed for the Hong Kong locations. Gould did not want more locations to open until the quality offered–both in terms of the product and service–was consistent with that offered in Canada. Overall, however, there was definite potential to open more locations successfully in Hong Kong.

Given that the pace of expansion in Hong Kong and Macau was slower than expected, Gould wondered if he should offer the expansion rights for the rest of the region (China and Taiwan) to someone else. Gould also wondered if the product was right for mainland China. There was no question that there was an opportunity to appeal to the growing Chinese middle class, but there were adverse logistical issues as well. While Hong Kong and China were close, there were fewer suppliers going into China. Moreover, large Western quick-service restaurants had had difficulty adjusting their menus to regional taste preferences across China. Gould recognized that opening a location in China would probably take a great deal of time and effort from his head office staff.

LESSONS FROM INTERNATIONAL MARKETS

This was not the first time the Company had encountered difficulties during expansion. NYF had experienced growing pains in some of the countries they had entered over the years, notably Australia and South Korea. A failure in Australia, for example, left Gould cautious about straying into foreign territory. "Australia should have been the perfect place for New York Fries," he remembered. "Both Canada and Australia have a British heritage and the people remember eating fresh chips." In addition, both Canada and Australia relied on shopping centres with food courts for respite from extreme temperatures and both shared a language and a similar culture. Unfortunately, the Australia venture, which lasted from 1998 to 2002, failed. Gould blamed the failure on a number of reasons, including a franchisee who micro-managed, real estate choices Gould had not approved of and the franchisee not having enough money to invest in the Australian stores. Gould hoped the franchisee would turn things around and recommended different courses of action, such as different locations and a different management style; however, after four years, Gould admitted defeat. He had given the franchisee too much control over decisions in the franchise agreement and he had taken the franchisee's word about the amount of cash that was available to invest in the venture. Just before head office pulled out, it considered opening wholly-owned locations in Australia because both Gould and Price believed it was the perfect market for NYF. Ultimately, however, they decided not to because it would drain too many resources.

The Australian failure left Gould reluctant, but not opposed, to international expansion. He tried to learn from his failures. In 2002, Gould changed the franchise agreement so that he retained control over key decisions and he demanded more money upfront from franchisees in order to ensure that adequate resources were available. As franchisees expanded, a portion of the franchise fee was returned to them.

South Korea was another example of the Company's less-than-successful forays into international expansion. In the 1990s, Gould was given an unsolicited offer by a potential franchisee. When Gould and Price assessed the business potential, it seemed plausible and the franchisee was believed to be well-financed; however, the South Korean location did not perform as hoped. The franchisee wanted the store to have more of a Korean design and taste, as opposed to adopting the NYF brand as planned. Part of the reason for this resistance to the brand could have been that this franchisee was older, in his 60s, and did not want to adopt the NYF strategy. Another reason could be that the first stores operated on street front properties instead of in shopping malls. In 2006, a new franchisee bought the Korean stores. At present, there were four stores in South Korea but that was still less than the six that Gould and Price felt would give NYF adequate market presence in the country. The new franchisee lacked some of the business-savvy of the other international franchise owners and required a time investment from head office. The opening of Hong Kong allowed NYF's head office to pay closer attention to South Korea's operations because travel costs could be shared between locations.

ISSUES BEFORE GOULD AND PRICE IN MAY 2011

"Over the next three days, we have many decisions to make," said Price. "We need to determine whether we should expand into China and/or India and we need to devise an expansion plan for South Street."

Gould nodded in agreement and shuffled through his notes and spreadsheets. A table comparing key indicators in existing and target countries caught his eye (see Exhibit 5).

"There is something else we should consider," added Gould. "I would like us to think about the strategic direction of NYF. We have been falling into our international expansion plans but what should our goal be? To be the number one purveyor of French fries and poutine? Or simply to maintain our NYF brand in current markets and start building the SSBC brand?"

The pair huddled around the boardroom table, intent on making these key decisions over the next three days before their franchisees from across Canada and around the world convened in Toronto.

EXHIBIT 1: Organization Chart

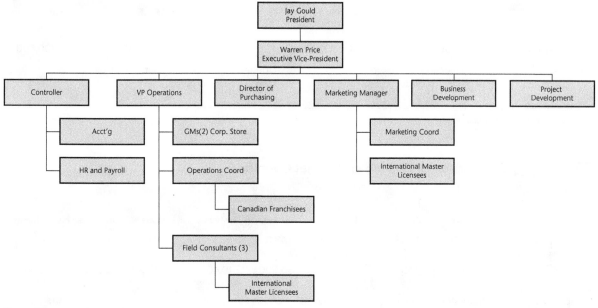

Source: Company documents.

EXHIBIT 2: Key International Events

1983	1987	1998	2001	2002	2004	2008
NYF Canadian rights purchased	NYF International rights purchased	NYF Australia and South Korea agreements* signed	NYF U.A.E. agreement* signed	Australia agreement ends	SSBC founded	NYF Hong Kong agreement* signed

* First store opens the same or next year.
Source: Company documents.

EXHIBIT 3: New York Fries Mission Statement

"As a franchisor, our goal is to increase our system-wide sales and maximize store profitability. In order to achieve this goal we employ the following strategies:

— Grow our store units by finding new markets in which to sell our products;

— Closely manage the delivery of fresh ingredients to our stores in order to offer a high-quality product to our customers;

— Be recognized as an outstanding franchisor by ensuring the operational and financial success of our franchisees; and

— Increase same store sales and customer counts by driving traffic with innovative marketing campaigns."

Source: Company marketing department.

EXHIBIT 4: International Presence In 2011

	South Korea	Bahrain	Macau	U.A.E.	Hong Kong
Locations	4	1	1	14	3
Sales—Cdn$	1,000,000	500,000	—	7,000,000	1,700,000
Notes	One location temporarily closed for building repair		Opened in May 2011	Three sub-franchised units under construction	

Source: Company documents.

EXHIBIT 5: Comparison of Existing and Target Countries

	Canada	China	India	South Korea	Bahrain	Macau	United Arab Emirates	Hong Kong
Population (millions)	34.0	1,337	1,189	48.8	1.2	.573	5.1	7.1
GDP/Capita (US$)	39,600	7,400	3,400	30,200	40,400	33,000	40,200	45,600
Vacancy of premier shopping malls	Saturated	Data coming	Contact with Canadian real estate manager	Store-front	Adequate	Adequate	Adequate	Adequate
Fast food entrants	Advanced	Early	Early	Mid	Mid	Advanced	Advanced	Advanced
2011 Index of Economic Freedom rating	6	135	124	35	10	19	47	1

Sources: Company documents; "The World Factbook," *Central Intelligence Agency,* www.cia.gov/library/publications/the-world-factbook/, accessed on April 16, 2011; "Top Ten of 2011," *2011 Index of Economic Freedom—The Heritage Foundation,* www.heritage.org/index/topten, accessed on April 16, 2011.

Ethiopian Airlines: Bringing Africa Together

In 2006, Ethiopian Airlines was named "African Airline of the Year."[1] A year later, the company gained further acclaim when it received the "Africa Business of the Year" award.[2] These achievements signalled that the company was on course for achieving the strategic plan it had formulated in 2005, which sought, among other things, to increase the company's annual passenger traffic to three million and to triple its annual revenue to $1 billion[3] by 2010.

Whereas Ethiopian Airlines (Ethiopian) boasted a global airline network, its strength lay in its pan-African network. By 2007, roughly 60 per cent of its 49 worldwide routes were in Africa. In fact, since Ethiopian's founding in 1945, it had worked diligently to bring Africans together. As carriers from Europe, the Middle East and Africa jockeyed for position in the rapidly growing aviation market of Africa, Yissehak Zewoldi, Ethiopian's vice president of alliances and corporate strategy, resolved to consolidate the airline's already strong foothold in the continent. He knew full well that achieving this goal would be no simple task, given the high operational costs and restrictive regulations characterizing air transportation in Africa.

Yamlaksira S. Getachew wrote this case under the supervision of Professor Paul W. Beamish solely to provide material for class discussion. The authors do not intend to illustrate either effective or ineffective handling of a managerial situation. The authors may have disguised certain names and other identifying information to protect confidentiality.

This publication may not be transmitted, photocopied, digitized or otherwise reproduced in any form or by any means without the permission of the copyright holder. Reproduction of this material is not covered under authorization by any reproduction rights organization. To order copies or request permission to reproduce materials, contact Ivey Publishing, Ivey Business School, Western University, London, Ontario, Canada, N6G 0N1; (t) 519.661.3208; (e) cases@ivey.ca; www.iveycases.com.

Copyright © 2014, Richard Ivey School of Business Foundation   Version: 2014-03-03·

One time permission to reproduce granted by Richard Ivey School of Business Foundation on April 22, 2014.

IVEY | Publishing

[1]"Ethiopian Airlines Crowned Africa's Best Carrier," *Angola Press,* September 21, 2006, www.ethiomedia.com/carepress/ethiopian_airlines_crowned.htmlaccessed August 14, 2013.

[2]*The African Times/USA* is a U.S.-based news journal that, among other things, recognizes best practices in Africa.

[3]All currency amounts are shown in U.S. dollars unless otherwise noted.

A handful of African carriers had been major players in intra-African aviation. Recent economic development and improved business relations among African countries had opened up the market for intra-continental aviation. As a result, major African airlines were rushing to capitalize on this opportunity. Kenya Airways, for example, had built an extensive African network. Similarly, by 2007, Ethiopian was flying to 28 destinations throughout the continent (see Exhibit 1). Zewoldi believed that the African market had much to offer, and tapping this potential would require expanding the airline's market base while ensuring greater efficiency. The challenge was that the demand for air transport between most African countries was insufficient to justify point-to-point connections.

In a bid to promote efficiency and serve even thinner markets profitably, Zewoldi and his team formulated a strategy of setting up multiple hubs across different regions of Africa, in addition to the existing main hub in Addis Ababa, Ethiopia. While this strategy, if successful, could set Ethiopian apart from its African competitors and catapult it into becoming a leading airline on the continent, it was also a risky proposition with much at stake. Clearly, success at the first new hub[4] would validate the viability of the strategy. As a result, it was vital to locate this hub where the probability of success would be the greatest and to carefully decide on the appropriate mode and level of ownership.

THE AFRICAN CIVIL AVIATION INDUSTRY

The history of commercial aviation in Africa dates back to the colonial times. Most colonial powers established commercial airlines connecting their colonies to their home countries. In East Africa, for example, East African Airways–formed jointly by three former British colonies, Kenya, Tanzania and Uganda–had been a major carrier in the region until it went out of business in 1977.[5] Similarly, Air Afrique, established by 11 former French colonies in West and Central Africa, had been at the forefront of the aviation industry in the region until its collapse in 2002.[6] The pioneering airlines in Southern and Northern Africa had remained relatively stable, registering long years of commendable performance. South African Airways, one of the leading carriers in Africa, had dominated the Southern African market since 1932. Similarly, the aviation industry in North Africa had featured, for decades, Royal Air Maroc, EgyptAir, Tunisair and Air Algerie, among others.

European-based airlines had traditionally dominated the African skies. Leveraging their prior imperial connections, airlines from France and Britain secured a commanding presence in markets spreading across their former colonies. While Air France established a firm presence in most West and Central African countries, British Airways built extensive networks in the northern and southern parts of the continent. In addition, Lufthansa and the now defunct Sabena maintained a presence in the African skies. Starting from the late 1980s and early 1990s, the African aviation industry had seen the introduction of a different breed of competitors from the Gulf region.

Over the years, the African market had proved difficult for African and non-African operators alike. Whereas about 26 African-based airlines provided intercontinental connectivity during the 1970s and 1980s, only nine such carriers had been in business since 2000.[7] Several factors were responsible. Airport charges, taxes and fuel costs were unduly

---

[4]Ethiopian's main hub was at Bole International Airport in Addis Ababa; here, "the first hub" refers to the new hub the company was looking to set up.

[5]East African Airways homepage, www.eastafricanairways.com/EAA/History.html accessed January 15, 2014.

[6]"World Airline Survey," *Flight International*, April 11, 1963, p. 508, www.flightglobal.com/pdfarchive/view/1963/1963%20-%200530.html, accessed August 15, 2013.

high in Africa and contributed to relatively higher operating costs for African carriers. For instance, a study comparing airport charges in 18 African countries with airport charges in a European country indicated the African airports charged, on average, 30 to 40 per cent more than the European airport. Similarly, the cost of fuel accounted for up to 45 to 55 per cent of the overall operational cost of African carriers–a figure up to 55 per cent greater than the global average.[8] Other factors that rendered the African aviation industry less attractive included underdeveloped infrastructures; limited access to capital, human, and technical resources; and governmental restrictions on access to markets.

These challenges notwithstanding, the industry afforded numerous opportunities. Over the past few years, the continent had registered an unprecedented rate of economic growth, which had facilitated trade and thereby an inflow of investment to Africa, opening up potential markets for the aviation industry. Ever-increasing economic ties across and beyond the continent, coupled with flourishing south-south trading among Africa, South America and Asia, prefigured a looming aviation bonanza. With a population nearing one billion and the rate of urbanization ever increasing, Africa looked ripe for a thriving aviation business. Its rapidly growing middle-class population also created potential market opportunities.

According to a 2007 report by the International Air Transport Association (IATA)[9] Africa registered an average annual passenger traffic growth rate of 5.6 per cent, placing the continent among the world's top aviation growth regions. That said, passenger traffic to and from Africa comprised only about 3 per cent of the world air traffic, indicating a potential for growth and further expansion. The African market had been served by carriers mostly from Europe, the Middle East and Africa. Major players included Air France, British Airways, Lufthansa German Airlines, Turkish Airlines and KLM-Royal Dutch Airlines from Europe; Emirates Airlines, Qatar Airways and Etihad Airways from the Middle East; and EgyptAir, Royal Air Maroc, Air Algerie, South African Airways, Ethiopian Airlines and Kenya Airways from Africa.

Yet, African carriers' performance, especially in terms of market share, remained mediocre. In fact, according to a 2007 report by the African Airlines Association (AFRAA), non-African carriers held a staggering market share of approximately 80 per cent of the overall passenger traffic to and from Africa, with the balance covered by a handful of African operators. Of these African carriers, only a few managed to consistently avoid losses.

To offset the relatively higher airline operating costs in Africa, most African carriers charged much higher fares per seat kilometre than their European, American and Middle Eastern counterparts. For example, average travel fare per seat kilometre in Africa was roughly four times that in Europe.[10] These higher fares clearly put African airlines at a stark competitive disadvantage.

In addition, most of the European and Gulf carriers serving the African market had a much greater capacity and a richer worldwide network to exercise their economies of scale advantage over their African competitors. Such advantage not only conferred a competitive

[7]EU-Africa Aviation Conference, Windhoek, Namibia, April 2–3, 2009.

[8]Heinrich C. Bofinger, "Unsteady Course: Challenges to Growth in Africa's Air Transport Industry," Africa Infrastructure Country Diagnostic, Background paper 16 (Phase II), The International Bank for Reconstruction and Development/The World Bank, Washington, DC, 2009.

[9]International Air Transport Association Annual Report 2007 63rd Annual General Meeting Vancouver, June 2007,

[10]"African Aviation Industry – Deep Dive Analysis by FastJet, Ethiopian Airlines, Kenya Airlines," Travopia, November 12, 2012, www.travopia.com/2012/11/african-aviation-industry-deep-dive-analysis-by-fastjet-ethiopian-airlines-kenya-airways.html, accessed January 15, 2014.

edge on their existing routes but also offered an incentive to expand connectivity that would, in turn, help sustain their edge.

The cost disadvantage was further compounded by, in general, the poor safety and security records of African carriers. In 2005, for example, 37 per cent of all fatal airline accidents occurred in Africa, making the continent the most unsafe place for flights. This figure was even more surprising when positioned in the context that Africa accounted for only 3 per cent of the world's airline traffic.[11] By 2006, only four African airlines had received an IATA Operational Safety Audit certificate, a certificate issued by the IATA after an assessment confirmed adherence to accepted safety standards and practices. Without this certification, airlines were hugely limited in their operations and route expansion. The disproportionate accident rate was attributed largely to an underdeveloped infrastructure, an aging fleet, lack of capacity to enforce standard safety precautions and lack of trained workers.

Another challenge facing African air transport was the restrictions most countries imposed on access to their skies by foreign operators. Generally, such restrictions were directed more toward African carriers than non-African carriers. In 1999, in an effort to deregulate air transportation services, 44 African countries signed an agreement called the Yamoussoukro Decision. Billed as the appropriate solution to several problems confronting African aviation, the agreement sought, inter alia, to open up national and regional air skies to foreign carriers and liberalize intra-African aviation service.[12] However, its implementation fell short of expectations, and the challenges it sought to address remained salient.

The African international aviation industry featured competition on both intra- and inter-continental levels. Competition in intercontinental routes was, in general, stiffer, with carriers from all around the globe jockeying for market share. Such competition was justified given that intercontinental travel accounted for more than 50 per cent of the flights to, from and within Africa. Despite its relatively lower share of the overall air traffic, the market for intra-African travel had grown at a healthy rate of 10.2 per cent between 2004 and 2007. Robust economic growth and increased intra-African trade and relations were among the many factors responsible for the surge in demand.

African carriers had a minority share in the intercontinental air travel market. The strategic orientations of most non-African carriers seemed to suggest that they were concerned less with ensuring point-to-point connectivity within Africa and more with connecting the continent to the rest of the world. Intercontinental air travel market growth stood at 11.4 per cent over the years between 2004 and 2007. While European carriers dominated the intercontinental flights to and from Africa, competitors from the Middle East had recently registered a rapidly increasing prominence.[13] The capacity and size of even the largest of the African carriers were nowhere near the capacity and size of their European and Middle Eastern counterparts.

---

[11]Harro Ranter, *Airliner Accident Statistics 2005: Statistical Summary of Fatal Multi-engine Airliner Accidents in 2005*, 2006, aviation-safety.net/pubs/asn/ASN%20Airliner%20Accident%20Statistics%202005.pdf, accessed January 10, 2014.

[12]Charles E. Schlumberger, Open Skies for Africa Implementing the Yamoussoukro Decision. The World Bank, Washington, DC, 2010, web.worldbank.org/WBSITE/EXTERNAL/TOPICS/EXTTRANSPORT/EXTAIRTRANSPORT/0,,contentMDK:22709045- pagePK:210058- piPK:210062- theSitePK:515181,00.html, accessed January 17, 2014.

[13]Heinrich C. Bofinger, "Unsteady Course: Challenges to Growth in Africa's Air Transport Industry," Africa Infrastructure Country Diagnostic, Background paper 16 (Phase II), The International Bank for Reconstruction and Development / The World Bank, Washington, DC, 2009.

Two recent developments were changing the African aviation landscape. The first was the proliferation of viable low-cost carriers (LCCs) in the African aviation market. Unlike in Europe and North America, the African aviation industry had traditionally remained unsuitable for LCCs. African LCCs were denied the success their counterparts enjoyed across the rest of the world because of their high cost of operation, restrictions on access to skies and relatively higher cost associated with leasing aircraft. In the rest of the world, most successful LCCs reduced their costs by flying to secondary airports. However, in Africa, the dearth of secondary airports rendered such an option impractical. Despite the odds, the industry's share of LCCs was steadily growing and such LCCs as Mango and 1Time were adapting by limiting their services to sub-regional destinations.

The second development was the incorporation of major African airlines into major global aviation alliances. For example, South African Airways was introduced to the Star Alliance in April 2006, and the SkyTeam alliance welcomed Kenya Airways in September 2007. These moves proved useful for both the African airlines and the associated global alliances. While the former gained access to a market to feed their intra-African flights, the latter secured connectivity to their respective members' vast pan-African networks.

HISTORY OF ETHIOPIAN AIRLINES

Ethiopian Airlines was founded in December 1945 as a joint venture between the then Ethiopian government and America's Trans World Airlines. Its maiden flight was from Addis Ababa to Cairo in April 1946. From the beginning, Ethiopian had a motto of "Bringing Africa Together," and, over the years, ensured connectivity to every part of the continent. In 2005, Ethiopian placed orders for 10 Boeing 787 Dreamliners – a move that would make it the first airline in Africa and the second in the world to operate these efficient planes. By 2007, the company operated a fleet of 35 aircraft,[14] which were among the youngest and most modern in the continent, flying to multiple destinations in Africa, Europe and the Middle East.

The airline had, for decades, been wholly owned by the Ethiopian government, and its consistent profitability over the years, even under difficult circumstances, challenged the notion that state-owned airlines do not work in the African aviation market. Within just a few years after the turn of the century, the African aviation industry saw an alarming streak of failure by several major, state-owned airlines. In 2002, Air Afrique went out of business. A year later, Nigeria Airways followed suit. In 2005, Ghana Airways collapsed, and Air Gabon had a similar fate in 2006. Ethiopian, however, turned a net profit in excess of $14 million in 2006 (see Exhibit 2), in the same year that African airlines overall suffered an operating loss of approximately $120 million.[15] Ethiopian's profits came from its passenger transportation service, cargo freight and services provided to other airlines.

Since 1956, Ethiopian had operated its own aviation academy, training pilots, technicians, crews and management professionals and thereby ensuring a consistent supply of human resources. Recently, the airline had been working on modernizing its fleets to improve customer satisfaction, promote safety and secure efficiency. In 2003, Ethiopian started using a newly erected airport terminal, built as part of the $130 million airport expansion project announced in 1999. By the turn of the century, a consensus had built up around the company's board of directors that Ethiopian had not grown to its potential, despite its long years of experience.

---

[14]Most were suitable for short-haul flights (a flight distance of under 5,600 km).

[15]AFRAA 2006 Annual Report presented at the 39th AFRAA annual general assembly on December 10, 2007.

In 2004, Ethiopian appointed Girma Wake as its chief executive officer. With his decades of experience in the aviation industry, both in Ethiopia and the Middle East, Wake was no stranger to the business. He brought with him a spirit of change and dynamism. Within a year, he oversaw the formulation of an ambitious five-year strategic plan. Strategies were developed to realize the plan, including the multi-hub strategy that sought to expand Ethiopian's African market base and profitably serve thinner markets. This multi-hub strategy aimed to add one or more hubs in different regions of Africa to its existing main hub at Bole International Airport.

THE MULTI-HUB STRATEGY

Similar to its economic development, Africa's aviation sector had remained underdeveloped. However, recent progress across multiple dimensions appeared to have changed this situation for the better. For example, Africa's rapid economic development was already attracting global attention. Similarly, its rising population, emerging middle-class and improving intra-Africa trade presented opportunities on which carriers could capitalize.

Cognizant of these opportunities, Zewoldi and his team designed a multi-hub strategy to tap into the huge potential of the African aviation market. Africa was the second largest and second most populous continent, comprising more than 50 countries. The continent hosted approximately 660 regional and domestic city-pairs,[16] of which the vast majority had no or insufficient connectivity.[17] For some flights within Africa, travellers were required to fly to another continent, such as to Europe. Yet, most city-pairs lacked sufficient market size to justify a direct connecting service. Hence, serving such markets would require the devising of a special mechanism.

Airlines used two common models of route network: the hub-and-spoke (HS) model and the point-to-point (PP) model. The HS model involved using a third location to connect flights between an origin and destination. The third location, the hub, served as a consolidation point to which flights connecting two points were routed. The PP model entailed direct connection of two locations without the need for a connecting flight at a third location.

The HS model required identifying a location, preferably centrally located, to collect flights from surrounding locations. This model essentially divided a journey into two, while reducing the total number of flights needed to connect locations (nodes) on the network. Please refer to Exhibit 3 to better understand the differences between the two models.

As shown in Exhibit 3, five locations (nodes) needed to be connected in both networks. Note that the PP network contained 10 connecting flights; whereas, the HS network used only four connecting flights to serve the same number of locations. In the case of the HS model, location C served as a hub through which all flights passed to connect with the other locations. Markets were collected from the rest of the locations and supplied to connecting flight at the hub. Zewoldi and the strategic planning team were convinced that this model would improve the economic feasibility of serving thinner markets as (1) each departing flight carried passengers flying to any of the remaining four nodes, thereby increasing the utilization of airline seat capacity, and (2) flights from the hub to each destination could access markets collected from the other locations.

In the PP model, the number of connecting flights is given as $\dfrac{[N(N-1)]}{2}$, where N represents the total number of locations; whereas, in the HS model, the number of

---

[16]A city-pair represents city combination of origin and destination for a flight.

[17]Air Transport Market Trends in Africa, AFRAA, 2011, www.afraa.org/index.php/media-center/publications/sg-speeches/sg-speeches-2011/232-air-transport-market-trends-in-africa-speech/file, accessed January 17, 2014.

connecting flights is a function of $(N - 1)$. The smaller number of flights to connect all the locations in the HS model facilitates more efficient use of resources. In addition, the marginal benefit of adding a route in the network is much greater for the HS model than for the PP model. That is, in the HS model, any additional route not only provides access to markets in the same route but also expands traffic flow along the network. The HS model also provides greater value to passengers. For example, an airline adopting the HS model operates fewer connecting flights than would be possible otherwise. The extra capacity can be deployed toward increasing the frequency of flights between locations. Hub connections also provide passengers with a wider choice of destinations. The greater pool of traffic and potential for increased load factor are likely to drive fares down.

However, the HS model is also likely to increase the average travel time for passengers, as flights need to be routed through the hub. For example, looking at Exhibit 3, the direct connection of A and B in the HS model makes for a shorter and likely a cheaper flight than a connection via C. The HS model also significantly increases the costs of coordination and scheduling by the airline running the hub. This increased coordination cost is likely to be passed on to customers in the form of increased fares. Likewise, a problem in one of the links affects customers in the entire network, possibly leading to dissatisfaction among passengers who may need to wait for hours or days until a connecting flight arrives.

Major airlines in North America had been using the HS model since 1975. Their European counterparts adopted the same model during the 1980s and 1990s. Ethiopian's move toward developing multiple hubs in Africa would be pioneering for African aviation. Zewoldi and his team understood that the strategy was to be implemented against the backdrop of a considerable initial investment requirement, restricted access to skies and the high costs of aviation operation in Africa. They needed to mobilize all of Ethiopian's strengths and tap into existing competencies. Understandably, the formation of subsequent hubs hinged on the success of the first hub. As a result, Zewoldi and his team needed to select a region where the probability of success was the greatest.

REGIONAL AVIATION MARKETS

Zewoldi knew that performance in the first hub would be strategically crucial, as it would set the tone for subsequent moves. Thus, he needed to ensure both a careful selection of location for the first hub and its proper management afterward. As the main hub of Ethiopian was located in Eastern Africa, the regions available for locating the new hubs were Northern, Middle, Western and Southern Africa. See Exhibit 4 and Exhibit 5 for the available regional options according to the UN geoscheme. Exhibit 6 shows the level of liberalization of air transport in each of these regions along with the traffic freedom rights Ethiopian exercises in each region.

Northern Africa

A home to more than 195 million people by 2007 (see Exhibit 5), Northern Africa was the largest sub-region of Africa. Between 2005 and 2007, its annual average population growth rate stood at 1.8 per cent. It comprised seven states that, in many ways, were more homogenous than states in other African sub-regions. The countries were religiously and culturally similar and shared the official language of Arabic.

The economic development of the countries in this region was among the fastest growing in the continent. Between 2005 and 2007, the region registered an average gross domestic product (GDP) growth rate of 5.77 per cent, higher than that of most regions of Africa.[18] This growth was due mainly to an abundant oil reserve in the region that had led to Libya, Algeria and Sudan being among Africa's major oil producers. In addition, greater access to skilled human power and better infrastructure encouraged investment in the region.

Most of the states in this region had airlines whose performances were on a par with the best in Africa. EgyptAir, for example, was among the best airlines on the continent and invited to join Star Alliance network in 2007. Its network stretched across Eastern and Northern Africa. Royal Air Maroc flew to numerous cities in West and North Africa. Air Algerie and Tunisair, from Algeria and Tunisia, respectively, were among the strongest, not just in the region but also in the continent.

For all its extensive route network in Africa, Ethiopian flew only to a single destination in North Africa–Cairo, Egypt. The region had some strategically appealing features to justify that location for Ethiopian's first hub. Greater economic activity across the region could easily translate to greater aviation demand. Its proximity to Europe was also a plus. As an underrepresented region in Ethiopia's network, North Africa also presented a new market and, thus, growth opportunities. However, the presence of strong carriers in the region could present a formidable challenge to building a favourable market share. In addition, lack of brand awareness in the region could require extensive promotion and initial periods of sub-standard performance.

Middle Africa

Comprising nine countries and a population of 118 million by 2007, the region known as Middle Africa presented a viable alternative for locating the first hub. Between 2005 and 2007, the region had registered an annual average population growth rate of 2.2 per cent. French was the working language in seven of the nine countries. The mineral wealth of the region was considerable. Angola was among the top producers of oil, gas and diamonds, while Gabon was among the continent's top iron producers. Extensive oil reserves and production in Cameroon, Gabon and Republic of the Congo were behind the region's impressive GDP growth of 8.28 per cent between 2005 and 2007. In fact, the region recorded the highest level of GDP growth of all regions in Africa between 2005 and 2007.

This region featured in the networks of most of the major airlines in Africa. For instance, continental giants such as South African Airways, Ethiopian and Kenya Airways were already flying to several cities in this region. By 2007, Ethiopian flew to six countries in the Middle African region: Chad, Gabon, Democratic Republic of the Congo, Republic of the Congo, Cameroon and Angola. Ethiopian's familiarity with this part of Africa would come in useful when operating a hub. In addition, the centrality of this region to the existing network of Ethiopian would make it an attractive alternative for the hub location, as centrality within a network was an important criterion for hub success. Similarly, its robust economic growth presented a clear opportunity for increased traffic in and across the region. After experiencing the collapse in 2006 of Air Gabon and a dismal performance of Cameroon Airlines, the region desperately needed a safe and reliable air transportation service. This condition also provided a level playing field for all outsiders to compete and win markets.

That said, inadequate and underdeveloped infrastructure and governmental restrictions to operate out of the region could make a move to this region difficult.

---

[18]The three-year GDP growth rate figures were collected from data from the African Development Bank, a development finance institution for promoting economic and social development.

Western Africa

The most populous of the regions under consideration was West Africa, home to about a third of the African population. The region was also the most densely populated. Its annual population growth rate over the three-year period between 2005 and 2007 averaged at 2.5 per cent. Of the 17 countries in the region, eight were French speaking, six were English speaking, two were Portuguese speaking and one was Arabic speaking.

The region was known for its vast potential of natural resources, including oil. Nigeria ranked among Africa's largest oil producers and exporters; Ghana's rich gold, diamonds and aluminum deposits had been the envy of many; and steel abounded in Guinea, Liberia, Mauritania, Nigeria, Senegal and Sierra Leone. Despite such wealth, the region experienced the lowest rate of GDP growth, with an average growth rate of only 4.64 per cent between 2005 and 2007. The plunge in the GDP growth rate was partly the result of large-scale social unrest and civil wars in many countries of the region.

By 2007, Ethiopian flew to six destinations in Western Africa: Mali, Senegal, Nigeria, Ghana, Côte d'Ivoire and Togo. The past couple of years had seen the demise of major airlines of the region. The then-mighty Air Afrique and the major airlines of Nigeria and Ghana went bankrupt, leaving an extensive vacuum for other airlines to fill. The region had also been traditionally served by European carriers such as Air France and Brussels Airlines, but they connected the region only to Europe, not to other regional locations.

As a viable alternative for the hub location, Western Africa presented several advantages. The huge population size could provide a large customer base and adequate access to human resource. In addition, the vast mineral wealth of the region would continue to attract investments and trade for the years to come. The sheer absence of a strong carrier operating out of this region could translate to the possibility of gaining market dominance. Its proximity to the South American and North American markets was also another appeal. However, the political instability in many countries of the region and the region's recently weak economic performance foreshadowed a risky road ahead. In addition, the states in this region had a longstanding desire to establish their own strong national carriers, which could limit Ethiopian's plans for forming and operating a hub there.

Southern Africa

Southern Africa featured five countries and had the smallest combined population of all the regions. Its annual average population growth rate was also the lowest, at approximately 1.4 per cent. English was the official language in all these countries. Like other regions in Africa, Southern Africa had rich reserves of natural resources, ranging from petroleum to diamonds to gold. The most developed economy in the whole of Africa, South Africa was among the most resource-rich countries in the world. Its gold, platinum and diamond reserves contributed to its growing economy. Likewise, Botswana was among the world's top producers of diamonds; Namibia was home to large supplies of diamonds, uranium and copper; and Lesotho had attractive petroleum reserves.

In terms of economics, the region's average GDP growth between 2005 and 2007 stood at 4.74 per cent, higher only than that of the Western Africa region. The aviation industry of the region was dominated by a single carrier – South African Airways (SAA). As one of the largest carriers in the continent, SAA had developed an extensive route network and a reputation for excellent performance. In 2006, the carrier diversified its business by setting up an LCC called Mango. However, SAA had not been as successful lately. Over the five years leading up to 2007, the company had suffered significant losses three times and was barely in the black for the remaining two years. This situation had led the company to contemplate a turnaround strategy.

By 2007, Ethiopian flew only to one destination in the Southern Africa region – Johannesburg. As a result, its limited presence in the region could pose a challenge for penetrating the market, should it decide to locate its first hub there. The recent substandard performance of SAA, however, could present an opportunity for Ethiopian to establish its presence in the region. The fairly developed infrastructure of the region was favourable for locating the first hub there. Yet, the smaller potential market size and the slower rate of economic growth could force Ethiopian to choose other regions over Southern Africa.

ENTRY MODE AND OWNERSHIP-LEVEL DECISIONS

In addition to the crucially important decision of location, Zewoldi knew that management and control of the first hub was important for success. The level of control exercised was, in turn, dependent on the degree of ownership maintained. The move would be the first of its kind for Ethiopian. It would also be pursued in a continent characterized by high level of uncertainty. Should Ethiopian go it alone, or should it partner with others and jointly own the first hub? If the company elected to go with the latter option, what share of ownership should it aim for? That is, should Ethiopian go for a majority share, a 50 per cent share or a minority share? Zewoldi considered his choices, knowing that Ethiopian's capital and asset levels had been steadily increasing over the years between 2005 and 2007 (see Exhibit 7).

EXHIBIT 1: Ethiopian Airline's Pan-African Network By 2007

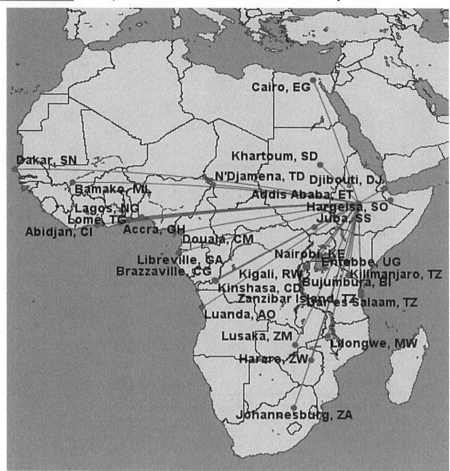

Source: Ethiopian Airlines and case writer.

EXHIBIT 2: Ethiopian Airlines' Summarized Performance, 2004/05 TO 2006/07

	2004/05	2005/06	2006/07
Consolidated Financial Statement			
Total Revenue (in millions of ETB*)	4,328	5,399	6,888
Total Expenditures (in millions of ETB)	3,950	5,162	6,690
Operating Profit (in millions of ETB)	377	237	198
Net Profit (in millions of ETB)	310	134	131
Airline Operating Statistics			
Performance Indicators			
Breakeven Load Factor (%)	52.20	52.77	51.64
Fleet (No. of Aircraft)	26	29	33
Fuel Cost (as a percentage of total operating costs)	0.32	0.37	0.39
Production			
Destination Cities	44	47	49
Available Seat Kilometres (millions)	7,473	8,973	11,357
Aircraft Departures	34,297	37,829	37,544
Traffic			
Passengers Carried(000s)	1,552	1,763	2,096
Passenger Seat Kilometres(millions)	4,965	5,833	7,243
Passenger Load Factor (%)**	66.64	65.02	63.8

* ETB = Ethiopian birr, the national currency of Ethiopia. The average exchange rate over the three-year period was US$ 0.11 = ETB 1.
**Passenger Load Factor (%) 5 Passenger Seat Kilometres / Available Seat Kilometres
Source: Ethiopian Airlines.

EXHIBIT 3: Connecting Five Nodes Via The Point-To-Point Model and The Hub-And-Spoke Model

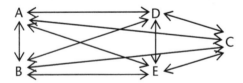

The Point-to-Point Network   The Hub-and-Spoke Network

Source: Case writer.

EXHIBIT 4: Map of Africa

AFRICA

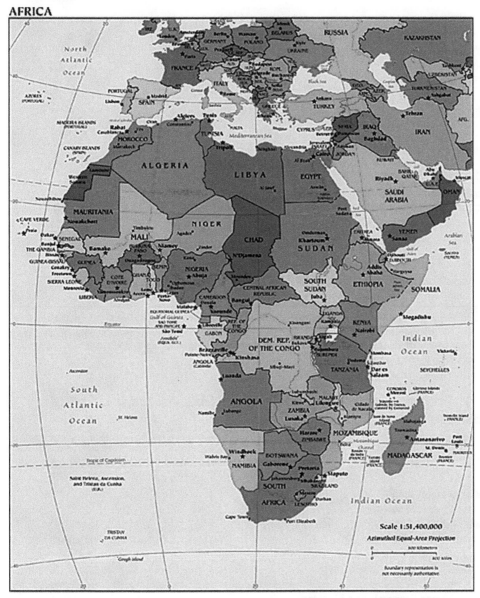

Source: www.cia.gov/library/publications/the-world-factbook/docs/refmaps.html, February 3, 2014.

EXHIBIT 5: Population and Economic Development Data On Africa's Regions (2007)

Region	Countries	Total population (in millions)	Average GDP (in US$ billions)	Average GNI Per Capita, PPP (International $*)
Northern Africa	Algeria, Egypt, Libya, Morocco, Sudan, Tunisia, Western Sahara	195	82.9	7,307
Western Africa	Benin, Burkina Faso, Cape Verde, Côte d'Ivoire, Gambia, Ghana, Guinea, Guinea-Bissau, Liberia, Mali, Mauritania, Niger, Nigeria, Saint Helena Ascension and Tristan da Cunha, Senegal, Sierra Leone, Togo	283	17.3	1,264
Middle Africa	Angola, Cameroon, Central African Republic, Chad, Democratic Republic of the Congo, Republic of the Congo, Equatorial Guinea, Gabon, Sao Tomé & Principe	118	14.4	3,942
Eastern Africa	Burundi, Comoros, Djibouti, Eritrea, Ethiopia, Kenya, Madagascar, Malawi, Mauritius, Mozambique, Rwanda, Seychelles, Tanzania, Uganda, Zambia, Zimbabwe	294	8.7	3,162
Southern Africa	Botswana, Lesotho, Namibia, South Africa, Swaziland	55	62.1	7,096

Note: GDP = gross domestic product; GNI = gross national income; PPP = purchasing power parity; International $= international dollar.

*According to a definition by the UN, "[a]n international dollar would buy in the cited country a comparable amount of goods and services a U.S. dollar would buy in the United States. This term is often used in conjunction with Purchasing Power Parity (PPP) data."

Source: Compiled by the authors using the United Nations data

EXHIBIT 6: Regional Economic Commissions, Air Transport Liberalization, and Traffic Freedom Rights (2007)

Regions	Regional Economic Commissions	Regional Air Transport Liberalization score*	Countries where Ethiopian has unlimited 3rd, 4th, 5th traffic freedom rights**
Northern Africa	The Arab Maghrib Union(AMU)- members: 5 Northern African countries	1	Algeria
Western Africa	The Banjul Accord Group(BAG)-members: 6 Western Africa countries	3	Burkina Faso, Cape Verde, Gambia, Ghana, Mali, Nigeria, Senegal, Togo
	West African Economic and Monetary Union(WAEMU)-members: 8 Western Africa countries	4	
Middle Africa	Central African Economic and Monetary Community(CEMAC)-members: 10 Middle and Eastern African countries	4	Congo Republic, Cameroon Equatorial Guinea
Southern Africa	Southern African Development Community (SADC)-members: 15 Southern and Eastern African countries	2	None

*Adapted from the World Bank's calculation. 1 = Least Liberal; 4 Most Liberal

**3rd freedom right: a right to carry passengers from a country of origin to a foreign country; 4th freedom right: a right to carry passengers from a foreign country to a country of origin; 5th freedom right: a right to fly between two foreign countries so long as the flight originates or ends in a country of registry.

Source: Compiled by the authors using date from the World Bank and Ethiopian Airlines.

EXHIBIT 7: Summary of Ethiopian Airlines' Balance Sheet Information (as of June 30, in millions of ETB)

	2005	2006	2007
Assets Employed			
Property, Plant, and Equipment	3,322	4,328	4,580
Investments	18	18	18
Standing Deposits	174	224	183
Differed Charges	92	120	120
Net Current Assets	441	332	391
Total Assets	**4,046**	**5,020**	**5,291**
Financed By			
Paid-up Capital	1,867	2,177	2,310
Contributions	44	45	47
Deferred Liabilities	1	3	9
Provision for Maintenance	—	—	265
Long-term Loans	2,134	2,796	2,659
Total Capital and Liabilities	**4,046**	**5,020**	**5,291**

Source: Ethiopian Airlines.

Palliser Furniture Ltd.: The China Question

In September 2003, Art DeFehr, president of Canada's second largest furniture company, Palliser Furniture Ltd. of Winnipeg, Manitoba, was pondering whether to significantly expand the company's relationship with China. Ever since Palliser set up a plant in Mexico in 1998, the company had faced increasing competitive pressures from Asia, especially from China.

THE MEXICO INVESTMENT 1998

In 1998, Palliser set up a leather furniture manufacturing facility in Saltillo, Coahuila, Mexico, to serve the mid-west and southern North American market. Palliser continued to ship products from its Winnipeg plants to the northern United States and Canadian markets. The Mexican facility would expand Palliser's leather manufacturing capacity, which was also part of its strategic shift from producing wood furniture to more leather products.

In 1997, DeFehr had considered the China option. Beginning in the mid-1990s, Taiwan furniture manufacturers started to establish plants in Mainland China, and China's household furniture exports to the U.S. market had increased quickly. However, in 1997, China was not making much leather furniture. This would have been a proactive move to respond to the emerging low-cost Asian furniture-manufacturing sector. DeFehr nonetheless chose Mexico over China for several reasons:

1. The Mexican location, which was close to the Texas border, would provide a lower distribution cost structure for Palliser. Prior to 1998, Palliser had difficulties absorbing

IVEY | Publishing

Jing'an Tang prepared this case under the supervision of Professor Paul W. Beamish solely to provide material for class discussion. The authors do not intend to illustrate either effective or ineffective handling of a managerial situation. The authors may have disguised certain names and other identifying information to protect confidentiality.

Richard Ivey School of Business Foundation prohibits any form of reproduction, storage or transmission without its written permission. Reproduction of this material is not covered under authorization by any reproduction rights organization. To order copies or request permission to reproduce materials, contact Ivey Publishing, Richard Ivey School of Business Foundation, The University of Western Ontario, London, Ontario, Canada, N6A 3K7; phone (519) 661-3208; fax (519) 661-3882; e-mail cases@ivey.uwo.ca.

Copyright © 2004, Richard Ivey School of Business Foundation   Version: 2011-09-21

One time permission to reproduce granted by Richard Ivey School of Business Foundation on April 22, 2014.

the higher freight cost when the company shipped products from Winnipeg, Canada, across the U.S.-Canadian border to the south.

2. At the time, China's leather furniture sector was small and inexperienced. Tanneries in China were not suitable for making leather furniture, and the leather had to be imported. Moreover, although there had been leather cutting and sewing workers in the garment business in China, they had little experience in producing leather furniture. In Mexico, there were more industry skills. One other major firm in the volume furniture business, Leather Trend, built products in Tijuana (a Mexican city near San Diego, California) and shipped across the continent to other cities in the United States. Other firms in Mexico were all very small businesses.

3. At that stage, the foreign investments in China were mainly joint venture operations. DeFehr wanted to own a business; he did not want a joint venture (JV) and he did not want to contract the work.

> I did not feel comfortable owning something in China. I still have certain discomfort. There are millions of examples of joint ventures in China. The JV partners were pushed out after some time. In contrast, in Mexico it was easy to wholly own a business.

4. Fourth, Palliser had manufactured its products mainly in Canada with only a small portion of products being assembled in the United States in 1997. As a first stage of expansion, Palliser considered Mexico an ideal choice because it was closer to the U.S. market, and it was more manageable compared with offshore sites.

Since being established, the Mexican facility had been working well, operationally. It started to ship products to the United States, especially to the southern states, in 1999. Because of reduced costs and similar quality, Palliser's Mexican-made products were well accepted.

There had been some problems however, with the Mexico investment. Palliser had issues with the Mexican taxation practices and had disagreements with the local taxation authorities. According to Kliewer, senior vice-president in finance,

> (Their) way of interpreting the law was just so discretionary. What they allow and what they don't allow were not clear. For example, the inflation adjustment was very problematic . . . It is a bit hard to plan for that. These are things you learned as you go on.

It had taken longer than planned to recover the initial investment. For instance, Palliser did not anticipate all the shipping costs accurately. The company had not anticipated the extra tariff fees associated with cross-border shipments leaving Mexico. Moreover, there had been other costs involved in shipping products across the Mexico-U.S. border because the trucks from Mexico could not cross the border; goods had to be transferred to U.S. trucks which resulted in extra charges. DeFehr called it a "friction cost." According to Palliser calculations, the friction costs of crossing the Canadian border were around US$1[1] for a leather sofa, but the friction costs for the same sofa built in Mexico would be US$12. (The friction costs from China would have been approximately $10.)

As another example, the order allocation process initially favored the Canadian facility. While the Mexico plant essentially produced the same products, orders were given to the Winnipeg plants first and the balance was allocated to Mexico. As a result, the Mexico plant had to fight with headquarters for orders. Palliser acknowledged and corrected the issue, a move that had a positive impact on the Mexican overhead recovery rate.

---

[1]All currency in Cdn$ unless otherwise specified.

It could also be noted that the decision to set up a facility in Mexico had relied upon the competitiveness resulting from the North American Free Trade Agreement (NAFTA). Palliser had yet to focus on how to lower the costs through changes in its Mexican supply chain. Mexico was, in a sense, trying to build its competitiveness on a more limited framework.

THE FURNITURE INDUSTRY SINCE 1998

Since the late 1990s, the world furniture industry had undergone tremendous change. The most significant trend was the rise of China. In 2002, China's total furniture output value was US$20 billion, accounting for 10 per cent of the world's total furniture output value. In the past five years, China's furniture export had grown at an annual rate of over 30 per cent. Countries with heavy demand for furniture products had flocked to China to make purchases. China's export of household furniture to the United States accounted for almost 40 per cent of the market, while exports to Japan accounted for about 15 per cent of Japan's total furniture demand. IKEA, the top selling furniture company in the world, had shifted its purchasing centre from Singapore to Mainland China.

With the prospect of cheaper labor and high-quality workers in China, American, Japanese and Italian firms had established factories in China. Natuzzi, an Italian firm who was the No. 1 furniture manufacturer in the world, built a plant in Shanghai. DeCoro, another Italian furniture company, set up a plant in DongGuan, Gongdong province. Taiwanese firms had also built more than 500 furniture plants in Mainland China. Three U.S. office furniture firms with annual production values of US$1.5 billion, US$2.7 billion and US$3 billion, respectively, had all constructed production bases in Shanghai. China's furniture capacity had increased dramatically. Guangdong province, the biggest furniture manufacturing province, produced one-third of China's total furniture production.

The rise of China had shifted the world furniture market competition structure. It had affected most furniture firm's profit margins. Natuzzi's income dropped 70 per cent, and sales dropped 10 per cent in the second quarter 2002. Firms in the North America furniture industry felt the pressure most. The market share of all household furniture imports in the U.S. domestic market increased between 1993 and 2002 from 20.4 per cent to 38.9 per cent, while the market share of all office furniture imports increased from 9.1 per cent to 23.8 per cent during the same period. U.S. furniture imports in 2002 grew 13 per cent to US$14.2 billion. China fuelled much of that growth, accounting for 40 per cent of total U.S. imports in 2002. That year also marked the fifth out of the last six years in which total Chinese furniture exports to the United States jumped 30 per cent or more (see Exhibits 1, 2, 3 and 4).

The contributing factors were multifold, including China's cheaper labor and comparable product quality and design. Palliser managers estimated that the labor cost in China was around US$3 day, in Mexico about US$32, while in Canada around US$90 a day. Chinese workers usually worked more than 10 hours a day, six days a week. There were no unions nor union pressure. The leather furniture business in China did not need to deal with any environmental problems, although there were many concerns with tannery operations. Chinese firms did not pay much income tax, nor did they bear many social costs, such as health and insurance costs for employees. The Chinese currency was pegged to the U.S. dollar and, to many people, was arguably undervalued. The combination of these factors gave China a strongly competitive position. Furniture from China could be 20 per cent to 30 per cent cheaper than the same products that were produced in North America. Exhibit 5 provides the comparison of cost bases for some wood furniture components.

Under the weight of the competitive pressure, many U.S. firms moved manufacturing sites offshore. In July 2003, some furniture makers in America jointly protested to the American government about the severe impact the Chinese furniture manufacturers were having on the American wood bedroom furniture industry. They submitted anti-dumping applications seeking industry protection.

Total Canadian shipments of furniture and bedding hit a record $4.76 billion in 2002, capping 10 years of almost continuous growth (see Exhibit 6). According to a survey conducted by Statistics Canada, there were 630 residential furniture and bedding manufacturers in Canada in 1999–the last year for which figures were available. Canada's furniture and bedding producers could be segmented into four categories: exporters, non-exporters, bedding producers and importers. The exporters were by far the largest group. While the 19 exporters did some business in Europe, South America and the Middle East, more than 95 per cent of all Canadian furniture exported was sold to U.S. retailers.

Canadian furniture producers were employing a variety of strategies to remain competitive in an increasingly uncertain North American economy. The impact of China had not been felt as deeply in Canada as it had been in the United States. Unlike their American counterparts, many of which had moved much of their production offshore, almost every one of the top 10 Canadian producers (see Exhibit 7) had recently made, or was making, a big investment in their business.

While others followed a balancing act to remain as low-cost manufacturers, some Canadian manufacturers became active importers, focusing on specialized lines not being produced domestically. Two examples illustrate this approach. Dorel Industries tried to develop a strong capability to source a wide variety of products designed by Dorel and manufactured in Asia. In 2002, the company established a new division called Dorel Asia, whose mission was to develop product suitable for North America that was built cheaply and efficiently in the Pacific Rim. A second company Shermag Inc., launched a new import division to expand its offerings of labor-intensive, traditionally styled bedroom and dining room furniture. These goods complemented the more technology-driven, casual contemporary furniture that Shermag made in its factories in Quebec and New Brunswick, Canada.

PALLISER'S STRATEGY SINCE 1998

Cost Leadership

The Mexico investment was part of Palliser's cost leadership strategy. Palliser negotiated with its Brazilian partners to be part of its supply chain for the Mexico plant. Brazil was the No. 1 source of leather in the world. Raw leather was delivered from Brazil to Mexico, where Palliser processed the leather (cutting and sewing) for redistribution to its U.S. and Canadian locations. Although it was more expensive than that in China, processing leathers in Mexico was still much cheaper than producing in Canada.

Quick Delivery

Quick delivery was another strategy. Purchasing from China meant a minimum delivery time of six to seven weeks, which translated into high inventory cost for those importers buying Asian products. Alternatively, Palliser focused on a custom manufacturing strategy with a delivery time of three weeks. Custom business was Palliser's premium business. The company was able to charge a slight premium for the service that could eliminate customers' inventory cost. According to DeFehr, Palliser was still making most of its money from the plants in Canada, which were strong at specialty order businesses. As the China threat developed, more and more competitors established factories offshore. However, in doing so, they became less flexible, either in time or in variety. For example, the cycle time of the specialty businesses of the Italian producers DeCoro and Natuzzi was around 90 days.

The quick delivery strategy had been working very well until September 11, 2001 (9/11). After 9/11, because the airlines cut their flights, airfares had risen, it became very expensive to ship leather from Brazil to Mexico by air. If shipping by ocean, the quick delivery advantages over China would soon disappear. Palliser was working with Brazilian suppliers seeking solutions.

Value Enhancement

Palliser was committed to delivering annual value improvements to its customers. For instance, if the company offered some products for $500 last year, it would try to offer the equal value of products at $400 this year. Such improvements were driven by process and product redesign. The first step was to identify those products where Palliser had absolute advantages or relative advantages in the North American market. Palliser still considered the North American market to be its first priority. Palliser considered developing a product using oak in Canada. Oak had a similar price around the world. Products could be built with a rustic and low grade of oak, with rough and simple machine-driven designs. By leveraging the low-cost material and leveraging the machine-driven design, the value would be similar to that produced in China.

At the same time, Palliser tried to remain a volume producer. Using Mexico and China to do cutting and sewing, Palliser was still doing low-price business. Beyond Mexico, the company was sourcing substantial quantities of finished goods from Asian countries, such as China, Thailand and Indonesia. Another way to enhance value was to produce machine-made and capital-intensive products instead of labor intensive-furniture. The new products that Palliser was going to produce were all less labor-intensive.

EQ3, a New Marketing Initiative

In the late 1990s, Palliser started a new marketing program called EQ3. Palliser realized that there was an opportunity in the market place, which had been underserved. A trend in the furniture industry was that consumers were becoming more fashion conscious, design conscious and more educated. EQ3 was a new concept that was designed to meet this market trend. It was not about one piece of furniture, but about everything in the home with fashionable designs. Palliser recruited some product managers from IKEA and designers from many regions over the world, such as Sweden, Hong Kong, and Italy. Most people in the new EQ3 team were in their late 20s and early 30s.

After two years of market research, Palliser introduced in-store EQ3 galleries through its traditional retailers in the United States and Canada in October 2001, but these galleries did not work well in the traditional stores channels which did not understand or draw in the target customer. In late 2002, Palliser started building new channels. The company set up the first two dealer-owned EQ3 stores—one in Toronto, Ontario, and the other in Grand Rapids, Michigan. These stores started offering a unique storefront with the new image, advertising, and catalogues, which customers could identify with. This distribution channel was developed outside of the traditional channel and had been very successful.

Motion Business

In the North American marketplace, the motion business was one of the fastest growing categories. Motion products referred to furniture that could be adjusted, such as recliners. Palliser started to make motion products at the same time it started to make leather furniture. Several years ago, Palliser's sales in motion products were around $26 million dollars. In 2003, sales were expected to be nearly $100 million.

Previously, motion products were mainly considered to be products that would go in the basement, not something that could be a focal point in the living room or family room. But in recent years, with better leathers and the popularity of leather furniture in the market place, furniture companies had been able to utilize leather to make motion products more attractive, fashionable and contemporary. People were willing to put them in their living room, family room and home theatres. Leather had made motion products more fashionable. For example, the leather recliner became one of the most popular household furniture for every American family and sofas and love seats were becoming more fashionable too.

On average, from a labor perspective, motion products required 25 per cent to 30 per cent more labor than standard products. Motion products were more technical and required more skill to produce.

Palliser had motion product factories in Winnipeg, Manitoba; Airdrie, Alberta and Saltillo, Mexico. The latter plant called "Las Colinas" was set up in 2000. Each of these factories operated at the same scale, but production costs in Mexico were much cheaper. The lower labor rate in Mexico might translate into a $75 savings for a sofa ($1,000 in retail value). If making the same product in Asia, the possible savings could be $120 to $130 dollars for a product with a retail value of $1,000.

Currently, Palliser realized advantages in the North American marketplace by offering good value in motion products with color options, good service, delivery and good quality. Traditionally, even the large Asian companies, which had considerable exports to North America, had not been successful in the motion business. The lengthy lead time had been a contributing factor, but in the last year, motion products were starting to come from Asia. For instance, DeCoro now produced motion products in China. In the last international furniture show, DeCoro displayed around 10 new motion product styles.

Palliser's approach to motion products was vinyl-leather match design. DeCoro's approach was all-leather style. By producing in China, DeCoro was able to provide the same product at a lower cost than Palliser offered. For example, Palliser could offer a leather-vinyl sofa at $999 retail, while DeCoro could offer $999 for an all-leather sofa retail. Thus, for the same product, DeCoro would have approximately a $200 advantage over Palliser's retail price. In the stationary category, several years ago, Palliser was providing leather-vinyl products. As a result of competition from Asia, which was offering all-leather products at the same price point, Palliser stopped producing leather-vinyl stationary products. The same shift might be anticipated in the motion product market.

Rach, director of motion products at Palliser, pointed out that contributing factors to cheap production in Asia were not only the leather for less money, but other components were cheaper too, such as the wood for the frame, the foam and the packaging materials.

PALLISER'S ASIAN PRESENCE

Palliser had several small factories in Indonesia, did contract work in Thailand and China, and had an office in Taiwan and two offices in Mainland China, (one in Shanghai and another in Guangzhou).

Taiwan

Furniture exports from Asia were driven by people from Taiwan, who developed the expertise first, starting around 20 years ago. Palliser set up an office in Taiwan in 1985. It mainly imported final furniture products to the North American market.

Taiwanese firms were the first investors to go to Mainland China. In contrast to Palliser, Taiwanese firms did not go to Indonesia because mainland China was closer and the culture was the same, therefore they preferred to invest in mainland. Also the Chinese had had a bad experience in Indonesia in the 1960s, and there had been a recent reoccurrence of this experience. Many Chinese people who were sent there to do quality work flew to Indonesia in the morning and flew back home to China at night. Some people considered Indonesia an investment place with a lot of uncertainty.

Indonesia

Palliser had several factories in Indonesia. Some were owned, some used 100 per cent contracting and others used partial contracting. Palliser provided loans to one of the plants in 1997 when the plant experienced financial difficulties during the Asian financial crisis. The loan ended up with Palliser's controlling interests in that factory. The other two plants were owned by Palliser. Compared with Palliser's production facilities in Canada and in Mexico, these operations were very small. The total investment amount was approximately Cdn$500,000. Indonesia was more like a training ground for Palliser in Asia. Palliser sent full-time Canadian staff to those local operations.

DeFehr had worked and kept in touch with Indonesia for almost 20 years, and he felt comfortable investing there. In terms of the risk concerns in Indonesia, DeFehr provided the following logic,

> By going to Indonesia, I separate myself from the face-to-face competition with these Chinese businesses for factory space, materials and other things. As a result, I am not competing with the best capital in the business. Will Indonesia be better than China in five years? I don't know, and you don't know either. So we make the bet . . . . We try to go to places that others might consider difficult. Because we are alone, you may get a little bit of a premium by being there.

Thailand and Mainland China

Beyond Indonesia, Palliser had a lot of contract work in Thailand as well. Local plants manufactured furniture components or finished products according to the design provided by Palliser.

Currently, Palliser contracted cutting and sewing work to a Chinese factory in Haiyin, a city south of Shanghai. The factory processed leather cover for its motion products. According to Rach, director of Palliser motion products,

> Chinese workers were very good at making leathers now. One of the advantages came from their larger tannery and their experience in the garment industry, especially the leather garment industry.

These leather covers were shipped back to Winnipeg, where they were upholstered. Almost $1 million of monthly sales were from Asia. Cutting and sewing covers from China had enabled Palliser to make a leather sofa at eight per cent to 10 per cent less than that in Canada. In retail, there is around one price point ($100) difference. That was the only component that Palliser outsourced from China for motion products. For a sofa with a total cost of $625, the cutting and sewing cost was around $250. It cost approximately $30 to $33 per seat to transport a sofa from China to North America.

DeFehr had certain concerns about doing business in China. Although many foreign firms had set up plants in China, few of them had been successful.

Finding the right partner was another concern. DeFehr felt that Chinese partners were not committed, long-term OEM suppliers. He was not comfortable building long-term relationships in China. This might be due to the fact that a level of trust had not been established yet.

DeFehr was also concerned about the product itself. If a product had a well- established brand, no one else could easily make it and sell to the market. But a sofa and chair usually were not branded products. People could easily imitate and sell them. Therefore, if the products were exclusive, either technologically or brand-wise, the partnership relationship could work. Most furniture products were not exclusive.

Realistically, Palliser could not ignore China anymore. The resources in China were phenomenal, both in labor quantity and quality. People in China were working more and more efficiently than people in the North America and in other developing countries. According to Tielmann, senior vice-president of marketing,

> If you look at India, Indonesia and Thailand, there are real differences. The value you get from China is one of the best worldwide. Another interesting thing was the Chinese Yuan, which was tied to the U.S. dollar. It had stayed that way for a while and might be that way for a long time yet. This could avoid currency fluctuations, which is different from Indonesia and Thailand. Also, the exchange rate was very advantageous for export.

TOP MANAGEMENT'S ASIAN EXPERIENCE

DeFehr had been to China many times, both on political and business issues. His first visit to China was with his family in 1983 as guests of the government. He had started visiting Taiwan regularly on furniture business since 1985. He had regularly visited Mainland China since 1992. Most recently, he had visited Beijing, Shanghai, Shenzheng, Dongguan, Qsingdao, Tianjin and other coastal cities. Those were cities where the Chinese furniture businesses were concentrated.

DeFehr had extensive experience with Asian culture. He had lived in Asia, but he had never lived in Mexico. His two children were born in Asia. He had lived in Bangladesh, Thailand, and he travelled to Cambodia, India and many other Asian countries. Asia, to DeFehr was very much home. However, because both of his parents were from the former Soviet Union and he had experienced dealing with communist governments, he did not think he was comfortable doing business in a communist environment.

Most members of Palliser's top management had been to China. As the director of motion products, Rach visited China more frequently. He went to China at least three times a year. As China's furniture business had become stronger in recent years, the top management team had shifted much more attention to Asia.

THE DECISION

Products from China had increasingly become threats to most furniture manufacturers in North America and the pressures on Palliser had been increasingly felt. In April 2003, Palliser conducted its first layoff in the Winnipeg factory.

Palliser had production facilities in Canada, Mexico and Indonesia, and the company experimented with cutting and sewing leather in China. DeFehr had to decide whether to significantly expand Palliser's relationship with China and discern what form that relationship might follow. Should it be an investment, either wholly or partly owned? Should it be through subcontracting? To build Palliser's competitive advantages, DeFehr summarized:

> What we are considering right now is how to take advantage of our particular organizational and geographic situation to counter the advantages that the people in lower cost environments have.

EXHIBIT 1: All Household Imports By Significant Countries in The U.S. Market (US$ millions)

	1998	1999	2000	2001	2002	CAGR
China	1,550.5	2,235.6	3,001.6	3,423.2	4,832.8	37.9%
Canada	1,301.4	1,584.7	1,837.4	1,744.2	1,739.6	16.4%
Italy	760.3	917.8	1,140.1	1,107.7	1,139.3	14.5%
Mexico	641.0	704.7	764.2	699.9	729.1	13.1%
Indonesia	323.1	407.3	450.7	445.4	492.0	16.0%
Taiwan	687.2	722.1	701.1	502.1	477.6	−7.5%
Malaysia	384.0	443.1	452.3	407.9	467.4	10.8%
Thailand	165.2	210.5	253.7	261.1	338.3	9.5%
Philippines	214.0	241.1	269.2	223.8	217.7	8.4%
Brazil	53.4	74.8	96.9	135.2	209.5	23.6%

CAGR—Compounded Annual Growth Rate.
Source: Company files.

EXHIBIT 2: Wood Household Imports By Significant Countries in The U.S. Market (US$ millions)

	1998	1999	2000	2001	2002	CAGR
China	794.0	1,141.0	1,650.7	1,897.6	2,893.6	40.1%
Canada	947.5	1,182.9	1,368.5	1,306.7	1,267.7	17.1%
Italy	306.4	392.6	460.4	453.6	484.3	15.2%
Malaysia	340.4	396.4	399.5	364.4	414.5	11.3%
Indonesia	254.6	332.2	373.4	376.7	414.2	19.2%
Mexico	353.7	371.9	392.8	372.2	372.1	10.8%
Thailand	149.7	188.2	225.8	226.7	297.7	9.7%
Taiwan	381.7	402.7	349.4	280.5	260.2	−8.7%
Brazil	52.0	70.3	92.6	126.1	187.9	23.3%
Philippines	83.9	99.6	118.6	109.8	109.2	15.0%

Source: Company files.

EXHIBIT 3: Upholstered Household Imports By Significant Countries in The U.S. (US$ millions)

	1998	1999	2000	2001	2002	CAGR
Italy	363.6	412.9	559.3	529.0	528.6	14.5%
China	46.6	83.6	127.6	172.8	312.9	53.8%
Mexico	111.8	139.0	170.5	172.3	208.6	27.3%
Canada	95.8	122.8	156.2	161.5	184.3	19.7%

Source: Company files.

EXHIBIT 4: Metal and Other Household Imports By Significant Countries in The U.S. Market (US$ millions)

	1998	1999	2000	2001	2002	CAGR
China	541.3	766.7	938.7	1,033.6	1,235.5	44.0%
Canada	181.9	185.4	205.2	167.7	183.4	13.0%
Taiwan	240.9	256.7	282.4	177.2	178.0	−6.0%
Mexico	150.6	164.8	171.0	126.2	121.0	8.0%
Italy	61.3	85.4	82.0	85.9	85.0	15.0%

Source: Company files.

EXHIBIT 5: Wood Furniture Cost Comparison

	American Made[1]	Chinese Made[2]	Difference
Bed headboard	100.00	89.00	11%
Nightstand	95.00	80.22	16%
Chest	109.00	88.76	19%
Entertainment centre	211.00	159.54	24%
Armoire	474.00	330.00	30%
Rolltop desk	275.00	181.50	34%

[1]Costs are as if the product were in a U.S. warehouse, ready to ship to retailers.
[2]For the Chinese, shipping is included.
Source: Furniture/Today, May 26, 2003.

EXHIBIT 6: The Canadian Furniture Market (Cdn$ millions)

	2002	2001	2000	2001–2002 Change	1997–2001 Change
Total industry shipments	4,760	4,307	4,106	10.5%	54.9%
Total exports	2,153	2,018	1,924	6.7%	87.9%
Export to the United States	2,036	1,911	N/A	6.5%	N/A
Total imports	1,443	1,252	1,134	15.3%	54.7%
Imports from the United States	489	509	N/A	−3.9%	N/A
Total domestic shipments	2,607	2,289	2,182	13.9%	34.2%

Source: Statistics Canada.

EXHIBIT 7: Canada's Top 25 Furniture and Bedding Producers (Cdn$ millions)

Rank	Company Name	Home Base	2002	2001	Change
1	Dorel Inds.	Montreal, Quebec	712.9	701.7	1.6%
2	Palliser Furniture	Winnipeg, Manitoba	518.8	493.6	5.1%
3	Shermag Inc.	Sherbrooke, Quebec	188.0	163.2	15.2%
4	Canadel Furniture	Louiseville, Quebec	155.0	135.0	14.8%
5	Sealy Canada	Toronto, Ontario	139.7	121.1	15.4%
6	Simmons Canada Inc	Mississauga, Ontario	130.9	120.1	9.0%
7	La-Z-Boy Canada Ltd.	Waterloo, Ontario	117.9	100.9	16.8%
8	Magnussen Home Furnishings	New Hamburg, Ontario	106.8	N/A	N/A
9	Gusdorf Canada	Montreal, Quebec	105.0	94.0	11.7%
10	South Shore Inds.	Sainte-Croix, Quebec	100.0	100.0	0.0%

Source: Furniture/Today, June 2, 2003.

Firstwell Corporation and the Production Mandate Question

In June 2011, Firstwell Corporation's operating committee met at its world headquarters in New York City to consider a proposal to rationalize the North American production and distribution of SUPER-CLOTH cleaning cloths. Due to increased consumer demand, the decision had been made to upgrade the equipment that converted the jumbo-sized rolls into consumer- and industrial-sized packages and quantities. At issue was where this upgraded processing equipment would be located.

Currently, most of the conversion took place in Buffalo, New York, using jumbo rolls supplied from Kingston, Ontario. The Buffalo facility then shipped the finished goods to six distribution centres around the United States (see Exhibit 1).

The Canadian division of Firstwell Corporation had proposed that all production and distribution of SUPER-CLOTH cleaning cloths take place from its Kingston facility. This arrangement would mean that \$4 million[1] in new equipment would be shipped to Kingston, the current SUPER-CLOTH workforce in Buffalo would be shifted to different responsibilities and Kingston would ship directly to the various distribution centres (see Exhibit 2). This proposal to grant a regional product mandate to Kingston had not gone unopposed. Management at the Buffalo plant felt it would be preferable to house the new converting equipment in its facility and to maintain its existing relationship with Kingston.

IVEY | Publishing

Professor Paul W. Beamish prepared this case solely to provide material for class discussion. The author does not intend to illustrate either effective or ineffective handling of a managerial situation. The author may have disguised certain names and other identifying information to protect confidentiality.

Richard Ivey School of Business Foundation prohibits any form of reproduction, storage or transmission without its written permission. Reproduction of this material is not covered under authorization by any reproduction rights organization. To order copies or request permission to reproduce materials, contact Ivey Publishing, Richard Ivey School of Business Foundation, The University of Western Ontario, London, Ontario, Canada, N6A 3K7; phone (519) 661-3208; fax (519) 661-3882; e-mail cases@ivey.uwo.ca.

Copyright © 2012, Richard Ivey School of Business Foundation   Version: 2012-02-28

One time permission to reproduce granted by Richard Ivey School of Business Foundation on April 22, 2014.

[1]All currency in U.S funds unless specified otherwise.

FIRSTWELL CORPORATION BACKGROUND

Firstwell Corporation (Firstwell) was a multinational enterprise with 80,000 employees, subsidiaries and operations in 50 countries, and worldwide annual sales in excess of $10 billion. During the past decade, Firstwell Corporation's sales outside the United States had climbed from about one-third to nearly one-half of total sales. This growth was a result of a conscious strategy of global expansion. The company was organized into four divisions and produced a variety of products familiar to consumers. Cleaning cloths were early products of the company and still formed a very important portion of the business. Developing other technologies and applying them to make problem-solving products was the basis on which Firstwell had been able to grow. Many new products were produced on an on-going basis.

Like its parent company, Firstwell Canada Inc. was a highly diversified company that manufactured thousands of different products for industry, business, the professions and the consumer. The head office and main plant were located in St. Thomas, Ontario, while sales and service were handled by centres across the country. Firstwell Canada was established in 1951, as part of the newly founded International Division. Additional subsidiaries were set up in Australia, Brazil, France, Germany, Mexico and the United Kingdom. Firstwell Canada employed about 2,000 people. In addition to operations in St. Thomas and Kingston, the company had manufacturing plants in Toronto, Hamilton and Windsor, Ontario, and in Winnipeg, Manitoba. Canada was the sixth largest of Firstwell Corporation's subsidiaries.

With the exception of two or three people from the worldwide organization, everyone working for Firstwell Canada was Canadian. The Canadian subsidiary annually lost 10 to 15 people to the worldwide organization. Although a high proportion of the professional group in Canada had, at some stage, a career goal to work in the worldwide organization, doing so was not a requirement. For example, several managers at the plant manager level and above had indicated a preference to stay in Canada despite offers from the worldwide organization.

Firstwell's global subsidiary network constituted subsidiaries that had varying degrees of specialization and autonomy. Traditionally, most subsidiaries operated fairly specialized operations with a modest level of autonomy. At the four extremes, foreign subsidiaries with a *world product mandate* enjoyed a high level of autonomy and administered highly specialized operations. Conversely, subsidiaries that operated as *general swing producers* were given little autonomy and did not specialize in the production of any particular products. Their future was often precarious and depended, in part, on their agility. Other types of subsidiaries included those with a *regional product mandate* (high specialization but low autonomy) and *miniature replica structures* (highly autonomous but unspecialized subsidiaries). Miniature replica structures typically persisted where market demand and manufacturing economies of scale were not sufficient to justify the establishment of a more specialized facility. Modifying a foreign subsidiary's mandate to increase either its autonomy or its specialization (or both) could be lucrative, both for the parent corporation (in terms of profitability) and for the affected subsidiary's managers (in terms of career development and potential bonus compensation), but such an undertaking was not without its challenges.

The Canadian subsidiary under the direction of its president, James Lavell, was expected to generate sales growth and to produce an operating income on Canadian sales. Increasingly, emphasis was being placed on achieving certain target market share levels. Within Canada, the 25 individual business units were split among eight groups, each of which operated as a profit centre. Variability existed in each with respect to the amount of divisional input from the United States.

At headquarters, the perception of the competencies of the Canadian subsidiary varied according to the business and functional area. For example, Canadian manufacturing and engineering had a solid reputation for getting things done. In terms of research, Canada specialized in three, to some extent, narrow areas. Several dozen scientists pursued research in these areas within Canadian laboratories.

The Canadian subsidiary did not have a critical mass in research and development (R&D) for all the technologies necessary to support SUPER-CLOTH. In addition, it had not been deemed feasible to move (or build) a pilot plant in Canada for SUPER-CLOTH testing purposes since pilot plants tended to serve a multitude of products.

The overall level of company harmonization between the two countries had risen. Some U.S. divisions were asking for more direct control over their businesses in Canada. The Canadian president needed to deal with these issues and to develop the necessary organizational response.

The Canadian subsidiary had placed much importance on building intercompany sales. More than 20 per cent of its sales were intercompany sales, and further increases were expected. Firstwell Canada's sales in 2011 were more than $500 million, while its after-tax earnings were in the range of 10 per cent (see Exhibits 3 and 4 for financial statements).

THE KINGSTON SUPER-CLOTH PLANT

The $5 million Kingston plant began operation in 2002, employing 22 people. The plant covered 36,000 square feet on a 78-acre site and was the first Canadian production facility for this product line. It was built to supplement the jumbo output of the Buffalo facility, which was nearing capacity. The plant was designed with sufficient capacity to produce enough cleaning cloths to eliminate imports, but with exports in mind. Over the next decade, the plant had expanded several times, and employment grew to 80 people. Throughout this period, the plant exclusively produced SUPER-CLOTH, a profitable, growing product line in a core business area. The total cleaning cloth market in which SUPER-CLOTH competed was estimated to be $60 million in the United States and nearly $5 million in Canada.

SUPER-CLOTH had a microfibre construction that absorbed nearly double the amount of moisture as a traditional cotton dishcloth. Microfibre dried quickly to reduce the potential for bacterial growth and was both washable and reusable.

SUPER-CLOTH products were made in sheet and roll shapes for use in a variety of applications in various industries, in addition to home use and use in the hotel and restaurant trade. Schools, hospitals and building maintenance personnel used a wide variety of SUPER-CLOTH cloths for cleaning maintenance. Other smaller hand-held cloths were used for cleaning painted surfaces. Several types of SUPER-CLOTH products were available for home use.

THE KINGSTON PROPOSAL

During the first decade of the 2000s, as the Kingston plant grew in size and experience, it began to develop its reputation as a workforce with a demonstrated ability to work effectively. With increased confidence came a desire to assume new challenges. An obvious area for potential growth was to take on more of SUPER-CLOTH's value-added function in Kingston, rather than shipping semi-finished goods to the United States. Around 2005, the Kingston managers advocated that they should begin supplying finished goods to the United States for certain mandated products; however, this approach was opposed by SUPER-CLOTH's manufacturing director at the time. He claimed that nothing would be saved because all the finished goods would need to be shipped to Buffalo anyway, for consolidation and distribution to the customer.

The United States-based manufacturing director also argued that mandating products could reduce the utilization of the larger, more expensive maker at Buffalo, which, in turn, would increase the unit burden costs on other products there. During this period, the Kingston facility operated as the swing maker, with utilization cycling, in an effort to keep the Buffalo facility fully loaded.

With a change in management came a willingness to take a fresh look at the situation. The new manager, J.K. Smith, insisted on being provided with a more complete analysis of all the delivery costs. To that end, a study was initiated in December 2010 to determine the cost of converting and packaging SUPER-CLOTH cleaning cloths in Kingston, rather than shipping the jumbo-sized rolls to Buffalo for converting and packaging. The task force struck in Canada was led by Randall Carson, the Kingston plant manager. Procedurally, any proposal would go first to Ed Monteith, manufacturing director for Canada, and Donald Carr, executive vice president of manufacturing for Canada. Once their agreement had been obtained, the Kingston plant manager would continue to champion the project through the Firstwell Corporation hierarchy, although someone such as Carr would facilitate the process.

The proposal would next go to the Building Service and Cleaning Products (BS + CP) division for review and agreement. If successful, the proposal would then be returned to Canadian engineering to develop an Authority for (capital) Expenditure, or AFE. This AFE would then be routed through senior Canadian management and the U.S. division and group levels. The final stage was for the AFE to be forwarded to the operating committee at the sector level for assessment (see Exhibits 5 and 6 for partial organizational charts for Firstwell Corporation Worldwide and Firstwell Corporation International).

The Kingston proposal acknowledged that Buffalo was a competently managed plant and that putting the new equipment in either location would reduce costs from their current levels. At issue was which location would generate the greater cost savings. The Kingston proposal argued that greater savings would occur in Kingston (see Exhibit 7) through a combination of reduced freight and storage costs, and faster and more efficient manufacturing. The Kingston proposal's overall approach was to emphasize what was best for shareholders on the basis of total delivered costs.

Overall employment needs were expected to increase by eight in Canada yet decline by at least double that in Buffalo (see Table 1).

Some of the modest employment increases in Canada could be traced to the small amount of manual converting in Kingston that would be automated under the proposed arrangement. When shipping costs were factored in, it was viable to convert a small quantity of cleaning cloths in Canada, even manually.

TABLE 1: Changes in Staffing for Each Proposal

Kingston Proposal

Add in Kingston	1 Maintenance
	3 Shippers
	4 Production Operators*
	8 persons @Labour Rate of US$13.18/hour
Delete in Buffalo	Maintenance ?
	Shipping/Receiving ?
	16.5 Production Operators

Buffalo Proposal

Add in Buffalo	6 Operators @US$15.43/hour

*In addition, 12 persons in manual conversion would now be shifted to automated conversion in Kingston.

The biggest reason for the small number of proposed new hires in Canada was the plan to discontinue manual converting in Kingston and to move those operators to the automated cleaning cloth area. The initial response to this move in Canada had, in several quarters, been less than enthusiastic. The Canadian business unit manager felt that he might now be required to pay a premium if purchasing from the United States. As well, he was concerned that some of his customers might notice a difference in performance. He felt the manually converted product from Kingston was of a slightly higher quality than the automatically converted product from Buffalo, New York. The Canadian business manager had built a higher market share for Firstwell Corporation in Canada than his U.S. counterparts, and he did not wish to see this market growth jeopardized.

A move from manual converting to automated converting would also have immediate implications for the operators. Currently, most of the manual cleaning cloth jobs were on a one-shift (i.e., a day shift) basis. A second, evening shift was sometimes required, but no one worked the midnight-to-morning shift. If the plant were automated, all operators would need to work a three-shift rotation to maximize machine utilization. In a non-union plant, with a 10-year tradition of day jobs in converting, and with a no-layoff policy, introducing a 24-hour work schedule could be an emotional issue for many workers. The task of selling it to the operators would fall on Carson.

THE BUFFALO RESPONSE

The Buffalo response was less a proposal, and more a reaction to the Kingston initiative. A variety of concerns, some old and some new, were raised. First, the increased production volume in Canada and the resultant re-exports to the United States would cause an increased vulnerability to currency fluctuations. Second, lengthening the supply distance would make it more difficult to guarantee delivery to U.S. customers.

Third, the Kingston plant would need to be interfaced with the Firstwell Corporation-USA computer-based materials management system to ensure effective transportation. This interface would require the Canadian information technology group to work with the logistics people to develop a program that would allow for cross-border integration of information.

Fourth, the cost of shipping finished goods to the branches would increase both in Kingston and in Buffalo. In Kingston the cost increase would result from the smaller volumes and the increased distances associated with shipping a single product line. In Buffalo, making up a truckload would take longer without the cleaning cloths.

Fifth, since SUPER-CLOTH converting was already well established in Buffalo, and savings would be realized wherever the new equipment was located, it was safer to keep the equipment where the manufacturing experience already existed, rather than relying on optimistic projections from Kingston.

CONCLUSION

In Europe, in part due to the distances involved, regional production mandates on various products had been granted as early as the 1990s by Firstwell Corporation. SUPER-CLOTH, in fact, was already being produced in Europe, Asia and Mexico. However, unlike these other production mandates, the Kingston proposal was to supply the core U.S. market. For the operating committee, the decision would come down to their level of confidence in the Kingston proposal.

EXHIBIT 1: Present Super-Cloth Product Flowchart

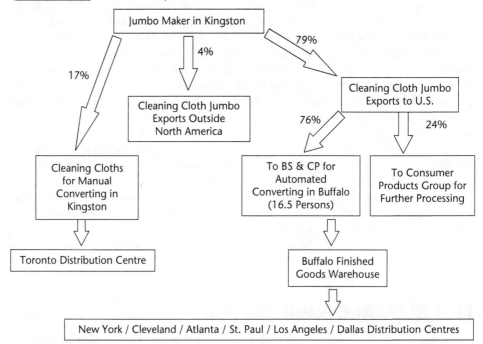

Source: Company records.

EXHIBIT 2: Proposed Super-Cloth Product Flowchart

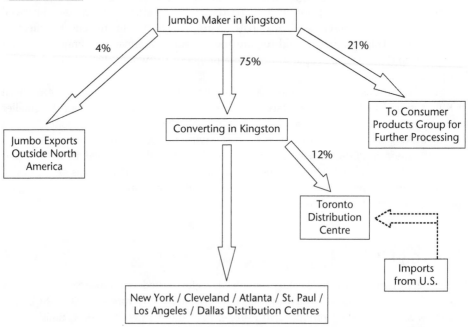

Source: Company records.

EXHIBIT 3: Firstwell Corporation Canada Inc. Consolidated Statement of Earnings and Retained Earnings for The Year Ended October 31, 2010 ($000S)

	2010	2009
Revenue		
Net sales*	$561,406	516,663
Other income	8,823	3,536
	570,229	520,199
Costs and expenses		
Cost of goods sold and other expenses	451,298	412,826
Depreciation and amortization	16,908	15,921
Interest	312	239
Research & development	1,876	2,010
	470,394	430,996
	99,835	89,203
Provision for income taxes	41,636	38,339
Net earnings for the year	58,199	50,864
Retained earnings—beginning of year	215,960	185,496
	274,159	236,360
Dividends	28,046	20,400
Retained earnings—end of year	$246,113	215,960
*includes net sales to parent and affiliated companies	106,773	89,709

Source: Company records.

EXHIBIT 4: Firstwell Corporation Canada Inc. Consolidated Balance Sheet as of October 31, 2010 ($000S)

	2010	2009
Assets		
Current Assets		
Interest bearing term deposits	$ 66,998	52,896
Accounts Receivable	73,524	69,631
Amounts due from affiliated companies	18,050	13,670
Other receivables and prepaid expenses	5,472	4,592
Inventories:		
Finished Goods and work in process	67,833	63,745
Raw materials and supplies	9,321	10,601
	241,198	215,135
Fixed Assets		
Property, plant and equipment—at cost	180,848	164,313
Less accumulated depreciation	85,764	75,676
Other Assets	9,590	8,856
	$345,872	312,628
Liabilities		
Current Liabilities		
Accounts payable	21,600	18,388
Amounts due to affiliated companies	18,427	17,985
Income taxes payable	9,394	12,437
Deferred payments	1,437	1,422
Other liabilities	20,832	18,367
	71,690	68,599
Deferred Income Taxes	14,669	14,669
	86,359	83,268
Shareholders' Equity		
Capital Stock		
Authorized—Unlimited shares issued and fully paid		
14, 600 shares	13,400	13,400
Retained Earnings	246,113	215,960
	259,513	229,360
	$345,872	312,628

Source: Company records.

EXHIBIT 5: Firstwell Corporation International—Partial Organization Chart

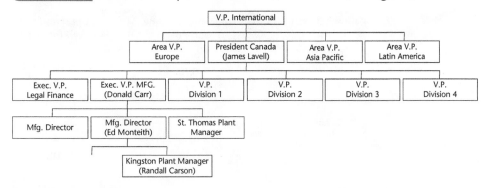

Source: Company records.

EXHIBIT 6: Firstwell Corporation Worldwide—Partial Organization Chart

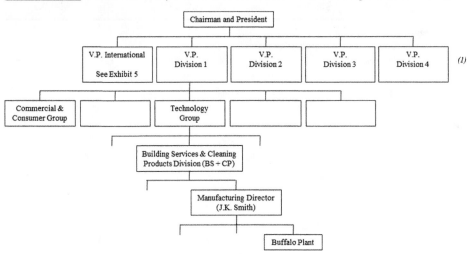

(1) Operating Committee made up of the four sector vice-presidents, the V.P. International and several other key executives.

Source: Company records.

EXHIBIT 7: Sample Unit Cost Comparison (US$ Per Case)

	Current Buffalo Operation	Upgraded Cutter Buffalo	Upgraded Cutter Kingston
Jumbo Cost Ex Kingston	$ 6.20	$ 6.20	$6.20
Jumbo Freight to Buffalo	$ 0.70	$ 0.70	
Jumbo Storage	$ 0.70	$ 0.70	$0.05
Jumbo Burden Absorption			($ 0.20)[1]
Input Cost to Converting	$ 7.60	$ 7.60	$6.05
Converting Waste	$ 0.95	$ 0.65	$0.45
Converting Labour	$ 1.35	$ 0.30	$ 0.15[2]
Variable Converting Overhead	$ 0.60	$ 0.45	$0.30
Fixed Converting Overhead	$ 1.00	$ 0.55	$0.85[3]
Packaging Supplies	$ 1.20	$ 1.20	$ 1.20
Finished Goods Warehouse/Material Handling	$ 0.45	$ 0.45	$0.25
Finished Goods Direct Charges	$ 1.15	$ 1.15	$0.90
Cost Including Converting	$14.30	$12.35	$10.15
Freight to Branch	$ 0.90	$ 0.90	$ 1.05
Cost Delivered to Branch	$15.20	$13.25	$11.20

[1]Volume savings through equipment usage.

[2]Lower than Buffalo due to faster equipment speed and smaller production teams.

[3]Higher than Buffalo due to larger investment in equipment.

Source: Company records.

Coral Divers Resort

Jonathon Greywell locked the door on the equipment shed and began walking back along the boat dock to his office. He was thinking about the matters that had weighed heavily on his mind during the last few months. Over the years, Greywell had established a solid reputation for the Coral Divers Resort as a safe and knowledgeable scuba diving resort that offered not only diving but also a beachfront location. Because Coral Divers Resort was a small but well-regarded, all-around dive resort in the Bahamas, many divers had come to prefer Greywell's resort to the other crowded tourist resorts in the Caribbean.

However, over the last three years, revenues had declined; for 2008, bookings were flat for the first half of the year. Greywell felt he needed to do something to increase business before the situation worsened. He wondered whether he should add some specialized features to the resort to help distinguish it from the competition. One approach would be to focus on family outings.

Rascals in Paradise (Rascals), a travel company that specialized in family diving vacations, had offered to help him convert his resort to specialize in family diving vacations. Rascals had shown him the industry demographics indicating that families were a growing market segment (see Exhibit 1) and suggested the changes that would need to be made at the resort. Rascals had even offered to create children's menus and to show the cook how to prepare the meals.

Another potential strategy for the Coral Divers Resort was to focus on adventure diving. Other resort operators in the Bahamas were offering adventure-oriented deep-depth dives, shark dives and night dives. The basic ingredients for adventure diving (i.e., reef sharks in the waters near New Providence and famous deep-water coral walls) were already in place.

Professors Paul W. Beamish and Kent E. Neupert prepared this case with assistance from Andreas Schotter solely to provide material for class discussion. The authors do not intend to illustrate either effective or ineffective handling of a managerial situation. The authors may have disguised certain names and other identifying information to protect confidentiality.

🛡 **IVEY** | Publishing

Richard Ivey School of Business Foundation prohibits any form of reproduction, storage or transmission without its written permission. Reproduction of this material is not covered under authorization by any reproduction rights organization. To order copies or request permission to reproduce materials, contact Ivey Publishing, Richard Ivey School of Business Foundation, The University of Western Ontario, London, Ontario, Canada, N6A 3K7; phone (519) 661-3208; fax (519) 661-3882; e-mail cases@ivey.uwo.ca.

Copyright © 2008, Richard Ivey School of Business Foundation   Version: 2011-09-21

One time permission to reproduce granted by Richard Ivey School of Business Foundation on April 22, 2014.

However, either of these strategies, creating a family vacation resort or an adventure diving resort, would require changes and additions to the current operations. Greywell was not sure whether any of the changes was worth the time and investment or whether he should instead try to improve on what he was already doing.

A final option, and one that he had only recently considered, was to leave New Providence and relocate elsewhere. At issue here was how much he might be able to recover if he sold Coral Divers Resort and whether better opportunities existed elsewhere in the Bahamas or around the Caribbean.

SCUBA DIVING INDUSTRY OVERVIEW

Skin diving was an underwater activity of ancient origin in which a diver swam freely, unencumbered by lines or air hoses. Modern skin divers used three pieces of basic equipment: a face mask for vision, webbed rubber fins for propulsion and a snorkel tube for breathing just below the water's surface. The snorkel was a J-shaped plastic tube fitted with a mouthpiece. When the opening of the snorkel was above water, a diver was able to breathe. When diving to greater depths, divers needed to hold their breath; otherwise, water entered the mouth through the snorkel.

Scuba diving provided divers with the gift of time to relax and explore the underwater world without surfacing for their next breath. Scuba was an acronym for self-contained underwater breathing apparatus. Although attempts to perfect this type of apparatus dated from the early 20th century, it was not until 1943 that the most famous scuba, or Aqualung, was invented by the Frenchmen Jacques-Yves Cousteau and Emil Gagnan. The Aqualung made recreational diving possible for millions of non-professional divers. Although some specially trained commercial scuba divers descended below 100 meters (328 feet) for various kinds of work, recreational divers never descended below a depth of 40 meters (130 feet) because of increased risk of nitrogen narcosis, an oxygen toxicity that causes blackouts and convulsions.

The scuba diver wore a tank that carried a supply of pressurized breathing gas, either air or a mixture of oxygen and other gases. The heart of the breathing apparatus was the breathing regulator and the pressure-reducing mechanisms that delivered gas to the diver on each inhalation. In the common scuba used in recreational diving, the breathing medium was air. As the diver inhaled, a slight negative pressure occurred in the mouthpiece, prompting the opening of the valve that delivers the air. When the diver stopped inhaling, the valve closed, and a one-way valve allowed the exhaled breath to escape as bubbles into the water. By using a tank and regulator, a diver could make longer and deeper dives and still breathe comfortably.

Along with scuba gear and its tanks of compressed breathing gases, the scuba diver's essential equipment included a soft rubber mask with a large faceplate; long, flexible swimming flippers for the feet; a buoyancy compensator device (known as a BC or BCD); a weight belt; a waterproof watch; a wrist compass and a diver's knife. For protection from colder water, neoprene-coated foam rubber wet suits were typically worn.

Certification Organizations[1]

Several international and domestic organizations trained and certified scuba divers. The most well-known organizations were PADI (Professional Association of Diving Instructors), NAUI (National Association of Underwater Instructors), SSI (Scuba Schools International)

---

[1]Information on the certifying agencies has been drawn from materials published by the various organizations.

and NASDS (National Association of Scuba Diving Schools). Of these, PADI was the largest certifying organization.

Professional Association of Diving Instructors The Professional Association of Diving Instructors (PADI), founded in 1967, was the largest recreational scuba diver training organization in the world. PADI divers comprised 70 per cent of all divers. The diving certificate issued by PADI through its instructors was acknowledged worldwide, thus enabling PADI-certified divers wide access to diving expeditions, tank filling, and diving equipment rental and purchase. Worldwide, PADI had certified more than 16.5 million recreational divers. In 2007, PADI International issued nearly 1 million new certifications.

In addition to PADI's main headquarters in Santa Ana, California, PADI operated regional offices in Australia, Canada, Switzerland, Japan, Sweden, the United Kingdom and the United States. PADI offices served more than 130,000 individual professional members and more than 5,300 dive centers and resorts in more than 180 countries and territories. Translations of PADI materials were available in more than 26 languages. PADI comprised four groups: PADI Retail Association, PADI International Resort Association, professional members and PADI Alumni Association. The three association groups emphasized the "three E's" of recreational diving: education, equipment and experience. By supporting each facet, PADI provided holistic leadership to advance recreational scuba diving and snorkel swimming to equal status with other major leisure activities, while maintaining and improving the organization's excellent safety record. PADI courses ranged from entry levels (such as scuba diver and open water diver certifications) to master scuba diver certification and a range of instructor certificates. Via its affiliate, Diving Science and Technology (DSAT), PADI also offered various technical diver courses, including decompression diving, Trimix diving and gas blending for deep sea diving. In 1995, PADI founded Project AWARE to help conserve underwater environments. Project AWARE information was integrated into most courses, and divers were offered the opportunity to exchange their standard certificate for an AWARE certificate by making a donation to the program when applying for a new certificate.

National Association of Underwater Instructors The National Association of Underwater Instructors (NAUI) first began operation in 1960. The organization was formed by a nationally recognized group of instructors known as the National Diving Patrol. Since its beginning, NAUI had been active worldwide, certifying sport divers in various levels of proficiency from basic skin diver to instructor. NAUI regularly conducted specialty courses for cave diving, ice diving, wreck diving, underwater navigation, and search and recovery.

Industry Demographics[2]

Scuba diving had grown steadily in popularity over the last 20 years. From 1989 until 2001, certifications had increased an average of 10 per cent each year; and increases had continued to be steady, despite more difficulties surrounding air travel because of the events of September 11, 2001, and the bleaching impact of climate change on coral reefs. In 2007, the total number of certified divers worldwide was estimated to be more than 22 million. The National Sporting Goods Association, which conducted an annual sports participation survey, projected the number of active divers in the United States at 2.1 million, and market share data from resort destinations showed 1.5 million active traveling U.S.-based scuba divers, not including resort divers.

---

[2]This section draws from results of surveys conducted by scuba diving organizations and publications for the years 1991 to 2007.

Approximately 65 per cent of the certified scuba divers were male, 35 per cent were female and about half of all scuba divers were married. Approximately 70 per cent of scuba divers were between the ages of 18 and 34, and approximately 25 per cent were between the ages of 35 and 49 (see Exhibit 2). Scuba divers were generally well educated: 80 per cent had a college education. Overwhelmingly, scuba divers were employed in professional, managerial and technical occupations and earned an average annual household income of $75,000, well above the national average. Forty-five per cent of divers traveled most often with their families, and 40 per cent traveled most often with friends or informal groups.

People were attracted to scuba diving for various reasons; seeking adventure and being with nature were the two most often cited reasons (identified by more than 75 per cent of divers). Socializing, stress relief and travel also were common motivations. Two-thirds of all divers traveled overseas on diving trips once every three years, whereas 60 per cent traveled domestically on dive trips each year. On average, divers spent $2,816 on dive trips annually, with an average equipment investment of $2,300. Aside from upgrades and replacements, the equipment purchase could be considered a one-time cost. Warm-water diving locations were generally chosen two to one over cold-water diving sites. Outside of the continental United States, the top three diving destinations were Cozumel in Mexico, the Cayman Islands and the Bahamas.

According to a consumer survey, the strongest feelings that divers associated with their scuba diving experiences were excitement and peacefulness. In a recent survey, these two themes drew an equal number of responses; however, the two responses had very distinct differences. The experience of excitement suggested a need for stimulation, whereas experience of peacefulness suggested relaxation and escape. Visual gratification (beauty) was another strong motivation for divers, as were the feelings of freedom, weightlessness and flying.

Under PADI regulations, divers needed to be at least 10 years old to be eligible for certification by the majority of scuba training agencies. At age 10, a child could earn a junior diver certification. Divers with this certification had to meet the same standards as an open water diver but generally had to be accompanied on dives by a parent or another certified adult. At age 15, the junior diver certification could be upgraded to open water status, which required a skills review and evaluation. Youth divers required pre-dive waiver and release forms signed by a parent or guardian until they reached age 18. Recently, PADI added a so-called bubble-maker program, which allowed children as young as age 8 to start scuba diving at a maximum depth of two meters (six feet). The program was conducted by PADI instructors in sessions that typically lasted one hour, and no pre-training was required. However, few dive centers had adopted the program because of the additional investment in special child-sized equipment and the low student-to-instructor ratio, which made the program uneconomical. On the other hand, children's programs increased the family friend-liness of scuba diving.

In general, most dive centers maintained a cautious approach to young divers, based on the concept of readiness to dive. An individual's readiness to dive was determined by physical, mental and emotional maturity. Physical readiness was the easiest factor to assess: Was the child large enough and strong enough to handle scuba equipment? A regular air tank and weight belt can weigh more than 40 lbs (18 kilograms). Mental readiness referred to whether the child had the academic background and conceptual development to under-stand diving physics and perform the arithmetic required for certification. The arithmetic understanding was needed to determine a diver's allowable bottom time, which required factoring in depth, number of dives and length of dives. Emotional readiness was the great-est concern. Would the junior diver accept the responsibility of being a dive buddy? Divers never dived alone, and dive buddies needed to look out for and rely on each other. Did young divers comprehend the safety rules of diving and willingly follow them? Most dive centers therefore accepted students from age 10, but the final determination of readiness to dive rested with the scuba instructor. Instructors were trained to evaluate the readiness of all students before completion of the course work and would only award a certification to those who earned it, regardless of age.

DIVING IN THE BAHAMAS[3]

New Providence Island, the Bahamas

New Providence Island was best known for its major population center, Nassau, a community whose early development was based on its superb natural harbor. As the capital of the Bahamas, it was the seat of government and home to 400 banks, elegant homes, ancient forts and a wide variety of duty-free shopping. Nassau had the island's most developed tourist infrastructure exemplified by its elegant resort hotels, casinos, cabaret shows and cruise ship docks. More than two-thirds of the population of the Bahamas lived on the island of New Providence, and most of these 180,000 people lived in or near Nassau, on the northeast corner of the island.

Because thousands of vacationers took resort-based diving courses (introductory scuba courses taught in resort pools), Nassau had become known as a destination for both an exploratory first dive and more advanced diving. As a result, many professional dive operations were located in the Nassau area (see Exhibit 3). Although all dive operations offered resort courses, many also offered a full menu of dive activities designed for more advanced divers. Within a 30-minute boat ride of most operations were shipwrecks, beautiful shallow reefs and huge schools of fish.

In contrast to the bustle of Nassau, the south side of New Providence Island was quieter and more laid back. Large tracts of pine trees and rolling hills dominated the central regions, while miles of white sand beach surrounded the island. At the west end of the island was Lyford Cay, an exclusive residential area. Nearby, the Coral Harbour area offered easy access to the sea. Although golf and tennis were available, the primary attractions were the good scuba diving and the top-quality dive operators.

The southwest side of the island had been frequently used as an underwater film set. The "Bond wrecks" were popular diving destinations for divers and operators. The Vulcan Bomber used in the James Bond film *Thunderball* had aged into a framework draped with colorful gorgonians and sponges. The freighter, Tears of Allah, where James Bond eluded the Tiger Shark in *Never Say Never Again*, remained a popular dive attraction in just 40 feet of water. The photogenic appeal of this wreck had improved with age as marine life increasingly congregated on this artificial reef.

Natural underwater attractions, such as Shark Wall and Shark Buoy, were popular dive spots. Drop-off dives, such as Tunnel Wall, featured a network of crevices and tunnels beginning in 30 feet of water and exiting along the vertical wall at 70 or 80 feet. Southwest Reef offered magnificent coral heads in only 15 to 30 feet of water, with schooling grunts, squirrelfish and barracuda. A favorite of the shallow reef areas was Goulding Cay, where Elkhorn coral reached nearly to the surface.

---

[3]The content in this section is based on information drawn from *The Islands of the Bahamas Dive Guide*, published by the Bahamas Ministry of Tourism, Commonwealth of the Bahamas, in conjunction with The Bahamas Diving Association, retrieved from http://www.bahamasdiving.com/6729/with.flash/html/index-5.html, accessed on April 10, 2008.

TYPES OF DIVING

A wide array of diving activities was available in the Bahamas, including shark dives, wreck dives, wall dives, reef dives, drift dives and night dives. Some illustrative examples follow.

Shark Diving

The top three operators of shark dives in the Caribbean were located in the Bahamas. Although shark diving trips varied depending on the dive operators, one common factor was shared by all shark dives in the Bahamas: the Caribbean reef shark (Carcharhinus perezi). When the dive boat reached the shark site, the sound of the motor acted as a dinner bell. Even before the divers entered the water, sharks gathered for their handouts.

Long Island in the Bahamas was the first area to promote shark feed dives on a regular basis. This method began 20 years ago and had remained relatively unchanged. The feed was conducted as a feeding frenzy. Sharks circled as divers entered the water. After the divers positioned themselves with their backs to a coral wall, the feeder entered the water with a bucket of fish, which was placed in the sand in front of the divers, and the action developed quickly. At Walker's Cay, in Abaco, the method was similar except for the number and variety of sharks in the feed. Although Caribbean reef sharks made up the majority of sharks seen, lemon sharks, bull sharks, hammerhead sharks and other species also appeared.

The shark feed off Freeport, Grand Bahama, was an organized event in which the sharks were fed either by hand or off the point of a polespear. The divers were arranged in a semi-circle with safety divers guarding the viewers and the feeder positioned at the middle of the group. If the sharks became unruly, the food was withheld until they calmed down. The sharks then went into a regular routine of circling, taking their place in line and advancing to receive the food. Although the sharks often came within touching distance, most divers resisted the temptation to reach out.

Shark Wall, on the southwest side of New Providence, was a pristine drop-off decorated with masses of colorful sponges along the deep-water abyss known as the Tongue of the Ocean. Divers positioned themselves along sand patches among the coral heads in about 50 feet of water as Caribbean reef sharks and an occasional bull shark or lemon shark cruised mid-water in anticipation of a free handout. During the feeding period, the bait was controlled and fed from a polespear by an experienced feeder. Usually six to 12 sharks were present, ranging from four to eight feet in length. Some operators made two dives to this site, allowing divers to cruise the wall with the sharks in a more natural way before the feeding dive.

The Shark Buoy, also on the southwest side of New Providence, was tethered in 6,000 feet of water. Its floating surface mass attracted a wide variety of ocean marine life, such as dolphin fish, jacks, rainbow runners and silky sharks. The silky sharks were typically small, three to five feet long, but swarmed in schools of six to 20, with the sharks swimming up to the divemaster's hands to grab the bait.

From the operator's standpoint, the only special equipment needed for shark dives were a chain mail diving suit for the feeder's protection, feeding apparatus and intestinal fortitude. The thrill of diving among sharks was the main attraction for the divers. For the most part, the dives were safe; only the feeder took an occasional nip from an excited shark.

Recently, shark feeding had come under attack from environmentalists for causing a change in the feeding behavior of sharks, which had led to the loss of their natural fear of humans. In addition, some rare but fatal accidents had been prominently exposed through TV news channels and newspapers. For example, in 2001, Krishna Thompson, a 34-year-old New York banker, lost a leg and very nearly his life, when he was attacked just off the beach at Lucaya Golf and Beach Resort in Freeport, Grand Bahama. Thompson successfully sued the resort for failing to warn guests that local dive operators sold shark-feeding tours at sites located less than a mile from the hotel beach. In April 2002, TV shark show daredevil Erich Ritter went into severe shock and nearly lost his left leg after he was bitten by a bull shark that he had attracted to shallow water with fish bait.

In spite of opposition from a small but well-funded group of U.S. dive industry insiders including PADI, DEMA, *Scuba Diving* magazine and *Skin Diver* magazine, the Florida Fish and Wildlife Conservation Commission banned shark feeding in 2001. However, shark feeding remained legal in the Caribbean, and despite its dangers, was on the rise. Divers participating in shark dives were required to sign waivers before the actual dive. As noted by the fine print in most life insurance and travel insurance policies, claims for scuba-related accidents were excluded.

Wreck Diving

Wreck diving was divided into three levels: non-penetration, limited penetration and full penetration. Full penetration and deep wreck diving should be attempted only by divers who have completed rigorous training and have extensive diving experience. Non-penetration wreck diving referred to recreational diving on wrecks without entering an overhead environment that prevented direct access to the surface. Divers with open water certification were qualified for this type of diving without any further training provided they were comfortable with the diving conditions and the wreck's depth. Limited penetration wreck diving was defined as staying within ambient light and always in sight of an exit. Full penetration wreck diving involved an overhead environment away from ambient light and beyond sight of an exit. Safely and extensively exploring the insides of a wreck involved formal training and mental strength. On this type of dive, a diver's first mistake could be a diver's last.

Wall Diving

In a few regions of the world, island chains, formed by volcanoes and coral, have been altered by movements of the earth's crustal plates. Extending approximately due east-west across the central Caribbean Sea was the boundary between the North American and Caribbean crustal plates. The shifting of these plates had created some of the most spectacular diving environments in the world, characterized by enormous cliffs, 2,000 to 6,000 feet high. At the cliffs, known as walls, divers could experience, more than in any other underwater environment, the overwhelming scale and dynamic forces that shape the ocean. On the walls, divers were most likely to experience the feeling of free motion, or flying, in boundless space. Many of the dives in the Bahamas were wall dives.

Reef Diving

Reefs generally were made up of three areas: a reef flat, a lagoon or bay, and a reef crest. The depth in the reef flat averaged only a few feet with an occasional deeper channel. The underwater life on a shallow reef flat could vary greatly in abundance and diversity within a short distance. The reef flat was generally a protected area, not exposed to strong winds or waves, making it ideal for novice or family snorkelers. The main feature distinguishing bay and lagoon environments from a reef flat was depth. Caribbean lagoons and bays could reach depths of 60 feet but many provided teeming underwater ecosystems in as little as 15 to 20 feet, making this area excellent for underwater photography and ideal for families because it was a no decompression stop diving site[4]. The reefs crest was the outer boundary that sheltered the bay and the flats from the full force of the ocean's waves. Since the surging and pounding of the waves was too strong for all but the most advanced divers, most diving took place in the protected bay waters.

FAMILY DIVING RESORTS

The current average age of new divers was 36. As the median age of new divers increased, families became a rapidly growing segment of the vacation travel industry. Many parents were busy and did not spend as much time with their children as they would have preferred. Thus, many parents who dived would have liked to have a vacation that would combine diving and spending time with their children. In response to increasing numbers of parents traveling with children, resort operators had added amenities ranging from baby-sitting services and kids' camps to dedicated family resorts with special facilities and rates. The resort options available had greatly expanded in recent years. At all-inclusive, self-contained resorts, one price included everything: meals, accommodations, daytime and evening activities, and water sports. Many of these facilities offered special activities and facilities for children. Diving was sometimes included or available nearby.

For many divers, the important part of the trip was the quality of the diving, not the quality of the accommodations, but for divers with families, the equation changed. Children, especially younger children, could have a difficult time without a comfortable bed, a television and a DVD player, no matter how good the diving promised to be. Some resorts that were not dedicated to family vacations, made accommodations for divers with children. Condos and villas were an economical and convenient vacation option. The additional space of this type of accommodation allowed parents to bring along a babysitter, and the convenience of a kitchen made the task of feeding children simple and economical. Most diving destinations in the Bahamas, the Caribbean and the Pacific offered condo, villa and hotel-type accommodations. Some hotels organized entertaining and educational activities for children while parents engaged in their own activities.

Because the number of families vacationing together had increased, some resorts and dive operators started special promotions and programs. On Bonaire, an island in the Netherlands Antilles, August had been designated family month. During this month, the island was devoted to families, with a special welcome kit for children and island-wide activities, including eco-walks at a flamingo reserve, snorkeling lessons and evening entertainment for all ages. In conjunction, individual resorts and restaurants offered family packages and discounts. Similarly, in Honduras, which had very good diving, a resort started a children's dolphin camp during summer months. While diving family members were out exploring the reefs, children aged eight to 14 spent their days learning about and interacting with a resident dolphin population. The program included classroom and in-water time, horseback riding and paddle boating.

Rascals in Paradise

One travel company, Rascals in Paradise (Rascals), specialized in family travel packages. The founders, Theresa Detchemendy and Deborah Baratta, were divers, mothers and travel agents who had developed innovative packages for diving families. According to Detchemendy,

---

[4]A decompression stop is a safety requirement for dives below 30 feet. It lasts typically between 1 to 5 minutes at 3 to 6 meters (10 to 20 ft). During the stop, "micro-bubbles" in the bloodstream that are present after every dive leave the diver's body safely through the lungs. If they are not given enough time to leave safely, it can cause the symptoms and injuries known as decompression sickness.

"The biggest concern for parents is their children's safety, and then what the kids will do while they're diving or enjoying an evening on the town." The Rascals staff worked with a number of family-run resorts all over the world to provide daily activities, responsible local nannies and child-safe facilities with safe balconies, playgrounds and children's pools.

Rascals also organized family weeks at popular dive destinations in Belize, Mexico and the Cayman Islands. Family week packages accounted for more than 50 per cent of Rascals' bookings each year. On these scheduled trips, groups of three to six families shared a teacher/escort, who tailored a fun program for children and served as an activities director for the group. Rascals' special family week packages were priced based on a family of four (two adults and two children, aged two to 11) and included a teacher/escort, one babysitter for each family, children's activities, meals, airport transfers, taxes, services and cancellation insurance (see Exhibit 4) but not airfare. For example, in 2007, a seven-night family vacation at Hotel Club Akumal, on the Yucatan coast, cost US$2,080 to US$3,100 per family. Rascals also packaged independent family trips to 57 different condos, villas, resorts and hotels, which offered scuba diving. An independent family trip would not include a teacher/escort and babysitter (see Exhibit 5) and a 7-night family trip to Hotel Club Akumal would cost between US$624 and US$1,779, depending on the season and the type of room. Here also, the airfare was not included.

Rascals personally selected the resorts with which the company worked. "We try to work with small properties so our groups are pampered and looked after," said Detchemendy. "The owners are often parents and their kids are sometimes on the property. They understand the characteristics of kids." Typically, Detchemendy and Baratta visited each destination, often working with the government tourist board to identify potential properties. If the physical structure were already in place, adding the resort to the Rascals booking list was easy. If modifications were needed, then Detchemendy and Baratta met with the property's management to outline the facilities needed to include the resort in the Rascals program.

Rascals evaluated resorts according to several factors:

- Is the property friendly toward children and does it want children on the property?
- How does the property rate in terms of safety?
- What facilities does the property have? Is a separate room available that could be used as a Rascals room?
- Does the property provide babysitting and child care by individuals who are screened and locally known?

A successful example of this approach was Hotel Club Akumal, in Akumal, Mexico. Detchemendy and Baratta helped the resort expand its market reach by building a family-oriented resort that became part of the Rascals program. Baratta explained:

In that case, we were looking for a place close to home, with a multi-level range of accommodations, that offered something other than a beach, that was family friendly, and not in Cancun. We found Hotel Club Akumal, but they didn't have many elements in place, so we had to work with them. We established a meal plan, an all-inclusive product and designated activities for kids. We went into the kitchen and created a children's menu and we asked them to install a little kids' playground that's shaded.

The resort became one of Rascals' most popular family destinations.

Rascals offered two types of services to resort operators interested in creating family vacations. One was a consulting service. For a modest daily fee plus expenses, Baratta or Detchemendy, or both, would conduct an on-site assessment of the resort, which usually took one or two days. They would then provide a written report to the resort regarding needed additions or modifications to the resort to make it safe and attractive for family vacations. Physical changes might include the addition of a Rascals room and child-safe play equipment and modifications to existing buildings and structures, such as rooms, railings and docks, to prevent child injuries. Rascals always tried to use existing equipment or equipment available nearby. Other non-structural changes could include the addition of educational sessions, play times and other structured times for entertaining children while their parents were diving. The report also included an implementation proposal. Then, after implementation, the resort could decide whether or not to list with Rascals for bookings.

Under the second option, Rascals provided the consulting service at no charge to the resort; however, any requests for family bookings were referred to Rascals. Rascals would then list and actively promote the resort through its brochures and referrals. For resorts using the Rascals booking option, Rascals provided premiums, such as hats and T-shirts, in addition to the escorted activities. This attention to the family differentiated a Rascals resort from other resorts. Generally, companies that promoted packages received net rates from the resorts, which were 20 per cent to 50 per cent lower than the rack rates. Rascals, in turn, promoted these special packages to the travel industry in general and paid a portion of its earnings out in commissions to other travel agencies.

Rascals tried to work with its resorts to provide packaged and prepaid vacations, an approach that created a win-win situation for the resort managers and the vacationer. Packaged vacations, also known as all-inclusive vacations, followed a cruise ship approach that allowed the inclusion of many activities in the package. For example, such a package might include seven nights' lodging, all meals, babysitting, children's activities and scuba diving. This approach allowed the vacationer to know, upfront, what to expect. Moreover, the cost would be included in one set price, so that the family would not have to pay for each activity as it came along. The idea was to remove the surprises and make the stay enjoyable. The resort operator could bundle the activities together, providing more options than might otherwise be offered. As a result, the package approach was becoming popular with both resort owners and vacationers.

In its bookings, Rascals required prepayment of trips, which resulted in higher revenues for the resort since all activities were paid for in advance. Ordinarily, resorts that operated independently might require only a two- or three-night room deposit. The family would then pay for the balance of the room charge on leaving, after paying for other activities or services they used. Although vacationers might think they had a less expensive trip this way, in fact, pre-paid activities were generally cheaper than a la carte activities. Moreover, purchasing individual activities potentially yielded lower revenues for the resort. Rascals promoted prepaid vacations as a win-win, low-stress approach to travel. Rascals had been very successful with the resorts it listed. Fifty per cent of its bookings were repeat business, and many inquiries were based on word-of-mouth referrals. All in all, Rascals provided a link to the family vacation market segment that the resort might not otherwise have access to. It was common for Rascals-listed resorts to average annual bookings of 90 per cent.

CORAL DIVERS RESORT

Coral Divers Resort (Coral Divers) had been in operation for 10 years. Annual revenues had reached as high as $554,000. Profits generally had been in the two per cent range, but for the past two years, the business had experienced losses. The expected turnaround in profits in 2007 had never materialized (see Exhibit 6). Although the resort was not making them rich, the business had provided an adequate income for Greywell and his wife, Margaret, and their two children, Allen, age 7, and Winifred, age 5. However, revenues had continued to decline.

From talking with other operators, Greywell understood that resorts with strong identities and reputations for quality service were doing well. Greywell thought that the Coral Divers Resort had not distinguished itself in any particular aspect of diving or as a resort.

The Coral Divers Resort property was located on a deep-water channel on the southwest coast of the island of New Providence in the Bahamas. The three-acre property had beach access and featured six cottages, each with its own kitchenette, a full bath, a bedroom with two full-sized beds and a living room with two sleeper sofas. Four of the units had been upgraded with new paint, tile floors, a microwave, a color TV and a DVD player. The two other units ranged from "adequate" to "comfortable." Greywell tried to use the renovated units primarily for families and couples and housed groups of single divers in the other units (see Exhibit 7). Also on the property was a six-unit attached motel-type structure. Each of these units had two full-sized beds, a pull-out sofa, sink, a refrigerator, a microwave and a television. The resort had the space and facilities for a kitchen and dining room, but neither a kitchen nor a dining room was in use. A small family-run restaurant and bar was available within walking distance.

Greywell had three boats that could each carry from eight to 20 passengers. Two were 40-foot fiberglass V-hull boats powered by a single diesel inboard with a cruising speed of 18 knots and a protective cabin with dry storage space. The third was a 35-foot covered platform boat. Greywell also had facilities for air dispensing, equipment repair, rental and sale, and tank storage.

Coral Divers Resort, which was affiliated with PADI and NAUI, had a staff of 11, including two boat captains, two mates, a housekeeper, a groundskeeper, a person who minded the office and the store, and four scuba diving instructors. Greywell, who worked full-time at the resort, was a diving instructor certified by both PADI and NAUI. The three other diving instructors had various backgrounds: one was a former U.S. Navy SEAL working for Coral Divers as a way to gain resort experience, another was a local Bahamian whom Greywell had known for many years and the third was a Canadian who had come to the Bahamas on a winter holiday and had never left. Given the size of the operation, the staff was scheduled to provide overall coverage, with all of the staff rarely working at the same time. Greywell's wife, Margaret, worked at the business on a part-time basis, taking care of administrative activities, such as accounting and payroll. The rest of her time was spent looking after their two children and their home.

A typical diving day at Coral Divers began around 7:30 a.m. Greywell would open the office and review the activities list for the day. If any divers needed to be picked up at the resorts in Nassau or elsewhere on the island, the van driver would need to leave by 7:30 a.m. to be back at the resort for the 9 a.m. departure. Most resort guests began to gather around the office and dock about 8:30 a.m. By 8:45 a.m., the day's captain and mate began loading the diving gear for the passengers.

The boat left at 9 a.m. for the morning dives that were usually "two tank dives," that is, two dives utilizing one tank of air each. The trip to the first dive site took 20 to 30 minutes. Once there, the captain would explain the dive, the special attractions of the dive, and tell everyone when they were expected back on board. Most dives lasted 30 to 45 minutes, depending on the depth. The deeper the dive, the faster the air consumption. On the trip down, divers were always accompanied by a divemaster, who supervised the dive. The divemaster was responsible for the safety and conduct of the divers while under water.

After the divers were back on board, the boat would move to the next site. Greywell tried to plan two dives that had sites near each other. For example, the first dive might be a wall dive in 60 feet of water, and the second might be a nearby wreck 40 feet down. The second dive would also last approximately 40 minutes. If the dives went well, the boat would be back at the resort by noon, which allowed time for lunch and sufficient surface time for divers who might be interested in an afternoon dive. Two morning dives were part of the resort package. Whether the boat went out in the afternoon depended on the number of non-resort guest divers contracted for afternoon dives. If enough paying divers were signed up, Greywell was happy to let resort guests ride and dive free of charge. If there were not enough paying divers, no afternoon dive trips were scheduled, and the guests were on their own to swim at the beach, sightsee or just relax. When space was available, non-divers (either snorkelers or bubble-watchers) could join the boat trip for a fee of $15 to $25.

Greywell's Options

Greywell's bookings ran 90 per cent of capacity during the high season (December through May) and 50 per cent of capacity during the low season (June through November). Ideally, he wanted to increase the number of bookings for the resort and dive businesses during both seasons. Adding additional diving attractions could increase both resort and dive revenues. Focusing on family vacations could increase revenues because families would probably increase the number of paying guests per room. Break-even costs were calculated based on two adults sharing a room. Children provided an additional revenue source since the cost of the room had been covered by the adults, and children under 10 incurred no diving-related costs. However, either strategy, adding adventure diving to his current general offerings or adjusting the focus of the resort to encourage family diving vacations, would require some changes and cost money. The question was whether the changes would increase revenue enough to justify the costs and effort involved.

Emphasizing family diving vacations would probably require some changes to the physical property of the resort. Four of the cottages had already been renovated. The other two also would need to be upgraded, which would cost $15,000 to $25,000 each, depending on the amenities added. The Bahamas had duties of up to 35 per cent, which caused renovation costs involving imported goods to be expensive. The attached motel-type units also would need to be refurbished at some point. The resort had the space and facilities for a kitchen and dining area, but Greywell had not done anything about opening these facilities.

The Rascals in Paradise people had offered to help set up a children's menu. He could hire a chef, prepare the meals himself or offer the concession to either the nearby restaurant or someone else. He would also need to build a children's play structure. An open area with shade trees between the office and the cottages would be ideal for a play area. Rascals would provide the teacher/escort for the family vacation groups, and it would be fairly easy to find babysitters for the children as needed. The people who lived on this part of the island were very family-oriented and would welcome the opportunity for additional income. From asking around, Greywell determined that between $5 and $10 per hour was the going rate for a sitter. Toys and other play items could be added gradually. The Rascals people had said that, once the program was in place, Greywell could expect bookings to run 90 per cent capacity annually from new and return bookings. Although the package prices were competitive, the attraction was in group bookings and the prospect of a returning client base.

Adding adventure diving would be a relatively easy thing to do. Shark Wall and Shark Buoy were less than an hour away by boat. Both of these sites featured sharks that were already accustomed to being fed. The cost of shark food would be $10 per dive. None of Greywell's current staff was particularly excited about the prospect of adding shark feeding to their job description. But these staff could be relatively easily replaced. Greywell could probably find an experienced divemaster who would be willing to lead the shark dives. He would also have to purchase a special chain mail suit for the feeder at a cost of about $15,000. Although few accidents occurred during shark feeds, Greywell would rather be safe than sorry. His current boats, especially the 40-footers, would be adequate for transporting divers to the sites. The other shark dive operators might not be happy about having him at the sites, but they could do little about it. Shark divers were charged a premium fee. For example, a shark dive would cost $115 for a two-tank dive, compared with $65 for a normal two-tank dive. He figured that he could add shark dives to the schedule on Wednesdays and Saturdays without taking away from regular business. Although he needed a minimum of four divers on a trip at regular rates to cover the cost of taking out the boat, 10 or 12 divers would be ideal. Greywell could usually count on at least eight divers for a normal dive, but he did not know how much additional new and return business he could expect from shark diving.

A third option was for Greywell to try to improve his current operations and not add any new diving attractions, which would require him to be much more cost efficient in his operations. For example, he would have to strictly adhere to the policy of requiring a minimum number of divers per boat, and staff reductions might improve the bottom line by five per cent to 10 per cent. He would need to be very attentive to materials ordering, fuel costs and worker productivity in order to realize any gains with this approach. However, he was concerned that by continuing as he had, Coral Divers Resort would not be distinguished as unique from other resorts in the Bahamas. He did not know the long-term implications of this approach.

As Greywell reached the office, he turned to watch the sun sink into the ocean. Although it was a view he had come to love, a lingering thought was that perhaps it was time to relocate to a less crowded location.

EXHIBIT 1: U.S. Population Demographics 1980, 1990 and 2000

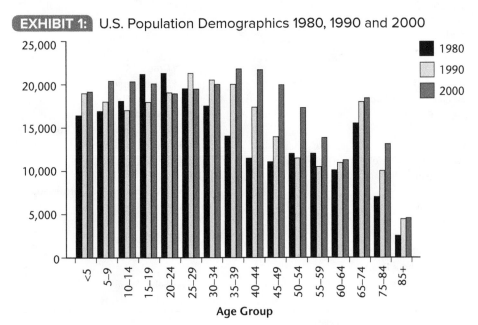

Note: Numbers are in the thousands

Source: U.S. Bureau of the Census, 2000. Retrieved from http://factfinder.census.gov/servlet/QTTable?
_bm=y&-geo_id=01000US&-qr_name=DEC_2000_SF1_U_DP1&-ds_name=DEC_2000_SF1_U, accessed on April 10, 2008.

EXHIBIT 2: US Diver Demographics: Age of Divers

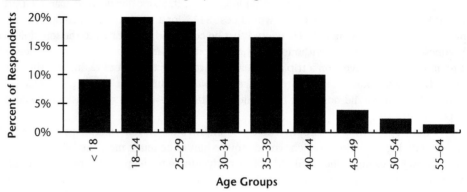

Source: PADI Diver Survey Results and Analysis.

EXHIBIT 3: Names and Location of Diving Operators in The Bahamas

Abaco
Above and Below Abaco
Brendal's Dive Center International
Dive Abaco
Dive Guana
Froggies Out Island Adventures, Ltd.
Treasure Divers

Andros
Coral Caverns Dive Resort
Kamalame Cay Resort
Seascape Inn
Small Hope Bay Lodge
Tiamo Resort

Bimini
Bill & Nowdla Keefe's Bimini Undersea
Scuba Bimini

Cat Island
Hawk's Nest Resort & Marina

Eleuthera/Habour Island
Cape Eleuthera Divers
Ocean Fox Divers
Valentine's Dive Center

Exuma
Exuma Scuba Adventures

Live-Aboard Dive Boats
Aqua Cat Cruises
Blackbeard's Cruises
Cat Ppalu Cruises
Explorer Ventures
Juliet Sailing and Diving
Nekton Diving Cruises
Sea Dragon
The Dream Team, Inc.

Long Island
Cape Santa Maria Beach Resort
Reel Divers at Grotto Bay
Stella Maris Resort Club

New Providence Island/Nassau
Bahama Divers Ltd.
Coral Divers Resort
Land Shark Divers
Stuart Cove's Dive South Ocean

San Salvador
Riding Rock Resort

Source: The Bahamas Diving Association membership.

EXHIBIT 4: Rascals in Paradise Pricing Guide—Rascals Special
Family Weeks

Destination	Price	Notes
Bahamas		
South Ocean Beach	$3,120 to $3,970	Lunch not included
Small Hope Bay	$3,504	Scuba diving included. Local host only.
Mexico		
Hotel Buena Vista	$2,150 to $2,470	
Hotel Club Akumal	$2,080 to $3,100	Lunch and airport transfer not included.

Note: Prices are based on a family of four with two adults and two children aged two and 11. Rates are per week (seven nights) and include (except as noted): accommodations, Rascals escort, meals, babysitter, children's activities, airport transfers, taxes and services, and a $2,500 cancellation insurance per family booking. Airfares not included.

EXHIBIT 5: Rascals in Paradise Pricing Guide*—Independent Family Trips

Destination	Price	Notes
Bahamas		
South Ocean Beach	$1,355 to $1,771	
Small Hope Bay	$2,860 to $3,560	All meals, bar service, babysitter and diving included.
Hope Town Harbour Lodge	$962 to $1,121	
Treasure Cay	$875 to $1,750	
Stella Maris, Long Island	$1,547 to $2,597	
Mexico		
Hotel Buena Vista	$1,232 to $1,548	All meals included
Hotel Club Akumal	$624 to $1,779	
Hotel Presidente	$1,120 to $1,656	
La Concha	$655 to $963	
Plaza Las Glorias	$632 to $1,017	

Note: Prices are based on a family of four with two adults and two children aged two and 11. Rates are per week (seven nights) and include accommodations and applicable taxes. These rates are to be used as a guide only. Each booking is quoted separately and the amount charged depends on season, type of accommodation, ages and number of children, meal and activity inclusions. All prices are subject to change. Some variations apply. Airfares not included.

EXHIBIT 6: Comparative Balance Sheets as at June 30 (US$)

	2007	2006	2005
Assets			
Current Assets			
Cash	$ 5,362	8,943	15,592
Accounts Receivable	2,160	8,660	2,026
Inventories	5,519	6,861	9,013
Prepaid Expenses	9,065	8,723	8,195
Total Current Assets	22,106	33,187	34,826
Fixed Assets			
Land	300,000	300,000	300,000
Building	200,000	200,000	200,000
Less: Accumulated Depreciation	(70,000)	(60,000)	(50,000)
Boats	225,000	225,000	225,000
Less: Accumulated Depreciation	(157,500)	(135,000)	(112,500)
Vehicles	54,000	54,000	54,000
Less: Accumulated Depreciation	(32,400)	(21,600)	(10,800)
Diving Equipment	150,000	150,000	150,000
Less: Accumulated Depreciation	(90,000)	(60,000)	(30,000)
Total Fixed Assets	579,100	652,400	725,700
Total Assets	**601,206**	**685,587**	**760,526**
Liabilities			
Current Liabilities			
Accounts Payable	1,689	4,724	1,504
Bank Loan	20,000	—	2,263
Mortgage Payable, current portion	25,892	25,892	25,892
Note Payable, current portion	40,895	40,895	40,895
Total Current Liabilities	**88,476**	**71,511**	**70,554**
Long-term Liabilities			
Mortgage Payable, due in 1996	391,710	417,602	443,494
Note Payable, 5-year	81,315	122,210	163,105
Total Long-term Liabilities	473,025	539,812	606,599
Total Liabilities	**561,501**	**611,323**	**677,153**

EXHIBIT 6: (Continued)

	2007	2006	2005
Shareholders' Equity			
Jonathan Greywell, Capital	44,879	44,879	44,879
Retained Earnings	(5,174)	29,385	38,494
Total Shareholders' Equity	39,705	74,264	83,373
Total Liabilities and Shareholders' Equity	$601,206	685,587	760,526
Revenue			
Diving and lodging packages	$ 482,160	507,670	529,820
Day diving	11,680	12,360	14,980
Certifications	5,165	5,740	7,120
Lodging	2,380	1,600	1,200
Miscellaneous	1,523	1,645	1,237
Total Revenues	502,908	529,015	554,357
Expenses			
Advertising and promotion	15,708	15,240	13,648
Bank charges	1,326	1,015	975
Boat maintenance and fuel	29,565	31,024	29,234
Cost of goods sold	762	823	619
Depreciation	73,300	73,300	73,300
Dues and fees	3,746	4,024	3,849
Duties and taxes	11,405	18,352	17,231
Insurance	36,260	34,890	32,780
Interest, mortgage, note and loan	40,544	40,797	41,174
Management salary	31,600	31,600	31,600
Office Supplies	12,275	12,753	11,981
Professional fees	11,427	10,894	10,423
Repairs and maintenance, building	15,876	12,379	9,487
Salaries, wages and benefits	196,386	194,458	191,624
Telephone and fax	9,926	9,846	7,689
Trade shows	14,523	14,679	14,230
Utilities	20,085	19,986	17,970
Vehicles, maintenance and fuel	12,753	12,064	11,567
Total Expenses	537,467	538,124	519,381
Net Income	(34,559)	(9,109)	(34,976)
Retained Earnings, beginning	29,385	38,494	3,518
Retained Earnings, ending	$ (5,174)	29,385	38,494

Note: Bahama$1 = US$1

EXHIBIT 7: Coral Divers Resort Pricing Guide—Family Dive Vacations

Destination	Duration	Price	Notes
Bahamas			
Coral Divers Resort		$1,355 to $1,455	Standard accommodations, continental breakfast and daily two-tank dive included.
Coral Divers Resort		$1,800 to $1,950	Deluxe accommodations, continental breakfast and daily two-tank dive included.

Note: Prices are based on a family of four with two adults and two children ages two and 11. Rates are per week (7 nights) and include accommodations and applicable taxes. Rates will be dependent on season, type of accommodation, ages and number of children. All prices are subject to change. Airfares not included. Prices dropped to $600 to $700 per week for the standard package and $800 to $900 for deluxe accommodation if diving was excluded.

Tavazo Co.

In June 2010, Naser Tavazo, one of the three owner/manager brothers of both Tavazo Iran Co. and Tavazo Canada Co., was considering the company's future expansion opportunities, including further international market entry. Candidate cities of interest were Los Angeles, Dubai, and other cities with large Iranian diasporas. Another question included where to focus on the value chain. Should the family business use its limited resources to expand its retailer business into more international markets, or to expand its current retailer/wholesale activities within Canada and Iran?

BACKGROUND

Tavazo was a family business operated by three brothers: Naser, Khosro and Parviz. The business was originally started by their grandfather. He had started his career as a gardener in Eastern Azerbaijan province in Iran in 1929 when he was 18 years old. Later, he moved to Tabriz, the capital city of the province, and dried his gardens' fruits using sunlight. From his small processing site, he distributed to small retail stores. Difficulties dealing with distributors led him to rent a store and sell dried fruits from his and neighboring gardens directly to customers. The store started with fruits such as apples, peaches and apricots. Then to the store's product list he added seeds, which he roasted in a big pan at the store.

As the store's business grew, he added nuts such as pistachios and cashews, which were not the products of Azerbaijan. Pistachios thrived in areas with cool winters and long,

Majid Eghbali-Zarch wrote this case under the supervision of Professor Paul W. Beamish solely to provide material for class discussion. The authors do not intend to illustrate either effective or ineffective handling of a managerial situation. The authors may have disguised certain names and other identifying information to protect confidentiality.

Richard Ivey School of Business Foundation prohibits any form of reproduction, storage or transmission without its written permission. Reproduction of this material is not covered under authorization by any reproduction rights organization. To order copies or request permission to reproduce materials, contact Ivey Publishing, Richard Ivey School of Business Foundation, The University of Western Ontario, London, Ontario, Canada, N6A 3K7; phone (519) 661-3208; fax (519) 661-3882; e-mail cases@ivey.uwo.ca.

Copyright © 2010, Richard Ivey School of Business Foundation   Version: 2011-09-21

One time permission to reproduce granted by Richard Ivey School of Business Foundation on April 22, 2014.

IVEY | Publishing

hot summers. They were drought resistant and very tolerant of high summer temperatures, but could not tolerate excessive dampness and high humidity. Central provinces in Iran, such as Kerman and Yazd, were the main sources of Iranian pistachio production. He purchased raw pistachios from the central provinces and displayed and sold them in the store after roasting them.

Their grandfather was 23 years old when he married. Later, his three sons joined him to grow the business. Meanwhile, the manufacturing site was equipped with drying machinery which burnt sulphur to dry the fruits, as well as roasting machinery for nuts and seeds.

In 1962, the grandfather passed away and his elder son, together with his teenage sons Naser, Khosro and Parviz, moved to Tehran, the capital of Iran. He bought a store in a prestigious location in Tehran, as well as a warehouse and manufacturing site in Karaj, a city 50 kilometres from Tehran, and started the same business his father had years ago. After Iran's 1979 revolution, the two younger sons came back from Italy, where they had completed their higher education. The unstable institutional environment and unfavourable job market in Iran led them to decide to continue their father's business, despite the fact it was unrelated to their education.

THE CURRENT SITUATION

By 2010, the family business was vertically integrated as grower, manufacturer, retailer and exporter. The current mark-up figures, as well as the sales contribution of each section in the value chain, are illustrated in Exhibit 1.

Historically, nuts and dried fruit had been considered commodities in Iran. The three partner brothers felt an advantage in continuing their ancestors' way of differentiating the Tavazo products and tried to provide nuts and dried fruits as a branded product as opposed to a commodity product. The store had loyal customers who came to Vali-E-Asr Street just to buy nuts from Tavazo.

In mid-March, before Nowrouz[1] the first day of the New Year in the Iranian calendar, the nuts and dried fruits market in Iran would experience a seasonal surge in demand in addition to the steady demand throughout the year. Iranians had been celebrating Nowrouz for more than 2,500 years. Families had the tradition of getting together, visiting senior family members, and exchanging gifts. Guests were served mostly nuts, cookies and fruit during the Nowrouz parties. Yalda night, the longest night of the year, was the other occasion that created a seasonal demand for Tavazo. The night was celebrated by going to the house of the eldest person in the family, eating nuts, and reading Hafiz[2] poems.

Growing

The company grew only a small portion of what it sold, and this mainly focused on fruits. Most supplies were purchased from gardeners and farmers across Iran. The relatively strong financial resources of the business, as well as its insistence on high-quality products, had made the company's network of suppliers a valuable asset. The company purchased the farmers' products months in advance of the harvest season. This was considered an

---

[1]Nowrouz is the Persian word for new Iranian year and means "the new day.",

[2]Hafiz was a prominent Iranian poet who lived from 1320 to 1389 AD. His poems are intriguing and complex. In addition to reading the poems, some Iranians open his poem book and use the random poem that comes up for fortune-telling purposes. Although the majority of Iranians do not believe in the ability of poems to predict the future, they still do it for fun.

advantage against rivals who could not do so for financial reasons. Also, Tavazo knew that high-quality products were not abundantly available. Farms or gardens with high-quality nuts and fruits were limited. Therefore, the company did its best to develop a long-term relationship with its suppliers so that they would see little advantage in switching to Tavazo's rivals.

As part of a heart-healthy diet, many people ate tree nuts with some regularity, either as a snack, as part of a recipe or as some kind of treat. Unlike many vegetable plants, nut trees grew for a long time before their first harvest. A walnut tree, for instance, performed best after 30 years and a pistachio tree took approximately seven to ten years to reach significant production. Year-to-year production levels were not consistent, even after a tree had reached its prime. Many nut trees that produced a large crop one year would have a smaller yield the following year in order to build up internal nutrients.

Iran's diverse climate and agricultural lands made it a source of high-quality agricultural products which shaped a significant pillar of the Tavazo business in Iran and later in international markets. Iran was the largest producer of pistachios in the world followed by the United States, Turkey, Syria, and China (see Exhibit 2). Pistachios were a major contributor to Tavazo's sales, accounting for about 20 per cent of total sales. Other nuts and fruits for which Iran had a substantive worldwide market share were berries, apricots, dates, cherries, apples, figs, almonds, and walnuts. Exhibit 3 illustrates Iran's worldwide rank in the production of select fruits and nuts.

Manufacturing/Processing

Dried fruits and nuts, the two main categories of Tavazo products, had different manufacturing processes.

For nuts, time was of the essence once they were picked. They needed to be hulled promptly for proper dehydration. If the outer shell was left on too long, the quality of the nut (and, in turn, the price it could command) would decline. The next stage was sorting the nuts and categorizing by size. Then, if some nuts such as pistachios were supposed to be roasted, they would go through the salting and roasting stage and eventually be ready for delivery to retail stores.

Tavazo conducted all manufacturing operations in-house. Advanced drying and roasting machines were acquired to keep the quality of the products to a high standard.

The manufacturing process for dried fruits was different to some extent. After the fruit was picked from the tree, collected and transported to the manufacturing site, it was washed, sorted, had its stones removed, and was chopped or sliced. Then it was spread in pots and placed in shelves in an area which was smoked by burning sulphur and other drying materials.

Tavazo Retail Store

Retailing was the main focus of Tavazo Co. in Iran. The Tavazo brothers believed that presenting and selling nuts and dried fruits was a special skill that only retailers specializing in nuts and dried fruits held. Therefore, they devoted a significant effort to presentation, in-store packaging and sales at the retail store. Customers could browse the store, choose a product, fill special Tavazo bags with the desired amount and have the bags sealed with a packaging machine available in the store. Also, they could choose among the gift packaging boxes or baskets offered in the Tavazo store. Exhibit 4 illustrates decorative handicraft pots and some gift boxes and baskets specifically designed for presenting Tavazo products at its store in Toronto. Gift boxes/baskets carried a modest additional cost for customers.

Tavazo Brand and the Case of Imitators

The store was known to offer slightly premium-priced products. However, customers who had quality as their first priority would choose Tavazo for their purchases both year-round and for special occasions. By 2010, the brand was more of a retail brand and did not have as much strength in the upstream of the value chain. However, Naser Tavazo believed that the company's relationship with growers and its tendency towards careful and high-quality manufacturing had a significant impact on its success in retailing. Focusing on customer satisfaction and excellent product quality made the Tavazo brand well known among nuts retailers in Tehran, a city which had about 10 million of the 70 million people in Iran.

Trained in a traditional business environment, the Tavazo brothers were not originally aware of the importance of brand management. While the performance of the Tavazo nuts store was strengthening the brand, imitators started to pop up all around Tehran using Tavazo as the name of their stores. After a short time, there were 28 such stores in Tehran and other cities in Iran. This caused the family to register the brand and take imitators to court. Naser Tavazo remembered a quote by one fake Tavazo store owner in court:

> Well, I thought every store that sold nuts should be named Tavazo!

The fake stores were banned from using the Tavazo name as a result. However, afterwards each used a prefix or suffix to Tavazo both to keep the name and to obey the lawful order of the court.[3] Further follow-ups required more legal expenditure, which was recognized as uneconomic at the time.[4]

Iran's Economy

After Iran's revolution in 1979, the economic as well as business environment in Iran became volatile. Many large companies were nationalized and the economy moved toward more government intervention. Later, the Iranian government tried to change its policy towards more privatization and encouragement of foreign firms investing in Iran, a policy that met with little success.

Iran's economy had been performing relatively strongly in recent years, supported by high oil prices and expansionary fiscal and monetary policies.[5] Notwithstanding this, many believed the growth was not proportionate to the country's resources and potential. Iran's economy was marked by reliance on the oil sector, which provided the majority of its revenue. After oil, which constituted 80 per cent of the country's revenue, chemical and petrochemical products, fruits and nuts, and carpets held the next rankings in the country's sources of revenue. As of 2009, the country's major export partners were China (16.6 per cent), Japan (11.9 per cent), India (10.5 per cent), South Korea (7.5 per cent), and Turkey (4.4 per cent), and the major import partners were the United Arab Emirates (15.1 per cent), China (13.5 per cent), Germany (9.7 per cent), South Korea (7.2 per cent), Italy (5.3 per cent), Russia (4.8 per cent), and India (4.1 per cent).

The country had been using a managed floating exchange rate regime since unifying multiple exchange rates in March 2002. The rial, the local currency, had been pegged to the U.S. dollar ever since. This policy made the exchange rate unrealistically low and caused imports to seem more profitable and attractive than local production and exports.[6]

---

[3]Examples of the new names were Tavazo-North and Tavazo-Bazaar.

[4]$200,000 to $300,000 was the estimated legal cost for the follow-up at that time.

[5]International Monetary Fund's Country Report No. 10/74, www.imf.org, accessed September 23, 2010.

[6]The inflation rate was 13.6 per cent as of 2009 and 25.6 per cent as of 2008. The local currency would depreciate against the U.S. dollar each year by approximately these figures, whereas the controlled exchange rate policy would not let it happen in reality.

ENTERING CANADA

In the 1990s, Tavazo Co. was steadily moving forward and although it had started exporting nuts, especially pistachios, to some countries like the United States, it had not planned any significant growth. In 1988, after their father passed away, the three brothers decided to leave Iran in search of a more stable and developed environment in which to live, and to further their children's education. They began to consider whether they could expand their business into a foreign market. Among the countries on their list were the United States and Canada, the two major destinations for the Iranian diaspora. Due to a lower government tariff on nuts and dried fruits, they chose Canada. The U.S. government had encouraged aggressive growth in domestic U.S. pistachio production during the past three decades, the result of which was a tariff of around 400 to 500 per cent on imported pistachios. Coupled with the increased global demand, pistachio production had jumped from 1,179 tons of production in 1978 to around 175,000 tons in 2009.[7] The Tavazo partners believed that by entering Canada, they would have access to its southern neighbor too.

A friend helped the family to go to Canada and believed that the overall living conditions as well as the business environment fitted their situation well. As a result, the three owner/manager partners of Tavazo Co., together with their families, immigrated to Canada in 1995 under the business immigration program. After their initial settlement and adjustment to life in Toronto, the brothers contemplated starting a similar business in Canada.

Since they did not have an already developed market in Canada, and since the majority of their products were to be imported from Iran in bulk, they had to consider a warehouse to store the imported products to be sold over time. To be exported, nuts and dried fruits were to be packed, kept in industrial fridges, and transported by ships equipped with fridges.[8] The destination warehouse had to have refrigerators too. The brothers bought a warehouse facility in Richmond Hill (a suburb of Toronto) and equipped it with the necessary requirements.

For some products, the manufacturing process was split between Iran and Canada. A major example was roasted pistachios. In order for the product to be of the highest quality, the roasting process was to be done as close to the point of sale as possible. Therefore, pistachios were refrigerated and transported from Iran to Canada, and the roasting process was done in the company's facility in Richmond Hill. An additional advantage was that raw nuts could be kept in the refrigerated warehouses for up to two years without changing taste or color. Later, they could be roasted based on the demand from the market.

The brothers started by wholesaling the imported products and distributing them to retail stores. Although the majority of the target retail stores at that stage were those with ethnic products, mainly Iranian and Afghan stores in Toronto, the Tavazo brothers did their best to familiarize others with their high-quality Iranian nuts and dried fruits as well. In 2010, on average 70 per cent of the Tavazo retail store customers were Iranians and 30 per cent were other nationalities. Naser Tavazo was surprised at the growth of the number of Chinese customers, who constituted around half of non-Iranian customers.

> We had participated in trade fairs in Canada and the United States during our stay in Canada. When we presented samples of Iranian high quality pistachios and dried fruits, some said they had not seen such large pistachios before and they doubted if they were really pistachios.

---

[7] http://faostat.fao.org.

[8] The products were exported to Canada through a trading company based in Iran.

Notwithstanding this, the Iranian diaspora in Toronto was a proper starting point. The majority of Iranians abroad knew the brand and the quality positioning that the company had. They understood that the premium-priced high quality of Tavazo products compared very well to the extant Iranian and American pistachios and nuts available in the market. Naser Tavazo noted:

> When we were in Iran, we had export orders from Canada that were very price sensitive. They requested very low priced pistachios regardless of the size and quality. When we offered higher quality pistachios, they were wondering if the market would pay for the higher price. It took time and effort since we entered Canada to establish a market receptive to higher quality and premium priced products.

Meanwhile, the Tavazo brothers had to consider the management of the Iranian side of the business. On one hand, Tehran's retail store was still active and manufacturing facilities in Karaj needed supervision and control. With the expansion of the business, someone needed to be physically present in Iran to facilitate the day-to-day issues that could come up. Good relations with suppliers was historically a valuable asset for the company, but needed close supervision and maintenance. Another need for a physical presence of a decision maker was plausible change in regulations (e.g. customs tariffs, or other restrictions) in Iran. On the other hand, the brothers had all moved to Canada with their families. They decided to solve the need for managing Iran's facilities in a rotating way. Each of the three brothers would spend four months of the year in Iran and the rest in Canada. The respective brother's family had the choice of staying in Canada, or having a trip to Iran to reconnect with family and friends.

Dealing with retailers had its own challenges and difficulties. Many retailers were grocery stores with a variety of products and were not as specialized in the presentation and sales to customers of nuts and dried fruits. Retailers' poor sales performance together with their financial weakness resulted in an increase in the number of non-sufficient funds (NSF) cheques received by Tavazo. Many of the products were returned as a result. A more important factor for Tavazo that made its relations with retailers weaker was the harm to the Tavazo brand. Weak presentation and shelving of Tavazo products in stores made the brand decline, which was not in accordance with what Tavazo had strived for over the years.

The difficulties of dealing with retailers led the brothers to think of having their own retail store, as they had in Iran. They knew that they should have the store somewhere on Yonge Street near where the majority of Iranians were residing and where the Iranian Plaza was located. A Thornhill store (near Richmond Hill) was chosen after an attractive offer was received. The store was decorated like the company's retail store in Iran and products were presented similarly. The company stopped distributing to the stores that were harming the brand through poor sales performance and presentation. Later, in 2010, the company's second retail store in Canada was inaugurated in Richmond Hill.

Exhibits 5 and 6 illustrate the statement of earnings and the balance sheet of the company in 2009.

Products

Nuts, dried fruits and vegetables, spices, cookies and other Iranian ethnic food products such as saffron and caviar were the main products of Tavazo in Iran and Canada. Exhibit 7 includes some rough estimates of the sales contribution of each category. Among the products, pistachios were the largest contributor in the sales figures.

COMPETITORS

Retailing accounted for the majority of the Tavazo business. No significant Iranian competitor existed. Of course, the remaining Tavazo imitators in Iran sometimes attracted uninformed new customers by claiming that they were the original Tavazo. In Canada, the closest retailer to Tavazo in terms of product presentation was Bulk Barn. The market and product positioning of the companies, however, was quite different. For example, in October 2010 the average retail price for natural, salted, unbranded pistachios was $26 per kilogram at Bulk Barn, while Tavazo sold its pistachios for $20–$30 per kilogram, depending on size.

In wholesale, there were a few companies in Canada which could be considered Tavazo's competitors.[9] Naser Tavazo, however, believed that the limited strength of the company in the wholesale area had made it more cooperative than competitive. In fact, North American Co. and Tavazo sometimes sold Iranian and American nuts and pistachios to each other.

THE FUTURE OF TAVAZO

After a successful entry into Canada, the Tavazo family business was contemplating further growth. The challenge was to determine the direction of future business expansion. One option was to exploit current geographic markets, expanding more inside Iran and Canada and focusing more on the upstream of its value chain as a wholesaler. Alternatively, the business could pursue more geographic diversification and entry into other international markets with or without Iranian diasporas.

Iranian Diasporas

For Tavazo, Iranian diasporas could be a solid starting point at the time of entry to a new geographic market. The Tavazo brand recognition among Iranians was an asset that differentiated the company from its export and retail competitors. Iran had a vast diaspora abroad. Some had gone abroad in search of higher education and quality of life. Others had done so for political reasons. The United States hosted over a million Iranians, whose socioeconomic characteristics were reported to be significantly above average.[10] The United Arab Emirates, due to its proximity to Iran and its being a convenient hub for Iranian businessmen and tourists, hosted some 400,000 Iranians. Canada was third with some 120,000 Iranians, followed by Qatar and Germany, with numbers fast approaching 100,000 each. Other countries with large concentrations included Sweden, with approximately 54,000 Iranians; the United Kingdom, home to some 43,000 Iranians; and Israel, home to some 48,000 Persian Jews.

Candidate Cities

By 2010, the three brothers had had frequent discussions about how to expand their business. Whenever they discussed more geographic expansion (see Exhibit 8 for the top pistachio importer nations in the world), cities such as Vancouver, Los Angeles, and

---

[9]North America Co., Genesis Co. and John Vince Co. were some examples.

[10]The percentage of Iranians over 25 years old who had obtained a bachelor's degree or higher, for example, was 57.2 per cent in comparison to 24.4 per cent for the rest of the U.S. population. Percentage-wise, Iranian-Americans held five times the number of doctorates than the national average. Also, the per capita average income for Iranian-Americans was 50 per cent higher than that of the nation (Source: Iranian Studies Group at the Massachusetts Institute of Technology).

Dubai were mentioned. Business expansion in the current geographic markets of Tehran and Toronto often had its proponents in the family discussions as well. While the brothers were aware of the match between the company's capabilities and the opportunities for further geographic diversification, they were often concerned with the financial and managerial resources required for diversification. They had the experience of entering Canada and were therefore aware that each market entry entailed initial set-up and market penetration costs.

Recently, on a trip to visit some family and friends in Los Angeles, the city with the largest population of Iranians in the United States, Parviz Tavazo had collected some data on start-up costs for a new store and discussed these with his brothers when he came back to Toronto. The monthly rental cost for a store in a decent neighborhood and the required warehouse space cost were $2,500 and $1,500, respectively. He had estimated some $20,000 for store renovation and decoration and around $30,000 as the required financials for store and warehouse inventory. Furthermore, for store management, one of the family members would have to move and live in the new location. The other major restriction for Tavazo in the U.S. market was the challenge of importing Iranian products (especially pistachios) into the United States.

Having the second-highest population of overseas Iranians, Dubai was the other alternative on the table. Apart from the Iranian diaspora there, many Iranians traveled to Dubai for business, vacations, and shopping. The number of Iranians travelling to Dubai was 970,000 in 2009. The generally rich Arab population of Dubai could contribute to the potential target market as well. The costs and challenges of starting and running a business in Dubai were to a great extent similar to those in Tehran.

A major disadvantage of Dubai for the Tavazo family was its rather similar living environment to Tehran. Although the city was famous in the Middle East for its modern infrastructure, attractive entertainment and fancy shopping malls, the higher education system was no stronger than in Iran, if not weaker. No members of the Tavazo family seemed interested in moving to Dubai on a permanent basis.

Family Business Limitation

As in every family business, the number of family members was considered to be a limited resource. The three partner brothers had four children between them, who were mostly university or college students. Only one of them had a business-related education. The three others were studying law and engineering. Further expansion of the business would probably require the family partners to bring in a non-family member partner or manager. The traditional family ambiance in the business would require a radical change and adjustment to accommodate a non-family member.

The Tavazo brothers had to decide whether to enter new geographic markets, or to focus on the current markets and expand within them as retailers. They could also vertically integrate and expand by focusing more on the wholesale side. As a family, they had to contemplate their limitations and strengths in order to exploit opportunities and respond to threats to the business that they had inherited from their grandfather.

EXHIBIT 1: Tavazo Co. Value Chain Price Mark-Ups and Current Business Focus

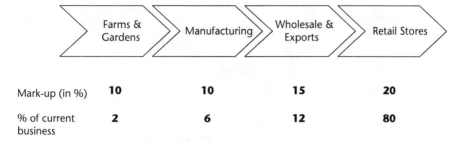

	Farms & Gardens	Manufacturing	Wholesale & Exports	Retail Stores
Mark-up (in %)	10	10	15	20
% of current business	2	6	12	80

EXHIBIT 2: Top Pistachio Producer Nations in the World

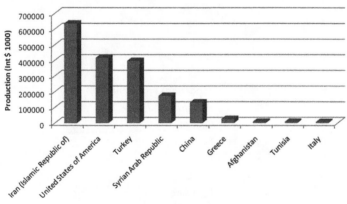

Top Production - Pistachios - 2008

Source: http://faostat.fao.org/site/339/default.aspx, accessed October 6, 2010.

EXHIBIT 3: Iran's Rank in Global Production of Nuts and Fruits

Global Production Rank (Value-based)	Commodity
1	Pistachios
1	Berries
2	Watermelons
2	Apricots
2	Cucumbers and gherkins
2	Dates
3	Cherries
3	Apples
3	Figs
4	Almonds, with shell
4	Walnuts, with shell
4	Indigenous sheep meat
6	Peas, dry
6	Hazelnuts, with shell
6	Chick peas
7	Peaches and nectarines
7	Tomatoes
7	Pumpkins, squash and gourds
7	Sour cherries
7	Onions, dry
7	Grapes
8	Tangerines, mandarins
8	Kiwi fruit
8	Oranges
8	Lemons and limes
8	Lentils
8	Spices
10	Potatoes
10	Persimmons
10	Tea
10	Natural honey
12	Plums and sloes
13	Melon seed
13	Eggplants (aubergines)

Source: http://faostat.fao.org.

EXHIBIT 4: Tavazo Company's Store Appearance and Gift Baskets

EXHIBIT 5: Tavazo Canada Co. Statement of Earnings (2009) (in '000)

Sales	$495
Cost of sales	$250
Gross margin	$245
Expenses	
Administrative and selling expenses	$ 70
Interest and bank charges	$ 5
Depreciation	$ 2
Total expenses	$ 77
Net profit (loss) before income taxes	$ 168

Note: Financial figures are estimates.

EXHIBIT 6: Tavazo Canada Co. Balance Sheet (2009) (in '000)

Current Assets	
Cash	$ 80
Accounts receivable	$ 10
Inventory	$ 60
Property, plant and equipment	$600
Subtotal	**$750**
Current Liabilities	
Bank indebtedness	$400
Accounts payable and accrued liabilities	$ 45
Subtotal	**$445**
Retained earnings	**$305**

Note: Financial figures are estimates.

EXHIBIT 7: Tavazo Canada Co. Product Sales Contribution

Product	Sales Contribution (%)
Pistachios	20
Almonds	10
Walnuts	15
Seeds	10
Hazelnuts	5
Cashews	5
Dried fruits, vegetable, spices, etc.	35

Source: Company estimates.

EXHIBIT 8: Top Pistachio Importing Nations (2007)

Rank	Area	Quantity (tons)
1	China, Hong Kong	55,031
2	Germany	41,373
3	China	29,915
4	Russian Federation	20,749
5	Netherlands	16,729
6	United Kingdom	15,040
7	Spain	13,101
8	Italy	11,533
9	France	11,073
10	Luxembourg	10,612
11	Belgium	9,235
12	India	7,777
13	Saudi Arabia	5,426
14	Mexico	4,879
15	Lebanon	4,613
16	Japan	3,742
17	Israel	3,478
18	Pakistan	3,359
19	Canada	3,241
20	Lithuania	3,180

Source: http://faostat.fao.org/site/342/default.aspx.

Canadian Solar

In late September 2009, Dr. Shawn Qu, CEO, president, chairman and founder of Canadian Solar, was constantly on the move. His company, a NASDAQ-traded solar cell and module manufacturer, had grown at a compound annual growth rate (CAGR) of 135.7 per cent over the last five years from $9.7 million in revenues in 2004 to $705 million in 2008 (see Exhibit 1 for key financials). The strong growth had been spurred by an increasing number of government incentive programs to encourage the adoption of solar photovoltaic (PV)[1] technology. For the past couple of years, solar energy was seen to be the world's fastest-growing industry. However, the credit crunch and global economic downturn combined with changes to Spain's incentive program had put the worldwide PV industry into over-supply for the first half of 2009. During the summer, demand changed again. Forecasts were exceeded, causing a temporary undersupply of ready-to-install solar modules. The fluctuating solar demand had caused analysts to change their financial outlook for Canadian Solar several times throughout 2009. In mid-2009, a Deutsche Bank analyst had predicted full-year sales to come in at $395 million with net losses at -$18 million, only to revise the outlook two months later to sales of $574 million and net income of $49 million.

Part of the increasing positive outlook was attributed to government incentive programs. Of particular interest to many players, including Canadian Solar, were proposed incentive programs in China and Canada. In Ontario, for example, the details of the provincial government's incentive program for green energy—the Feed-in Tariff (FIT) program—had

Jordan Mitchell wrote this case under the supervision of Professor Paul W. Beamish solely to provide material for class discussion. The authors do not intend to illustrate either effective or ineffective handling of a managerial situation. The authors may have disguised certain names and other identifying information to protect confidentiality.

Richard Ivey School of Business Foundation prohibits any form of reproduction, storage or transmission without its written permission. Reproduction of this material is not covered under authorization by any reproduction rights organization. To order copies or request permission to reproduce materials, contact Ivey Publishing, Richard Ivey School of Business Foundation, The University of Western Ontario, London, Ontario, Canada, N6A 3K7; phone (519) 661-3208; fax (519) 661-3882; e-mail cases@ivey.uwo.ca.

Copyright © 2010, Richard Ivey School of Business Foundation   Version: 2011-09-21

One time permission to reproduce granted by Richard Ivey School of Business Foundation on April 22, 2014.

IVEY | Publishing

[1]Solar photovoltaic (PV) technology is one of the main types of solar electric power. It is the main focus of this case.

just been released with specific requirements for domestic content. Although registered as a Canadian company, Canadian Solar had the bulk of its production operations in China; namely, seven facilities dedicated to the manufacture of different solar PV components. And, even though the company's "bases" were in China and Canada, 89.5 per cent of 2008 revenues came from Europe. Company management expected that to change rapidly as they were planning or had already established new sales offices in South Korea, Japan, China, Italy, Spain, Germany, the United States and Canada.

When looking at the relatively nascent and rapidly growing solar PV industry replete with a mix of diverse competitors, Qu and other Canadian Solar senior managers wondered how best to compete in the increasingly "global" PV industry.

SOLAR ENERGY

Solar energy was divided into three main categories: solar electric, solar thermal and concentrating solar. Solar electric converted the sun's energy into electricity and solar thermal used the sun for heating or cooling. Concentrating solar power mixed solar electric and solar thermal as it used small optical mirrors to collect solar energy and convert the sunlight to heat. The heat was then applied to a liquid or gas to turn a turbine, thereby creating electricity.

The other important distinction in solar energy was between "grid-tied" and "off-grid" applications. Grid-tied applications were solar-electric systems that were connected to an electricity utility grid (in nearly all jurisdictions, electricity utility grids were heavily regulated by government bodies and were often separate from electricity providers). Grid-tied applications were either "ground mount" or "rooftop"—ground mount applications were typically in a field or desert area and were either solar PV or concentrating solar power. Grid-tied rooftop projects ranged from one kilowatt to 10 kilowatts (kW) on residential homes to larger projects of 10 kilowatts to five megawatts (MW) on commercial buildings.

Off-grid applications were defined as a system completely independent of the main electricity grid. Off-grid applications ranged from tiny solar cells in pocket calculators to solar-thermal systems for hot water tanks in residential homes. In the last few years, off-grid applications had become popular for road lights, signs and parking meters whereby a solar module was placed on top of the apparatus to provide power at night through a battery. Off-grid applications were also seen as one solution to providing power in isolated rural areas.

PHOTOVOLTAIC CELLS[2]

The main tenet of solar-electric power was the photovoltaic (PV) cell, which used the "photovoltaic effect" to generate electricity. When sunlight hit a PV cell, electrons bounced from negative to positive, thus producing electricity. In order to generate electricity, a PV cell required a semiconductor material and positive and negative poles.[3]

The most common semiconductor material for PV cells was silicon.[4] For most solar applications, the silicon was refined to 99.9999 per cent purity, which was known as 6N silicon (the number "6" referred to the number of "9s"). Companies such as Canadian Solar

---

[2]This section draws upon *SBI*, "The U.S. Solar Energy Market in a World Perspective," March 2008, pp. 2–30.

[3]Phosphorous was often used as the negative pole and boron was often used as the positive pole.

[4]Silicon was found in sand, rocks or soil as silicon oxide ($SiO2$); the process for manufacturing silicon involved heating silicon oxide with a carbon material like coke or coal at high temperatures to remove the oxygen.

had commercialized products with lower grades of silicon for solar applications. For example, upgraded metallurgical-grade silicon (UMG-Si) was one such type of lower grade silicon. It was 99.999 per cent pure (or 5N for five "9s"). UMG-Si was a bi-product of the aluminum smelting business and historically had been less expensive than 6N silicon.

The three types of PV cells were polycrystalline ("poly"), monocrystalline ("mono") and amorphous ("thin-film"). Poly PV cells used silicon in its refined state whereas mono took the refinement a step further, thus creating higher efficiency (the drawback with mono PV was the higher cost of production vs. poly). The third type, thin-film, was substantially different in that it did not have crystalline silicon, but rather a painted or printed semi-conductor. There were six main types of materials used in thin-film, although three had not yet been proven to be commercially viable.[5]

The basic process of constructing a crystalline PV cell began by forming cylindrical ingots from the semi-conductor material. The ingots were then cut into very thin disc-shaped wafers. The wafer was etched with hydrofluoric acid and washed with water, creating a PV cell. To create a usable "solar module" (also called a "solar panel"), a series of PV cells were placed in between a sheet of glass held in by an aluminum frame and plastic backing connected to a cable plug. In most installations, a number of modules were used to make up an array. The array was then connected to an inverter (to convert the electricity from direct current (DC) to alternating current (AC)).

Solar modules were rated by their capacity in watts (W). Most solar PV modules were rated between 80W and 250W. Larger solar modules (200W +) weighed approximately 20 kilograms and were sized 1.6 meters long, one meter wide and four to five centimeters thick. Solar efficiency–the amount of sunlight energy converted to electricity–ranged between 12 and 18 per cent for most PV modules. However, breakthroughs were constantly being achieved–as of mid-2009, the highest PV cells had efficiency ratings slightly above 23 per cent. As a general rule of thumb, one to two per cent efficiency was deducted from the rating of the cell to determine the rating of the module (i.e. an 18 per cent efficient cell would have a 16-17 per cent efficient module).

The cost of PV cells was a constantly moving target. In securing contracts with large volumes, it was common for PV manufacturers to offer discounts of 10-30 per cent on the price of a module. In large-scale projects, many buyers saw PV modules more as a commodity product and were largely concerned with the price per watt. From 2007 to 2009, the selling price of a solar PV (from a PV module manufacturer to a customer) had increased slightly from $3.50 per watt to around $4 before dropping to approximately $2.50 per watt (put another way, the price for one 200W solar PV crystalline module was about $500 as of mid-2009).

A major driver behind the price of solar PV was the price of silicon. A temporary silicon shortage around mid-2008 pushed the spot price of silicon to over $500 per kilogram (up from around $25 per kilogram in 2004). However, by mid-2009, that price had fallen to around $60 per kilogram.[6] As the supply of silicon increased along with greater manufacturing efficiencies, the cost for crystalline PV modules was expected to fall below $1 per watt in two to three years.

Many industry insiders debated whether thin-film modules held more promise given their lower cost versus poly and mono modules. As of August 2009, the price of thin-film was

---

[5]The six types of materials used in thin-film technology were: amorphous silicon (a-Si); copper indium diselenide (CIS); copper indium gallium diselenide (CIGS); cadmium telluride (CdTe); gallium arsenide (GaAs); and thin-film silicon.

[6]Edgar Gunther, "Solar Polysilicon Oversupply until 2013?" August 3, 2009, http://guntherportfolio.com/2009/08/solar-polysilicon-oversupply-until-2013, accessed August 18, 2009.

reported at $1.76 per watt versus $2.50 per watt for silicon modules.[7] Despite silicon's current higher price, crystalline silicon supporters often pointed to the fact that thin-film would have trouble competing as the price of crystalline modules dropped. Additionally, poly and mono crystalline silicon modules typically enjoyed higher efficiencies than thin-film and required less space, fewer mounting systems and less cabling for the same power output.

In addition to the cost of the module itself, the cost of installation ranged from $4 to $8 per watt. Developers of utility-scale PV projects also had to be mindful of the real estate cost and electricity transmission costs. All tallied, the cost of solar PV was between 0.15 and 0.35 per kilowatt-hour (kWh) versus non-renewable sources of energy between 0.03 and 0.15 per kWh. As scale efficiencies grew along with technological breakthroughs, many insiders felt that the cost of solar would be competitive with non-renewable sources in a three to five year time horizon (this was referred to in the industry as reaching "grid parity").

THE GLOBAL SOLAR INDUSTRY

In 2008, solar PV experienced its largest increase to date by growing 5.6 gigawatts (60.8 per cent) to 14.73 gigawatts (GW) in 2008.[8] (On a global level, solar power accounted for under one per cent of all electricity generation.) Geographically, total installed capacity was split: 65 per cent in Europe, 15 per cent in Japan and eight per cent in the United States. In 2008, the strongest market was Spain, which represented nearly half of the installations due to its aggressive Renewable Energy Feed-in Tariff (referred to as REFIT or FIT) program, which guaranteed electricity rates for certain renewable projects. Even though Spain dominated the PV market in 2008, the Spanish government had placed a 500MW cap on annual installations for the next two years, given uncontrollable growth. Thus, Spanish PV installations were expected to drop substantially in 2009. Germany was the second largest market, capturing 26.7 per cent of worldwide installations during the year (Germany was one of the first countries in the world to introduce a FIT program). Other leading solar countries were the United States (six per cent of worldwide installations), South Korea (five per cent), Italy (4.9 per cent) and Japan (four per cent).

The future of the global PV market largely hinged on government initiatives and renewable support schemes. The European Photovoltaic Industry Association (EPIA) predicted two scenarios: a moderate scenario without heavy government incentives; and a policy-driven scenario with some support initiatives present. Under the first scenario, EPIA projected that cumulative solar PV power would equate to 54.8GW in 2013 (representing a CAGR of 30 per cent). The second scenario resulted in global installed PV power being 85.8GW by 2013 (CAGR of 42.3 per cent). Exhibit 2 shows some highlights from different world markets and Exhibit 3 gives EPIA's moderate and policy-driven scenarios for the top 13 markets.

Germany was expected to be the top market for the next few years, given the government's continuing Renewable Energy Law (*Erneuerbare-Energien-Gesetz* or EEG). As a successor to an earlier law passed in 1991, the EEG came into effect in 2000 as part of Germany's aim to derive 12.5 per cent of the country's energy from renewable sources by 2010 (the goal was surpassed in 2007 when Germany reached 14 per cent and was modified to reach a new goal of 27 per cent renewable by 2020). In 2009, the EEG was updated–for PV solar, the feed-in rates were between €0.33 and €0.43 per kWh ($0.46 to $0.60 per kWh) depending on the size of the project. The EEG called for those rates to decrease by eight to 10 per cent in 2010

---

[7]Quote from www.solarbuzz.com, accessed August 11, 2009.

[8]By comparison, the global installed capacity of wind power grew by 29 per cent from 93.9GW in 2007 to 121.2GW in 2008.

and nine per cent after 2011 but guaranteed the rates for a period of 20 years.[9] Despite the decreasing feed-in rates over the next few years, the EPIA believed that the rates were sufficient to encourage installations. Furthermore, PV solar was expected to remain strong as a result of high public awareness and support of renewables, the skilled PV industry and accessible financing opportunities through Kreditanstalt für Wiederaufbau (KfW).[10]

The story of Spain's boom and subsequent bust had become a hot topic in the solar industry. Through laws in 2004 and 2007, the Spanish government created an attractive Feed-in Tariff (FIT) giving up to €0.44 per kWh ($0.62 per kWh) for solar projects installed before September 2008. In spite of the original cap of 400MW, the country was flooded with demand for projects and in an 18-month period (from the passing of the 2007 law to September 2008), about 3GW of PV solar energy were installed. The heavily unanticipated installations were estimated to cost taxpayers about $26.4 billion, causing a public backlash against the government.[11] In 2008, the Spanish government placed a new cap of 500MW on installations and backed off the Feed-in Tariffs to €0.32 to €0.34 per kWh ($0.45 to $0.48 per kWh).[12] Despite the new cap, Spain was seen as a key market in the long term due to its government's high renewable target (the government wanted 20 per cent of consumed energy to come from renewables by 2020).[13]

Prior to the boom in Germany and Spain, Japan had had one of the strongest solar PV markets in the world up until 2006, when the government stopped supplying subsidies. The majority of its PV installations were in residential applications (different from other markets where commercial applications were the norm). Recently, the government had set new targets of reaching over 50GW of installed PV power by 2030 and had implemented national and regional support mechanisms. The country's Feed-in Tariff schemes promised an initial rate of 50 yen per kWh ($0.50 per kWh) for solar installations.[14]

The U.S. market also held great promise given President Obama's support of renewable energy and several state programs targeted at rolling out renewables. California, Arizona, New Mexico, Texas, Vermont and several other states had or were in the process of enacting incentives and stimulus programs. In 2010 many expected that the United States would enact a federal incentive program—one source suggested that the bill would guarantee a 10 per cent return over 20 years for renewable projects under 20MW.[15] Nearly all of the PV manufacturers had set up offices in the United States given the future potential in what many believed would become the world's largest market by the middle of the next decade.

[9]"Act Revising the Legislation on Renewable Energy Sources in the Electricity Sector and Amending Related Provisions–Renewable Energy Sources Act–EEG 2009," www.erneuerbare-energien.de/inhalt/42934/3860, accessed August 18, 2009.

[10]*European Photovoltaic Industry Association (EPIA),* "Global Market Outlook for Photovoltaics until 2013," March 2009, p. 7.

[11]Paul Voosen, "Spain's Solar Market Crash Offers a Cautionary Tale About Feed-In Tariffs," August 18, 2009, www.nytimes.com/gwire/2009/08/18/18greenwire-spains-solar-market-crash-offers-a-cautionary-88308. html?pagewanted=2, accessed August 18, 2009.

[12]"Spain Makes Changes to Solar Tariff," September 29, 2008, www.renewableenergyworld.com/rea/news/article/2008/09/spain-makes-changes-to-solar-tariff-53698, accessed August 18, 2009.

[13]"Plan de Energías Renovables 2011-2020," http://www.plane.gob.es/plan-de-energias-renovables-2011-2020, accessed August 17, 2009.

[14]*Energy Matters,* "Japan Announces Solar Feed In Tariffs," February 25, 2009, www.energymatters.com.au/index.php?main_page=news_article&article_id=335, accessed August 17, 2009.

[15]James Murray, "US lawmakers outline plan for feed-in tariff bill," *Business Green,* August 5, 2009, http://www.businessgreen.com/business-green/news/2247352/lawmakers-outline-plan-feed, accessed August 19, 2009.

A number of other policies and support mechanisms had also been implemented or were in the design phase in countries as far-reaching as Italy, Greece, France, Israel, South Korea, China and Canada.

In Canada, the main program was Ontario's FIT, announced in early 2009 with a start date of October 1, 2009. Ontario's FIT would replace the 2006 Standard Offer Program, which gave PV solar rates of C$0.42 per kWh and other renewable sources rates of C$0.11 per kWh.[16] In North America's first FIT program, renewables could garner between Cdn$0.08 and Cdn$0.802 per kWh depending on the scale of the project. Smaller-scale solar rooftop systems for residential homes would receive the highest rates, between Cdn$0.539 and Cdn$0.802 per kWh. Larger-scale solar (less than 10MW) would receive Cdn$0.443 per kWh. The program called for domestic content to make up 40 per cent on projects less than 10kW and 50 per cent of the project cost on projects over 10kW (after January 1, 2011, domestic requirements would rise to 60 per cent). See Exhibit 4 for more details on Ontario's FIT program.

In July 2009, the Chinese government announced major subsidies for utility-scale solar projects. The conditions of receiving the subsidies required that the project have a minimum of 300kW peak, and be built in one year with longevity of 20 years. The subsidy would be 20 yuan ($4) per watt with the overall goal of reaching 10GW of installed power by 2020.[17]

PLAYERS IN THE GLOBAL PV MARKET

Globally, there were hundreds of PV cell and module manufacturers. On the supply side of PV manufacturers, there were raw material suppliers for goods such as silicon, glass, substrates, metal and cables as well as specialized equipment manufacturers to make solar components such as furnaces, sawing machines, printing machines and laminators. On the buyer side of PV manufacturers, there were several potential customers. Consumer electronics, automotive and industrial product companies integrated solar cells into their products for resale (examples ranged from solar cells in garden lamps through to cells used on marine buoys). For grid-tied applications, the typical customers were project developers, utility companies, solar installation companies, distributors, wholesalers, governments, construction companies and building owners.

Barriers to entry were considered fairly low due to the low capital requirements and medium-low technological know-how to make a PV module. However, product warranties were one barrier that was becoming more important. For example, smaller manufacturers struggled to sell modules for use in bank-financed large-scale projects because of requirements from the banks for greater assurances that 25-year product performance warranties would be upheld. Some analysts also predicted more vertical integration both from silicon producers, specialized suppliers of PV cells and customers (such as project developers). Complementary players such as inverter manufacturers or rack suppliers were not considered to pose an immediate vertical integration threat.

The top 10 producers accounted for 55.3 per cent of PV module sales in 2008. Exhibit 5 shows the market shares of both PV module and PV cell producers. Some observers divided the market into three groups based on geography, market strength, size and quality perception. The first group competed on the basis of price and used China as a manufacturing base, the second was made up of up-start companies with a point of technological differentiation,

[16]"Ontario's Standard Offer Contracts," March 22, 2006, www.energyalternatives.ca/content/SOC.htm, accessed August 18, 2009.

[17]Jim Bai and Leonora Walet, "China offers big solar subsidy, shares up," *Reuters*, July 21, 2009.

and the third consisted of Japanese electronic firms with established brand names. The market could also be divided simply into: more recent start-ups and established incumbents.

A powerful contingent of emerging PV module companies were the four companies which used China as their primary manufacturing base: Suntech, Yingli Green, Trina Solar and Canadian Solar. All were vertically integrated in that they produced ingots, wafers, cells and modules and used their access to low-cost labor for a cost advantage. Canadian Solar's management believed its company to be unique in that it combined elements of Western management and engineering with a low-cost Chinese production base.

Of the specialized start-ups, two main groups of companies existed: those producing complete PV modules and those focusing on the production of PV cells only. PV module start-ups competed more on tailored propositions, customer relationships and service, technological differences and price. For example, First Solar used Cadmium Telluride as a semi-conductor, which allowed it to deliver a lower price per watt. SunPower competed by offering solar systems complete with inverters for easy residential and commercial installation. Both U.S. companies had the majority of their production in low-cost Asian countries, namely Malaysia and the Philippines.

Up-starts such as Germany's Q-Cells and Solar World, Taiwan's Motech and Gintech and China's JA Solar produced PV cells only and sold the cells to module producers. Q-Cells had surpassed Sharp in terms of total PV cell production in the last couple of years. The five PV cell companies competed on technology, relationships with module producers and price.

Of the incumbents, Japanese electronics multinationals such as Sharp, Kyocera and Sanyo all had long histories developing PV solar. They typically competed on the strength of their brand recognition, research and development, strong distribution and in some cases, exclusive rights with large-scale customers. Sharp had begun developing PV solar in 1959 and had dominated the world market for much of the last 50 years. While Sharp had historically sold mono and poly crystalline PV, they had begun investing in thin-film technology in 2005. In addition to its four plants in Japan, the company produced PV solar products in the United States, the United Kingdom and Thailand. To expand production even further, Sharp was seeking joint venture partners to build solar module factories in other countries (in late 2008, the company inked a deal with Italy's Enel for a joint venture plant in Italy).

Japan's second largest PV solar manufacturer, Kyocera, produced a range of PV products in a network of factories split between Japan, China, the Czech Republic and Mexico. Japan's third major player, Sanyo, produced nearly all of its PV offerings in its home country. It had invested heavily in developing its own thin-film technology (called HIT for Heterojunction with Intrinsic Thin-layer), which it claimed had the highest efficiency of any solar PV cell in the world (its efficiency was 23 per cent).[18] Sanyo sold its complementary batteries with its PV solar products and had reorganized its business to satisfy its master plan of becoming a "leading provider of environment and energy-related products."[19] Sanyo's strong position in PV solar and related products was one of the key reasons for Panasonic taking a key ownership stake in Sanyo in late 2008.[20]

Other multinationals also participated in PV solar, namely, Japan's Mitsubishi, Britain's BP and U.S. companies General Electric and Chevron. Mitsubishi began developing PV solar technology in the 1970s and offered complete packages including the PV module and

---

[18]"Sanyo Develops HIT Solar Cells with World's Highest Energy Conversion Efficiency of 23.0%," May 21, 2009, http://us.sanyo.com/News/SANYO-Develops-HIT-Solar-Cells-with-World-s-Highest-Energy-Conversion-Efficiency-of-23-0-, accessed August 16, 2009.

[19]Sanyo Annual Report 2008, December 31, 2008, p. 9.

[20]"Panasonic and SANYO Agree to Capital and Business Alliance," http://sanyo.com/news/2008/12/19-1.html, accessed August 17, 2009.

inverter. As of 2009, Mitsubishi claimed to have one of the highest efficiencies of any poly PV cell (18.9 per cent).[21] Its production capacity was about 200MW. BP Solar also had about 30 years of history in the solar industry. With a capacity of 200MW, it produced poly and mono PV cells and modules in five plants located in Australia, Spain, the United States, India, and China. However, in a recent move to focus on its core business of petroleum, its parent company, BP, had announced that it would be closing factories in Australia, Spain and the United States and shifting to a mix of its lower cost plants and sub-contractors in China.[22] (Shell divested its solar operations in 2006 and 2007—the majority of the assets were purchased by Germany's SolarWorld.[23])

BACKGROUND ON CANADIAN SOLAR

Canadian Solar was established by Qu in October 2001 in Markham, Ontario. In tandem, a production facility in Changshu, China, registered as CSI Solartronics was set up as a wholly owned subsidiary. Qu, a graduate of applied physics at Tsinghua University (B.Sc.) and the University of Manitoba (M.Sc.), had completed a doctoral degree in material science from the University of Toronto (Ph.D) and extensive post-doctorate work on semiconductor optical devices and solar cells. In 1996, he joined Ontario Hydro (now Ontario Power Generation) as a research scientist, where he worked on the development of a next-generation solar technology called Spheral Solar™. In 1998, he joined ATS (Automation Tooling Systems), working in several capacities such as product engineer, director for silicon procurement, solar product strategic planning as well as technical vice president for one of ATS's subsidiaries.

Qu left ATS to establish Canadian Solar; he commented on the opportunity he saw at the time:

> In 2001, solar was still a very small industry. A lot of my colleagues from the PhD program in applied physics were involved in fibre optics for the telecommunications industry. I believed that solar had great prospects and thought I could easily spend my career in the solar industry. Because solar was such a small part of ATS, it did not get a lot of management attention. Around 2000, I started thinking of starting my own company and worked on the business plan. At that time, the major players were small solar divisions in multinationals. My idea largely focused on areas that I felt they were not addressing: rural electrification with solar, the low-cost production of solar cells and solar modules, building integrated solar products and consumer solar products. It just so happened the first product was a consumer solar product for the automotive industry.

Canadian Solar's first contract was to manufacture and sell a solar charger to Audi-Volkswagen for use in its automobiles being manufactured in Mexico. Audi-Volkswagen required that Canadian Solar became ISO9001 and ISO16949 certified. Management saw the certification as an essential part of raising Canadian Solar's quality credibility in the early stages of the company. Canadian Solar established two additional solar module manufacturing plants in Suzhou, China, incorporated as separate companies: CSI Solar Technologies in August 2003; and CSI Solar Manufacturing in January 2005. The company purchased solar

---

[21]"Mitsubishi Electric Breaks Own Record With World's Highest Conversion Efficiency Rate Of 18.9% For Multi-Crystalline Silicon Photovoltaic Cells," February 18, 2009, www.mitsubishielectricsolar.com/news, accessed August 19, 2009.

[22]Ed Crooks, "Back to petroleum," *Financial Times*, July 7, 2009.

[23]Terry Macalister, "Big Oil lets sun set on renewables," *The Guardian*, December 11, 2007, www.guardian.co.uk/business/2007/dec/11/oil.bp, accessed August 19, 2009.

cells and silicon raw materials from a small group of companies such as Swiss Wafers (Switzerland), Kunical (United States), Luoyang Zhong Gui (China) and LDK (China).

While continuing to supply Audi-Volkswagen (eventually receiving the accolade of class A supplier), Canadian Solar's management saw a great opportunity to develop solar modules for electricity generation for residential and commercial applications in 2004. Qu commented:

> In early 2004 with the change of Germany's FIT program, I identified a major increase in demand for solar PV modules for buildings. Within three to four months, we were able to switch gears to large solar modules. The decision to spin-off the company from ATS in 2001 when we did was vital–had I waited until 2004, I would not have had the time to build the team and capabilities to make this switch into larger solar modules.

By the end of 2004, nearly three-quarters of Canadian Solar's sales were derived from selling standard solar modules to distributors and system integrators based in Germany, Spain and China. The company made initial contact with its customers through international trade shows. By the end of 2005, the top five customers accounted for 68.2 per cent of total sales. Most sales were made with non-exclusive, three-month sales contracts. It was normal that the customer paid 20 to 30 per cent of the purchase as prepayment and the remainder in advance of the shipment from China. In China, sales of solar modules were associated with development projects in conjunction with Chinese governmental organizations and the Canadian International Development Agency (CIDA)–for example, in the spring of 2005, the company installed a demonstration power plant in a rural area of the province of Jiangsu.

With sales of standard solar modules accelerating, Canadian Solar turned to venture capital (VC) funding. Qu stated: "Up until 2005, we had grown without any VC involvement. We received an investment from HSBC and Jafco Ventures [a VC from Japan with $350 million under management] and then started preparing for an IPO." In November 2006, the company listed on the Nasdaq, raising $115.5 million. The proceeds were to be used to purchase and prepay for solar cells and silicon (35 per cent); expansion into solar cell manufacturing (45 per cent); and general funding purposes (20 per cent). The initial public offering (IPO) enabled it to expand into solar cell manufacturing, resulting in the following facilities: CSI Solarchip for solar cells and modules; and CSI Advanced and CSI Luoyang for solar modules. By the end of 2007, the company had established four solar cell production lines, taking total cell capacity to 120MW.

Canadian Solar's management established a sales office of two people in Phoenix, Arizona, and a European office of three people near Frankfurt, Germany in December 2007. All sales in Spain were done through an independent distributor. As Qu said: "We serviced these growing markets from China and Canada. The decision to open up the offices in 2007 was a logical move given that the majority of sales were coming from those markets." On the production side, the company expanded to seven factories including a solar module manufacturing site in Changshu and an ingot and wafer manufacturing site in Luoyang. The continued expansion in China was complemented by a high-profile BIPV (Building Integrated Photovoltaic) module roof project as part of the Beijing 2008 Olympic Games. At the close of 2008, the company was recognized as one of the top 10 fastest-growing companies in China by Deloitte Asia, given its sales had more than doubled from $302.8 million in 2007 to $705 million in 2008.

In 2009, the company underwent a number of changes in its international configuration. To respond to market opportunity in South Korea, it established a two-person sales office. In Canada, it established an international development office of three people in Ottawa to focus specifically on projects in Latin America and the Middle East, given its working history with CIDA. In the United States, the company moved the Phoenix office to San Ramon, California, to be located closer to the heart of the U.S. solar movement and to take advantage of the favorable Californian incentives. It opened a warehouse at the office site to store finished solar modules. In China, it opened a PV research and development facility at its head office in Suzhou. As of the end of 2008, the company had 3,058 employees: 2,742 in manufacturing, 251 in general and administrative, 36 in research and development and 29 in sales and marketing.[24]

CANADIAN SOLAR'S MODEL

The company described itself as an "inverted flexible vertical integration business model." This meant that the company had higher capacity as it went further downstream in the manufacturing process of each component of a solar module. Graphically, this could be illustrated as:

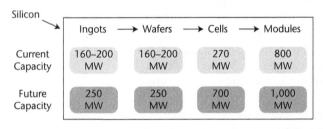

The rationale behind the "inverted vertical integration" model was to allow for flexibility in short-term demand shifts by purchasing ingots, wafers and cells from other manufacturers and to free the company from the capital investment required to have equal capacity of each component. The company believed that it would lead to a lower manufacturing cost base in the long term as well as superior production yields, better inventory control and efficient cash management.

Canadian Solar also had been one of the first solar companies to initiate a recycling process for reclaimable silicon from discarded, broken or unused silicon wafers and ingots at two of its plants in Suzhou and Changshu. The process involved a substantial amount of labour and analysts believed that Canadian Solar had a competitive advantage in recycling silicon. However, in the 2008 Annual Report, the company stated: "As a result of the oversupply of silicon materials that developed in the fourth quarter of 2008, we expect this aspect of our operation to be less significant in the foreseeable future."[25] The company also became a member of the Belgian organization PV CYCLE in mid-2009. PV CYCLE promoted a take-back and recycling of PV modules that had reached the end of their useful life.[26]

Products

Canadian Solar offered a portfolio of products ranging from 0.3W to 300W. It split its offerings into two main divisions: standard and specialty. The company used both its own branding and manufactured white label products for other OEMs. With a few exceptions, all products were standardized for the global market. The company offered three types of products:

1. Standard: Standard modules were used for both ground mount and rooftop systems and were available in both mono and poly.
2. e-Modules: e-Modules were a recent product introduction which were aimed at providing a lower-cost product for smaller roof-top systems. e-Modules were lower cost because they used upgraded metallurgical-grade silicon (Umg Si) instead of pure silicon.
3. BIPV (Building Integrated Photovoltaic): Finally, BIPV were intended to be used as a building material in a roof, skylight or façade.

Standard modules were all tested and certified by various international standards. Product performance warranties were normally 25 years depending on the product. Prices were negotiated on the quantity ordered but were between $2 and $3 per watt. Margins ranged from 13 to

---

[24]Canadian Solar Annual Report 2008, 20-F, www.sec.gov, December 31, 2008, p. 74.

[25]Canadian Solar Annual Report 2008, 20-F, www.sec.gov, December 31, 2008, p. 30.

[26]"Canadian Solar Becomes Member of PV Cycle," July 21, 2009, http://phx.corporate-ir.net/phoenix.zhtml?c=196781&p=irol-news, accessed November 20, 2009.

18 per cent for standard and e-Modules and were 15 to 20 per cent on BIPV products. Canadian Solar's strategy was to maintain comparable prices to its primary Chinese competitors.

Specialty products included items to be used in battery chargers, GPS tracking systems, street and traffic lights, garden lights, marine lights and other home systems. Prices varied greatly depending on the level of customization—margins were usually around 15 to 20 per cent for specialty items.

Production Facilities

The company produced all of its products in its seven plants in China. The seven factories had been set up because of Chinese government incentives to establish operations in specific jurisdictions. For example, the Luoyang factory, located approximately eight hours by road from the central offices of Suzhou, was set up at the request of the government-owned silicon supplier in Luoyang.

In late 2008, Canadian Solar's then vice president of corporate and production development, Robert Patterson, was asked if production facilities would be opened closer to areas of demand:

> Not yet. We got our hands full in terms of how fast we're growing and also our capital requirements going into our current plants. We'd probably have to stabilize our current supply stream and then we would address whether we'd want to do assembly plants in various locations. If you're based in China, you have an advantage on an assembly basis, mainly because of the labour content of a solar cell or solar module. So, it would be a future thing, not ruled out.[27]

Sales Offices

Canadian Solar had seven sales offices outside of China (domestic Chinese sales were done primarily from Suzhou and Shanghai). In mid-2009, the company opened an office in Kitchener, Ontario, and shifted its official headquarters there from Markham. The Kitchener office (eight people) was responsible for the development of Canadian sales with a focus on the Ontario market, given the recently introduced FIT program. The Ottawa office (four people) was the international sales office for projects in the Middle East and Latin America and initially also housed the company's investor relations manager. Opportunities in the Middle East and Latin America were developed through a combination of trade shows, bids on public tenders and CIDA-sponsored development projects.

The United States was primarily covered through the 10-person facility in San Ramon, California, which included business development managers and a warehouse. Additionally, there was a sales representative located in a satellite office in New York State.

The company's office in Munich, Germany, was responsible for the coordination of all sales efforts in Europe. The top five German customers accounted for just over half of the company's corporate sales. The customers were utility-scale developers and distributors of roof-top solar projects. With a total of 15 people, the office was responsible for managing the independent sales agent in Spain as well as establishing new offices.

Canadian Solar served the Asian market through its sales forces at the principal Chinese office in Suzhou and offices in Seoul, South Korea (two people), and Tokyo, Japan (eight people). In Japan, due to the popularity of solar PV in residential applications, Canadian

[27]Interview with Robert Patterson, VP corporate & production development, by Mark Osborne, Photovoltaics International, December 3, 2008, www.pv-tech.org/solar_leaders_video_clips/_a/canadian_solar_vp_robert_patterson_talks_umg_si_product_lines_150mw_plus.

Solar was developing a complete systems package, which included the solar PV modules, racking systems, inverter and monitoring devices.

Marketing

Due to the small size of the PV industry, the company focused on building its brand through industry tradeshows and publications such as *Photon International* and *PV Technology*. In early 2009, the company had recently re-branded itself to emphasize its "Canadian" roots by changing its logo to read "Canadian Solar" instead of the previous "CSI" (standing for "Canadian Solar International"). Hanbing Zhang, the company's director of global marketing, explained:

> No one really understood what CSI meant—with Canadian Solar, we don't need to explain. As a country, Canada is well received around the world. People from all over have a connection to Canada; for example, Koreans send their kids to learn English in Canada and many Europeans have relatives in Canada. It is seen as a peaceful and environmentally aware country. By emphasizing the Canadian image, we can further differentiate from the other Chinese manufacturers.

Development Projects

In addition to its role as a producer, Canadian Solar was becoming more active in the development of both ground-mount and rooftop commercial projects. Typically, Canadian Solar partnered with a solar developer, system integrator or utility to carry out the tasks involved in commercial solar development such as engineering, construction, financing, negotiation of the power purchase agreements (PPAs) and the operation of the solar project.

In its largest project to date, in 2009 Canadian Solar formed a strategic alliance with China-based Guodian Power Development to build and operate two 50MW PV power plants in China. Historically, most of Canadian Solar's development projects had been focused on providing power to rural areas in China.[28]

Financials

For the past three years, Canadian Solar posted losses. In 2008, the net loss was $9.4 million. The global economic crisis caused the company to have higher than normal interest expenses on short-term loan facilities, increases in the allowance for doubtful accounts and a major inventory write-down (caused by both a weakening in demand and the rapidly declining price of silicon).

In June 2009, Deutsche Bank analysts projected Canadian Solar's revenues to be $395 million with a loss of $18 million and wrote:

> [Canadian Solar] is a smaller, upstream solar PV company, struggling with weak fundamentals in a highly competitive industry where capital is still a constraint for its solar PV customers amidst a credit contraction environment. Upside risks include: a rapid demand rebound, minimal average sales price declines, a weakening U.S. dollar and more favorable policy and incentive programs. Downside risks include: gauging end demand for company products amidst industry demand destruction, rapid average sales price declines/high input costs dislocating business model assumptions, capital constraints hindering operational flexibility and managing currency dislocations.[29]

---

[28]Canadian Solar Prospectus, October 12, 2009, www.sec.gov, p. 5.

[29]"Canadian Solar: Notes from the Deutsche Bank alternative energy conference," *Deutsche Bank*, June 10, 2009, p. 3.

However, by August 2009, Deutsche Bank had raised its estimates to revenues of $574 million and net income of $49 million for 2009, stating:

> Canadian Solar posted 2Q09 results well ahead of expectations on strong shipments growth [in markets like the Czech Republic, Korea and Italy], further aided by favorable FX trends (i.e., $0.14 contribution to EPS) and prior inventory write-downs... we believe the company is gaining share in new markets.[30]

Deutsche Bank rated the stock a "hold" and Oppenheimer rated it an "outperform." As of September 25, 2009, Canadian Solar's stock price closed at $16.74 (the 52-week range was from $3.00 to $19.91).

CONSIDERATIONS GOING FORWARD

Some industry observers believed that the solar PV industry needed to regroup and get back to basics. Consultants from BCG wrote:

> In order to thrive in and not merely survive the harsh reality of today's market, PV suppliers need to take a critical look at their business model and operations... . To negotiate this far more challenging environment, PV suppliers will need to refocus their attention on the basics: relative cost position, go-to-market effectiveness, and an understanding of key market segments and channels.[31]

Having been on a track of dynamic growth since inception, it was now Canadian Solar's opportunity to strategically think about any changes to its international strategy. Qu stated:

> In terms of the solar industry, the first step is to determine the market and follow the renewable policies closely. For the next two to three years, we've determined that we will be focusing on 10 countries: Canada, China, Germany, Spain, Italy, France, Czech Republic, South Korea, Japan and the United States.

> There is plenty of competition. First, the established players such as Sharp and Sanyo have powerful brands. From a technology standpoint, a company like FirstSolar clearly has a different product with their thin-film technology and the question is, "Which technology wins?" The other U.S. competitor is SunPower, which has high efficiency and a high price premium. Out of the Chinese producers, Suntech is slightly different than others since they combine Australian engineering with Chinese production much like we combine Canadian engineering with Chinese production. The other potential threat is the possibility that some upstream silicon makers will adapt their business models to start producing modules downstream. After the financial crisis, I think the industry realizes that silicon is not precious and there could be an increasing trend for silicon producers to move downstream to capture more value.

> When I look back at my original business plan, we've greatly exceeded our initial revenue projections. The business has changed substantially from its initial focus—this illustrates that one of the key skills in this industry, and any start-up for that matter, is the ability to see changes in the marketplace and adapt the business accordingly.

---

[30]"Canadian Solar: New market penetration drives solid shipments," *Deutsche Bank*, August 6, 2009, p. 1.

[31]"Back to the Basics: How Photovoltaic Suppliers Can Win in Today's Solar Market," *The Boston Consulting Group*, p. 1.

EXHIBIT 1: Canadian Solar Financials

USD million, Years ended Dec. 31	2006	2007	2008
Net Revenues	**68.2**	**302.8**	**705.0**
Cost of revenues	55.9	279.0	634.0
Gross Profit	**12.3**	**23.8**	**71.0**
Operating expenses:	0.0	0.0	0.0
Selling expenses	2.9	7.5	10.6
General and administrative expenses	7.9	17.2	34.5
Research and development expenses	0.4	1.0	1.8
Total operating expenses	11.2	25.7	46.9
Income (loss) from operations	**1.1**	**−2.0**	**24.1**
Other income (expenses):			
Interest expense	−2.2	−2.4	−11.3
Interest income	0.4	0.6	3.5
Loss on change in fair value of derivatives	0.0	0.0	0.0
related to convertible notes	−8.2	0.0	0.0
Gain on foreign currency derivative assets	0.0	0.0	14.5
Debt conversion inducement expense	0.0	0.0	−10.2
Foreign exchange gain (loss)	−0.5	2.7	−20.1
Other−net	0.4	0.7	0.0
Income (loss) before income taxes	−9.0	−0.4	0.5
Income tax benefit (expense)	−0.4	0.2	−9.9
Net loss	−9.4	−0.2	−9.4
Loss per share−basic and diluted	−0.5	0.0	−0.3
Shares used in computation−basic and diluted	19.0	27.3	31.6
Total current assets		219.9	339.0
TOTAL ASSETS		**284.5**	**570.7**
Total current liabilities		59.2	172.7
TOTAL LIABILITIES		**158.2**	**238.6**
Total stockholders' equity		126.3	332.2
TOTAL LIABILITIES AND STOCKHOLDERS' EQUITY		**284.5**	**570.7**

Source: Canadian Solar Annual Report, 20-F, www.sec.gov, December 31, 2008, p. 54.

EXHIBIT 2: Highlights From World Markets

Country	Comments
Germany	Leading market for solar PV with strong financing available
	Over 40,000 people were employed in the PV sector
	The Renewable Energy Law (Erneuerbare-Energien-Gesetz or EEG) promised rates of $0.46 to $0.60 per kWh for solar PV with digression in 2010 and 2011
	The country had some of the world's largest solar parks (e.g. the 40MW Waldpolenz Solar Park)
	Over 100,000 roof-top solar PV applications had been installed
Spain	Historical strength had been on utility-scale solar parks
	The Spanish market would undergo a major decrease in 2009 and 2010 due to the government's cap of 500MW
	Potential growth beyond 2013 was still seen to be strong due to experience with renewables and long-term targets

EXHIBIT 2: (Continued)

Country	Comments
Japan	Historical strength had been with solar PV on residential homes due to the "Residential PV System Program," which ended supplying subsidies in 2006
	In December 2008, the government was renewing its focus on solar with the aim to have solar power installed on 70 per cent of new homes. Furthermore, it wanted 14GW of installed PV power by 2020
United States	The Investment Tax Credit (ITC), state programs and the potential of a federal-level FIT were expected to boost solar PV in 2010 and beyond
	The challenge was seen to be a lack of financing
	The United States had some of the world's largest solar PV parks (e.g. Nellis Solar Power Plant, NV 15MW)
	California was the leading state for solar roof installations due to programs such as the "Million Solar Roofs" vision and the "California Solar Initiative"
Italy	The country had a competitive FIT program and a net-metering scheme (allowing PV system owners to get credits for their produced electricity)
	Italy had no cap for PV installations
South Korea	The country's FIT program was seen as promising; however, the devaluation of the Korean currency and the placement of a cap of 500MW on the FIT in October 2008 were expected to dampen the number of installations
	Observers believed that strong political support for solar PV still existed and expected the market to grow in 2010
France	The government had a favorable FIT program for BIPV; however, the growth had been stalled by long administrative procedures to connect the systems to the grid
	France was expected to adopt a FIT program for non-BIPV applications for commercial roofs, which would be the source of its growth over the next few years
Czech Republic	The Czech government introduced a FIT program in 2008 and was one of the premiere Eastern European growth countries for solar PV
Portugal	Portugal had several large-scale PV and concentrating solar power plants but had not yet introduced a FIT program or similar incentive scheme
Greece	Greece was seen to have one of the most favorable FIT programs in Europe
	The country had a pipeline of 3.5GW of PV projects
	Bureaucracy and lengthy administrative procedures were seen to be barriers for installations in 2008
Israel	Solar-thermal (solar water heaters) were very popular, being present in 90 per cent of Israeli homes
	Israel was extensively used for research and development due to the country's high level of solar irradiance
	A FIT scheme was passed in 2008 and the market was expected to grow
India	India was expected to develop slowly but held great potential due to efforts for both on and off-grid projects (off-grid projects were a specialty area for project developers—e.g. Shell Solar had had a division dedicated to off-grid solar PV development in India)
China	The new incentive program was expected to boost solar PV applications both for residential, commercial and utility-scale applications
Canada	Ontario's solar PV applications were expected to grow under the proposed FIT program
	The FIT program required that for projects up to 10kW, the minimum domestic content was 40 per cent and for projects greater than 10kW, the domestic content was 50 per cent for projects with a commercial operation date prior to January 1, 2011. For projects thereafter, domestic content needed to be 60 per cent

Source: Compiled by case writer.

EXHIBIT 3: EPIA Predictions by Market

Country	Type	2006	2007	2008	2009E	2010E	2011E	2012E	2013E
Belgium	EPIA Moderate	2	18	48	100	70	80	90	100
	EPIA Policy-Driven				175	125	130	140	160
Czech Republic	EPIA Moderate	0	3	51	80	90	110	140	170
	EPIA Policy-Driven				100	160	200	220	240
France	EPIA Moderate	8	11	46	250	340	600	900	1,000
	EPIA Policy-Driven				300	500	850	1,200	1,400
Germany	EPIA Moderate	850	1,100	1,500	2,000	2,000	2,300	2,600	3,000
	EPIA Policy-Driven				2,500	2,800	3,200	3,600	4,000
Greece	EPIA Moderate	1	2	11	35	100	100	100	100
	EPIA Policy-Driven				52	200	450	700	900
Italy	EPIA Moderate	13	42	258	400	600	750	950	1,250
	EPIA Policy-Driven				500	800	1,100	1,400	1,600
Portugal	EPIA Moderate	0	14	50	40	50	100	160	230
	EPIA Policy-Driven				50	80	180	350	500
Spain	EPIA Moderate	88	560	2,511	375	500	500	550	800
	EPIA Policy-Driven				375	500	600	650	1,500
Rest of Europe	EPIA Moderate	12	17	28	120	140	200	300	450
	EPIA Policy-Driven				250	325	400	525	625
Japan	EPIA Moderate	287	210	230	400	500	700	1,000	1,100
	EPIA Policy-Driven				500	1,000	1,200	1,500	1,700
USA	EPIA Moderate	145	207	342	340	1,000	1,200	1,500	2,000
	EPIA Policy-Driven				1,200	3,000	3,400	3,900	4,500
China	EPIA Moderate	12	20	45	80	100	300	600	1,000
	EPIA Policy-Driven				100	150	600	1,200	2,000
India	EPIA Moderate	12	20	40	50	60	80	120	300
	EPIA Policy-Driven				100	200	250	300	600
South Korea	EPIA Moderate	20	43	274	100	150	220	300	400
	EPIA Policy-Driven				200	350	450	700	1,000
Rest of the World	EPIA Moderate	153	125	126	250	300	300	300	350
	EPIA Policy-Driven				400	600	800	1,000	1,600
TOTAL	**EPIA Moderate**	**1,603**	**2,392**	**5,559**	**4,620**	**6,000**	**7,540**	**9,610**	**12,250**
	EPIA Policy-Driven				**6,802**	**10,790**	**13,810**	**17,385**	**22,325**
CUMULATIVE	**EPIA Moderate**	**6,770**	**9,162**	**14,730**	**19,350**	**25,350**	**32,890**	**42,500**	**54,750**
	EPIA Policy-Driven				**21,532**	**32,322**	**46,132**	**63,517**	**85,842**

Source: European Photovoltaic Industry Association (EPIA), "Global Market Outlook for Photovoltaics until 2013," March 2009, p. 6.

Case 27 | CANADIAN SOLAR

EXHIBIT 4: Ontario's Feed-in Tariff (FIT) Program

Renewable Fuel	Size tranches	Contract price cent/kWh
Biomass	≤ 10MW	13.8
	> 10MW	13.0
Biogas		
On-farm	≤ 100kW	19.5
On-farm	> 100kW ≤ 250kW	18.5
Biogas	≤ 500kW	16.0
Biogas	> 500kW ≤ 10MW	14.7
Biogas	> 10MW	10.4
Waterpower	≤ 10MW	13.1
	> 10MW ≤ 50MW	12.2
Landfill gas	≤ 10MW	11.1
	> 10MW	10.3
Solar PV		
Any type	≤ 10kW	80.2
Rooftop	> 10kW ≤ 250kW	71.3
Rooftop	> 250kW ≤ 500kW	63.5
Rooftop	> 500kW	53.9
Ground mounted	≤ 10MW	44.3
Wind		
Onshore	Any size	13.5
Offshore	Any size	19.0

Domestic Content Requirements: The minimum requirements of Ontario-based content: 40% for MicroFIT (projects less than 10kW) and 50% for FIT (projects over 10kW) for projects reaching commercial operation by the end of 2010. For projects with commercial operation after January 1, 2011, domestic content increases to 60%.

	Designated Activity	Qualifying Percentage
1.	Silicon that has been used as input to solar photovoltaic cells manufactured in an Ontario refinery.	10%
2.	Silicon ingots and wafers, where silicon ingots have been cast in Ontario and wafers have been cut from the casting by a saw in Ontario.	12%
3.	The crystalline silicon solar photovoltaic cells, where their active photovoltaic layer(s) have been formed in Ontario.	10%
4.	Solar photovoltaic modules (i.e. panels), where the electrical connections between the solar cells have been made in Ontario, and the solar photovoltaic module materials have been encapsulated in Ontario.	13%
5.	Inverter (to convert the electricity from direct current (DC) to alternating current (AC)), where the assembly, final wiring and testing have been done in Ontario	9%
6.	Mounting systems, where the structural components of the fixed or moving mounting systems have been entirely machined or formed or cast in Ontario. The metal for the structural components may not have been pre-machined outside Ontario other than peeling/roughing of the part for quality control purposes when it left the smelter or forge. The machining and assembly of the mounting system must entirely take place in Ontario (i.e. bending, welding, piercing, and bolting).	9%
7.	Wiring and electrical hardware that is not part of other designated activities (i.e. items 1, 2, 3, and 5 of this table), sourced from an Ontario supplier.	10%
8.	All on- and off-site labour and services. For greater certainty, this designated activity shall apply in respect of all contract facilities.	27%
	Total	**100%**

Source: Ontario Power Authority, http://fit.powerauthority.on.ca, accessed October 30, 2009.

EXHIBIT 5: Market Shares and Gross Profits by PV Module Producers

2008 Rank	PV Supplier	HQ	2008 % of Total MV Shipments	2008 Gross Profit (%)
1	Suntech	China	7.2	23.7
2	Sharp	Japan	7.2	16.0
3	First Solar	U.S.	6.9	54.4
4	Yingli Green Energy	China	4.4	21.9
5	Kyocera	Japan	4.2	25.9
6	Sunpower	U.S.	3.4	25.3
7	Trina Solar	China	3.3	19.7
8	Sanyo	Japan	2.8	15.8
9	Canadian Solar	Canada/China	2.6	10.7
10	Solar World	Germany	2.6	N/A
	Top 10 Total		**44.7**	
	Others		**55.3**	
	Total Module Shipments in GWs		**6.3**	

Source: IMS Research and company files.

N/A = not available

Market Shares PV Cell Producers

2008 Rank	2007 Rank	PV Supplier	HQ	2007 % of Total MW	2008 % of Total MW	08/07 % Change	2007 % of Total $	2008 % of Total $	08/07 % Change
1	1	Q-Cells	Germany	10.9	9.4	48	14.5	12.2	43
2	4	First Solar	U.S.	5.8	8.3	144	6.2	9.0	147
3	2	Suntech	China	10.2	8.2	37	9.0	7.2	36
4	3	Sharp	Japan	9.0	8.0	51	8.0	7.3	56
5	6	Motech	Taiwan	4.9	4.8	67	4.1	4.0	70
6	5	Kyocera	Japan	5.7	4.6	37	5.0	4.0	38
7	10	JA Solar	China	3.7	4.6	108	4.6	5.8	117
8	9	Yingli Green Energy	China	4.0	4.5	93	3.3	3.8	95
9	12	Gintech Energy	Taiwan	3.1	4.4	144	2.6	3.6	141
10	8	Solar World	Germany	4.7	4.0	44	4.9	3.8	32
		Top 10 Total		**62.0**	**60.8**	**67.0**	**62.0**	**60.6**	**67.0**
		Others		**38.0**	**39.2**	**75**	**38.0**	**39.4**	**77**
		Cell & Panel PV Total		**3.57GW**	**6.0GW**	**70**	**$8.1b**	**$13.85b**	**71**

Source: "Japanese solar cell manufacturers losing market share, says IC Insights," July 22, 2009, www.pv-tech.org/news/_a/ japanese_solar_cell_manufacturers_losing_market_share_says_ic_insights.

Canadian National Railway Company: Culture Change (A)[1]

INTRODUCTION

As he walked around one of Canadian National Railway Company's (CN) railway terminals, E. Hunter Harrison, executive vice president and chief operating officer, noticed there were few employees at their stations. Harrison had been promoted from his position as director, president and chief executive officer of Illinois Central Railroad Company (Illinois Central), which had been acquired by CN on February 11, 1998. While Harrison had expected to be let go after Illinois Central was integrated into CN, Paul Tellier, CN's president and chief executive officer (CEO), convinced him to play a key part in the transformation of the firm: Tellier would run the company and Harrison would run the railroad. Harrison accepted and began reviewing CN's operations across the country.[2]

It was an early afternoon in mid-1998, and Harrison was puzzled. He asked his managers what was going on, and they replied that they had a policy called "early quits," which allowed employees to go home early–up to four hours early for every eight hour shift.

Ken Mark wrote this case under the supervision of Professor Stewart Thornhill solely to provide material for class discussion. The authors do not intend to illustrate either effective or ineffective handling of a managerial situation. The authors may have disguised certain names and other identifying information to protect confidentiality.

This publication may not be transmitted, photocopied, digitized or otherwise reproduced in any form or by any means without the permission of the copyright holder. Reproduction of this material is not covered under authorization by any reproduction rights organization. To order copies or request permission to reproduce materials, contact Ivey Publishing, Ivey Business School, Western University, London, Ontario, Canada, N6G 0N1; (t) 519.661.3208; (e) cases@ivey.ca; www.iveycases.com.

Copyright © 2013, Richard Ivey School of Business Foundation   Version: 2013-09-06

One time permission to reproduce granted by Richard Ivey School of Business Foundation on April 22, 2014.

[1]This case has been written on the basis of published sources only. Consequently, the interpretation and perspectives presented in this case are not necessarily those of Canadian National Railway Company or any of its employees.

[2]Judy Johnson, Les Dakens, Peter Edwards, Ned Morse, *SwitchPoints: Culture Change on the Fast Track to Business Success,* John Wiley & Sons Inc., Hoboken, N.J., 2008, p. xxix. Adapted from E. Hunter Harrison, *Change, Leadership, Mud and Why: How We Work and Why,* Vol. 2, Canadian National Railway Company, 2008.

IVEY | Publishing

Harrison was astounded. "That has got to stop today," he said, as he walked away. As Harrison was leaving, a supervisor walked beside him and said, "Mr. Harrison, it's worse than this at the other terminals." "Where," Harrison asked? The supervisor replied, "Everywhere!"[3] In that instant, Harrison knew he had to deal with the problem of "early quits."

Later, Harrison learned about another practice that was resulting in reduced productivity: the practice of easing into the workday. Even though the shifts should have started by 7:30 a.m. sharp, it was typical for supervisors to wait until everyone was present before handing out the assignments. In some cases, it would take until 8:15 a.m. before the crews were ready to head out for the day's work. Harrison wondered if he could address this issue of late starts as the first step towards dealing with the bigger issue of "early quits."

CANADIAN NATIONAL RAILWAY COMPANY

After nearly a century of expansion starting in the 1830s, Canada's privately-owned railways were bankrupt. Many lines were built in anticipation of business that never materialized. The lines that were built did not follow common standards and rail cars often could not move between sets of tracks owned by competitors.

The Private Railways were Nationalized

Between 1918 and 1923, the Canadian government started taking control of these troubled railways, creating Canadian National Railways (CNR). In addition to operating a nationwide railway, CNR had interests in radio broadcasting, hotels and steamships. While some of these assets were sold off, such as the radio broadcasting system which later became the Canadian Broadcasting Corporation, CNR continued to operate in multiple industries until well after it was privatized.

As it was a government-funded entity–with 100,000 employees–CNR's strategic decisions were guided by government policies and the prevailing party's political agenda. Government support allowed CNR to expand its rail network outside of the major cities but there were no real efforts to run CNR as a profitable enterprise. Other policies, such as the requirement that rail cars be purchased from Canadian manufacturers, meant that expenses consistently exceeded sales. In the nearly 70 years that CNR was government run (renamed CN in the 1960s), it was evident that the Crown corporation had become a bloated, loss-making operation:

> In 1986, CN's long-term debt exceeded Cdn$3.4 billion,[4] and interest charges alone surpassed $1 million a day. The railroad was burdened with hundreds of miles of business track that went to specific customers and carried extremely low volume, but the government would not abandon it. One-third of the track carried less than one per cent of the business. CN was profitable in some years, but those profits occurred mostly when the railroad could jettison little-used track or large numbers of employees. . . . As the railway struggled to lower costs, it quickly became a burden on the taxpayers. . . . Canada's national dream had become a national nightmare. Taxpayers were bailing out CN decade after decade, to the tune of tens of billions of dollars.[5]

[3]Ibid.

[4]All currencies in Canadian dollars unless otherwise stated.

[5]Judy Johnson, Les Dakens, Peter Edwards, Ned Morse, *SwitchPoints: Culture Change on the Fast Track to Business Success*, John Wiley & Sons Inc., Hoboken, N.J., 2008, p. 5. Adapted from E. Hunter Harrison, *Change, Leadership, Mud and Why: How We Work and Why*, Vol. 2, Canadian National Railway Company, 2008.

Two developments in the 1980s ignited efforts to reform CN. U.S. and Canadian railroads were deregulated, which allowed for greater competition, and high interest rates in the 1980s prompted firms to be more cognizant of their working capital costs. Deregulation was a significant move. It allowed prices to be set at market rates, removing subsidies for unprofitable lines, but while the number of employees fell from 51,000 to 38,000, the company lost more than $1 billion in 1992.[6]

The Turnaround Begins at CN

As the top bureaucrat in the Canadian government, Tellier was tasked with turning around CN. Instead of following advice to proceed gradually, Tellier made significant changes immediately after assuming the post of president and CEO:

> Tellier didn't know the old-fashioned way of running a railroad. But his years in politics made him a master at overcoming bureaucracy. . . . Tellier and his team quickly focused on the core business and sold off nearly 9,000 miles of track—an astonishing one-third of the rail network. They also disposed of CN's nonrailroad assets, including a hotel in Paris and the CN Tower. And they eliminated redundant processes that wasted time and money. In less than four months, five senior executives were gone and not replaced. The entire CN payroll was cut by about one-third, including about 11,000 jobs over three years. Tellier reorganized his executive team and reduced management layers from as many as a dozen to only five between himself and the front line. He made it clear: Bureaucracy in CN was history, everyone must pull his own weight, and no one had guaranteed employment. . . . The sense of urgency and focus on the bottom line translated into immediate results. Within three years, the operating ratio dropped from the high 90s to the high 80s[7]. CN's net income grew 3.5 times, from a loss in 1992 of $68 million to $204 million.[8]

When CN was privatized in 1995, as a sign of the confidence they had in their firm, employees bought enough shares to own more than 40 per cent of the outstanding shares, the highest employee shareholder percentage of any North American railroad.[9] A 1997 book on the CN IPO story recounted:

> Throughout CN, a competitive spirit took hold. Workers seemed proud to serve not a government bureaucracy, but a customer-driven, investor-driven railway. The privatization, Tellier says, had been "a tremendously powerful instrument in our transformation. Our people have become more bottom line-oriented. They want to see a higher share price and our performance improved." In short, the revolution in CN's corporate culture was well underway. Its rewards would soon prove dramatic.[10]

---

[6]Ibid, p. 6.

[7]Operating ratio is defined as the percentage of operating expenses to net sales. CN's historical operating ratios can be found in Exhibit 1.

[8]Judy Johnson, Les Dakens, Peter Edwards, Ned Morse, *SwitchPoints: Culture Change on the Fast Track to Business Success*, John Wiley & Sons Inc., Hoboken, N.J., 2008, pp. 6–7. Adapted from E. Hunter Harrison, *Change, Leadership, Mud and Why: How We Work and Why*, Vol. 2, Canadian National Railway Company, 2008.

[9]Ibid, p. 8.

[10]Harry Bruce, *The Pig That Flew*, Douglas & McIntyre Ltd., Vancouver, B.C., 1997, p. 154. Quoted in Judy Johnson, Les Dakens, Peter Edwards, Ned Morse, *SwitchPoints: Culture Change on the Fast Track to Business Success*, John Wiley & Sons Inc., Hoboken, N.J., 2008, p. 9.

CN's Transformation Continues as a Publicly-owned Firm

In 1998, CN and Canadian Pacific Railways were the two major railroads in Canada. CN had achieved record revenues and profits in 1997 along with record shipping volume. In its security filings, CN had stated that it had "achieved one of the most significant turnarounds in recent railway history and reached, several years ahead of time, the targets set at the time of its initial public offering."[11] CN was the only coast-to-coast network in North America[12], with 15,300 route miles of track in Canada and the United States and that achieved 119.5 billion revenue ton miles.[13]

By 1998, its operating ratio had fallen to 81.5 per cent, a dramatic improvement in six years (see Exhibit 1) and generated $10.7 billion in cash from operations. CN had an investment grade credit rating and had an EV/EBITDA[14] ratio of 9.3 times in March 1998, compared to a range of 8.0 times to 9.0 times for its peers,[15] Class 1 railroad stocks. See Exhibit 2 for CN's operating statistics from 1995 to 1997.

CN was in the midst of implementing trip planning and monitoring technology, named Service Reliability Strategy (SRS) that would help improve utilization and track customer shipments. The company was investing in new fuel-efficient trains to boost reliability and decrease maintenance costs. Tellier continued to cut costs, reducing another 1,500 miles of track in 1997. In six years, CN had reduced its track network by one third.

On the employee front, labour productivity had increased by 17 per cent in 1997. CN's metric for labour productivity was based on revenue ton miles per average number of employees. It continued to cut its workforce, reducing its number of employees by 750 in 1997. These improvements had not come at the expense of safety. In 1997, CN was the top-ranked railroad in North America based on safety performance, defined by train accidents per million train miles.[16] CN's employees were represented by the Canadian Auto Workers Union, or CAW (6,400 employees), the Brotherhood of Locomotive Engineers and the United Transportation Union (5,820 employees), and the Canadian Council of Railway Unions (4,700 employees). In 1998, the CAW had been given a mandate to strike, with arbitration a possibility.[17]

Its operations were divided into three corridors: East, West, and Transcontinental. CN's traffic in its Eastern Service Corridor (Atlantic Canada, Montreal, Toronto, and Chicago), consisted of intermodal[18] shipments and industrial (aluminum, steel, chemical, and plastic products), forest, and automotive products. CN's Western Service Corridor ran from Thunder Bay and Chicago to the west coast of Canada. It transported grain, coal, sulphur and fertilizers, as well as products that were transferred from shipments originating in the Eastern Service Corridor. The Transcontinental Service Corridor stretched from Halifax to the farthest western ports, Prince Rupert and Vancouver.

---

[11]CN, Annual Information Form, 1997, page 2.

[12]CN, Annual Information Form, 1997, page 6.

[13]One revenue ton mile equals one ton of goods shipped one mile for which CN is paid. For example, there are no revenue ton miles generated when CN moves empty trains from one yard to another.

[14]EV/EBITDA = Enterprise value / Earnings before interest, taxes, depreciation and amortization.

[15]Glynn Williams, "Canadian National Railway Company," TD Newcrest Investment Research, March 2, 1998, pp. 1 and 9.

[16]CN, Annual Information Form, 1997, pages 2 and 3.

[17]Lafferty, Harwood and Partners Ltd., "The Comparative Investment Merit of the Two Railroads Namely Canadian National and Canadian Pacific", Montreal, Quebec, July 1998, page 16.

[18]Intermodal shipments involve more than one mode of transport, for example ship to truck to rail.

CN was organized into three business units: Merchandise, which included industrial and forest products; Bulk, which encompassed commodities such as grain, coal, sulphur and fertilizers; and intermodal and automotive, which managed intermodal traffic and the shipment of automotive parts.

CN's strategic plan in 1998

Building upon a turnaround effort that was gaining momentum, CN had three priorities for 1998: leveraging its franchise, extending its reach and improving service. It aimed to take advantage of growing shipments among the three countries in the North American Free Trade Agreement, extending its ability to serve customers in Canada and the United States. Information technology investments targeted service improvement and the communication of these service objectives to employees. A key enabler of the strategic plans was the purchase of Illinois Central, a U.S. railway in early 1998.

The Purchase of Illinois Central and the Outlook for 1998 and Beyond

In February 1998, CN purchased Illinois Central for US$1.8 billion.[19] Instead of expanding east or west, Tellier, recognizing the positive impact the North American Free Trade Agreement would have on Canada and United States, looked to re-orientate the railway's focus to a north-south axis. In its budget for 1998, Illinois Central was targeting an operating ratio of 60.9 per cent. It was one of the most efficient railroads in North America. An analyst stated:

> Illinois Central Corporation is a class act. It has great profit margins. Last year it had revenues of US$700 million and net income of US$150 million, which is a profit margin of 21 per cent. This compares with CN's profit margin last year (1997) of just under 10 per cent.[20]

Tellier talked about the importance of Illinois Central's team, especially Harrison:

> When I came to CN, I knew very little about railroads, but a lot about people. Over the years, I'd developed the skill of quickly figuring out who could make things happen. . . . I was always looking for that future talent. I found a pool of it in a regional U.S. railroad known as Illinois Central. . . . So when we put the deal together, I made sure that Hunter and his leadership team agreed to join the CN team. Retaining Hunter Harrison was probably one of the best decisions I took as CEO of CN.[21]

E. Hunter Harrison

Harrison began his career with St. Louis-San Francisco Railway in 1964, working as a carman-oiler (labourer). Following several promotions, he left St. Louis-San Francisco to join Burlington Northern Railroad and then Illinois Central in 1989. Harrison had transformed

---

[19]The US dollar was worth $1.42 Canadian in March 1998.

[20]Lafferty, Harwood and Partners Ltd., "The Comparative Investment Merit of the Two Railroads Namely Canadian National and Canadian Pacific", Montreal, Quebec, July 1998, page 7.

[21]Judy Johnson, Les Dakens, Peter Edwards, Ned Morse, *SwitchPoints: Culture Change on the Fast Track to Business Success*, John Wiley & Sons Inc., Hoboken, N.J., 2008, p. 9. Adapted from E. Hunter Harrison, *Change, Leadership, Mud and Why: How We Work and Why*, Vol. 2, Canadian National Railway Company, 2008.

Illinois Central into one of the top railways by focusing on five guiding principles: service, cost control, asset utilization, safety and people.

He built on these guiding principles, introducing the concept of "precision railroading," which shifted the railroad's focus from maximizing utilization per car to minimizing shipment time per load. Waiting for a rail car to fill up before sending it on its way seemed like a great way to ensure fuel efficient transportation of goods. But problems emerged when shipment delays–while waiting for loads to fill up–resulted in idle rail cars, overdue shipments and irate customers. Minimizing shipment time per load had the potential to result in decreased shipping times and increased availability of rail cars, boosting revenues and profits.

As chief operating officer, Harrison began visiting CN's rail yards across the country. It was in one of these rail yards that he first learned of the issue of "early quits." In the 1990s, there were North American railroads whose unions had won concessions for eight hours' pay for six hours' work. In contrast, at CN, supervisors had granted "early quits" to employees, believing that the incentive of having half of a typical workday off would motivate employees to perform better at their jobs. CN managers believed that allowing "early quits" demonstrated that management cared for their employees.[22]

Dressed and Ready

Another practice that had taken root at CN involved easing into the workday. Morning shifts were scheduled to begin at 7:30 a.m. While employees arrived at 7:30 a.m., they would typically have a cup of coffee, change into their work clothes, chat with their coworkers and then wait to receive their daily assignments from a supervisor. Once the days tasks had been sorted out, employees would gather the necessary equipment and safety gear, take time for another cup of coffee and then begin the day's work. For a 20-person crew taking up to 45 minutes each morning, lost productive time could total 15 hours before the shift started.

There were many crews operating in this manner across the organization. Support for this practice of late starts was not universal. There were a few crew members who would have preferred to have started on time, at 7:30 a.m. sharp, but since the majority of workers preferred the option of starting off slowly, this practice had become ingrained into the work culture. CN supervisors, many of whom had been crew members before they were promoted, did not discourage this practice, believing that the crews could make up for lost time during the work day.

Harrison and his team identified the morning routine as an opportunity to change behaviour and to set the stage to tackle the even more costly and pervasive issue of early quits. Their goal was to ensure employees were dressed and ready for work at the start of each shift. The challenge for the individual shift supervisors was translating this objective into new employee behaviour.[23]

---

[22]Judy Johnson, Les Dakens, Peter Edwards, Ned Morse, *SwitchPoints: Culture Change on the Fast Track to Business Success*, John Wiley & Sons Inc., Hoboken, N.J., 2008, pp. xxx–xxi. Adapted from E. Hunter Harrison, *Change, Leadership, Mud and Why: How We Work and Why*, Vol. 2, Canadian National Railway Company, 2008.

[23]Ibid, p. xxix.

EXHIBIT 1: CN—Historical Operating Ratios

Year ended December 31	1997		1996		1995	
Dollars in millions	Amount	% of revenue	Amount	% of revenue	Amount	% of revenue
Labour and fringe benefits	$1,431	32.90%	$1,381	34.60%	$1,477	37.40%
Material	316	7.30%	297	7.40%	318	8.00%
Fuel	335	7.70%	314	7.90%	277	7.00%
Depreciation and amortization	200	4.60%	194	4.80%	231	5.80%
Operating taxes	186	4.30%	171	4.30%	192	4.90%
Equipment rental	219	5.00%	216	5.40%	194	4.90%
Net car hire	116	2.70%	108	2.70%	117	3.00%
Purchased services	363	8.30%	348	8.70%	354	9.00%
Casualty and insurance	103	2.40%	85	2.10%	52	1.30%
Other	276	6.30%	271	6.80%	302	7.60%
Operating ratio	3,545	**81.50%**	3,385	**84.70%**	3,514	**88.90%**
Special charges			381		1,453	
Total operating expenses	$3,545		$3,766		$4,967	

Source: CN Annual Report 1997, pages 25 and 28.

EXHIBIT 2: CN—Operating Statistics

Year ended December 31	1997	1996	1995
Rail operations			
Freight revenues ($ millions)	4,255	3,886	3,844
Gross ton miles (billions)	228.4	208.3	204.1
Revenue ton miles (RTM) (millions)	119,534	107,470	105,487
Route miles (includes Canada and the U.S.)	15,292	17,124	17,918
Operating expenses excluding special charges per RTM (cents)	2.97	3.15	3.33
Freight revenue per RTM (cents)	3.56	3.62	3.64
Carloads (thousands)	2,547	2,315	2,295
Freight revenue per carload ($)	1,671	1,679	1,675
Diesel fuel consumed (Canadian gallons in millions)	272	259	256
Average fuel price ($/Canadian gallon)	1.23	1.22	1.08
Revenue ton miles per Canadian gallon of fuel consumed	439	415	412
Locomotive bad order ratio (%)	10.1	11.2	10
Freight car bad order ratio (%)	3.7	4	5.2
Productivity			
Operating ratio excluding special charges (%)	81.5	84.7	88.9
Freight revenue per route mile ($ thousands)	278	227	215
Revenue ton miles per route mile (thousands)	7,817	6,276	5,887
Freight revenue per average number of employees ($ thousands)	187	161	143
Revenue ton miles per average number of employees (thousands)	5,243	4,466	3,914

EXHIBIT 2: (continued)

Year ended December 31	1997	1996	1995
Rail operations			
Employees			
Number at end of year	21,081	21,589	23,999
Average number during year	22,800	24,064	26,951
Labour and fringe benefits per RTM (cents)	1.2	1.29	1.4
Injury frequency rate per 200,000 person hours	1.6	2.1	2.5
Accident rate per million train miles	2.2	3	2.6
Financial			
Debt to total capitalization ratio (% at end of year)	33	33.1	41
Return on assets at end of year (%)	7.4	6.2*	5.4*

Certain of the 1996 and 1995 comparative figures have been reclassified in order to be consistent with 1997 presentation.

*Based on the adjusted results.

Source: CN Annual Report 1997, page 19.

Project HUGO at LHSC: Leading Urgent Change in Healthcare

On the morning of September 6, 2011, Susan Johnson took a deep breath as she entered the parking lot of the London Health Science Centre (LHSC). She had just launched her children into a new school year. Johnson smiled as she recalled the excitement and anticipation on their faces at their fresh start back to school. Her smile lessened as her thoughts turned to the monumental change leadership task that lay ahead. Today would bring a public announcement by the senior management team that "her" Project HUGO would be live in all LHSC hospitals by April 2013.

Johnson was the director of Pharmacy Services at LHSC. Over the past year, she had been planning for the launch and implementation of Project HUGO, an acronym for Healthcare Undergoing Optimization. HUGO would be one of the most complex, expensive and challenging projects ever undertaken by the hospitals in London and region. HUGO would transform the way care was delivered, from patent registration to patient discharge. When fully implemented, the physicians, nurses and other healthcare providers would be using a fully electronic patient record (EPR) in place of the current paper-based system at all London hospitals and the nine smaller regional hospitals that partnered with LHSC.

Johnson knew that HUGO would bring some operational efficiency, but the main rationale for the project was to ensure patient safety and quality of care. HUGO was ultimately about preventing medical errors and saving lives. She also knew that the implementation of HUGO would be very challenging, including the risks of running over budget, missing deadlines and not getting everyone on board.

Just the previous week, in the hallway, she had run into a physician whom she had thought would have been a supporter of HUGO. Yet, surprisingly, the physician had stated,

Professor Cara Maurer wrote this case solely to provide material for class discussion. The author does not intend to illustrate either effective or ineffective handling of a managerial situation. The author may have disguised certain names and other identifying information to protect confidentiality.

This publication may not be transmitted, photocopied, digitized or otherwise reproduced in any form or by any means without the permission of the copyright holder. Reproduction of this material is not covered under authorization by any reproduction rights organization. To order copies or request permission to reproduce materials, contact Ivey Publishing, Ivey Business School, Western University, London, Ontario, Canada, N6G 0N1; (t) 519.661.3208; (e) cases@ivey.ca; www.iveycases.com.

Copyright © 2012, Richard Ivey School of Business Foundation   Version: 2013-07-26

One time permission to reproduce granted by Richard Ivey School of Business Foundation on April 22, 2014.

IVEY | Publishing

"Susan, I believe that we will have electronic order entry very soon, but you know, I will never enter my own orders. My secretary will do this for me. I'm not a data entry clerk."

Johnson knew that diverting this process to clerical staff would dilute the gains in safety. She also recalled a conversation with the dean of the medical school who had stated unequivocally that by introducing electronic order entry medical students would not learn how to prescribe orders and properly care for patients. "This is 'cookbook' medicine," the dean had said. "I treat my patients as individuals. Standardization will not work!"

THE GLOBAL HEALTHCARE INDUSTRY AND THE NEED FOR CHANGE

The global healthcare industry provided healthcare services and products, including medical equipment, pharmaceuticals and biotechnology. Services could be broadly divided into hospital activities, medical and dental practice, and other medical services, such as those delivered by registered dieticians and optometrists. In many countries, healthcare was one of the largest industries and often one of the most inefficient. In many countries, healthcare consumed about 10 per cent of gross domestic product (GDP).

Although healthcare spending absorbed more than US$1.7 trillion per year in the United States and more than Cdn$175 billion in Canada, premature mortality in North America remained higher than in many other developed countries. Most medical records were still stored on paper, which precluded the coordination of care or routine measurement of quality, and often led to critical, often fatal, medical errors. Recent media reports had highlighted the tragic consequences of medical errors:

- "Deaths of 3 Babies in Indiana Spotlight Medication Mix-ups"–*Boston Globe*, September 23, 2006

- "Quaids Sue Blood-thinner Manufacturer"–*Los Angeles Times*, Dec 5, 2007

- "Heparin Overdoses Hit Babies in Texas Hospital"–*Wall Street Journal*, July 9, 2008

- "3 Philadelphia Infants Die After Mix-up at Hospital Pharmacy"–*Philadelphia Inquirer*, June 1990

- "Two Die in Hospital Dialysis Mix-Up"–*National Post*, March 19, 2004

- "Hospital Error, Woman Dies"–*BBC*, Wednesday, April 4, 2001

In addition to these alarming media reports, the academic literature also painted a bleak picture. The Institute of Medicine published findings of widespread medical errors in its report, *To Err Is Human*.[1] The report suggested that as many as 98,000 Americans died every year as a result of medical error. A subsequent Canadian study[2] echoed these findings, reporting that 7.5 per cent of patients admitted to hospital had experienced an adverse event. Of those patients, 37 per cent were considered to have experienced preventable events, and 21 percent had died as a result of their adverse events. Across key steps in the medication process, different types of errors occurred with different frequencies. Errors were classified into ordering errors, transcription errors, dispensing errors, and administration errors (see Exhibit 1).

---

[1]Institute of Medicine, *To Err Is Human: Building a Safer Healthcare System*, National Academy Press, Washington, D.C., 1999.

[2]G. Ross Baker et al., "The Canadian Adverse Events Study: The Incidence of Adverse Events among Hospital Patients in Canada," *The Canadian Medical Association Journal*, 2004, vol. 170, no. 11, pp. 1678-1689.

BACKGROUND ON THE ORGANIZATIONS

Included in the HUGO project were a total of 11 hospitals, all located in and around London, Ontario, in southwestern Ontario, Canada. These hospitals included London Health Sciences Centre, St. Joseph's Health Care London and nine smaller regional hospitals (see Exhibit 2). In total, HUGO would affect more than 10,000 staff members across the different hospitals and sites.

LHSC, one of Canada's largest acute-care teaching hospitals, cared for the most critically ill patients and the most medically complex cases in the region. In 2010, 150,000 patients visited the emergency departments, 700,000 patients visited outpatient departments and 40,000 patients were admitted. LHSC was the largest employer in London, with more than 2,200 doctors and medical students, almost 3,500 nurses, 500 clinical staff (such as pharmacists, nutritionist and physiotherapists), and approximately 7,000 other staff and volunteers. It encompassed the South Street Hospital, University Hospital, Victoria Hospital and Children's Hospital, Byron Family Medical Centre and Victoria Family Medical Centre, and was home to the Fowler Kennedy Sport Medicine Clinic, Canadian Surgical Technologies and Advanced Robotics (CSTAR), Lawson Health Research Institute, Children's Health Foundation and London Health Sciences Foundation.

St. Joseph's Health Care London (St. Joseph's) was a major patient care, teaching and research centre. It included St. Joseph's Hospital, Parkwood Hospital, Mount Hope Centre for Long-Term Care, Regional Mental Health Care London and Regional Mental Health Care St. Thomas. Annually, more than 500,000 patients visited the outpatient clinics at St. Joseph's, 20,000 surgeries were performed and 41,000 urgent care cases administered. St. Joseph's more than 5,000 staff members included almost 1,500 physicians, residents and medical students and 1,100 nursing and allied health professionals.

Both LHSC and St. Joseph's had newly appointed chief executive officers, who were redefining the vision for their organizations (see Exhibit 3). While the organizations were slightly different in some ways, both organizations were "obsessed" with quality of care and patient safety.

Johnson knew that staff differed and could be categorized into physicians, nurses and allied health professionals. Because physicians were independent and not regular employees of the hospital, hospital administration was permitted only limited direct influence over physicians' workflow. Physicians were more likely than nurses or allied health professionals to switch hospitals several times in their careers. They often compared the performance of their hospital with the performance of other hospitals in Ontario and Canada. Many physicians resisted change in their routines and resented purely administrative tasks. This group valued independence, time, money and professional prestige. Physicians were ultimately responsible for the patient healthcare that was ordered. Nurses were employees of the hospital where they worked and typically remained at the same place of work for a longer duration than physicians. They valued excellence in patient care, time efficiency and consistent and ongoing employment. The age and tenure of nurses ranged widely, with some senior nurses having been employed for several decades. The group of allied health professionals was the most diverse group of hospital staff, including several smaller groups of professionals, such as pharmacists, physiotherapists, occupational therapists, dieticians, lab technicians, radio technicians and massage therapists. These professionals were driven by their ability to provide safe and effective care for patients in an efficient manner. They were also concerned with communications with both physicians and patients. For all three groups, the ability to access patient records from anywhere in the hospital and before seeing a patient would significantly improve their ability to provide high-quality, effective care in an efficient manner.

SUSAN JOHNSON

Susan Johnson had taken on the role as director of Pharmacy at LHSC six months earlier. She had been trained as a clinical pharmacist and had gained related experience in multiple areas over almost 20 years. She had practiced clinical pharmacy in pediatric specialty areas, general surgery, gastrointestinal medicine, infectious disease and adult intensive-care programs. Additionally, she had spent two years as a pharmacist in a teaching family medicine clinic, providing pharmaceutical care to an ambulatory patient population. In 2000, Johnson became the coordinator of Pharmacy Operations at St. Joseph's Health Care in London, Ontario. In this administrative role, she had played a key role in the implementation of smart infusion systems, a purchasing system and a pharmacy information system.

In 2008, Johnson had established the new Medication Safety Department at St. Joseph's Health Care and had been its coordinator for 19 years. In this role, she had implemented several medication safety initiatives, including Medication Reconciliation, a high-alert medication safety program and had introduced an independent double-check system. In 2009, she had established the new Department of Clinical Informatics at London Health Sciences Centre and St. Joseph's Health Care. Over the two years that Johnson was director, this department had grown to a staff of 20 full-time equivalents.

Previously, she had received her bachelor of science degree in pharmacy from the University of Toronto and her master's degree in health studies (Leadership) from Athabasca University.

HISTORY OF ELECTRONIC PATIENT RECORDS AT LHSC

HUGO was LHSC's second attempt to implement an electronic patient record (EPR) system. From 2003 to 2005, a monumental effort had been undertaken to implement computerized provider order entry (CPOE) and clinical documentation. Information technology staff, not clinical staff, had driven this project. Several consultants from the United States had been "parachuted in" to the organization to build the system. In the spring of 2005, the project was over-budget and had failed to meet key deadlines. Clinicians had considered the system cumbersome and unsupportive of patient care. Hence, they were frustrated by the system before it had even been launched, and they had clearly indicated they would never use it. The project was put on indefinite hold and had remained dormant until 2009; however, the organizational memory of the failed attempt to introduce EPR had stayed alive in the minds of the many staff who had remained at the hospital.

In 2009, under Johnson's leadership, a new team was formed, the Clinical Informatics Team. This team was staffed with clinicians, including nurses, pharmacists and nutritionists, and was tasked with the design, implementation, education and training of the clinical systems. This team acted as advocates for the clinical staff and for the use of technology to enhance quality of care and patient safety. They also played key roles as translators between the information technology staff and clinical staff, two groups that often used very different language.

In 2010, with the Clinical Informatics Team on the ground and two Toronto hospitals reporting successful CPOE implementations, the London hospitals experienced renewed interest in a second try at implementing CPOE. A report was released that compared Canadian hospitals' adoption of new technology. London, typically a national leader, was starting to fall behind much smaller Canadian hospitals. In addition, reports were emerging from every major organization regarding the tremendous gains in patient safety being realized as a result of the implementation of an electronic patient record. Under President Obama, the U.S. administration had invested billions of dollars in U.S. hospitals for electronic patient records. Expected to follow suit was Canada Health Infoway, a federally funded government organization created to foster and accelerate adoption and implementation of electronic health records.

PROJECT HUGO

Senior leadership at the hospital had asked Johnson to determine what it would take to launch a full electronic patient record project at LHSC. In response, she had completed an extensive analysis of the change effort required, the human and physical resources needed and the proposed roll-out plan. The estimated cost of HUGO was more than $25 million. Part of this cost was the technology that was new, sophisticated and expensive. The scope of Project HUGO was massive, considering the number of hospitals and staff involved. The amount of data that would be processed electronically instead of manually was also staggeringly high. Information on approximately seven million patient visits was already stored, and new information would be added quickly, due to rapidly increasing health care needs.

Johnson's plan included an aggressive time schedule that would see the project roll-out occur over a 24-month period, beginning in October 2012. At least 100 additional staff members would need to be hired, and the current clinician workflow would need to change dramatically.

Workflows in hospital healthcare systems were highly complex, resulting in inefficiencies and room for error. A process analysis, from a physician ordering a medication to the administration of the drug to the patient, showed the involvement of at least five people and 24 key steps (see Exhibit 4). HUGO would shorten this process considerably (see Exhibit 5). Handwritten orders that were often illegible added to the risk of serious errors (see Exhibit 6). HUGO would eliminate the need to decipher poorly written orders and would produce easily readable and traceable medication orders (see Exhibit 7).

LHSC, St. Joseph's and the regional hospitals already had in place the foundational components of the EPR; however, to achieve the promise of a fully functional and integrated EPR, further development was necessary. All of the programs would require significant process redesign and changes in clinicians' behaviour and thinking. Systems, structures and processes would need to be aligned and intentionally designed to achieve the desired outcomes.

The project included two main components. The first was computerized provider order entry (CPOE) (by physician, nurse, or practitioner), the second was a closed-loop medication administration process (CLMP), which included electronic medication administration records (eMAR) and closed-loop medication administration (CLMA).

CPOE referred to the process by which a physician or other healthcare provider entered orders (e.g., lab test, X-rays, medications) directly into the computer rather than handwriting the orders on a paper chart. CPOE decreased delays in order completion, reduced errors related to handwriting, allowed order entry at either point-of-care or off-site and provided both automated error-checking and alerts. Alerts would occur when a physician ordered a drug that a patient was known to be allergic to or ordered a test that had already been completed (see Exhibit 8).

CLMP and eMAR put the power of technology at the patient's bedside. Patients received a barcoded patient identification band when admitted to the hospital. When a nurse or a therapist administered a medication, they used the list of medications on the eMAR and verified that the patient was given the correct medication by scanning each dose at the bedside. Next, the nurse or therapist scanned the patient's armband to verify that each patient received the correct medication. In the case of an incorrect match between patient and medication, the safety software issued a warning. Lastly, the nurse scanned her own identification badge. The administration of the medication was then automatically documented on the patient's electronic record.

The broad adoption of electronic patient record systems was widely believed to lead to major healthcare savings, a reduction in medical errors and improved health.[3] A patient's blood type, prescribed drugs, medical conditions and other aspects of medical history could be accounted for much more quickly. At the very least, an EPR could save time at the doctor's office. At most, quick access to records could save lives in an emergency situation when questions need to be answered quickly during the emergency decision-making process. For example, during such tragic events as 9/11 and Hurricane Katrina, the benefits of electronic record keeping were highlighted. The injured were more easily treated and may have had better outcomes than those whose paper records had been destroyed.

Despite the staggering costs and the magnitude of this organizational change challenge, the senior leadership team had decided that the potential gains in quality of patient care and patient safety were too great to delay any further, and hence, had recently approved Project HUGO.

A 50:50 CHANCE

While Johnson knew that getting HUGO off the ground was a monumental challenge, she also knew that the results would be well worth the effort. She had spent much of the last four years researching the causes of medication errors and advocating for changes to the system. She knew that HUGO wasn't about efficiency or saving money; it was about saving lives. She thought about the media headlines that were burned into her memory forever. She knew that all of those tragedies could have been prevented by systems like HUGO.

Yet, Johnson was also acutely aware of the many factors that could have a serious negative impact on the adoption of this project. She also knew that the odds of success were not in her favour, with up to 50 per cent of CPOE projects typically failing because of resistance from clinicians. She remembered reading about Cedars Sinai Hospital in California. In 2002, the organization had been forced to scrap a $34 million system when physicians had "walked out" of the hospital and refused to work until the system was removed.[4] Many reasons had been noted for why EPR systems had failed (see Exhibit 9).

Thinking back to her prior conversations with physicians, Johnson knew that the clinicians she had worked with on a daily basis had their own personal reasons for resisting HUGO. And it was not just physicians that Johnson had heard from while working on the HUGO proposal. Nurses were also vocal in their opposition. They had cared for patients for many years using pen and paper (often even just a paper towel), which they felt had worked just fine. These nurses claimed that mistakes did not happen to them because they had perfected the manual processes. Johnson was reminded of a report from a hospital that noted in the first six months after the implementation of barcoded medication administration, a total of 746 medication errors had been avoided. Most of these errors would have gone unnoticed by nursing staff. Even Johnson's own pharmacy staff and other allied health

---

[3]Richard Hillestad et al., "Can Electronic Medical Record Systems Transform Health Care? Potential Health Benefits, Savings and Costs," *Health Affairs*, 2005, vol. 24, no. 5, pp. 1103–1117.

[4]Cedars-Sinai Doctors Cling to Pen and Paper, by Ceci Connolly, *Washington Post*, 2005, March 21, 2005; page A01.

providers had reservations about HUGO. Most staff believed that the physicians would find a way to deflect order entry responsibility to a pharmacist or nurse and thus resented the expected increase in their workload.

"Resistance to change is normal," Johnson thought, but she could not help but wonder whether the timing was right to embark on HUGO. Within the clinical areas, staff was dealing with pressing issues. Infection transmission of antibiotic-resistant organisms was at an all-time high, and staff felt they were being blamed for poor infection control practice. Wait times in the emergency departments were much longer than in any other hospital in Canada; patients were waiting up to three days for a bed after a physician's decision to admit them. In addition, the information technology (IT) services were being outsourced to the United States, and many of the expert technical staff that LHSC needed to rely on had been laid off. Staff throughout the organization was exhausted, morale at an all time low and sick time was at record levels.

HOW TO MAKE HUGO WORK (AND STICK)

Johnson was well aware of the magnitude of the organizational change challenge that she faced. She knew that the implementation of an EPR was like a hurricane whipping through an organization. Everything that staff once knew would change.

"The happy excitement for the new school year that my children feel could not be more different from the not so joyous anticipation of HUGO for hospital staff", Johnson thought.

EXHIBIT 1: Effect of Health Information Technology at Key Stages in the Process of Medication Use

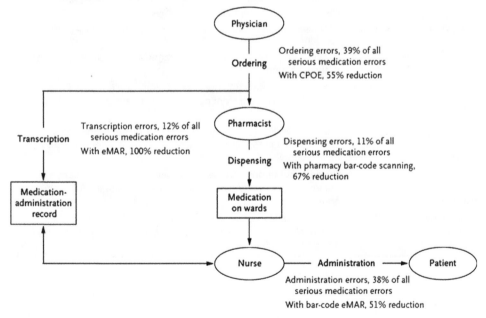

Source: Eric G. Poon, et al, "Effect of Bar-Code Technology on the Safety of Medication Administration," *New England Journal of Medicine*, 2010, vol. 362, pp. 1698–1707.

EXHIBIT 2: Summary of Hospitals Involved in Project HUGO

Organization	Type	Bed Count	Description
London Health Sciences Centre	**Acute-care teaching and research hospital**	**998**	Provides the broadest range of patient services of any hospital in Ontario (offering care in 51 different specialties) Provided care to more than 1 million patients in the past year, including the most medically complex and critically ill patients in the region Home to South Street Hospital, University Hospital, Victoria Hospital, Children's Hospital, Byron Family Medical Centre, Victoria Family Medical Centre, London Regional Cancer Program, Fowler Kennedy Sport Medicine Clinic, CSTAR (Canadian Surgical Technologies & Advanced Robotics) and Lawson Health Research Institute
St. Joseph's Health Care	**Major patient care, teaching and research centre**	**1,278**	Provides a broad range of patient care, including outpatient, long-term, regional mental health, rehabilitation, palliative, veterans and specialized geriatric services Home to St. Joseph's Hospital, Parkwood Hospital, Regional Mental Health Care (London & St. Thomas), Mount Hope Centre for Long-Term Care, the Ivey Eye Institute and Lawson Research Institute
LHSC/SJHC provides services to the following regional hospitals, including the operation of a shared electronic health information management system.			
Alexandra Hospital	Community healthcare provider	35	An acute- and continuing-care hospital offering a variety of services, including medical, day surgery and therapy to more than 20,000 patients annually Serves Ingersoll and the surrounding area
Listowel & Wingham Hospital Alliance	Community healthcare provider	LMH: 47 WDH: 34	Composed of Listowel Memorial Hospital (LMH) and Wingham and District Hospital (WDH) Provides numerous services including Medicine, Emergency, Oncology and Surgery to the areas of Listowel and Wingham
Middlesex Hospital Alliance	Community healthcare provider	SMGH: 54 FCHS: 16	Composed of Strathroy Middlesex General Hospital and Four Counties Health Services; serves a combined area of 58,000 residents Focuses on providing outpatient, diagnostic and ambulatory care to the surrounding community
South Huron Hospital Association	Community healthcare provider	19	Serves approximately 19,000 clients within the Municipality of South Huron and adjacent communities, offering both acute and chronic care
St. Thomas Elgin General Hospital	Community health care provider	166	Provides medicine, surgery, obstetrics, pediatrics, anesthesia, emergency and family medicine services to St. Thomas and to Elgin County, which is a catchment area of 89,000 residents
Tillsonburg District Memorial Hospital	Community healthcare provider	51	Provides numerous care services, including medicine, surgery, emergency and mental health to the residents of the Tillsonburg area
Woodstock General Hospital	Community healthcare provider	113	Serving a catchment area of more than 54,000 residents, WGH provides a host of services, including critical care, surgery, ambulatory care and rehabilitation

Source: LHSC Internal Documentation.

EXHIBIT 3: Organizational Vision Statements

London Health Sciences Centre's Vision

Source: LHSC Internal documentation.

St. Joseph's Health Care's Vision

From the shortest visit to the longest stay, we earn complete confidence in the care we provide, and make a lasting difference in the quest to live fully.

Source: St. Joseph's Health Care, London http://www.sjhc.london.on.ca/missionvisionvalues

EXHIBIT 4: Current Medication Workflow

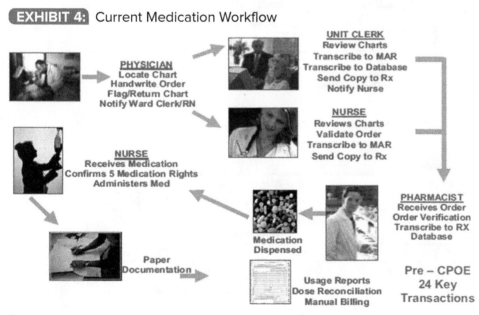

Note: RN = registered nurse; MAR = medical administration record; Rx = pharmacy; CPOE = computerized provider order entry.

Source: LHSC Internal Documentation.

EXHIBIT 5: Proposed HUGO Workflow

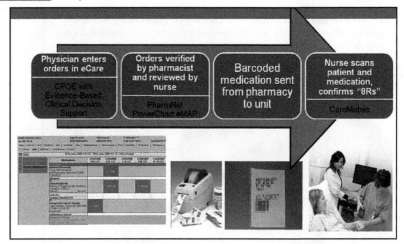

Note: CPOE = computerized provider order entry; eMAR = electronic medical administration record
Source: LHSC Internal Documentation.

EXHIBIT 6: Sample Handwritten Medication Order

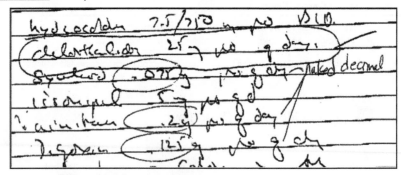

Source: LHSC Internal Documentation.

EXHIBIT 7: Sample HUGO Medication Order

		Order Name	Status	Details
Medications				
☑	🔲66^	amiodarone	Ordered	200 mg, TAB, PO, Daily, Routine, 11/12/08 9:00:00 EST
☑	🔲66^	chlorthalidone	Ordered	25 mg, TAB, PO, Daily, Routine, 11/12/08 9:00:00 EST
☑	🔲66^	digoxin	Ordered	0.125 mg, TAB, PO, Daily, Routine, 11/12/08 9:00:00 EST Record apical pulse prior to administration.
☑	🔲66^	levothyroxine (Synthroid)	Ordered	0.075 mg, TAB, PO, Daily, Routine, 11/12/08 9:00:00 EST
☑	🔲66^	lisinopril	Ordered	5 mg, TAB, PO, Daily, Routine, 11/12/08 9:00:00 EST
☐	🔲66^	acetaminophen-HYDROcodone (Vicodin 5/500)	Incomplete	PO, BID (2 times a day), 11/11/08 21:00:00 EST

Source: LHSC Internal Documentation.

EXHIBIT 8: Changes for Clinicians

	Today	With Electronic Patient Record
Physician Orders	• Orders are handwritten on paper. • Handwriting is often difficult to decipher! • No automatic alerts or warnings if dose is wrong or patient is allergic to the drug. • Physician must have the chart in their hands to write the order.	• Physician can order medications for any patient, anywhere, anytime because they access the chart through a computer. • Handwriting legibility is a non-issue. • Dose-range checking, rules and evidence ensure safe, high-quality care. Physician receives a warning if the drug ordered is inappropriate.
Medication Administration	• Nurse manually writes new orders to paper administration record. • Nurse administers medication with no double check or safety net. • Nurse documents administration manually on the paper record.	• Medications appear directly on electronic medication administration record. • Medications, patient and nurse are barcoded to automatically confirm that they are correct. • Nurse finally has a check at the bedside!
Processes and policies	• In the paper world, many policies and processes are not adhered to, particularly if they are not perceived by staff to be important. For example, medications must be administered within one hour of the time they are due. This time required is not tracked carefully in a paper world and no repercussions result when a dose is given early or late.	• In the electronic world, the nurse will receive a warning when a dose is late or early. If the dose is not given, an incident report is generated, leading to an explanation being required by the nurse.

Source: LHSC Internal Documentation.

EXHIBIT 9: Top 10 Reasons Computerized Provider Order Entry (CPOE) Efforts Fail

Reason	Description	Mitigation Strategy
1. Motivation for implementation is driven by anything but patient care	The purpose of implementation must be quality of care and safety (not an information technology [IT] or administrative project). Cannot be perceived to be "forced."	Promotion of CPOE as a process of medical management and not merely the entry of orders.
2. Lack of clarity in CPOE vision	The organization must have a shared vision regarding the purpose of CPOE.	Implementation of a clear communication and change strategy. Why is change needed?
3. Lack of visible leadership support	Senior leadership is not visibly supportive of the change.	Senior management must have an unwavering commitment to the change and all behaviours must reflect this commitment.
4. Costs are underestimated	Organizations forget about the ongoing costs of ownership. They must account for temporary decreases in productivity.	The organization must consider the total costs of ownership. Extra staffing is required during the go-live process to reduce the impact of decreased productivity. Consider a decrease in patient admissions and volume?
5. Workflow and processes are not accurately and completely mapped and understood.	Organizations do not fully appreciate the complexity of current workflow processes. Staff is often tempted to simply recreate their paper/manual processes in the electronic world.	The organization must consider the total costs of ownership. Extra staffing is required during the go-live process to reduce the impact of decreased productivity. Consider a decrease in patient admissions and volume?

EXHIBIT 9: (continued)

Reason	Description	Mitigation Strategy
6. Value to users not apparent	Clinicians must understand the value proposition. Clinicians cannot see the CPOE as clerical work.	Use decision-support and evidence-based order sets. Demonstrate that the benefits of the system cannot be provided by the paper-based processes.
7. Project management methodology is not followed to enhance speed to implement. The mistaken belief that hospitals can do it on their own!	Requires very tight project management and accountability	Budget included for senior project manager. Recruitment criteria will include experience with CPOE implementation. We will engage Cerner to assist in our implementation — they have successfully converted 53 CPOE projects and have more than 60 CPOE projects in progress.
8. Technology	Consider usability, system performance, sign on, clicks. Device deployment and access.	Sign-on strategy will be in place before go-live. Clinical informatics, IT staff and clinicians will design interfaces to ensure usability. Planning on two devices per nurse!
9. Training and support removed too soon	Require "live" help at the elbow.	Will have 24/7 support on site for 6 weeks (planned). Will have specific physician help line.
10. No optimization process	Need a plan for rapid action and change after the go-live date to deal with unexpected issues. Need a plan to optimize the system based on feedback.	IT staff will support the system 24/7 after the go-live date. For ongoing optimization issues an e-suggestion box will be in place. Clinical Informatics team will be deployed to interact with teams.

Victoria Heavy Equipment Limited

Brian Walters sat back in the seat of his Lear jet as it broke through the clouds en route from Squamish, a small town near Vancouver, British Columbia, to Sacramento, California. As chairman of the board, majority shareholder, and chief executive officer, the 51-year-old Walters had run Victoria Heavy Equipment Limited as a closely held company for years. During this time it had become the second-largest producer of mobile cranes in the world, with 2007 sales of $150 million and exports to more than 30 countries. But in early 2008 the problem of succession was in his thoughts. His son and daughter were not ready to run the organization, and he personally wanted to devote more time to other interests. He wondered about the kind of person he should hire to become president. There was also a nagging thought that there might be other problems with Victoria that would have to be worked out before he eased out of his present role.

COMPANY HISTORY

Victoria Heavy Equipment Limited (Victoria) was established in 1917 in Victoria, British Columbia, to produce horse-drawn log skidders for the forest industry. The young firm showed a flair for product innovation, pioneering the development of motorized skidders and later, after diversifying into the crane business, producing the country's first commercially successful hydraulic crane controls. In spite of these innovations, the company was experiencing severe financial difficulties in 1970 when it was purchased by Brian Walters Sr., the father of the current chairman. By installing tight financial controls and paying close

Paul W. Beamish and Thomas A. Poynter wrote this case solely to provide material for class discussion. The authors do not intend to illustrate either effective or ineffective handling of a managerial situation. The authors may have disguised certain names and other identifying information to protect confidentiality.

IVEY | Publishing

Ivey Management Services prohibits any form of reproduction, storage or transmittal without its written permission. Reproduction of this material is not covered under authorization by any reproduction rights organization. To order copies or request permission to reproduce materials, contact Ivey Publishing, Ivey Management Services, c/o Richard Ivey School of Business, The University of Western Ontario, London, Ontario, Canada, N6A 3K7; phone (519) 661-3208; fax (519) 661-3882; e-mail cases@ivey.uwo.ca.

Copyright © 2008, Ivey Management Services   Version: (A) 2008-04-15

One time permission to reproduce granted by Richard Ivey School of Business Foundation on April 22, 2014.

attention to productivity, Walters was able to turn the company around, and in 1977 he decided that Victoria would focus exclusively on cranes, and go after the international market.

At the time of Brian Walters Sr.'s retirement in 1990, it was clear that the decision to concentrate on the crane business had been a good one. The company's sales and profits were growing, and Victoria cranes were beginning to do well in export markets. Walters Sr. was succeeded as president by his brother James, who began to exercise very close personal control over the company's operations. However, as Victoria continued to grow in size and complexity, the load on James became so great that his health began to fail. The solution was to appoint an assistant general manager, John Rivers, through whom tight supervision could be maintained while James Walters' workload was eased. This move was to no avail, however. James Walters suffered a heart attack in 1992 and Rivers became general manager. At the same time, the young Brian Walters, the current chairman and chief executive officer, became head of the U.S. operation.

When Brian Walters took responsibility for Victoria's U.S. business, the firm's American distributor was selling 30 to 40 cranes per year. Walters thought the company should be selling at least 150. Even worse, the orders that the American firm did get tended to come in large quantities, as many as 50 cranes in a single order. This played havoc with Victoria's production scheduling. Walters commented, "We would rather have 10 orders of 10 cranes each than a single order for 100." In 1997, when the U.S. distributor's agreement expired, he offered the company a five-year renewal if it would guarantee sales of 150 units per year. When the firm refused, Walters bought it, and in the first month fired 13 of the 15 employees and cancelled most existing dealerships. He then set to work to rebuild, only accepting orders for 10 cranes or less. His hope was to gain a foothold and a solid reputation in the U.S. market before the big U.S. firms noticed him.

This strategy quickly showed results, and in 1998 Walters came back to Canada. As Rivers was still general manager, there was not enough to occupy him fully, and he began travelling three or four months a year. While he was still very much a part of the company, it was not a full-time involvement.

VICTORIA IN THE EARLY 2000S

Victoria entered the early 2000s with sales of approximately $75 million and by 2007, partly as a result of opening the new plant in California, had succeeded in doubling this figure. Profits reached their highest level ever in 2005, but declined somewhat over the next two years as costs rose and the rate of sales growth slowed. Financial statements are presented in Exhibits 1 and 2. The following sections describe the company and its environment in the early 2000s.

Product Line

The bulk of Victoria's crane sales in the late 1990s and early 2000s came from a single product line, the LTM 1000, which was produced both in its Squamish facility (the firm had moved from Victoria to Squamish in the early 1920s) and its smaller plant in California, built in 2001. The LTM 1000 line consisted of mobile cranes of five basic sizes, averaging $750,000 in price. Numerous options were available for these cranes, which could provide uncompromised on-site performance, precision lifting capabilities, fast highway travel, and effortless city driving. Because of the numerous choices available, Victoria preferred not to build them to stock. The company guaranteed 60-day delivery and "tailor-made" cranes to customer specifications. This required a large inventory of both parts and raw material.

Walters had used a great deal of ingenuity to keep Victoria in a competitive position. For example, in 2004, he learned that a company trying to move unusually long and heavy logs from a new tract of redwood trees in British Columbia was having serious problems with its existing cranes. A crane with a larger than average height and lifting capacity was required. Up to this point, for technical reasons, it had not been possible to produce a crane with the required specifications. However, Walters vowed that Victoria would develop such a crane, and six months later it had succeeded.

Although the LTM 1000 series provided almost all of Victoria's crane sales, a new crane had been introduced in 2006 after considerable expenditure on design, development and manufacture. The $975,000 A-100 had a 70-tonne capacity and could lift loads to heights of 61 metres, a combination previously unheard of in the industry. Through the use of smooth hydraulics even the heaviest loads could be picked up without jolts. In spite of these features, and an optional ram-operated tilt-back cab designed to alleviate the stiff necks which operators commonly developed from watching high loads, sales of the A-100 were disappointing. As a result, several of the six machines built were leased to customers at unattractive rates. The A-100 had, however, proven to be a very effective crowd attraction device at equipment shows.

Markets

There were two important segments in the crane market—custom-built cranes and standard cranes—and although the world mobile crane market was judged to be $945 million in 2007, no estimates were available as to the size of each segment. Victoria competed primarily in the custom segment, in the medium-and heavy-capacity end of the market. In the medium-capacity custom crane class Victoria's prices were approximately 75 per cent of those of its two main competitors. The gap closed as the cranes became heavier, with Victoria holding a 15 per cent advantage over Washington Cranes in the heavy custom crane business. In heavy standard cranes Victoria did not have a price advantage.

Victoria's two most important markets were Canada and the United States. The U.S. market was approximately $360 million in 2007, and Victoria's share was about 15 per cent. Victoria's Sacramento plant, serving both the U.S. market and export sales involving U.S. aid and financing, produced 60 to 70 cranes per year. The Canadian market was much smaller, about $66 million in 2007, but Victoria was the dominant firm in the country, with a 60 per cent share. The Squamish plant, producing 130 to 150 cranes per year, supplied both the Canadian market and all export sales not covered by the U.S. plant. There had been very little real growth in the world market since 2002.

The primary consumers in the mobile crane industry were contractors. Because the amount of equipment downtime could make the difference between showing a profit or loss on a contract, contractors were very sensitive to machine dependability, as well as parts and service availability. Price was important, but it was not everything. Independent surveys suggested that Washington Crane, Victoria's most significant competitor, offered somewhat superior service and reliability, and if Victoria attempted to sell similar equipment at prices comparable to Washington's, it would fail. As a result, Victoria tried to reduce its costs through extensive backward integration, manufacturing 85 per cent of its crane components in-house, the highest percentage in the industry. This drive to reduce costs was somewhat offset, however, by the fact that much of the equipment in the Squamish plant was very old. In recent years, some of the slower and less versatile machinery had been replaced, but by 2007 only 15 per cent of the machinery in the plant was new, efficient, numerically controlled equipment.

Victoria divided the world into eight marketing regions. The firm carried out little conventional advertising, but did participate frequently at equipment trade shows. One of the company's most effective selling tools was its ability to fly in prospective customers from all over the world in Walters' executive jet. Victoria believed that the combination of its integrated plant, worker loyalty, and the single-product concentration evident in their Canadian plant produced a convinced customer. There were over 14 such visits to the British Columbia plant in 2007, including delegations from China, Korea, France and Turkey.

Competition

As the world's second largest producer of cranes, Victoria faced competition from five major firms, all of whom were much larger and more diversified. The industry leader was the Washington Crane Company with 2007 sales of $600 million and a world market share of 50 per cent. Washington had become a name synonymous around the world with heavy-duty equipment and had been able to maintain a sales growth-rate of over 15 per cent per annum for the past five years. It manufactured in the United States, Mexico and Australia. Key to its operations were 100 strong dealers worldwide with over 200 outlets. Washington had almost 30 per cent of Canada's crane market.

Next in size after Victoria was Texas Star, another large manufacturer whose cranes were generally smaller than Victoria's and sold through the company's extensive worldwide equipment dealerships. The next two largest competitors were both very large U.S. multinational producers whose crane lines formed a small part of their overall business. With the exception of Washington, industry observers suggested that crane sales for these latter firms had been stable (at best) for quite some time. The exception was the Japanese crane producer Toshio which had been aggressively pursuing sales worldwide and had entered the North American market recently. Sato, another Japanese firm, had started in the North American market as well. Walters commented:

> My father laid the groundwork for the success that this company has enjoyed, but it is clear that we have some major challenges ahead of us. Washington is four times our size and I know that we are at the top of their hit list. Our Japanese competitors, are also going to be tough. The key to our success is to remain flexible—we must not develop the same kind of organization as the big U.S. firms.

Organization

In 2001, a number of accumulating problems had ended Brian Walters' semi-retirement and brought him back into the firm full time. Although sales were growing, Walters saw that work was piling up and things were not getting done. He believed that new cranes needed to be developed, and he wanted a profit-sharing plan put in place. One of his most serious concerns was the development of middle managers, given a perceived lack of depth. The root cause of these problems, Walters believed, was that the firm was overly centralized. Most of the functional managers reported to Rivers, and Rivers made most of the decisions. Walters concluded that action was necessary: "If we want to grow further we have to change."

Between 2001 and 2004 Walters reorganized the firm by setting up separate operating companies and a corporate staff group. In several cases, senior operating executives were placed in staff/advisory positions, while in others, executives held positions in both operating and staff groups. Exhibit 3 illustrates Victoria's organizational chart as of 2005.

By early 2006 Walters was beginning to wonder "if I had made a very bad decision." The staff groups weren't working. Rivers had been unable to accept the redistribution of power and had resigned. There was "civil war in the company." Politics and factional disputes were the rule rather than the exception. Line managers were upset by the intervention of the staff VPs of employee relations, manufacturing, and marketing. Staff personnel, on the other hand, were upset by "poor" line decisions.

As a result, the marketing and manufacturing staff functions were eradicated with the late-2007 organizational restructuring illustrated in Exhibit 4. The services previously supplied by the staff groups were duplicated to varying extent inside each division.

In place of most of the staff groups, an executive committee was established in 2006. Membership included the president and head of all staff groups and presidents (general managers) of the four divisions. Meeting monthly, the executive committee was intended to evaluate the performance of the firm's profit and cost problems, handle mutual problems such as transfer prices, and allocate capital expenditures among the four operating divisions. Subcommittees handled subjects such as research and development (R&D) and new products.

The new organization contained seven major centres for performance measurement purposes. The cost centres were:

1. Engineering; R&D (reporting to Victco Ltd.)
2. International Marketing (Victoria Marketing Ltd.)
3. Corporate staff.

The major profit centres were:

4. CraneCorp. Inc. (U.S. production and sales)
5. Victco Ltd. (supplying Victoria with components)
6. Craneco (Canadian production and marketing)
7. Victoria-owned Canadian sales outlets (reporting to Victoria Marketing Ltd.)

The major profit centres had considerable autonomy in their day-to-day operations and were motivated to behave as if their division was a separate, independent firm.

By mid-2007, Brian Walters had moved out of his position as president, and Michael Carter, a long-time employee close to retirement, was asked to take the position of president until a new one could be found.

Walters saw his role changing.

If I was anything, I was a bit of an entrepreneur. My job was to supply that thrust, but to let people develop on their own accord. I was not concerned about things not working, but I was concerned when nothing was being done about it.

In the new organization Walters did not sit on the executive committee. However, as chairman of the board and chief executive officer, the committee's recommendations came to him and ". . . they constantly tried me on." His intention was to monitor the firm's major activities rather than to set them. He did have to sit on the product development subcommittee, however, when "things were not working . . . there was conflict . . . the engineering group (engineering, R&D) had designed a whole new crane and nobody, including me, knew about it." Mr. McCarthy, the VP of engineering and R&D, called only five to six committee meetings. The crane his group developed was not to Walters' liking. (There had been a high turnover rate in this group, with four VPs leaving since 2005.) Recognizing these problems, Walters brought in consultants to tackle the problems of the management information system and the definition of staff/line responsibilities.

In spite of these moves, dissatisfaction still existed within the company in 2008. The new organization had resulted in considerable dissension. Some conflict centred on the establishment of appropriately challenging budgets for each operating firm and even more conflict had erupted over transfer pricing and allocation of capital budgets. In 2007-08, even though requested budgets were cut equally, lack of central control over spending resulted in over expenditures by several of the profit and cost centres.

The views of staff and the operating companies' presidents varied considerably when they discussed Victoria's organizational evolution and the operation of the present structure. Diane Walters, the president of Victoria International Marketing, liked the autonomous system because it helped to identify the true performance of sections of the company. "We had separate little buckets and could easily identify results." Furthermore, she felt that there was no loss of efficiency (due to the duplication of certain staff functions within the divisions) since there was little duplication of systems between groups, and each group acted as a check and balance on the other groups so that "manufacturing won't make what marketing won't sell." Comments from other executives were as follows:

> The divisionalized system allowed me to get closer to my staff because we were a separate group.
> We ended up with sales and marketing expertise that was much better than if we had stayed under manufacturing.
> If you (run the firm) with a manufacturing-oriented organization, you could forget what people want.
> In a divisionalized system there was bound to be conflict between divisions, but that was not necessarily unhealthy.

Some executives saw the decentralized, semi-autonomous operating company structure as a means of giving each person the opportunity to grow and develop without the hindrance of other functional executives. Most, if not all, of the operating company presidents and staff VPs were aware that decentralization brought benefits, especially in terms of the autonomy it gave them to modify existing practices. One senior executive even saw the present structure as an indicator of their basic competitive stance, "Either we centralize the structure and retract, or we stay as we are and fight with the big guys." With minimal direction from Brian Walters, presidents were able to build up their staff, establish priorities and programs, and essentially, were only held responsible for the bottom line.

Other executives believed that Victoria's structure was inappropriate. As one put it, "The semi-independence of the operating companies and the lack of a real leader for the firm has resulted in poor co-ordination of problem solving and difficulty in allocating responsibility." As an example, he noted how engineering's response to manufacturing was often slow and poorly communicated. Even worse, the executive noted, was how the priorities of different units were not synchronized. "When you manufacture just one product line all your activities are inter-related. So when one group puts new products first on a priority list, while another is still working out bugs in the existing product, conflict and inefficiencies have to develop."

The opposing group argued that the present organization was more appropriate to a larger, faster growing and more complex company. As one senior executive put it, "We're too small to be as decentralized as we are now. All of this was done to accommodate the Walters' kids anyway, and it's now going to detract from profitability and growth." Another executive stated that rather than being a president of an operating company he would prefer to be a general manager at the head of a functional group, reporting to a group head. "If we had the right Victoria Heavy Equipment president," he said, "we wouldn't need all these divisional presidents." Another continued,

> Right now the players (divisional presidents and staff VPs) run the company. Brian Walters gives us a shot of adrenaline four or six times a year, but doesn't provide any

active leadership. When Brian leaves, things stop. Instead, Brian now wants to monitor the game plan rather than set it up for others to run. As we still only have an interim president (Carter), it is the marketplace that leads us, not any strategic plan or goal.

THE NEW PRESIDENT

Individual views about the appropriate characteristics of a new president were determined by what each executive thought was wrong with Victoria. Everyone realized that the new president would have to accommodate Brian Walters' presence and role in the firm and the existence of his two children in the organization. They all generally saw Brian as wanting to supply ideas and major strategies, but little else.

All but one of Victoria's executives agreed that the new president should not get involved in day-to-day activities or in major decision making. Instead, he should "arbitrate" among the line general managers (subsidiary presidents) and staff VPs and become more of a "bureaucrat-cum-diplomat" than an aggressive leader. As another put it, "The company will drive itself; only once in a while he'll steer a little."

THE 2008 SITUATION

Due to the proliferation of subprime mortgages in the U.S. and the subsequent decline in real estate and construction, industry analysts predicted a decline of 10 per cent in world crane sales, which totalled 1,200 units in 2007, and as much as a 30 per cent decrease in the North American market in 2008. Victoria's sales and production levels were down. Seventy-five shop floor employees had been laid off at Squamish, bringing total employment there to 850, and similar cuts were expected in Sacramento. Worker morale was suffering as a result, and the profit sharing plan, which had been introduced in early 2007 at Walters' initiative, was not helping matters. In spite of the optimism conveyed to workers when the plan was initiated, management had announced in October that no bonus would be paid for the year. Aggravating the problem was the workforce's observation that while certain groups met their budget, others did not, and hence all were penalized. This problem arose because each bonus was based on overall as well as divisional profits.

Many of the shop-floor workers and the supervisory staff were also disgruntled with the additions to the central and divisional staff groups, which had continued even while the workforce was being reduced. They felt that the paperwork these staff functions created was time-consuming and of little benefit. They noted, for example, that there were four or five times as many people in production control in 2008 as there were in 2002 for the same volume of production. In addition, they pointed out that despite all sorts of efforts on the part of a computer-assisted production control group, inventory levels were still too high.

Brian Walters commented on the 2008 situation and his view of the company's future:

What we are seeing in 2008 is a temporary decline in the market. This does not pose a serious problem for us, and certainly does not impact on my longer term goals for this company, which are to achieve a 25 per cent share of the world market by 2012, and reach sales of $375 million by 2021. We can reach these goals as long as we don't turn into one of these bureaucratic, grey-suited companies that are so common in North America. There are three keys for success in this business—a quality product, professional people and the motivation for Victoria to be the standard of excellence in our business. This means that almost everything depends on the competence and motivation of our people. We will grow by being more entrepreneurial, more dedicated, and more flexible than our competitors. With our single product line we are also more focused than our competitors. They manage only by the numbers–there is no room in those companies for an emotional plea, they won't look at sustaining losses to get into a new area, they'll turn the key on a loser . . . we look at the longer term picture.

"The hazard for Victoria," Walters said as he looked out of his window toward the Sacramento airstrip, "is that we could develop the same kind of bureaucratic, quantitatively oriented, grey-suited managers that slow down the large U.S. competitors." "But that," he said, turning to his audience, "is something I'm going to watch like a hawk. We need the right people."

EXHIBIT 1: Victoria Balance Sheet for the Years 2003–2007 ($000s)

	2003	2004	2005	2006	2007
ASSETS					
Current Assets					
Accounts receivable	$12,492	$11,940	$14,664	$15,768	$16,426
Allowance for doubtful accounts	(439)	(465)	(423)	(445)	(474)
Inventories	31,729	36,637	37,047	38,439	40,567
Prepaid expenses	178	156	234	159	193
Total current assets	43,960	48,268	51,522	53,921	56,712
Advances to shareholders	1,950	1,950	1,950	1,950	1,950
Fixed assets: property plant and equipment	10,260	10,470	10,312	11,029	11,083
Total assets	$56,170	$60,688	$63,784	$66,900	$69,745
LIABILITIES AND SHAREHOLDERS' EQUITY					
Current Liabilities					
Notes payable to bank	$11,599	$12,328	$13,887	$15,241	$16,998
Accounts payable	14,568	17,029	15,814	15,697	16,479
Accrued expenses	1,611	1,678	2,613	2,251	1,732
Deferred income tax	628	600	594	612	517
Income tax payable	817	1,038	918	780	774
Current portion of long-term debt	1,368	1,336	1,300	1,332	1,354
Total current liabilities	$30,591	$34,009	$35,126	$35,913	$37,854
Long-term debt	9,426	9,165	9,030	9,007	9,171
Total liabilities	40,017	43,174	44,156	44,920	47,025
SHAREHOLDERS' EQUITY					
Common shares	300	435	442	585	652
Retained earnings	15,853	17,079	19,186	21,395	22,068
Total shareholders' equity	16,153	17,514	19,628	21,980	22,720
Total liabilities and shareholders' equity	$56,170	$60,688	$63,784	$66,900	$69,745

EXHIBIT 2: Victoria Income Statement for the Years 2003–2007 ($000s)

	2003	2004	2005	2006	2007
Revenue					
Net sales	$95,079	$116,566	$129,519	$142,329	$151,414
Costs and Expenses					
Cost of sales	73,857	89,755	95,994	107,727	113,712
Selling expense	11,205	13,851	16,402	17,155	19,656
Administrative expense	4,026	5,800	8,235	8,692	10,557
Engineering expense	2,013	2,533	2,748	2,923	3,163
Gross income	3,978	4,627	6,140	5,832	4,326
Income taxes	1,621	1,921	2,445	2,257	1,881
Net income	$ 2,357	$2,706	$ 3,695	$ 3,575	$ 2,445

EXHIBIT 3: Victoria Organizational Structure, 2001–05

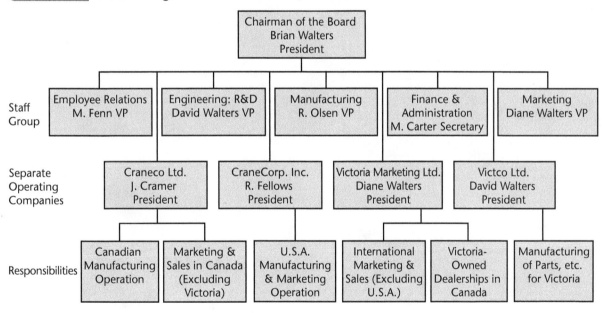

EXHIBIT 4: Victoria Organizational Structure, Late 2007

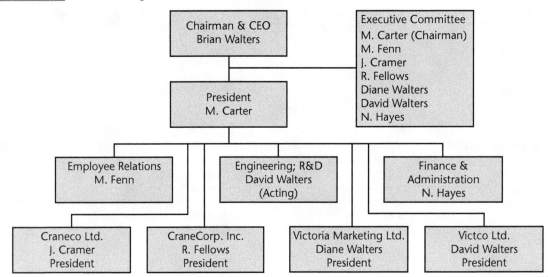

Enerplus Corporation: Assessing the Board Invitation

Sue MacKenzie called herself a "thermal girl." The expression referred to her expertise in the black art of using steam to coax oil from the Earth's reluctant crust. Graduating with an engineering degree from McGill, Montréal-raised MacKenzie found herself in the high-risk, high-reward, rough-and-tumble of Alberta's oil and gas industry. During her fourteen years with Amoco, MacKenzie acquired oil and gas development skills which she complemented with an MBA from the University of Calgary, deepening her understanding of the business side of the industry. A strong leader, MacKenzie was charged with progressively greater technical and executive challenges during her career. As a desire to volunteer and add value were also part of her personal makeup, MacKenzie served on a number of nonprofit association and advisory boards. After 25 years in the industry, MacKenzie decided on a midcourse career correction by very deliberately shedding her executive responsibilities in favor of nonprofit, coaching and mentoring work.

In 2011, MacKenzie received an invitation to join the board of Enerplus Corporation, an oil and gas producer based in Calgary, Canada (see Exhibit 1). She was interested and intrigued, but also cautious. She reasoned this could be an opportunity to add value to this organization while increasing her own knowledge of the energy sector. At the same time, however, corporate board service was not without financial and personal risks. She had to convince herself that the needs of the Enerplus board and her skill set and experience would be a good match. She had to consider whether the time and financial commitment of board service would be consistent with her new direction towards nonprofit

Professor Malcolm Munro and Professor P. Michael Maher wrote this case solely to provide material for class discussion. The authors do not intend to illustrate either effective or ineffective handling of a managerial situation. The authors may have disguised certain names and other identifying information to protect confidentiality.

Richard Ivey School of Business Foundation prohibits any form of reproduction, storage or transmission without its written permission. Reproduction of this material is not covered under authorization by any reproduction rights organization. To order copies or request permission to reproduce materials, contact Ivey Publishing, Richard Ivey School of Business Foundation, The University of Western Ontario, London, Ontario, Canada, N6A 3K7; phone (519) 661-3208; fax (519) 661-3882; e-mail cases@ivey.uwo.ca.

Copyright © 2012, Richard Ivey School of Business Foundation   Version: 2013-07-24

One time permission to reproduce granted by Richard Ivey School of Business Foundation on April 22, 2014.

IVEY | Publishing

work. She also had to convince herself she could handle a corporate board service challenge. The board asked for a reply soon. MacKenzie had to consider how to undertake a thorough assessment of this complicated issue and decide if she would accept this opportunity to serve.

BACKGROUND

Susan MacKenzie was born in Ontario and moved with her parents and two brothers to Montréal when she was very young. After high school, her keen analytical mind led her to the highly-regarded McGill Faculty of Engineering where she obtained a bachelor's degree in mechanical engineering. Her career in the oil and gas industry began when she joined Amoco Canada Petroleum Company in 1983. Her fourteen years with Amoco drew her into a variety of engineering and leadership roles in natural gas, and conventional oil and heavy oil exploitation. Her last years with Amoco were spent working on development of the Wolf Lake heavy oil project in northern Alberta.

In energy industry parlance, conventional oil is more accurately referred to as light crude oil. In the Hollywood versions, a "wildcatter" nails together an oil rig. After many days of nervous drilling, a gusher comes in and blows light crude oil one hundred feet in the air. Gushers don't occur when mining heavy crude. With much greater density, heavy crude has to be diluted to flow easily in pipelines. As might be expected, extracting heavy oil from the earth presented difficult engineering challenges. MacKenzie worked with various enhanced oil recovery techniques that included injecting steam into the underground oil deposits to decrease the oil's viscosity enabling it to flow more easily to the producing well. This is referred to as *in situ* oil recovery, a term that generally described the "in place" extraction of oil from those parts of the vast Athabasca oil sands deposit too deep to traditionally mine.

In 1997, with a proven track record of oilsands development and production, MacKenzie was lured by Petro-Canada. Petro-Canada was a government-owned corporation founded in 1975 to enable Canadians to benefit from rising oil prices. Over the years, Petro-Canada became a large player in traditional oil exploration and recovery, oilsands development and East Coast offshore oil production. Among her roles at Petro-Canada, MacKenzie was appointed vice-president of *in situ* development and operations, where she was responsible for Petro-Canada's *in situ* operations and development and for identifying and developing additional *in situ* production sources. Petro-Canada's MacKay River operation was an active Athabasca oilsands development site. In addition to the decade she spent in development of the company's oilsands resources, MacKenzie had spent her last two years with Petro-Canada as vice-president of human resources.

Throughout these very busy years, MacKenzie still found time to serve on a variety of nonprofit boards including ones in support of a school for children with learning disabilities, a university engineering advisory council, a condominium strata council and a golf course. In an interview, MacKenzie explained she was motivated by a desire to assist others, a commitment to lifelong learning and a variety of interests. She recognized the considerable satisfaction she derived from these activities and eventually contemplated leaving the corporate world to do more nonprofit work as well as coaching and mentoring. The decision was not easy since leaving the corporate world could be risky financially. However, after careful thought, MacKenzie and her husband concluded their finances were adequate. With no children at home and her husband's full support, Mackenzie believed it would be manageable. When Petro-Canada merged with Suncor in 2009, MacKenzie saw this as her opportunity to make a graceful exit and departed the company.

SHIFTING TO A DIFFERENT GEAR

When MacKenzie left Petro-Canada, she held off involvements of any sort for the first six months to enable her to shift to a different gear. With the benefit of this reflective period, MacKenzie targeted board level participation in two nonprofit organizations whose work resonated deeply with her. As a result, in early 2010 she was invited to join the boards of both the Calgary Women's Emergency Shelter and Safe Haven Foundation. She observed however that she had managed to fend off the temptations presented by numerous business opportunities which had come her way. Even so, she sensed a desire to continue to contribute and stay engaged in the industry. As MacKenzie described it, "I felt the desire to keep my oar in the water."

Unexpectedly in early 2010, MacKenzie was contacted by the CEO of Oilsands Quest, an exploration and development company with assets predominantly in the neighboring province of Saskatchewan. Oilsands Quest needed a chief operating officer to advance a small *in situ* development project. MacKenzie made it clear she would only consider participation in the relative short-term—the attraction for MacKenzie was that she considered it "a project-oriented opportunity—in and out." MacKenzie took on the job despite knowing it was inconsistent with her new career direction. However, within a few months, Oilsands Quest's project timing became constrained and uncertain, and with the understanding of its board, MacKenzie resigned in September 2010. This was soon followed by an appointment as Executive-in-Residence at the Banff Centre, which drew her back to her chosen path. Her main responsibility was to assist the Centre's executive leadership development activities group and provide advice on how to connect with the business community, as well as provide coaching to program participants.

THE ENERPLUS TRANSITION

Enerplus was a company in transition. It had been an "income trust"—a corporation that bought existing oil and natural gas reserves, produced and sold the product, and paid investors accordingly, a business model that was supported by certain tax advantages. However, in October 2006, the Canadian government announced a change to tax policy that, coupled with an increasingly challenging business environment, encouraged income trusts like Enerplus to reconfigure their business models to include generation of cash through higher risk and capital-intensive activities like drill bit exploration, as different from solely acquiring and exploiting proven reserves. Mirroring the change in skills required within the organization itself to accomplish this shift, the Enerplus board required new blood and people with strong asset exploitation skills to provide additional insight into this new higher-risk business environment.

As part of its attention to governance process and board effectiveness, the Enerplus board of directors undertook an annual assessment of skills required and skills resident within the board membership. As a result, with the business model shift and the knowledge that two directors were retiring from the board by the end of 2012, the board charged its corporate governance and nominating committee to hunt for replacements with strong asset exploitation skills. The board needed to recruit two new people immediately to give them time to gain experience before the retiring members left.

By chance, the Enerplus vice-president of corporate services, Jennifer Koury, had come to know Sue MacKenzie when MacKenzie was the vice-president of human resources at Petro-Canada. They'd known each other for many years, served on an industry HR committee and advisory board together, and teamed up to develop an external mentoring program for executives in their respective companies. As MacKenzie commented, "Jen and I would occasionally go for coffee or lunch to share insights and pick each other's brains on work issues–I know I very much valued and trusted her opinions and views. I suspect she did likewise. You could say she was a part of my HR network."

Maintaining that relationship proved mutually beneficial when Jen Koury suggested MacKenzie's name as a potential board candidate to the CEO, Gordon Kerr. A highly regarded executive within Calgary's oil and gas industry, Kerr had held a number of senior positions with Enerplus and other companies and was appointed as a director in May 2001. With Kerr's agreement, Koury soon called MacKenzie and asked if she was interested in learning more about a potential board opportunity. About a week after sending her resume to Enerplus, MacKenzie received a request to meet Kerr for lunch to explore possible mutual interests.

MACKENZIE'S INITIAL REACTION

When first asked about submitting her resume and the prospect of a board invitation, MacKenzie professed to be intrigued, but not overly excited. She felt complimented, but acknowledged serving on a corporate board had never been a burning career aspiration. It would be an opportunity to have an excellent learning experience, share her knowledge, and stay engaged at a strategic level in the energy industry, but it was not particularly consistent with her new career direction. Still, she saw her new career path as less structured and, in that sense, corporate board service could be a "fit" for her. MacKenzie knew if she secured a board appointment, she would receive some financial compensation, but she felt the intangible benefits were far more compelling. In effect, she viewed the opportunity more favorably from a personal development perspective and less as a career step. With no critical downside so far, MacKenzie decided to treat the situation seriously and allow it to develop.

For her first meeting with Gordon Kerr, MacKenzie resolved to be generally familiar with the Enerplus business, its corporate governance practices (see Exhibit 2), strategic drivers, and major risks it might be facing as well as the business background of Kerr, the CEO. Enerplus' website provided the information she needed. She wanted to know enough to ask informed questions when meeting with Kerr. As an executive in the industry, MacKenzie knew of Enerplus, but aside from her colleague, the VP of corporate services, she had few personal contacts in the company or the board. Kerr and the directors on its then 13-member board were known to her generally as a highly respected group.

THE LUNCH

MacKenzie and Kerr met for lunch at the storied Calgary Petroleum Club, a prestigious downtown members-only place where in past years many oil and gas joint-ventures, as well as mergers and acquisitions, had been sealed with a handshake. Kerr described the changing Enerplus corporate environment and discussed the need to replace two board members. He quickly made known his interest in discussing options with MacKenzie and determining if there might be a match. Kerr particularly stressed Enerplus was in need of someone who understood asset development and had technical work experience in it. Acknowledging their currently all-male board, Kerr also believed MacKenzie could bring new perspectives to the board table. When MacKenzie indicated her interest in hearing more, Kerr said he would have further discussions with the board and would get back to her soon. When they parted, Sue MacKenzie knew she had a lot to think about.

One week after the meeting with Kerr, MacKenzie received an invitation to lunch at Enerplus to meet the chair of the Enerplus board and the chair of the corporate governance and nominating committee. It registered on MacKenzie at the time that the promptness of the invitation following her earlier meeting with Kerr suggested both board chairs had likely been consulted in advance regarding her general suitability. MacKenzie decided for the upcoming meeting it was time to ramp up her research on Enerplus, examine potential downside risks much more closely and begin preparing a set of very specific questions.

MACKENZIE'S RESEARCH AND RISK ASSESSMENT

MacKenzie resolved to take an analytical risk-averse approach: research, analysis, advice-seeking, and risk assessment. To prepare for her next interview, she began by accessing investor reports for Enerplus from SEDAR (see Exhibit 3) and from the Enerplus website (see Exhibit 4). SEDAR was an acronym for the System for Electronic Document Analysis and Retrieval, an electronic system of the Canadian Securities Administration for filing disclosure documents of Canadian public companies and investment groups. From SEDAR, MacKenzie was able to obtain a much clearer fix on the Enerplus financial situation from an investor perspective. On the Enerplus website she found executive and board member biographies. The Enerplus board was a very impressive group (see Exhibit 5).

She also looked more closely at her own background as it related to the needs of both the corporation and the board. While MacKenzie was an expert in heavy oil development, she had broad experience in asset exploitation generally, from land purchases right through producing operations. She had had technical and profit/loss responsibility for the full value chain, understood the technical requirements, the drivers, and the pressures. She saw no problems here. MacKenzie also reasoned that with the transition, the company might be facing succession issues and as anywhere, executive compensation would be a big topic. Her match with the Enerplus board's needs would be strengthened as she had been the senior management representative on Petro-Canada board's management resources and compensation committee and had worked on executive compensation for several years.

As for the downside risks, MacKenzie first thought about the adequacy of Enerplus Directors and Officers (D&O) liability insurance to cover costs in the event of a legal action against the board. She professed not to be overly concerned about the liability issue. From other corporate involvements, including having sought legal counsel on the adequacy of D&O protections in the past, she was sure a company the size of Enerplus would have adequate D&O protection coverage and up to current corporate standards. Nonetheless, not wishing to risk her "retirement nest egg," MacKenzie decided to ask about the matter. She also resolved to ask the chairs to characterize the Enerplus approach to enterprise risk management and the board's process in overseeing those risks.

Another consideration was the director shareholder requirements. Enerplus required each director to maintain a minimum share ownership level equal to a multiple of their annual retainer, and to reach this level within a prescribed timeline subsequent to board appointment. MacKenzie would be tying up more than Cdn$100,000. Relative to her financial situation, this was not egregious by any stretch but at the same time it represented an opportunity cost. "If I use this cash to meet my shareholder requirements," she asked herself, "then what am I not funding and am I happy with that?"

There was also the matter of time commitment. This raised a host of questions with no easy answers. Was she prepared to dedicate the time required for board service? She understood this was a different game from nonprofit board service; on a corporate board, at the end of the day your responsibility was to the corporation. Complex problems often demanded significant time to thoroughly address. Not all of that time would be slotted into a convenient pre-determined schedule—MacKenzie would have to be prepared to react and adjust on an as-needed basis. She also knew she would not be satisfied with being just a board member; she would want to be a good one. Completing the Institute for Corporate Directors training program would be a must; finding time to meet with mentors would be important. She knew she would dedicate whatever time was required to improve her ability to do the job well and viewed that as a basic necessity.

What impact would this have on her other desired pursuits? Board service was hard work and you had to be passionate about it; time spent there would not be available for other things. For a start, MacKenzie would have to prepare for and attend monthly meetings. This meant she and her husband would have to put on indefinite hold a year-long round-the-world trip they had been contemplating since their mutual retirement, a troubling sacrifice. In general, she had to think about the collateral impact on her husband and family. Her husband's unconditional support was a must.

MacKenzie viewed serving on the Enerplus board as a long-term commitment of at least five years. MacKenzie knew she had a ton of energy, and whatever she was involved with she would commit plenty of time to it—the real reflection point was whether she wanted to commit the time to this particular cause.

Finally, MacKenzie confessed she had real doubts about her ability to serve and thought very hard about the matter. The board was a group of highly seasoned exceptionally qualified energy and financial services experts who in turn served on many other corporate boards; she knew she would have to be ready to contribute, to add value. MacKenzie sought the advice of mentors who were former board members of Petro-Canada, and several other friends who were corporate board members. They were very supportive and argued she understood board operations and the difference between governance and management; they attested she would be a good board member and would make a strong contribution.

When asked if she had any concerns about being the only woman on the board, MacKenzie commented she had plenty of experience in male-dominated environments, including growing up with two brothers. Her confidence in this regard had shown up early when she opted for the then highly male-dominated engineering program at McGill. In her 25 year career in the oil and gas business, MacKenzie observed she had grown accustomed to working in male-dominated environments and had found her own way to thrive in them. In her opinion, successful women who are senior leaders become less concerned over the years about the male majority. As MacKenzie put it, "Over time, you get better at being comfortable with who you are and what you bring to the table in *any* environment."

THE BOARD INVITATION AND MACKENZIE'S FINAL THOUGHTS

In an Enerplus conference room on the 30th floor of Dome Tower in downtown Calgary, MacKenzie met the chair of the Enerplus board and the chair of the board's corporate governance and nominating committee. MacKenzie went well-prepared with many questions in hand. Her mindset was not on "selling" herself; she would let them decide if she could add value, make a contribution and otherwise be a good match for the company. Instead, MacKenzie mainly concerned herself with whether the company would be a good match for her. She wanted more insight regarding how Enerplus board service would meet her personal needs for learning and career development.

She knew the meeting would not result in an offer on the spot. If they decided in her favor, the chair of the corporate governance and nominating committee would likely recommend her appointment at a future full meeting of the board. As expected, the Enerplus people ended the meeting pleasantly, thanked MacKenzie for her time, and offered the customary remarks about "having some decisions to make." MacKenzie thought the outcome was uncertain, but needed to think about what to do if an invitation was extended.

In the days that followed, MacKenzie concluded the major issue for her was whether taking on this board role was really consistent with why she had engineered a departure from the business in the first place. MacKenzie recalled she had purposefully left to spend more time on nonprofit, coaching and mentoring work. Would those, still be the *main* things in her life? She asked herself if her rationale for departing the corporate world was still relevant, or if staying connected to it had become more important to her now that she was away.

A few weeks after the meeting, MacKenzie received a phone call from the board chair informing her he was authorized by the board to offer her an appointment, and detailed some of the terms. He explained that if she accepted, the appointment would be made promptly, the board having the authority to appoint up to three board members between annual general meetings (AGM). Board members appointed in such a manner would be required to stand for election by the corporation's shareholders at the next AGM in 2012.

For Sue MacKenzie, the thermal girl, it was decision time.

Emeritus Professor Malcolm C. Munro and Professor P. Michael Maher are from the Haskayne School of Business, University of Calgary.

EXHIBIT 1: Enerplus Corporation Home Page

Source: www.enerplus.com, accessed July 5, 2012.

EXHIBIT 2: Enerplus Corporate Governance

Source: www.enerplus.com/responsibility/corporategovernance/corporate-governance-overview.cfm, accessed May 25, 2012.

EXHIBIT 3: System for Electronic Data Analysis and Retrieval (SEDAR)

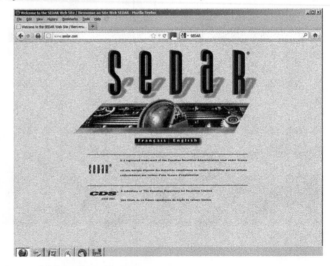

Source: www.sedar.com, accessed May 25, 2012.

EXHIBIT 4: Enerplus Finances

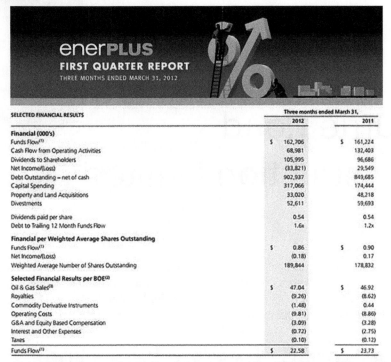

SELECTED FINANCIAL RESULTS	Three months ended March 31,	
	2012	2011
Financial (000's)		
Funds Flow[1]	$ 162,706	$ 161,224
Cash Flow from Operating Activities	68,981	132,403
Dividends to Shareholders	105,995	96,686
Net Income/(Loss)	(33,821)	29,549
Debt Outstanding – net of cash	902,937	849,685
Capital Spending	317,066	174,444
Property and Land Acquisitions	33,020	48,218
Divestments	52,611	59,693
Dividends paid per share	0.54	0.54
Debt to Trailing 12 Month Funds Flow	1.6x	1.2x
Financial per Weighted Average Shares Outstanding		
Funds Flow[1]	$ 0.86	$ 0.90
Net Income/(Loss)	(0.18)	0.17
Weighted Average Number of Shares Outstanding	189,844	178,832
Selected Financial Results per BOE[2]		
Oil & Gas Sales[3]	$ 47.04	$ 46.92
Royalties	(9.26)	(8.62)
Commodity Derivative Instruments	(1.48)	0.44
Operating Costs	(9.81)	(8.86)
G&A and Equity Based Compensation	(3.09)	(3.28)
Interest and Other Expenses	(0.72)	(2.75)
Taxes	(0.10)	(0.12)
Funds Flow[1]	$ 22.58	$ 23.73

Source: www.enerplus.com/investor/financial/reports.cfm, accessed May 25, 2012.

EXHIBIT 5: Enerplus Board of Directors

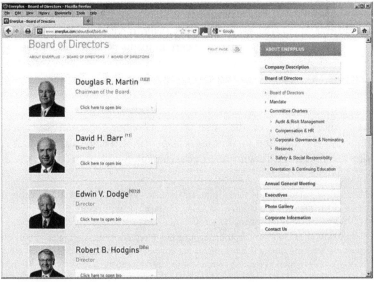

Source: www.enerplus.com/about/bod/bod.cfm, accessed May 25, 2012.

CASE

32

Currie Road Construction Limited (A)

In December 2008, Martin Cook, president of Currie Road Construction Limited, a British Columbia-based road construction and maintenance firm, was contemplating U.S. market entry. Having investigated the opportunity to establish an operation in Houston, Texas, Cook now needed to make his decision.

THE B.C. ROAD CONSTRUCTION AND MAINTENANCE INDUSTRY

The construction and maintenance of Canada's highways and roads fell under the jurisdiction of the provincial and municipal governments. In B.C., for example, the primary government funding agency responsible for the construction and maintenance of the major transportation structures (i.e., highways, roads, bridges) was the Ministry of Transportation and Infrastructure (MTI). As well, each municipal government (e.g., City of Victoria) was also responsible for constructing and maintaining certain roadways in its respective jurisdiction.

With the 2010 Winter Olympic Games slated to be held in the Vancouver area, the B.C. Road Builders and Heavy Construction Association, which represented approximately 100 road construction and maintenance companies in B.C., acknowledged that the transportation and infrastructure projects associated with the Games had been a boon to the Association's members. However, the onset of an economic recession was now casting a shadow of uncertainty over the continuing prosperity of the industry in B.C. More specifically, with the forecasted downturn in government revenues, it was unclear whether

⚜ IVEY | Publishing · Professor Paul Beamish prepared this case solely to provide material for class discussion. The author does not intend to illustrate either effective or ineffective handling of a managerial situation. The author may have disguised certain names and other identifying information to protect confidentiality.

Richard Ivey School of Business Foundation prohibits any form of reproduction, storage or transmission without its written permission. Reproduction of this material is not covered under authorization by any reproduction rights organization. To order copies or request permission to reproduce materials, contact Ivey Publishing, Richard Ivey School of Business Foundation, The University of Western Ontario, London, Ontario, Canada, N6A 3K7; phone (519) 661-3208; fax (519) 661-3882; e-mail cases@ivey.uwo.ca.

Copyright © 2011, Richard Ivey School of Business Foundation   Version: 2011-09-21

One time permission to reproduce granted by Richard Ivey School of Business Foundation on April 22, 2014.

the MTI would be in a position to continue funding major improvements to B.C.'s road infrastructure. A competing perspective suggested that the Canadian federal and provincial governments would follow the example of their American neighbors and accelerate infrastructure spending in an effort to stimulate economic recovery.

Competition in the road construction industry was fierce. Exhibit 1 presents market share data and the contract value for a majority of the road construction work awarded by MTI in 2008. This was only for new construction work awarded by the MTI, and excluded work tendered by the municipal governments. The industry was fragmented among many competitors.

A tendering process was used by both the MTI and municipal governments to award work to contractors. A tender document was broken down into specific stages where a cost was assigned for each stage (i.e., stage one–survey stake out; stage two–shrubbery removal; stage three–direct excavation). A unit cost was attached to each stage so that if a cost overrun occurred that was beyond the control of the contractor, then MTI would pay the contractor for the overrun. A contract was awarded on a lowest cost basis among those contractors who prepared a tender for a specific job. There was no limitation on the number of jobs a contractor could bid for as long as the company was qualified (i.e., total dollar value of work the company could do per year) and the qualification associated with each tender call (i.e., assets of company) was satisfied. As a result, often as many as ten companies bid on one job at a time in B.C., thus making it extremely difficult to gain market share.

In order to stay profitable, construction companies had a number of options. The first was to invest in costly capital equipment. This was critical in this labor-intensive industry because equipment breakdowns were a major reason for cost overruns on a job. A second option was to integrate vertically backwards into the commercial end of the industry. This involved owning an asphalt production plant and/or a sand and gravel operation. Large amounts of money were required as well as a strategic decision to compete in a related industry. The third option was to compete in markets other than B.C. (i.e., the U.S., Ontario, Alberta). With this option the firm risked an incomplete understanding of the market, the competitors and the customer (i.e., government agencies responsible for road construction /maintenance have varying specifications and methods of doing business in each province or state). The final option was to diversify into an unrelated industry (e.g., concrete, housing, or transportation). This option also involved a great deal of risk because of market unfamiliarity and the large amounts of capital required.

Background Information on Cook

Cook graduated from the University of Manitoba with a Bachelor of Science degree in 1984 and immediately accepted a job as an Asphalt Engineer with Shell Canada Limited (SCL). It was in the asphalt division that Cook established a working relationship with David Thomas that would have a significant effect on both their future careers within SCL. By the early 1990's, Cook was elevated to the position of Asphalt Sales Manager for Western Canada. Not totally satisfied with the constraints of a large corporation, he turned down two excellent promotional opportunities within SCL.

In 1994, Cook and Thomas discussed the possibility of entering into business together in the asphalt-related products market. The business would supply road asphalt and other oil-based by-products to the consumer. On January 1, 1995, Cook and Thomas left SCL and formed a company called Costal Asphalt Limited (Costal). They each contributed their personal savings of $30,000 into this company. As Cook said: "When we left Shell we did not know where we were going. We had to first find a place to set up our plant and then find the necessary financing. However, we knew we had a good idea."

Development of Costal Limited

Cook and Thomas approached the B.C. Ministry of Small Business, Technology and Economic Development and the Federal Business Development Bank for financial support for Costal. They were turned down because their proposal was determined to be infeasible. The banks also would not provide any financing because Cook and Thomas had no personal assets for use as collateral. However, they were able to get financial support from Mark Currie and Evan Clarry, owners of Currie Road Construction Limited. The deal was structured so that Currie Road Construction owned 51 per cent of Costal and Cook and Thomas 49 per cent. After payment of a $200,000 loan to Currie and Clarry, the equity position would become 50 per cent Currie, 25 per cent Cook and 25 per cent Thomas. It took one and one-half years to repay the original $200,000 loan.

In 1997, Costal entered into a joint venture with an investor (Jake Garner) to purchase a profitable road construction company, A.A. McLeod Construction Limited (McLeod), in the Queen Charlotte area in British Columbia. Garner was responsible for the day-to-day operations and management of the firm.

From 1997 to 2000, Cook and Thomas concentrated primarily on expanding Costal operations by opening up terminals in Calgary and Edmonton. McLeod continued to be profitable under Garner's direction. Costal's success to this point was attributed mainly to the dedication of Cook and Thomas. It was not unusual for either partner to work seven days a week, fifteen hours a day. During this period, Cook's responsibilities included answering the phone, pouring 425°F asphaltic product into 25 kilogram containers in the shop and taking care of financial matters as well as "pounding the pavement to drum up business." This hard work paid off for Cook and Thomas–Costal was profitable from its inception. Over this period, their management skills and business know-how increased enormously.

In 2000, Cook and Thomas wanted to further vertically integrate forward. They attempted to purchase a profitable road construction company in Victoria (similar in size to McLeod), but the deal fell through. At the same time, Currie Road Construction was offered for sale. Currie and Clarry had received a serious offer from a British-based company to purchase Currie; however, they desired to sell it to Canadian investors if they could be found. Cook and Thomas saw this as an excellent opportunity to become fully integrated in the road construction industry in B.C. Because Currie was a major customer for Costal product, a change of ownership could jeopardize this account. Also, the purchase of Currie by another firm could have a negative effect on Costal's operations since Currie owned 50 per cent of Costal. Up to this time, Currie and Clarry were silent partners in Costal; they never interfered with the management of Costal and McLeod and the valuable long-term assets on Currie's balance sheet.

Currie Road Construction Limited

Currie Road Construction was one of the oldest and largest road maintenance and construction companies based in B.C. Its history dated back to 1933 when Eugene Boyle built the foundations upon which Currie would grow and prosper for the next 75 years. During that time, Currie participated in building such large projects as the Trans Canada Highway and the Alaskan Highway. The company enjoyed enormous success in the '60s and '70s when governments were spending huge amounts of money to build Canada's transportation infrastructure. However, during the late 1970s and early 1980s Canada's infrastructure was nearing completion and the industry was shifting away from new construction of road systems to reconstruction and maintenance of the existing road networks.

Cook and Thomas decided that with the purchase of Currie Road Construction, Cook would leave Costal and become president of Currie. There was too much at stake to allow someone else to run the company for them; this was a major acquisition that could cause the collapse of everything they had achieved to date if not managed properly.

On November 15, 2000, Cook took over total control of Currie's operations. During the negotiations to purchase Currie for $21.2 million, Currie had indicated that he expected Currie to make a profit of $1 million for the fiscal year (ending March 31) of 2001. However, much to Cook's surprise, Currie experienced a net operating loss of $1.3 million instead.

Despite the poor performance in 2000, Cook believed that Currie was still a good deal. The company owned valuable pieces of real estate (e.g., two golf courses) whose potential value was enormous. As well, Currie owned and operated asphalt production plants in key strategic locations in the province, and owned valuable land north of Vancouver that contained large amounts of aggregate used in the construction process and in the asphalt production plants. Having an asphalt supply was extremely important in the road construction business.

Cook identified some critical problems with Currie's operations initially. A glaring problem was that they were still competing heavily in the highway road construction segment of the market, yet they were losing money. Currie had failed to recognize that the market was undergoing a change from new highway construction to reconstruction and road maintenance. Road construction placed much greater emphasis on earth-moving (excavating, drilling, blasting) than road maintenance, where the emphasis was more on grinding and recycling. In addition, Currie's equipment was old and tended to break down. This led to cost overruns and reduced profit margins on all jobs.

Another problem was that Currie was an old company which had old ways of doing business. The majority of the senior level management had been with the company for over 30 years; in fact, a lot of them had started out as equipment operators and worked their way up into management. Currie lacked fresh "blood" in the organization; the environment was changing dramatically and management was not able to realize this or keep up with it.

The employees of Currie were very dedicated and loyal to the company. A great majority were immigrants who had worked for Currie for many years. However, Cook noticed that some of the older employees had become comfortable and complacent with their positions and hence their motivation had dropped. As Cook stated: "We had a lot of old employees who were getting late in their years and did not have too much drive. It was imperative that we get their productivity to increase dramatically."

For the next three years, Cook concentrated on restructuring the organization in terms of personnel and operations. The key was to identify those people in management who were able to make the quantum leap from the "old school" to the "new school." Those who were not able to adapt had to retire. Also, Currie had to re-orient itself in the market by making the transition from the heavy construction end of the business to the road maintenance end where the profit margins were higher.

By 2004, Cook felt that he had molded Currie into a more aggressive and stronger competitor in the road construction market. He had removed all the older management that could not adapt to Currie's new environment and, as a result, the senior management staff was much leaner and more aggressive. Secondly, Cook hired two key people to the management staff: one brought valuable experience to the commercial side of the business and the other to the equipment operations area. Finally, Cook had rationalized the operations in some areas and expanded efforts in other areas.

Cook identified six key strategic decisions that were made:

1. Entered into a joint venture operation with a successful and experienced sand and gravel company to develop Currie's 500 acres of gravel deposits north of Vancouver.

2. Made a commitment to become the leader in the pavement maintenance market in B.C. This required investing in specialized technologies required to engage in activities such as recycling, road surface scarifying and pavement profiling. Recycling was a process whereby the existing pavement surface was removed (i.e., by grinding machines or by using back hoes to completely tear it up) and used along with virgin aggregate to form a new recycled mix of asphalt. The new mix was then re-laid on the roadway using the usual procedures. This process required additional equipment installed in the asphalt production plant. Pavement profiling was a process whereby a machine (i.e., a grinder) with a large rotating drum containing carbide teeth planed the surface of the road to various depths. The material removed from the road could be used in a recycled asphaltic mixture or it could be used as subgrade material in another project. This process was used to remove surface distress appearing in the pavement. As well, it corrected the pavement profile to allow for proper drainage and to correct curb heights. Road surface scarifying was a process in which a machine heated up the pavement and removed the surface distress. The removed material was treated with an emulsion to rejuvenate its properties and then re-laid.

3. Increased Currie's presence in the road calcium segment of the market. Calcium was sprayed on dirt roads to control the amount of dust.

4. Obtained operating authority to transport petroleum products (for Currie and commercially) in Alberta and several surrounding northern U.S. states.

5. Rationalized Currie's operations in Burnaby, moving away from road construction and concentrating on supplying materials (i.e., asphalt and aggregate) and carrying out winter operations (i.e., snow removal and sanding).

6. Purchased a road surfacing company in Alberta. This made Currie one of the dominant firms in this market.

These changes had a positive effect on Currie's income statement. Exhibit 2 presents a financial summary of Currie's performance from 2001 to 2008. Since 2003, Currie had been a profitable company.

A major burden upon Currie's profitability was the interest owing on the $20.0 million loan. The original plan was to repay the bank the entire debt by 2006. However, owing to the economic deceleration associated with the stock market slowdown between 2000 and 2002, Currie was not able to make any interest payments until 2007. Cook was able to get the bank to agree to capitalize the interest payments over that time.

In 2004, Currie was able to sell some property in order to pay off some of the outstanding debt. As well, the company seemed to be going in the right direction, and as Cook stated: "We were able to see faintly the light at the end of the tunnel."

The Proposed Houston Division

In the summer of 2007, Cook had business dealings with Brad Carlyle. Carlyle worked for a pipeline construction company in the Calgary area. Prior to this job, he worked in Houston supervising the expansion of a rapid transit system. In December 2007, Carlyle arranged to have lunch with Cook. Over lunch, Carlyle told Cook about the opportunities that he saw in the Houston market. Carlyle knew that Currie was looking to expand its operations and he felt that the Houston market was one area that Currie should seriously consider. Currie Road Construction had previously only worked in the U.S. as a subcontractor on several road rehabilitation projects.

Carlyle indicated to Cook that he wanted to return to Houston. He believed that he was capable of developing a successful division in this market for Currie. Carlyle had made some valuable contacts within both the government and the construction industry that would be very beneficial. As well, he knew the market and the way it functioned. Cook was impressed with Carlyle's enthusiasm and his belief in the Houston market. Although Carlyle did not have a civil engineering background and was not totally comfortable with road construction techniques, Cook had full confidence in his ability to 'learn on the job'. Cook indicated that he would get back to Carlyle very soon.

As a result of this meeting, Cook and Thomas decided that it would be worthwhile to spend a few days in the Houston market in order to get a better feeling for its potential. None of Currie's senior management people had experience in this market. In mid-January, 2008, Cook, Thomas and Carlyle spent three days in Houston meeting with Texas Department of Transportation (TxDOT) officials and touring the area. During this brief stay, a large amount of positive information was gathered about the prospects of entering this market. The TxDOT officials were excited about Currie entering the market because a recent combines investigation found that a large number of the old established road construction firms were guilty of price fixing and collusion. As a result, they were barred from bidding work for one to two years.

Texas was also undergoing growth and government officials realized that improvements to the infrastructure were required to ensure this growth. As a result, the government had made it a priority to upgrade the highways, bridges and roadways throughout the state. Cook and Thomas were astonished at the amount of money budgeted to infrastructure upgrading. It was approximately US$1,400 million a year, roughly 4.5 times more than the amount allocated by the MTI in B.C.

Even more enticing about this market was the fewer number of competitors compared with the competition in B.C. The average number of contractors bidding per job was approximately four.

Further discussion regarding the Houston market took place between Cook, Thomas and Carlyle. More visits to Houston followed.

The main reason to enter this market according to Cook was because: "It offered an opportunity to get better utilization out of our specialized machinery. Instead of having our grinding machines and scarifiers sit idle during the winter months, we could find work for them in Houston. Additionally, there were only five firms identified by the Asphalt Recycling & Reclaiming Association as being headquartered in the state of Texas."

Cook's orientation for the Houston market was to concentrate primarily on the road maintenance activities of pavement grinding and scarifying operations where Currie was strongest. It was thought that by going in small, Currie could get a better understanding of the market, make some key contacts in government and develop a good reputation within the industry by doing quality work. Because the road maintenance techniques which Currie possessed were more advanced than those in use in Texas, the company realized it would take a little time to demonstrate their merits to the key government contacts. Currie planned to eventually reproduce its B.C. operations in Texas, where there were no companies totally vertically integrated. Once Currie was established in Texas, it would be able to compete in the nearby surrounding states: Florida, Georgia, North and South Carolina, Tennessee, Alabama and Louisiana.

The proposed organizational chart for the Houston operations is presented in Exhibit 3. Carlyle would report directly to Cook on all matters concerning operations. If the entry took place, Cook planned to spend time overseeing the move to Houston. However, after operations were running, Cook did not plan on spending much time in Houston because Currie did not have much slack in the management ranks. The existing people were all so extended that U.S. entry would have to be delayed if Brad Carlyle, or someone like him from outside existing management, was not available.

Subsequent Thinking

Early in the Fall of 2008, it appeared that the prospect of expanding into the Texas market might be de-railed by the collapse of global credit and equity markets, as well as the rapid onset of an economic recession. However, the dramatic downturn in the U.S. economy prompted federal lawmakers to consider implementing unprecedented stimulus spending in order to revive the economy and to avoid an impending depression. By February 2009, the U.S. Congress was anticipated to sign into force the American Recovery and Reinvestment Act which would inject more than $100 billion into infrastructure spending. Approximately $27 billion of this infrastructure spending was earmarked for highway and bridge construction. More than $4.5 billion of this was slated for projects approved by the TxDOT. The TxDOT's commissioners were anxious to quickly identify "shovel-ready" projects and scheduled nearly $2.75 billion worth of project bid dates to occur between April and December 2009 (see Exhibit 4 for the monthly gross value of projects subsequently scheduled for tender throughout 2009). Exhibit 5 lists a sample of the types of projects that were being subsequently scheduled for tender in April 2009. With the broad slowdown in the economy, competition for these lucrative projects was expected to be fierce.

At the same time, Canadian lawmakers were beginning to consider similar stimulus spending. Cook informally learned that the B.C. government was considering more than $880 million in infrastructure spending, although the timelines for implementation were not as aggressive as they were in Texas and it was unclear how much would be directed to the MTI for road construction and maintenance projects.

Although Currie's primary strength was in road maintenance, the decision was made to get involved in the road construction end of the business if Currie entered the Texas market. There were two reasons for this strategy. The first was to generate some cash flow in order to cover the operating expenses until the grinding and scarifying operations picked up. Secondly, according to information provided by Carlyle, the market appeared to be made of gold; it offered easy access to abnormal profits.

Although little public data were available, the competition in this market was primarily family-owned companies. These firms were cash rich and were not accustomed to much competition. As Cook described them: "They are a bunch of old-time southern contractors who are financially very strong and wealthy, primarily from the price fixing that had occurred." One additional key player in the market was ARRON, a subsidiary of Petro Oil, one of the largest corporations in the United States.

If they proceeded, Cook and Carlyle decided that Currie would buy new equipment since abnormal profits seemed to be present. While Currie would normally lease and/or rent equipment for new operations initially in order to minimize investment in a new market, this would reduce profit margins slightly. It was felt that Currie could be competitive and easily make even more than four per cent net profit on revenue with new equipment.

Carlyle felt there would be no problem locating supervisors and equipment operators given the rising rate of unemployment. Due to the large population growth occurring in the southern states and the minor influence of labor unions, Carlyle felt he would be able to hire blue-collar employees at about half the wage rate that Currie was paying its employees in B.C. Carlyle would be responsible for hiring all the blue-collar employees; however, he would require Cook's approval in hiring supervisors.

If Currie decided to enter this market, the Houston subsidiary would utilize Currie's existing centralized control systems. In 2006, Currie had paid $30,000, and invested a further $140,000, for a fully integrated job costing/receivable/ledger cost reporting and accounting system which was one of the most comprehensive of any firm in the industry. For each of the 200 active accounts that Currie was working on, it received a monthly cost analysis (see Exhibit 6, for example). This allowed the company to see costs broken down by sub-category on each job for the current month, to date, to complete, and forecasted final–all versus the original plan. For *any* given job, it might be several years before all of the relevant costs had been accounted for and the accounts closed off.

In light of the rapid developments associated with the anticipated economic stimulus spending in both B.C. and Texas, Cook realized that if he were to enter the U.S. market at all, he would have to decide soon.

EXHIBIT 1: 2008 Market Share Ranking (MTI)*

Total Contracts 682		Total Value $697,354,600	Total Tonnes 4,455,751	
Rank	Contractor	Contracts	$ Value	Market %
1	ARC Holdings Ltd.	46	130,963,194	18.78
2	TCN Construction	14	66,876,306	9.59
3	Arvac Construction	14	41,353,128	5.93
4	Jean Ltd.	7	35,286,143	5.06
5	Pey Ltd.	7	24,756,088	3.55
6	Atlas Construction Ltd.	4	22,873,231	3.28
7	RAC Paving	25	22,524,554	3.23
8	Dunn Construction	28	20,711,432	2.97
9	Alden Ltd.	18	19,177,252	2.75
10	Currie Road Construction	14	18,828,574	2.70
11	Gant Paving Ltd.	4	17,852,278	2.56
12	Lyee Construction Ltd.	11	17,364,130	2.49
13	Rant Construction Ltd.	28	16,945,717	2.43
14	Rome Construction Ltd.	11	16,039,156	2.30
15	Ram Brothers Construction	4	14,435,240	2.07

* Figures may be disguised

Source: Company files.

EXHIBIT 2: Currie Road Construction Limited Financial Summary (Yearly) ($'000)

Year	Current Assets	Current Liabil.	Long-Term Debt	L.T.D. Interest	Revenue	Net Income	F.A. Purch.
March 2001*	10,962	9,074	17,948	—	13,798	−2,740	1,146
March 2002	12,012	11,292	19,450	1,802	44,760	4,248	0
March 2003	12,058	8,646	23,836	2,780	42,318	306	2,674
March 2004	10,228	7,940	21,002	3,262	46,866	7,438	2,272
March 2005	10,126	5,728	20,560	3,908	46,534	2,050	3,990
March 2006	20,956	14,102	22,056	4,190	59,568	4,338	4,164
Feb. 2007	18,578	7,176	25,910	4,210	69,404	2,288	3,390
Feb. 2008	25,966	16,290	13,654	3,326	81,842	1,480	4,618

* 2001 values are for an eight-month period.

Source: Company files.

EXHIBIT 3: Proposed Organization Chart: Houston, 2009

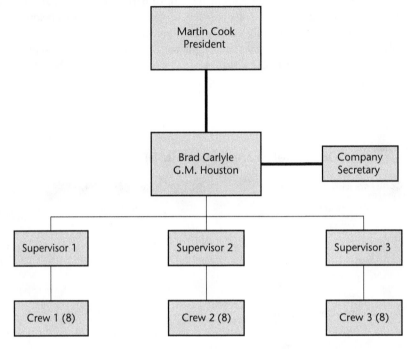

Source: Company files.

EXHIBIT 4: Gross Estimated Value of Transportation Infrastructure Scheduled for Bidding in Texas During 2009

Month scheduled for bidding	Estimated gross value of projects
April	$ 397,026,973
May	$ 151,320,643
June	$ 1,256,350,277
July	$ 258,887,573
August	$ 260,255,403
September	$ 118,414,267
October	$ 52,717,115
November	$ 198,285,487
December	$ 57,499,031
Total:	**$2,750,756,768**

Source: Company files.

EXHIBIT 5: Sample of Transportation Infrastructure Projects Scheduled for Bidding in Texas During April 2009

District	County	Highway	Project ID	Estimated value	Project description
Tyler	Anderson	US 84	12301034	$ 6,491,332	WIDEN ROADWAY
Odessa	Andrews	SH 115	54801036	$ 5,604,394	REPAIR ROADWAY
Wichita Falls	Archer	SH 25	13705028	$ 3,763,273	WIDEN ROADWAY
Amarillo	Armstrong	US 287	4203038	$ 13,712,239	REPAIR ROADWAY
Corpus Christi	Bee	US 181	10007045	$ 3,999,719	RESURFACE ROADWAY
Waco	Bell	SH 317	1505043	$ 1,671,882	RESURFACE ROADWAY
Waco	Bell	SH 201	353402002	$ 1,840,469	INTERSECTION
Austin	Blanco	US 281	25301047	$ 1,261,109	RESURFACE ROADWAY
Houston	Brazoria	SH 35	17803138	$ 5,258,533	RESURFACE ROADWAY
Houston	Brazoria	FM 524	100402014	$ 2,402,836	RESURFACE ROADWAY
Bryan	Brazos	SH 21	11604096	$ 1,414,670	RESURFACE ROADWAY
Bryan	Brazos	FM 60	50601093	$ 1,554,118	RESURFACE ROADWAY
Bryan	Brazos	FM 1179	131601053	$ 461,440	RESURFACE ROADWAY
Brownwood	Brown	US 67	5406090	$ 2,251,374	RESURFACE ROADWAY
Bryan	Burleson	FM 60	64803046	$13,606,472	WIDEN ROADWAY
Atlanta	Cass	SH 77	27703024	$ 3,320,478	WIDEN ROADWAY
Atlanta	Cass	SH 43	56901048	$ 1,409,474	WIDEN ROADWAY
Lubbock	Castro	FM 1055	129101012	$10,533,348	REPAIR ROADWAY
Beaumont	Chambers	SH 61	24203068	$ 1,631,534	RESURFACE ROADWAY
Beaumont	Chambers	IH 10	50803090	$ 1,241,392	RESURFACE ROADWAY
Childress	Childress	CR	92508017	$ 2,157,148	REPLACE BRIDGE
San Antonio	Comal	FM 306	310601012	$ 8,532,728	REBUILD ROADWAY
Wichita Falls	Cooke	IH 35	19402088	$ 3,580,759	RESURFACE ROADWAY
Waco	Coryell	US 84	5503023	$14,282,449	CONSTRUCT LANES
Dallas	Dallas	FM 1382	104702044	$ 2,246,574	TRAFFIC SIGNAL
San Angelo	Edwards	SH 55	23502043	$ 3,306,441	CONSTRUCT BRIDGE
Houston	Fort Bend	US 90A	2706055	$ 1,740,866	RESURFACE ROADWAY
Houston	Fort Bend	FM 521	11103054	$ 1,178,514	RESURFACE ROADWAY
Houston	Fort Bend	SH 36	18801036	$ 1,901,213	REPAIR ROADWAY
Houston	Fort Bend	FM 1093	125802031	$ 1,453,262	RESURFACE ROADWAY
Houston	Fort Bend	FM 3155	322301009	$ 294,857	RESURFACE ROADWAY
Bryan	Freestone	FM 80	45603015	$ 6,239,325	REPAIR ROADWAY
San Antonio	Frio	FM 140	74804036	$ 1,258,462	CURB & GUTTERS

Source: Company files.

EXHIBIT 6: Currie Road Construction Ltd. Cost Analysis for Period Ended _____

Cost for Month		Cost to Date		Cost to Complete		Forecasted Final		Planned*		Variance
Unit	Cost	Unit	Cost	Unit	Cost	Unit	Cost	Unit	Cost	
100 — Contract Costs										
110 — Construction Costs										
198 — Cost of Operations										
200 — Traffic Control										
Quantity										
Man Hours										
Labor										
Man Hours										
Supervisor										
Permanent Materials										
Other Construction Costs										
Equipment										
TOTALS										
210 — Erosion Control										
Quantity										
Man Hours										
Labor										
Permanent Material										
Other Construction Costs										
Equipment										
TOTALS										
220 — Lump Sum Construction										
Quantity										
Man Hours										
Labor										
Permanent Material										
Other Construction Costs										
Equipment										
Hired Equipment and Operator										
Hired Equipped/Operated										
Minority Business Enterprises										
TOTALS										

*Equals original bid cost

Source: Company files.

Sobey's Inc: A Strategic Approach to Sustainable Seafood Supply

By 2013, there was a growing awareness that business must take action to shift the economy towards a sustainable future. Many businesses had begun to explore possible ways to reduce their firm's environmental footprint, and the public's expectation of business was rising on topics such as waste management, genetically modified products and food safety, to name a few. While Sobey's Inc., one of Canada's largest food retailers, had initiated a number of energy-reducing and waste-minimizing programs, the real challenge was to harness the efforts of its supply chain since in-house operations constituted only about 10 per cent of the retailer's overall environmental footprint. At the top of Sobey's agenda was to develop a sustainable seafood strategy, a task that fell to David Smith, vice-president, Sustainability.

While data collection, metric selection, employee incentives and customer education were important parts of this emerging strategy, a central decision was what products to choose to sell or not to sell. Certain major competitors had announced that they would sell only "certified sustainable" seafood–an approach strongly advocated by well-known environmental organizations, such as the World Wildlife Fund. Sobey's, on the other hand, decided that to abandon uncertified seafood would not only hamper Sobey's bottom line but also would eliminate its ability to push the very fisheries that needed more guidance towards better practices. Yet, to continue to sell "red zone" seafood was very controversial and could jeopardize Sobey's standing as a leader in sustainable practices–an outcome that

IVEY | Publishing

Professor Anthony Goerzen wrote this case solely to provide material for class discussion. The author does not intend to illustrate either effective or ineffective handling of a managerial situation. The author may have disguised certain names and other identifying information to protect confidentiality.

This publication may not be transmitted, photocopied, digitized or otherwise reproduced in any form or by any means without the permission of the copyright holder. Reproduction of this material is not covered under authorization by any reproduction rights organization. To order copies or request permission to reproduce materials, contact Ivey Publishing, Ivey Business School, Western University, London, Ontario, Canada, N6G 0N1; (t) 519.661.3208; (e) cases@ivey.ca; www.iveycases.com.

Copyright © 2014, Richard Ivey School of Business Foundation   Version: 2014-02-24

One time permission to reproduce granted by Richard Ivey School of Business Foundation on April 22, 2014.

could have serious negative consequences in the marketplace. In this context, Smith had to implement a sustainable seafood strategy by year-end 2013.

A HISTORY OF SOBEY'S

A proudly Canadian company with more than 100 years in the food business, Sobey's Inc. was a wholly owned subsidiary of Empire Company Ltd., headquartered in Stellarton, Nova Scotia. One of only two national grocery retailers in Canada, Sobey's owned or franchised more than 1,300 food stores in all 10 provinces under retail banners that included Sobey's, IGA *extra*, IGA, Foodland, FreshCo, Price Chopper and Thrifty Foods, as well as Lawton's Drugs stores. The company's private label brands, Compliments and Signal, encompassed more than 3,800 products.

Sobey's began in 1907 when John William Sobey (JW) started a meat delivery business in Stellarton, Nova Scotia. With a horse-drawn cart, JW purchased and collected livestock from local farmers for resale. In 1924, this family business was expanded from meat and a few local vegetables to a full line of groceries. By 1939, Sobey's had established a chain of six stores in and around Pictou County, and by 1947, JW's son, Frank, opened the first modern Sobey's supermarket in Atlantic Canada. As Sobey's continued to expand through Atlantic Canada, Frank's three sons, Bill, David and Donald, became active in the company, taking over management in 1971 with Bill as president, David as executive vice-president and Donald heading up the growing investment company, Empire Inc. In 1987, Sobey's sales reached $1 billion, and in this same year, the company opened a new store in Guelph, Ontario, its first store outside Atlantic Canada. Then in 1998, the company tripled its size to become a national company when it acquired The Oshawa Group, a Toronto-based supplier to Canada's IGA stores. On its 100th anniversary in 2007, Sobey's was taken private by majority shareholder Empire Company Limited, and in September of that year, Sobey's expanded its presence in British Columbia through the acquisition of Thrifty Foods. In 2010, the company launched FreshCo, a discount food retailer in Ontario, and by 2012, Sobey's Inc. was a $16 billion company with more than 1,300 corporate and franchised stores across Canada (see Exhibit 1).

In 2012, Sobey's had more than 97,000 employees and was committed to building sustainable worth for customers, employees and shareholders through its focus on innovation and superior customer service in food retailing. Its core retail food formats (i.e., Sobey's, IGA, Foodland, FreshCo, Price Chopper and Thrifty Foods), which served approximately 10 million customers every week, were based on their knowledge of the distinct markets they served and were designed to ensure that they had the right offering in the right-sized stores for each individual market–from full-service to convenience format–each tailored to satisfy the unique occasion-based food shopping needs of their customers.

A PRIMER ON BUSINESS SUSTAINABILITY

"The accelerating deterioration of the human environment and natural resources, and the consequences of that deterioration for economic and social development" were cited as the reason in the mid-1980s to establish the United Nations World Commission on Environment and Development, more commonly referred to as the Brundtland Commission after its chair and former Norwegian Prime Minister Gro Harlem Brundtland. The Brundtland Commission presented the idea that the environment and development were not separate from one another; "sustainable development" was a new concept at that time.

The Brundtland Commission argued that "environment" is where we live and "development" is what we all do—"the two are inseparable." Thus, sustainable development was defined as "development that meets the needs of the present without compromising the ability of future generations to meet their own needs."[1] This definition was at the heart of Sobey's formal sustainability strategy discussions and was combined with the definition formulated by the Food Marketing Institute, which was "business and personal strategies and practices that promote the long-term well-being of the environment, society and the bottom line."[2] Both definitions addressed the earth's "carrying capacity," a concept based on the ecological fact that excessive consumption of resources or degradation of the environment would threaten the earth's ability to support future generations.

Most Fortune 500 companies had made some kind of commitment to sustainable development, and over $3 trillion in assets under professional management in the United States were in sustainable and/or responsible investing.[3] The measurement of business sustainability often encompassed the concept of a "triple bottom line," which included social and environmental performance in addition to traditional financial measures. Yet, precise measurement tools of sustainability remained undeveloped and difficult to use. This void gave rise to "greenwashing" where companies trumpet their small, relatively insignificant moves towards sustainability to fool stakeholders.[4] To improve credibility, many businesses began to use third-party organizations to audit their sustainability reports. According to Ernst & Young, 25 per cent of businesses had their sustainability report validated in part or in full and a further 42 per cent planned to have their reports successfully audited within five years.[5]

SUSTAINABILITY AND THE SEAFOOD INDUSTRY

According to the United Nations Food and Agriculture Organization (FAO), the world seafood harvest in 2005 consisted of 93.3 million tonnes captured in wild fisheries (i.e., around 2.5 trillion fish) plus 48.1 million tonnes produced by fish farms, directly or indirectly employing over 200 million people. Fish was an important source of food for over 1 billion people worldwide—particularly in developing countries—who depend on fish as their primary source of protein.

Overfishing and illegal fishing, however, threatened both livelihoods as well as global food security. The collapse of the Grand Banks cod fishery off the east coast of Canada was a good example; despite the fact that the Atlantic cod fishery had been an essential part of the European and emerging North American economies for over 1,000 years, Canadian cod stocks collapsed in the early 1990s due to overfishing. The fishery, which had once brought in 800,000 tonnes of fish a year and supported 40,000 livelihoods in Canada alone, was lost

---

[1]www.unep.org/geo/geo4/report/01_Environment_for_Development.pdf, accessed September 8, 2012.

[2]www.fmi.org/industry-topics/sustainability, accessed September 6, 2012.

[3]Steve Lopresti and Pamela Lilak, "Do Investors Care About Sustainability?" Pricewaterhouse Coopers, March 2012, www.pwc.com/us/en/corporate-sustainability-climate-change/publications/investors-and-sustainability.jhtml, accessed September 6, 2012.

[4]Tiffany D. Gallicano, "A Critical Analysis of Greenwashing Claims," Public Relations Journal 5.3, 2011, www.prsa.org/intelligence/prjournal/documents/2011gallicano.pdf, accessed September 6, 2012.

[5]"Six Growing Trends in Corporate Sustainability," Ernst & Young Global Limited, November 2011, www.ey.com/US/en/Services/Specialty-Services/Climate-Change-and-Sustainability-Services/Six-growing-trends-in-corporate-sustainability_overview, accessed September 6, 2012.

when the cod were fished to the point of commercial extinction. Despite the closing of the fishery, however, deliberate and large-scale violations by both Canadian and foreign vessels continued, often in the form of "by catch." In fact, a great deal of overfishing occurred in this way where fish were caught *en masse* and unprofitable species were thrown back into the ocean. A 2005 study, for example, estimated that 1.3 million tonnes of fish (over 10 per cent of the total catch) were discarded annually.[6] According to some estimates, 85 per cent of the world's fisheries had been pushed to their biological limits by overfishing, pollution and climate change and that the current stocks of commercially fished wild species would collapse by 2048.[7]

While fish farming, or aquaculture, offered some hope for seafood as a future food source, this method also was not without significant challenges. Critics pointed out that many types of farmed fish put pressure on wild fisheries since it took as much as three kilograms of fishmeal, which came from the same ocean feed stocks pursued by wild fish (e.g., anchovies, sardines, etc.), to yield one kilogram of farmed fish. Furthermore, farmed fish were often held in ocean pens in densities that did not occur in the wild, thereby creating new risks of parasites and other infections that threatened wild stocks.[8]

As a result, the seafood industry–from producer to retailer–had come under growing pressure to adopt sustainable practices as various environmental groups succeeded at putting sustainable seafood on the business agenda. Smith stated, "We saw that it was time to do something. But the trigger was Walmart in 2006 who announced that, within five years, they would only sell "certified" sustainable seafood. That put it on the radar for everyone."

Despite assurances by vocal advocates of sustainable practices that retailers would experience superior profitability for sustainable seafood, industry veterans[9] stated categorically that this was simply not the case, suggesting instead that the primary incentive for retailers was that of supply risk management, i.e., the future availability of healthy fish stocks for society rather than of current retailing profitability for individual retailers.

SOBEY'S APPROACH TO SUSTAINABLE SEAFOOD STRATEGY

Sobey's approach to sustainability was shaped by its desire to improve environmental performance through reasonable, practical and environmentally responsible business practices that are in the long-term best interests of its customers, employees, suppliers and communities. In this process, Sobey's developed various initiatives that were both cost-saving and also reduced their environmental impact including the reusable Green Bag for Life, in-store energy conservation programs and LEED® standards to guide store and distribution centre construction, to name a few. Yet, driving more fundamental changes towards greater sustainability in food retailing was challenging since these initiatives could not interfere with operating or financial goals and must be consistent with overall corporate strategy. Further, initiatives to improve sustainability had to be consistent with corporate strategy and could not interfere with profit targets.

------

[6]European Union, "Commission Proposes to End Waste of Fisheries Resources," *Europa*, March 28, 2007, www.europa.eu/rapid/press-release_IP-07-429_en.htm?locale=en, accessed September 30, 2012.

[7]Kimberly Davis, "Wild-Caught Seafood," *Wildlife Conservation, Endangered Species Conservation*, World Wildlife Fund, 2012, www.worldwildlife.org/industries/wild-caught-seafood, accessed September 26, 2012.

[8]Monterey Bay Aquarium, *Turning the Tide: The State of Seafood*, 2nd ed., Monterey Bay Aquarium, Monterey, CA, 2011.

[9]This assertion is based on interviews with individuals who preferred to remain anonymous.

At the top of Sobey's agenda was to push its seafood supply chain towards greater sustainability, a process that had begun in 2008. Yet, in 2013, mainstream consumers were neither actively demanding sustainable seafood nor willing to pay a premium price when retailers did offer it. According to Smith,

> At Sobey's, we pride ourselves on being customer driven but, frankly, the mainstream consumer is not in the store saying "Gee, I want sustainable seafood." Our experience shows that mainstream buyers are not going to pay a premium, they are not going to suffer a performance inadequacy in either taste or quality, and they are not going to be inconvenienced to get it. Yet to become truly sustainable, we can't focus just on the 5 to 10 per cent niche of "green" customers—we need to reach the mainstream buyer.

Sobey's decided that it did not want to communicate with consumers on this until it could provide information and substantive options. Therefore, the starting point was to work with the seafood supply chain to create transparency by capturing data and developing new measurement systems, a process that began in 2008. Key pieces of information had to be developed including baselines, benchmarks and targets that would make environmental performance data visible to management and those involved in day-to-day operations. Initially, Sobey's purchasers had no idea where their seafood actually came from.

According to Smith,

> Most of our first level suppliers (i.e., agents, consolidators and warehouses) didn't know either. We had all been focused on cost, quality, food safety and service so other aspects beyond that were not even considered previously. So we began filling in these gaps by requiring our seafood suppliers to provide data on the origins of their products, and this information was matched with assessments of those fisheries to allow us to see which were in good shape and which were facing significant sustainability issues.

A key question in Sobey's sustainable seafood strategy, however, was how to use this emerging data on seafood origins and fishery health. Many competitors (e.g., Loblaw's "certified only" approach) appeared to be migrating towards a policy of offering seafood that had an "eco label" as "certified sustainable" by a given non-governmental organization (see Exhibit 2 for a brief summary of competitors' approaches to sustainable seafood and Exhibit 3 for Greenpeace's summary of retailers' sustainable seafood offerings). At Sobey's, however, according to Smith, "We decided to go a very different path. To us, to be responsibly sourced means that we can sell everything except species that are facing significant issues—and we would still consider selling even those "red label" species as being responsibly sourced if there's an improvement plan in place."

The logic behind this thinking was that seafood sustainability could be arrayed on a continuum; that is, certain species that have no sustainability issues at all represent the species with a "green" or "certified sustainable" rating, while other species that have some issues or are clearly under threat would be "yellow" or "red" species, respectively. In Sobey's view, to focus only on certified sustainable seafood would be simply to pick the low-hanging fruit, ignoring the areas that were in most need of attention. Further, there were widely differing ideas of how to go about rating fisheries and great challenges in completing this task; for example, in the 15 years since the Marine Stewardship Council (MSC) launched its widely respected wild seafood certification scheme, only about 12 per cent of wild seafood caught legally had been certified. In fact, most of the "certified" volume that was considered "green" was, in fact, already well managed prior to being certified. Further, the vast majority of MSC certified seafood tonnage came from developed economy fisheries

(North America and Western Europe), indicating that virtually all emerging economy fisheries were still uncertified and that many faced significant issues, thereby earning a "red" listing. Yet, Smith believed,

> By maintaining engagement with "red" species producers, by sourcing from them, encouraging improvements to be made and maybe helping them build their capacity—we consider that responsible because we are making an improvement to get at the issues. The alternative approach is to follow Greenpeace, for example, who asks companies to stop sourcing from fisheries that are facing significant sustainability issues. Our belief is that this is the wrong approach because you lose your influence and the fishery management practices in place won't change because these suppliers will always find less discerning markets to sell to—often developing countries—and then there is no change in behaviour.

Smith admitted,

> In the wrong hands, this kind of approach could be an excuse for greenwashing. But that's certainly not the way Sobey's operates and not the way I operate. We are working very hard to drive change and to support change where it is already happening. Further, because this effort has got to be driven by people who are on the water and know the business, we have begun working with Sustainable Fisheries Partnership—SFP,[10] whose experience and model is based on doing improvements or fisheries improvement plans.

Unlike many other non-governmental organizations, SFP did not engage in campaigns or provide eco-labels. Instead, it was a business-focused, donation-based, non-profit organization that was attempting to provide powerful information tools as well as a methodology to allow companies to directly engage with natural resource suppliers to achieve improvement. SFP was available to Sobey's[11] to work on its supply chain, to provide a metric system, to facilitate engagement with suppliers and to provide some guidance and advice to Sobey's executives.

To achieve the goal of responsibly sourced seafood, an important challenge was to migrate this effort so that it was part of every employee's day-to-day activities; this would require educating staff and management about the specific goals and highlighting each employee's role in advancing sustainability at Sobey's. To this end, Sobey's implemented an employee e-Learning module on sustainable seafood that was completed by over 2,000 staff. Overall, Sobey's believed its sustainable seafood strategy was a superior approach. According to Smith,

> There were two benefits to our approach; one is that it's about the science—we are dealing with the critical issues, not working around the edges. The other benefit is that it's more financially responsible: how do you explain to your merchants, who are on the hook every week to meet their sales and profit goals, "yeah, sorry remember all those species you used to sell, well sorry, they are not certified. You can only sell something else." And how do you explain to your customers, "you know all that great seafood you used to buy, sorry, you can't have that anymore." This paints you into a corner financially. You've created a huge risk for yourself and, environmentally, you're not even creating the needed impact.

---

[10]www.sustainablefish.org. accessed September 12, 2012.

[11]Other significant clients were McDonald's, Walmart, Tesco, Disney and Highliner.

To improve customers' knowledge of the origins of its seafood, Sobey's initiated a web-based traceability program called ThisFish.[12] This hugely successful initiative generated over 27 million media impressions when it was launched in October 2012 – Sobey's biggest media campaign ever. Further, in the quest for greater understanding of the opportunities to develop a sustainable seafood policy, Sobey's conducted a survey with 1,000 seafood eating consumers across Canada. They found, according to Smith,

> [People were still in] a state of confusion but with an interest in becoming part of the solution. Consumers seem to want to protect long-term viability of the oceans but don't know how to do it. They want to be informed and want us to help them. So it appears there is a latent demand–but they are largely silent because they are confused. I think people would like to do the right thing but there is so much to learn about things like ratings lists (e.g., red, yellow, green) from organizations like the Monterey Bay Aquarium, Sea Choice, the Ecology Action Centre and the Marine Stewardship Council.[13] Our objective is to make it easy and take all the work out of it so that customers don't have to memorize "eco labels" and all that kind of stuff–they can simply trust that anything in our seafood department is responsibly sourced. So people can feel good about buying at Sobey's; this will drive loyalty, because they will recognize us for the work we have done without their having to really get into the weeds on all this.

Yet an important consideration for Smith was,

> There is a risk of bad optics if you continue to engage in some of these difficult areas because it's hard to explain to people. It's very easy to give them an "eco label" to look for. It's riskier in terms of the "court of public opinion" and perhaps by the people who are ill-informed. But once we explain it, I think people will get it.

---

[12]*Go to www.ThisFish.info and enter the code T001118 to view a particular BC-sourced halibut sold in Ontario stores.*

[13]See, for example, www.montereybayaquarium.org; www.seachoice.org; www.ecologyaction.ca; and www.msc. org. The MSC is currently the biggest and most common certification system used in the world. Its blue logo, based on guidelines from the FAO, certifies that a product comes from a fishery that does not harm the surrounding environment while maintaining a sufficient fish population.

EXHIBIT 1: Sobey's Corporate Financial Data

Sobeys Income Statement		
CDN$ in millions	**2012**	**2011**
Sales	16,045	15,756
EBITDA*	802	794
Adjusted EBITDA	789	775
Operating Income	476	473
Adjusted Operating Income	463	455
Net Earnings, net of minority interest	304	297
Adjusted Net Earnings, net of minority interest	293	281

*EBITDA: earnings before interest, taxes, depreciation and amortization.
Source: Empire Company Ltd., 2012 Annual Report.

Sobeys Balance Sheet	
CDN$ in millions	**2012**
Total Assets	6,328
Liabilities	
Short Term Liabilities	16
Long Term Liabilities	976
Total Liabilities	991
Total Equity	5,337
Total Liabilities and Equity	6,328

Source: ThompsonOne, https://www.thomsonone.com, accessed September 10, 2012.

EXHIBIT 2: Competitors' Approaches to Sustainable Seafood

Overwaitea Food Group Overwaitea is a supermarket chain that operates in communities across Western Canada. In 2012, Greenpeace ranked Overwaitea as the top performer in seafood sustainability, the first and only time a company has ever received a green rating. The company's sustainable seafood guidelines include a wide selection of sustainable seafood products, awareness programs and a commitment to transparency.[14] The company works with SeaChoice in order to improve its existing seafood selections, and in 2011, it stopped promoting red list species. It has committed to preserving the livelihood of all seafood species for the future.[15] At Overwaitea retail locations, sustainable products are marked by SeaChoice logos in order to better inform the consumer. It is currently the only Canadian supermarket to have removed open net-pen farmed salmon from its stores. According to vice-president Carmen Churcott, "Sustainability has been a journey for us in all areas of our business, and when it comes to sustainable sourcing, it's been a real partnership with suppliers."[16] By 2015, it hopes to carry only "sustainably sourced" seafood products.

Loblaw Companies Loblaw, Canada's largest food retailer, aims to carry only seafood from sustainable sources by the end of 2013. The company is currently in partnership with organizations such as World Wildlife Foundation Canada, the MSC and other groups in order to achieve this goal. In 2011, the company more than tripled the number of sustainable seafood products sold from 22 to 73 and implemented a vendor questionnaire in order to evaluate the impact of their purchases. The company has also been working with its vendors to find sustainable alternatives wherever possible. Loblaw's packaging and customer communication channels have been used to educate consumers about sustainable seafood and related issues. By 2012, the company's goal was to convert all existing sources to MSC-approved producers, where they existed.[17]

Safeway Inc. Safeway is North America's second biggest supermarket chain. Safeway Canada aims to carry only sustainably sourced seafood products by 2015. In 2008, the company created an internal team to focus on the issue of sustainability in the seafood sector. In 2011, Safeway partnered with SeaChoice and adapted its branding policy to encourage consumers to select sustainable seafood options. Also in 2011, the company's suppliers all completed a sourcing assessment to help determine the production methods and practices used in procuring seafood products. Safeway is currently working with suppliers in order to help them transition to sustainable seafood practices. The company is actively seeking sustainable alternatives wherever possible. Moreover, the company's employee training program helps to facilitate its sustainable seafood endeavours.[18] Safeway's seafood policy is continuously evolving but does not currently include all products containing marine ingredients such as pet food.

Metro Inc. Metro is a Canadian food retailer that operates in Ontario and Quebec. It is the third largest grocery chain in Canada. Metro's sustainable seafood policy reflects several guiding principles. In 2009, it created a work committee that helps select sustainable products and reduces the company's effects on marine life. Its policy is guided by scientific studies, independent studies and organizations such as Greenpeace. In 2010, the company produced a code for its suppliers to hold them accountable to lawful and ethical practices wherever possible. The company is committed to transparency and providing all possible information to its consumers. In September 2010, the company removed seven threatened species from its shelves and is currently in the process of removing another seven threatened species. Metro will expand its policy to include all products containing marine ingredients in 2014. Uniquely, the company's private label brand not only signifies that a product is sustainably sourced, it also lists information about the product's procurement methods to better inform the consumer.[19] Furthermore, the company considers the local economies it sources its products from in its decision making whenever possible.[20]

[14]Overwaitea Food Group, "Sustainable Seafood Policies," January 19, 2013, www.owfg.com/sustainable-seafood, accessed September 10, 2012.

[15]Living Oceans Society, "SeaChoice Partners with Overwaitea Food Group on Bold Sustainable Seafood Project," January 19, 2013, www.livingoceans.org/, accessed September 10, 2012.

[16]Overwaitea Food Group, "Overwaitea Food Group Tops Greenpeace Sustainable Seafood Rankings," June 28, 2012, www.owfg.com/sustainable-seafood, accessed January 19, 2013.

[17]Loblaw, "Loblaw Sustainable Seafood Commitment," 2012, January 18, 2013, www.loblaw.ca/seafood, accessed September 10, 2012.

[18]Safeway, "Sustainability Seafood Policy," January 20, 2013, www.safeway.ca/community/seafood.html, accessed September 10, 2012.

[19]"Sustainable Fisheries at Metro: Summary of the Efforts and Progress Made," Metro, May 2012.

[20]"Sustainable Fisheries – FAQ," Metro, January 20, 2013.

EXHIBIT 2: (continued)

Walmart Walmart, a U.S. corporation, is the world's biggest retailer. Walmart Canada aims to carry only wild-caught fish and frozen fish that meet MSC minimum standards. Moreover, the company expects its farm-raised seafood products to be a result of Best Aquaculture Practices. Lastly, it will source canned tuna only from an International Seafood Sustainability Foundation member. These goals are set to be completed by the end of 2013. The company's seafood sustainability plan includes working with suppliers to improve their environmental performance and dropping suppliers who refuse to adhere to minimum standards. The company is also working with vendors to improve its packaging to make labels more transparent.[21] Walmart's policies do not include other products that include seafood ingredients such as pet food and sauces. The company is currently in partnership with the MSC, SFP and the World Wildlife Fund.

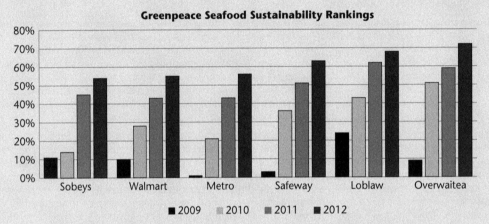

Greenpeace Seafood Sustainability Rankings

Source: Adapted by the author from www.greenpeace.org/canada/en/campaigns/ocean/Seafood/Get-involved/2012-supermarket-ranking/, accessed September 10, 2012.

---

[21]"Sustainable Seafood Policy," Walmart Canada, March 2010.

EXHIBIT 3: Greenpeace's Red List Species Sales by Selected Organizations

Legend: ● = Still sold in supermarkets; ◑ = Some product categories removed

Species	Overwaitea	Loblaw	Safeway	Metro	Walmart	Sobeys
Monkfish		●		●		●
Hake		●	●	●		●
Rockfish/Red fish	●	●	◑	◑		●
King crab		●	●	●		●
Alaska pollock	◑	●	●	●	●	●
Fraser River sockeye	●	●	●	●	●	●
Tropical shrimp and prawns	●	●	●	●	●	●
Farmed Atlantic salmon		●	●	●	●	●
Atlantic sea scallops	●	●	●	●		●
Haddock	●	●	●	●		●
Atlantic cod	●	●	●	●	*discontinued but may still be found in store	●
Yellow fin tuna		◑	◑	●	●	●
Atlantic halibut		●		●		●
Swordfish				●		
Arcticsurf clams				●		●
Chilean sea bass						●

● Still sold in supermarkets ◑ Some product categories removed

Source: Adapted by the author from www.greenpeace.org/canada/Global/canada/report/2012/10/GP-English-REDLIST-FIN.pdf, accessed September 10, 2012.

CASE
34

Online Piracy: Jaywalking or Theft?

In September 2009, Brian Lee purchased a computer game developed by a major company and, like some other customers, was experiencing difficulty running it. The source of the problems was a highly restrictive system of digital rights management (DRM),[1] which, while more or less universally disliked, was causing serious technical problems for a minority of users. Lee began to share his experience on the company's message board and was soon engaging in a debate about online piracy with a company representative. He was curious about piracy in the file-sharing age and wondered why it would be wrong to download a pirated version of the game with the DRM circumvented.

THE DIALOGUE

Brian: I have been a loyal supporter of your company for over a decade, but that is going to change. I pre-ordered your newest game and since it arrived a week ago, I have tried repeatedly to run it but my DVD-ROM drive will not recognize the disc. Updating drivers at the request of technical support did not fix the problem. In fact, technical support insinuated that I must be using a pirated version, which is outrageous. Many people on this message board are experiencing problems running the game and yet for the most part our

IVEY | Publishing

Alex Beamish and Professor Paul Beamish wrote this case solely to provide material for class discussion. The authors do not intend to illustrate either effective or ineffective handling of a managerial situation. The authors may have disguised certain names and other identifying information to protect confidentiality.

Richard Ivey School of Business Foundation prohibits any form of reproduction, storage or transmittal without its written permission. Reproduction of this material is not covered under authorization by any reproduction rights organization. To order copies or request permission to reproduce materials, contact Ivey Publishing, Richard Ivey School of Business Foundation, c/o Richard Ivey School of Business, The University of Western Ontario, London, Ontario, Canada, N6A 3K7; phone (519) 661-3208; fax (519) 661-3882; e-mail cases@ivey.uwo.ca.

Copyright © 2009, Richard Ivey School of Business Foundation   Version: 2012-10-03

One time permission to reproduce granted by Richard Ivey School of Business Foundation on April 22, 2014.

[1]DRM is a broad term for methods of controlling access to digital material. Examples of DRM include FairPlay for iTunes, which prevented songs purchased from the iTunes Store from playing on competitors' digital music players; region codes on DVDs; installation limits and online activation requirements in computer games; and copying and printing restrictions in e-books.

computers are perfectly capable according to the box's specifications. It seems that many of the difficulties customers are experiencing result from the new system of DRM employed by the game. When it was announced months ago that the game would use this form of DRM, some were skeptical, particularly because it entailed an installation limit of five times. Yet we all expected to play the game through at least once! The retailer from which I purchased the game will not issue a refund or allow an exchange for a different game. It did permit me to swap for another copy of the same game in case the first copy was defective, but I did so and my problems remained. Also, when I tried to sell the game, I discovered that the used computer games market is now virtually non-existent due to DRM. Thus, I am out $60 and hours of time and I will never give business to your company again.

Customer Support: Dear Brian, we regret that you are experiencing this problem. It has come to our attention that a minority of users (approximately two per cent) are having trouble running the game because of DRM conflicts. We encourage you to stay in touch with technical support until a solution is reached. We are aware of the unpopularity of what seems like a draconian anti-piracy system and can assure you that our decision to use it was not taken lightly. We deemed it necessary after our games were pirated 50,000 times in 2008. That equates to 50,000 stolen games–50,000 lost sales! We deeply regret the problems our customers face due to DRM, but we believe their frustration is better directed at the pirates who have forced us to take these measures.

Brian: Technical support has stopped replying to my e-mails. Nonetheless, I would like to respond to one of your points; namely, where you claim you lost 50,000 sales in 2008 after your games were "stolen" 50,000 times. It is incorrect to equate an illegal game download with a game stolen off a store shelf, because in the latter instance each game stolen represents a physical and likely irretrievable loss for the company, whereas software piracy entails illegal duplication. While piracy certainly cuts into your company's profits, you cannot assume that each user of a pirated software program would have purchased the retail version if a pirated version was unavailable.

Customer Support: I acknowledge that an illegally downloaded piece of media does not equate perfectly with a lost sale. However, I will in turn point out a misconception that many piracy advocates believe–that if they are morally obligated to pay for content, it should merely be the materials cost (e.g. a couple dollars for a DVD, booklet and case). But this neglects to factor in all the labor involved in the creation of the content and it suggests that intellectual property itself is worthless. How is a record company supposed to pay salaries if it receives money for the raw materials cost of CDs but not also for the creativity on the CDs? As Mark Helprin writes in Digital Barbarism: "The advocates of 'music sharing' think that, because the Beatles, half of whom are dead, have hundreds of millions, or perhaps even billions of dollars, and the people who would filch a song or two may have to buy their salad one tomato at a time and use milk crates as chairs, these expropriations are somehow mathematically justified. They aren't, and not merely because their cumulative effect has destroyed the music industry. . . . It doesn't matter if you steal a lot or a little, or if you get away with it, or not: theft is ugly."[2] I regret your problems, but I stand firm in my belief that piracy is always wrong.

Brian: I do believe intellectual property is of monetary value, and indeed I have never used pirated content. However, this is the first time I have been unable to run purchased content. While I have been waiting (hopefully not in vain) for a patch to fix the game, I have researched online piracy and have learned some surprising facts. Your assertion that "piracy is always wrong" is probably off the mark. In Free Culture, Lawrence Lessig defines four different types of file sharers: a) those who "use sharing networks as substitutes for

---

[2]Mark Helprin, *Digital Barbarism*, HarperCollins, New York, 2009.

purchasing content"; b) those who "use sharing networks to sample music before purchasing it"; c) those who "use sharing networks to get access to copyrighted material that is no longer sold or that they would not have purchased because the transaction costs off the Net are too high"; and d) those who "use sharing networks to get access to content that is not copyrighted or that the copyright owner wants to give away."[3] Of course, type A is unambiguously wrong, and type D is perfectly acceptable. The grey area falls within types B and C. Some think it not unreasonable that users illegally download and "sample" a program or album before buying it and admittedly, doing so quickly eliminates many weak, overpriced products from consideration. Also, some who sample products will then buy them and a few of these converted pirates would never have known about these products had they been unavailable in pirated form. As for acquiring content no longer manufactured or commercially available but still copyrighted, I see no harm in this. Waiting for content with a "dead copyright" to enter the public domain is increasingly unrealistic considering the average copyright term in the United States has ballooned from 32 years in 1973 to 95 years in 2003.[4] In addition, it can be next to impossible to locate copyright holders of dormant works.

By the way, are there any updates on the patch?

Customer Support: We are actively working on a patch, although if we are unsuccessful we might arrange for a refund or a coupon for our products.

As for type B file sharing, I find this sense of entitlement preposterous and I doubt there is conclusive evidence that pirates often purchase works they have illegally sampled. Type C file sharing also involves a sense of entitlement. Indeed, pirates are abetted by a sense of entitlement that coincides with the new potential for massive accumulation of content and information. This sense of entitlement, Mark Helprin believes, stems from a faulty belief in endless, ubiquitous wealth; the relative youth of the anti-copyright movement and its adherents; the view that intellectual property is not property; and the expectation of paying for media not with cash, but through subjection to nonstop commercials, banners and other advertising intrusions.[5] It is plain to see that there is a slippery slope in both types B and C. Conscientiously sampling content with a genuine willingness to buy good content turns into carelessly "sampling" everything and buying nothing. Rigorously searching the web and store bargain bins for an old underground album before downloading a pirated version as a last resort quickly degenerates into conducting a 30-second web search, conveniently concluding the album is commercially unavailable and downloading an illegal copy. Besides, there are legal means for acquiring rare content, such as EBay. The point is that types B and C quickly become type A. Ultimately, we can fret about the details but it is fair to conclude that piracy is utterly harmful not only to content creators, but also to users. Increased piracy drives up prices and necessitates measures that occasionally cause problems for paying customers such as yourself. Nobody likes intrusive DRM, but the fact remains that a mere four per cent of video games entering production will earn a profit.[6] Worldwide, more than a third of all software used in 2007 was pirated, causing lost revenues to the software industry of approximately $48 billion,[7] and DRM is a logical response to this reality. Critics of DRM hold that because DRM is sometimes circumvented,

---

[3]Lawrence Lessig, *Free Culture*, Penguin Books, United States, 2005.

[4]Ibid.

[5]Mark Helprin, *Digital Barbarism*, HarperCollins, New York, 2009.

[6]Koroush Ghazi, "PC Game Piracy Examined," June 2009, www.tweakguides.com/Piracy_1.html.

[7]Note that pirated software does not include pirated music or movies. *Business Software Alliance*, "Online Software Scams: A Threat to Your Security," October 2008, www.bsa.org/files/Internet_Piracy_Report.pdf.

it should cease to exist. By this logic, because locks on houses are often broken, we should not bother to lock our houses.[8] The point of DRM is deterrence, and it performs this function more or less admirably.

Brian: But at what cost? DRM can undoubtedly be expensive and tricky to maintain for companies, and the drawbacks for consumers are even worse. Much of the DRM used in games, for example, is so intrusive that it remains on a user's computer after a game is uninstalled. If it retains the potential to collect information about a user's computer after the user has removed the program, is it much better than malware?[9] Installation limits are also troubling. Users are constantly formatting their hard drives or uninstalling programs to free up space, and a limit of three or five installations is unfair. Of course, I am posting here simply because of the impasse DRM has brought me to and I sense that in time we will look back on most of these anti-piracy measures with disbelief. Remember DRM audio CDs? They suffered a quick demise after it was discovered that Sony BMG was including rootkits on their DRM CDs, causing potential security vulnerabilities for customers' computers.[10] More recently, Steve Jobs, the driving force behind Apple, has identified the folly of DRM in iTunes and has succeeded in relaying his opinion to the big four record companies, who control the distribution of 70 per cent of the world's music,[11] so that the iTunes Store is now DRM-free. Fairplay, iTunes's DRM, used to mean that only iPods could play tracks purchased from iTunes, that tracks purchased from iTunes would not play on competing music players, and that there were other limitations such as only being able to access purchased tracks on a maximum of five computers. Unsurprisingly, many other digital music players and online music stores employed their own systems of DRM. Yet the vast majority of worldwide music sales were still in the form of CDs and thus were DRM-free, so it was silly and overly complex for music distributed online, which comprised a small portion of music sales, to be saddled with these different forms of DRM. Even Bill Gates himself criticized DRM, saying it has "huge problems."[12]

Customer Support: DRM is not perfect, and the anti-piracy measures of the future will undoubtedly look different from those used now. But no good comes of piracy and necessary steps need to be taken to prevent it.

Brian: Is it entirely true that no good comes of piracy? While I recognize the harm caused by piracy, it has brought certain inadvertent benefits. Jeff Raikes, when he was president of the Microsoft Business Division, stated, "Our number one goal is that we want people to use our product. If they're going to pirate somebody, we want it to be us rather than somebody else. . . . What you hope to do is over time you hope to convert them to licensing the software, legally licensing it."[13] Regarding the competition in China between Microsoft Windows and Linux, a free open source operating system, Bill Gates said, "It's easier for our software to compete with Linux when there's piracy than when there's not."[14]

---

[8]Koroush Ghazi, "PC Game Piracy Examined," June 2009, www.tweakguides.com/Piracy_1.html.

[9]Malware, also known as malicious software, is software made to break into or disrupt a user's computer without the user's permission. The term encompasses viruses, trojan horses, spyware, rootkits, etc.

[10]Robert McMillan, "Settlement Ends Sony Rootkit Case," *PC World*, May 23, 2006, www.pcworld.com/article/125838/settlement_ends_sony_rootkit_case.html.

[11]Steve Jobs, "Thoughts on Music," February 6, 2007, www.apple.com/hotnews/thoughtsonmusic.

[12]Cyrus Farivar, "CE-Oh no he didn't! . . ." *Engadget*, December 14, 2006, www.engadget.com/2006/12/14/ce-oh-no-he-didnt-part-xxi-gates-tells-consumers-to-ditch-dr.

[13]*Computer Business Review*, "Microsoft admits piracy benefits," March 16, 2007, www.cbronline.com/news/microsoft_admits_piracy_benefits.

[14]David Kirkpatrick, "How Microsoft conquered China," *CNN Money*, July 17, 2007, http://money.cnn.com/magazines/fortune/fortune_archive/2007/07/23/100134488.

And generally speaking, have not many of the technological and cultural milestones in the West been inextricably linked to piracy? Consider Hollywood, born of pirates evading the patent laws of Thomas Edison, the inventor of filmmaking.[15] What about the United States, which neglected to recognize foreign copyrights for the first hundred years of its existence?[16] How about extensive "borrowing" and refining by Disney?[17] It was Rupert Murdoch who said that without Napster, there was no Internet, and we can see that high-speed Internet boomed due to Napster.[18] In Canada, Bell had 51,000 high-speed Internet customers when Napster launched in June 1999. By 2002, this number had jumped to 1.1 million.[19] Consider the iPod now. Hank Berry, former Napster CEO, said, "Without Napster, there is no iPod, period. . . . Remember that the iPod launched two years before the iTunes store was around, so you have a two-year period where essentially the only source of music for people's iPods was people doing their own ripping from their own CD collection and getting things from Napster or some other service."[20] I could go on—Youtube, cable television, radio, VCRs, CD burners, tape recorders; all these technologies owe a debt to piracy, and many could not have thrived without it.

Customer Support: I cannot say I share your utopian vision of piracy. I will grant that much of the technology we use today is or was associated with piracy, but whether we should be proud of this is another question. You seem to champion piracy and imply that theft is a key driver of innovation. Indeed, there are many likeminded individuals on the web and you would find a better reception for your views at the Pirate Bay, the famous torrent[21] indexing site. In case you were unaware, BitTorrent has taken the baton of file sharing from the older generation of peer-to-peer (P2P) programs like Napster and while there are plenty of sites from which to download torrents, none is as famous as the Pirate Bay, which is the centre of an anti-copyright, counter-culture movement touting "freedom of information" to justify facilitating massive piracy. But if you ask me, the four men who own the Pirate Bay are just masquerading as revolutionaries and their grievances about the supposed greed of corporate America lose credibility when you consider that the site racks up millions of dollars a year in ad revenues, not to mention donations. They do not simply promote and facilitate piracy, they get rich off of it. And as a result, they have been sentenced to serve a year in jail and pay millions of dollars in fines. As a matter of fact, following their sentencing the "business" has been sold to a gaming company for nearly $8 million. The company, Global Gaming Factory X, promises that the Pirate Bay will introduce legitimate business models with which to pay content owners, but the owners of the Pirate Bay seem to tell a different story, suggesting the sale will not affect the site.[22] Only time will tell. Suffice it to say, I find it repugnant to see my company's work available on the Pirate Bay for free under the pretence of "freedom of information." The fact that the Pirate Bay has

---

[15]Lawrence Lessig, *Free Culture*, Penguin Books, United States, 2005.

[16]Ibid.

[17]Ibid.

[18]*The Globe and Mail*, "Download Decade," 2009, www.theglobeandmail.com/news/technology/download-decade.

[19]Ibid.

[20]Ibid.

[21]A torrent is a small file that contains the metadata needed to download a larger file (e.g. a game or movie) from a network of users. BitTorrent is the protocol through which torrents function, and some sources estimate that BitTorrent traffic accounts for half of all the traffic on the Internet.

[22]*CBC News*, "Pirate Bay site sold to Swedish gaming company," June 30, 2009, www.cbc.ca/arts/music/story/2009/06/30/pirate-bay-sold-gaming-company.html.

many loyal fans hardly legitimizes it—is it surprising that people flock to its banner after using it to steal thousands of dollars of free content? You even have a Norwegian socialist party launching filesharer.org, a website where users are supposed to post their mug shots to demonstrate they are "criminals" like the owners of the Pirate Bay. I doubt the pro-piracy movements, political or otherwise, offer coherent, realistic plans for intellectual property rights. What they do offer is a tired communitarian philosophy, or worse—anarchy.

Brian: Geez, why are we talking about anarchy? I'm still trying to get my computer game working.

Customer Support: Fair enough. But my little rant is due to the fact that if my company cannot generate revenues, people like me lose their job.

Brian: Nobody wants you to lose your job. But can we get back to my problem? On Google, I searched for the name of the game plus the word "torrent" and was astounded at the depth of matches. The torrent sites offer a version of the game that is complete, yet cracked, so that the DRM is removed.[23] This means that following a few hours' download time, I could install a pirated copy of your game and it would probably play successfully (since there is no potential for a DRM incompatibility), not to mention present fewer hassles than the retail version. I am somewhat confounded that BitTorrent is resilient to the legal problems that defeated Napster, but I would wager that BitTorrent survives because the standard BitTorrent client does not feature a built-in search engine for torrents (these must be downloaded from a site like the Pirate Bay) and because torrents only contain metadata and not "real data."

Companies do not seem to be giving enough thought to the future of the relationship between the Internet and intellectual property. In my view, this is where our focus should lie, so I have compiled a list of technological and other ways that content could be protected from piracy. In fact, I have created a new message board thread because this is such an important topic (see Exhibit 1).

At this juncture, I must say that it has been weeks since I first notified technical support of my problems and that the assistance I have received has been disappointing, if not unethical. When I first explained my problem, tech support provided me with a customer complaint number and asked a question about my computer hardware, then received a response, sent another question, received another response and stopped replying. When I e-mailed to ask why they stopped responding, they gave me a new customer complaint number, started asking the same questions as before and again stopped replying. They have issued four customer complaint numbers now and I suspect they keep placing me at the top of the queue so that I give up trying. They have never apologized or indicated a serious effort to fix my problem, and especially disconcerting is their suggestion that I am using a pirated version and that this must be the source of my difficulties (ironically, a pirated version would probably play fine). As a former part-time business student, I detect a weakness in your service recovery. In fact, in my view, it is so bad that it is bordering on immoral. I found an old ethics textbook which says that the minimal moral obligation of a business organization toward customers is "Accurately labeled, safe goods and services of good value. Adequate customer information. Respect promises on delivery and performance."[24]

Customer Support: I take issue with your claim that the company has conducted itself unethically in response to your problem. We care deeply about customers' concerns, though unfortunately technical support is overstretched and cannot always provide

---

[23]To crack software is to modify it in order to remove protection such as the requirement of CD checks or serial numbers.

[24]Frederick Bird and Jeffrey Gandz, *Good Management: Business Ethics in Action*, Prentice-Hall Canada Inc, Scarborough, Ontario, 1991, p. 111.

immediate assistance. I can assure you we are operating in accordance with ethical standards. But remember, if users object to the glitches, installation limits and other hassles brought on by DRM in games, they should not forget that the pirates are the offending party, not us.

Brian: Whatever you say! Did you read the new thread about ways to cut down on online piracy?

Customer Support: Yes, I read it over and it's interesting stuff. At this time I regret to inform you that due to cash flow issues, we cannot issue a refund. Furthermore, we have been unsuccessful in developing a patch. Thank you for your understanding.

EXHIBIT 1:   A Few Ways to Reduce Piracy

The first way to reduce piracy is to launch an attack against file-sharing technologies such as BitTorrent. The idea of stifling technology in order to protect copyrights is not unprecedented in recent decades. Jack Valenti, when he was president of the Motion Picture Association of America, was virulently opposed to VCRs, calling them "tapeworms": "When there are 20, 30, 40 million of these VCRs in the land, we will be invaded by millions of 'tapeworms,' eating away at the very heart and essence of the most precious asset the copyright owner has, his copyright."[1] Quashing file-sharing technologies would be an overreaction, causing technological regression, and is impractical. Much more realistic is the prospect of Internet service providers (ISPs) blocking access to file-sharing sites like the Pirate Bay and, as I understand, that site is blocked in Denmark. One problem with this measure is that torrent indexing sites are almost ubiquitous; another is that some ISPs are reluctant to offer restrictive access to the Internet because it undermines the free, limitless nature of the technology. France just narrowly rejected legislation to enact a three-strikes policy whereby users who illegally download copyrighted content would be warned twice before their Internet was cut off. A common means by which ISPs reduce traffic is "throttling," where download speeds of BitTorrent users are mitigated, and this is inadvertently an anti-piracy measure. Finally, it is evident that monitoring piracy on the Internet and then pursuing the culprits is incredibly unpopular—witness the notorious efforts of the Recording Industry Association of America to sue casual P2P users for hundreds of thousands of dollars.

There is, of course, the DRM question. DRM has arguably proven unsuccessful with digital music but is still a factor in PC games, e-books (e.g. to control copying and printing), Blu-rays and DVDs (e.g. region codes), operating systems, and even ring tones. The very fact of my writing this post speaks to one of DRM's shortcomings—inconveniencing legitimate customers, whether through bogging down the experience or stopping it altogether. An alternative to the sort of DRM that irritates computer gamers is selling games through Steam, an online distribution system (somewhat like an iTunes for games) that requires users to log in and for some games be connected to the Internet. This could be considered "DRM-lite." Most games sold on Steam do not use a separate system of DRM; hence, most do not have installation limits or disc checks (since Steam games are all downloaded), and do not leave remnants of DRM on the computer after removal.

Bundling software with new computers is an effective method of combating software piracy. Another good method is cloud computing, in which software functionality lies on a vendor's server instead of on a local PC.[2] Another possibility is software asset management, which helps users keep track of software licenses. The potential rise of streaming media services offering a vast archive of high-quality media could mitigate the appeal of downloading media illegally (and perhaps with lower quality) through BitTorrent. Last.fm is an innovative Internet radio site that streams free music with ads, and offers a premium service for a small subscription fee. Spotify streams free ad-supported music to computer users and is experimenting with a subscription model for mobile phone users. These business models accept that the current generation, rightly or wrongly, feels entitled to music for free or for dirt cheap.

Moving on, there are ways to protect content that are rooted more in ideology than technology. Does overpriced content significantly increase piracy rates? Certainly some users engage in piracy out of a belief that big business does not need or deserve their money. However, the correlation between price and piracy rates is difficult to gauge for general Western populations. On the other hand, many users in the developing world are simply too poor to pay for content, whether it costs $2 or $20, and unsurprisingly the highest software piracy rates in the world are in Georgia (95 per cent), Bangladesh (92 per cent), Armenia (92 per cent) and Zimbabwe

---

[1]Lawrence Lessig, *Free Culture*, Penguin Books, United States, 2005.

[2]Sixth Annual BSA-IDC Global Software Piracy Study, May 2009, http://global.bsa.org/globalpiracy2008/index.html.

EXHIBIT 1: (continued)

(92 per cent), while the lowest piracy rates are in North America (21 per cent) and Western Europe (33 per cent).[3] Finally, globalization means that emerging markets will increasingly value legitimate software, and will be more active in cracking down on intellectual property violations. This seems to be playing out in China right now.

It is plausible that some tweaking of copyright laws is in order. For example, Canada has not updated its copyright law since 1997, two years before the release of Napster.[4] As well, some argue that people need to change their perceptions about piracy—should it remain illegal to download "abandonware," that is, software no longer sold or supported and for which no one is actively asserting copyright ownership? The following system could be implemented for users who want to draw from, or publishers who want to make available, orphan works: "In the absence of a claimant, a notice could be posted on a universal copyright internet notice board. After a reasonable time and no response, a potential user or publisher could be granted permission to use or publish, with royalties held in escrow for yet another period, until they were claimed. And if they were not claimed, they could be directed to a fund of some sort, or revert to the payer. These simple steps would make orphan works available and protect the copyright holders at the same time."[5] Are copyright terms in general too long? In the United States, the only software that has entered the public domain due to copyright expiration is software published before 1964 that was not renewed in its copyright during its 28th year following publication; for unpublished software, the copyright lasts 70 years plus the life of the author, regardless of when it was written.[6] Hopefully Creative Commons[7] will grow in popularity so that content creators can conveniently permit their work to be available to others with minimal restrictions if they so desire. New possibilities for abandonware and orphan works, as well as the availability of a more flexible copyright, could reduce the scope of what is considered piracy and copyright infringement.

More sample or trial versions[8] of software, music and movies could reduce piracy rates to a small degree. Evolving attitudes, perhaps influenced through educational initiatives, could present purchasing content as classy and pirating as reprehensible. The public should be informed that pirated content frequently comes with malware, and that unpaid taxes on pirated content can hurt communities.

To end, I would like to share a scheme proposed by Harvard law professor William Fisher to solve the problem of online piracy: "Under his plan, all content capable of digital transmission would (1) be marked with a digital watermark. . . . Once the content is marked, then entrepreneurs would develop (2) systems to monitor how many items of each content were distributed. On the basis of those numbers, then (3) artists would be compensated. The compensation would be paid for by (4) an appropriate tax."[9] Thus, users would simply download what they wanted and taxes would compensate content creators according to how much their work was downloaded. Lawrence Lessig has proposed a slight modification to this scheme.

---

[3]Ibid.

[4]*The Globe and Mail*, "Download Decade," 2009, www.theglobeandmail.com/news/technology/download-decade.

[5]Mark Helprin, *Digital Barbarism*, HarperCollins, New York, 2009.

[6]Stephen Fishman, *The Public Domain: How to Find and Use Copyright Free Writings, Music, Art & More*, NOLO, 2008.

[7]Creative Commons is a non-profit organization devoted to providing a "some rights reserved" alternative to the traditional "all rights reserved" copyright.

[8]Trial versions generally offer limited features and/or expire after a specified term.

[9]Lawrence Lessig, *Free Culture*, Penguin Books, United States, 2005.

Barrick Gold Corporation– Tanzania[1]

By March 2009, Canadian mining company Barrick Gold Corporation (Barrick) had only been operating in the Lake Victoria Zone in Tanzania for a decade. In the same year, Barrick had adopted a new name for its business in Tanzania, African Barrick Gold plc (ABG), which was also listed on the London Stock Exchange. The company was widely considered to be one of the more "responsive" global corporations in the mining industry.[2] Its extensive mining activities in the region employed thousands of local people, and Barrick was engaged in social development projects in various Tanzanian communities.[3] By October 2010, the company operated four main gold mining sites in the country.[4]

Despite Barrick's efforts to support social development initiatives in the Lake Victoria Zone over the past decade, discontent and resistance at one of its mining sites in North Mara still remained. This area posed challenges. A key question was why the tension and violence had not stopped in certain mining sites in the North Mara mining area, and whether there was much more Barrick could reasonably be expected to do to resolve the problem.

IVEY | Publishing

Professors Aloysius Newenham-Kahindi and Paul W. Beamish wrote this case solely to provide material for class discussion. The authors do not intend to illustrate either effective or ineffective handling of a managerial situation. The authors may have disguised certain names and other identifying information to protect confidentiality.

Richard Ivey School of Business Foundation prohibits any form of reproduction, storage or transmission without its written permission. Reproduction of this material is not covered under authorization by any reproduction rights organization. To order copies or request permission to reproduce materials, contact Ivey Publishing, Richard Ivey School of Business Foundation, The University of Western Ontario, London, Ontario, Canada, N6A 3K7; phone (519) 661-3208; fax (519) 661-3882; e-mail cases@ivey.uwo.ca.

Copyright © 2010, Richard Ivey School of Business Foundation   Version: 2011-09-21

One time permission to reproduce granted by Richard Ivey School of Business Foundation on April 22, 2014.

[1]This case has been written on the basis of published sources only. Consequently, the interpretation and perspectives presented in this case are not necessarily those of Barrick Gold Corporation or any of its employees.

[2]www.barrick.com/CorporateResponsibility/BeyondBorders/default.aspx, accessed March 24, 2009.

[3]www.barrick.com/News/PressReleases/PressReleaseDetails/2010/Barrick-Named-to-Dow-Jones-Sustainability-World-Index-for-Third-Consecutive-Year/default.aspx, accessed September 27, 2010.

[4]www.tanzaniagold.com/barrick.html, accessed October 1, 2010.

BACKGROUND ON TANZANIA

Tanzania was a developing country located in East Africa, with a total land size of 945,087 square kilometres. It had one of the highest levels of unemployment and poverty in Sub-Saharan Africa. Its economy was heavily dependent on agriculture, which accounted for half of the gross domestic product (GDP), provided 85 per cent of the country's exports and employed 90 per cent of the work force. Topography and climatic conditions, however, limited cultivated crops to only four per cent of the land area. Industry was mainly limited to processing agricultural products and light consumer goods.

Like most developing nations, Tanzania had a very weak national institutional and legal system. It also had a very high rate of corruption.[5] The country needed support from foreign direct investment (FDI) and transnational corporations (TNCs) in order to promote businesses, employment, and other opportunities for its citizens. Tanzania wanted its institutions to be more transparent and accountable, and to regulate the activities of FDI and TNCs in addressing the country's social and ecological issues. Both local and international not-for-profit organizations (NFOs), however, had continued to create a significant impact with respect to promoting responsive behaviour in corporate governance practices, positively influencing all involved stakeholders and other social actors to address social issues.

Following independence in 1961, Tanzania opted for a socialist command economic and institutional system, with socialist policies (*"Ujamaa"* in Swahili*)* being implemented in 1967. The emphasis of these policies was to promote co-operative institutions and collective villages with the aim of building an egalitarian society, eliminating ethnic and gender barriers, and creating a common language of Swahili for all. Within the practice of Ujamaa, the country had managed to unite its ethnic groups under a common language, with the result that the central government had created strong post-colonial nationalistic ideologies, unity, ethnic harmony and peace among its people. Compared to many post-colonial Sub-Saharan African countries that went through civil and ethnic strife and conflicts after independence in the 1960s and 1970s, Tanzania under Ujamaa appeared to be a successful model.

Towards the end of the 1980s, however, Tanzania began to experience significant economic stagnation and social problems. To combat these issues, in the early 1990s the government sought to privatize its economy and reform its institutions in order to attract foreign investment. The introduction of the famous post-Ujamaa Investment Act of 1997 was intended to encourage free market and trade liberalization in the country. Investment in various private sectors such as mining, tourism, fishing, banking and agriculture under foreign-owned TNCs served to bolster the country's reforms by creating employment opportunities for the local economy.

As the country continued to privatize and reform its national institutional and legal systems, many foreign companies sought to invest in its economy. The Tanzania Investment Centre (TIC) was created in the early 2000s as a tool for identifying possible investment opportunities and aiding potential investors in navigating any procedural barriers that might exist during the process of investment in the country.[6] The liberalization of the banking industry in 2002, for example, saw the former Ujamaa Cooperative and Rural Development Bank replaced by the Commercial Rural Development Bank (CRDB) and the National Microfinance Bank (NMB), which promoted community investments across the country. In February 2009, the Tanzania Private Sector Foundation (TPSF) was created with

---

[5]See data on Tanzania at www.transparency.org.

[6]www.tic.co.tz, accessed April 1, 2009.

the aim of strengthening the entrepreneurial culture among its citizens by providing communities and individuals across the country with entrepreneurial business ideas and grants. In June 2009, the government started an ambitious national resolution under the so-called "Kilimo Kwanza" policies (meaning "Agriculture First" in Swahili) to boost the standard of living among the *eighty per cent* of citizens who relied on agriculture for their livelihood.[7] It was based on Green Revolution principles aimed at boosting Tanzania's agriculture into the modern and commercial sector, and mobilizing for-profit organizations (FPOs) such as local private businesses and foreign-owned TNCs in the country to increase their investment engagement with the agriculture sector, both at the macro and micro levels (i.e. along with local communities).

In order to ensure that there was sufficient security and peace for private and foreign-owned investors (i.e. TNCs), in 2005 the government introduced a new entity called "Tanzania Security Industry Association." The association was based on local, professional private security firms and groups whose main tasks were to safeguard business firms' activities rather than letting the firms rely on local police forces. The largest and best-known local security firm was "Moku Security Services Limited," based in Dar Es Salaam, which had over 13,000 employees across the country. Other security groups with over 400 employees were "Ultimate Security Company," "Dragon Security," "Tele-security Company Limited," and "Group Four Security Company." Private security employees were mainly retired army and police officers; young people who had lost their previous jobs following the collapse of the Ujamaa policies that provided "jobs for everyone and for life"; and individuals who sought better remuneration in the security sector than in the government public sector. However, due to increased demand for better security across businesses, many foreign-owned TNCs sought the services of security firms from abroad, mainly from South Africa's professional security firms such as the South African Intruder Detection Service Association (SAIDS). Some security personnel had combat experience, which helped them handle sophisticated forms of crime and intrusion.

The Tanzanian economy continued to grow and create job opportunities, training and innovative development prospects for its people. Earlier, the country had introduced new mining legislation such as the Mining Act of 1998 and the Mining Regulation Act of 1999 in order to harmonize investment relations between FDI and local interests. However, in April 2010 the government passed another new mining Act, following consultations with civil society groups such as the Foundation for Civil Society Tanzania (FCST), companies and other stakeholders. The legislation of a new mining Act imposed a new form of royalties that required all TNCs and local companies to be listed in the country and gave the state a stake in future projects.[8]

The country possessed vast amounts of natural resources like gold, diamond, copper, platinum, natural gas, and zinc deposits that remained underdeveloped. It was one of the more peaceful countries in Sub-Saharan Africa. In order to attract and protect the interests of FDI and TNCs and, of course, its own people, Tanzania had attempted to harmonize its investment practices and labour legislation. In order to create responsible institutional policies, in February 2010 the National Assembly of Tanzania enlisted a group of local environmental and toxicity experts to investigate environmental and toxic effects on the people and livestock in the North Mara gold mine in Tarime District, Mara Region, by the Tigithe River.[9]

---

[7]www.actanzania.org/index.php?option=com_content&task=view&id=121&Itemid=39, accessed February 12, 2010.

[8]www.mining-journal.com/finance/new-tanzanian-mining-act, accessed September 27, 2010.

[9]www.dailynews.co.tz, accessed February 10, 2010.

For a number of reasons, Tanzania was a willing host nation for FDI. The country needed the input of TNCs in order to create employment and prosperity. In return, Tanzania could provide TNCs with low-cost labour and a readily available labour force. Low labour costs were an opportunity to support a host nation's development policy in attracting FDI and ultimately in creating a knowledge-based society in the midst of the globalization challenges that were faced by so many developing countries. Furthermore, Tanzania continued to create a local business environment in conjunction with various TNCs' global business interests in order to generate sustainable development policies and practices. It also engaged in market development initiatives that represented innovative learning opportunities and entrepreneurship ventures for its citizens.

LAKE VICTORIA BACKGROUND

Tanzania's Lake Victoria was surrounded by the three East African countries of Kenya, Tanzania and Uganda. The lake itself was named after the former Queen of England, Queen Victoria, and stood as the world's largest tropical lake and the second-largest freshwater lake after Lake Superior in North America. Covering a total of 69,000 square kilometres, the lake was as large as the Republic of Ireland and lay in the Rift Valley of East Africa, a 3,500-mile system of deep cracks in the earth's crust, running from the Red Sea south to Mozambique. Lake Victoria was the source of the Nile River, which passed through the Sudan and Egypt and finally reached the Mediterranean Sea.

Lake Victoria Zone in Tanzania

The Lake Victoria Zone consisted of the three regions of Mwanza, Mara (formerly called Musoma) and Kagera (formerly called Bukoba), and was one of the most densely populated regions in Africa. Population growth around Lake Victoria was significantly higher than in the rest of Sub-Saharan Africa. During the last five decades, population growth within a 100-kilometre buffer zone around the lake had outpaced the continental average, which had led to growing dependency and pressure on the lake's resources.

Prior to the mining extraction boom in the early 1990s and following the collapse of Ujamaa, most people living in this region were mainly engaged in rudimentary forms of fishing, agricultural farming and keeping cattle, as well as other forms of co-operative activities that had been engineered by the country's former Ujamaa policies. Irrigation was limited to a small scale and often used rudimentary technologies to support both individual and co-operative farming activities. Noted for its temperate climate, the area had a mean temperature of between 26 and 30 degrees Celsius in the hot season and 15 and 18 degrees Celsius in the cooler months. The area was rich with tropical vegetation and fruits such as bananas, mangoes, corn, pineapple and many others. The lake was essential to more than 15 million people, providing potable water, hydroelectric power, and inland water transport, as well as support for tourism and wildlife.

The area remained one of the most fertile for farming activities and continued to attract immigrants from other regions of the country, as well as from Tanzania's neighbors in the war-torn populations of Burundi, Rwanda and the Democratic Republic of Congo. The presence of hundreds of TNCs engaged in various activities in the area was the main "draw" for these immigrants, who came seeking employment and new sources of livelihood.

The resulting population increase in the Lake Victoria Zone created several problems with respect to the lake and the environment. According to a report by World Watch Institute in Washington, D.C., the once clear, life-abounding lake had become murky, smelly and choked with algae. It had been reported that:

The ecological health of Lake Victoria has been affected profoundly as a result of a rapidly growing population, clearance of natural vegetation along the shores, a booming fish-export industry, the disappearance of several fish species native to the lake, prolific growth of algae, and dumping of untreated effluent by several industries. Much of the damage is vast and irreversible. Traditional lifestyles of lakeshore communities have been disrupted and are crumbling.[10]

As a result of the overuse of natural resources in the area, the traditional lifestyles of the lakeshore communities were significantly disrupted, a situation that prompted both social and ecological concerns for the area and its residents.

The fishing industry was badly affected in the region following the introduction of Nile perch (Lates Niloticus) and Nile tilapia (Oreochromis Niloticus) into the lake. For example, in the 1980s a survey of the lake revealed an abrupt and unexpected increase in numbers among the Nile perch, constituting 80 per cent of all fish in the lake. In spite of working harder, local fishermen caught fewer fish since the populations of smaller fish, which traditionally had been the fishermen's primary source of livelihood, became decimated. In addition, the big oily Nile perch, generally referred to as "Mbuta," swam too far out in the open waters for the little local fishing boats and was too big to be caught in the locals' unsophisticated nets.

In response to an increased international demand for the Nile perch, commercial fishing fleets owned by foreign firms displaced local fishermen and many women in lakeside communities who worked as fish processors. The processing of fish, traditionally performed by women, was gradually taken over by large filleting plants. The women resorted to processing fish waste, commonly referred to as *mgongo-wazi*, or "bare-back" in Swahili. The waste, comprised of fish heads, backbones and tails, was sun-dried and then deep-fried and sold to local people who were drawn to its low price and nutritional value. Many fishermen were forced to look for alternative sources of livelihood, mainly seeking employment in extractive mining corporations and other industries as manual labourers.

The water hyacinth posed another threat to the health of Lake Victoria. With the deceptive appearance of a lush, green carpet, the hyacinth was in fact a merciless, free-floating weed, reproducing rapidly and covering any uncovered territory. First noticed in 1989, the weed spread rapidly and covered areas in all three surrounding countries. It formed a dense mat, blocking the sunlight from reaching the organisms below, depleting the already-low concentrations of oxygen and trapping fishing boats and nets of all sizes. The hyacinth was also an ideal habitat for poisonous snakes and disease-carrying snails that caused bilharzias. The government, in partnership with other international agencies, had tried desperately to control the weed. Its most promising approach involved harvesting the hyacinth and using it either for compost or for biogas production.

The health implications associated with the declining state of the lake were extensive. Dumping untreated sewage in the lake and nearby rivers exposed people to waterborne diseases, such as typhoid, cholera and diarrhea, and chronic forms of malaria. The Lake Victoria Zone was known to have the most dangerous types of malaria in the world. As fish prices soared, protein malnutrition became a significant threat for communities living in the zone. Lack of regular income also meant that many people in the area could not afford to be treated for waterborne typhoid, yellow fever, and various forms of tropical worms such as tapeworms and hookworms.

---

[10]www.cichlid-forum.com/articles/lake_victoria_sick.php, accessed April 1, 2009.

Mining in Tanzania

Gold mining activities around the Lake Victoria Zone in Tanzania started during the German colonial period in 1894, when Tanzania was called Tanganyika. The First and Second World Wars accelerated the demand for gold production in the region and, following the introduction of Ujamaa in 1967, mining became a state-directed activity. By nationalizing the industry, the government hoped to capture more benefits from mining through the creation of local employment, direct spending on social services for mining communities, and higher budget revenues from having a direct stake in the business. However, despite these high hopes, the mining sector failed to stimulate the industrialization of the country's economy. During Ujamaa, the production of gold declined significantly due to limited government funding and limited technological know-how within the industry. Mining activities that were performed illegally by small-scale operators contributed to several environmental and social problems.[11]

The collapse of Ujamaa in the 1990s, however, resulted in new opportunities for the country to attract mining companies from Canada, the United Kingdom, Australia and South Africa, all of whom were interested in gold exploration and development activities. Following successful exploration mining activities that began in 1995, Barrick invested in Tanzania in 1999 at the Lake Victoria Zone. It acquired gold reserves in the Bulyanhulu mine, located in northwest Tanzania, East Africa, approximately 55 kilometres south of Lake Victoria and approximately 150 kilometres from the city of Mwanza; Buzwagi near Kahama District; Tulawaka in Biharamulo, Kagera Region; and later at the North Mara gold mine in the northwestern part of Tanzania in Tarime District of Mara Region, approximately 100 kilometres east of Lake Victoria and 20 kilometres south of the Kenyan border.

According to the Tanzanian Mineral Authority and Tanzania Chamber of Minerals and Energy (TCME), since 2000 production of gold had been growing, making the Lake Victoria Zone one of the most attractive areas for employment opportunities as well as for business opportunities in other industries. Tanzania was Africa's third-largest producer of gold, after Ghana and South Africa.[12] Tanzania was also richly endowed with other minerals, including cobalt, copper, nickel, platinum group metals, and silver, as well as diamonds and a variety of gemstones. The energy sector was dominated by natural gas. Commercial quantities of oil had yet to be discovered. In 2008, TCME reported that a total of US$2 billion in the past decade had been injected into the Tanzanian economy by mining TNCs, and in total mining TNCs had paid the government over US$255 million in taxes within the same period.[13]

In 2002, Tanzania joined the African Union's development blueprint, an endeavour that was governed by the New Economic Partnership for African Development (NEPAD), to oversee an African Mining Partnership (AMP) with global mining corporations. The goal of this partnership was to promote sustainable development and best-practice guidelines for African governments as a way to ensure that their mining laws protected ecological and community welfare while maximizing remittances from the mining TNCs to the government budgets in a transparent and accountable way.

The country did, however, develop competitive tax packages and incentives to attract TNCs to invest in high-risk and complex exploration areas such as the Lake Victoria Zone. The government did not devise a practical and engaging strategy to utilize mining resources and revenues paid by TNCs to support the local communities that were situated around mining sites and who had lost their livelihood, homes, health, natural resources and

---

[11]www.douglaslakeminerals.com/mining.html, accessed February 26, 2009.

[12]www.mineweb.co.za/mineweb/view/mineweb/en/page67?oid=39782&sn=Detail, accessed May 1, 2009.

[13]Ibid.

recreation with little or no compensation.[14] Also, the government did not come up with a concrete strategy to deal with the chronic sewage and environmental issues in the area.

Like any TNC engaged in extractive mining activities in a developing country such as Tanzania with so many social problems and legal and institutional weaknesses, Barrick had faced conflicting pressures with regard to the way it engaged in locally based community social partnership (see Exhibit 1). Such partnerships were meant to address the social problems of unemployment, poverty, diseases and environmental concerns in a sustainable way. Barrick strictly followed Western legal and property approvals to legitimize its mining activities in the country. It also continued to face challenges with respect to its efforts to strike a balance between its global strategies and those of the local subsidiary operations in Tanzania. Mineral wealth continued to fuel and prolong violent behaviour by local communities mainly in North Mara, thus failing to diversify economic growth and contribute to the development of communities in the Lake Victoria Zone. Corruption and weak institutional capabilities to enact or enforce the democratic, transparent and agreed-upon rules and laws that governed the operation and taxation of mining activities were a source of ongoing problems.[15] Also, some local communities did not see the potential benefits of large corporations in their communities.

BARRICK GOLD CORP IN TANZANIA

As a gold producer on the world stage, Barrick used advanced exploration technological systems for its mining development projects.[16] The company owned one of the world's largest gold mineral reserves and a large land position across its subsidiary mining extraction activities. These were located across the five continents of North America, South America, Africa, Australia and Asia. As one of the largest Canadian mining companies, Barrick shares were traded on the Toronto and New York stock exchanges and on other major global stock index centres in London, as well as on the Swiss Stock Exchanges and the Euronext-Paris. It was a shareholder-driven firm. Barrick invested in Tanzania in 1999, following the completion of exploration activities that had started in 1995. The company's initial mining activities were limited to Bulyanhulu in Kahama Dictrict until 2004, when it expanded to other areas surrounding the Lake Victoria Zone.

Socialization was part of the corporate culture used to manage human resources (HRM)[17] in Tanzania. Each mining site had a training department. Barrick recruited university graduates who worked on administrative activities in corporate offices, and assigned manual labourers to mining sites to work along with expatriates and locals who had experience in mining activities. Also, the company was involved in developing the so-called Integrated Mining Technical Training (IMTT) program, a joint project with the Tanzania Chamber of Minerals and Energy and the Tanzanian government. The goal was to offer locals the skills they needed to participate in the country's burgeoning mining sector and to reduce the industry's reliance on foreign-trained expatriates.[18] Barrick used its Global

---

[14]"The Challenge of Mineral Wealth in Tanzania: using resource endowments to foster sustainable development," International Council on Mining & Metals, 2006.

[15]www.revenuewatch.org/our-work/countries/tanzania.php, accessed May 1, 2009.

[16]www.tanzaniagold.com/barrick.html, accessed, May 1, 2009.

[17]www.barrick.com/CorporateResponsibility/Employees/AttractingRetaining/default.aspx, accessed April 24, 2009.

[18]www.barrick.com/Theme/Barrick/files/docs_csr/BeyondBorder2008July.pdf#page=4, accessed September 27, 2010.

Succession Planning Program (GSPP) that provided expatriates with a chance to increase their knowledge and expertise by transferring them into assignments at other Barrick sites in Tanzania, and sites in other countries where the company operated.[19] The major role of GSPP was to instill the corporate culture through the training of employees regarding various mining technology skills, and to run the company's daily practices in accordance with the corporate business interests of the company.

Mission, Vision and Values

Given the questionable reputation of some global mining corporations with respect to sustainable development projects in developing societies, Barrick's core vision and values were to continue finding, acquiring, developing and producing quality reserves in a safe, profitable and socially responsible manner. Barrick claimed to promote long-term benefits to the communities in which it operated and to foster a culture of excellence and collaboration with its employees, governments and local stakeholders.

The company followed global corporate social responsibility standards as part of its larger global business strategies, using the vocabularies of business ethics, human rights and development. Among these strategies, the company placed significant emphasis on its social relationships with local communities and the right to operate in their land.[20]

Building Social Development Initiatives

Barrick was committed to making a positive difference in the communities where it operated. The company focused on responsible behaviour as its duty, as well as creating opportunities to generate greater value for its shareholders, while at the same time fostering sustainable development in the communities and countries where it operated. As a global TNC, Barrick strove to earn the trust of its employees, of the communities where its subsidiary operations were based, of the host nations' governments, and of any other persons or parties with whom the company was engaged in the sustainable development of mineral resources.[21]

In 2008, the corporation established a locally based mining institution in Moshi, Kilimanjaro Region. The aim of the institute was to provide training skills and opportunities for Barrick's mining sites and other mining TNCs in the country.[22] Local individuals involved in the training program included fresh university graduates in engineering and geology, and dedicated individuals from local communities where Barrick operated. Such an initiative supported Barrick's sense of corporate responsibility towards these two groups of people by providing tangible benefits to their communities in the form of employment opportunities and co-operative relationships.

Yet among community leaders and NFOs, there was clear discontent regarding the various foreign companies:

"The government has not addressed the role of foreign companies in our communities. Some communities have been compensated by the government to clear land for the mining company, but some did not receive any money. Most communities would tell

---

[19]www.barrick.com/CorporateResponsibility/Employees/AttractingRetaining/default.aspx, accessed September 27, 2010.

[20]www.barrick.com/CorporateResponsibility/OurCommitment/default.aspx, accessed September 27, 2010.

[21]www.barrick.com/CorporateResponsibility/default.aspx, accessed March 25, 2009.

[22]www.ippmedia.com/ipp/guardian/2008/04/11/112164.html, accessed February 13, 2009.

you what was given to them by the government, which is very little. They cannot build a house and send children to school and so on. They feel their livelihood is gone forever."

"The mining corporation does not compensate people nor does it explain why it is operating in our communities. Of course, these companies have official binding contracts and the right to operate in our communities from the government. Local communities are in despair . . . the government is nowhere to be seen! The people are angry with the government and the mining company."

"People are not happy with the government. They are aware of the extent of corruption among the government officials in the region and districts, but they cannot confront the government the way they are now confronting the mining company. They think that the company might be more sympathetic to them than the government would be with respect to offering them jobs and other opportunities."

"The company has initiated several development projects in our communities [North Mara] in education, health and infrastructure. But we do not have jobs to access these better equipped services (education and health) nor essential means to support us to build community enterprises where we could apply our local skills in many activities. Though the company is doing very good projects here, we are still unhappy with the company. Our problems are long-term; they need serious engagement with us."

"The company discharges water to the land, which is causing lots of environmental problems on our farms such as land erosion and polluting of the rivers. We have more mosquitoes, snakes and snails at the moment than any time in our lives because of stagnant water caused by the company's water discharge. The exploration and explosive activities conducted at night on mining sites have caused shockwaves, panic and sleepless nights among neighborhood villages, making big cracks on community farms and land."

Two community leaders (representing local stakeholders' interests) commented:

"The other night we were all suddenly shaken by the mining blast tremor. Initially, we thought it was the so-called earthquake ("Tetemeko la Ardhi" in Swahili). What is on all the people's minds here in Bulyanhulu is, 'When will all this end?'"

"We need a mutual partnership with foreign companies investing in our communities. There are so many potential benefits we can get from the company with respect to jobs and skill development; also, the company can learn a lot from us when it comes to negotiation strategies with our communities. If the company responds positively to our concerns, we will strive to protect its business interests here and it will operate in harmony in our communities. But the government needs to sit with local communities and tell them why the government has allowed the company to come to practice mining in their land and tell us what potential benefit it will bring in our communities. For the time being, the company is left to itself to address these issues with the local communities."

Amid this climate of discontent among the native Tanzanians, Barrick's mining operations were subject to some hostilities from local stakeholders. In response, the company put into place several CSR initiatives that were aimed at developing sustainable benefits within the communities and around its business operations in the core mining sites of Tulawaka, Bulyanhulu and Buzigwa. Two NFO officials in Mwanza cut to the nature of the problem:

"The company initially attempted to collaborate with local communities and the local government to address the social and ecological issues during its initial stage of entry into the country. But it was not easy to find serious stakeholders right away. Because of the nature of the local institutions, it was also not easy to have things done quickly due to the degree of bureaucracy and the culture of corruption."

"The recent protests in North Mara from local communities can be resolved only if the government, company and other social awareness groups sit together to address this situation. Shooting protestors, closing the mining site and sending employees home without pay won't solve the problem in the long run. And the company's legal insistence of its right to operate in the communities isn't enough to convince these angry communities."

"The company is not wrong at all . . . it has followed all legal procedures and has the right to be here [in the Lake Victoria Zone], but for local communities, legal papers are NOTHING. The company finds people very unpredictable. The answer is so simple: it is all about deep understanding, integration, and building a trusting relationship."

"Mining companies are granted too many tax contracts and subsidies in order to create jobs. During this process, it is very possible for companies to avoid paying taxes that would actually benefit poor countries. There are often 'secret contracts' with corrupt government officials. The lack of institutional capacity is also a major problem; the people have not been made to see how these companies can benefit our poor societies. That's why there is still so much poverty, and that's why communities around the mining sites are angry and desperate."

Several local communities felt they were isolated when it came to the social issues that concerned them, e.g., land issues, compensation, employment, and how the presence of the company in their communities would benefit them generally. According to community leaders, few projects were initiated by the company within the various neighbourhood communities, and the ones that were enacted showed a lack of any significant sense of local ownership and influence; they did not possess the diverse forms of institutional infrastructure that fostered accountability values in communities and in the management of the company itself. As a consequence, local communities lost interest in pursuing most of the developmental projects that Barrick had initiated.

Following community tensions with Barrick between 2007 and 2009, a different strategy was developed. Implementing a locally based interaction model that promoted mutual partnership with communities seemed like the best strategic legitimacy approach. In early 2009, Barrick encountered discontent from the local communities, as well as from the local media, activists groups and lobby groups, who felt that the company had not done enough to promote sustainable and inclusive development in the communities where it operated. Barrick's new mining site at North Mara was featured several times in the media.[23] Two local NFOs commented on the dispute:

"The government needs to educate its people as to what benefits TNCs would bring to its citizens; the mining company is extracting our natural resources, causing environmental degradation and pollution, and displacing people, all with a lack of accountability, and is not doing enough for the host communities to create prosperity, jobs, local innovation and entrepreneurship initiatives."

"The source of discontent is from local communities and small-scale miners who feel neglected by the government. We strongly feel that their livelihoods have been

---

[23]Several protests by local communities against Barrick's mining activities in Tanzania had been reported. See www.protestbarrick.net/article.php?list=type&type=12, accessed February 17, 2009.

destroyed with little or no compensation. They also feel that the government and local authorities have been giving foreign investors much attention at the expense of local people. Corruption and lack of accountability on the government side is the source of all these problems. The company is caught in the middle!"

Creating a Corporate Responsive Agenda

Barrick developed a responsive initiative to deal with the company's challenges in its international business activities abroad, including Tanzania. It established a community department in all four mining areas to oversee development initiatives. It also adopted standardized global CSR strategies as part of its larger international and localization business strategies, stating that "as a global corporation, we endorse the definition of Corporate Social Responsibility as proposed by the World Bank—Corporate Social Responsibility is the commitment of business to contribute to sustainable economic development—working with employees, their families, the local community and society at large to improve the quality of life, in ways that are both good for business and good for development."[24]

1. Education in partnership with local communities

Through its newly established community department, Barrick had made a concerted attempt to identify self-employment opportunities to the communities around the Bulyanhulu gold mine. In partnership with local governments, NFOs and communities, the company had used educated locals to promote a broad array of social entrepreneurship skills in a variety of areas such as finance, accounting and marketing (see Exhibit 2).

The communities surrounding the mine needed a great deal of support in terms of education in order to be able to exploit the area's potential. By 2008, Barrick had committed to working closely with eight villages before expanding to another eight villages along the Bulyanhulu-Kahama road in Bulyanhulu. Seven of the eight villages were in the Bugarama ward and one was in the Mwingilo ward, but all were located in the Bulyanhulu mining area.

2. Community-based entrepreneurship

In collaboration with local community authorities, Barrick went on to assist several community groups that already possessed local skills and entrepreneurship initiatives and which had local resources to generate business activities. Other community development projects had also been started and were engineered under the same procedure of governance.

3. Health

Barrick committed itself to upgrading the Sungusungu Health Centre into what became called the Nyamongo Hospital in the Bulyanhulu area under the so-called phase I. Organized by the Evangelical Lutheran Church in the area, several NFOs had entered into an agreement with the local District Office and the Village Councils to provide health care that was affordable to the many local residents to treat diseases such as malaria, waterborne diseases, typhoid, yellow fever and other epidemiology problems. The community trust committed $30,000 towards beds and fittings and for a general upgrade to the hospital. Barrick's overall

---

[24]www.barrick.com/CorporateResponsibility/Ethics/PoliciesStandards/default.aspx, accessed February 17, 2009.

objective was to make health services available to many disadvantaged communities, and to attempt to curb the number of deaths that occurred among pregnant women when they travelled from the poor communities to the district hospital.

4. Environment

The Lake Victoria Zone was one of the most densely populated areas in Sub-Saharan Africa, but it was also one of the most polluted and environmentally affected places in the world. Barrick, in cooperation with local government authorities, had been working to provide opportunities to the residents of the mining areas to orient themselves with mining operations. The company was creating environmental awareness in order to create local "ambassadors" who could then go out and speak positively about the mining sites to other communities. Adequately addressing the issues of water toxins on rivers and the lake and land degradation had been the major challenge for Barrick.

Protests from so-called "secondary" stakeholders that included local communities, artisanal miners, peasant farmers and their families, and local not-for-profit organizations (NFOs) had occurred to address specific social, environmental, and land heritage and resettlement issues. All these stakeholders had widely varying claims, interests and rights. In addition, subgroups and individuals with multiple and changing roles and interests existed. They included manual mining workers who felt they had been unfairly dismissed from their jobs with little or no compensation, and felt unjustly treated by either Barrick or the Tanzanian labour court system. Local communities also had expressed anger at the level of noise caused by heavy machines during mining explorations at night and the extent of the company's impact on land in their neighborhoods. There were also individuals, mainly unemployed youths, who were engaged in intrusion, vandalism and theft at the mining sites.

Barrick had relied on the Tanzanian anti-riot police force, known as "Field Force Unit" (FFU), to quell large-scale mob criminal behaviour and demonstrations at the mining sites. Also, Barrick had relied on the Tanzanian legal system and government to protect its business activities in the region. However, the behaviour of the FFU, the weak government institutional system, and the loyalty of administrative workers to Barrick had increased anger, frustration, and resentment among communities, small-scale artisan miners and NFOs. The FFU had been regarded by local communities as brutal and uncompromising during confrontations. Responses by the FFU had even led to death,[25] long-term imprisonment of community campaigners' leaders, intimidation and harassment.[26] The government had been viewed as lacking vision and leadership to reap the benefits of the mining activities in the region and had been criticized for failing to protect the interests of its citizens.

CONCLUSION

By 2010, a variety of corporate social responsibility (CSR) initiatives were established based on ABG's commitment to building a sustainable relationship with local communities. The overall aim was to ensure that the company would build mutual respect, active partnerships, and a long-term commitment with its secondary stakeholders who tended to have disparate goals, demands and opinions. Mutual respect, it was argued, was important if

---

[25]A recent incident at a Barrick mining site in the Mara region had led the Tanzanian FFU to kill an intruder (see www.protestbarrick.net/article.php?list=type&type=12, accessed April 17, 2009).

[26]For the behaviour of Tanzania's FFU in quelling demonstrations, see www.protestbarrick.net/article.php?id=369, accessed April 17, 2009.

such relationships were to be lasting, beneficial and dynamic. In addition, the company had used its social development department in each of the mining sites to develop practical guidelines in order to facilitate the implementation of its organizational values and mission, including building long-term relationships of mutual benefit between the operations and their host communities, and to avoid costly disputes and hostilities with local stakeholders.[27] Although significant progress and successful collaborations had evolved across local communities at its mining sites, African Barrick Gold still faced serious, unique problems and increased pressure to manage conflicts and reconcile stakeholders' demands in places such as North Mara.

---

[27]Further CSR programs are available at www.barrick.com/CorporateResponsibility/default.aspx, accessed February 24, 2009.

EXHIBIT 1: Three Types of Engagement Behaviors

Dimension	Transactional	Transitional	Transformational
Corporate Stance	"Giving Back" Community Investment	"Building Bridges" Community Involvement	"Changing Society" Community Integration
Communication	One-Way	Two-Way	Two-Way
# of Community Partners	Many	Many	Few
Nature of Trust	Limited	Evolutionary	Relational
Frequency of Interaction	Occasional	Repeated	Frequent
Learning	Transferred from Firm	Transferred to Firm	Jointly Generated
Control over Process	Firm	Firm	Shared
Benefit & Outcomes	Distinct	Distinct	Joint

Source: F. Bowen, A. Newenham-Kahindi and H. Irene, "Engaging the Community: A Synthesis of Academic and Practitioner Knowledge on Best Practices in Community Engagement," Canadian Research Network for Business Sustainability, Knowledge Project Series, Ivey School of Business, 1:1, 2008, pp. 1–34.

EXHIBIT 2: Barrick Spending on Corporate Social Responsibility in Tanzania

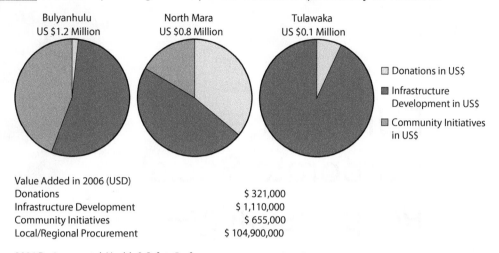

Bulyanhulu
US $1.2 Million

North Mara
US $0.8 Million

Tulawaka
US $0.1 Million

☐ Donations in US$

◼ Infrastructure Development in US$

▨ Community Initiatives in US$

Value Added in 2006 (USD)	
Donations	$ 321,000
Infrastructure Development	$ 1,110,000
Community Initiatives	$ 655,000
Local/Regional Procurement	$ 104,900,000

2006 Environmental, Health & Safety Performance

Note: Total amount of money in U.S. dollars spent on health & safety training and emergency response training in 2006

Source: www.barrick.com/Theme/Barrick/files/docs_ehss/2007%20Africa%20Regional%20Rpt.pdf, accessed April 30, 2009.

EXHIBIT 3: Total Amount of Money Spent on Community Development Projects, 2006

COMMUNITY	2006	2005	2004	2003
Donations in US$				
Bulyanhulu	20,193	14,000	410,000	485,000
North Mara	294,220	50,000	0	0
Tulawaka	6,778	7,662	5,894	n/a
Infrastructure Development in US$				
Bulyanhulu	631,222	3,570,000	4,374,000	572,000
North Mara	389,384	360,000	350,000	100,000
Tulawaka	89,020	43,697	6,250	n/a
Community Initiatives in US$				
Bulyanhulu	519,793	609,000	0	0
North Mara	135,015	0	not measured	
Tulawaka	304	0	0	n/a
Regional Purchases of Goods & Services in US$				
Bulyanhulu	65,600,000		not measured	
North Mara	37,700,000		not measured	
Tulawaka	1,600,000		not measured	

Source: www.barrick.com/Theme/Barrick/files/docs_ehss/2007%20Africa%20Regional%20Rpt.pdf, accessed April 30, 2009.

FIJI Water and Corporate Social Responsibility— Green Makeover or "Greenwashing"?[1]

"Bottled water is a disaster, for several reasons. First there's the issue of the sustainability of underground aquifers, from where much of the bottled water is drawn. And then there's the carbon footprint. Water is heavy, and transporting it around the world uses a lot of energy."

Jeff Angel, Total Environment Centre, Sydney, Australia[2]

"We survived before we had water in bottles. It is unnecessary. When you see water imported from Fiji in plastic bottles, you know it's bad for the environment all round."

Lee Rhiannon, Australia's Greens MP[3]

IVEY | Publishing

James McMaster and Jan Nowak wrote this case solely to provide material for class discussion. The authors do not intend to illustrate either effective or ineffective handling of a managerial situation. The authors may have disguised certain names and other identifying information to protect confidentiality.

Richard Ivey School of Business Foundation prohibits any form of reproduction, storage or transmission without its written permission. Reproduction of this material is not covered under authorization by any reproduction rights organization. To order copies or request permission to reproduce materials, contact Ivey Publishing, Richard Ivey School of Business Foundation, The University of Western Ontario, London, Ontario, Canada, N6A 3K7; phone (519) 661-3208; fax (519) 661-3882; e-mail cases@ivey.uwo.ca.

Copyright © 2009, Richard Ivey School of Business Foundation   Version: 2011-09-21

One time permission to reproduce granted by Richard Ivey School of Business Foundation on April 22, 2014.

---

[1]This case has been written on the basis of published sources only. Consequently, the interpretation and perspectives presented in this case are not necessarily those of FIJI Water LLC. or any of its employees.

[2]"Disaster in a bottle," *Sydney Morning Herald*, April 24, 2007.

[3]Kelly Fedor, "Greens call for ban on bottled water," *Livenews.com*, March 22, 2008.

"I think the world is slowly going insane. No thanks but I prefer water in bottles, that way you know it's clean and you know, healthy. Not a sacrifice people should make when plastic bags are still rampant. Those Greens are extremists and I don't see this 'tap water alternative' ever being viable."

Anthony L, N.S.W.[4]

"Consumers who choose FIJI Water will actually be helping the environment by taking carbon out of the atmosphere with every purchase."

Thomas Mooney, senior vice-president, sustainable growth,
FIJI Water, Los Angeles, California[5]

2008 was a trying year for FIJI Water LLC., a U.S.-based company that marketed its famous brand in more than a dozen countries out of its bottling plant located in the Fiji Islands. The company was facing some complex challenges to achieve its goal of a carbon negative outcome at its production plant and in the transportation of its products, and to convince its consumers and other stakeholders that it was leading the industry in carbon footprint disclosure and offset. The environmental protest against bottled water in general, and FIJI brand in particular, in the United States, United Kingdom and other developed countries was gathering steam as the message on the carbon impact of bottled water was more and more widely publicized to consumers. FIJI Water was singled out as a primary example of "water insanity" due to the fact that the product was shipped from a remote island in the South Pacific to its main markets thousands of miles away. In response to this protest, the company launched a new promotion campaign under a slogan "every drop is green," only to be immediately accused by environmentalist groups of engaging in green-washing activities. The claim was also challenged by government watchdogs in some countries where FIJI Water was sold.

At the same time, the company's relationships with the Fiji government were at the lowest point. The government accused FIJI Water of transfer price manipulations and seized hundreds of containers carrying FIJI brand water. After assessing the company's contribution to the Fiji economy, the government tried to impose a hefty tax on exported water and the company took the drastic action of laying off its employees in Fiji to pressure the government to repeal the initial 20-cents-a-litre tax that would have greatly reduced FIJI Water's profitability by increasing its tax bill by about FJ$50 million per year. The company intensified its PR activities, focusing on its contributions to the local communities, to show how good a corporate citizen it was in Fiji.

THE PRODUCT CONCEPT AND COMPANY BACKGROUND

The product concept was developed in the early nineties by David Gilmour, the Canadian-born owner and founder of Fiji's renowned Wakaya Island Resort. Simply put, the concept was to bottle Fiji natural artesian water and market it both locally and internationally as a unique and exotic product. An important aspect of the product concept was to bottle the water straight from the source–the source being an old artesian aquifer containing tropical rainwater, filtered for 450 years through layers of volcanic rock. The aquifer was found in

---

[4]A reader's comment posted on Livenews.com on March 22, 2008.

[5]"FIJI Water Becomes First Bottled Water Company to Release Carbon Footprint of Its Products," Press Release from FIJI Water, April 9, 2008, www.bevnet.com.

the Yaqara Range of the Nakauvadra Mountains. Being separated by 1,500 kilometres of ocean, far away from major polluting sources, and being formed before any industrial activity could contaminate it, the water could only be of the purest quality and of distinct taste. Moreover, this silica-rich water was attributed anti-aging and immunity-boosting properties. The product was expected to appeal to health-conscious and image-oriented consumers.[6]

To extract and bottle Fiji's artesian water, in 1993 Gilmour founded a company under the name Nature's Best. In 1995, the company's name was changed to Natural Waters of Viti Ltd. The first bottling plant was built in 1996 at the cost of FJ$48 million at Yaqara in Ra, on land sub-leased from the Yaqara Pastoral Company. The plant was built where the source of artesian water had been found.[7] The site was in a remote and underdeveloped rural area of the island of Viti Levu that was poorly served with public infrastructure. The unpolluted, pristine location of the water source and factory guaranteed that the artesian water was of the highest purity. However, the site's remoteness from the capital city of Suva, where Fiji's main port is located, entailed higher road transport costs compared to other alternative mineral water sources. In 1996, FIJI Water LLC corporate headquarters was established in Basalt, Colorado, to handle the product distribution in the United States, which was intended to be the main market for FIJI Water.

The production process began with the extraction of the water from a bore-hole. The water was then channelled through a pipe into the factory, treated and bottled in four bottle sizes: 0.33, 0.5, 1.0 and 1.5 litres. Using imported bottle caps, PET resin and labels, the bottles were manufactured by the company on its premises and were filled with water during the same production cycle. Bottles were packed into cartons for shipment to domestic and international markets. The cartons were made in Fiji by Golden Manufacturers.[8]

Rising demand for FIJI Water led to the construction of a new 110,000-square-foot, state-of-the-art bottling plant, completed in 2000. Demand continued to build in the 2000s, leading to the airlifting of a new bottling line in 2004 to help increase capacity to more than 50 million cases a year. The design and construction of the factory was regarded as among the best in the world, with high-quality and high-speed production capability.

In 2004, the company was sold by its main shareholder, David Gilmour, to Roll International Corporation for an undisclosed price. Roll International was controlled by one of Hollywood's richest couples, Stewart and Lynda Resnik.[9] Following this acquisition, FIJI Water's corporate headquarters was moved to Los Angeles. While the Fiji Islands-based operation focused on mineral water extraction, bottling and transportation within Fiji, the corporate headquarters handled marketing and logistics functions worldwide. The new owner expanded the Fiji plant's production capacity by adding a new (third) bottling line in 2006. In 2007, the state-of-the-art factory could churn out more than a million bottles of FIJI Water a day.[10]

---

[6]James McMaster and Jan Nowak, "Natural Waters of Viti Limited–Pioneering a New Industry in the Fiji Islands," *Journal of the Australian and New Zealand Academy of Management*, 9:2, 2003 (Special Edition on Management Cases).

[7]Reserve Bank of Fiji, "Natural Waters of Viti Limited," Briefing Paper, August 2001, p.1; and Ed Dinger, "Fiji Water LLC," International Directory of Company Histories, 74, 2003.

[8]Ibid.

[9]Roll International also owned such companies as POM Wonderful, which produced and marketed juices and fresh pomegranates; Telesfora, the largest online flower shop in the world; Paramount Farms, the largest grower and producer of pistachios and almonds in the world; and Paramount Citrus, a leader in the California orange and lemon markets (www.roll.com).

[10]Charles Fishman, "Message in a Bottle," *Fast Company*, 117, July/August 2007, p. 110.

As of 2008, FIJI Water marketed its bottled mineral water in about a dozen countries in North America (including Mexico and the Caribbean), Asia-Pacific, Europe and the Middle East. It was marketed as FIJI Natural Mineral Water in Europe and as FIJI Natural Spring Water in Australia. The two main markets for the product were the United States and Australia.

In the latter part of 2008, the bottling plant at Yaqara had about 400 employees. Of the total number of employees, only about 10 per cent were employed with the administration, finance and management sections; the rest were factory-floor workers. The company employed only a handful of expatriates and placed an emphasis on the hiring, training and advancement of the inhabitants of nearby villages, most of whom had little or no employment opportunities prior to Natural Waters of Viti Ltd. locating its factory at Yaqara. The company claimed to be one of the highest paying employers in Fiji.[11]

THE GLOBAL MARKET FOR BOTTLED WATER— CONSUMPTION TRENDS

Sales of FIJI Water in the domestic market were relatively very small. More than 90 per cent of all production was exported. Therefore, for FIJI Water global trends in bottled water consumption and demand were of paramount importance.

Since the beginning of the last decade, the beverage product category had been shaken by rapidly changing consumer preferences that had led to a radical shift away from traditional beverages and toward "New Age" products, like bottled water. In fact, bottled water had been the fastest growing segment of the entire beverage business. As Exhibit 1 shows, between 2002 and 2007 the world's bottled water consumption was increasing by 7.6 per cent annually and by 2007 reached close to 50 billion gallons (approximately 185 billion litres). As a result, by 2007 bottled water had become the second largest beverage category, after soft drinks.

As Exhibit 1 also indicates, the United States was the world's leading consumer of bottled water in 2007. Americans drank 8.8 billion gallons of bottled water, as compared to 5.8 billion consumed by Mexicans and 4.8 billion consumed by Chinese. Altogether, the top 10 consuming nations accounted for 73 per cent of the world's bottled water consumption in 2007. However, it should be pointed out that China's consumption grew the fastest among the top three consumers in the world between 2002 and 2007, at the compound annual rate of 17.5 per cent, which was twice the world's average. Therefore, China was expected to become the largest consumer of bottled water in the world in the next decade. Another emerging big consumer of bottled water was India. Although not among the leading bottled water consuming nations in 2007, India had experienced one of the fastest growth rates in the world during the period shown in Exhibit 1, even faster than China.[12]

When per capita consumption was taken into account, the nations' ranking looked different (see Exhibit 2). In 2007, the United Arab Emirates, Mexico and Italy showed the highest consumption per person in the world, and the United States was ranked ninth, with only a slightly higher consumption per capita than Hungary and Switzerland. It is noteworthy that Australia and the United Kingdom, two markets of interest to FIJI Water, were not among the biggest consumers of bottled water in the world, neither in terms of total consumption nor per capita.

---

[11]Company website: www.fijiwater.com.

[12]"The Global Bottled Water Market. Report 2007," Beverage Marketing Corporation, January 2008.

In 2007, Europe and North America were the biggest regional markets for bottled water, accounting for 30.9 and 30.7 per cent of the world's sales volume, respectively. Asia accounted for 24.3 per cent and the rest of the world accounted for 14.1 per cent.[13]

FIJI WATER'S INTERNATIONAL MARKET EXPANSION

While responding to those world market trends, FIJI Water had made its strategy revolve around capturing international market opportunities and strongly positioning the brand in large and growing markets for bottled water, but markets that were not overly price competitive, as FIJI Water, right from the beginning, was designed to be a premium brand. The first, and critical, international market to conquer was the United States.

Conquering the U.S. Market

To begin its international market expansion, FIJI Water was first launched in California in 1997, using Los Angeles and Palm Beach as a beach head for a subsequent and gradual roll-out of the product across the United States. In 1998, the company entered the sophisticated New York market, firmly positioning itself on the East Coast. At the same time, FIJI Water was also introduced to the Canadian market, starting with the country's West Coast. The North American market provided the company with tremendous growth opportunities. The U.S. market in particular was so embracing that after about five years of the product's presence there, FIJI Water had achieved the second selling position in the U.S. market among imported still water brands, and in 2008 it had climbed to the number one position among imported bottled waters in the United States.[14] Such a strong market position had been achieved in the market where competition was fierce and which was characterized by industry consolidation and the increasing dominance of major soft drink companies in bottled water marketing, such as Coca Cola and PepsiCo, which had entered the market with their own proprietary brands, Dasani and Aquafina, respectively. At the same time, FIJI Water had benefited from the overall beverage market trend that had shown a major shift in beverage consumption preferences in the United States.

As Exhibit 3 shows, the per capita consumption of bottled water in the United States increased from 13.5 gallons in 1997, when the FIJI Water brand was introduced to the U.S. market, to 29.3 gallons in 2007, thus more than doubling. This was part of the exponential growth trend in bottled water consumption over a longer period, although growth clearly accelerated after 1990.[15]

The above shifts in the consumption of beverages could be linked to changing lifestyles and growing concerns of the effects of sweetened carbonated drinks on people's health. The baby boom generation, which constituted about a third of the total population in North America, had become obsessively health-conscious and fitness-oriented. Bottled water had become popular among the younger generation as well. Over the last decade, bottled water had gained a reputation of not only being healthy but also a fashionable, elegant and "trendy" drink.

---

[13]Ibid.

[14]"FIJI Water Becomes First Bottled Water Company to Release Carbon Footprint of Its Products," Press Release from FIJI Water, April 9, 2008, www.bevnet.com.

[15]"The Global Bottled Water Market. Report 2007," Beverage Marketing Corporation, January 2008.

In 2007, total U.S. bottled water sales surpassed 8.8 billion gallons, a 6.9 per cent advance over 2006's volume level. That translated into more than 29 gallons per person, which meant U.S. residents drank more bottled water annually than any other beverage, other than carbonated soft drinks (CSDs). While CSDs still had volume and average intake levels more than twice as high as those of bottled water, the soft drink market had been struggling because of competition from bottled water. Per capita consumption of bottled water had been growing by at least one gallon annually, thereby more than doubling between 1997 and 2007. In 2007, U.S. consumers spent $15 billion on bottled water, more than on iPods or movie tickets.[16]

As Exhibit 4 shows, sales of non-sparkling bottled water by far exceeded sales of its sparkling counterpart. Also, between 2000 and 2007, non-sparkling water's sales grew faster than those of sparkling water. At the same time, it is noteworthy that imported bottled water constituted only a little more than two per cent of the total sales of this product category, and imports tended to fluctuate widely from one year to another. The biggest sellers in the U.S. market were local brands, such as Arrowhead, Poland Spring, Zephyrhills, Ozarka, Deer Park, and Ice Mountain. The market was dominated by four large companies: Nestlé, Coca Cola, PepsiCo and Danone. Nestlé had the largest market share of all–in 2007 the company's brands of bottled water accounted for 26 per cent of total sales of the product category.[17]

During the product's introduction into the U.S. market, FIJI Water LLC was responsible for the marketing and logistics of FIJI brand. The company had two senior VPs, in charge of the East Coast and the West Coast, respectively, reporting to the company's CEO, Mr. Doug Carlson.[18]

The successful launch of FIJI Water in the United States was attributed to a skillful marketing strategy and the high quality of the people who drove the initial marketing campaign.[19] FIJI Water LLC's marketing personnel were able to differentiate the FIJI brand in a crowded market where about 400 brands of bottled water competed with each other. This was mainly achieved through unique product positioning, innovative packaging, premium-product pricing, effective distribution, and image-creating publicity. The latter had elevated this otherwise mundane commodity to celebrity status.

Due to its light mineralization, FIJI Water was characterized by a smooth taste and no aftertaste. The light mineralization also gave the water a clean, pure taste. Many U.S. consumers instantly liked the taste of the water and, having tried it, repurchased the product in preference to the more mineralized waters. FIJI Water had been top-rated in taste tests sponsored by such influential magazines and guides as Chicago Magazine, Cook's Illustrated Buying Guides, and Men's Health. Taste therefore was one of FIJI Water's main advantages over other bottled water brands. The company continued to educate the consumer about the difference between purified, spring and artesian bottled water.[20] In addition to superb taste, the water had a high level of silica, the ingredient that was believed to promote rejuvenation and anti-aging. Another distinct aspect of the product was its purity, stemming from the fact that the source of the water was a virgin, unpolluted ecosystem, located 1,500 kilometres away from any metropolitan and industrial area, and the fact that the water was 450 years old, thus formed before industrial pollution could affect its purity. All this added

---

[16]Fishman, "Message in a Bottle," July/August 2007, p. 110.

[17]Ibid., p. 115.

[18]McMaster and Nowak, "Natural Waters of Viti Limited–Pioneering a New Industry in the Fiji Islands," 2003, p. 42.

[19]Paul Yavala, "Fiji Water Travels," *The Fiji Times*, November 2000, p. 4.

[20]www.fijiwater.com.

to the mystique that the product seemed to be surrounded by in the minds of consumers. Due to FIJI Water's superb taste, purity and mystique, a premium-product positioning had been followed right from the beginning.

Although of paramount importance, the product content was only part of the successful marketing equation. Another important element was packaging. For many years, all bottles containing natural water were the same—round, with paper labels. Packaging, one of the most fundamental ways to differentiate a product, was not used as such a tool in bottled water markets. Over the last decade, both companies and consumers had discovered the power of packaging in bottled water brand positioning and imagery. FIJI Water had utilized the power of packaging to its benefit. Natural Waters of Viti Ltd. was the first company in the industry to use a square bottle and this had become the product's signature trait. Furthermore, since FIJI was the only brand that came from a tropical paradise—not a cold, mountainous region—the packaging reflected that in an artful and compelling way: consumers could see that immediately when they looked at the unique square bottle bearing bright, three-dimensional graphics.[21]

FIJI Water's packaging was initially designed by a New York-based advertising agency and had been refined several times since its original design. When the brand was introduced to the U.S. market, its square-shaped bottle was unique and had great appeal to consumers. The gold border on the label gave an image of quality. The blue cap was colour-coordinated with the blue waterfall and the blue-green colours in the see-through labels. Consumers had reported favourably on the attractive label with the Pacific image and see-through waterfall. Later on, the company had redesigned the labelling and added new features to the bottle's front and back labels. The front label, in addition to the brand name, featured a pink hibiscus flower, a national flower of the Fiji Islands. In a new version of the bottle design, the inside of the back label, instead of a waterfall, displayed a large palm frond, which was amplified when the bottle was filled with water, and the outside of that label explained the water's distinct characteristics, such as its remote and pristine source and its unique mineral composition. In fact, in 2008 FIJI Water had four different outside back labels, each of which illustrated a unique image and communicated a different part of the FIJI Water story; they included: "bottled in Fiji," "what ecosystem is your water from," "what is artesian water," and "untouched by man."

Similarly to packaging, a premium-price policy reinforced the product's high-quality image. Anyway, high freight costs between Fiji and the United States would have made a low- or even medium-price policy impossible. FIJI Water's price was higher than that of most brands offered to U.S. consumers. For example, in the Californian market, FIJI Water was positioned slightly below Perrier but above Evian.

Another important factor that had contributed to FIJI Water's success in the U.S. market was its distribution. Having good distributors was important in that it enabled the brand to be well-placed in and readily available to the market. While in Fiji the company used exclusively Coca Cola Amatil to distribute its product, in the U.S. market the product was sold by numerous distributors, including wholesalers, retail chains and individual retailers. In addition to stores, the product was sold on the premises of many high-end restaurants and hotels. The product was also available online in the continental United States. To support the brand's continued growth, FIJI Water LLC had expanded distribution beyond exclusive retailers to include mass merchandisers, convenience stores, drug stores, and even gas stations.[22] This intensification of distribution might sound like a contradiction of the

---

[21]Nancy Christy, "Age of enlightenment," *Beverage Aisle*, August 2001.

[22]Heather Landi, "Paradise in a Bottle," *Beverage World*, November 2007, p. 24.

product's exclusive positioning, but the company representatives claimed that it was all part of "the affordable luxury" strategy.

Destined for the U.S. market, FIJI Water was shipped from the ports of Suva or Lautoka on Viti Levu to three major distribution centres in the United States–Los Angeles, New Jersey and Miami. It was then distributed throughout most of the United States. Initially, the physical distribution to and within the United States was contracted out to specialized logistics firms, which delivered the product to a variety of distributors who then carried it through their distribution channels. Occasionally, these logistics firms delivered the product directly to consumers. In 2000, FIJI Water entered into an exclusive distributorship agreement with Cadbury Schweppes. This partnership was crucial to FIJI Water's aggressive expansion and success in the U.S. market, where the FIJI brand was available at tens of thousands of outlets. Canadian shipments were sent to Vancouver, the only location where the product was initially available. In 1999, FIJI Water appointed Brio Industries Inc. as Canada-Wide Master Distributor of the FIJI brand.[23] In 2008, the U.S.-market distributorship agreement with Cadbury Schweppes was extended to cover Canada also. Since February of that year, FIJI Water had been exclusively distributed by Cadbury across Canada among grocery, convenience, drug and most other retail stores.[24]

Building an image of the high quality, uniqueness and class of the product was another aspect of this successful marketing campaign. At the beginning, FIJI Water did very little "formal" or paid advertising, which included only some printed advertisements placed in in-flight magazines, such as those of Air Pacific. The brand achieved an explosive growth early on, mostly through word-of-mouth advertising, free product placement and targeted sampling. According to Thomas Mooney, senior vice-president of sustainable growth, the company continued its focus on introducing new customers to the brand and converting them to "brand evangelists." While doing so, FIJI Water targeted locations and venues that resonated with the brand's premium image. Said Mooney: "It's different to get a bottle of water after walking off the subway than it is to get a bottle at an after-party following the Oscars."[25] In fact, the product had received a lot of publicity through movies, as Hollywood celebrities, such as Tom Cruise, Pierce Brosnan, Whoopi Goldberg and Vin Diesel, and popular singers, such as Michael Bolton, Tina Turner and Jessica Simpson, had eagerly endorsed the product. FIJI Water had also become a favourite at the dining tables of some of New York's better restaurants and hotels, including Jean Georges, Four Seasons Restaurant, Pierre Hotel, Trump International Hotels & Towers, the Carlyle and the Paramount. And there were celebrity chefs using FIJI Water as a cooking ingredient in their kitchens, such as "Sam the Cooking Guy," an Emmy-Award winning TV show.

In 2007, the company launched a new marketing campaign, aiming at communicating the core benefits of FIJI Water. Revolving around the theme "untouched," the campaign followed an integrated marketing communication approach, combining advertising, PR, direct marketing, product placements and event marketing. The advertising part of the campaign used a striking blue-colour creative copy that brought out the pristine nature, magical allure and mystery that the Fiji Islands embodied. The advertising campaign was developed by FIJI Water's in-house creative agency and used both out-of-home (OOH) and print media.[26]

---

[23]"Brio Industries Inc. Appointed Canada-Wide Master Distributor of Fiji Water," *Business Wire*, Vancouver, British Columbia, April 15, 1999, http://findarticles.com/p/articles/mi_m0EIN/is_1999_April_15/ai_54381790.

[24]"Canadians Have a Taste for FIJI Water," FIJI Water Press Release, Toronto, Ontario, March 10, 2008, www.nkpr.net/pressreleases/FW_Cadbury_Schweppes_Release.pdf.

[25]Heather Landi, "Paradise in a Bottle," *Beverage World*, November 2007, p. 24.

[26]FIJI Water Press Releases, www.fijiwater.com, accessed July 23, 2008.

In sum, the secret of FIJI Water's success in the United States seemed to lie in its marketers' ability to elevate the world's simplest drink to celebrity status. FIJI Water was much more than just pure, good-tasting liquid. It was a promise of good health, refinement, status, and exclusivity. It evoked images of unspoiled natural beauty and purity. It was a tropical paradise captured in a bottle!

Expanding into the Australian Market

With the tremendous success achieved by FIJI Water in the United States, the firm entered the Australian market in 2003 from a position of strength. As shown earlier, Australia was not among the leading bottled water consuming countries. However, the country's relatively large market and, more importantly, its proximity to Fiji made it an attractive market to enter. Moreover, before the product was launched in Australia, many Australians visiting Fiji had a chance to develop a taste for FIJI Water. It was common to see Australian vacationers returning from Fiji carrying cartons of FIJI Water with them back home. This created awareness of, and even pent-up demand for, the product before it was officially launched.

The product was initially introduced to select hotels and restaurants, before becoming available in gourmet, deli and independent convenience stores. In 2005, FIJI Water gained national distribution in more than 400 Coles supermarkets, and in 2007 FIJI Water's Australian subsidiary signed a national distribution agreement with Cadbury Schweppes Australia.[27] At that time, Cadbury Schweppes had a national market share of about eight per cent, with its Cool Ridge, Spring Valley Twist and FIJI Water brands.

The Australian bottled water market had sustained a high growth rate in the past decade and was predicted to continue to grow strongly in the next one. FIJI Water was emerging as a major brand in the premium market segment and was facing stiff competition. The Australian bottled water market was very competitive, and it was also less consolidated than the U.S. market. In Australia, about one thousand brands of bottled water competed for market share. Coca-Cola Amatil's Mount Franklin was Australia's leading water brand and was sourced from select Australian springs.

According to the Australasian Bottled Water Institute (ABWI) website, consumer research suggested that although bottled water was consumed in Australia by people of varying age groups and occupations, a large majority of them tended to be young singles and couples, in particular females, aged between 14 and 35 years. In terms of psychographics, bottled water consumers could be described as being more health-conscious, progressive and socially aware.[28]

Another Fiji company, whose brand name was Island Chill, with a very similar bottle design to FIJI Water, successfully entered the Australian market a few years after FIJI Water's launch there. Island Chill also contained silica and had been well-received in the Melbourne market. Although Melbourne was initially Island Chill's primary sales focus area, the brand was expanding to other Australian cities. The noticeable similarities in bottle shape and label design between the FIJI Water and Island Chill brands had led to a trademark dispute between the two companies in both Australia and the United States. According to the Island Chill website's press centre, in February of 2007 the Federal Court of Australia ruled in favour of Island Chill, dismissing FIJI Water's

---

[27]"National Packaging Covenant," FIJI Water (Australia) Pty Ltd., Annual Report, July 2006–June 2007, South Yara, Victoria, Australia.

[28]www.bottledwater.org.au.

complaint against Island Chill.[29] In the United States, the dispute was settled outside of court in June of 2008, when Island Chill agreed to remove the hibiscus flower from its bottle's label.[30]

Experiencing a Backlash in the U.K. Market

One year after FIJI Water entered the Australian market, it made an attempt to crack the U.K. market. The company launched FIJI brand through the supermarket chains Waitrose and Selfridge's, department stores Harvey Nichols and Harrods, and a number of specialty stores carrying whole-food products.

Soon after the brand had arrived in Britain, FIJI Water gained the reputation as the best-travelled bottled water in the country.[31] The fact that the product had to travel 10,000 miles to reach the British consumer could not escape the attention of environmentalist and conservation groups, in a country where quality of tap water was among the highest in the world. In a newspaper article published in 2004, an official from the Food Commission was reported to have said that "it was ludicrous to bring water from the other side of the world when essentially the same product was available out of the tap."[32] At the same time, it was noted that the most popular French bottled water brands–Evian and Vittel–travelled "only" between 400 and 460 miles to reach Britain. As a result of this backlash, FIJI Water had so far been largely unsuccessful in penetrating the U.K. market. Moreover, FIJI Water's appearance in the United Kingdom had fuelled the debate around the environmental impact of bottled water.

In 2008, British environmentalists and conservationists took up the war against bottled water. They were joined by some political leaders and government officials as well. For example, the mayor of London and the CEO of Thames Water Authority launched a campaign called "London on Tap" to encourage consumers to order tap water in restaurants.[33] Their message to consumers was that using less bottled water would help tackle climate change by cutting carbon emissions with its production, storage, transport and disposal. Campaign partners included London Remade, the Crafts Council and WaterAid, and the supporters included Friends of the Earth and London Sustainability Exchange.

On January 18, 2008, the BBC broadcast a TV special that featured FIJI Water in a Panorama documentary called "Bottled Water–Who Needs It?" It gave a critical analysis of the negative impact the success of the U.K. bottled water industry was having on the environment.[34] It pointed out that, "In the UK last year we spent nearly £2 billion buying bottled water, yet a billion people around the world don't have access to safe drinking water" and that, "Sales of bottled water have boomed in recent decades, growing 200-fold from the 1970s. But a litre of one of the UK's most popular French mineral waters generates up to 600 times more CO2 equivalent than a litre of Thames tap water."[35] The programme travelled to Fiji, where they visited the FIJI Water bottling plant, Fijian villages and hospitals, noting that one in three Fijians did not have access to safe tap water. The documentary was

---

[29] www.islandchill.com/press.html.

[30] "Island Chill and Fiji Water end trademark dispute," *FOODBEV.COM*, June 24, 2008.

[31] "Bottle of water that has travelled the world," *The Daily Telegraph*, November 3, 2004.

[32] Ibid., p. 3.

[33] Hannah Marriott, "Bottled water under fire: how industry responded," *PRWeek (UK)*, February 21, 2008.

[34] The documentary can be accessed from http://news.bbc.co.uk/2/hi/programmes/panorama/7247130.stm.

[35] Ibid.

wrapped up with the following statement: "Indeed FIJI Water would make the case that if you really care about the plight of Fijians, you should buy FIJI Water as it provides jobs and income for the islands. But tell people here on the street that we buy bottled water from Fiji and most will still roll their eyes and ask: Why?"[36] The 2008 BBC Panorama story focusing on FIJI Water had 3.5 million viewers!

Growing concerns about bottled water's harmful effects on the environment might have caused a reversal of a growing trend in bottled water consumption in the United Kingdom. For the first time in years, a nine per cent drop of retail sales of bottled water was reported in the first quarter of 2008.[37] This was largely attributed to an Evening Standard campaign to get Londoners to turn to tap water instead of buying expensive and environmentally harmful bottled water. A fifth of diners in London restaurants were reported to opt for tap water. The government's Food Standards Agency banned bottled water from its offices. This move was followed by a growing number of Whitehall departments doing the same, including Downing Street. Food and health lobby group "Sustain" launched a campaign for government departments and official bodies to turn to tap water. The campaign's director, Richard Watts, believed it had worked. He said: "This looks to be the first ever recorded fall in bottled water sales. It is a significant development. The message about bottled water being unnecessary, expensive and damaging to the environment is finally getting through."[38]

WORLDWIDE CONTROVERSIES OVER BOTTLED WATER'S IMPACT ON THE ENVIRONMENT

In the last 10 years, the high sustained global growth rate of bottled water sales of about eight per cent per annum had been a triumph of modern marketing and a dynamic, profitable segment of the beverage market for the growing number of producers. FIJI Water had been very successful in gaining market share in this rapidly growing industry. Advertising campaigns had promoted bottled water as a healthy alternative to high-calorie CSDs and purer alternative to tap water. The advertisements focused on its pristine pureness, safeness and better taste compared to tap water. However, conservationists pointed out that the price of bottled water was about 500 to 1000 times higher than that of tap water. Since the launch of FIJI Water in the United Kingdom, the bottled water industry had been under attack in the media and FIJI brand had been singled out for criticism by environmental groups and by a BBC documentary that had been widely broadcast.

The Swiss-based conservation group World Wide Fund for Nature had published a research study it funded, which found that bottled water was often no healthier or safer to drink than tap water and it had used the findings to argue strongly that bottled water was not only environmentally unfriendly but also a waste of money.[39] Another watchdog, Corporate Accountability International, had mounted a campaign called "Think Outside the Bottle."[40] The group advocated ending state contracts with bottled water suppliers, promoting water systems and improving the quality of water infrastructure.

---

[36]Ibid.

[37]Lucy Hanbury, "Bottled water sales dry up as London turns to tap," *Evening Standard*, April 14, 2008.

[38]Ibid.

[39]Catherine Ferrier, "Bottled Water: Understanding a Social Phenomenon," Discussion Paper commissioned by WWF, April 2001.

[40]"Corporate Accountability International: Challenging Abuse, Protecting People," www.stopcorporateabuse.org.

According to Janet Larsen's article "Bottled Water Boycotts," in 2007 city governments, high-class restaurants, schools, and religious groups from San Francisco to New York to Paris were ditching bottled water in favour of tap water.[41] The U.S. Conference of Mayors, which represented some 1,100 American cities, discussed at its June 2007 meeting the mayors' role in promoting the consumption of municipal tap water and many city councils were banning the purchase of bottled water for their employees. In the same year, New York City launched a campaign to persuade people to cut back on bottled water and return to tap water. San Francisco's mayor banned city employees from using public money to buy imported water, while Chicago's mayor imposed a five-cents-a-bottle tax on plastic bottles to compensate for the financial burden bottled water caused for municipal waste disposal systems.[42] It was somewhat ironic that in the United States, more than a quarter of bottled water was just purified tap water, including Pepsi's top-selling Aquafina and Coca-Cola's Dasani.

FIJI WATER'S "CARBON NEGATIVE" CAMPAIGN

In response to the environmentalists' criticism, in 2008 FIJI Water LLC launched a "carbon negative" PR campaign, claiming that it was the first bottled water company to release carbon footprint of its products.[43] It had also joined the Carbon Disclosure Project Supply Chain Leadership Collaboration and had started working with the Carbon Disclosure Project (CDP), the world's largest investor coalition on climate change, to disclose its own and its suppliers' carbon emissions. As measurement is the first step to managing and reducing carbon emissions, FIJI Water Company estimated its total annual carbon footprint at 85,396 metric tons of CO2eq. This was for the base year ending June 30, 2007.[44]

While measuring its carbon footprint, FIJI Water calculated its carbon emissions across every stage in the product lifecycle: starting from producing raw materials for packaging, through transporting raw materials and equipment to the plant, manufacturing and filling bottles, shipping the product from Fiji to markets worldwide, distributing the product, refrigerating the product in stores, restaurants, and other outlets, to disposing/recycling the packaging waste. It estimated that about 75 per cent of its carbon emissions resulted from the operations of supply chain partners. The company also looked at carbon emissions from its administrative and marketing activities. At the same time, the company launched a product-specific emissions disclosure via a website (www.fijigreen.com). The website provided consumers with access to product lifecycle emissions data and analysis for each of the company's products. The company's senior VP for sustainable growth, Mooney, argued that "the only way consumers can turn their good environmental intentions into good decisions is to give them the information they need regarding the emissions associated with the products they buy."[45]

As part of its "carbon negative" campaign, FIJI Water was planning to offset its total carbon footprint by 120 per cent, by removing from the earth's atmosphere not only all the emissions its activities produced, but also an additional 20 per cent. In that sense, the

---

[41]Janet Larsen, "Bottled Water Boycotts," Earth Policy Institute, 2007.

[42]Lucy Siegle, "It's just water, right? Wrong. Bottled water is set to be the latest battleground in the eco war," *The Observer*, February 10, 2008, p. 30.

[43]"FIJI Water Becomes First Bottled Water Company to Release Carbon Footprint of Its Products," April 9, 2008, www.bevnet.com.

[44]Ibid.

[45]Ibid.

company's impact on carbon emissions would be negative. To achieve this goal, FIJI Water had undertaken a number of steps towards sustainable growth. These steps included:

- reducing packaging by 20 per cent
- supplying at least 50 per cent of the energy used at its bottling plant with renewable energy
- optimizing logistics and using more carbon-efficient transportation modes
- restoring degraded grasslands in the Yaqara Valley by planting native tree species
- supporting recycling programs for plastic PET bottles

According to a company press conference held in April 2008, FIJI Water had already implemented several measures to reduce its carbon emissions. By optimizing its logistics, the company had reduced trucking miles by 26 per cent on average. FIJI Water's 1.5-litre bottle had been redesigned to reduce the packaging by seven per cent. The company had also managed to reduce motor fuel consumption in Fiji by 50 per cent by using more fuel-efficient trucks in transporting its products from the plant to ports.[46]

All in all, the above sustainable growth commitment provided FIJI Water with an opportunity to use that commitment as a PR pitch: the sale of every bottle of FIJI Water would result in a net reduction of carbon in the atmosphere! In other words—"every drop is green," as the company's website emphasized.

CONSERVATIONISTS' ATTACKS ON FIJI WATER'S GREEN MAKE-OVER

Conservation groups had not been impressed by FIJI Water's claim that it was going carbon negative. It was perceived as pure greenwashing at its best. The 10th Edition of the Concise Oxford English Dictionary recognizes the word "greenwash," defining it as "Disinformation disseminated by an organisation so as to present an environmentally responsible public image." Greenwashing was defined in law in Australia by the Competition and Consumer Commission that ensured compliance with the Commonwealth Trade Practices Act 1974. The Act contains a general prohibition on "conduct that is misleading or deceptive or is likely to mislead or deceive." Section 53 of the Act prohibits a corporation from representing that "goods or services have sponsorship, approval, performance characteristics, accessories, uses or benefits they do not have."

Conservation groups argued that the new website launched by FIJI Water in 2008 to sell its carbon negative message failed to provide a detailed description of the actual calculation of its carbon footprint and its reduction by the measures that were promised to be implemented in the future. At the same time, the groups pointed to the basic carbon footprint advantages of consuming local tap water. They argued that the new slogan "every drop is green" was straightforward greenwashing pushed to its limits.

The Food and Water Watch website posted a blog, entitled "Greenwashed: FIJI Water Bottles the Myth of Sustainability," about FIJI Water's carbon negative claim that summarized the response of the environmental watchdogs.[47] The website stated: "Corporate attempts to label their products as 'green' for the sake of turning a fast buck are nothing

---

[46]"FIJI Water Becomes First Bottled Water Company to Release Carbon Footprint of Its Products," FIJI Water Press Release, Los Angeles, April 9, 2008, www.bevnet.com.

[47]www.foodandwaterwatch.org/blog/archive/2008/05/02/greenwashed-fiji-water-bottles-the-myth-of-sustainability.

new. Corporations exist, after all, in order to make money, and capitalizing on whatever is capturing the public's collective imagination is often the best way of doing so. But *Fiji Artisanal Water*'s entree into the green movement strikes us as particularly suspect. The company has recently launched *fijigreen.com*, a website outlining the ways in which their *water* is 'good for the environment.' If you're anything like us, you are probably wondering how this claim could be true. It can't."[48]

The Greenwash Brigade (part of the Public Insight Network), a U.S. organization of environmental professionals that are dedicated to exposing "greenwash" as they examine eco-friendly claims by companies, was quick to respond to FIJI Water's claim that it was going carbon negative. In an article by Heidi Siegelbaum on June 6, 2008, titled "FIJI Water by the numbers," she summarized FIJI Water's environmental impact by the following numbers:

- 5,500 miles per trip from Fiji to Los Angeles;
- 46 million gallons of fossil fuel;
- 1.3 billion gallons of water;
- 216,000,000 pounds of greenhouse gases.[49]

And she commented: "FIJI is using staggering amounts of energy, water, and fossil fuels to take a naturally occurring product (which is not regulated like drinking water here in the US), put it in an inherently problematic container and then have that forever-container tossed into landfills or incinerators all over America (and Asia, where we have a healthy export market for plastics)."[50]

Tony Azios summarized the reaction in the United States to the response of bottled water companies to the environmental protests, as follows: "Even as bottled water companies continue to see increased sales, the recent raft of negative media coverage and activist campaigns against the industry has caused a product once seen as fundamentally green and healthy to lose some of its luster. Now, brand-name bottlers are scrambling to reposition their products by upping their green credentials to fend off further consumer backlash fermenting in churches, college campuses, and city halls across the country."[51]

Rob Knox, in his article titled "Green or Greenwashing? FIJI Water," was also not convinced that "every drop is green."[52] His evaluation of the green makeover was that it was greenwashing. Knox reported: "[. . .] In March they took out a massive booth at the Natural Products Expo, part of a larger 'hey we're green now' campaign by the company. The booth featured a gigantic banner proclaiming 'every drop is green'."

He continued: "Allow me free reign to mock FIJI for a moment. Let's discuss what every drop of FIJI Water is—and here's a hint, it's not green. Every drop of FIJI Water is imported from Fiji. That's right, the Fiji that is an island in the middle of the Pacific Ocean, thousands of miles from the mainland United States. This company takes water, which can be found in rather large quantities in the US, all the way from Fiji to your neighborhood. Every drop of FIJI Water represents thousands of miles in completely unnecessary transportation and hundreds of gallons of fuel, all so you can drink expensive water from a pretty bottle."[53]

---

[48]Ibid.

[49]Heidi Siegelbaum, "Fiji Water by the numbers," June 6, 2008.

[50]Ibid.

[51]Ibid.

[52]Robert Knox, "Green or Greenwashing? Fiji Water," www.greenopia.com/USA/news/15063/7-16-2008/Green-or-Greenwashing?-Fiji-Water.

[53]Ibid.

In 2007, Pablo Päster, an engineer and MBA, claimed to have undertaken a thorough and exhaustive study of the cost of bringing a litre of FIJI Water to America that was reported about on the Treehugger website in an article by Lloyd Alter entitled "Pablo Calculates the True Cost of Bottled Water." His study found that, "In summary, the manufacture and transport of that one kilogram bottle of FIJI Water consumed 26.88 kilograms of water (7.1 gallons), .849 kilograms of fossil fuel (one litre or .26 gallons) and emitted 562 grams of Greenhouse Gases (1.2 pounds)."[54]

RELATIONS WITH THE FIJI GOVERNMENT

Natural Waters, the Fiji Islands-based production subsidiary of FIJI Water LLC, played an important role in the Fiji economy, particularly as a source of export earnings. While in 1998 FIJI Water brand exports ranked 14th among product categories exported from Fiji,[55] its position among exports had climbed to number two in 2007, bringing FJ$105 million in export earnings.[56] Only sugar, whose exports in 2007 stood at FJ$185 million, brought more export revenues than bottled water, which was virtually all accounted for by FIJI Water. Since export revenues from sugar had been on the decline since 2000, there was a possibility that bottled water would soon become the number 1 export earner for Fiji, provided the Fiji government did not do any harm to the rapidly growing bottled water industry. The stand-off between Fiji's bottled water companies and the government over the 20-cents-per-litre export duty and excise in 2008 might put a brake on this industry's growth and erode a substantial part of Fiji's export earnings. In 2007, bottled water accounted for almost 10 per cent of Fiji's total export revenues.[57]

Taxation Issues

Over the last decade, the Fiji government had observed the rapid growth of a new export industry led by FIJI Water.[58] When Natural Waters of Viti Ltd. was established, it applied to the government for financial incentives under the Tax Free Factory Scheme and was granted a thirteen-year tax holiday from the government. Also, it was granted approval to import the plant and equipment for its factory free of import duty.[59]

The success of FIJI Water was very evident to all citizens of Fiji as they observed the large number of trucks transporting containers of bottled water to the ports of Lautoka and Suva using the Queens highway. FIJI Water received positive media reports and was a sponsor of the Fiji Exporter of the Year Awards. A film was made about the company's past growth and plans for the future, and was broadcast several times on the local TV station Fiji One.

It was not until 2008 that the government started to review the potential tax contribution that could be levied on the bottled water industry. FIJI Water appeared to provide little direct benefits to government revenue because of the tax-free status granted by earlier

---

[54]www.treehugger.com/files/2007/02/pablo_calculate.php.

[55]McMaster and Nowak, "Natural Waters of Viti Limited–Pioneering a New Industry in the Fiji Islands," 2003.

[56]Fiji Islands Bureau of Statistics, "Key Statistics: Overseas Merchandise Trade," March 2008, p. 71.

[57]Ibid.

[58]According to Fiji Times (August 12, 2008, p. 2), FIJI Water accounts for 98 per cent of bottled water exports from Fiji.

[59]McMaster and Nowak, "Natural Waters of Viti Limited–Pioneering a New Industry in the Fiji Islands, 2003."

governments. One could argue that the damage caused to the national roads and bridges by the huge number of heavily laden trucks carrying FIJI Water might have exceeded the road and fuel tax, and that the citizens of Fiji were subsidizing FIJI Water. The bottling plant of FIJI Water was fully automated with state-of-the-art equipment and featured a highly capital-intensive production process employing a relatively small workforce given the volume of exports.

On July 4, 2008, without any prior consultation with the industry, the Fiji government imposed a twenty-cents-per-litre export duty on all mineral water exports and the same level of excise duty on mineral water sold for domestic consumption.[60] This new tax was put into effect by amending the Customs Tariff Act (Amendment) (No 3) Promulgation 2008 And Excise Act (Amendment) (No 1) Promulgation 2008.[61]

The local media reported that the interim finance minister, Mahendra Chaudhry, said, "The main purpose of this new duty was to stimulate conservation of our scarce natural resources."[62]

These new taxes came into effect on July 1, 2008. In a press statement released on July 20 by Fiji Islands Revenue and Customs Authority chief executive officer, Jitoko Tikolevu, it was announced that: "Should there be a change in the rates in the future as decided by government, the Authority will refund any excess revenue collected from these taxes."[63]

Based on FIJI Water's export levels, the new export tax would result in the company paying many millions to the government coffers. In 2006, FIJI Water exported 119,000,000 litres of bottled water to the United States. Applying a tax of 20-cents-per-litre to this level of export to the United States would result in a tax bill of FJ$24 million to FIJI Water just for its exports to one market. It was likely that FJIJ Water could end up paying as much as FJ$50 million for the new tax. [64]

FIJI Water and the nine other companies immediately mounted a campaign against the new tax. They first threatened to cease production and to lay workers off. They issued press releases that argued the new tax would destroy the whole industry and greatly undermine foreign investor confidence, which was already at a low level. The 10 bottled water companies formed an industry association and appointed a spokesperson to lead the media campaign. They argued that this sudden decision by the Cabinet was made without thorough analysis of the economic costs and benefits. They stated that the government did not have detailed information on company costs and profitability and that the firms could not absorb the ill-conceived new tax that would have a major negative impact on the whole economy. It would be the death knell of this new export industry and would greatly reduce export earnings and foreign exchange earnings, and lead to job losses and slower economic growth. They pointed out that it would undermine the government's economic development strategy, which was based on increasing the level of investment and export-oriented growth.

The new industry association comprising 10 firms—Warwick Pleass, FIJI Water, VTY, Mr Pure, Island Chill, Aqua Pacific, Diamond Aqua, Tappoos Beverage, Fresh Spring Limited and Minerals Water of Fiji—lobbied the members of the Military Council and the media and gained strong support of the local newspapers. The main local newspaper, The Fiji Times, published an editorial in July 2008 calling for the sacking of the interim minister of finance,

---

[60]"Cabinet Approves Tariff, Excise Act," *Fiji Times*, July 4, 2008.

[61]Ibid.

[62]Ibid.

[63]"Duty on Bottled Water Remains," *Fiji Times*, July 20, 2008.

[64]FIRCA Press Release, July 21, 2008, www.frca.org.fj/docs/firca/press_releases/Press Release 21.07.pdf

who was seen as the architect of this new tax. The bottled water industry was required to make its submissions to the Finance Ministry on the new tax.

A critical issue was the likely impact of this new tax on both foreign and local investment. It was seen as moving the goal posts after the start of the game. Foreign investor confidence was already at a very low level because of the military takeover of the democratically elected government in December 2006. Investors are not attracted to a country where the taxation environment can alter dramatically overnight without consultation.

On July 23, 2008, Natural Waters of Viti Limited laid off about 400 workers and shut down operations along with five other major exporting companies. The following day, The Fiji Times, the leading local newspaper, published an editorial comment on the so-called "Water Debacle."[65] The editorial stated that: "the closure of FIJI Water's operations yesterday shows what happens when governments take draconian measures to impose unrealistic taxes on large corporate entities. This major contributor to the national economy has closed its doors, sent staff home and deprived the nation of $3 million in export revenue per week." The editorial continued, stressing the importance of FIJI Water operations for the livelihood of workers and their families, for tax revenues, as well as for retail revenues in the nearby towns of Rakiraki and Tavua. It also pointed out the impact of the plant closure on dockworkers and drivers."[66]

Also the following day, a spokesperson for the bottlers, Jay Dayal, said they had decided to take legal action, as their patience had been exhausted. The bottlers had filed for a judicial review over the government decision to impose the 20-cents-per-litre tax.[67] On the same day, FIJI Water released a statement saying that the lawsuit was caused by the lack of movement by the interim government on the imposition of tax by Fiji Islands Revenue and Customs Authority (FIRCA), pending a final decision by the interim Cabinet. "Unfortunately, FIJI Water must take this action because we have now reached a critical juncture where we can no longer effectively operate our business," the statement said. "We have neither sold nor exported any product since July 1, forcing us to cancel multiple port calls from various shipping lines. As long as the crisis continues, the nation of Fiji will continue to lose approximately FJ$3 million in export revenue each week (more than FJ$150 million annually)."[68]

Behind the scenes, the bottlers were very active in seeking the support of the media and key decision makers, trade unions, village leaders and local chiefs as well as lobbying interim ministers and members of the Military Council. One of the bottlers described the tax-induced crisis as "like a war had broken out or a bomb had exploded." There were tens of millions of dollars at stake that could be collected from the bottlers.

On July 25, 2008, the Fiji government made an announcement that it had decided to drop the new tax. This decision by interim Prime Minister Commodore Voreqe Bainimarama was praised by the proprietors of water bottling companies.[69] Immediately after the announcement of the repeal of the tax, the major bottled water-exporting companies resumed production and re-employed the hundreds of workers who had been laid off.[70]

---

[65]"Water Debacle," *Fiji Times*, July 24, 2008.

[66]Ibid.

[67]"FIJI Water bottlers file suit against government, Association says 20-cent tax will kill industry," Radio New Zealand International, www.rnzi.com.

[68]"Fiji Water Shuts down Operations," *Fiji Daily Post*, July 24, 2008.

[69]Margaret Wise, "Sigh of Relief as State Drops Tax," *Fiji Times*, July 25, 2008.

[70]"Bottled Water Back in Action," Fiji Live website, July 24, 2008.

FIJI Water had for a number of years been a sponsor of the Fiji Exporter of the Year Awards, an annual event to celebrate successful exporters. On August 3, 2008, FIJI Water's local CEO, David Roth, announced the company's decision to withdraw its sponsorship of the Awards because of the lack of support of FTIB during the taxation dispute.[71] David Roth said: "Fiji Islands Trade and Investment Bureau (FTIB) did not provide any support or assistance towards the bottled water industry during this struggle, and in fact FTIB's chairman publicly supported the imposition of the unreasonable and draconian excise and export duties, in spite of many of us trying to explain to him that his assumptions about our businesses were simply incorrect." Roth added that the company's decision to withdraw had nothing to do with its attitude toward others in government.[72]

In November 2008, the Fiji government re-introduced the disputed water tax as part of the 2009 budget in a different form. It was called "water resource tax" and was progressive depending on the amount of water extracted. For extractions up to 4,999,999 litres it was set at 0.11 cents per litre; for extractions between 5,000,000 and 9,999,999 litres it was 0.22 cents per litre; and an extraction volume of 10,000,000 litres or more would attract a tax of 0.33 cents per litre.[73] The tax was to be imposed only on extracted (artesian) water; companies engaged in the bottling of rainwater or purified tap water would be exempt from the tax. The tax was supposed to be collected from January 2009. It was expected that the Fiji government would collect F$1.5 million through the water extraction tax.[74]

Transfer Pricing

In January 2008, the government became concerned that FIJI Water was engaging in transfer price manipulations, selling the water shipments produced in Fiji at a very low price to the company headquarters in Los Angeles. It was feared that very little of the wealth generated by the company was coming into Fiji as foreign reserves from export earnings, which Fiji badly needed to fund its imports. Seemingly, FIJI Water was funnelling most of its cash to the United States.

As a result of these concerns, FIRCA decided to take action against FIJI Water and it halted exports in January 2008 at the ports by putting 200 containers loaded with FIJI water bottles under armed guard, and issued a statement accusing FIJI Water of transfer price manipulations. FIRCA's chief executive, Jitoko Tikolevu, said, "The wholly US-owned Fijian subsidiary sold its water exclusively to its US parent at the declared rate, in Fiji, of US$4 (NZ$5) a carton. In the US, though, the same company then sold it for up to US$50 a carton."[75]

Natural Waters of Viti Ltd. immediately filed a lawsuit against FIRCA with the High Court of Fiji. The High Court issued an interim order, allowing the company to resume shipment of the embargoed containers upon payment of an F$5 million bond to the Court.[76]

The U.S. ambassador to Fiji, Larry Dinger, issued a barely veiled threat to Fiji. "The example [the authority] and the interim government set regarding fair and impartial treatment in this case will surely have a major impact on global perceptions of Fiji's investment climate. American companies have to receive fair and impartial treatment around the

---

[71]"Fiji Bottlers Reconsider Boycott Decision," Fiji Live website, August 3, 2008.

[72]Ibid.

[73]PriceWaterhouseCoopers, 2009 Fiji Islands Budget Summary, November 21, 2008.

[74]"$1.5 million expected from water tax," Fiji Live website, November 21, 2008.

[75]Michael Field, "Fiji-US row brews over water exports," *The Dominion Post*, January 21, 2008.

[76]"High Court set to rule in Fiji Water case," *Fiji Times*, February 8, 2008.

world. That applies in Fiji, too. 'Rule of law' and a 'level playing field' are critically important factors when there are commercial disputes, and those elements have a major impact in decisions by foreign investors, including American investors, on where they will direct their funds," he stated.[77]

A press release by FIRCA, issued in January 2008, noted that FIJI Water had received advice from international law firm Baker & McKenzie, which conducted an economic study on transfer pricing and declared what the company was doing in Fiji was fair. FIRCA rejected the claim by stating that: "FIRCA will not passively accept the verdict of Baker & McKenzie without itself having access to the information on which same is based, and to the instructions on which same is based, and without the opportunity to conduct its own transfer pricing study based on such matters and upon the profitability of Natural Waters of Viti Limited."[78]

The FIJI Water dispute with the government over transfer pricing attracted the attention of the University of the South Pacific economist Sukhdev Shah, who published an article on "The true cost of water" in the Fiji Times on January 24, 2008, to give the general public a lecture on the complexities of transfer pricing. He stated that: "Multinational companies as represented by FIJI Water are capable of spreading their risks across countries where they do business. They do this by shifting most of their profits and asset holdings to their affiliates in low-tax countries that are also considered safe. Given a choice between US and Fiji, FIJI Water would definitely take a bet on the US—partly for the reason of lower tax obligation but mostly because it can be a safe-haven."[79]

RELATIONS WITH THE LOCAL COMMUNITY

The company had recognized the importance of establishing and maintaining good relations with the five neighbouring Fijian villages that were the traditional landowners of the Yaqara basin, where the bottling plant was located. These villages were: Draunivi, Togovere, Naseyani, Nananu and Rabulu. FIJI Water's bottling plant drew most of its workforce from these villages. It employed a young workforce and most of the workers had not previously had a wage job but had been engaged in subsistence farming and fishing activities. The company provided its staff with on-the-job training in operating the sophisticated production line. In return, its workers showed a lot of enthusiasm, loyalty, and pride in working for the company. Through strong leadership, FIJI Water had established an excellent work environment with good interpersonal relationships among the workforce. The company supported children's education. To assist the children in getting an early start, it had constructed a kindergarten classroom in each village to provide early childhood education. The company had also provided the pre-schools with equipment, educational material, teacher training and other support.

In March 2002, the company voluntarily established an independently administrated community development trust fund and allocated FJ$275,000 to it. The trust fund was established after a series of negotiations with the members of the community. It was designed to support village projects to improve the hygiene and sanitation of the community. Through this fund, the company intended to finance projects to supply potable water to the villages and reticulate it to the households. It also aimed at supporting projects to reduce pollution and improve hygiene. Through improving the quality of hygiene and

---

[77]Field, "Fiji-US row brews over water exports," January 21, 2008.

[78]"Press Release," Fiji Islands Revenue & Customs Authority, January 11, 2008, p. 3.

[79]Sukhdev Shah, "The true cost of water," *Fiji Times*, January, 24, 2008

sanitation, it was hoped to improve the health of the villagers and of the workforce of the company.[80]

As a result of the above-described trust fund, Draunivi and Togovere were first provided with clean, safe drinking water. The water supply project was then extended in 2008 to cover three other villages in the vicinity of the bottling plant–Naseyani, Nananu and Rabulu.[81] Moreover, in the same year, FIJI Water teamed with the Rotary Club in Suva to fund the Pacific Water for Life Trust. The Trust provided funds for developing the infrastructure, expertise and skills needed to supply clean, safe and sustainable water to more than 100 communities, schools, health centres and nursing stations throughout Fiji.[82]

Natural Waters of Viti Ltd. was a strong believer in contracting out. It had contracted out services to a local company that employed tens of people in the following functions: transport of workers to and from work; security office to guard the factory; the preparation of food for workers in the canteen; ground maintenance; and laundry.

In recognition of FIJI Water's involvement in local community development in Fiji, in 2004 the U.S. State Department honoured the company with the Award for Corporate Excellence for Outstanding Corporate Citizenship, Innovation and Exemplary International Business Practice. The award was presented to FIJI Water founder David Gilmour by Secretary of State Colin Powell in October 2004, who remarked, "Fijians take special pride in their island's tranquil beauty and Fiji Water has matched their passion with action . . . More than a good corporate citizen, Fiji Water is a good neighbour to all the people of Fiji."[83] Ironically, two months later FIJI Water was sold by Gilmour to Roll International.

WHAT NEXT?

In 2009 and beyond, FIJI Water will continue facing complex CRS challenges. It will have to live up to its promise of becoming a carbon negative company. Any attempt to engage in greenwashing will be quickly identified and protested by environmental groups. Keeping true to its slogan "every drop is green" will require substantial new investment in a renewable energy plant and equipment and in tree-planting offset activities.

FIJI Water's tax-free concession granted by the Fiji government for 13 years in 1995 came to an end in October 2008 and the company will be required to pay corporate tax in Fiji. The new water resource tax, although much lower than the draconian 20-cents-a-litre excise, is nevertheless likely to erode the company's profitability by adding about FJ$1 million to its costs every year. This is expected to coincide with a slow-down of growth or even stagnation of FIJI Water sales in its main markets due to the global recession.

Maintaining good relations with the Fiji government will be vital. A series of ads sponsored by FIJI Water, placed in the popular daily Fiji Times in late 2008 and early 2009, was focused on letting the public (and the government!) know how good a corporate citizen the company is. The ads highlighted FIJI Water's contribution to creating new jobs, improving education and raising standards of living in Fiji. In January 2009, FIJI Water donated US$0.5 million to Fiji's National Disaster, Relief and Rehabilitation Fund, which was created by the prime minister's office in the aftermath of devastating floods.[84] Clearly, FIJI Water was making efforts to live up to its good corporate citizenship claim. But is it enough to

---

[80]McMaster and Nowak, "Natural Waters of Viti Limited–Pioneering a New Industry in the Fiji Islands."

[81]www.fijiwater.com.

[82]Ibid.

[83]"Here's to you: Fiji Water," *Beverage World*, March 8, 2007.

dispel government officials' and ordinary citizens' doubts about FIJI Water's positive contribution to the local economy and community?

Designing and implementing a sustainable growth strategy and a socially and environmentally responsible marketing plan will require dealing effectively with the promise to go carbon negative as well as meeting the demanding needs of customers, clients and other stakeholders. Will FIJI Water be able to successfully navigate through these rough waters of corporate social responsibility? What should it do to breathe new life into this otherwise clever marketing strategy?

James McMaster is a professor at the Graduate School of Business, The University of the South Pacific, and Jan Nowak is a professor at the Central European University Business School.

---

[84]"Fiji Water donates to PM's Relief Fund," Press Release, Fiji Government On-line, January 27, 2009.

EXHIBIT 1: Global Bottled Water Market Leading Countries' Consumption and Compound Annual Growth Rates, 2002–2007

Rank, 2007	Countries	Consumption in Millions of Gallons		CAGR* 2002/07
		2002	2007	
1	United States	5,795.6	8,823.0	8.8%
2	Mexico	3,898.6	5,885.2	8.6%
3	China	2,138.4	4,787.8	17.5%
4	Brazil	2,541.8	3,621.1	7.3%
5	Italy	2,558.2	3,100.9	3.9%
6	Germany	2,291.5	2,743.2	3.7%
7	Indonesia	1,622.5	2,400.6	8.2%
8	France	2,225.6	2,283.2	0.5%
9	Thailand	1,277.0	1,533.1	3.7%
10	Spain	1,191.4	1,284.0	1.5%
	Top 10 Subtotal	**25,540.7**	**36,462.2**	**7.4%**
	All Others	9,054.2	13,407.3	8.2%
	WORLD TOTAL	**34,594.9**	**49,869.6**	**7.6%**

* Compound annual growth rate.

Source: "The Global Bottled Water Market. Report 2007," Beverage Marketing Corporation, January 2008.

EXHIBIT 2: Global Bottled Water Market Per Capita Consumption by Leading Countries, 2002–2007

Rank, 2007	Countries	Consumption in Gallons Per Capita	
		2002	2007
1	United Arab Emirates	35.2	68.6
2	Mexico	37.7	54.1
3	Italy	44.2	53.3
4	Belgium-Luxembourg	32.7	39.5
5	France	37.1	35.8
6	Germany	27.8	33.3
7	Spain	29.7	31.7
8	Lebanon	24.9	29.3
9	United States	20.1	29.3
10	Hungary	13.5	28.5
11	Switzerland	24.2	28.2
12	Slovenia	18.8	25.2
13	Austria	20.9	25.0
14	Czech Republic	21.1	24.6
15	Croatia	14.9	24.3
16	Saudi Arabia	23.8	24.1
17	Cyprus	21.4	24.0
18	Thailand	20.1	23.6
19	Israel	12.4	23.2
20	Portugal	19.9	22.4
	GLOBAL AVERAGE	**5.6**	**7.6**

Source: "The Global Bottled Water Market. Report 2007," Beverage Marketing Corporation, January 2008.

EXHIBIT 3: U.S. Bottled Water Market Per Capita Consumption, 1997–2007

Year	Gallons Per Capita	Annual % Change
1997	13.5	—
1998	14.7	8.3%
1999	16.2	10.2%
2000	16.7	3.5%
2001	18.2	8.6%
2002	20.1	10.6%
2003	21.6	7.2%
2004	23.2	7.5%
2005	25.4	9.7%
2006	27.6	8.4%
2007	29.3	6.4%

Source: "The Global Bottled Water Market. Report 2007," Beverage Marketing Corporation, January 2008.

EXHIBIT 4: U.S. Bottled Water Market Volume and Growth by Segment, 2000–2007

	Non-sparkling		Domestic Sparkling		Imports		Total	
Year	Volume*	Change	Volume*	Change	Volume*	Change	Volume*	Change
2000	4,443.0	—	144.2	—	137.9	—	4,725.1	—
2001	4,917.3	10.7%	144.0	−0.1%	123.9	−10.1%	5,185.3	9.7%
2002	5,487.5	11.6%	149.5	3.8%	158.7	28.0%	5,795.7	11.8%
2003	5,923.9	8.0%	152.6	2.1%	193.3	21.8%	6,269.8	8.2%
2004	6,411.3	8.2%	166.8	9.3%	228.6	18.2%	6,806.7	8.6%
2005	7,171.4	11.9%	185.0	10.9%	182.5	−20.2%	7,538.9	10.8%
2006	7,899.9	10.2%	189.3	2.3%	164.3	−10.0%	8,253.5	9.5%
2007	8,435.7	6.8%	201.2	6.3%	186.0	13.2%	8,823.0	6.9%

*Millions of gallons.

Source: "The Global Bottled Water Market. Report 2007," Beverage Marketing Corporation, January 2008.

Alta and SAIT: A Potential Private-Public Partnership

In November 2012, Gerry Darichuk, president of Alta Injection Molding (Alta), sat in his Calgary office, reflecting on the conversation he just had. A representative of the Ministry of State for Western Economic Diversification had just contacted Darichuk about an ambitious private-public partnership (P3) project in which Alta could partner with the Southern Alberta Institute of Technology (SAIT) and the government of Canada.

Since 1990, Alta's business had specialized in composite plastic manufacturing, prototyping, mold design and manufacturing.[1] The P3 project would explore alternative methods for promoting diversification in Alberta's manufacturing sector. The proposed partnership would allow SAIT students to see how private enterprise responded to market needs, get experience with state of the art equipment, and apply cutting-edge materials developed for new-age plastic mold injection manufacturing processes. In return, Alta would house and have full access to Cdn$3.5 million worth of specialized equipment, which would be jointly owned by both Alta and SAIT.

Darichuk and his sons had developed a unique business model for bringing innovative products to market. Alta had developed the capability to take ideas brought to them by inventors and nurture those ideas through the entire R&D and production stages of the value chain. This model helped hundreds of individuals and firms develop innovative products and get them to market. The products they helped develop ran the gamut of the market, from reusable coffee filters for single cup coffee brewers, to a welding handle that could withstand the harsh Alberta elements without breaking, to sophisticated oil field equipment.

Michael Roberts and Travis Guay wrote this case solely to provide material for class discussion. The authors do not intend to illustrate either effective or ineffective handling of a managerial situation. The authors may have disguised certain names and other identifying information to protect confidentiality.

This publication may not be transmitted, photocopied, digitized or otherwise reproduced in any form or by any means without the permission of the copyright holder. Reproduction of this material is not covered under authorization by any reproduction rights organization. To order copies or request permission to reproduce materials, contact Ivey Publishing, Ivey Business School, Western University, London, Ontario, Canada, N6G 0N1; (t) 519.661.3208; (e) cases@ivey.ca; www.iveycases.com.

Copyright © 2013, Richard Ivey School of Business Foundation   Version: 2013-11-20

One time permission to reproduce granted by Richard Ivey School of Business Foundation on April 22, 2014.

☒ IVEY | Publishing

[1]Industry Canada, "Alta Injection Molding," 2011, www.ic.gc.ca/app/ccc/srch/prfl.do?sbPrtl=&prtl=1&estblmnt No=123456162775&profile=cmpltPrfl&app=sold&lang=eng, accessed December 25, 2012.

Darichuk had a straight-shooting, blue-collar personality. He considered himself a quintessential entrepreneur and a man of the free market. His business models had been built on innovation, quick response and a strong belief that the market knew best. Darichuk's business was not just about making money. He prided himself on helping to build the province's manufacturing sector, and he was committed to creating wealth, jobs and opportunities for the people of Alberta. He strongly believed in the power of the free market to accomplish this and had no sympathy for government handouts or subsidies.

Darichuk wondered whether the bureaucratic mindset of a post-secondary institution would be compatible with a private enterprise's "get-it-done" school of thought. Because private and public sectors had different funding systems and structures, how would these differences affect Alta's bottom line? By being part of this P3 project, he wondered if his business could still maintain its aggressiveness in the marketplace by quickly capitalizing on opportunities as they arose. How would the three players in this P3 project get what they wanted out of the partnership without compromising the goals of the other partners? Were there steps Darichuk could take to ensure the partnership would allow the government and SAIT to achieve their goals without interfering with his business, and vice versa? Darichuk realized that although this P3 project could be the start of a model that could be used across the country for businesses, institutions and government to work together, he did not want to threaten his business's ability to respond quickly to market demands.

THE MANUFACTURING SECTOR IN ALBERTA

The public policy motivation for the P3 project was to help diversify the Alberta economy towards a more manufacturing-based economy. The manufacturing sector of Alberta consisted mainly of petroleum and coal processing, chemical production, forestry, electronics manufacturing and plastics processing. In 2011, the manufacturing industry represented 6.8 per cent of the total employment in Alberta.[2] Compared to the leading manufacturing provinces of Ontario and Quebec, this was quite low. Ontario and Quebec had 14 per cent and 13.5 per cent of total employment in manufacturing, respectively. Overall, however, the Canadian national average was 11.5 per cent.[3] While Alberta led all other western provinces in terms of per capita manufacturing sales,[4] the real backbone of its thriving economy had been based on its lucrative petroleum and gas industries.

A major concern for the government of Alberta was that despite the growth of the oil and gas sectors, the manufacturing industry had seen a decline in the contribution to Alberta's GDP from 2001 to 2011, with total output of goods and services produced dropping from 8.6 per cent to 6.8 per cent of the total economic output. More worrisome than this relative decrease in the manufacturing sector's contribution to the economy were the overall employment statistics in manufacturing. In this rapidly growing province, employment in the manufacturing sector had remained nearly unchanged over the past 10 years. In 2011 there were 141,000 people engaged in manufacturing, compared to 139,800 in 2001. Over this 10-year period, the Alberta manufacturing industry had grown by less than 1 per cent.[5]

---

[2]Government of Alberta, "Industry Profiles," *Manufacturing Industry*, 2010, p. 3, http://eae.alberta.ca/documents/profiles/industry-profile-manufacturing.pdf, accessed January 13, 2013.

[3]Statistics Canada, "Trends in Manufacturing Employment," 2009, 75-001-X, p. 10, www.statcan.gc.ca/pub/75-001-x/2009102/pdf/10788-eng.pdf, accessed January 16, 2013.

[4]Statistics Canada, "Manufacturing Industries," *Canada Yearbook*, 2008, p. 303, www.statcan.gc.ca/pub/11-402-x/2008000/pdf/manufacturing-fabrication-eng.pdf, accessed January 16, 2013.

[5]Government of Alberta, p. 4, http://eae.alberta.ca/documents/profiles/industry-profile-manufacturing.pdf, accessed January 13, 2013.

The reasons for the lack of growth in Alberta's manufacturing sector did not appear to be as straightforward as they were in other parts of North America. Growth in Alberta's manufacturing sector was primarily restrained by the inability of firms to attract qualified employees. Firms often had to forgo potential growth because they were not able to get skilled workers. Thus, Albertans employed in the manufacturing sector were not subject to poor wages but rather received salaries that were higher than the other industrial-focused provinces in Canada (see Exhibit 1).[6] The question was if there was a strong demand for workers, and workers could make more than the national average salaries in the manufacturing industry, then why had the manufacturing industry remained nearly stagnant over the past decade?

The major driver of wages and the employment shortage in Alberta was the oil and gas boom that had been developing around the Alberta oil-sands industry. This industrial sector had more than doubled in size from 2000 to 2010. Next to Saudi Arabia and Venezuela, Alberta had the third largest proven oil reserves in the world, and accounted for 80 per cent of Canada's total natural gas supply.[7] The energy sector contributed nearly 25 per cent of the province's GDP.[8]

In 2012, the average weekly salary for the oil and gas sector was $2,010, which earned some Albertans an annual salary of $104,547.[9] This meant the average oil and gas salary was 65 per cent greater than the average salary a worker in the manufacturing industry could earn. With the incentive to earn a strong income, it was hard to attract Alberta's skilled workers to the manufacturing industry.

From a public policy perspective, the government had been interested in capturing as many of the economic gains as possible from the oil and gas sector and transferring that wealth into the general economy. A white paper published by PricewaterhouseCoopers revealed that within Alberta, approximately one third of the real GDP from the oil sands should flow to industries outside the oil and gas sector over a 20-year period starting in 2000.[10]

To a certain degree, this prediction came true in Alberta, but only for a limited number of industries. The construction industry, for example, witnessed a boom, as spending on housing and infrastructure took place to support the growing energy sector. In addition, many companies in the industrial manufacturing sector that directly supplied oil and gas field equipment in the form of machinery or metal fabrication had also seen significant growth, with employment levels more than doubling since the late 1990s.[11] Unfortunately, the aspiration of using the oil and gas boom to generate success and growth for a broad range of industrial sectors for Alberta had so far been largely unfulfilled.

[6]Statistics Canada, "Employment, Earnings And Hours," *Estimates of Employment and Average Weekly Earnings for All Employees by Industry,* 2012, 72-002-X, p. 92–113, www.statcan.gc.ca/pub/72-002-x/72-002-x2012010-eng. pdf, accessed January 16, 2013.

[7]Government of Alberta, "Oil and Gas," 2012, p. 1, www.albertacanada.com/files/albertacanada/oil-and-gas-profile.pdf, accessed January 13, 2013.

[8]Alberta Economic Development Authority, "The Alberta Economy," *Percentage Distribution of GDP by Industry–2009,* https://aeda.alberta.ca/albertaeconomy/Pages/default.aspx, accessed January 16, 2013.

[9]Statistics Canada, "Employment, Earnings and Hours," *Estimates of Employment and Average Weekly Earnings for All Employees by Industry–Alberta,* 2012, 72-002-X, p. 113, www.statcan.gc.ca/pub/72-002-x/72-002-x2012010-eng.pdf, accessed January 17, 2013.

[10]PricewaterhouseCoopers, "Alberta Industry Sector Performance and Prospects," *Industry Performance and Drivers,* 2009, p. 21, www.albertacanada.com/ABIndustrySector.pdf, accessed December 21, 2012.

[11]PricewaterhouseCoopers, "Alberta Industry Sector Performance and Prospects," *Oil Patch Activity Spills Over to Other Sectors,* 2009, p. 11, www.albertacanada.com/ABIndustrySector.pdf, accessed December 21, 2012.

THE ROOT CAUSE

The most significant problem facing the manufacturing sector in particular, and many other sectors in general, was the lack of skilled labour. The problem, however, went beyond a simple lack of employable people. The population of Alberta was growing, but not necessarily in a way that could supply sectors demanding skilled labour.

The education and training sector was not supplying the market with enough new, locally educated graduates. Alberta was the only province in Canada that saw a decline in enrollment in post-secondary participation over the past decade.[12] Alberta students leaving high school could choose jobs that earned them an immediate strong income rather than spending long periods of time in academic institutions or apprenticeship programs that would help them work towards building a sustainable long-term career.

In addition, until recently, federal immigration policies did not favour skilled labourers that were in immediate demand in the Alberta economy. Instead, the system was more geared to family sponsorship or to attracting independently wealthy individuals. However, recent changes in the federal immigration system allowed some businesses to sponsor skilled individuals.[13]

THE REAL DOWNSIDE

With Alberta's dependence on the oil and gas industry, the economic success of Alberta was influenced by fluctuations in oil prices and some changes in natural gas prices. While many of the current oil and gas projects were long term and not immediately affected by the price of oil, government tax revenue was directly tied to oil prices. Exhibit 2 demonstrates fluctuations in the price of oil from 2008 to 2012. Given the revenue variability of the province's key economic driver, the government of Alberta had been under considerable pressure to create a strategy that could diversify the province's economy and encourage more sustainable methods of growth.[14]

Yet a fundamental part of Alberta's strategic puzzle had been overlooked. The province risked its long-term capability of sustaining a strong economy because it was so dependent on natural resources. The province suffered from what is often called the Dutch disease. "This Dutch disease phenomenon might be seen as one particular mechanism explaining the so-called natural resource curse, i.e., the observation that countries [or provinces] rich in natural resources tend to exhibit poor performance in terms of economic development."[15]

Without the capability of developing a more diverse economy, many of the value-added components of the oil and gas industry had to be exported, which accounted for 70 per cent of Alberta's total exports.[16] The truth about Alberta's productive oil and gas sector was that the profits from this industry were often not reinvested to further develop the

[12]PricewaterhouseCoopers, "Alberta Industry Sector Performance and Prospects," *Underscoring the Need to Invest in Innovation*, 2009, p. 15, www.albertacanada.com/ABIndustrySector.pdf, accessed December 21, 2012.

[13]Government of Canada, "Citizenship and Immigration Canada," *Investors, Entrepreneurs and Self-Employed Persons*, 2010, www.cic.gc.ca/english/immigrate/business/index.asp, accessed January 22, 2013.

[14]Sustainable Prosperity, "Alberta well-advised to pursue economic diversification," 2011, www.sustainable-prosperity.ca/article1890, accessed April 8, 2013.

[15]M. Beine, C.S. Bos and S. Coulombe, "Does the Canadian Economy Suffer from Dutch Disease?" *Resource & Energy Economics*, 34(4), 2012, p. 469.

[16]Government of Alberta, "Industry And Economy," *Energy*, 2012, http://alberta.ca/industryandeconomy.cfm, accessed January 16, 2013.

Province.[17] Instead, other regions and countries were acquiring Alberta's energy and investing in the development of their own economies.

The solutions that were needed to keep the cash-cow energy sector sustainable could not be addressed because of a lack in supporting industries. For Alberta's economy to be more diversified, it had to be innovative and forward-looking. This was extremely challenging to accomplish without an innovative manufacturing sector.[18]

Alison Redford, the premier of Alberta, stated, "It's investing in our post-secondary institutions in a different way, attracting researchers from across the country and around the world, that will really allow us to use the financial resources that we have to accelerate Alberta to a much more technologically and knowledge-based economy than we have ever been before."[19]

FOSTERING INNOVATIVE MANUFACTURING

Exhibit 3 shows the R&D intensiveness of Alberta's manufacturing sectors. The government of Alberta believed that the solution to sustainable homegrown industrial growth and diversification was to find a way to direct the profits from the oil and gas cash-cow industry towards more R&D-intensive industries. These could include petroleum and coal processing, chemical manufacturing, high-tech plastics and rubber products, and machinery or electronics manufacturing. In fact, the government believed that the Alberta oil-sands industry and the entire accompanying infrastructure could serve as an ideal customer for innovative and R&D-intensive firms in these industries.[20] The key was to get them to grow.

Outside of the oil and gas industry, Alberta did not have a strong R&D mentality. As a percentage of GDP, businesses in Alberta were well below the national average in terms of R&D spending and were ranked last among the four largest provinces in terms of such R&D activities.[21] In particular, the oil and gas industry had been hungry for supporting industries to offer solutions that could help improve their exploration processes in a more efficient and sustainable fashion.[22]

CURRENT APPROACH OF THE GOVERNMENT OF ALBERTA

Fostering investment in more R&D-intensive industries was not a new challenge for the government of Alberta. Over the past several decades, the government had committed considerable resources to this end. When business had not initiated R&D activities, the

[17]J. Byrne, "The World Is Leaving Canada's Carbon Economy Behind," *IPolitics Insight*, 2013, www.ipolitics.ca/2013/03/14/the-world-is-leaving-canadas-carbon-economy-behind/, accessed January 16, 2013.

[18]Canadian Manufacturers & Exporters. "Manufacturing in Alberta," 2012, www.albertacanada.com/files/albertacanada/AIS-Neil-Kaarsemaker.pdf, accessed January 16, 2013.

[19]Canadian Broadcasting Corporation, "Alison Redford's Budget Strategy" [video file], www.cbc.ca/player/News/ID/2329516845/, accessed January 27, 2013.

[20]Government of Alberta, "Policies and Regulations," 2013, http://albertacanada.com/business/industries/rpb-policies-and-regulations.aspx, accessed January 16, 2013.

[21]PricewaterhouseCoopers, "Alberta Industry Sector Performance and Prospects," *Underscoring the Need to Invest in Innovation*, 2009, p. 15, www.albertacanada.com/ABIndustrySector.pdf, accessed December 21, 2012.

[22]Government of Alberta, "Oil and Gas," 2012, p. 2, www.albertacanada.com/files/albertacanada/oil-and-gas-profile.pdf, accessed January 14, 2013.

government initiated its own R&D-intensive ventures. For instance, the government of Alberta funded SMART Technologies through the Alberta Innovates initiative. This company was known for its SMART Board, an interactive whiteboard that could be used in various educational or collaborative environments. SMART Board had also been showcased in television programs such as *The West Wing* and *CSI*.[23]

The government also tried to incentivize private firms to invest more in R&D by providing a 10 per cent provincial R&D tax credit. For several reasons, however, this credit did not have much impact. First, the policies associated with the R&D tax credit made it quite challenging for businesses to receive when the company was involved in a partnership with a firm outside of Alberta.[24] In addition, the tax credit, when used in combination with the Federal Investment Tax credit, was substantially reduced.[25]

As another incentive, the government had set up the Alberta Enterprise Corporation. This government agency had been endowed with $100 million in venture capital to help invest in firms that could potentially bring new technology to commercialization sooner.[26] The provincial government's current approach had been to make capital readily available for Albertan companies so that they could become innovative.

Over the past few years, it became clearer that investing in government-led businesses and providing tax credits and venture capital—in a province "swimming" in oil money—was not solving the fundamental problem: something was holding back innovation in the manufacturing sector. This fundamental problem was the systemic lack of skilled labour available for this sector. Without people who were willing to participate, there could be no innovative industries.

ADDRESSING THE PROBLEM

For the past two decades, the government of Canada has developed collaborative partnerships between federal or provincial government bodies and private enterprises to develop the country's labour force. A federal government report suggested that in order for these projects to be successful, the government must:

- change their current thinking so that the collaborative partnerships would be planned and carried out with a more "horizontal" mindset;

- engage business owners and organizations with a concrete value proposition to encourage their participation; and,

- establish fundamental management practices and the appropriate culture within the public sector, which would enable the collaborative partnership to flourish.[27]

---

[23]Alberta Innovates, "Calgary's SMART Technologies: An Industry Game-Changer," 2010, www.industrymailout .com/Industry/LandingPage.aspx?id=573949&p=1, accessed January 23, 2013.

[24]Alberta Chamber of Commerce, "Improving Alberta's Research and Development Tax Credit," *Partnerships as a Catalyst R&D Investment and Commercialization*, p. 2, www.abchamber.ca/wp-content/uploads/2012/02/Improving Alberta R D tax credit.pdf, accessed January 17, 2013.

[25]Alberta Chamber of Commerce, "Improving Alberta's Research and Development Tax Credit," *Investment Tax Credit Reform*, p. 1, www.abchamber.ca/wp-content/uploads/2012/02/Improving Alberta R D tax credit.pdf, accessed January 17, 2013.

[26]PricewaterhouseCoopers, "Alberta Industry Sector Performance and Prospects," *Executive Summary*, 2009, p. i, www.albertacanada.com/ABIndustrySector.pdf, accessed December 21st,2013.

[27]J. Armstrong and D. Lenihan, "From Controlling to Collaborating: When Governments Want to Be Partners," *New Directions–Number 3*. The Institute of Public Administration of Canada. 1999, p. 10.

Traditionally, there were three core forms of private-public partnerships.[28] The first was via client-contractor partnerships wherein the government established a set of tasks it wanted performed and then paid the partner to complete such items. Only some components of a genuine partnership emerged with this approach, such as sharing of rewards or information and perhaps some of the risk; however, power or decision-making authority was not shared.

Intergovernmental partnerships were another form of collaborative effort; they included some form of cost sharing. In most cases, federal or provincial governments defined an outline and funding for a given project. The other partner then undertook the design and delivery of the specific program. This type of arrangement was closer to a genuine partnership because there was some shared gain, risk and decision-making.

The third form of private-public partnership which could be established was through the use of collaborative partnerships. In this case, both parties aimed more at working together. The downside to this approach however, was that roles and responsibilities were often less clear because an arrangement would go beyond the contractual model, as some situations required higher levels of collaborative planning and shared decision-making.

P3 partnerships tend to be less at arm's length than traditional partnerships, which are most often based on defined contracts for the delivery of goods or services. Government-based partnerships tend to require shared decision-making, where "the government and its partner negotiate a framework of outcomes, principles, objectives and indicators . . . . The flexibility built into these partnerships amounts to a delegation of some decision-making authority to non-governmental actors. Exactly how much, of course, depended on the agreement."[29]

PRIVATE SECTOR INFLUENCES[30]

A private-public partnership is a formal agreement (or set of agreements) for the government agencies and private firms or organizations to work together to promote a mutually beneficial outcome. They demand a different kind of management approach, one based on trust, consensus building and conflict resolution, as opposed to command and control.

From the private sector's perspective, a collaborative partnership called for long-term commitment from senior decision-making staff. Having this type of involvement ensured the stability of the partnership. However, the success of public partnerships required an equal effort from both parties. Private partners were often resistant to getting involved in such agreements because government funding and commitment could change suddenly with political fortune or the immediate demands of the voting public. Private partners found it hard to trust that government agencies would support the partnership over the long term. "This is not a result of bad relations between individuals at the community or regional level but of bad practices within the public sector as a result of changing senior officials and ministers, changing delivery methods, management styles, and priorities."

A critical first step in ensuring a collaborative partnership's success consisted of "setting strategic objectives. For collaborative partnerships to work, multiple, often-competing objectives and priorities need to be balanced. Effective collaborative partnerships require a mechanism for collaborative planning." In order to accomplish these objectives, partners must engage in a collaborative mindset that is often foreign to both the public and private

---

[28]Ibid. pp. 14–15.

[29]Ibid. pp. 54–55.

[30]All quotes in this section are from Armstrong and Lenihan, 1999.

partners. Inter-organizational communication, consensus building, and the delegation of accountability and responsibility are key to meeting strategic objectives. These take time and require considerable planning. As noted by the Institute of Public Administration of Canada:

> A more collaborative outlook thus required a major shift in the traditional culture of the public sector, from its role as unquestioned monopoly to a more open team of diverse players, from a provider focus to a client focus, from a closed system with clear boundaries to a borderless network.[31] In essence, a more decentralized approach would allow for more of a bottom-up influence from front-line service providers, citizens or stakeholder groups.

A NEW SOLUTION

The province of Alberta, in cooperation with the government of Canada, had begun to seek solutions to Alberta's labour shortage. Part of that solution was to foster homegrown talent that could become the next generation of Alberta innovators. Darichuk and his sons' highly innovative composite plastic business offered a potential starting point.

Advances in the composite plastics industry have led to innovative plastic products that have been displacing applications traditionally dominated by metal and glass. The driving technology in this industry was the evolution of polymers, a primary chemical input in plastic products, into engineered resins, a higher-performing type of polymer that increased a product's strength and made it lighter in weight.[32] Darichuk was in the composite plastic business and was using this technology to create some of the most innovative products in the province. Teaming up with Alta offered the government a potential first step to fostering a homegrown industrial base.

ALTA

Darichuk became involved in the plastics industry in 1994, and crafted a growth-orientated strategy right from the start. He was proud to say, "Every time we get an extra dollar in this place, we spend it on a new machine." Darichuk's plastic mold injection equipment was housed in a 12,000-square foot plant in the northeast part of Calgary. Darichuk had involved all four of his sons in his businesses, and they all shared the same mindset of embracing innovation and providing prompt service. His sons Brett and Joel began to oversee Alta's daily operations as Darichuk senior began to transition into retirement.

Alta had the most advanced computer-aided design (CAD) program in western Canada, which was bought from a software company in Germany. This software not only allowed them to develop plastic injection mold designs but also put a heavy emphasis on detailed flow analyses for maximum efficiencies in production situations. Once a suitable 3D design had been developed using the CAD software, Alta machined a plastic-composite model. To create any product, be it a plastic golf tee or a high-tech piece of military equipment, a specific mold made of steel needed to be designed by Alta's computer engineers and machined by Alta's skilled machinists.

Once a successful mold had been created, it was set into a plastic injection machine, and a composite plastic product was produced. Runs varied from a few prototypes (for

---

[31]Ibid. p. 24.

[32]Industry Canada, "Industry Profile for the Canadian Plastic Products Industry," p. 1, www.ic.gc.ca/eic/site/plastics-plastiques.nsf/eng/pl01383.html, accessed January 13, 2013.

initial marketing and test purposes) to the mass production of millions of items. Alta offered its clients a variety of resins used in plastic mold injection, such as nylon, polystyrene, urethane, thermoplastic polyurethane (TPU), polypropylene, high-density polyethylene (HDPE) and low-density polyethylene (LDPE), which were added to glass fiber metals or nanofibers for enhanced properties in the application. These newly engineered resins allowed innovators to resolve industry problems from a completely new perspective.

ALTA'S VALUE PROPOSITION

Alta generated revenue throughout the value chain. A fully funded project might yield Alta project-based revenue for their services. However, not all clients had the ability to fund their own projects, so Alta offered shared-ownership agreements on the patents and injection molds, with the financial aid of angel investors. By participating in a joint-ownership agreement, Alta generated long-term profits from successfully developed projects. Exhibit 4 illustrates the percentage of Alta's revenue that was generated either through royalties or one-off, small-batch production.

Since founding his first company, Darichuk had focused on serving the needs of local clients first and foremost. Alta had developed a start to finish production chain facility, which allowed local businesses and individuals to take new and innovative products to market. By focusing on local clients, Alta slowly began building an international reputation. Firms from all over the world sought out Alta's fully integrated design and production facilities.

Since there were very few other competing firms in Alberta, the market forced Alta to do everything in house. "If we didn't make the mold we lost control, so we had to go into the steel business. Once we were making the mold then we had to get into the design business and then once we went through that, we went into the prototype business. It wasn't us pushing into the market, the market was pulling us."[33]

Except for the creation of a basic website, Darichuk had never spent a dollar on marketing. However, demand for Alta's expertise had grown to such an extent that it had developed three significant categories of clients. Darichuk referred to the first group as the multinational enterprise (MNE) corporate sector. These were clients like General Dynamics, Meggitt, Flexpipe, 3M, Plastifab, Slumberger, Honeywell and TransCanada. These large multinational corporations sought out Alta's highly innovative in-house services. There were very few other players who had start to finish capabilities to solve problems using state-of-the-art plastic injection molding with the new materials now entering the manufacturing arena. For example, TransCanada requested that Alta develop a plastic-composite alternative for pipeline protection. This type of project had great potential for Alta and the Alberta economy.

The second group of clients was the small corporate sector. Darichuk referred to this category as the situational inventors that typically work for a company: "they see a solution to a problem that their industry faces." A good example is a 23-year-old welder who was part of a SAIT program in Calgary. In the wintertime, this tradesman broke half a dozen welding handles per week. When he realized that this was normal in the industry, he became irritated by unnecessary material expenses, and approached Brett Darichuk. After exchanging thoughts and ideas about the product, they eventually created a more durable and weather-resistant welding handle. The welder was able to patent the invention and market it. He has since gone on to invent and market several other welding-related products, with a major international distributor carrying them.

---

[33]Gerry Darichuk (President of Alta Mold Injection) in discussion with the author, December 17, 2012.

The third category of clients consisted of the 400 or so individuals that approached Alta every year and sought help in bringing an idea from concept to commercialization.[34] This group was comprised of people from every walk of life with the idea that they think would solve a need in the market. Most of the ideas brought to Alta did not amount to much; the Darichuks referred to these ideas as "brain hiccups" because they had very little commercial viability. However, 5 to 10 per cent were exceptional and went on to commercialization. Ideas for Alta ranged from dental appliances to cattle prods, radio-frequency identification (RFID) cow tags, oil valve devices, medical devices and many more that were being used in the market place.

THE TURNKEY APPROACH TO INNOVATION

Darichuk and his sons strove to make Alta a source of "Turnkey Innovation." This meant that the company was able to walk anyone through the entire innovation process and no client needed to leave Alta's facilities during the process. This included all printed packaging the retailers demanded when carrying the products within their distribution chain. To accomplish this, Alta had created its seven-step product-development model (see Exhibit 5). All products developed at Alta went through this seven-step series to ensure success. As Darichuk argued, "If you're going to take an invention from conception to commercialization, you got to go through all these phases. If they leave for any one of them, they may never come back."[35]

This seven-step turnkey approach to innovation had allowed Alta to produce more commercially viable patents than the University of Calgary, University of Alberta, SAIT and its equivalent institution in Edmonton (NAIT, the Northern Alberta Institute of Technology) combined. In February 2012, this small Alberta company caught the eye of the provincial and federal government as they were looking for a new solution to help diversify Alberta's manufacturing sector. Using federal money and a provincially funded education institute, SAIT, the governments approached Alta to join them in partnership.

SAIT POLYTECHNIC

For many years, Darichuk had been involved with Rotary International, a volunteer-based organization.[36] Through his local club, Darichuk met Irene Lewis, President of SAIT. When Darichuk was approached by the federal government and asked to consider the possibility of partnering with SAIT, Darichuk felt confident and comfortable with Lewis as the other decision-maker involved in this project. In 2010 and 2012, Lewis was nominated for the Top 100 of Canada's Most Powerful Women.[37]

In 2006, Lewis was faced with the task of developing a new 10-year plan for SAIT. The outcome of the plan was to shape SAIT into a competitive technical institute guided by three priorities: to act as a leader in learning, to have an entrepreneurial outlook, and to provide a world-class service culture. As an institution that had over 77 certificate programs, two degree programs, and 2,300 faculty and staff that provided training to more than

---

[34]Ibid.

[35]Ibid.

[36]Rotary International, "About Us," 2013, www.rotary.org/en/AboutUs/Pages/ridefault.aspx, accessed January 16, 2013.

[37]SAIT Polytechnic, "SAIT's President One of Canada's Most Powerful Women," www.sait.ca/about-sait/news/news/2012-12-6-saits-president-one-of-canadas-most-powerful-women.php, accessed December 6, 2012.

71,000 students every year,[38] Lewis believed these priorities provided graduates with a rich education that would equip them with the necessary skills to solve the problems of the future. Lewis saw this opportunity to partner with Alta as a way to partially fulfill this new mission and provide an educational experience at SAIT that was distinct from traditional models.

The connection between Alta and SAIT was actually part of a longer relationship between the two organizations that they had had for over a decade. Through the Applied Research and Innovative Services department, students were introduced to a real manufacturing setting. For the past several years, students enrolled in this faculty had been part of the development process of innovation. Through the goodwill between Lewis and Darichuk, students visited Alta on a field trip. This new project would make the experience a much more significant part of their academic training. Students and faculty would have greater, long-term exposure to Alta's innovation process, and consequently a deeper commitment.

With access to a company that could not be found anywhere else in SAIT's vicinity, students could develop their ideas and bring them into Alta's innovation process, which Darichuk referred to as the "dream weaver." Alta consulted with SAIT students and challenged their imaginations as Alta shared its industrial experience and knowledge. For instance, SAIT students developed a radio-frequency identification tag (RFID). It was enclosed in a plastic casing that was designed with Alta. It could be attached to the ears of cows so ranchers or farmers could easily track their herds.[39] SAIT students enrolled in one of the Applied Research and Innovative Services programs would undoubtedly receive a rich education complemented by the chance to work with industry experts in Alta.

FEDERAL FUNDING

This unique opportunity to expand one of SAIT's programs was primarily motivated by a $3.5 million dollar investment for SAIT to purchase equipment that would remain in Alta's facility. The federal investment was on behalf of the Western Economic Diversification Canada (WD), a department within the Canadian government. The WD was founded in 1987 with a mandate to support the development and diversification of the economy of western Canada. Overall, the WD envisioned itself as a leader in creating a more diversified western Canadian economy that had strong, competitive, innovative business communities.[40]

Western Economic Diversification Canada provided services for business, not-for-profit organizations, academic/research projects and communities, and was a natural champion of private-public partnerships.[41] Universities and other post-secondary institutions, research institutes, industry associations and other not-for-profit organizations were all eligible to apply for WD's direct agreement programs.[42]

---

[38]SAIT Polytechnic, "About SAIT," 2012-12-20, www.sait.ca/about-sait.php#What%20is%20Polytechnic%20 Education?,

[39]Innovation in Action, "RFID Project Prep," 2012, www.industrymailout.com/Industry/LandingPage .aspx?id=902428&p=1, accessed December 23, 2013.

[40]Western Economic Diversification Canada, "The Department," 2012, www.wd.gc.ca/eng/36.asp, accessed December 21, 2012.

[41]Western Economic Diversification Canada, "Services," 2011, www.wd.gc.ca/eng/37.asp, accessed December 21, 2012.

[42]Western Economic Diversification Canada, "Western Economic Diversification Canada Programs," 2012, www.wd.gc.ca/eng/16.asp, accessed November 11, 2012.

Funding from the WD also sought to accomplish larger goals such as increasing trade and export opportunities resulting from increased participation in domestic and international markets. In addition, WD tried to facilitate the commercialization of technologies, in an attempt to strengthen community innovation and capacity-building by bringing people, communities, ideas and resources together.[43]

THE ALTA & SAIT P3

The P3 would include $3.5 million worth of funding to allow SAIT to purchase new state-of-the-art manufacturing equipment. Alta would have to front some capital in order to have co-ownership of the equipment. Once the equipment was acquired, the machinery would be housed in Alta's production facility. Alta would have access to the equipment, while SAIT students would gain exposure to plastic-manufacturing processes and have the opportunity to be connected to company leaders and distribution channels through Alta's large network.

Private-public partnerships had the potential to create something that otherwise would be beyond the reach of a private enterprise or be subject to slow implementation due to the layers of bureaucracy if handled solely by a government institution. However, Darichuk understood that these partnerships were not without complications and risks. One of the most significant obstacles was the difference in mindsets that existed between government, public institutions and private industry. For instance, the primary goal of a private enterprise was to earn profits in both the short term and long term. A publically funded academic institution, on the other hand, was concerned about funding, student enrollment and success, and faculty research outcomes.

Darichuk had established Alta to meet the needs of local clients. As a business owner, Darichuk did not want to compromise his ability to meet demand, and potentially the reputation of his business, if SAIT expected to use the equipment when it was most convenient for them. Darichuk had created a successful private enterprise because he recognized that a business required not only a responsive decision-making process in order to adapt to client needs and emerging industry trends, but also the freedom to do so.

Darichuk was concerned about whether this P3 would ultimately harm his businesses viability both in the short and long term. Darichuk reaffirmed his belief that when businesses received government aid, they were no longer operating as an autonomous entity, but rather as a guided agent on behalf of the government. Government or public institutions in this case were concerned with meeting their own interests, which were derived from a completely different set of metrics. For government and public institutions, their objective was to provide a solution, in the short-term, that satisfied stakeholders.

Although this P3 partnership involved Alta, SAIT, the government of Alberta and the government of Canada, there were also different stakeholders to consider. While less directly involved, the broader Alberta business community and the taxpayers were also significant stakeholders. If this P3 proved to be successful, it could provide a template for other Alberta-based business to collaborate with publically funded post-secondary institutions.

This could prove advantageous to businesses that were willing to partner with the public sector, because not only would their own business benefit from the increase in

[43]Western Economic Diversification Canada, "Western Diversification Program," 2012, www.wd.gc.ca/eng/301. asp, accessed November 28, 2012.

public exposure, they would also be seen as leaders in diversifying Alberta's economy. For taxpayers, this P3 and potentially others of the same nature would provide tangible evidence of public funds that created favourable, close-to-home returns. However, regardless of the potential benefits that this 3P could bring to Alberta's greater business environment, Darichuk questioned if it was Alta's responsibility to be the type of business that forged the way for others.

It was also clear to Darichuk that profit was not the main motive for publically funded institutions. Rather, they were concerned with creating programs for students and research opportunities for faculty. Successful students and research output were the measures of success. Private industry, on the other hand, was concerned with profits, market share and customer satisfaction to ensure long-term sustainable growth. If Darichuk entered this P3, would Alta still be able to act as a business, or would it encounter new constraints that otherwise would not be presented if he did not participate in the P3?

From a government perspective, the P3 would aid in the diversification of Alberta's economy. For SAIT, the P3 provided the institution with a unique competitive advantage over other technical post-secondary institutions because of the potentially close access to state-of-the-art-machinery and industry expertise. The faculty and graduates of this program could become the next generation of inventors, entrepreneurs and even investors that Alta needed in order to continue to drive its business.

Darichuk and his sons had established a profitable business that revolved around a seven-step approach to innovation that embraced a turnkey approach. In essence, this process distinguished Alta from its competitors. Could Alta's ability to carry out the seven-step process be compromised if machines started to be occupied by SAIT students?

Darichuk wondered what steps he could take if he entered into the P3 to ensure his business could continue to operate as a private enterprise while SAIT, and the provincial government, achieved their goals. "Our rewarding structures are very much different, but can we meld the agendas to a common cause?"

Since the proposed P3 stated that Alta would house the equipment for which SAIT received funding, what steps would Darichuk have to consider to ensure that if a divorce was needed, it could occur smoothly? How could he ensure that the machinery in his factory was put to the most efficient uses and not subjected to the pet projects of SAIT faculty members? As these thoughts came to mind, Darichuk wondered if it was even worth the time, effort and risk to be part of this P3 in the first place.

As a man that believed strongly in the power of the free market and had experienced its wrath and rewards for many years, Darichuk was still very unsure about committing to such a non-traditional business partnership. Although he was comforted in knowing that Lewis, his long-time acquaintance, would be the point of contact for SAIT, her role in the partnership was not indefinite. Like all leadership roles, there would come a time for the current leader to step down and pass the decisions on to the next suitable candidate. It was not only Lewis's limited time in this proposed partnership that Darichuk was concerned with, it was also his own. If Darichuk made this sort of commitment, it would be his sons that would have to handle the future challenges, as well as enjoy potential rewards. From a fundamental level, Darichuk evaluated this partnership on the premise that reward had to outweigh costs; however, this P3 was merely in the proposal stages, and it would take a few years for all the intricacies to emerge.

However, as a shrewd businessman, Darichuk could also see that if P3s grew, his firm stood to gain from localizing the returns on the natural resources extracted from the land. His company and his approach to innovation could become a driving force in this capital-rich province.

EXHIBIT 1: 2012 Manufacturing Industry Average Salaries

	Average Weekly Wage	Average Annual Wage
Canada	$ 1,021.28	$ 53,106.56
Alberta	$ 1,213.32	$63,092.64
Ontario	$1,048.66	$54,530.32
Quebec	$ 951.55	$49,480.60

Source: Statistics Canada, "Employment, Earnings And Hours," *Estimates of employment and average weekly earnings for all employees by industry,* 2012, 72-002-X, pp. 92–113, www.statcan.gc.ca/pub/72-002-x/72-002-x2012010-eng.pdf, accessed January 16, 2013.

EXHIBIT 2: 2008–2012 Crude Oil Prices (US$)

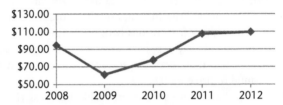

Source: Figures for 2008 to 2012 from Organization of the Petroleum Exporting Countries website, www.opec.org/opec_web/en/data_graphs/40.htm, *accessed February 18, 2013.*

EXHIBIT 3: Subsectors of Alberta's Manufacturing Industry

Column A (*Less R&D-Intensive*)	Column B (*More R&D-Intensive*)
Food	Petroleum & Coal Products
Beverage & Tobacco Products	Chemicals
Textiles	Plastics & Rubber Products
Wood Products	Non-metallic Mineral Products
Paper	Fabricated Metal Products
Printing & Related Activities	Machinery
Furniture & Related Products	Computer & Electronics
	Electrical Appliances & Components
	Transportation Equipment

Source: Adapted from Statistics Canada, "Manufacturing Sales, By Subsector, By Province and Territory (Monthly)," Canada, 2012, www.statcan.gc.ca/tables-tableaux/sum-som/l01/cst01/manuf32n-eng.htm, accessed February 13, 2013.

EXHIBIT 4: Percentage of Total Revenue Derived From Clientele Types

Percentage of Total Revenue Derived from Clients

Client	Royalties	One-Offs
Corporate Sector (MNEs)	60%	30%
Small Corporate Sector	30%	30%
Individuals	10%	40%

Source: Gerry Darichuk (President of Alta Mold Injection) in discussion with the author, December 17, 2012.

EXHIBIT 5: Alta's Seven-Step Product Development Model

1. The Idea	The company or individual has thought of a concept to solve a problem or improve a process, so they approach Alta for solutions. The client must have identified a real market for the product and be able to demonstrate an ability to bring the product to market. Clients must also be able to demonstrate that they have secured the funding for the project. While generally this portion is the sole responsibility of the client, Alta has used it resources and network to help clients secure funding or provided them with potential market leads.
2. Drawing	Using a state-of-the-art CAD program, a 3D illustration of the concept is developed together with the client's input. "First you get a brain idea. Next you get it drawn out; then you have to go to a 3D drawing." With the 3D image created, Alta can start researching similar patents to find out if the concept has already been invented.
3. The Prototype	A physical representation of what the client envisioned is created, and then adjustments are made to its dimensions and looks. "The prototype is only good as a dimensional vision; it has no structural integrity with the environment." This is an iterative process that is often repeated several times before agreement is reached with the client on the final prototype. The goal is to match the client's needs and desires with a product that will be efficient to manufacture. Often, small design changes considerably decrease manufacturing expenses.
4. Testing	Very small batches of the product are produced using different combinations of composite plastics. The goal is to find the materials that will allow the product to stand up to the needs of the client. The product is tested for its ability to withstand different torsion, tension and compression loads, as well its resistance to temperature variations, and chemicals to which it will be exposed. Permeability may also be tested. Testing is a repetitive process, as fixing one problem may cause another. Once again, the goal is to use the most efficient material combinations that will satisfy the client's needs.
5. Product Combinations	Based on the test results, Alta creates up to 10 variations of the same product but with different technical characteristics, at which point, the client takes the products and tests them in their field.
6. Product Evaluation	Testing the product in its intended environment often leads to flaws that were not previously considered. The product is then tweaked further and re-tested in its intended environment until a satisfactory result can be achieved.
7. Production	Once the product can withstand its environmental conditions, Alta builds a final production mold, and production commences on the product. Alta's facilities handle relatively small production runs as well as mass-production runs of a product.

Source: Gerry Darichuk (President of Alta Mold Injection) in discussion with the author, December 17, 2012.

CASE

38

IMAX: Larger Than Life[1]

In Daytona, Florida, John watched a racecar going at more than 100 miles per hour crash into a concrete barrier. John ducked to escape the debris that appeared to be flying straight at him. A few moments later John was virtually within a racecar, next to the driver, zooming at more than 120 miles per hour around the racetrack. For the next half an hour, John experienced in three dimensions and on a larger-than-life scale crashing cars, dizzying turns, efficient pit crews, shining metal, burning rubber, swirling gas fumes and screaming fans. Finally, as the overhead lights at the theater gradually lit up, the audience sitting around John started applauding. John had just witnessed a screening of the IMAX movie *NASCAR*.

NASCAR set a box-office record as an original IMAX 3D film with the highest grossing opening weekend and the highest per-screen average. At $21,579, *NASCAR's* per-screen average was higher than that of the weekend's top 10 films.[2] Reports of *NASCAR's* box-office success would have surely pleased Richard Gelfond and Bradley Wechsler, the co-CEOs of IMAX Corporation.

IVEY | Publishing

Anil Nair wrote this case solely to provide material for class discussion. The author does not intend to illustrate either effective or ineffective handling of a managerial situation. The author may have disguised certain names and other identifying information to protect confidentiality.

Richard Ivey School of Business Foundation prohibits any form of reproduction, storage or transmission without its written permission. Reproduction of this material is not covered under authorization by any reproduction rights organization. To order copies or request permission to reproduce materials, contact Ivey Publishing, Richard Ivey School of Business Foundation, The University of Western Ontario, London, Ontario, Canada, N6A 3K7; phone (519) 661-3208; fax (519) 661-3882; e-mail cases@ivey.uwo.ca.

Copyright © 2009, Richard Ivey School of Business Foundation · · · · · · · · · · · Version: 2011-09-21

One time permission to reproduce granted by Richard Ivey School of Business Foundation on April 22, 2014.

---

[1]This case has been written on the basis of published sources only. Consequently, the interpretation and perspectives presented in this case are not necessarily those of IMAX or any of its employees.

[2]IMAX press release, March 14, 2004.

INTRODUCTION

Gelfond and Wechsler had bought IMAX along with Wasserstein Perella Partners from the original owners in 1994 for $80 million. They took it public the same year to raise capital to fund IMAX's growth. For investors in IMAX, the years since then had been like a ride on a rollercoaster in the IMAX film *Thrill Ride:* exciting peaks when movies achieved commercial and critical acclaim, and scary drops when analysts questioned whether a niche player such as IMAX would be able to achieve consistent growth or even survive.

NASCAR's success at the box office was evidence that the co-CEOs' efforts to reach a new audience–distinct from those typically attracted to IMAX's educational documentaries–might work. Another movie that was indicative of IMAX's emerging strategy was *The Polar Express. The Polar Express* was the first time a Hollywood movie would be released simultaneously in commercial multiplexes and IMAX theaters. *NASCAR* and *The Polar Express* were symbolic of the direction in which Gelfond and Wechsler had pushed the company to achieve faster growth and higher margins. The two-pronged strategy involved expanding the reach of IMAX by (a) going beyond its cloistered museum environments into multiplexes and (b) presenting Hollywood films in IMAX format.

Despite the success of *NASCAR* and *The Polar Express*, IMAX faced several questions about its future:

- Could IMAX thrive as a niche player that made large format films and systems?

- Would increasing the number of Hollywood movies released in IMAX format save the firm or dilute the IMAX brand?

- Should Hollywood movies be released simultaneously in regular and large format?

THE BACKGROUND SCORE

Since the first moving images flickered in a dark theater, movies have captivated audiences around the world. About the time that people were getting familiar with programming their VCRs and learning to enjoy movies on the small television screen, a small group of people was developing a technology to project movies on giant screens. The idea for IMAX originated in 1967 when the success of a multi-screen theater system at the Montreal Expo led filmmakers Graeme Ferguson, Robert Kerr and Roman Kroitor to create a large format movie system. IMAX was founded as the only company in the world that was involved in all aspects of large format films. The first IMAX film premiered in 1970 at the Fuji Pavilion in Osaka, Japan.

IMAX was listed in the NASDAQ exchange in 1994 and achieved a market capitalization of $196 million in the first year itself.[3] As of December 12, 2008, market capitalization was down to $125 million. There were about 295 theaters showing IMAX movies in 40 countries, with almost 60 per cent of the theaters in North America.[4] Almost 50 per cent of the theaters were located in museums, aquariums, zoos and other institutions, and about the same percentage had the IMAX 3D technology. The IMAX movie library at the end of 2007 stood at 226 films; some produced by IMAX, many others produced by independent filmmakers or studios such as Time-Warner. In 2007/2008, some of the well-known films to be released in IMAX included *Harry Potter and the Order of the Phoenix, Shine a Light*–a film about the Rolling Stones by the famous film director Martin Scorcese–and *The Spiderwick Chronicles*.

---

[3]S. N. Chakravarty, "A really big show," *Institutional Investor*, 35:10, October 2002, p. 20.

[4]Hoover's, www.Hoovers.com.

THE IMAX STORY

Scope of IMAX

The company's main sources of revenues were long-term theater system lease and maintenance agreements, film production and distribution, and theater operations. Given its scope of operations, IMAX could be considered a part of three different industries: Photographic Equipment and Supplies (SIC code 3861), Motion Picture and Video Tape Production (SIC code 7812), and Motion Picture and Video Distribution (SIC code 7822). IMAX was a relatively small firm compared to a rival studio such as Disney/Pixar or a theater chain such as Regal Entertainment.

In 2007, it generated $59.12 million (51.04 per cent of total revenue) from IMAX systems sales, $36.57 million (31.57 per cent of total revenue) from films and $16.58 million (14.31 per cent of total revenue) from theater operations.[5] Order trends suggested that newer agreements were for 3D systems. The theater leases were generally for 10 to 20 years and renewable by the customer. As part of the lease, IMAX advised customers on theater design, supervised the installation of the system, trained theater staff and maintained the system.[6]

Inside IMAX

Hardware: The Film Technology IMAX films were printed on films that were 10 times larger than the 35 mm films that were used in traditional multiplexes and were projected on screens that were (on average) eight stories high (approximately 88 feet) and 120-feet-wide, or in domes that were 81 feet in diameter. Please see Exhibit 1 for a comparison of 35 mm and IMAX film sizes.

IMAX theaters were designed so that projected images stretched up to the peripheral vision of the viewer, thus the viewer was completely immersed in the scene. Each frame of an IMAX film had 15 sprocket holes to guide it through projectors (compared to four in each frame of a 35 mm film). The films were projected to screens by IMAX-designed projectors that had special features–a higher shutter speed, rolling loop motion and vacuum to hold the film to the lens.[7] IMAX projectors used 15,000-watt bulbs, whereas the regular 35 mm projectors used bulbs between 3,000–4,000 watts. The projectors were cooled by circulating more than 50,000 cubic feet of air and nine gallons of distilled water per minute. These features of the IMAX projection system produced images on-screen that were brighter and sharper than those found in conventional movie theaters.

IMAX had developed the skills, knowledge and capabilities to design and assemble the critical elements involved in its projector and camera systems, though most of the components were purchased from vendors with whom it maintained long-term relationships. Strict quality control of components and end products had ensured an average service time of 99.9 per cent for its equipments installed in theaters. Company personnel visited each theater for servicing the systems; the projection systems were serviced every three months and the audio systems were serviced once a year.

In 2007, IMAX spent almost five per cent of its sales revenue on Research and Development, and 50 of its 318 employees were involved in it. The company had spent about

---

[5]Annual Report, 2007.

[6]Annual Reports.

[7]*Computer-Aided Engineering*, 15:8, 1996, pp. 8–9.

$12.6 million in R & D in the past three years.[8] It had also received grants from Ontario Technology Fund for its R & D, and held 46 patents and had seven patents pending in the United States.[9] IMAX had successfully developed 3D cameras and projection systems to produce realistic 3D images. The audience used polarized or electronic glasses that split the images for the left and right eye by using liquid crystal shutter lenses that were controlled by an infrared signal and opened and shut 48 times per second in coordination with the projector to create a 3D effect. Another example of the firm's technological capabilities was a lightweight 3D camera that it had developed to shoot a movie about the International Space Station in space. IMAX worked with MSM Design, a small firm owned by Marty and Barbara Mueller, and developed a camera that weighed only 90 pounds, compared to the traditional IMAX 3D cameras that weighed 228 pounds.[10] IMAX 3D projectors were also capable of projecting 2D images. The visuals were supported by six-channel digital audio that typically produced 12,000 watts of realistic, distortion-free sound. The sound systems were developed by Sonics Associates Inc., a subsidiary in which IMAX had 51 per cent ownership. The company had even developed a 3D directional sound technology that offered location and depth to the audio. A testament to IMAX's technological prowess was the 1997 Oscar Award it received for Scientific and Technical Achievement.[11]

Because of its larger size, printing and distributing IMAX films was costlier than 35 mm films. IMAX had developed digital cameras and projectors that it planned to install in theaters starting in 2008 so that it could produce and distribute its movies in digital format. While the conversion to digital format required substantial upfront investment, it was expected that this shift would allow IMAX to lower its operational costs (of film production and distribution) significantly.

Software: IMAX Films The motion picture industry produced several types of movies: horror, adventure, comedy, romantic comedy, family, drama and documentaries. Of these, the documentary segment was considered so significant that the Motion Picture Association of America (MPAA) in its annual Oscar Award ceremony gave out separate awards for these films. While the large format film itself was a unique feature of IMAX, it had also differentiated itself by its library of films and locations. IMAX films were often educational and entertaining, and involved documentaries of natural and scientific wonders such as the Grand Canyon, space stations, etc. An IMAX film, *Fires of Kuwait*, was nominated for an Academy Award in 1993.

By locating itself in prestigious venues such as the Smithsonian Institution in Washington, Liberty Science Center in New Jersey, Museum of Science and Industry in Chicago, and Port Vell in Barcelona, Spain, the firm had created a unique brand image. In an interview with CNN, co-CEO Gelfond noted IMAX's advantage: "IMAX is also a brand, so we don't have to pay the same kind of talent that Hollywood has to pay, which is really a huge percentage of the costs. Once you take those costs down and you look at just making the film with the world around you as the talent, you get into much more manageable budget ranges. A typical two-dimensional film at IMAX is about $5 million; a typical 3D film at IMAX is about $10 million."[12] Hollywood studios would have to pay a major star (such as

---

[8]Annual Report, 2007.

[9]Annual Report, 2007.

[10]"Cam programming helps design 3d IMAX movie camera for NASA," *Computer Aided Engineering*, 19:3, March 2000, p. 10.

[11]W. C. Symonds, "Now showing in IMAX: Money!; The giant-screen technology will even bag an Oscar," *Business Week*, 3520, March 31, 1997, p. 80.

[12]D. Michael, "Bigger is better: IMAX knocking competition down to size," *CNN*, November 6, 1998, www.cnn.com/SHOWBIZ/Movies/9811/06/imax/index.html?iref=newssearch, accessed March 23, 2008.

Tom Cruise or Eddie Murphy) more than $10 million for a movie. While top movie stars were celebrities and drew huge compensation, many others involved in the production, distribution and marketing of a film were neither well known nor highly paid. In 2007, according to the Bureau of Labor Statistics (BLS), the median salary for an actor in the motion picture and video industry was about $17 per hour.[13] Some of these talents had formed unions, such as the Screen Artists Guild, to negotiate higher wages for their labor. The disruption of TV programming in spring 2008 caused by the brief Writers Guild strike was suggestive of the power such groups had on studios.

Besides stars, the other major cost of movie-making was the marketing. It was estimated that a studio spent almost 30-50 per cent of the total cost of production and distribution of a movie in its marketing. According to the Motion Picture Association of America (MPAA), the average cost of making and marketing a movie rose to more than $106 million in 2007, with marketing budgets averaging $36 million.[14] The marketing of the movie was done through several channels such as TV, the press, theaters, websites and promotions with retailers. Please see Exhibit 2 for average spending in each media. For example, most kids' movies released by studios such as Disney and SKG Dreamworks were promoted through tie-ups with restaurants such as McDonald's and Burger King, and also toy manufactures and other retailers. The Hollywood business model used the awareness created by the presence of stars and substantial marketing budgets to draw large audiences into theaters in the opening weekend itself.[15] To achieve high ticket sales on opening weekends, large numbers of prints of the movie were distributed. In contrast, traditionally, IMAX had not marketed its films aggressively. The company did have a sales force and marketing staff at its offices in Canada, the United States, Europe, Japan and China to market its theater systems. The movies were sold to theaters separately; as such, there was no national marketing or advertising.[16] Unlike Hollywood movies that had short lifespans in the theater circuit and were then withdrawn for release on DVD and pay-per-view format, IMAX films were often shown in theaters for years after their release. In recent years, IMAX films had received some marketing support. For example, for IMAX movie *Everest*, producer Greg MacGillivray spent $2 million in marketing and reportedly saw a 20-45 per cent increase in box-office revenues at each theater. Moreover, IMAX's alliances were helping in cross-promoting its movies. For example, for its *T-Rex: Back to the Cretaceous* 3-D movie, it had a month-long promo on Showtime that was also shown in Imaginarium stores in malls across the United States.[17] The increasing number of Hollywood movies that were released in IMAX format allowed IMAX to ride on the coat-tails of marketing campaigns launched by the studios.

IMAX films were often produced by the firm or partially or fully financed by other parties. The firm hired the talent for the film on a project-by-project basis. Most of the post-production work was performed at David Keighley Production, a wholly-owned subsidiary of IMAX. IMAX (and any investors or sponsors) shared the ownership rights for a film, while usually IMAX controlled the distribution rights. As a result, IMAX had the distribution rights to the largest number of large format films. The distributor received a percentage of

---

[13]www.bls.gov/oes/current/naics4_711500.htm, accessed December 23, 2008.

[14]M. Marr, "Now playing: Expensive movies; Average cost of a film tops $100 million for first time; Valenti set to leave MPAA," *The Wall Street Journal*, March 24, 2004, p. B. 4, www.mpaa.org/researchStatistics.asp, accessed December 23, 2008.

[15]Adam Leipzig, "How to Sell a Movie (or Fail) in Four Hours," *The New York Times*, November 13, 2005.

[16]D. Oestricher, "IMAX hopes for big run with Matrix," *The Wall Street Journal*, June 18, 2003, p. b5c.

[17]T. L. Stanley, "IMAX lands showtime, GTE for 1st X-Promo," *Brandweek*, July 13, 1998, 39:28, p. 5.

the theater box office revenues. IMAX films often remained in distribution for four or five years. (Please see Exhibit 3 for box office revenues for IMAX films.)

Generating Growth

IMAX used a two-pronged strategy to maintain its growth. First, it had sought to expand beyond its institutional environment by opening IMAX theaters within multiplexes or converting existing multiplexes' screens to IMAX format. Second, it had launched Hollywood films in IMAX format.

An IMAX Near You While early IMAX theaters were mostly located in institutional settings such as museums and aquariums, to reach a wider audience IMAX had engaged in alliances with commercial movie theater owners.[18] It grew rapidly during the late 1990s as theater owners such as AMC, Cinemark and Regal went on a building spree and bought IMAX systems to install in their multiplexes. According to Wechsler, this strategy backfired when IMAX could not escape the crisis that hit the theater industry in the late 1990s because of the overbuilding during that decade. As many theater-owners filed for bankruptcy, IMAX had to engage in belt-tightening of its own because of its receivable problems. Moody's downgraded IMAX's debt of $200 million senior notes from Ba2 to B2 and a $100 million note from B1 to Caa1 because of the risk of default by customers. In response, IMAX cut $14 million in overhead, laid off 200 employees and bought back $90 million of its debt.[19] Debt remained a critical problem for IMAX (please see Exhibits 4, 5 and 6 for IMAX financials).

In recent years, IMAX entered into partnerships with AMC and Regal Cinemas to screen IMAX films in multiplexes using its MPX technology. MPX technology allowed IMAX and theater-owners to convert traditional theaters to IMAX format.[20] It was estimated that it now cost only $175,000 to retrofit a multiplex and another $500,000 to install the IMAX system.[21] Regal Cinemas had built IMAX theaters in several markets and waited to see how they performed before adding more.[22] In March 2008, it signed another agreement with IMAX for 38 more theaters, bringing the total number of Regal IMAX theaters to 52 by 2010. Regal theaters would charge $2.50-5.00 more than their regular feature admission for IMAX films.[23] In December 2007, IMAX signed a deal with AMC to install 100 IMAX digital theaters systems in 33 markets, thereby substantially increasing its presence in the U.S. market. IMAX had identified 655 multiplexes without an IMAX nearby.[24] However, IMAX co-CEO Wechsler had stated that he did not expect IMAX theaters to be ubiquitous but exclusive, like flying first-class; while co-CEO Gelfond had suggested that the IMAX experience would be so unique that it could not be replicated at home. Consistent with

---

[18]L. Gubernick, Hollywood Journal: Hollywood think bigger–your favorites, only taller: Can re-released movies breathe life into IMAX," *The Wall Street Journal*, February 15, 2002, p. W. 5.

[19]Z. Olijnyk, "One giant leap," *Canadian Business*, 75:17, September 16, 2002, pp. 46-48.

[20]D. Oestricher, "IMAX hopes for big run with Matrix," *The Wall Street Journal*, June 18, 2003, p. b5c.

[21]Katy Marquardt, "Imax Parlays a Huge Screen and 3-D Tech into an Experience You Can't Duplicate at Home. Coming soon to a multiplex near you," *US News and World Report*, Feb. 6, 2008, www.usnews.com/articles/business/2008/02/06/imax-parlays-3-d-tech-into-an-experience-you-cant-duplicate-at-home.html, accessed December 23, 2008.

[22]*The Wall Street Journal*, 2000.

[23]B. Pulley, "The really big screen," *Forbes*, 172:13, December 22, 2003, p. 222.; *The Wall Street Journal*, 2003.

[24]D. Oestricher, "IMAX hopes for big run with Matrix," *The Wall Street Journal*, June 18, 2003, p. b5c.

this vision, the theater agreement that it recently signed gave AMC territorial exclusivity.[25] Unlike past agreements where theaters chains bought the system from IMAX, the newer agreements required the partner theater chain to make the investment for retrofitting the theater, while IMAX paid for the system installation in return for revenue-sharing on future ticket sales. Analysts expected that such agreements (and digital conversion) would lower IMAX's capital requirements and help it pay off its debt.[26]

Go West IMAX!

Another strategic move by IMAX to ensure its growth was the conversion of Hollywood movies into IMAX format. IMAX had developed a patented digital re-mastering (DMR) technology that allowed it to convert traditional 35 mm films such as *Harry Potter, Spiderman, Antz* and *The Simpsons* into the large-screen format and even develop 3D versions of such movies. The development of this technology was critical because merely projecting a 35 mm film on the large IMAX screen would have produced a grainy picture. According to co-CEO Gelfond, the firm invested millions of dollars to sharpen the resolution of the converted pictures and it took more than five years to develop the technology.[27] The re-mastering of *Apollo 13* took 16 weeks, while *The Matrix Revolutions* was re-mastered as it was being produced, allowing for near-simultaneous theater and IMAX releases. As IMAX had worked out the teething problems with this technology, the costs of conversion had come down. For each print, it now cost $22,500 to convert a standard two-dimensional film and $45,000 to convert a 3-D film. It was expected that moving to a digital format would further lower the conversion costs. If the conversion succeeded at the box office, more studios might be willing to spend the extra money to convert their standard 35 mm films to IMAX format.[28] This would also attract theater chains to open new IMAX screens. Though IMAX made only seven per cent of the box office revenue from reformatted films by other studios, compared to the nearly 30 per cent that it made on its own movies,[29] the conversion of Hollywood movies might allow IMAX to survive, according to co-CEO Gelfond.[30] An announcement to launch the *Harry Potter* movie on IMAX resulted in an almost 11 per cent surge in its stock price that day. Gelfond noted that IMAX could continue making educational films that could be screened in theaters during daytime for families, students and tourists, while its reformatted Hollywood movies could be screened in the evening. In an interview with Amusement Business, co-CEO Wechsler noted that the IMAX strategy of moving into the commercial movie business would hopefully expand the core audience.[31] "Our research tells us that a lot of people will pay that extra $3 to $5," Gelfond said in an interview with USA Today.[32]

[25]Katy Marquardt, "Imax Parlays a Huge Screen and 3-D Tech Into an Experience You Can't Duplicate at Home. Coming soon to a multiplex near you," *US News and World Report*, February 6, 2008, www.usnews.com/articles/business/2008/02/06/imax-parlays-3-d-tech-into-an-experience-you-cant-duplicate-at-home.html, accessed December 23, 2008.

[26]Ibid.

[27]S. N. Chakravarty, "A really big show," *Institutional Investor*, 35:10, October 2002, p. 20.

[28]The Wall Street Journal, 2000; Institutional Investor, 2002.

[29]D. Lieberman, "IMAX supersizes its plans for future flicks," *US Today*, December 16, 2002, www.usatoday.com/tech/news/techinnovations/2002-12-16-IMAX_x.htm, accessed December 23, 2008.

[30]Z. Olijnyk, "One giant leap," *Canadian Business*, 75:17, September 16, 2002, pp. 46-48.

[31]N. Emmons, "IMAX may turn toward mainstream," *Amusement Business*, 112:49, December 4, 2000, p. 1, pp. 20-21.

[32]D. Lieberman, "IMAX supersizes its plans for future flicks," *US Today*, December 16, 2002, www.usatoday.com/tech/news/techinnovations/2002-12-16-IMAX_x.htm, accessed December 23, 2008.

The first full-length Hollywood movie released on IMAX was *Fantasia* 2000 in January 2000.[33] The classic *Beauty and the Beast*, which had a 20-week show on 67 IMAX screens in 2002, generated $32 million in revenue.[34] The first live action commercial movie to be launched in IMAX format was *Apollo 13*, which generated an additional $2 million in revenue. Later, *Star Wars* was released on IMAX followed by *The Matrix Reloaded*, which generated $11.7 million.[35] These movies were released in IMAX after their theatrical release.[36]

As more Hollywood movies were converted to IMAX format, the studios had to decide whether these should be released simultaneously in theaters and IMAX format. Could the expansion into IMAX theaters cannibalize the traditional theatrical revenues? It was found that almost 90 per cent of *The Matrix Reloaded* IMAX viewers had seen the movie in theaters earlier. *The Polar Express*, which was released simultaneously in IMAX and traditional theaters during the 2004 Christmas season, was a big hit with $45 million in revenues in the IMAX format.[37] On December 12, 2008, the movie *The Day the Earth Stood Still* was released simultaneously on IMAX and multiplex screens. At $31 million, the movie had the highest box office gross over a weekend. More than $3.8 million (about 12 per cent) of the total revenue came from IMAX theaters. Notably, the average revenue per IMAX theater was $30,800, compared to the national average theater revenues of $8,100.[38] Such track records should give more studios the confidence to release their movies simultaneously in commercial and IMAX theaters.

INDUSTRY DYNAMICS

Motion picture production and distribution was part of the service sector of the economy and included firms such as Disney/Pixar, MGM, Regal Entertainment, Lions Gate and Carmike. Many of the production and distribution companies were now part of other, larger, diversified firms. For example, Columbia Pictures was now part of Sony, Warner Brothers was a subsidiary of Time-Warner, Paramount Studios was part of Viacom and Pixar and Miramax were part of Disney. Over the years, media firms had sought to vertically integrate their operations by owning not only the production facilities but also distribution networks.

Film production remained a risky business. Only one in 10 films ever recovered its investment from domestic theater release; and only six out of 10 movies ever recouped the original investment. Competition among movies within the same genre was so high that studios scheduled releases carefully to avoid direct competition. Thus, release dates were announced several years in advance and production was designed around preferred holiday release dates such as Thanksgiving, July 4th, Memorial Day weekends or the first weekend of May.

---

[33]R. Ricklefs, "IMAX hopes to take cast screen into mainstream—a new 'fantasia' tests film strategy of Canadian firm," *The Wall Street Journal*, December 10, 1999, p. 1.

[34]D. Oestricher, "IMAX hopes for big run with Matrix," *The Wall Street Journal*, June 18, 2003, p. b5c.

[35]T. Lowry, "Now playing at IMAX: Hit movies" *Business Week*, 3807, November 11, 2002, p. 46.; N. Sperling, "IMAX executives hoping Warner's 'The Matrix' is 'the one'," *Amusement Business*, 115:46, 2003, pp. 24-25.

[36]T. King, "Hollywood Journal: When a 'Sure thing' Isn't—Even the $20 million stars can't guarantee a hit; trying to ignore 'Pluto'," *The Wall Street Journal*, October 11, 2002, p. w11.

[37]W. D. Crotty, "IMAX's screen gets bigger," The Motley Fool, September 15. 2005, www.fool.com/investing/general/2005/09/15/imaxs-screen-gets-bigger.aspx?terms=Imax+screen+gets+bigger&vstest=search_042607_linkdefault, accessed December 23, 2008.

[38]"Imax rises as consumers embrace large screens," *Associated Press*, December 16, 2008, http://biz.yahoo.com/ap/081216/imax_mover.html?.v=1, accessed December 23, 2008.

IMAX films faced competition from other films produced by studios such as Pixar/Disney that were targeted for families or children. Within the large format film segment, Iwerks was the only rival to IMAX.[39] Iwerks was founded in 1986 and continued to be involved in all aspects of large format films and simulation rides. It produced films in the 15/70 and 8/70 formats; however, the focus of the firm was more on ride simulation packages located in theme parks, zoos, museums and other destinations. Iwerks had received two Academy Awards for Scientific and Technical Achievement. In 2002, Iwerks merged with SimEx (a firm founded in 1991), which was involved in ride simulation and animation production. Another firm, Megasystems, which was involved in the development of large format projection systems, production and consulting in marketing, operations and technical services, had discontinued its projection system production and was renamed Pollavision. Pollavision was now only involved in consulting (and maintenance) services for large format film theaters.[40]

Technology Trends

Potential IMAX viewers could consume many alternative sources of entertainment such as live plays, sport events, TV programs, the Internet, etc. Please see Exhibits 7 and 8 for admissions, prices and time spent on alternative entertainment sources. Viewers might choose to watch a movie on DVD, pay-per-view or video on demand rather than at the theater. The development of high-definition DVD recording, big-screen TVs and cheaper home theater projection and sound systems posed an even bigger threat to box office ticket sales. Please see Exhibit 9 for DVD sales trends in the United States. According to one estimate, almost 85 per cent of a film's revenue now came from home viewing through various channels such as DVD/VHS, cable and TV.[41] Yet, it had been found that the success of secondary sources such as DVD sales and rentals was a function of the movie's box office success.[42] According to Jack Valenti, former president of MPAA, 50 per cent of DVD viewers and almost 38 per cent of VCR movie-users were frequent moviegoers. He said, "People who love movies are eager to watch them again in different environments."[43]

The development of new technologies, such as cheaper high definition camcorders, as well as the proliferation of new distribution channels such as cable, satellite and the Internet, had also created opportunities for new independent firms to enter the industry. One such firm that leveraged its knowledge of computer technology to develop blockbuster animated films was Pixar. New firms might enter one or more parts of the film industry value chain–talent management, production, post-production, distribution, etc. Specialists in post-production processes had emerged who were responsible for editing, special effects, media transfers, subtitling, etc. However, entry into all aspects of the value chain simultaneously had been rare. A recent example of such an entry was SKG Dreamworks, a studio that was started by film industry veterans Spielberg, Katzenberg and Geffen.

Such technological changes had also increased the potential for piracy. According to the Motion Picture Association of America, the U.S. film industry lost more than $3 billion annually because of piracy. Section 8, Article 1 of the U.S. Constitution offers Congress the power to offer copyright protection. The Copyright Act of 1976 that was amended in 1982 offers

---

[39]C. Booth, "IMAX gets bigger (by getting smaller)," *Time*, June 29, 1998, 151:25, pp. 48–49.

[40]www.pollavision.com, accessed December 23, 2008.

[41]E. J. Epstein, "Hollywood's death spiral," *Slate*, July 25, 2005.

[42]Bruce Orwall, "A Dud at Theaters Will Be a Dud DVD," *The Wall Street Journal*, November 26, 2005, p. A2.

[43]J. Valenti, MPAA Press Release, 2002.

strong penalties for copyright violations. Please see www.copyright.gov/title17 for recent development in copyright law. Violations were considered felonies and were subject to federal criminal charges and civil lawsuits. The Motion Picture Association was working closely with the U.S. Congress to enforce sentencing guidelines and improve copyright protection as newer technologies emerged and posed fresher challenges. According to Karen Randall of Vivendi, whose production *The Hulk* was released on the Internet by pirates before its theatrical release, the FBI was very cooperative and aggressive in pursuing the case.[44]

Other Trends

IMAX had to cease screening its movie *Volcanoes of the Deep Sea* in some parts of the United States, as certain religious groups were offended by its position on, and depiction of, evolution.[45] Concerns about violence and sex in movies had generated considerable efforts to organize and lobby political action to regulate the industry. For example, Tipper Gore and Lynn Cheney (spouses of former vice-presidents Al Gore and Dick Cheney, respectively) had worked hard to curtail the levels of violence, sex and vulgar language found in popular media.[46]

Another trend that might help firms such as IMAX was the increased consumption of educational entertainment. Ever since Sesame Street succeeded in educating and entertaining kids simultaneously, the "edutainment" market had grown as parents increasingly sought out play activities for their children that were educational. This trend had been attributed to increasing belief among parents that in a knowledge economy, their kids' success might depend on education. The widespread popularity among parents of the concept of the "Mozart effect"–a finding that babies that listened to Mozart recordings in the womb or at early stages after birth had richer cognitive development–was seen as evidence of their desire to produce smart kids.[47] Other trends that were driving this growth could include higher education levels of parents and overscheduled kids and parents.[48] As a result, zoos, museums, software, TV shows and toys were all redesigning their products to entertain and educate.

According to IMAX, more than 20 per cent of IMAX audiences were school groups. About 70 per cent of IMAX viewers were between 19 and 65 years of age, and the majority were college- or university-educated, with an average household income of more than $70,000, and with 33 per cent earning more than $100,000.[49] MPAA offered a more fine-grained analysis of demographic data on movie attendance. It reported that 12-24 year olds (38 per cent of admissions) had the largest attendance for feature films in theaters in 2007, followed by the 25- to 39-year-olds group (29 per cent of admissions).[50] The 12-24-year-olds were also frequent moviegoers (at least one movie per month), representing 41 per cent of frequent moviegoers. IMAX needed to figure out a way to attract this demographic.

---

[44]S. McBride and B. Orwall, "Movie industry steps up drive against pirates," *The Wall Street Journal*, January 27, 2004, p. B1.

[45]Cornelia Dean, "A new test for IMAX: The Bible vs. the volcano," March. 19, 2005.

[46]Richard Goldstein, "Scary Move: When Both Parties Team Up to Target Hollywood, Be Afraid. Be Very Afraid!" *Village Voice*, October 3, 2000 p.20.

[47]Jeffrey Kluger and Alice Park, "The Quest For A Superkid," *Time*, April 22, 2001 www.time.com/time/nation/article/0,8599,107265-1,00.html, accessed December 23, 2008.

[48]R. White, "That's Edutainment," White Hutchinson Leisure & Learning Group, 2003.

[49]www.IMAX.com.

[50]J. Valenti, MPAA Press Release, 2002.

U.S. and Global Market

In 2007, 603 movies were released in the United States and collected revenues of $9.6 billion.[51] According to the MPAA, there were 1.4 billion movie theater attendances in the United States in 2007.[52] Jack Valenti, former president of the MPAA, noted that Americans had the highest per capita movie attendance in the world at 5.3 films a year. By excluding those who did not see at least one movie a year, the per capita attendance rose to 8.6 films per year.[53] Exhibit 10 displays theater revenues, average U.S. ticket prices, attendance annual growth rate, consumer price index (CPI) and growth of the U.S. economy. Theater-owners realized that ticket prices could not go up forever, as this might drive away more viewers; so they tried to generate revenue by screening more commercials before showing the feature film. According to some experts, release of big budget franchise movies or sequels of popular movies attenuated the adverse impact of the economy on theater attendance.

Movies were now increasingly becoming a global industry. More than 5000 films were released worldwide in 2007, with seven billion attendances and annual global box office revenues estimated at $26.7 billion.[54] The Asia-Pacific region had the largest share of the global market. While Hollywood movies had always enjoyed an international audience, with globalization and the increased movement of people across national borders movies from other regions such as Hong Kong and India were also finding an international audience. For Hollywood movies, a significant part of the revenues now came from outside the United States. Please see Exhibit 11 on domestic and foreign sources for the top 10 films in 2007.

THE LARGER ISSUES

At this point in its evolution, IMAX faced two critical questions. Would IMAX lose its differentiation if it exhibited too many Hollywood movies? Greg MacGillvray, who had made several films in the IMAX format, including the highly successful *Everest,* argued that IMAX ran the risk of losing its brand identity as it moved into non-educational entertainment films. He said: "There's also been a slight brand erosion given that these films have not been really educational experiences, but more entertainment experiences." According to MacGillvray, IMAX's own research showed that the brand's trustworthiness was rooted in the fact that IMAX grew up in institutional settings.[55]

Another question that the present co-CEOs had faced for several years was: Should IMAX be sold to a larger studio such as Sony, Disney or Time-Warner? That is, was it too small to survive on its own? Some analysts had speculated that IMAX was ripe for acquisition. Co-CEO Gelfond had once stated, "Someday it will make sense for IMAX to be part of a studio."[56]

The author would like to thank Professors Barbara Bartkus, Alan Eisner, Jim Key, participants at a case writing workshop organized by the Society for Case Research, and students at Old Dominion University for comments on earlier versions of the case. Thanks also to Lee-Hsien Pan for his research assistance.

[51]US Entertainment Industry: 2007 MPAA statistics. See also, M. Marr, "Now playing: Expensive movies; Average cost of a film tops $100 million for first time; Valenti set to leave MPAA," *The Wall Street Journal,* March 24, 2004, p. B. 4.

[52]James Jaeger, The Movie Industry, www.mecfilms.com/moviepubs/memos/moviein.htm, accessed December 23, 2008.

[53]2007 movie attendance study, MPAA.

[54]2007 International Theatrical Snapshot, MPAA; www.mpaa.org/International%20Theatrical%20Snapshot.pdf, accessed March 4, 2009.

[55]P. Waal, "Call in the barbarians," *Canadian Business,* 73:17, September 18, 2000, pp. 85-87.

[56]P. Waal, "The plot quickens," *Canadian Business,* 71:11, June 26-July 10, 1998, pp. 51-57.

EXHIBIT 1: IMAX Film Size

Film Frames Actual Size

15/70mm

Standard 70mm

Standard 35mm

Source: IMAX, with permission.

EXHIBIT 2: Average Marketing Spending on Various Media, 2007

Newspapers	12.9 %
Network TV	16.1 %
Spot TV	13.7 %
Internet	5.3 %
Trailers	4.9 %
Other Media (cable TV, radio, magazines, billboards)	24.5 %
Other Non-media (production/creative services, exhibitor services, promotion & publicity, market research)	22.6 %

Source: www.mpaa.com.

EXHIBIT 3: Box Office Revenues for IMAX Movies (in Millions of $)

Rank	Title	Studio	Gross-to-date	Year
1	*Everest*	MFF	$ 87.18	1998
2	*Space Station 3-D*	IMAX	$ 77.10	2002
3	*T-Rex: Back to the Cretaceous*	IMAX	$53.14	1998
4	*Fantasia 2000*	BV	$52.26	2000
5	*Mysteries of Egypt*	IMAX	$40.59	1998
6	*Deep Sea 3-D*	WB	$ 37.09	2006
7	*Magnificent Desolation*	IMAX	$26.67	2005
8	*Beauty and the Beast*	BV	$25.49	2002
9	*NASCAR 3D: The IMAX Experience*	WB	$ 21.58	2004
10	*Sea Monsters: A Prehistoric Adventure*	NGC	$20.05	2007

Source: www.boxofficemojo.com. IMAX box office receipts have only recently started being tracked.

EXHIBIT 4: IMAX Corporation Annual Balance Sheet (in thousands of dollars)

Period Ending	31-Dec-07	31-Dec-06	31-Dec-05	31-Dec-04
Assets				
Current Assets				
Cash and Cash Equivalents	16,901	25,123	24,324	28,964
Short-Term Investments	–	2,115	8,171	–
Net Receivables	25,505	26,017	89,171	19,899
Inventory	22,050	26,913	28,294	29,001
Other Current Assets	2,187	3,432	3,825	2,279
Total Current Assets	**66,643**	**83,600**	**153,785**	**80,143**
Long-Term Investments	59,092	65,878	–	59,492
Property Plant and Equipment	23,708	24,639	26,780	28,712
Goodwill	39,027	39,027	39,027	39,027
Intangible Assets	4,419	3,782	6,030	3,931
Accumulated Amortization	–	–	–	–
Other Assets	10,928	6,646	9,756	7,532
Deferred Long-Term Asset Charges	4,165	3,719	10,806	12,016
Total Assets	**207,982**	**227,291**	**246,184**	**230,853**
Liabilities				
Current Liabilities				
Accounts Payable	74,267	69,720	62,057	62,724
Short/Current Long-Term Debt	–	–	–	–
Other Current Liabilities	–	–	–	–
Total Current Liabilities	**74,267**	**69,720**	**62,057**	**62,724**
Long-Term Debt	160,000	160,000	160,000	160,000
Other Liabilities	–	–	–	–
Deferred Long-Term Liability Charges	59,085	55,803	44,397	50,505
Minority Interest	–	–	–	–
Negative Goodwill	–	–	–	–
Total Liabilities	**293,352**	**285,523**	**266,454**	**273,229**
Stockholders' Equity				
Common Stock	122,455	122,024	121,674	116,281
Retained Earnings	(213,407)	(184,375)	(144,347)	(160,945)
Other Stockholder Equity	5,582	4,119	2,403	2,288
Total Stockholder Equity	**(85,370)**	**(58,232)**	**(20,270)**	**(42,376)**

Source: Annual Reports.

EXHIBIT 5: IMAX Corporation Annual Income Statement (in thousands of dollars)

Period Ending	31-Dec-07	31-Dec-06	31-Dec-05	31-Dec-04
Total Revenue	115,832	129,452	144,930	135,980
Cost of Revenue	74,673	76,902	73,005	70,062
Gross Profit	41,159	52,550	71,925	65,918
Operating Expenses				
Research & Development	5,789	3,615	3,264	3,995
Selling General and Administrative	44,705	42,527	39,503	36,066
Non-recurring	562	1,073	−859	−639
Others	547	1,668	911	719
Total Operating Expenses	51,603	48,883	42,819	40,141
Operating Income or Loss	(10,444)	3,667	29,106	25,777
Income from Continuing Operations				
Total Other Income/Expenses Net	(933)	1,036	1,004	265
Earnings Before Interest and Taxes	(11,377)	4,703	30,110	26,042
Interest Expense	17,093	16,759	16,773	16,853
Income Before Taxes	(28,470)	(12,056)	13,337	9,189
Income Tax Expense	472	6,218	934	(255)
Minority Interest	0	0	0	0
Net Income from Continuing Ops	(28,942)	(18,274)	12,403	9,444
Non-recurring Events				
Discontinued Operations	2,002	1,425	1,979	800
Extraordinary Items	0	0	0	0
Effect of Accounting Changes	0	0	0	0
Other Items	0	0	0	0
Net Income	(26,940)	(16,849)	14,382	10,244

Source: Annual Reports.

EXHIBIT 6: IMAX Corporation Cash Flow Statement (in thousands of dollars)

Period Ending	31-Dec-07	31-Dec-06	31-Dec-05	31-Dec-04
Net Income	(26,940)	(16,849)	14,382	10,244
Cash Flows Provided By or Used In Operating Activities				
Depreciation	17,738	16,872	15,867	14,947
Adjustments to Net Income	(3,520)	10,349	(8,678)	(4,577)
Changes in Accounts Receivables	675	(11,106)	(8,324)	(6,673)
Changes in Liabilities	4,781	4,399	(11,749)	(6,830)
Changes in Inventories	(1,603)	57	(383)	(283)
Changes in Other Operating Activities	2,648	(9,659)	(1,545)	4,583
Total Cash Flow from Operating Activities	(6,221)	(5,937)	1,786	11,411
Cash Flows Provided By or Used In Investing Activities				
Capital Expenditures	(2,150)	(1,985)	(1,597)	(320)
Investments	2,115	6,396	(7,818)	393
Other Cashflows from Investing Activities	(702)	2,105	(1,301)	(1,435)
Total Cash Flows from Investing Activities	(737)	6,516	(10,716)	(1,362)
Cash Flows Provided By or Used In Financing Activities				
Dividends Paid	—	—	—	—
Sale Purchase of Stock	420	286	3,633	558
Net Borrowings	(1,714)	—	—	(29,769)
Other Cash Flows from Financing Activities	—	—	786	800
Total Cash Flows from Financing Activities	(1,294)	286	4,419	(28,411)
Effect of Exchange Rate Changes	30	(66)	(129)	44
Change in Cash and Cash Equivalents	($8,222)	$799	($4,640)	($18,318)

Source: Annual Reports.

EXHIBIT 7: Substitute Activities to Movies in 2007

	Activity	Attendance (in millions)	Average Ticket Price (in $)
1	Movies	1400	6.88
2	Theme Parks	341	35.30
3	Ice Hockey/NHL	21	44.60
4	Basketball/NBA	22	46.75
5	Football/NFL	17	65.25
6	Baseball/MLB	77	23.50

Source: MPAA, www.mpaa.com.

EXHIBIT 8: Media Consumption Based on Hours Per Person Per Year

Filmed Entertainment	2003	2004	2005	2006	2007
Cable & Satellite TV	886	909	980	997	1,010
Broadcast TV	729	711	679	676	676
Consumer Internet	153	164	169	177	181
Home Video (DVD & VHS)	60	67	63	62	64
Box Office	13	13	12	12	13
In-flight Entertainment & Mobile Content	5	8	10	13	18
Subtotal	1,846	1,872	1,913	1,937	1,962
Other Entertainment					
Broadcast & Satellite Radio	831	821	805	778	769
Recorded Music	187	196	195	186	171
Newspapers	195	192	188	178	172
Consumer Magazines	122	125	124	121	119
Consumer Books	108	108	107	108	108
Video Games	76	78	73	76	82
Subtotal	1,522	1,520	1,492	1,447	1,421

Source: MPAA, www.mpaa.com.

EXHIBIT 9: DVD Consumption in the United States (in millions of units)

	Rental DVDs	Sell-through DVDs	Total DVDs	Avg. Price of DVD
2007	171.2	1,084.6	1,255.8	22.11
2006	180.2	1,129.0	1,309.2	22.29
2005	179.0	1,114.5	1,293.6	21.20
2004	149.3	1,063.3	1,212.6	20.32
2003	105.4	768.3	873.6	20.15

Source: MPAA, www.mpaa.com.

EXHIBIT 10: Theater Box Office Revenues, Average U.S. Attendance, Price and Economy

Year	Revenue (in billions $)	Ticket price (in $)	Attendance (in billions)	GDP Growth (in %)	CPI Inflation (in %)
1990	5.02	4.22	1.19	1.9	5.4
1991	4.80	4.21	1.14	−0.2	4.2
1992	4.56	4.15	1.10	3.3	3.0
1993	4.89	4.14	1.18	2.7	3.0
1994	5.18	4.08	1.24	4.0	2.6
1995	5.27	4.35	1.21	2.5	2.8
1996	5.81	4.42	1.32	3.7	3.0
1997	6.21	4.59	1.35	4.5	2.3
1998	6.76	4.69	1.44	4.2	1.6
1999	7.31	5.06	1.44	4.5	2.2
2000	7.46	5.39	1.38	3.7	3.4
2001	8.12	5.65	1.44	0.8	2.8
2002	9.27	5.80	1.60	1.6	1.6
2003	9.16	6.03	1.52	2.5	2.3
2004	9.21	6.21	1.48	3.6	2.7
2005	8.83	6.41	1.38	2.9	3.4
2006	9.14	6.55	1.39	2.8	3.2
2007	9.63	6.88	1.40	2.0	2.8

Source: National Association of Theater Owners (NATO), www.natoonline.org; Bureau of Economic Analysis, www.bea.gov; and Bureau of Labor Statistics, www.bls.gov.

EXHIBIT 11: Domestic and Overseas Revenues for 2007 (in millions of dollars)

Rank	Title	Domestic	Overseas	World
1	*Pirates of the Caribbean: At World's End*	309.4	649.0	958.4
2	*Harry Potter and the Order of the Phoenix*	292.0	645.0	937.0
3	*Spider-Man 3*	336.5	548.9	885.4
4	*Shrek the Third*	321.0	470.4	791.4
5	*Transformers*	319.1	382.0	701.1
6	*Ratatouille*	206.4	409.5	615.9
7	*I Am Legend*	256.4	327.6	584.0
8	*Simpsons Movie, The*	183.1	342.4	525.5
9	*300*	210.6	246.0	456.6
10	*National Treasure: Book of Secrets*	220.0	234.0	454.0

Source: www.worldwideboxoffice.com.